Border Security

Border Security

Second Edition

James R. Phelps

Jeffrey Dailey

Monica Koenigsberg

CAROLINA ACADEMIC PRESS

Durham, North Carolina

Library of Congress Cataloging-in-Publication Data

Names: Phelps, James R., author. | Dailey, Jeffrey D., author. | Koenigsberg,
    Monica, author.
Title: Border security / James R. Phelps, Jeffrey Dailey, and Monica
    Koenigsberg.
Description: Second edition. | Durham, North Carolina : Carolina Academic
    Press, LLC, [2018] | Includes bibliographical references and index.
Identifiers: LCCN 2017046548 | ISBN 9781611638219 (alk. paper)
Subjects: LCSH: Border security. | Border security--United States. | United
    States--Emigration and immigration--Government policy. | Smuggling--United
    States--Prevention. | Human trafficking--United States--Prevention.
Classification: LCC JV6035 .P44 2017 | DDC 363.28/50973--dc23
LC record available at https://lccn.loc.gov/2017046548

e-ISBN 978-1-53100-643-3

Carolina Academic Press, LLC
700 Kent Street
Durham, North Carolina 27701
Telephone (919) 489-7486
Fax (919) 493-5668
www.cap-press.com

Contents

Part Two
Border Security and Transnational Crime

x CONTENTS

Part Three
US Border Security Today

Preface to the First Edition

Homeland security is *Border Security*!

We could argue that the more secure the border the more secure the homeland. We could also argue that a porous or open border offers better relations, and therefore better security than does a closed border. Consider Germany—a country that has been at war with its neighbors so many times in the past two centuries that you could expect it to be completely cordoned off and isolated by those who have been attacked by Germans, or who have invaded and conquered the country. Yet in today's world, just a quarter century after the fall of the Berlin Wall, any citizen or resident of the European Union can cross into, pass through, or even choose to move and work in Germany without having to pass through a border checkpoint or immigration process. Yet Germany today is arguably the most militarily and economically secure country on the European mainland. Germans, even with their problems with immigrants and neo-Nazis, still have one of the most secure homelands in the world. Why is the lack of border enforcement not a problem for Germany, but such a major problem for the U.S. and many other countries? This is one of the questions raised and answered in this text.

Where is the U.S. border? Some point south, others point north. Alaskan residents point east toward Canada and west toward Russia. I tell people that the border is in Des Moines, Iowa, just to see their faces get that screwy look. The reality is that the U.S. border really is in Des Moines. The city has an international airport, and therefore is a Port of Entry for travelers to enter and depart the U.S. Within the airport itself there is a boundary between where a person is within the U.S. and still outside of it, even though they are well within the confines of the territorial landmass of the country. The same can be said for any international airport anywhere in the world. This was recently demonstrated when Eric Snowden, the whistle blower of NSA fame, flew to Russia, and even though he was on the ground in Moscow, was still outside of the country itself and could not be arrested and extradited because he had not crossed through immigration and customs for admission and inspection. Therein lies the quandary of where a country's international borders begin and end. With the exception of a very small number of island nations, this question vexes all countries.

How much border security is enough security and at what point docs border security become so obstructive to economy that society suffers? These questions are raised and sometimes answered in this text. So too is the history of borders and border security, the interaction between nations over time, and the unique open border experiment that is ongoing within the European Union.

The fence being erected in places along the U.S.-Mexico border is not the first barrier between nations and will not be the last. However, in an attempt to provide security for the U.S. homeland, how much strain can the country put on our relationship with our southern neighbor and second largest trading partner before security efforts become counterproductive? This question is just as difficult to answer, as the question of how much crime is acceptable in a society. Answering such questions often results in offending the sensibilities and riling the emotions of everybody with a vested interest in any part of the answer to the question. This book will undoubtedly result in similar arguments but I must question the worth of a book that doesn't engender discussion.

Can America secure the homeland? Does a porous border threaten the homeland? Both questions can be answered if we ask and answer a qualifier: to what extent? If the U.S. wants a totally secure country, then fences, walls, free-fire dead zones are going to be needed along all our borders, including within airports and along over 95,000 miles of shoreline. Aircraft that stray off course will have to be shot down. Ships that come too close to territorial waters will need to be sunk. Communications that allow political and religious thought from perspectives that originate outside of the borders will need to be stifled. We would have to be willing to implement and accept Google China and the North Korean method of isolation. All the necessities required to produce true homeland security are anathema to a free people.

This textbook is about the politics of borders, the delineation of boundaries and the location and effectiveness of barriers. As a textbook it is not the answer to all the questions that arise about securing borders, yet it will drive the development of innumerable questions for other authors and researchers to attempt to answer. We look forward to incorporating those arguments and discussions in future editions.

There are several perils to being apolitical when writing a textbook. I do not mean that we modify our writing so as not to offend but that we take no side, politically, on any of the subjects discussed. We have tried our best to be as relevant as we could while still maintaining maximum neutrality in writing the text, yet still providing complete coverage of sensitive issues and developing proposed solutions to politically charged problems. One peril that we have experienced is that anybody of importance in any political administration simply cannot put a career on the line by writing an endorsement or foreword to your work. This becomes problematic when every administration in the recent past has maintained a position (in direct opposition to existing federal law) that drives development and maintenance of border porosity by political *fiat*.

When my co-authors and I came to an agreement that we would take on this effort, we decided not to gloss over the bare realities of U.S. border security efforts. We did not want the history or the politics of administrations to influence the writing we produced, or to allow for the falsification of statistics or manipulation of reported data. It was more important to us that we produced an apolitical work that reflects the realities of today in light of the long history of U.S.-Mexico and U.S.-Canada relationships.

Another point that we hope you will find appropriate in this *Border Security* text is that we haven't neglected the incorporation of history in this book. The three of us have determined that without a thorough understanding of how the present border security situation developed, without comprehension of what efforts throughout human history have resulted in success and failure, it would be impossible for students of border and homeland security, as well as students of political and international relations and those who study borderlands, to develop effective strategies for the future. Our students, and we hope your students as well, will become the future leaders of the homeland security effort, the defenders of our national integrity, and perhaps even the political movers and shakers of tomorrow. Too many times have today's political leaders acted unilaterally on mythological versions of historical events to the detriment of nations, societies, cultures and the lives of America's defenders, on the international stage and in our own back yards. The students who are exposed to this text won't suffer from the disease of *mythification* of the past.

Determining what subjects to incorporate into this effort was difficult for us. Determining how much to write, while maintaining a textbook perspective of inclusiveness of relevant materials is no easy task. We appreciate your feedback and recommendations on where we should expand and reduce the content and concepts. At some point in writing about each of the included topics it was necessary to draw a line and say that we had enough relevant information to conclude the reader would understand the concept. To go further would belabor a point, or extend into the realm of a whole new book on that particular subject.

There is one other point necessary to address in this preface. As the very first textbook on the subject, *Border Security* took over two years to write. We had been collecting information and performing interviews for at least three years prior to Carolina Academic Press asking us to write this text. Some of the information included is, of course, a bit aged in a world where from month to month the fiscal arguments between political parties lead to changes in border security policy implementation, hiring freezes result in reduced border staffing, drug cartels morph and change tactics, and the dependency on energy imports is reduced even while under free trade agreements industrial manufacturing takes flight to other countries.

We are certain that you will find *Border Security* useful in your classes and as an excellent text for new classes that you are developing.

James R. Phelps, Ph.D.
San Angelo, Texas, USA
November 22, 2013

Foreword

My immediate response to the authors of *Border Security* upon being asked to pen the foreword to the 2nd edition was "I would consider it a privilege." *Border Security* stands alone as an authoritative and cogent textbook in the field of 'forward deployed' homeland security, that is, the protection of the sovereign borders of the United States across the multiple-domain frontier of land, sea, air, and cyberspace. No other academic textbook presently exists that comes anywhere near its comprehensive, clear, concise, and fair treatment of this subject matter. While somewhat similar works exist, they tend to be overly specialized with a sole emphasis on terrorism or illegal migration concerns, politicized with some sort of agenda in mind, or have fallen prey to critical revisionism or political alternative discourse.

This work, however, being solely educationally focused in its intent and intentionally written from inception as a textbook, does not suffer from such limitations. Instead, it strives to offer an 'honest broker' perspective—as much as is humanly possible—on the subject of historical and contemporary border security and, as a result, has immense classroom utility for both introductory and advanced topical teaching purposes. In addition, this textbook deftly achieves the appropriate balance between theory and practice and academic and professional considerations, which is an exceedingly difficult task to pull off in an almost 500 page text.

My association with the work spans four years, having been an early manuscript reviewer of it in draft form, an editorial reviewer, and later having reviewed it in the journal *Homeland Security Affairs*. I've also used the textbook in a graduate level course on *Narcos, Illicit Trafficking, and the Border* as an early foundational reading with excellent student feedback concerning its efficacy for such an intended use. I found the 1st edition of work to be an excellent product and, from my close reading of the 2nd edition galleys, I believe this new and updated version will follow in that tradition.

The new edition has been expanded by roughly eighty pages, with a slightly different format that incorporates a 'Key Words and Concepts' listing at the beginning of each chapter and 'Questions for Further Consideration' towards the end as student learning and teaching aids. Sections of the work on energy security have had major updates as have immigration issues and statistics now available from the Obama administration era. Further, recent historical events—the erection of the Hungarian border fence, for example—and present US/Mexico border policy considerations—such as the new Trump presidential administration's stance on expanding border wall construction—have been incorporated into the manuscript. With these changes in mind, I believe that both the scholar and the student will find the new and even further polished 2nd edition of *Border Security* to be a superb textbook that will facilitate both classroom and distance learning in a critical subfield of homeland security studies.

Robert J. Bunker, Ph.D.
Claremont, California, USA
November 2, 2017

Past Minerva Chair
Strategic Studies Institute
U.S. Army War College
Carlisle, Pennsylvania, USA

Acknowledgments

Completing this book has been a long journey for the three of us and there are innumerable individuals without whose assistance we would have long ago died in the Southwest deserts. At the risk of missing people, we want to specifically recognize a few who have been most beneficial. It goes without saying that Beth Hall and Keith Sipe at Carolina Academic Press took a chance on us when they accepted our initial book idea. Thank you for guiding us through the process. Also at Carolina Academic Press we want to thank Grace Pledger for the skill she put into producing the final product you hold in your hands. To all the other people at CAP, we offer our thanks — you are a great publishing team who really look after your authors.

The research that went into writing the first edition took several years to accomplish. We gathered the materials over three years, starting in 2009, and published the first edition in 2014. This second edition has taken us another three years of monitoring government activities, requesting FOIA data from CBP and fighting to maintain consistency of the data they provided as the constantly changing policies of the Obama Administration made gathering real statistics nearly impossible, then watching the changes in the first year of the Trump Administration and trying to keep up with the rapidly evolving landscape of U.S. Border Security.

Bringing it all together would have been impossible were it not for several friends, faculty, and students. We want to thank, in particular, retired Senior Border Patrol Agents Randy Rigsby and his assistant David Estevis of the San Angelo Border Patrol Station who started us along this dusty trail. They were instrumental in sharing with us their love for the U.S. Border Patrol and their experiences in border security. So too were two Customs and Border Patrol Pilots, Special Agents Jon Herron and Andrew Duff. More importantly, recently retired Border Patrol Agent Cliff Crumley from the Rio Grand Valley and CBP Officer Tom Grady from the El Paso POE were instrumental in guiding us through the constant ups and downs of CBP morale and real-world happenings over the past four years. The tales of air interdiction, hunting cocaine submarines, and the cooperation they received from Mexican law enforcement were essential to our grasp of the subject matter contained in this book. The information these six guided us to is matched by the assistance of Homeland Security Investigations and Enforcement and Removal Operations Special Agents across west Texas. Due to the nature of their occupations it isn't possible to reference them by name, but the men and women of HSI/ICE who helped us have our thanks.

The number of law enforcement agents across the Southwest who assisted us in innumerable ways cannot be counted. From Del Rio Chief of Police (interim) Fred Knoll, who guided us through his border community and arranged for us to speak at length with his senior officers about cross-border crime, to the individual Border Patrol Agents sitting at remote border sites who took the time to answer our questions, we owe you our thanks. To the residents of the border communities around the United States who offered their insight into local issues we also owe a debt of gratitude. We also need to thank the director and staff of the Border Patrol Museum in El Paso, Texas, for their long hours in helping us put together rare photos that are included in this work. Additional thanks go to Thom Phelps for his rendering of the Maginot and Siegfried Lines and to Christy Anzelmo for her reproduction of innumerable graphs and charts from UNODC and DOJ data in a quality adequate for printing.

Most importantly of all, we owe a huge thanks to our students. Your questions, and your answers to our questions, made this book possible. We hope that future students across the country learn much from your contributive efforts to this project.

There are a number of places in this text where we cite information from law enforcement professionals who currently work in the field — putting their lives on the line defending the borders of our country. Due to the nature of the material provided, we have consolidated their materials into generalizations and identified the authors as anonymous to protect their employment with various agencies. You took the biggest step in helping us with this effort and we owe you a great debt. Perhaps a day will come when we can publically acknowledge your assistance. Until then — you will have to settle for a beer when we occasionally meet.

Author Biographies

James Phelps is semi-retired professor teaching Homeland Security, Emergency Management, Cybersecurity and Cyber Conflict, Security Studies, GIS, WMD, Strategy and Critical Thinking for a number of online universities at the graduate (and sometimes undergraduate) level. He earned his B.A. in History from the University of Southern Colorado (2003), an M.A. in History from Sam Houston State University (2005), and remained there for his doctorate in Criminal Justice (2008). A retired U.S. Navy Senior Chief Machinist's Mate—submarines, he served the United States for over 21 years in the Navy Nuclear Power program, including 7 years holding both enlisted and commissioned status as a Limited Duty Officer. His military duty included serving on three nuclear powered submarines, two surface ships, and a SEAL Team. The undergraduate and graduate programs he developed in Homeland and Border Security for Angelo State have been recognized as some of the very best in the nation. He has developed Master's Degrees in Diplomacy and in Security Studies, and a Ph.D. in Security and Strategic Studies for a university in Dubai, where he taught in the 2016–2017 academic year. Among other books, his text, *What Happened to the Iraqi Police: Applying Lessons in Police Democratization Efforts in West Germany and Japan* (2010), also published by Carolina Academic Press, has proven to be prophetic in post-U.S. Iraq.

Jeff Dailey is an Associate Professor in the Department of Security Studies and Criminal Justice at Angelo State University. He teaches graduate courses in the Intelligence, Security Studies, and Analysis program. He also teaches in ASU's Homeland Security program. He has a background working in military intelligence, primarily SIGINT, with Army and Air Force intelligence groups, both CONUS and overseas. His Ph.D. is in Criminal Justice from Sam Houston State University in Huntsville, TX (2002). He earned his M.S. in Criminal Justice (1994) from Eastern Kentucky University. He also attended Florida Atlantic University where he earned his B.A.S. in Computer Systems and a B.S. in Physics. He has co-authored books on Texas Probation, Border Security, and the Sexual Abuse of Female Inmates and authored several book chapters.

Monica Koenigsberg is an Associate Professor of Criminal Justice in the Department of Security Studies and Criminal Justice (DSSCJ) at Angelo State University in San Angelo, Texas. Earning a B.S. in Administration of Justice from Wichita State University (1990), an M.C.J. (Criminal Justice) from the Graduate School of Public Affairs at the University of Colorado at Denver (1998), and a Ph.D. in Criminal Justice from Sam Houston State University (2008). She is a former commissioned police officer (Kansas) and a former prison officer (Colorado Peace Officer). Dr. Koenigsberg participated in the curriculum reorganization of the undergraduate Criminal Justice program at ASU and developed the graduate program in Criminal Justice which cross-lists elective courses with the Homeland Security master's program. Dr. Koenigsberg's dissertation, *Mediated Images of Crime and Justice: A Grounded Theory Methodology Examination of One Strand of Discourse* indicates her interest in both qualitative methodology and perceptions of crime and justice. Other interests include exploring the nexus of incarceration and society as well as media depictions relating to the criminal justice system, its denizens and workers.

Part One

Defining Borders

"The border is a line of barbwire and spiked pillars that seems only to serve as a symbol of one man's futile lifetime endeavors, his attempts to define Mother Nature's boundaries, as well as man's national claims to a piece of what no human can ever call his own possession. Men will always be willing to fight and die in follies of nationalism, but they will never be able to continually control their own borders."

—Lee Morgan (quoted in Vulliamy, E. (2010). *Amexica*, p. 108)

Arizona-Mexico Border Fence, Donna Burton/CBP.gov.

Chapter 1

Barriers, Boundaries, and Borders

Key Words and Concepts

Accretion

Barriers

Berlin Wall

Borders

Boundaries

Cession

Conquest

Dispute Resolution

Harmonized Tariff Schedule

USITC

Introduction

Border security is clearly a component of national security. While policy may vary with each administration, the overall importance of border integrity, no matter where a port of entry may be, is an imperative component of national policy. How effectively border integrity and security are provided directly affects all citizens, legal residents, and those who want to profit from violating internationally accepted rules on national

A medallion marks the spot where the U.S. and Mexican borders meet. Photo by James R. Tourtellotte/cbp.gov.

sovereignty. To understand what a border is, it is necessary to establish several basic definitions. We could easily say that a border is a line drawn on a map. Or a wall is a barrier and boundaries are restrictions placed on people to establish norms for a society to abide by. Unfortunately, such definitions are simplistic and fail to demonstrate the reality of what borders, boundaries, and barriers are. This chapter uses practical examples to help establish a common perspective of what borders are and how boundaries and barriers are used to reinforce the political demarcations we see as lines on maps. To do this it is necessary to provide a series of basic lessons in geography, cartography, oceanography, international law, and economics.

This book makes use of several learning styles to enhance the reader's grasp of the topics under discussion. You will see throughout the book breakout sections that reinforce the overall lessons of each chapter. You will also find history lessons to help explain how the issues of borders, boundaries, and barriers have helped to establish and shape the world we live in today. Border security is not simply a matter of building walls or stationing a large number of troops along a line drawn across a desert. Nor is it a simple matter of enforcing the large numbers of state, federal, and international laws and conventions that constantly change. Understanding the concept of border security requires a holistic view of the wide variety of issues that affect the human condition in all parts of the world.

We begin this exploration of border security with a story about how two diametrically opposed political ideologies converted their cooperation during wartime into a fifty-year political conflict that tore apart a continent, and in particular, the country of Germany.

East and West Germany

From 1940 to 1944 Nazi Germany and Italy occupied and controlled nearly the entire European mainland. To counter this occupation, the military forces of Great Britain, the United States, the free French, the free Polish, and the Union of Soviet Socialist Republics (aka the Soviet Union) among others, allied with each other to conduct a combined assault on German and Italian military forces from three different directions. These unlikely allies came from entirely different political ideologies — the Western countries being democracies or republics, while the Soviet Union was a socialist dictatorship. Across the duration of the Second World War the heads of the Allied powers met to determine the best approach to defeat Germany and Italy, and how to divide Germany and Italy after the war to preclude them ever again becoming a military threat to their neighbors.

At the end of the Second World War the Allied forces divided the occupation of Germany along pre-determined lines. The selection of these boundaries was made years before Germany was invaded and, in several instances, military forces from the United States and Britain had to vacate conquered territory so the Soviet army could take over per the prior agreements. Between the Soviet, US, and UK forces existed

Occupation of Germany, 1945. University of Texas.

formal boundaries that each occupier was supposed to maintain. However, that was not the reality driven by political necessity at the war's end.

The Soviet army began forcing hundreds of thousands of Germans out of Poland, Czechoslovakia, and the eastern portion of Germany. These ethnic Germans found their way into US- and UK-occupied territory. This continued for years. Often, the Soviets would assist the refugees in bypassing regulated crossing points. It was impossible to prevent this mass exodus from one occupied zone to another, no matter the number of troops deployed or the regulations implemented.

As political tensions between the former Allies rose, an "Iron Curtain" fell across Europe, resulting in the division of Germany into two occupied countries, West and East Germany. Even the capital city of Berlin was divided. As the people who had remained in the East began to realize the draconian domination being imposed by the Soviets, and the complete lack of freedom they were being subjected to, another exodus began. This time the Soviets attempted to prevent people from leaving, building a barrier across Berlin and eventually through the entire country. The goal of the Berlin Wall (and the fence between East and West Germany) was not to keep people out, but to keep people in. East Germany became a prison on the scale of a nation.

What were originally boundaries between occupation forces became barriers to human and commercial traffic, and ultimately morphed into a formal border between two politically and economically divergent countries. The fence between East and West Germany (and the wall between East and West Berlin) became physical barriers, protected with mine fields, wire fence that could only be cut with a torch, guard towers, lights, and armed forces with orders to shoot-to-kill people trying to leave, rather than potential invading forces. The Communist East German government, and its backers in the Soviet Union, felt that a barrier was necessary between themselves and their Western counterparts for a variety of reasons including the prevention of the departure of thousands upon thousands of Germans from under their totalitarian control to freedom in the West.

The barrier known as the Berlin Wall finally came down in November 1989. The effect of bringing the peoples of East and West together, along with the dissolution of the border and ultimate reunification of the two countries into a single Federal Republic of Germany (*Bundesrepublik Deutschland*) has not been without difficulties. There remains animosity and the perception of lower respect expressed toward those from the eastern portion of the country. Professional law enforcement officers who participated in the reunification process have reported, twenty years after the fact, that they see East Germany as lazy and uncivilized; essentially a *Mauer im Kopf* (Wall in the Head) still exists for about 10 percent of the country's population.[1]

After fifty years of isolation, the people found a way to exercise control over their own lives. As German President Christian Wulff stated during the 20th anniversary celebrations of the Wall's demise, "No wall can permanently withstand the desire for freedom.... The violence of the few does not withstand the quest for freedom of the many."[2]

The separation between East and West Germany was a political and economic barrier that has left remnants of "otherness" in some people's minds. A physical, political, and economic wall had separated people of the same ethnicity, language, and culture for nearly fifty years. Twenty years after that barrier came down there are still political, social, and cultural repercussions.

What happened to the boundaries between the military and political forces in post-World War II occupied Germany is just one of many examples where politically designated boundaries have shifted over time into barriers. Understanding that the border issues faced by any particular country today are neither new nor unique is fundamental to comprehending border security in the modern world. Therefore, this book is divided into major parts that address the development of standard definitions and backgrounds appropriate to our world. It then takes a focused look at a variety of issues, from security and crime to economics and the lack of electronic borders in the Internet. The book concludes with specific attention to the borders of the United Sates with Canada and Mexico. We begin in this chapter with general and specific definitions.

Geographic Barriers, Boundaries, and Borders

There are significant differences among barriers, boundaries, and borders. Each has separate and unique functions, while all are common components of the modern political and economic demarcations that separate countries, states, and counties. Natural barriers and boundaries make some of the best borders because of the inherent difficulties in crossing them. Geography provides the best examples of natural barriers and therefore natural borders.

Barrier: a material object that blocks or is intended to block passage. A natural formation or structure that prevents or hinders movement or action. Can also be manufactured structures intended to prevent passage such as solid walls, electric fences, and minefields.

Boundary: anything that indicates or fixes a limit or extent. Can be political, economic, legal, physical, or mental.

Border: an outer part or edge, perimeter, periphery, or rim. Commonly used to delineate national and political boundaries.

Geography has long been a barrier to movement and in much of the world it still is. Take, for instance, the Himalaya mountain system. Running west to east, these 1,500 miles (2,500 km) of long rock wall vary in width from 250 miles (400 km) in the west to 93 miles (150 km) in the east. Originating when the Indian tectonic plate (moving northwest) impacted the Eurasian continent about 40 to 50 million years ago, the Himalayan system acts as a physical barrier separating China from Pakistan, India, Nepal, and Bhutan among others. The mountains are so massive that they create their own weather systems and the rivers that originate in the Himalaya drainage basin provide water to half the world's population across eighteen countries.

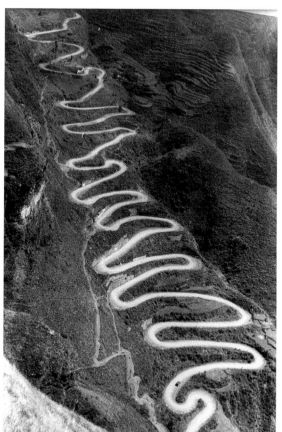

Ledo & Burma Roads, Assam, Burma, China in 1944–45. Department of Defense, Department of the Army.

Long considered impenetrable, the Himalayas have frequently been transited for economic and military purposes. One branch of the Silk Road transits the Hindu Kush between China and Pakistan and then proceeds into India along what is known as the Karakoram Highway. As early as the first century CE, India was receiving silk along this road in exchange for sandalwood and spices. This road is still open and used as a means of commerce between India, Pakistan, Afghanistan, and western China. Yet it does not directly cross the Himalayan range, instead weaving around the western side, across several very high plateaus and passes, and through river valleys. It is not now and has never been a route available for the mass movement of commodities or people.

As recently as the Second World War, the Himalayas were

Map of the Caucasus region. Source: CIA.

crossed for military purposes. The Chinese built the 717-mile (1,154 km) "Burma Road" across the eastern edge of the Himalayan range to ship British supplies into China in an effort to stop and then push back the Japanese invaders. Under diplomatic pressure from the Japanese, the British shut down the Burma Road in 1940, cutting off supplies to the Chinese military.

After Japan declared war on Britain in December 1941, they overran Burma in 1942, forcing the British back into India and cutting off all military supplies to the Chinese. This led the United States to pressure the British to reopen a supply route to China, leading to the construction of the Ledo Road connecting to the old Burma Road in Wandingzhen, Yunnan, China. This route reopened the supply line to the Chinese military with the first trucks reaching China on January 28, 1945.[3] It is no longer in use and has since become ruins due to time, neglect, and weather.

Today there are nearly no land crossings over the Himalayas and few air routes that cross them. Until the very recent past, the high mountains of the Himalayas also protected countries such as Nepal and Tibet from outside influence or invasion. Clearly, large mountain ranges make effective barriers, boundaries, and borders between peoples, philosophies, and economies.

Many other mountain ranges have acted as natural barriers, boundaries, and borders. The Pyrenees Mountains are a natural barrier between France and Spain and have long established the Iberian Peninsula as a separate political and economic entity. The Alps protect Switzerland from encroachment. The Carpathian Mountains have, until recently, served as a barrier to invasion into traditionally Slavic lands by northern Europeans and Asians.

The Caucasus Mountains provide a natural barrier between Russia and the nations of Georgia and Azerbaijan, and have long been a source of acrimonious dispute between the nations and peoples who inhabit the region. Formed by the collision of the northward-moving Arabian tectonic plate and the Asian landmass, these mountains are a natural barrier and therefore a natural border running from the Black Sea to the Caspian Sea. Within the country of Azerbaijan is the community of Khinalug, the oldest continuously inhabited village in the world with a history stretching back over five thousand years. The high altitude and remoteness of Khinalug have protected it during the innumerable wars across the region over the past three thousand years.[4]

The Andes are the world's longest continuous mountain range, running 4,300 miles (7,000 km) north to south along the west coast of South America. Unlike the Himalayas, the Andes are volcanic in origin; they were formed by the subduction of the Antarctic plate and Nazca Plate under the South American Plate. This has resulted in the deposition of large amounts of valuable mineral ores, including gold, silver, and copper, along the length of the range. These nearly impenetrable mountains form a natural physical barrier, and therefore a natural border between the Pacific and Atlantic countries of South America. Chile, Peru, Ecuador, and Colombia all lie along the western slopes while Argentina, Bolivia, Brazil, and Venezuela lie along the eastern slopes. The Amazon River, the second largest in the world, has its origins in the Andes.

Other natural geographical barriers include oceans, rivers, and straits. The United States of America has long considered itself immune from attack by other nations because of the North Atlantic and Pacific Oceans. This has generally been true since the end of the War of 1812 with Britain. Only rarely have the vast expanses of these two large oceans been crossed by military forces and terrorists. The South Atlantic and Pacific Oceans equally protect the countries of South America from invading armies. Other than when the British colonized Australia and New Zealand, these two island nations have never been invaded. Until about five hundred years ago, the large oceans were natural barriers to the movement of humans and commercial goods. However, with the opening of the invasion and trade routes by Christopher Columbus between Europe and the Americas in 1492 CE, mankind has made tremendous advances in transoceanic travel.

Depending upon their size, rivers and other bodies of water also make excellent boundaries, barriers, and borders. The Rhine River originates in the Swiss Alps and flows north, bisecting Europe. This major river has long been a barrier to east and west movement. This 766-mile (1,233 km) river was the boundary of the Roman Empire and served as a natural barrier for Rome to invasion by the Germanic peoples. Nineteen centuries later, the river would prove to be a major obstacle to invasion of Germany by Allied forces during the First and Second World Wars.

The Rio Grande River (known in Mexico as the Rio Bravo del Norte) has long been a natural barrier, boundary, and border between Texas and Mexico. It is also one of the most important natural barriers in North America, establishing more than half of the international border between the United States and Mexico. As the major water supply for numerous cities and thousands of square miles of agricultural land, less than one-fifth of the river's water actually reaches the Gulf of Mexico. In some areas water levels have been reduced so low that the river is nearly dry and can be easily crossed on foot or by vehicle.

The Rio Grande River

The Rio Grande rises in Rio Grande National Forest, San Juan County, Colorado (at 37° 47′ N, 107° 32′ W), as a clear, spring- and snow-fed mountain stream twelve thousand feet above sea level. Its origin is at the Continental Divide in the San Juan Mountains. The river cuts through the middle of New Mexico to the site of El Paso and Ciudad Juárez, at the junction of the states of Chihuahua and Texas. At that point, because of the Treaty of Guadalupe Hidalgo (1848), which terminated the Mexican War, the Rio Grande becomes the boundary between the United States and Mexico. It forms the western or southern border of the Texas counties of El Paso, Hudspeth, Presidio, Brewster (where the river's sweeping curve gives Big Bend National Park its name), Terrell, Val Verde, Kinney, Maverick, Webb, Zapata, Starr, Hidalgo, and Cameron. The river empties into the Gulf of Mexico (at 25° 57′ N, 97° 09′ W).

Depending on how it is measured, the Rio Grande is the twenty-second longest river in the world and the fourth or fifth longest in North America. It drains more than forty thousand square miles in Texas alone. In the late 1980s the population along its banks exceeded five million. The river flows for 175 miles in Colorado and 470 miles in New Mexico. Though the length from its headwaters in Colorado to the Gulf of Mexico varies as its course changes, in the late 1980s, according to the International Boundary and Water Commission, its total length was 1,896 miles. The official border measurement ranges from 889 to 1,248 miles, depending on how the river is measured. In a sense, the Rio Grande is two streams. It dwindles to nearly nothing at Presidio, and only water from the Río Conchos, coming out of Mexico, sustains its journey to the Gulf. Its principal tributaries are the Pecos, Devils, Chama, and Puerco rivers in the United States, and the Conchos, Salado, and San Juan in Mexico. Major cities and towns alongside the river are Santa Fe, Albuquerque, Socorro, Truth or Consequences, Mesilla, and Las Cruces in New Mexico, and El Paso, Presidio, Del Rio, Eagle Pass, Laredo, Rio Grande City, McAllen, and Brownsville in Texas. In Mexico the primary towns and cities are Ciudad Juárez, Ojinaga, Ciudad Acuña, Piedras Negras, Nuevo Laredo, Camargo, Reynosa, and Matamoros. Mexican states bordered by the Rio Grande are Chihuahua, Coahuila, Nuevo León, and Tamaulipas. In 1980 Ciudad Juárez was the largest city on the Rio Grande as well as on the international boundary, and El Paso, Texas, was the second largest city on the border. The two cities would constitute one of the world's major metropolitan areas if the Rio Grande did not divide them. — The Handbook of Texas, Texas Historical Association[5]

Other natural bodies of water also provide barriers, boundaries, and borders. In North America, the Great Lakes and St. Lawrence River comprise a large portion of the border between the United States and Canada. Straits narrow both ends of the Mediterranean Sea, at Gibraltar in the west, between Spain (Europe) and Morocco (Africa), and the Bosporus and the Dardanelles in the east, separating Europe and Asia. These straits act as barriers between continents and natural choke points by which commerce can be restricted in time of war.

The 99-mile (169 km) wide Taiwan Strait separates the Republic of China (Taiwan) from the People's Republic of China (mainland China). This narrow body of water is all that has kept the Communist government of China from invading and forcibly bringing democratic Taiwan back under the control of what the United Nations recognizes as the proper government of the Chinese people.

One of the most famous bodies of water to act as both barrier and border is the English Channel. While it is the smallest of the shallow seas that surround Europe, this 350-mile (560 km) long body of water has acted throughout history as both barrier and challenge to all manner of peoples. It varies from 150 miles (240 km) wide in the

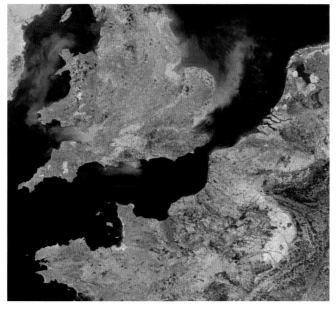

The English Channel, NASA, 2003.

west to a mere 21 miles (34 km) wide at the Strait of Dover. The English Channel is a fickle barrier when it comes to invading forces. It was not a major obstacle to the Roman, Norman, Saxon, and Dutch invasions of Britain, yet prevented the Spanish Armada, Napoleon, and Nazi Germany from doing the same. It has not proved an obstacle to the British invading the European mainland on many occasions.

This natural water barrier has also proved a challenge to human ingenuity of all types. An American and a Frenchman in a hot air balloon completed the first crossing of the Channel by air on January 7, 1785, between Dover and Calais.[6] Matthew Webb, the first person known to swim the Channel, did so along the same 21-mile gap in 21 hours and 45 minutes on August 25, 1875.[7]

The third type of natural geographical barriers that make for excellent boundaries and borders are deserts. About one-fifth of the world's surface is considered desert. The Sahara literally divides the African continent. Below this massive desert is equatorial (or sub-Saharan) Africa and above it is North (or Mediterranean) Africa. Not all deserts are hot and dry like the Sahara. There are also semiarid, coastal, and cold deserts. The Nearctic areas of North America, including large parts of Utah, Montana, Nevada, Arizona, and Texas; Greenland; Russia; and north Asia are all semiarid deserts. A cold desert would include the continent of Antarctica and the upper reaches of Greenland. The best example of a coastal desert is the Atacama of Chile, the driest place on Earth.[8]

What makes deserts natural barriers and good boundaries between nations is the amount of resources and specialized animals or transport equipment it takes to cross them. Deserts are naturally dry, averaging less than 10 inches (25 cm) of rainfall per year,[9] and there are few animals, humans included, who can survive long without access to water. Therefore, those who control the limited water sources in a desert region control the entire area. This is the reason that watering holes (called an oasis in the Sahara and Middle East) are so jealously guarded by the tribes who maintain and utilize them.

Creosote bush, USGS, n.d.

Deserts are not simply dry. They also suffer from temperature extremes detrimental to human life. Hot deserts, like the Sahara and those in the US Southwest, can reach temperatures of 113°F (45°C) in the daytime, have daily temperature spans in excess of 25°F (14°C), and frequently drop below freezing at night during winter months, particularly in high mountain deserts. This poses the need for a person crossing a desert region to take precautions against not only dehydration, but also heatstroke and heat exhaustion, while simultaneously carrying enough protection to keep from suffering hypothermia at night. These temperature extremes and natural dryness result in a unique mix of flora and fauna.

In North America, the desert regions acting as important barriers, boundaries, or borders are essentially found across the entire Southwest of the United States and northwest expanse of Mexico. Across this region are found several major deserts stretching from Laredo, Texas, to San Diego, California, including the Sonoran and Chihuahuan. One of the primary plants that identify North American desert regions is the shrub *Larrea Tridentata* (*Larrea Divaricata*), also known as the creosote bush. Ecologists and cartographers work together to establish the natural boundaries of different geographical features, such as deserts, by mapping the range of particular desert plants and then overlay that data on traditional political maps. This produces a unique perspective of the expanse a

Desert landscape with saguaro cacti (Carnegiea gigantea) near Tucson, Arizona. BLM, n.d.

desert covers. When the cartographer (mapmaker) adds in political boundaries, such as state and international borders, it becomes clear that it takes a tremendous effort to attempt to cross the United States–Mexico border on foot.

Natural geography can make an excellent barrier, boundary, or border between human populations. This is not without problems. Rivers change their paths. Movement of tectonic plates result in changes to mapped locations. Deserts expand and contract with changes in climate. And humans are ingenious creators of methods to turn disadvantage into advantage when it comes to their natural environment. Most of the world's major cities could not exist were it not for human inventions such as the high-rise apartment complex, mass transportation systems, and exploitation of natural resources for essentials such as heat, clothing, and cooking. This has led our species to derive other means than natural barriers as boundaries between what we consider ours and what others consider theirs. In many cases, it is the natural resources provided by the barrier itself that drive us to expand boundaries and limit access to other peoples. Into these discussions come the diplomat, politician, and lawyer.

Political Boundaries, Barriers, and Borders

We cannot simply establish any rules we want, erect any boundaries or barriers, or invoke any method that comes to mind when we address the issue of border security. Society and the social order simply don't work that way. Social systems are organized around a concept referred to as the "social contract." This concept is as old as philosophy itself, yet the greatest exposé on the subject comes from Jean Jacques Rousseau in his 1762 work *The Social Contract*. The very idea that a "people" have come to an agreement to abide by certain rules and conventions implies that at some point those "people" came together and determined amongst themselves that such a social order was to their mutual benefit. As such, all power of government stems from the people themselves. This is a core component of the constitutional republic of the United States.

National borders are established in a variety of ways. Countries begin with the people sensing commonality amongst themselves and uniqueness from others. Frequently, that commonality stems from a combination of language and ethnicity. Sometimes religion will play a part. This becomes the core component of the political entity that grows and establishes relationships with neighboring groups. Over time, fixed, identifiable limits are placed on which group controls a given area politically. This can evolve from simple understanding by the groups of the limits of their dominance or be forcibly established through military force. Formal arrangements are usually concluded by treaty, a formal agreement between two or more states in reference to peace, alliance, commerce, or other international relations, usually formalized through some sort of signed document.

Understanding how national borders are derived requires understanding the origin and evolution of the modern law of nations. The history of the modern law of nations begins with the emergence of independent nation-states from the ruins of the medieval Holy Roman Empire, which was based on the claims to universal authority of the Pope as the spiritual, and the Emperor as the temporal, head of the Christian nations of Europe. The idea of a central universal authority precluded the need for rules addressing diplomatic intercourse between sovereign states, principles of territorial sovereignty, jurisdiction, treaty-making, state responsibility, and other aspects of modern interstate relations.

Similar conceptions of secular and spiritual empire are found in Chinese, Japanese, Thai, African, and Islamic empires. Modern Islamic fundamentalist terrorism derives its origins from an era of Muslim conquest of neighboring peoples and the division of the world into two entities, those countries under Moslem rule (*dar al Islam*) and the rest of the world (*dar al Harb*). As each of these universalist ideologies and approaches to international relations encountered their neighbors and each other, and their ascendancy was challenged, the need arose to deal with each other on a basis of equality and mutual respect for sovereignty.

Returning to Europe as the example, the dissolution of the Holy Roman Empire into separate, frequently rebellious states, coupled with the Reformation, made it necessary for the newly emerging independent states to develop a system of rules that could govern their mutual relations. For the sources of these legal relations, they drew predominantly upon Roman law and canon law. The professional clerks who ran the governments of the emerging states and city republics relied heavily upon Justinian's *Corpus Juris* as their source for development of their legal codes. England and the Scandinavian countries remained outside of this orientation toward Roman law, forming their own legal systems based on their histories and cultures. To this day the ancient Roman law has strongly influenced international legal rules, for example those governing acquisition of territorial title.

It was during the post-Holy Roman Empire era in Europe that two different forms of law developed: civil law on the mainland and common law in England. A second contributor to the development of the modern law of nations was a move toward increased international trade. The international law merchant collected and collated various standards from international trade transactions, leading to compilations of maritime law that gained international acceptance. It was the intensification of international trade, the improvements in navigation and military techniques, and the discovery of many distant lands by the Europeans that stimulated further development of international practices and the emergence of modern conceptions of a law of nations. The Hanseatic League in northern Europe, comprising more than 150 trading cities and centers, established a network of commercial and diplomatic relations to regulate standards and customs. City-republics in Italy, such as Venice, Genoa, and Florence, developed the practice of sending ambassadors to other city-states, resulting in the establishment of the concept of diplomatic relations. This was all driven by the increase in trade and the need to establish commercial treaties. Coupled with the discovery and subjugation of distant lands and peoples by European conquerors, the rise in conflicting claims to territory and the rights of passage on the seas stimulated the development of new practices and principles. The rise and evolution of the modern nation-state, from the late eighteenth century to the early twentieth century, corresponds with the absolute claims to legal and political supremacy, and the ascendance of effective international law, which has essentially been derived from the will of nations.

Modern international law and the codification of the territorial integrity and existing political independence of nation-states is not yet even one hundred years old. The idea was long in development but not codified until the creation of the League of Nations following the end of the First World War. The League not only condemned external aggression against other nations, but also imposed on aggressors economic and military sanctions by the international community. Concurrent with the establishment of the League was the first International Labor Organization, which addressed improvement in working conditions and social welfare on a worldwide scale. This era was also the time frame when the Permanent Court of International Justice came into being as a major attempt to substitute permanent and organic methods of peaceful and legal settlement of disputes in place of imposition of force to solve international disagreements.

These efforts at peaceful resolution of international disputes, and standardization of regulation of working conditions, collapsed with the onset of the Second World War. The establishment of the United Nations at the end of World War II brought the modern era of international relations, from which we derive the current system of the law of nations. The world no longer operates from the perspective of mutual respect and abstention in the internal affairs of other nations, instead moving to the UN model of organized cooperation. This effectuated the creation of financial organizations such as the International Monetary Fund, organizations that deal with distribution of food and other resources to peoples in need, universal standards of health and welfare, cooperation in means and manner of international communications and transport, and even the sharing of outer space and the ocean bed. Modern in-

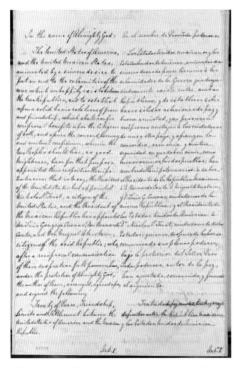

The first and last pages of the Treaty of Guadalupe-Hidalgo establishing the border between the United States and Mexico. The formerly Mexican lands north of the border were ceded to the United States following the U.S.-Mexican War (1846–48), Library of Congress.

ternational law is no longer predominantly a system of interstate diplomatic norms but now spans all economic and social aspects of the lives of nations.

This understanding of the origin and evolution of the law of nations necessitates the establishment of the identity of states. A state is a "legal personality" or an "international legal person" in proper terms.[10] The *Convention on Rights and Duties of States* (1933) defines in Article 1, "The state as a person of international law should possess the following qualifications: (a) a permanent population; (b) a defined territory; (c) government; and (d) capacity to enter into relations with the other states." Article 2 reads, "The federal state shall constitute a sole person in the eyes of international law." The United States is a signatory to this treaty and has further defined a state as "an entity that has a defined territory and population under the control of a government and that engages in foreign relations."[11]

Two different theories explain when a state becomes a state. One says that it is recognition of the "state" by other, already established, and recognized states that decides whether an entity is a state. The other theory looks to the establishment of facts that meet the criteria of statehood as laid down in recognized international law. Therefore, a state may exist without being recognized by other states. The primary function of international recognition is to declare that one country acknowledges the other state's political existence and as such is willing to treat that entity as an international person, with the rights and obligations of states.

Collectively, the governmental powers of a state are referred to as its sovereign powers. The fullest measure of sovereign powers is exercised by a state over its land territory. This leads to the institution and recognition of borders between nations. Sovereign powers are also extended to the airspace above the country, and the adjacent territorial waters.

There are many ways in which states can acquire more territory. They include:

Accretion. This is the expansion of a state's territory by operation of nature, for example the gradual shifting of the course of a river, volcanism resulting in creation of new landmass, and rivers laying down silt in their drainage basins.

Cession. This involves the transfer of sovereignty by means of an agreement between the ceding and the acquiring state(s). It is a derivative mode of acquisition. The consent of the population of the ceded territory is not essential to the validity of the cession. Recently this process is seen occurring because of the will of the people through a plebiscite, such as the creation of Timor-Leste in South East Asia and the Republic of South Sudan in Africa.

Conquest. This occurs when one country acquires the territory of another through the complete and final subjugation through military force and a declaration of the conquering state's intention to annex it. This is rare, as a treaty of cession generally carries out most annexation of territory after a war.

Borders between countries frequently span land, rivers, and lakes. In the Restatement, Second, Foreign Relations Law of the United States (1965), these boundaries were defined in subsection 12: "(1) The boundary separating the land areas of two states is determined by acts of the states expressing their consent to its location. (2) Unless consent to a different rule has been expressed, (a) when the boundary between two states is a navigable river, its location is the middle of the channel of navigation; (b) when the boundary between two states is a non-navigable river or a lake, its location is the middle of the river or lake." Boundaries on oceans fall under a separate rule of law, the Law of the Sea.

The Law of the Sea

"A law of the sea is as old as nations, and the modern law of the sea is virtually as old as modern international law. For three hundred years it was probably the most stable and least-controversial branch of international law. It was essentially reaffirmed and codified as recently ... as 1958. By 1970 it was in disarray."

— Henkin (1979)[12]

The United Nations Conference on the Law of the Sea in 1958 adopted four conventions: (1) on the Territorial Sea and the Contiguous Zone, (2) on the High Seas, (3) on the Continental Shelf, and (4) on Fishing and Conservation of the Living Resources of the High Seas. These documents, however, gave rise to significant disputes between countries, particularly as concerned the natural resources on the sea floor beyond a nation's contiguous zone. In 1977 a Third Conference on the Law of the Sea was convened and in 1982 produced a new treaty with a variety of additional provisions.

As of 20 September 2011, the current convention consists of three specific components to which countries agree by signature and/or ratification: (1) United Nations Convention on the Law of the Sea, (2) the Agreement relating to the implementation of Part XI of the Convention and (3) the Agreement for the implementation of the provisions of the Convention relating to the conservation and management of straddling fish stocks and highly migratory fish stocks. Of the UN member nations, 169 have ratified Part 1, 141 Part 2, and 78 Part 3. Most notably, the United States has not agreed to the convention in whole and only agreed by signature in 1994 to the implementation of Part XI of the Convention, but the Senate never ratified the treaty. Concerning Part III of the Convention, the United States signed the treaty in 1995 and the Senate ratified the agreement in 1996. Part XI of the Convention deals with access to and control of resources in the "Area," meaning "the seabed and ocean floor and subsoil thereof, beyond the limits of national jurisdiction."[13] Part I establishes the law of international boundaries and rights of passage for all nations in all waters, something the United States, as the preeminent naval power in the world, would rather not have to abide by.

Essentially, the United Nations Convention on the Law of the Sea establishes the territorial waters of a country as extending twelve miles from the low-tide water line of the country's landmass, including any islands. The contiguous zone is limited to twenty-four nautical miles from the low-tide water line (essentially doubling a country's territorial waters) and a state: 1. In a zone contiguous to its territorial sea, described as the Contiguous Zone, the coastal State may, according to Article 33, "exercise the control necessary to: (a) prevent infringement of its customs, fiscal, immigration or sanitary laws and regulations within its territory or territorial sea; (b) punish infringement of the above laws and regulations committed within its territory or territorial sea."[14]

The Convention also identifies the exclusive economic zone of a country as extending two hundred nautical miles from the low-tide water line. The purpose of exclusive economic zones as defined in Article 56 is to reserve to the state the "sovereign rights for the purpose of exploring and exploiting, conserving and managing the natural resources, whether living or non-living, of the waters superjacent to the seabed and of the seabed and its subsoil and with regard to other activities for the economic exploitation and exploration of the zone, such as the production of energy from the water, currents and winds."[15]

Waters that are not parts of exclusive economic zones, the territorial sea, or the internal waters of a State, or in the archipelagic waters of an archipelagic State are considered the high seas. For hundreds of years international law saw the high seas as belonging to everyone or to no one. Under the UN Convention, Article 87, the high seas "shall be reserved for peaceful purposes." The historic perception of freedom of the seas is codified in Article 87 as:

> 1. The high seas are open to all States, whether coastal or land-locked. Freedom of the high seas is exercised under the conditions laid down by this Convention and by other rules of international law. It comprises, inter alia, both for coastal and land-locked States:

(a) freedom of navigation;

(b) freedom of overflight;

(c) freedom to lay submarine cables and pipelines, subject to Part VI;

(d) freedom to construct artificial islands and other installations permitted under international law, subject to Part VI;

(e) freedom of fishing, subject to the conditions laid down in section 2;

(f) freedom of scientific research, subject to Parts VI and XIII.

2. These freedoms shall be exercised by all States with due regard for the interests of other States in their exercise of the freedom of the high seas, and also with due regard for the rights under this Convention with respect to activities in the Area.[16]

Clearly, the laws governing borders, limits to economic activities, and transit of the oceans are extensive and detailed. The reader wishing more information about maritime and border law should refer to texts on international law.

Economic Boundaries, Borders, and Barriers

Territorial boundaries have long acted as economic boundaries. The sovereignty of a state implies the right to regulate commerce through taxation, tariffs, and prohibitions. This is one of the fundamental core considerations of being an independent nation. As the world becomes more globalized, the barriers to trade are constantly being modified, or eliminated. This also changes the fundamental nature of the control that countries exercise over their economic systems.

One of the key components of the US Constitution is the "Commerce Clause" in Article I, section 8: "The Congress shall have the power.... To regulate commerce with foreign nations, and among the several States, and with the Indian tribes." Congress exercises this power through passage of laws and imposition of taxes, duties, imposts, and excises. To better address the growing international trade experienced in the early twentieth century, the Congress established the US Tariff Commission in 1916. The Trade Act of 1974 changed the name of the organization to the US International Trade Commission (USITC).

The USITC is an independent, nonpartisan, quasi-judicial federal agency with broad investigative powers on matters of trade. The Commission is a national resource where trade data are gathered and analyzed. The data are provided to the President and Congress as part of the information on which US trade policy is based.

USITC activities include:

- Determining whether US industries are materially injured because of imports that benefit from pricing at less than fair value or from subsidization;
- Directing actions, subject to Presidential disapproval, against unfair practices in import trade, such as patent, trademark, or copyright infringement;
- Making recommendations to the President regarding relief for industries seriously injured by increasing imports;

- Advising the President whether agricultural imports interfere with price-support programs of the US Department of Agriculture;
- Conducting studies on trade and tariff issues and monitoring import levels; and
- Participating in the development of uniform statistical data on imports, exports, and domestic production and in the establishment of an international harmonized commodity code.

The USITC performs several functions. It carries out investigations in countervailing duty and antidumping, which involve either subsidies provided to foreign companies through government programs or the selling of foreign products in the United States at less than fair value, in concert with the US Department of Commerce. The Commerce Department determines whether the alleged subsidies or dumping are occurring and, if so, at what levels (called the subsidy or dumping "margin"). The USITC determines whether the US industry is materially injured because of the dumped or subsidized imports. If the Commerce Department's final subsidy or dumping determination and the Commission's final injury determination are both affirmative, the Commerce Department issues an order to the US Customs Service to impose duties.

The USITC also assesses whether US industries are being seriously injured by fairly traded imports and can recommend to the President that relief be provided to those industries to facilitate positive adjustment to import competition. Relief could take the form of increased tariffs or quotas on imports and/or adjustment assistance for the domestic industry. The USITC makes determinations in investigations involving unfair practices in import trade, mainly involving allegations of infringement on US patents and trademarks by imported goods. If it finds a violation of the law, the USITC may order the exclusion of the imported product from the United States. The Commission is neither a policymaking body nor a court of law. It does not negotiate trade agreements.

Through its research program, the USITC conducts objective studies on many international trade matters. The President, the Senate Committee on Finance, or the House Committee on Ways and Means generally requests these. The USITC has an extensive library of international trade resources called the National Library of International Trade, which is open to the public during agency hours.

The USITC is responsible for continually reviewing the Harmonized Tariff Schedule (HTS) of the United States, a list of all the specific items that are imported into and exported from the United States and for recommending modifications to the HTS that it considers necessary or appropriate. The HTS includes all provisions enacted by Congress or proclaimed by the President in a 99-chapter, 3,214-page document (as of 2012). An example of the restrictions on trade with other countries can be found in Chapter 2, which deals with the subject of Meat and Edible Meat Offal. In addition to limiting tonnage, tariffs are placed on specific products based on weight, type of product, preparation, and country of origin.

A notable item in Table 1.1 is that Canada and Mexico have no limits on the quantity of meat they can export to the United States. This came about because of the North American Free Trade Agreement (NAFTA), a treaty between the three

Table 1.1 Meat Export Limitations

Country	Quantity (metric ton)
Canada	No limit
Mexico	No limit
Australia	378,214
New Zealand	213,402
Japan	200
Argentina	20,000
Uruguay	20,000
Other countries or areas	64,805

Consolidated from HTS 2017, Section 1, Chapter 2.

countries that went into effect January 1, 1994. Because of NAFTA, all nontariff barriers to agricultural trade between the United States and Mexico were eliminated, some immediately and others over a five- to fifteen-year period. A previous free trade agreement between the United States and Canada was incorporated into NAFTA.

While there are many benefits to removing trade barriers between countries, there are also significant problems. Low standards of living in one country result in lower wages for workers, putting companies in a position where the relocation of a factory from countries with higher standards of living and, therefore, higher wages, becomes more profitable in the lower-wage country. This "increasing the bottom line" improves the financial reports of companies, at the cost of lost employment in the original country. This is not a one-way street when trade barriers are lifted.

Agribusiness in the United States is extremely efficient in producing food, resulting in low food prices. This is exported to countries like Mexico where traditional food production methods can be costly and labor intensive. The result is increased exports for US agribusiness and a loss of agricultural jobs in an inherently poor country. This is not all bad, as the longer growing season in Mexico allows for US and Canadian consumers to have continual access to previously seasonally limited fruits and vegetables. The evolution and implementation of NAFTA will be expanded upon in later chapters.

More recently free trade agreements and identification of a country with "most favored nation" trading status has been used to reward countries for taking actions requested by another nation, or for agreeing to provide better access to export markets. Many of the past economic and communication barriers between states are being eroded in this manner. That erosion causes change, which may be beneficial to a nation but always impacts some individuals negatively.

Economic barriers between countries can be used to protect native businesses. The move toward free trade, the protection of a country's industrial and employment base can erode, while other industries grow to provide for different demands in the recipient countries. Globalization of trade is rapidly breaking down economic barriers among countries worldwide. The result is that borders have begun to change in function and purpose.

Ultimate in Borderless Regions

International conventions and treaties also provide for the exploration and use of territory for the benefit of all. The Antarctic Treaty of 1959 provides that Antarctica "shall be used for peaceful purposes only" (Article 1) and, to that end, the treaty prohibits military installations, maneuvers, and weapons tests. This includes the testing of nuclear devices and explosions of all kinds. Provisions of the treaty also provide for the free exchange of scientific information and personnel, however there are no general provisions addressing jurisdiction over persons in Antarctica.

Another area where there is agreement on free access and use is Space. There is even a treaty addressing access to space and celestial bodies, restricting any country from claiming territorial jurisdiction over any area or celestial body.

Treaty on Principles Governing the Activities of States in the Exploration and Use of Outer Space, Including the Moon and Other Celestial Bodies

Done at London, Moscow, and Washington, January 27, 1967,
18 U.S.T. 2410, T.I.A.S. 6347, 610 U.N.T.S. 205

Article 1. The exploration and use of outer space, including the moon and other celestial bodies, shall be carried out for the benefit and in the interests of all countries, irrespective of their degree of economic or scientific development, and shall be the province of all mankind.

Outer space, including the moon and other celestial bodies, shall be free for exploration and use by all States without discrimination of any kind, on a basis of equality and in accordance with international law, and there shall be free access to all areas of celestial bodies.

There shall be freedom of scientific investigation in outer space, including the moon and other celestial bodies, and States shall facilitate and encourage international co-operation in such investigation.

Article 2. Outer space, including the moon and other celestial bodies, is not subject to national appropriation by claim of sovereignty, by means or use of occupation, or by any other means.

Astronaut Edwin E. "Buzz" Aldrin, lunar module pilot, walks on the surface of the moon near the leg of the Lunar Module "Eagle" during the Apollo 11 extravehicular activity. Astronaut Neil A. Armstrong, commander, took this photograph. It is the only photo of both astronauts in the same image during the first moon landing. You can see Armstrong's reflection in Aldrin's facemask. NASA, July 1969.

Resolving Boundary and Border Disputes

There are numerous avenues available to states that have experienced boundary or border violations. The method of remedy is dependent upon the treaties the state is party to, the nature of the violation, and the severity with which the encroachment is seen.

The United States went to war with Mexico in 1846 over a variety of issues, including disputes over where the border was between Mexico and the recently acquired State of Texas. Another reason for the war was to acquire the lands between the Louisiana Purchase and the Pacific Coast. Mexico was soundly defeated during the two-year war and thus was forced to enter into negotiations with representatives of the United States. The result was the Treaty of Guadalupe-Hidalgo in 1848 in which Mexico ceded California, Nevada, Utah, Arizona, most of New Mexico and Colorado, and formerly claimed lands north of the Rio Grande River.

Industrialists in the United States later identified a section of Mexican land necessary for the construction of a southern trans-continental railroad from the Mississippi to

California. The ambassador to Mexico entered negotiations to purchase this 29,670-square-mile region for the United States. The result was a treaty now known as the Gadsden Purchase (after James Gadsden, then the ambassador to Mexico) or *Venta de La Mesilla* in Mexico. The Senate and Mexico ratified the treaty, with minor changes, in 1854. The Gadsden Purchase resulted in the border between the United States and Mexico being firmly established and remaining so today.

Other disputes may go to national or international courts for resolution. As an example, the International Tribunal for the Law of the Sea resolves disputes over access to mineral resources on the seabed in regions not reserved to any state or territory. Disputes over the delimitation of boundaries along continental shelf between States with opposite or adjacent coasts are resolved first in the International Court of Justice (provided the states in dispute recognize the Court's authority), or through negotiation, or through application to the UN for an arbitral or special tribunal to determine an equitable outcome.

The statements above imply that the dispute will be solved peacefully. This is not always the case. Historically, countries have come to blows over border and boundary disputes. It is only the recent past that has seen a move to negotiation and arbitration to resolve such disputes. There are many instances, even recently, where one country has invaded another to put a stop to border violations.

Responding to the continuous launching of rockets from inside Lebanon at Israeli border towns, Israel invaded Lebanon on July 12, 2006, and remained in the country for 34 days. The militant group Hezbollah fired the rockets at Israeli towns as a diversion to a planned attack on a border patrol of Israeli Defense Forces on the Israel side of the border. Responding,

Falklands Campaign (distances to bases), 1982, Department of History, United States Military Academy.

Israel attacked militant compounds in southern Lebanon and launched a naval blockade of the country. The United Nations brokered a ceasefire between the belligerents that went into effect the morning of August 14, 2006. However, Israel would not lift the naval blockade of Lebanon for another three weeks. The conflict over this military violation of an established border resulted in the deaths of more than twelve hundred people, mostly Lebanese civilians; severely damaged Lebanese civil infrastructure that included the Beirut airport; and displaced more than a million people. Israeli forces remained in Lebanon until early October, when Lebanese Army forces began moving into the occupied zone. As of this writing, no effort has been made by either Lebanon or the United Nations to disarm the Hezbollah militant forces in southern Lebanon.

Another recent dispute that ended in a military conflict over who possessed a territory is the Falklands War of 1982. The conflict was the result of a protracted historical confrontation regarding the sovereignty of the Islands. The long-standing dispute resulted in the Argentine invasion and occupation of the Islands on April 2, 1982. The British government dispatched a naval task force to engage the Argentine Navy and Air Force and retake the Islands by amphibious assault.

On the evening of April 3, 1982, Britain's UN Ambassador Sir Anthony Parsons put a draft resolution to the UN Security Council. The next day, the council adopted Resolution 502 condemning the hostilities and demanding immediate Argentine withdrawal from the Islands, with ten votes in support, one against, and four abstentions. The UK received further political support from the Commonwealth of Nations and the European Economic Community. The latter also provided economic support by imposing economic sanctions on Argentina. Argentina itself was politically backed by many countries in Latin America and the Non-Aligned Movement.[17]

The resulting conflict lasted 74 days and ended with Argentine forces surrendering on June 14, 1982, and the return of the Islands to British control. The conflict itself is notable as it was the only post-World War II conflict in which Britain has been involved without allied military aid. It is the first employment of nuclear submarines against surface warships and the first demonstration of the ability of British ships and aircraft to travel great distances in a very short time frame.

The successful defeat of the Argentine forces has not resolved the territorial dispute. Argentina has asserted that the Falkland Islands are Argentine territory since the 19th Century and, as of 2017, showed no sign of relinquishing the claim. The claim was added to the Argentine Constitution after its reformation in 1994. As such, the Argentine government characterized their initial invasion as the re-occupation of its own territory, while the British government saw it as an invasion of a British dependent territory.[18]

Disputes over borders and boundaries can be resolved through a variety of methods, from courts to tribunals to the employment of outright force. Another method of resolving continued border violations is for a state to erect barriers.

Barriers

"Fixed fortifications are a monument to the stupidity of man."

—General George S. Patton, Jr.[19]

As noted earlier in this chapter, barriers are material objects that block or are intended to block passage. Although natural formations make the best barriers, in the modern era most country borders are artificial delimitations drawn by politicians on maps. This has resulted in the need, in some instances, to erect physical barriers to prevent, or limit, unwanted incursions across borders.

Perhaps the iconic man-made physical barrier is the Great Wall of China, a series of fortifications running generally east to west through the entire northern part of China. The wall, made of stone, brick, tamped earth, wood, and other materials, was erected to protect the Chinese Empire and its associated states from intrusions and military incursions by various nomadic peoples in Mongolia and Siberia. The Wall was built between 220 and 206 BCE by Qin Shi Huang, the first Emperor. The original wall has long since deteriorated and has been rebuilt and reinforced many times throughout history.

One of the functions of the Great Wall was border control, such as checkpoints and customs collection centers. The Great Wall also allowed China to control emigration from the north. It is 5,500.3 miles (8,851.8 km) long, with actual wall sections comprising 3,889.5 miles (6,259.6 km) of that total length, the remainder consisting of trenches and natural defensive barriers such as hills and rivers.

Great Wall of China near Jinshanling. Jakub Hatun, Wikipedia.

The "Apartheid Wall," East Jerusalem, by delayed gratification,
free to use with attribution. Flickr, 2006.

Throughout history, including the 20th and 21st centuries, walls and fences have been built to control entry and departure of people, to regulate commerce, collect tariffs and taxes, and to prevent invasion. Hadrian's Wall was the northernmost extent of the Roman Empire, built as a series of fortifications across the isle of Great Britain in CE 122. Other historic barriers include the Siegfried Line and Maginot Line, a series of fortifications intended to prevent France from invading Germany and vice versa. This chapter opened with a discussion of the Berlin Wall, arguably the premier 20th Century effort to incarcerate an entire nation under a failed economic and political ideal. Walls and fences serve a wide variety of purposes, mostly political in nature and with limited benefit to all concerned.

The most contentious wall in recent history has been the wall being built by Israel to isolate Jewish settlements from encroachment by the native Palestinians living in the West Bank. Israel has been building communities throughout the land seized in a previous conflict under a variety of initiatives, with frequent starts and stops as part of the ongoing and often stalled peace process with the peoples of the occupied territories. The Israelis refer to the wall as the "separation" or "security fence." Opponents to the structure refer to it as the "Apartheid Wall." Regardless of the name, the function is clear — to prevent terrorists, particularly suicide bombers and snipers, from launching attacks against the Jewish population.

The Israeli government perceives there is a clear justification and purpose to the wall. According to Natan Sharansky, Minister of Housing and Construction, and therefore the government agent in charge of the initial construction of the wall,

> When Israel's free society was defending itself against an unprecedented campaign of terror, most of the international community was calling for an end of the "cycle of violence" and a return to the negotiating table. When the Palestinian terrorists struck ... Israel was condemned for imposing "collective punishment" on the Palestinian population. When Israel chose to target individual terrorists with precision air strikes, its actions were condemned as illegal extrajudicial assassinations. It seemed that in eyes of many, the Jews had a right to defend themselves in theory but could not exercise that right in practice ... our government understood that there were three options to maintain an acceptable level of security for our citizens. The first was to wage a total war against Palestinian terror using weapons that would claim many innocent Palestinian lives. The second was to keep our reserves constantly mobilized to defend the country. The third option was to build the security fence.[20]

Modern manufactured barriers work on a small, or local, scale, but tend to be inefficient or cost-prohibitive on a large scale. The border between the United States and Canada is almost entirely devoid of barriers to movement. The border between the United States and Mexico has several natural barriers to movement including the aforementioned Rio Grande River and the extensive deserts. These have proved to be insufficient to stop the movement of contraband and people into the United States from Mexico. Thus, significant efforts are being expended in developing and constructing barriers of various types to control illegal crossings. With the advent of the administration of President Donald Trump there is a major effort underway to construct a more significant barrier between the United States and Mexico. Only five days into the start of his administration President Trump issued his fourth Executive Order: *Border Security and Immigration Enforcement Improvements*, which clearly states its intent as, "To direct executive departments and agencies to deploy all lawful means to secure the Nation's southern border, to prevent further illegal immigration into the United States, and to repatriate illegal aliens swiftly, consistently, and humanely" and "secure the southern border of the United States through the immediate construction of a physical wall on the southern border, monitored and supported by adequate personnel so as to prevent illegal immigration, drug and human trafficking, and acts of terrorism"[21] [reprinted in its entirety below].

Conclusion

Any barrier constructed to restrict illegal movement also hinders legal crossings and restricts the free flow of commerce. This is the conundrum facing engineers and politicians alike—how to build barriers to keep out those not wanted, while allowing the maximum possible legal movement of people and commodities. This is the fundamental quandary facing all nations throughout history.

Throughout this text the successes and the failures in establishing border security will be identified. Current problems associated with border security and how they affect decisions by policymakers are key to understanding the issues of establishing effective and efficient security along a country's borders. No country stands apart from the rest of the world. Even the isolated North Korean Communist dictatorship is dependent upon foreign aid to feed its people. For this interrelationship between countries, particularly when dealing with economic issues, we use the term "globalization." Where there is cross-border interaction, there is both dependence and the opportunity to influence. This will become obvious and by the end of the book you should have a much better understanding of what borders, barriers, and boundaries are, as well as how they influence politics, culture, and economies worldwide. Securing a state's borders, whether by establishing economic or political boundaries, or the construction of physical barriers, is the subject of the remainder of this text. In the next chapter the history of border security is examined.

Questions for Further Consideration

1. When thinking of geologic and geographic barriers, such as oceans, rivers, mountains, and deserts, which is the most effective barrier to human movement?
2. With the construction of the "Chunnel" under the English Channel, the Island and European continent were connected. Would a similar system of roads and tunnels be an effective way to connect China and India? Why or why not?
3. "Globalization" is a term widely used throughout this book. Is there a solution to the problem globalization presents to national sovereignty?

Chapter 1 Endnotes

1. ZDF "Wochen Journal" (5 November 2009). "Große Zustimmung zur Wiedervereinigung." Weekly TV show. Archived and referenced by Wikipedia: Berlin Wall, Available at: https://en.wikipedia.org/wiki/Berlin_Wall

2. Associated Press (13 August 2011). "Germany Marks Construction of the Berlin Wall." Retrieved 21 December 2011 from: http://www.foxnews.com/world/2011/08/13/germany-marks-construction-berlin-wall-1271894147/.

3. Churchill, W. (1953) *The Second World War*, vol. VI, chap. 11. NY: Houghton Mifflin.

4. The history of Khinalug is an example of the many geographically isolated communities throughout the world. This information was taken from the Ketsh Khalkh of Azerbaijan website: http://www.xinaliq.az/.

5. Metz, Leon C. "RIO GRANDE," Handbook of Texas Online (http://www.tshaonline.org/handbook/online/articles/rnr05), accessed December 31, 2011. Austin, TX: Texas State Historical Association.

6. "Blanchard, J. P. F." Encyclopedia Britannica. Available online at: https://www.britannica.com

7. Elderwick, D. (1987). *Captain Webb — Channel Swimmer*. Studley, Warwickshire, England: Brewin Books Ltd.

8. "Desert Biomes" (n.d.). University of California Museum of Paleontology available at: http://www.ucmp.berkeley.edu/exhibits/biomes/deserts.php.

9. "Desert," Encyclopedia Britannica.

10. Henkin, Pugh, Schachter, & Smit (1980). *International Law: Cases and materials*. St. Paul, MN: West Publishing. Except as otherwise noted, references to the development and implementation of International Law throughout this chapter are devolved from this excellent (if dated) legal text.

11. Restatement, Second, Foreign Relations Law of the United States (1965). Available at: https://home.heinonline.org/titles/American-Law-Institute-Library/Restatement-Second-Foreign-Relations-Law-of-the-United-States/?letter=R

12. Henkin (1979). *How Nations Behave*, 2nd. ed. Columbia University Press, (p. 212).

13. United Nations Convention on the Law of the Sea (1982). Available at: http://www.un.org/depts/los/convention_agreements/texts/unclos/unclos_e.pdf. Current status on the signatory nations to the Convention can be found at: http://www.un.org/depts/los/reference_files/status2010.pdf.

14. Ibid.

15. Ibid.

16. Ibid.

17. "A Chronology of Events during the Falklands Conflict of 1982." Falkland Islands Information. Retrieved 24 December 2011. Available at: http://www.falklandswar.org.uk/chron.htm

18. "Argentine Foreign Office 11 February 2010." Cancilleria.gov.ar. Retrieved 9 June 2010. "Falklands sovereignty is "non-negotiable," says PM." BBC. 23 December 2011. Retrieved 24 December 2011. "Argentina to Reaffirm Sovereignty Rights over The Falkland Islands." National Turk. Retrieved 7 January 2012. Constitución Nacional: "La Nación Argentina ratifica su legítima e imprescriptible soberanía sobre las Islas Malvinas, Georgias del Sur y Sandwich del Sur y los espacios marítimos e insulares correspondientes, por ser parte integrante del territorio nacional."

19. This statement by General George S. Patton, Jr., was directed to comments about the Siegfried Line, an invasion barrier between Germany and France built between the First and Second World Wars.

20. Sharansky, N. and R. Dermer (2004). *The Case for Democracy*, New York: Public Affairs, (p. 214).

21. The White House, Office of the Press Secretary, January 25, 2017. Executive Order: *Border Security and Immigration Enforcement Improvements*. Available at: https://www.whitehouse.gov/briefing-room/presidential-actions/executive-orders?term_node_tid_depth=51

Appendix to Chapter 1
Donald Trump's Fourth Executive Order

The White House
Office of the Press Secretary
For Immediate Release   January 25, 2017
Executive Order: Border Security and Immigration Enforcement Improvements

EXECUTIVE ORDER

BORDER SECURITY AND IMMIGRATION
ENFORCEMENT IMPROVEMENTS

By the authority vested in me as President by the Constitution and the laws of the United States of America, including the Immigration and Nationality Act (8 U.S.C. 1101 et seq.) (INA), the Secure Fence Act of 2006 (Public Law 109-367) (Secure Fence Act), and the Illegal Immigration Reform and Immigrant Responsibility Act of 1996 (Public Law 104-208 Div. C) (IIRIRA), and in order to ensure the safety and territorial integrity of the United States as well as to ensure that the Nation's immigration laws are faithfully executed, I hereby order as follows:
Section 1. Purpose. Border security is critically important to the national security of the United States. Aliens who illegally enter the United States without inspection or admission present a significant threat to national security and public safety. Such aliens have not been identified or inspected by Federal immigration officers to determine their admissibility to the United States. The recent surge of illegal immigration at the southern border with Mexico has placed a significant strain on Federal resources and overwhelmed agencies charged with border security and immigration enforcement, as well as the local communities into which many of the aliens are placed.
Transnational criminal organizations operate sophisticated drug- and human-trafficking networks and smuggling operations on both sides of the southern border, contributing to a significant increase in violent crime and United States deaths from dangerous drugs. Among those who illegally enter are those who seek to harm Americans through acts of terror or criminal conduct. Continued illegal immigration presents a clear and present danger to the interests of the United States. Federal immigration law both imposes the responsibility and provides the means for the Federal Government, in cooperation with border States, to secure the Nation's southern border. Although Federal immigration law provides a robust framework for Federal-State partnership in enforcing our immigration laws — and the Congress has authorized and provided appropriations to secure our borders — the Federal Government has failed to discharge this basic sovereign responsibility. The purpose of this order is to direct executive departments and agencies (agencies) to deploy all lawful means to secure the Nation's southern

border, to prevent further illegal immigration into the United States, and to repatriate illegal aliens swiftly, consistently, and humanely.

Sec. 2. Policy. It is the policy of the executive branch to:

(a) secure the southern border of the United States through the immediate construction of a physical wall on the southern border, monitored and supported by adequate personnel so as to prevent illegal immigration, drug and human trafficking, and acts of terrorism;

(b) detain individuals apprehended on suspicion of violating Federal or State law, including Federal immigration law, pending further proceedings regarding those violations;

(c) expedite determinations of apprehended individuals' claims of eligibility to remain in the United States;

(d) remove promptly those individuals whose legal claims to remain in the United States have been lawfully rejected, after any appropriate civil or criminal sanctions have been imposed; and

(e) cooperate fully with States and local law enforcement in enacting Federal-State partnerships to enforce Federal immigration priorities, as well as State monitoring and detention programs that are consistent with Federal law and do not undermine Federal immigration priorities.

Sec. 3. Definitions. (a) "Asylum officer" has the meaning given the term in section 235(b)(1)(E) of the INA (8 U.S.C. 1225(b)(1)).

(b) "Southern border" shall mean the contiguous land border between the United States and Mexico, including all points of entry.

(c) "Border States" shall mean the States of the United States immediately adjacent to the contiguous land border between the United States and Mexico.

(d) Except as otherwise noted, "the Secretary" shall refer to the Secretary of Homeland Security.

(e) "Wall" shall mean a contiguous, physical wall or other similarly secure, contiguous, and impassable physical barrier.

(f) "Executive department" shall have the meaning given in section 101 of title 5, United States Code.

(g) "Regulations" shall mean any and all Federal rules, regulations, and directives lawfully promulgated by agencies.

(h) "Operational control" shall mean the prevention of all unlawful entries into the United States, including entries by terrorists, other unlawful aliens, instruments of terrorism, narcotics, and other contraband.

Sec. 4. Physical Security of the Southern Border of the United States. The Secretary shall immediately take the following steps to obtain complete operational control, as determined by the Secretary, of the southern border:

(a) In accordance with existing law, including the Secure Fence Act and IIRIRA, take all appropriate steps to immediately plan, design, and construct a physical wall along the southern border, using appropriate materials and technology to most effectively achieve complete operational control of the southern border;

(b) Identify and, to the extent permitted by law, allocate all sources of Federal funds for the planning, designing, and constructing of a physical wall along the southern border;

(c) Project and develop long-term funding requirements for the wall, including preparing Congressional budget requests for the current and upcoming fiscal years; and

(d) Produce a comprehensive study of the security of the southern border, to be completed within 180 days of this order, that shall include the current state of southern border security, all geophysical and topographical aspects of the southern border, the availability of Federal and State resources necessary to achieve complete operational control of the southern border, and a strategy to obtain and maintain complete operational control of the southern border.

Sec. 5. Detention Facilities. (a) The Secretary shall take all appropriate action and allocate all legally available resources to immediately construct, operate, control, or establish contracts to construct, operate, or control facilities to detain aliens at or near the land border with Mexico.

(b) The Secretary shall take all appropriate action and allocate all legally available resources to immediately assign asylum officers to immigration detention facilities for the purpose of accepting asylum referrals and conducting credible fear determinations pursuant to section 235(b)(1) of the INA (8 U.S.C. 1225(b)(1)) and applicable regulations and reasonable fear determinations pursuant to applicable regulations.

(c) The Attorney General shall take all appropriate action and allocate all legally available resources to immediately assign immigration judges to immigration detention facilities operated or controlled by the Secretary, or operated or controlled pursuant to contract by the Secretary, for the purpose of conducting proceedings authorized under title 8, chapter 12, subchapter II, United States Code.

Sec. 6. Detention for Illegal Entry. The Secretary shall immediately take all appropriate actions to ensure the detention of aliens apprehended for violations of immigration law pending the outcome of their removal proceedings or their removal from the country to the extent permitted by law. The Secretary shall issue new policy guidance to all Department of Homeland Security personnel regarding the appropriate and consistent use of lawful detention authority under the INA, including the termination of the practice commonly known as "catch and release," whereby aliens are routinely released in the United States shortly after their apprehension for violations of immigration law.

Sec. 7. Return to Territory. The Secretary shall take appropriate action, consistent with the requirements of section 1232 of title 8, United States Code, to ensure that aliens described in section 235(b)(2)(C) of the INA (8 U.S.C. 1225(b)(2)(C)) are returned to the territory from which they came pending a formal removal proceeding.

Sec. 8. Additional Border Patrol Agents. Subject to available appropriations, the Secretary, through the Commissioner of U.S. Customs and Border Protection, shall take all appropriate action to hire 5,000 additional Border Patrol agents, and all appropriate action to ensure that such agents enter on duty and are assigned to duty stations as soon as is practicable.

Sec. 9. Foreign Aid Reporting Requirements. The head of each executive department and agency shall identify and quantify all sources of direct and indirect Federal aid or assistance to the Government of Mexico on an annual basis over the past five years, including all bilateral and multilateral development aid, economic assistance, humanitarian aid, and military aid. Within 30 days of the date of this order, the head of each executive department and agency shall submit this information to the Secretary of State. Within 60 days of the date of this order, the Secretary shall submit to the President a consolidated report reflecting the levels of such aid and assistance that has been provided annually, over each of the past five years.

Sec. 10. Federal-State Agreements. It is the policy of the executive branch to empower State and local law enforcement agencies across the country to perform the functions of an immigration officer in the interior of the United States to the maximum extent permitted by law.

(a) In furtherance of this policy, the Secretary shall immediately take appropriate action to engage with the Governors of the States, as well as local officials, for the purpose of preparing to enter into agreements under section 287(g) of the INA (8 U.S.C. 1357(g)).

(b) To the extent permitted by law, and with the consent of State or local officials, as appropriate, the Secretary shall take appropriate action, through agreements under section 287(g) of the INA, or otherwise, to authorize State and local law enforcement officials, as the Secretary determines are qualified and appropriate, to perform the functions of immigration officers in relation to the investigation, apprehension, or detention of aliens in the United States under the direction and the supervision of the Secretary. Such authorization shall be in addition to, rather than in place of, Federal performance of these duties.

(c) To the extent permitted by law, the Secretary may structure each agreement under section 287(g) of the INA in the manner that provides the most effective model for enforcing Federal immigration laws and obtaining operational control over the border for that jurisdiction.

Sec. 11. Parole, Asylum, and Removal. It is the policy of the executive branch to end the abuse of parole and asylum provisions currently used to prevent the lawful removal of removable aliens.

(a) The Secretary shall immediately take all appropriate action to ensure that the parole and asylum provisions of Federal immigration law are not illegally exploited to prevent the removal of otherwise removable aliens.

(b) The Secretary shall take all appropriate action, including by promulgating any appropriate regulations, to ensure that asylum referrals and credible fear determinations pursuant to section 235(b)(1) of the INA (8 U.S.C. 1125(b)(1)) and 8 CFR 208.30, and reasonable fear determinations pursuant to 8 CFR 208.31, are conducted in a manner consistent with the plain language of those provisions.

(c) Pursuant to section 235(b)(1)(A)(iii)(I) of the INA, the Secretary shall take appropriate action to apply, in his sole and unreviewable discretion, the provisions of section 235(b)(1)(A)(i) and (ii) of the INA to the aliens designated under section 235(b)(1)(A)(iii)(II).

(d) The Secretary shall take appropriate action to ensure that parole authority under section 212(d)(5) of the INA (8 U.S.C. 1182(d)(5)) is exercised only on a case-by-case basis in accordance with the plain language of the statute, and in all circumstances only when an individual demonstrates urgent humanitarian reasons or a significant public benefit derived from such parole.

(e) The Secretary shall take appropriate action to require that all Department of Homeland Security personnel are properly trained on the proper application of section 235 of the William Wilberforce Trafficking Victims Protection Reauthorization Act of 2008 (8 U.S.C. 1232) and section 462(g)(2) of the Homeland Security Act of 2002 (6 U.S.C. 279(g)(2)), to ensure that unaccompanied alien children are properly processed, receive appropriate care and placement while in the custody of the Department of Homeland Security, and, when appropriate, are safely repatriated in accordance with law.

Sec. 12. Authorization to Enter Federal Lands. The Secretary, in conjunction with the Secretary of the Interior and any other heads of agencies as necessary, shall take all appropriate action to:

(a) permit all officers and employees of the United States, as well as all State and local officers as authorized by the Secretary, to have access to all Federal lands as necessary and appropriate to implement this order; and

(b) enable those officers and employees of the United States, as well as all State and local officers as authorized by the Secretary, to perform such actions on Federal lands as the Secretary deems necessary and appropriate to implement this order.

Sec. 13. Priority Enforcement. The Attorney General shall take all appropriate steps to establish prosecution guidelines and allocate appropriate resources to ensure that Federal prosecutors accord a high priority to prosecutions of offenses having a nexus to the southern border.

Sec. 14. Government Transparency. The Secretary shall, on a monthly basis and in a publicly available way, report statistical data on aliens apprehended at or near the southern border using a uniform method of reporting by all Department of Homeland Security components, in a format that is easily understandable by the public.

Sec. 15. Reporting. Except as otherwise provided in this order, the Secretary, within 90 days of the date of this order, and the Attorney General, within 180 days, shall each submit to the President a report on the progress of the directives contained in this order.

Sec. 16. Hiring. The Office of Personnel Management shall take appropriate action as may be necessary to facilitate hiring personnel to implement this order.

Sec. 17. General Provisions. (a) Nothing in this order shall be construed to impair or otherwise affect:

(i) the authority granted by law to an executive department or agency, or the head thereof; or

(ii) the functions of the Director of the Office of Management and Budget relating to budgetary, administrative, or legislative proposals.

(b) This order shall be implemented consistent with applicable law and subject to the availability of appropriations.

(c) This order is not intended to, and does not, create any right or benefit, substantive or procedural, enforceable at law or in equity by any party against the United States, its departments, agencies, or entities, its officers, employees, or agents, or any other person.

DONALD J. TRUMP

THE WHITE HOUSE,
January 25, 2017.

Chapter 2

Border Security in History

Key Words and Concepts

Great Wall of China	Korean Demilitarized Zone
Hadrian's Wall	Maginot Line
Iron Curtain	Siegfried Line

Introduction

Early peoples living in caves likely symbolized their early living and sleeping quarters with stone markers or a few, strategically placed, possessions. Conceivably, livestock enclosures for domesticated stock may mark the inception of property needing care and protection from predators of many kinds. Providing shelter for families and their domestic animals, these delineations separate groups from each other and provide a sense of security in vulnerable times. If we define borders as in Chapter 1 of this book, as an outer part or edge, perimeter, periphery, or rim, then livestock enclosures exist as early barriers, or symbolic borders, providing some protection for people and property from robbers and thieves.

This then evolved into a system of providing a means of identifying and defending the boundaries of communities, such as villages and small cities, usually through the building of fortifications. Over time this expanded to include markings delineating the boundaries of empires. When the age of great empires came to an end, the rise of independent city-states drove a return to a simpler time of using natural barriers as city boundaries and erecting walls where nature failed to provide a border. The reentry of civilizations into an era of national identity led to the establishment of borders to define the territory claimed by one group in relation to other groups and became a necessity, even when those borders were indefensible. Today we have reached

The Great Wall of China. Wikicommons.

a point where borders are essentially lines drawn on maps rather than walls erected for national security, at least in most cases. The oldest evidence for establishment of borders can still be found in archeological sites where walls are unearthed.

The Ancient World

The history of fortification is not merely a study of how humans have devised increasingly sophisticated ways of making a place of refuge more secure. A fortified place is much more than a last-ditch defense. It also has many positive uses. Fortifications play a role as active instruments of policy. A fortress or walled city had two chief advantages: it allowed a small force to resist a larger opposing force, at least long enough to enable a more effective and substantial resistance, and secondly, it allowed for poorly trained forces to hold out against a better trained enemy.[1] The basic principle of fortification is to put a barrier between defender and attacker. The number of obstacles and the sophistication of their arrangement may vary and evolve over time but the principle is as valid today against nuclear attack as it was when the walls of Jericho were erected more than twelve thousand years ago.[2]

Nature usually plays a key role in shaping the appearance and definition of borders, whether they are of a city, national, or continental scale. It is up to the ingenuity of humans to draw on the natural resources around their territory, or what they hold most essential to their survival, in the construct of borders and therefore the development of appropriate fortifications. This starts by defending the home. Next, one defends the community. Third, nations and empires defend their territorial boundaries. Numerous walled cities, castles and forts, and structures such as the Great Wall of China all attest to this fundamental principle throughout history, no matter where humans have established communities.

The earliest forms of defensive works of which we have any real knowledge or evidence are those broadly known as hill forts. These earth enclosures can be found across Europe from the Atlantic to the Urals, in Afghanistan, in the Deccan Plateau in India, throughout North America, and in New Zealand. While they are similar in detail it would be foolish to try to suggest a common derivation. The idea of digging a ditch around a hill and piling up the earth, perhaps with the addition of a wooden palisade, occurred independently to widely dispersed peoples. The subsequent refinements and additions associated with the development of walled cities or redoubts, also sprang from equally random inspiration as sedentary tribes had to adapt to new threats.

The first improvement made by prehistoric builders of hill forts was to add obstacles for an attacker to have to overcome. These obstacles could have been of such a nature that the attacker would be funneled into a narrow area where the defender would have the advantage of concentrating their efforts to repel an attack. They may have increased the depth of a ditch and may even have flooded it so that a simple bridge would allow normal access but lifting of that bridge would deter the ability of an attacker to penetrate the rampart. The science of archeology indicates that what may seem to be simple earth ramparts can be more complex than they appear on the surface. Some contain a reinforcing core of stone, loosely piled on the ground and then covered with dirt from the ditch. Others have traces of timber set in stone foundations against the revetment, essentially being a reinforced stockade. Others have palisading with walkways along the top for guards or defenders.[3]

While the tribes of northern Europe and North America were furrowing ground and piling earth into hill forts, the peoples of the Nile River valley and the Fertile Crescent, who had much greater human resources to draw upon, were erecting massive walled cities and temples.

The Walled City

The idea of surrounding early cities with walls was widespread. Examples can be found in China, Korea, Japan, and across the Middle East. In many cases the dating of early walled cities in Asia is difficult, as subsequent structures were built upon the foundations of previous structures. Early Rome was walled and walls were maintained and expanded around the city as it expanded. Walled cities even existed in North, Central, and South America.

Spanning from very early history to modern times, walls have been a near necessity for every city. Uruk in ancient Sumer (Mesopotamia) is one of the world's oldest known walled cities. Dating to the early second millennium BCE, tales of the building of Uruk by the king Gilgamesh were consolidated sometime around the eighteenth century BCE, making this the oldest narrative tale yet discovered. In the Epic of Gilgamesh, tablet 1, the king builds the wall of Uruk-Haven:

He carved on a stone stela all of his toils,
and built the wall of Uruk-Haven,
the wall of the sacred Eanna Temple, the
holy sanctuary.
Look at its wall which gleams like *copper* (?),
inspect its inner wall, the likes of which
no one can equal!
Take hold of the threshold stone—it dates
from ancient times!
Go close to the Eanna Temple, the
residence of Ishtar,
such as no later king or man ever equaled!
Go up on the wall of Uruk and walk
around,
examine its foundation, inspect its brick-
work thoroughly.
Is not (even the core of) the brick structure
made of kiln-fired brick,
and did not the Seven Sages themselves lay out its plans?
One league city, one league palm gardens, one league lowlands, the open area
(?) of the Ishtar Temple,
three leagues and the open area (?) of Uruk it (the wall) encloses.[4]

Tablet 1, The Epic of Gilgamesh.
British Museum.

Uruk would later become the city of Ur and grow into the capital city of the Sumerian Empire in southern Mesopotamia. The remains of the original walls supposedly built by Gilgamesh are standing to this day.

As more cities arose across the Fertile Crescent, in Egypt, and across the Middle East between the Egyptian and Assyrian Empires, more cities built walls to delineate their boundaries and provide fortifications to protect their inhabitants. One famous city of this era was Jericho, on the west bank of the Jordan River. Jericho is one of the oldest continuously inhabited cities in the world, with evidence of settlement dating back to 10,000 BCE. Archeological evidence indicates that by 9400 BCE the city had grown to more than seventy homes and held a population more than one thousand. The most striking aspect of this ancient city was a massive stone wall nearly 12 feet tall and more than 6 feet wide at its base. Included within the wall was a tower more than 12 feet tall with an internal staircase of twenty-two stone steps.[5] Although the city of Jericho was abandoned and relocated periodically throughout history, the remains of the original city provide ample evidence of the early efforts to defend communities from invaders through construction of defensive walls that clearly delineated a boundary the community could defend.

Records of the early Assyrian monarchs tell that walled cities were common and that the walls were reinforced with towers topped by crenellation. Archeology has expanded our knowledge of these structures at sites in ancient Babylon, northern Syria, ancient Troy, and Judea. The city of Troy, which controlled the entrance to the Black

Sea from the Mediterranean and was an important trading center, was built and rebuilt many times. The last of these cities, built about 1500 BCE, is generally known as the Sixth City and is the city written about by Homer. Its wall was massive and sloped outward on its face, thus giving not only great stability but also superior resistance to attack by the means available at the time. The wall was provided with square towers and had several unique gate designs including an overlapping of walls so that any invader would have to make several 90-degree turns while under constant attack from above.[6]

An early wall that requires mention was the Median Wall between the Tigris and Euphrates rivers. This structure was almost 50 miles (80 km) long. Built about 800 BCE it was intended to repulse the advance of the Medes from their territory in the uplands of Persia. However, when the Medes and the Chaldeans united at the end of the seventh century BCE, they overwhelmed the Assyrians. "The Median Wall was a relatively short-lived structure of which little is known, but it seems to have been one of the earliest attempts to … [provide] a sizable barrier rather than relying on individual fortified sites."[7]

Defense from invaders in Judean times, the eighth century BCE, included city walls. The Broad Wall, rediscovered in 1970, delineated and defended Old Jerusalem in the time of King Hezekiah and later was rebuilt after Babylonians laid siege and destroyed the city and temple. This original barrier wall supposedly extended to the first temple and enclosed the outlet of the tunnel of Gichon, providing a reliable water source for the city when it came under siege by the Assyrians under King Sennacherib. Isaiah[8] describes a vision of the Old Jerusalem city wall being breached. He calls for the destruction of houses for materials to reassemble and fortify the wall in that time of great challenge. As Isaiah promised, the City of David did not succumb to the invaders, having access to fresh water while a sudden plague depleted the Assyrians.

Later, the city did fall to Nebuchadnezzar II of Babylon. Later King Artaxerxes would send Nehemiah[9] to survey and rebuild the city of Jerusalem, including the city wall. A description of the restoration of the city gates and the Broad Wall are found in the biblical book of Nehemiah. Yet the city of Jerusalem, capital of Judea, would not remain standing as subsequent invaders repetitively breached the walls.

City-states, islands of civilization in the world long before the Common Era, constructed barriers such as Athens' Long Wall to delineate ultimate, last-ditch protection barriers. Athenians built their wall to extend to their port at Piraeus. Their barrier wall around the city was sufficient to protect the inhabitants from external forces, but left the city cut off from its harbors. Around 450

The Broad Wall in the old city of Jerusalem, 23 January 2009. Wikicommons.

BCE during a war with Sparta, two long walls were built between the city of Athens and the ports at Piraeus and Phalerum to ensure that Athens proper would not be cut off from its naval assets and trade. During the Peloponnesian War of 432–404 BCE, the long walls became crucial to the defense of Athens. The city maintained a supply line through its maritime commerce, even while Sparta ravaged Athenian farms outside the city walls. Ultimately the city was forced to surrender to Sparta when it suffered defeat at sea and the port of Piraeus was blockaded, cutting off all supplies to the city.[10]

The early era of city-states came to an end with the rise of the Alexandrian Empire and later the Roman Empire. This resulted in massive building projects as ever-greater-sized cities were walled and boundaries of entire empires were set in stone to define borders and provide security from invaders.

Hadrian's Wall

The expanding Roman Empire brought the idea of masonry fortifications to lands that hitherto had known only wooden stockades and earthworks. The first Roman colonial settlements were towns, intended to control traffic on the roads and subjugate the local peoples. When a colony was founded, among the first structures built was a wooden tower that acted both as a watchtower and as a defensive redoubt. This was later supplemented with smaller city towers, walls, and gates. As a district gradually

The remains of Milecastle 39 (coordinates 55° 0′ 13.12″ N, 2° 22′ 32.74″ W) on Hadrian's Wall; near Steel Rigg, looking east from a ridge along the Hadrian's Wall Path. Milecastle 39 is also known as Castle Nick. Wikicommons/Adam Cuerden, June 2007.

came under Roman control, masons were brought in to convert existing structures to stone. Hard roads were then laid; barracks and other structures were converted to stone buildings.[11]

One of the principal tasks of the legions stationed at the extreme reaches of the Empire was its defense, particularly against the tribes of Northern Europe and Britain. Along the empire's borders, the legions built *limes*, or fortified frontiers, each usually consisting of a ditch, rampart, and palisade, backed by towers and forts. One of the more important was the lime that ran some 300 miles (480 km) from the Rhine River at *Rigomgus* (Remagen) to the Danube at *Castra Regina* (Regensburg). On the island of Britain where distances to be guarded were shorter and the terrain more favorable, a more substantial work was produced.[12]

Today a UNESCO World Heritage Site, Hadrian's Wall (*Vallum Aelium*) was a defensive fortification in Roman Britain. Construction began in 122 CE during the rule of the Emperor Hadrian as one of two wall structures built across northern Britain, between the last outposts of the Roman Empire and the barbarian Scots north of the walls. The second wall, known as the Antonine Wall, was built to the north of Hadrian's Wall and spanned approximately 39 miles (63 km), and was about 15 feet wide and 10 feet high. The Antonine Wall and its forts were abandoned after only twenty years, but the more southern Hadrian's Wall was continuously manned until the Empire withdrew from Britain in 410 CE. Hadrian's Wall is 73 miles long (120 km) and varies in width and height depending upon the materials used in construction. At points the wall measured 20 feet high and at other points as short as only 10 feet. The wall was accompanied by ditches, berms, and forts (some fourteen to seventeen depending on the reference cited) along its length but was, probably, not simply a fortification for defense but a means to control trade, impose taxes, and minimize smuggling and immigration. There were many forts along the wall with gates to allow persons to pass through, which were manned by five hundred to one thousand soldiers each. These soldiers were not Legionnaires, but auxiliary troops consisting of both infantry and cavalry.[13]

While no portion of the Hadrian's Wall remains completely intact, some sections have reconstructions depicting how the wall may have appeared in its original form. Whether it had a wall walk and crenellations is questionable but the wall was obviously impressive in its original condition and with the numbers of troops that manned its length. Hadrian's Wall ultimately failed to prevent invasions of Britain from the north. The troops that garrisoned the forts along the wall intermarried with the locals and established families. As the Roman Empire lost strength and ultimately abandoned Britain, these soldiers, not being Roman citizens or Legionnaires, remained behind as farmers and craftsmen. The wall itself was later quarried as a source of ready cut stone for use in other construction projects and efforts to protect it were not started until the 1800s.

During the third century CE the Alemanii, natives outside of areas under Roman control, began to raid the Roman territories in northern Europe, including the Isle of Britain, with greater frequency and ferocity. The Saxons, invading by sea, had the advantage of mobility and surprise and were, therefore, extremely dangerous. To meet this threat the Saxon Shore was delineated and forts were built in strategic

Aurelian wall—ancient fortifications in Rome. Wikimedia Commons, Lalupa.

locations from Norfolk to Portsmouth in England and from Bordeaux to Ostend on the Continent. Although the historical records tend to have significant gaps, it appears that the English forts and some of the continental forts may have been under a single command structure. These Saxon Shore forts were relatively simple structures spread along the coastline to act as garrisons of troops and watchtowers to provide temporary delaying action while full legions were called upon to repel the invaders.[14]

The problems of the Saxon Shore were just one of the many difficulties that beset the later period of the Roman Empire. With much of the Roman military power located at extended distances from the city itself, once an invader had circumvented existing defenses, the road to Rome was essentially unguarded. Recognizing the threat an undefended Rome offered to invaders, the Emperor Aurelian mounted punitive expeditions against European tribes outside of the bounds of the empire and in 271 CE began construction of a new wall to encompass all of Rome.[15]

Aurelian's Wall was of wholly new construction and was designed to maximize the advantages of terrain. Securing the principal bridge across the Tiber River, a salient on the west band of the river enclosed its bridgeheads as well as a rise of ground from which they might be commanded. Similarly, the line of wall along the east side of the river took in commanding features and guarded all possible lines of approach. The wall was soundly constructed of a core of concrete made from volcanic tufa bound with cement and faced with tiles. It was generally 12–13 feet thick at the base and 20 feet in height, with a parapet on the outer side providing a protected walkway for sentries and defenders. The number of existing structures incorporated into the wall, or ruthlessly cleared away, demonstrates evidence of Aurelian's intent to site Rome's defenses along the best tactical setting. Tombs, dwellings, public buildings, and monuments were all razed if they were in the way of the wall. Eighteen gateways were constructed to allow access to the city through the wall, of which nine remain intact.[16]

Historical records indicate that it took about ten years to complete construction of Aurelian's Wall, well within expectations for such a massive undertaking. While Aurelian died before the wall was finished, his successor, Probus, continued construction until his assassination in 282 CE. The Emperor Diocletian and his successors made several changes to the original wall including raising its height to about 55 feet in some areas. The total reconstruction effort was not completed before Constantine invaded and overwhelmed the defenders of Rome in 312 CE. Constantine completed some of the construction of the wall but the final work was not completed until the time of the Emperor Honorius (395–423 CE).[17]

Aurelian's Wall was put to the test in 408 CE when Alaric the Goth besieged Rome. The wall proved too substantial for the Goths to defeat and they subsequently retreated after being paid off by the citizens of Rome. Two years later Alaric returned and succeeded in breeching the wall, spending three days looting the city before withdrawing. Known as the Sack of Rome, this event shocked the Mediterranean world and is generally considered to be the end of Rome's dominance in Europe and the Mediterranean world.[18]

The Great Wall of China

Other empires also built walls to keep out invaders, regulate trade, and prevent the smuggling of contraband. Arguably, the most famous wall in ancient history that was constructed as both a border and a barrier was the Great Wall of China.[19] As with all border fortifications, the Great Wall is not a single wall, but a series of fortifications built over many centuries along different geographic lines to provide protection from different threats. There have been four major walls:

    208 BCE (the Qin Dynasty)
    First century BCE (the Han Dynasty)
    1138–98 CE (the Five Dynasties and Ten Kingdoms Period)
    1368–1620 CE (from Emperor Hongwu until Emperor Wanli of the Ming Dynasty)

The Great Wall of China is a series of stone and earthen fortifications built, rebuilt, and maintained between the fifth century BCE and the sixteenth century CE to protect the northern borders of the Chinese Empire during the rule of successive dynasties. The most famous is the wall built between 220 BCE and 200 BCE by the first Emperor, Qin Shi Huang, as it was the wall that defined what was to become China.

The Chinese were already familiar with the techniques of wall building by the time of the Spring and Autumn Periods, which began around the seventh century BCE.

During the Warring States Period from the fifth century BCE to 221 BCE, the states of Qi, Yan, and Zhao all constructed extensive fortifications to defend their own borders. Built to withstand attack by forces equipped with small arms such as swords and spears, these walls were made mostly by stamping earth and gravel between board frames.

Qin Shi Huang conquered the Warring States and unified China in 221 BCE, establishing the Qin Dynasty. The Qin Wall was built during the reign of the first Emperor. This wall was constructed by the joining of several regional walls built by the Warring States. It was located much farther north than the current Great Wall and very little remains of it. Intending to impose centralized rule and prevent the resurgence of feudal lords, the Emperor ordered the destruction of the wall sections that divided his empire along the former state borders. To protect the empire against intrusions by the Xiongnu people from the north, he ordered the building of a new wall to connect the remaining fortifications along the empire's new northern frontier.

Transporting the large quantity of materials required for construction was difficult, so builders always tried to use local resources. Stones from the mountains were used over mountain ranges while rammed earth was used for construction in the plains. The peasants who died working were buried inside the wall, later to be unearthed by

Map of the Great Wall of China. Wikimedia commons —
Jan, Michel/Michaud, Roland/Michaud, Sabrina.

archaeologists. There are no surviving historical records indicating the exact length and course of the Qin Dynasty walls. Most of the ancient walls have eroded away over the centuries and very few sections remain today. It is estimated that many as one million people died building the wall under the Qin Dynasty.

The Great Wall concept was revived again during the Ming Dynasty. The Great Wall that can still be seen today was built following the Ming army's defeat by the Oirats in the Battle of Tumu in 1449 CE. The primary purpose of the wall was not to keep out people, as much of the wall could be easily scaled, but it was built to ensure that semi-nomadic people on the outside of the wall could not cross with their horses or return easily with stolen property. In other words, the Great Wall of China that we know today was built as a means of border control.

The Ming had failed to gain a clear upper hand over the Mongols after successive battles and the long-drawn-out conflict was taking a toll on the empire. The Ming adopted a new strategy to keep the nomadic Mongols out by constructing walls along the northern border. Acknowledging the Mongol control established in the Ordos Desert, the wall followed the desert's southern edge instead of incorporating the bend of the Huang He.

Unlike the earlier Qin fortifications, the Ming construction was stronger and more elaborate due to the use of bricks and stone instead of rammed earth. As Mongol raids continued periodically over the years, the Ming built on a much larger scale and

The Great Wall of China, 2005, Wikimedia commons — Nagyman.

with longer-lasting materials (solid stone used for the sides and the top of the wall) than any of the three previous walls. They devoted considerable resources to repair and reinforce the walls. Sections near the Ming capital of Beijing were especially strong.

Toward the end of the Shun Dynasty, the Great Wall helped defend the empire against the Manchu invasions that began around 1600 CE. Under the military command of Yuan Chonghuan, the Ming army held off the Manchus at the heavily fortified Shanhaiguan pass, thus preventing the Manchus from entering the Liaodong Peninsula and the Chinese heartland. The Manchus were finally able to cross the Great Wall in 1644 CE, when the gates at Shanhaiguan were opened by Wu Sangui, a Ming border general who disliked the activities of rulers of the Shun Dynasty. The Manchus quickly seized Beijing and defeated the newly founded Shun Dynasty and remaining Ming resistance, to establish the Qing Dynasty. Under Qing rule, China's borders extended beyond the wall and new lands were annexed by the empire, so construction and repairs on the Great Wall were discontinued.

The Great Wall is the world's longest man-made structure, stretching approximately 4,160 miles (6,700 km) from Shanhaiguan in the east to Lop Nur in the west, along an arc that roughly delineates the southern edge of Inner Mongolia. In addition to being the longest man-made structure, it is also the largest man-made structure ever built in terms of surface area and mass. At the height of its importance to the protection of China, more than one million soldiers guarded the Ming Wall. It has been estimated that somewhere in the range of two to three million Chinese died as part of the centuries-long project of building the wall.

Overcoming Walls

Before the development of high quality gunpowder weapons, when confronted with a wall, an attacker had five options: retreat, establish a siege and hope that disease and starvation would wear down the defenders, go over the wall, go under the wall, or go through the wall. Siege has been the most common practice in history. If the attacker can find sufficient provisions for their forces in the surrounding countryside, the walls provide an excellent prison from which the defenders have no escape and only the supplies stored within to wait out the attackers. Going over a wall, through it, or under it all require the construction and placement of siege weapons such as portable towers and battering rams, or the employment of sappers to undermine the walls. These took time, sufficient local materials, and skilled artisans, not all of which were readily available in all conditions.[20]

Following the Jewish revolt in 66 CE, the Romans under Titus employed towers, boring tools, rams, and missile-throwing engines to take Jerusalem. Stone-throwing engines were in action on both sides of the city walls. The Jews pursued the policy of active defense, making frequent sorties to attack the Roman siege engines and their defending troops. Titus responded by building three massive wooden towers close to the city walls and high enough to command the defenders along the top of the wall. The towers were lined with iron plating to prevent the enemy from using fire to destroy them. Using suppressing fire to keep the defenders back, other siege engines were brought up and eventually the outer wall of the city was breached. The Romans entered the city while the defenders withdrew to a second, inner wall. More siege engines eventually breached this wall as well, but it took days of hand-to-hand combat before the Romans could move their siege engines to bear on the final defensive wall, that of the Upper City and the Temple Mount. The Jews mustered 340 stone-throwing engines and were extremely active in defense, even tunneling out of the city and under the Roman engines to undermine them. Titus then pulled back his forces, consolidated his gains, and after sealing off the city, mounted another attack on the Temple itself, taking it after an extremely bloody battle. Ultimately, the Temple was destroyed so thoroughly that no stone was left standing, as a punishment to the Jews. Eleven thousand defenders died during the siege and 97,000 Jews were led into captivity. This was the beginning of the Jewish diaspora.[21]

Reverting to Natural Barriers as Borders in Europe

If you look at a map today and compare it with maps from one hundred or two hundred years ago you will see that national borders are fluid, as are the consolidations of political or religious entities that make up the various countries and empires in each different era. As some populations expand and others contract, as governments struggle with each other over control of new resources, as wars are fought over inheritances and territory, so too do the borders between states change. While societies and empires have always tried to define their borders as "fixed in stone" time has demonstrated that even iconic borders, such as the Great Wall of China, are much more fluid than their stone structures indicate. No better example of this fluidity in borders exists than Europe from the end of the Western Roman Empire through the present day.

Between the end of the Roman Empire and the establishment of modern Europe, the map delineating borders between countries and principalities changed so frequently that it is amazing anyone could keep track of to whom they owed political allegiance or where they were supposed to pay taxes. After the fall of the Roman Empire, the former single political entity was divided into four provinces and subdivided into thirteen dioceses for administration under the Roman Catholic Church. Borders between the various provinces and dioceses were sometimes established along rivers, other times paralleled mountain ranges and sometimes were simply lines drawn between political entities with no geographical basis to the decisions. Additionally, some of the dioceses were essentially independent of provincial control. This particular organization may have made good political sense from the perspective of administration, religious domination of the people, and control over entirely different socio-economic systems of production. When the Tartars and Cossacks were pushed into Europe because of pressure from the east, and the Mohammedans swept west after the establishment of Islam, the political system in Europe was unable to rapidly adjust to border incursions, invasions, and mass migrations.

It was not just pressure from the east that brought about change in European borders. Differences in the interpretation of Christianity resulted in a split between the Eastern Orthodox and Roman Catholic churches, splitting Europe along a north to south axis. Later, the Protestant Reformation would also contribute to another schism that would rend Europe from east to west.

Religious wars, fights over territories and rich resources, combat against invaders, and wars over succession to imperial thrones would shape the borders of Europe for more than one thousand years after the Roman Empire ceased to exist. There was even combat over which Pope was the real Pope, between different dioceses and within provinces. Later the Crusaders set forth to retake the Holy Land from the Muslims and even greater changes to the European map resulted.

By 1660 the Western European countries of England, Spain, and France were well established with relatively well-defined borders. Yet with the French Revolution and subsequent rise of Napoleon, the borders of France began to move eastward and resulted in a move by England and Russia to limit the span of Europe under French control. This led to numerous wars that ultimately resulted in the well-set borders of Western Europe by 1871. Yet the territorial ambitions of others would lead the Austrian and Hungarian monarchies to join the Austro-Hungarian Empire spanning southeast Europe and the German Empire to coalesce across north central Europe. Germans and Austrians, along with the Italians, faced with Czarist Russia to their east and well-established colonial powers to their west and north, found Europe too tight for their likings and began expanding their territorial control into Africa and Asia as colonial powers, frequently coming into conflict with pre-existing colonies established by the Dutch, French, English, and Spanish, not to mention the Chinese, Koreans, Japanese, and Siamese peoples who were already there with their own sense of self and nationality.

Fundamentally, European countries in the late nineteenth century would define their borders based on a combination of geography and language. The border between Spain and France was well established by the Pyrenees Mountains. Yet the border between France and Italy was questionable, even though the Alps made a formidable barrier. The Rhine River would be a natural boundary between France and Germany but the language spoken by those on the West Bank of the Rhine would determine their incorporation into the German Empire. More language differences would result in the creation of separate political entities that became known as the Low Countries in the northern space between France and Germany.

Even the map of 1911 Europe is essentially unrealistic, as within ten years the entire continent would be redrawn and then redrawn again by 1938 and even again by 1945. While the boundaries and borders established in 1945 would remain relatively constant, with the collapse of the Soviet Union in 1989, all Eastern Europe would once again see the cartographers working overtime to change borders, add and delete countries, and change names from year to year through the end of the twentieth century. Borders are clearly fluid and the lines drawn on a map today may be meaningless tomorrow.

The Ever-Changing
North American Borders

The Spanish, French, Russians, and British colonized North America in subsequent efforts to find a direct route to Asia that did not require traveling around the southern tip of Africa. The result of different efforts to establish colonies in North, Central, and South America over four centuries would result in the displacement and genocide of the native peoples and a never-ending conflict over access to the rich mineral resources of the continents. Frequent change in the Americas was tied to the fortunes of the colonial powers' home countries and their associated conflicts over territory and power on the European continent.

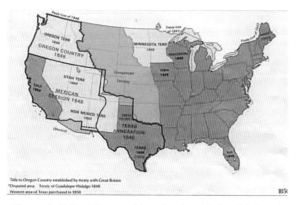

The early United States of America. The National Atlas of the United States of America (Arch C. Gerlach, editor). Washington, D.C.: U.S. Dept. of the Interior, Geological Survey, 1970. Courtesy of the University of Texas Libraries, The University of Texas at Austin.

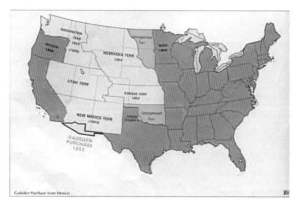

U.S. Territorial Expansion 1850–1860. The National Atlas of the United States of America (Arch C. Gerlach, editor). Washington, D.C.: U.S. Dept. of the Interior, Geological Survey, 1970. Courtesy of the University of Texas Libraries, The University of Texas at Austin.

With the Treaty of Paris (1783) between the United States and Great Britain, the original thirteen colonies gained control of all lands from the Eastern seaboard to the Mississippi River.[22] The new country, the United States of America, gained control over vast lands, increasing territorial possessions by more than 100 percent at the expense of the existing tribal peoples who had aligned themselves with their British allies. The new country found itself bounded on the west and south by Spanish lands and the north by British Canada.

The City of New Orleans controlled the mouth of the Mississippi River and, therefore, all commerce entering or leaving the river. Recognizing the vulnerability this situation presented to the growing population and economy of the lands west of the Appalachian Mountains, President Thomas Jefferson dispatched James Monroe and Robert Livingston to France to negotiate the sale of New Orleans to the United States. France, under Napoleon Bonaparte, had recently reacquired the territory back from Spain in 1800 in the hope of building an empire in North America. A slave revolt in Haiti and an impending war with England, however, led France to abandon these plans. When Napoleon offered to sell the entire Louisiana territory to the US ambassadors for only $5 million more than they were prepared to pay for New Orleans alone, Madison and Livingston jumped at the opportunity without consulting with President Jefferson or the Congress, signing the purchase treaty on April 30, 1803.[23]

The Louisiana Purchase did not define the specific territory being ceded to the United States and previous agreements between Spain and France had also ignored describing the actual lands encompassed in their various treaties. This posed a problem between the United States and Spain, which was finally resolved by the Adams-Onís Treaty of 1819. Differences over the legality of the sale by Napoleon to the United States, as well as between what was originally considered part of the Louisiana Purchase by the United States and what was subsequently settled by the Adams-Onís Treaty, would ultimately lead to the Texas Revolution and later the War with Mexico.[24]

Another disputed area to arise from the Louisiana Purchase was the ownership of Oregon Country, the realm of the Pacific Northwest that would ultimately be divided between the United States and Britain along the 49th parallel by the Oregon Treaty of 1846.[25] While providing some fundamental basics of borders for the expanding United States, these treaties would not actually settle all the disputes over various components of what was to become the country as it is currently defined.

Before coming into possession of all the lands now considered either part of the United States, or one of the many territorial possessions of the country, the Americans would fight a second war with Great Britain, a war with Mexico, and a war with Spain. Additionally, there would be purchases of territory from Czarist Russia and the forced capitulation of the Kingdom of Hawaii, along with several other treaties including the Gadsden Purchase in 1853 and treaties that dispossessed natives of their lands.

The Return to Walls and Fences

Following the end of the First World War, with the signing of the Treaty of Versailles in June 1919, the French military commanders, recognizing that there would ultimately be a resurgent Germany bent on revenge for the punitive and demeaning demands enumerated within the Treaty, came to a determination that the future of France would be one of military defense. At its most basic the concept became 'build a wall and keep them out.' Marshal Pétain, under this premise, gained control of France in 1919, due primarily to his heroic defense of Verdun during the war. His prodding of the Army General Staff caused study of the various defense options open to them. After much debate, in December 1925 the Higher War Council reached a decision and adopted Pétain's proposal of a continuous line of defense to keep the Bosch (Germans) on their side of the border.[26]

The Maginot Line

André Maginot, in 1925, was appointed minister of war. He was a politician who had enlisted as a private in 1914, had been seriously wounded at Verdun, and afterward returned to his political career. His experience at Verdun convinced him of the validity behind Pétain's thoughts on a continuous line of defense and he threw his considerable expertise behind the idea. The Commission for Fortified Regions was established and exploratory drillings and feasibility studies were undertaken to determine the route that a fixed and fortified wall would take on the border with Germany. Maginot, by 1920 had obtained the necessary parliamentary approval of funds, and construction of the defensive works was started. This modern return to walls and fixed fortifications would become known as the Maginot Line.[27] Ten years later it would be proved one of the most expensive military blunders and flawed doctrines in history as the Germans simply drove around the fortifications with such swiftness France would be forced to surrender after only one-and-a-half months of combat.[28]

Although always referred to as a 'line,' the Maginot Line was a deep defensive zone extending from 3–6 miles back from the actual frontier with Germany. The actual frontier along every river bridge and road was defended by a pillbox or fortified house, depending on the terrain, along with minefields and anti-tank traps. All road junctions were prepared for the installation of obstacles and mines should there be indications of a potential invasion. Behind the initial line was, about 1¼ miles further back, another line of concrete blockhouses equipped with anti-tank guns, machine guns, grenade-throwers, and about thirty defenders who had fixed communication lines with the main defensive positions to their rear. Another 2–3 miles behind the advanced posts was the main line of resistance, a mixture of casemates and ouvrages, and a deep dry ditch. Interestingly, the actual casemates and ouvrages, although massive in appearance, were lightly armed with artillery or mortars. The main defensive structures of the Maginot Line were dependent upon mobile field artillery units stationed to their rear that could be called upon depending on where an attack was taking place.[29]

The debacle of 1940 was due to a variety of issues. The problem with the Maginot Line was not the concept, but the limitations placed on construction of fixed fortifications by the terrain, politics, and finances. With the onset of the Great Depression, there simply were insufficient funds to fully wall in the eastern border of France. Cost-cutting measures left only enough resources to establish the defensive line from the south of the Ardennes Forest to just north of the Swiss border. Even this line would be significantly incomplete by the time the Second World War started. Because of Marshall Pétain's assertion that the terrain of the Ardennes was virtually impassable to tanks, the French were lulled into believing they were safe from attack through the forest.[30] As early as the initial decision to build the border fortification in the 1920s, French politicians were concerned that their allies, the Belgians, might misunderstand any French effort to fortify the Franco-Belgian border. Building fortifications here could conceivably have been interpreted as a lack of faith in the Franco-Belgian alliance or, worse, a desire to sacrifice the Belgians to the German wolves. However,

The West Wall and the Maginot Line, 1940. Thom Phelps.

many Belgians saw the fortification of the Franco-German border as a deliberate attempt to direct any German attack through Belgium and, therefore, the Belgians began building their own fortifications along the border with Germany, as well as establishing several fortified defensive cities that would prove difficult to overcome.[31]

The final component of the failure to construct a defensive line from the Franco-Swiss border to the English Channel was the issue of terrain. The question of the water table near Flanders raised the problem of deep excavation in the area and therefore, an inability to construct massive concrete and earth fortifications along that portion of the border. Concurrently, what the line was protecting had to be taken into consideration. The purpose of the northeastern portion of the Maginot Line was to protect the industrial zones of France. Pétain argued that there was little point in completing any fortifications beyond the Ardennes as the use of planned demolitions to destroy bridges and roads would prevent a modern army from maneuvering through the area.[32] Ultimately, this ideology and a failure to recognize the speed and mobility advantages of tank warfare would result in France falling to German invasion in 1940.

The Siegfried Line

With France building massive fortifications to its west and the Communist Revolution in Russia occurring to its east, Germany saw the need to build walls of its own to protect its borders. East of Germany was Poland, a traditional antagonist of the Prussian-dominated country. The Germans determined to establish a protective barrier running between the Oder and Warthe Rivers, east of Frankfurt, and just west of a line between the cities of Schroerin on the Warthe and Zullichau on the Oder to the south. This provided a physical barrier to protect Berlin should the country be invaded from the east. By the time construction began on the Oder-Warthe Bend (the East Wall), many of the numerous streams, lakes, ponds, and swamps in the area had already been harnessed to form natural barriers to invasion. The planned defensive East Wall was never completed. Instead, it was used extensively to test different types of fortification structures, combinations of terrain modification, and military tactics to defeat such obstacles.[33]

Border defenses in the east were of less importance than defenses in the west. Faced with France and Belgium both building extensive border fortifications along the western German frontier, the Weimar Republic began installing light fortifications in depth to the east of the Rhineland. At the time this was referred to as the West Wall. Like the French in the 1920s, the Germans weighed the pros and cons of a continuous line of fortifications and chose to install instead a series of light fortifications in depth. Faced with a rapidly changing political situation and major financial hurdles, the German General Staff compromised on what sort of fortifications to place along the borders with France, Luxembourg, and Belgium, settling for terrain modification in conjunction with holding defenses that could be reinforced should the country be attacked.[34]

When Hitler came to power, Germany assumed an aggressive campaign of expansion, annexing Austria, seizing the Sudetenland in Czechoslovakia and later the remainder of the country, as well as preparing to invade Poland. Before the

German armies could move forward with the invasion of Poland, a significant effort was needed to provide border security along the western frontier to prevent the French, Belgians, and British from invading Germany in response to a move into Poland. This required a considerable effort to upgrade the defenses of the West Wall or at least make it appear impregnable. This was accomplished by diverting 90,000 soldiers and 440,000 construction workers from the Autobahn projects. Under the direction of Hitler's road builder, Fritz Todt, beginning in May 1938, construction on the West Wall shifted into high gear. Constructing a combination of 'Limes,' taking their name from the original Roman system of defense, adding concrete 'dragon teeth' and using the terrain to advantage, a border fortification stretched from Aachen in the north to the Rhine River and then along the Rhine to the border with Switzerland.[35]

Approaches to bridges were fortified and roads were lined with visible barricades. Structures like those tested in the East Wall were erected along with several major defensive positions that matched those of the Maginot Line. Extensive use was made of barbed wire and tank traps. The equipment installed on the border defenses of the frontier with Czechoslovakia, recently annexed by Germany, was stripped and sent to the West Wall. Most importantly, using skillful propaganda, Hitler convinced the world the West Wall was significantly stronger than it was.[36] When Germany invaded Poland on September 1, 1939, both France and Great Britain were dragged into the war by their treaty obligations to come to Poland's aid. The French would attempt a half-hearted invasion of Germany through the West Wall, only to find a whole new and fearsome defensive component—minefields. During their brief foray into the German lines the French managed to recover several samples of the anti-personnel and anti-tank mines, the capabilities of which far exceeded anything in either the French or British inventory.[37] These technological advances kept France from successfully invading Germany in response to Germany's invasion of Poland.

The Siegfried Line (West Wall), as it was now called, was comparable to the Maginot Line in depth, but significantly longer and had a greater number of fortified bunkers. It was probably deepest around the city of Aachen. Five years after the start of World War II, the Americans and British would penetrate the Siegfried Line as rapidly as the Germans drove around the Maginot Line at the beginning of the war. In an era of modern warfare, the protection of the border from land incursions was insufficient and a considerable portion of the border protection involved the establishment of air defense capabilities. The advent of air defense along the Siegfried Line as a component of border security and the German development four years later of ballistic missiles, would determine the long-term policies of countries faced with border security issues for most of the remainder of the twentieth century.

The Wall to Keep People In

Not all border walls were to keep invaders out. A wall spanned the length of Europe for more than 40 years, splitting Germany in two, to keep people from leaving. Best described by the former Prime Minister of Britain in a speech before forty thousand people at Westminster College in Fulton, Missouri, in the United States, on March 5, 1946, Winston Churchill said, "From Stettin in the Baltic to Trieste in the Adriatic, an iron curtain has descended across the continent."

Fearful that continued interaction of people within the Soviet Union and those of Western ideologies, Joseph Stalin decreed that the East would be sealed off from the West through the erection of an ideological, military, political, and physical barrier. This post-World War II establishment of an Iron Curtain across Europe would last for 45 years, until multi-party politics was restored in Eastern Europe and the Berlin Wall was torn down.[38]

East of the Iron Curtain were the countries connected to or politically and economically influenced by the former Soviet Union. This included East Germany, Czechoslovakia, Poland, Hungary, Bulgaria, Romania, and Albania (until 1960 when it aligned with China). While Yugoslavia was Communist politically it was not considered to be a part of the Eastern Bloc or behind the Iron Curtain. Josip Broz Tito, the president of Yugoslavia at the time, could maintain access with the West while leading a Communist country. The other countries to the west of the Iron Curtain had democratic governments.

The Iron Curtain was a physical fence that stretched for thousands of kilometers to separate Eastern and Western countries and it was especially strong in Germany, where the division of Berlin by a concrete-and-barbed-wire wall became an unmistakable symbol of the forced separation of politically free and communist totalitarian societies. Physically, the Iron Curtain took the form of border defenses. In certain regions, the Iron Curtain was nothing more than a plain chain link fence when in other places it was a highly-guarded area that only people carrying special government permissions could approach.

While the iconic image of the Iron Curtain was the Berlin Wall, a much more extensive series of border fortifications were

The Iron Curtain. Alex Chubarov, 2013. Accessed at: http://www.allrussias.com/soviet_russia/legacy_3.asp. Used with permission.

erected along the length of the international borders between Warsaw Pact and North Atlantic Treaty Organization countries. This series of structures was not intended to prevent NATO invasion of the Warsaw Pact but to keep people from leaving the Soviet-dominated countries in a continuing drain of intellectual power and skilled labor for the better opportunities offered by democratic societies. East German soldiers were under orders to shoot people attempting to defect, even women and children.[39]

Communications in the modern world would ultimately result in the fall of the Iron Curtain. Television and radio simply made the physical barriers separating the Eastern Bloc countries from their Western counterparts moot. There was no way to prevent the continuous bombardment of audio and visual images of the "good life" experienced under democracy and capitalism from permeating the regions behind the Iron Curtain. On June 12, 1987, then-President Ronald Reagan challenged the General Secretary of the Communist Party of the Soviet Union, Mikhail Gorbachev, in a speech commemorating the 750th anniversary of the establishment of Berlin, saying,

> We welcome change and openness; for we believe that freedom and security go together, that the advance of human liberty can only strengthen the cause of world peace. There is one sign the Soviets can make that would be unmistakable, that would advance dramatically the cause of freedom and peace. General Secretary Gorbachev, if you seek peace, if you seek prosperity for the Soviet Union and Eastern Europe, if you seek liberalization, come here to this gate. Mr. Gorbachev, open this gate. Mr. Gorbachev, tear down this wall![40]

Hungary effectively disabled its physical border defenses with Austria on August 19, 1989, and in September 13,000 East German tourists, recognizing nothing was

One of the last remaining stretches of the Iron Curtain, maintained as part of the Möedlareuth Museum. Mödlareuth, Freilichtmuseum, 2002, Andreas Praefcke. Wikimedia Commons.

stopping them from escaping Soviet domination, simply left by going through Hungary to Austria.[41] Realizing what had happened, the Hungarians prevented many more East Germans from crossing the border and returned them to Budapest. These East Germans flooded the West German embassy and refused to return to East Germany. The East German government responded by disallowing any further travel to Hungary but allowed those already there to return. This triggered a similar incident in neighboring Czechoslovakia. On this occasion, the East German authorities allowed them to leave, provided they use a train that transited East Germany on the way. Protest demonstrations broke out all over East Germany in September 1989, prompting longtime leader of East Germany, Erich Honecker, to resign on October 18, 1989. Egon Krenz replaced him a few days later. The protest demonstrations grew considerably by early November. The movement neared its height on November 4 when half a million people gathered at the Alexanderplatz demonstration in a rally for change in East Berlin's large public square and transportation hub.

Meanwhile, the wave of refugees leaving East Germany for the West had increased and had found its way through Hungary via Czechoslovakia (or via the West German Embassy in Prague). This mass exodus was tolerated by the new Krenz government and in agreement with the communist Czechoslovak government. Easing the complications, the Politburo, led by Krenz, decided on November 9 to allow refugees to exit directly through crossing points between East Germany and West Germany, including West Berlin. The same day, the ministerial administration modified the proposal to include private travel. The new regulations were to take effect the next day.

However, due to an error by Günter Schabowski, the party boss in East Berlin and the spokesman for the Socialist Unity Party of Germany (Sozialistische Einheitspartei Deutschlands, SED) controlled Politburo, an uncontrolled opening of the border would occur a day early.[42]

Shortly before a November 9 press conference, Schabowski was handed a note announcing the changes but was given no further instructions on how to handle the information. These regulations had only been completed a few hours earlier and were to take effect the following day, to allow time to inform the border guards. However, nobody had informed him of the planned timeline.[43] He read the note out loud at the end of the conference. One of the reporters, by most accounts NBC's Tom Brokaw, asked when the regulations would take effect. After a few seconds' hesitation, Schabowski assumed it would be the same day based on the wording of the note and replied, "As far as I know effective immediately, without delay."[44] After further questions from journalists, he confirmed that the regulations included the border crossings toward West Berlin, which he had not mentioned until then.

After hearing the broadcast, East Germans began gathering at the wall and at the six checkpoints between East and West, demanding that border guards immediately open the gates.[45] The surprised and overwhelmed guards made many hectic telephone calls to their superiors about the problem. At first, they were ordered to find the "more aggressive" people gathered at the gates and stamp their passports with a special stamp that barred them from returning to East Germany, in effect revoking their citizenship. This still left thousands of people demanding to be let through "as Schabowski said we can."[46] None of the East German authorities would take personal responsibility for issuing orders to use lethal force to prevent the opening of the gates so the vastly out-numbered soldiers had no way to hold back the huge crowd of East German citizens. At 10:45 p.m., November 9, 1989, the guards yielded, opening the checkpoints and allowing people through with little or no identity checking. The Iron Curtain that had divided the European continent for nearly half a century succumbed to the will of the people to be free.

The Last Great Twentieth-Century Border Wall

While the Iron Curtain was falling across Europe and the Berlin Wall was going up to divide a city, in Asia ideological differences between the Soviet Union's client state in the north of the Korean peninsula and the United States' client state to the south, would result in a war that, as of this writing, has lasted more than sixty-three years and claimed more than three million lives. Although the active combat phase of the Korean War only lasted from June 25, 1950, until an armistice was signed July 27, 1953, no peace treaty has ever been completed between the warring states. Instead, a 2.5-mile (4 km) wide, 160-mile (250 km) long demilitarized zone has been erected to separate the opposing forces.

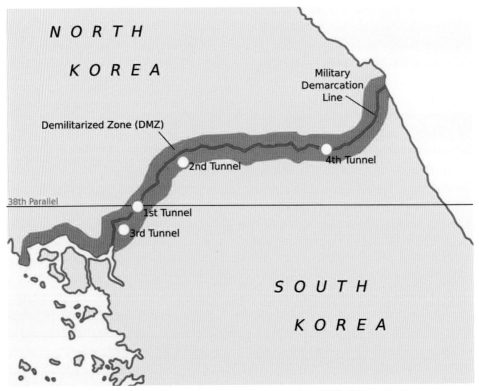

The Korean Demilitarized Zone. Rishabh Tatiraju, September 2012. Wikimedia Commons.

The demilitarized zone (DMZ) was created as each side agreed to move their stalemated forces back 2,000 meters (2,200 yards) from the front lines, creating a buffer zone between the troops. Today, the Military Demarcation Line (MDL) goes down the center of the DMZ and indicates exactly where the front was when the agreement was signed. Since the signing of the Armistice Agreement, the DMZ has been continuously monitored by the Neutral Nations Supervisory Commission (NNSC) consisting of representatives of the Swiss and Swedish Armed Forces. Either side of the DMZ the military forces of North and South Korea maintain a tenuous compromise guarding against active aggression, or the perception of aggression. The Armistice Agreement specifies the exact numbers of troops from each side that may be inside the DMZ at any given time and the weapons they may have. Forces from both countries conduct patrols within the DMZ but they may not cross the MDL. Both countries maintain numerous checkpoints along and within the DMZ.[47]

Sporadic outbreaks of violence, incursions (primarily by the North) across the MDL, and other events have resulted in the deaths of more than five hundred South Korean and North Korean soldiers, fifty U.S. soldiers, and numerous sailors from both sides between 1953 and the present.[48] The DMZ is the most heavily militarized border in the world, with significant forces arrayed against each other, in a constant state of readiness to respond to combat operations by the other side.[49]

Inside the DMZ, near the western coast of the peninsula, Panmunjom is the home of the Joint Security Area (JSA). Originally the only connection between North and South Korea, this changed in 2007 when a Korail train crossed the DMZ to the North on the new Donghae Bukbu Line built on the east coast of Korea.[50] At Panmunjom there are several buildings on both the north and the south side of the Military Demarcation Line. Only a handful straddle the MDL. The Joint Security Area is the location where all negotiations since 1953 have been held, including statements of Korean solidarity, which have generally amounted to little except a slight decline in tensions. The MDL goes through the conference rooms and down the middle of the conference tables where the North Koreans and the United Nations Command (primarily South Koreans and Americans) meet face to face.[51]

Though generally calm, the DMZ has been the scene of much saber rattling between the two Koreas over the years. Several small skirmishes have occurred within the Joint Security Area since 1953. The Axe Murder Incident in August 1976 involved the attempted trimming of a poplar tree that resulted in two deaths (Americans Capt. Arthur Bonifas and 1st Lt. Mark Barrett) and Operation Paul Bunyan, when the tree in question was subsequently removed by the Americans. Beforehand, the soldiers of both sides were permitted to go back and forth across the MDL inside of the JSA, a privilege since revoked because of this incident.[52]

Another incident occurred on November 23, 1984, when a Soviet tourist, who was part of an official trip to the JSA (hosted by the North), ran across the Military Demarcation Line (MDL) shouting that he wanted to defect. North Korean troops immediately chased after him opening fire. Border guards on the South Korean side returned fire eventually surrounding the North Koreans as they pursued the Russian national. One South Korean and three North Korean soldiers were killed in the action. The defector was not captured.[53]

North Korea has made at least four attempts to tunnel under the DMZ. Although the "official" position of the North Koreans has been that the tunnels were for coal mining, no coal has ever been discovered in the tunnels, which are bored through solid granite. The tunnels all run in a North-South configuration and have no branch tunnels. The engineering of the tunnels has consistently improved with each subsequent construction. The first three tunnels were discovered through information gained from North Korean defectors.[54]

In an era of nuclear weapons, the Korean DMZ is an anachronism reminding us of the ancient efforts by empires to protect themselves from outsiders. Should military hostilities break out again on the Korean peninsula, the DMZ would be meaningless in an era of stealth bombers, aircraft carriers, submarines, paratroops, and thermonuclear-tipped ballistic missiles.

A New Century Spawns New Walls

With the continuing turmoil in the Middle East and North Africa there has been a movement to return to the use of walls of all types along many borders in Europe and the Middle East. Saudi Arabia is building a high-tech fence along the border with Iraq that will include thermal imaging and battlefield radar to prevent the entrance of ISIS fighters.[55] Israel has constructed an extensive fence along the border with Egypt.[56]

Hungary built a 13-foot-tall barbed-wire-and-mesh fence along 325 miles of its border with Serbia and Croatia to prevent the free access to the European Union (EU)

Israel-Egypt Border Fence. Wikimedia, available for reuse.

Hungary Border Fence. Wikicommons, available for reuse.

by migrants in illegally entering Hungary wanting to claim asylum in accordance with international and European Law. This border was constructed because the EU was acting too slowly to address the migration problem from Middle East countries in conflict and Hungary could not continue providing support for the massive millions of immigrants entering its country.[57]

The continued use of fences as barriers between countries is indicative that the need for border security is imperative for national sovereignty and prevention of un-controlled migration. We can expect this trend of construction of new and extensive fencing to continue for the foreseeable future.

Conclusion

From the earliest days of human society, a border has been necessary to identify the boundaries of territory and provide security for members of the society. As civilizations grew, expanded, and came into conflict, the delineation of a border was insufficient, resulting in a need to establish barriers to invasion by raiders and conquering armies. Thus, came the development of walled cities, building of border fences, and, ultimately, the imposition of electronic surveillance systems to monitor cross-border traffic. Frequently, border security has been as much about regulation of trade and control of moving populations as it has been about physical security of cities and nations. Today, it is a combination of all aspects associated with the control of territory for the good of a recognized population.

If three thousand years of civilization has demonstrated anything, it has clearly pointed out that borders are fluid. Borders change as populations move and societies transform. Economics, politics, religion, and conflict are all factors affecting modern borders and driving them to change. Existing borders between modern countries are rarely static for more than a few decades and in rare instances, a century or so. Borders may soon become an anachronism in a world where industry, religion, and transportation are globalized, forcing a new reality on the human community.

Questions for Further Consideration

1. Hadrian's Wall is a classic example of what happens when people from different cultures and ethnicities interact across a fixed fortification. Is a similar process underway across the American Southwest?
2. Civilization has thousands of years' experience with fixed fortifications. What commonalities have all these "walls" experienced?
3. With the fall of the Berlin Wall (and the Iron Curtain) in 1989 the reunification of East and West Germany became inevitable. Sooner or later a similar event will occur on the Korean Penninsula. Under what conditions will the barriers between North and South Korea be eliminated?

Chapter 2 Endnotes

1. Hogg, I. (1981). *The history of fortification*. New York: St. Martin's Press.
2. Ibid.
3. Ibid.
4. Kovacs, M. G. (trans.) (n.d.) *The Epic of Gilgamesh*. Tablet 1. Accessed 2012-09-24 at: http://www.ancienttexts.org/library/mesopotamian/gilgamesh/tab1.htm.
5. Mithen, S. (2006). *After the ice: A global human history, 20,000–5000 BC* (1st Harvard University Press pbk. ed.) (p. 59). Cambridge, MA: Harvard University Press.
6. Hogg (1981).
7. Ibid. (p. 18).
8. Bible, New International Version (NIV, 1984), Isaiah 22:9–10.
9. Bible, NIV (1984), Nehemiah 3:16–32.
10. Fine, J. (1983). *The Ancient Greeks: A Critical History*. Cambridge, MA: Harvard University Press.
11. Hogg (1981).
12. Ibid.
13. Everitt, A. (2009) *Hadrian and the Triumph of Rome*. New York: Random House.
14. Hogg (1981).
15. Ibid.
16. Ibid.
17. Ibid.
18. Ibid.
19. Information on the Great Wall of China has been consolidated from a variety of sources including: Slavicek, L. C., G. J. Mitchell, J. I. Matray (2005). *The Great Wall of China*. New York: Infobase Publishing.; Evans, T. (2006). *Great Wall of China: Beijing & Northern China*. Bucks, England: Bradt Travel Guides; Pletcher, K. (2010). *The Geography of China: Sacred and Historic Places*. Buffalo, NY: Britannica Educational Publishing: The Rosen Publishing Group; Mooney, P. and C. Karnow (2008). *National Geographic Traveler: Beijing*. Washington, D.C.: National Geographic Books; Edmonds, R. L. (1985). *Northern Frontiers of Qing China and Tokugawa Japan: A Comparative Study of Frontier Policy*.

Chicago: University of Chicago, Department of Geography; Research Paper No. 213 (pp. 38–40).

20. Hogg (1981).

21. Whitson, W. (Trans.) (1737). The Works of Falvius Josephus. Book VII. Last accessed 2012-10-05 at http://www.sacred-texts.com/jud/josephus/index.htm.

22. Morris, R. (1983). *The Peacemakers: The Great Powers and American Independence.* Boston: Northeastern University Press.

23. Fleming, T. J. (2003). *The Louisiana Purchase.* John Wiley and Sons.

24. Haynes, R. V. (2010). *The Mississippi Territory and the Southwest frontier, 1795–1817.* Lexington, KY: University of Kentucky Press.

25. *Treaty between Her Majesty and the United States of America, for the Settlement of the Oregon Boundary* and styled in the United States as the *Treaty with Great Britain, in Regard to Limits Westward of the Rocky Mountains.* Library of Congress.

26. Hogg (1981).

27. Ibid.

28. Shirer, W. L. (1960). *The rise and fall of the Third Reich.* New York: Simon and Schuster.

29. Hogg (1981).

30. Kaufmann, J. E. and H. W. Kaufmann (1997). *The Maginot Line: None shall pass.* London: Praeger.

31. Hogg (1981). Kaufmann (1997).

32. Hogg (1981).

33. Kaufmann, J. E. and H. W. Kaufmann (2003). *Fortress Third Reich: German fortifications and defense systems in World War II.* Cambridge, MA: Da Capo Press.

34. Ibid.

35. Ibid.

36. Ibid.

37. Ibid.

38. Iron Curtain. Encyclopedia Britannica.

39. E. German 'license to kill' found. BBC News. Accessed 2012-10-06 at http://news.bbc.co.uk/2/hi/europe/6943093.stm.

40. "Remarks at the Brandenburg Gate." Ronald Reagan Presidential Foundation. Archived from the original on 22 June 2008. Retrieved 6 October 2012.

41. Meyer, Michael (13 September 2009). "The picnic that brought down the Berlin Wall." *LA Times.* Retrieved 6 October 2012.

42. Sarotte, M. E. (1 November 2009) "How it went down: The little accident that toppled history." *Washington Post.* Retrieved 6 October 2012.

43. Sebetsyen, V. (2009). *Revolution 1989: The Fall of the Soviet Empire.* New York: Pantheon Books.

44. Ibid.

45. Sarotte (2009).

46. Sebetsyen (2009).

47. Kirkbride, W. A. (1985). *The road to Panmunjom: Facts about the Korean DMZ.* Elizabeth, NJ: Hollym International.

48. Nanto, D. K. (18 March 2003). *North Korea: Chronology of provocations, 1950–2003.* Congressional Research Service: RL30004.

49. Kirkbride (1985).

50. "Trans-Korean Railway." *Korean Rail Technology* (English). September 2007. Retrieved 6 October 2012.

51. Kirkbride (1985).

52. Ibid.

53. Nanto (2003).

54. Panmunjom Visitors Center, North Korea.

55. Gayle, D. (15 January 2015). "The Great Wall of Saudi Arabia: Kingdom plans to build a 600-mile barrier from Jordan to Kuwait in response to the threat of an invasion by ISIS." Mail Online. Available at: http://www.dailymail.co.uk/news/article-2912334/The-Great-Wall-Saudi-Arabia-Kingdom--plans-build-600-mile-barrier-Jordan-Kuwait-response-threat-invasion-ISIS.html

56. Lamb, F. (21 April 2012). "How Many Walls Will Secure the Zionist Occupation of Palestine?" Almanar TV. Available at: http://archive.almanar.com.lb/english/article.php?id=53159

57. BBC: Europe. (15 September 2017). "Migrant crisis: Hungary's closed border leaves many stranded." Available at: http://www.bbc.com/news/world-europe-34260071

Chapter 3

Border Security Agency Operations

"[T]he bloody events transpiring along the trailing edges of the United States are the country's best-kept secrets. Only along the border can the death of fourteen men, women, and children not make headline news. Only along the border can a frustrated American citizen sling an AK-47 over his shoulder to protect his property and hardly garner a second glance. Only along the borders can a foreign military cross onto U.S. soil, open fire on a U.S. federal agent with assault rifles, and then head home without suffering the slightest repercussion, which is exactly what happened to me in the spring of 2002 while stationed at the Ajo Border Patrol Station in Why, Arizona."

—Alex Pacheco, from *On the Line: Inside the Border Patrol*, 2004

Key Words and Concepts

BORSTAR
BORTAC
Bracero Program
Chinese Exclusion Act(s)
Customs and Border Protection
Enforcement and Removal Office
Geary Act
Homeland Security Investigations
Operation Gatekeeper

Operation Hold the Line
Operation Safeguard
Operation Stonegarden
Operation Wetback
US Border Patrol
US Customs and Immigration Service
Immigration and Customs Enforcement
Immigration Reform and Control Act
(IRCA)

Introduction

Secure borders in every country play an extremely important role in maintaining economic vitality and commerce. National borders are natural gateways for imported and exported goods, and play a primary role in international tourism and business. Borders also provide access into the country through both major and minor (clandestine) entry points. Control of those borders is the key to mitigating the risk posed by the penetration of unwanted or dangerous people and goods into the country. The Department of Homeland Security has been tasked with managing the legal movement of goods and people across America's borders, and with protecting these same borders from illegal infiltration.

Linewatch — Chula Vista Sector — 1964. © U.S. Border Patrol Museum. Used with permission.

US Border Security Agencies before the Advent of Homeland Security

All the agencies within the Department of Homeland Security (DHS) have an historical organizational basis that predates the advent of DHS. Fully understanding today's operations and organization of those agencies assigned to border security operations necessitates we review their origins.

Border Patrol

The United States Border Patrol (USBP) is an American federal law enforcement agency that enforces laws and regulations for the admission of foreign-born persons (aliens) to the United States, as codified in the Immigration and Nationality Act of 1965, also known as the Hart-Celler Act. It is an agency operating within US Customs and Border Protection (CBP), and is one of the many agencies working under the umbrella of the Department of Homeland Security (DHS). US Customs and Border Protection currently has more sworn, armed law enforcement officers than any other agency within the United States.

The Border Patrol was founded on May 28, 1924, as an agency of the United States Department of Labor to prevent illegal entries along the Mexico–United States border and the United States–Canada border. The first two border patrol stations were in El

Paso, Texas, and Detroit, Michigan. The government initially only provided each Border Patrol agent a badge and revolver. Recruits furnished their own horse and saddle, but Washington supplied oats and hay for the horses and a $1,680 annual salary for the agents. The agents did not have uniforms until 1928.

Additional Border Patrol operations were established along the Gulf Coast in 1927 to perform crewman control and insure that non-American crewmen departed on the same ship on which they arrived. Additional Border Patrol stations were temporarily added along the Gulf Coast of Florida and the Eastern Seaboard during the Cuban Missile Crisis in the 1960s.

The primary mission of the US Customs and Border Protection agency in the Department of Homeland Security is securing the nation's borders. According to DHS, its measure of "border miles under effective control" applies to the entire 8,607 miles for which the Border Patrol is responsible, which includes approximately 2,000 miles along the United States–Mexico border. "Border miles under effective control" is defined by CBP as meaning "when the appropriate mix of personnel, equipment, technology and tactical infrastructure has been deployed to reasonably ensure that when an attempted illegal entry is detected, the Border Patrol has the ability to identify, classify and respond to bring the attempted illegal entry to a satisfactory law-enforcement resolution."

Mounted Inspectors, usually called "mounted guards," of the United States Immigration Service patrolled the border to prevent illegal crossings into this country as early as 1904, but their efforts were undertaken only when resources (available men and horses) permitted. The "mounted guards" did not wear uniforms, other than a badge, which at the time was the only thing that came with the job. They were given the impressive sum of twenty-four dollars a month, which was not bad money in those days, but out of that, they had to supply their own horses, their own guns, their own clothes, and their own ammunition. They had to feed their horses and pay for their own food from their monthly salary. The inspectors operated out of El Paso, Texas, and they patrolled as far west as California. They worked their own hours, and their own patrol routes. Somewhat surprisingly, the biggest problem with illegal immigration along the southern border with Mexico in 1904 was not Mexicans trying to cross the border. The Mounted Inspectors spent most of their time primarily trying to restrict the flow of illegal Chinese immigrants into the country, who came both for the California Gold Rush (which had started in 1848) as well as opportunities for work. The Chinese were a special case, partially due to the increasing numbers of Chinese entering the country, and partially due to the media of the time. Newspapers devoted article after article to the "yellow peril," as it was called, referring to the influx of Chinese. The more media coverage of the Chinese, the more public opinion turned against them, with a concomitant increase in public pressure for the mounted guards to locate them.

The California Gold Rush (1848–55) began on January 24, 1848, when gold was found by James Marshall at Sutter's Mill near Coloma, California. The first to hear confirmed reports of the Gold Rush were the people in Oregon, the Sandwich Islands (Hawaii), and Latin America. These were the first to start flocking to California in late 1848. All told, the news of gold brought some 300,000 people to the state from the rest of the United States and abroad.[1] Of the 300,000, some traveled by ship, and some came from the east overland on the California Trail (running from Missouri westward with the Mormon and Oregon Trails until it diverged at Ft. Hall on the Snake River to California) and the Gila River trail (which roughly follows the Gila River westward from Santa Fe, New Mexico, to San Diego, California, along the Gila River).

The gold-seekers, called "forty-niners" (as a reference to 1849), often faced substantial hardships on the trip. While most of the newly arrived were Americans from the East, the Gold Rush attracted tens of thousands from Latin America, Europe, Australia, and China. About half of the "forty-niners" came by ship, including Europeans, Australians, Chinese, Americans from the East Coast, and those from Latin America, and about half by land. Those coming overland to the gold fields originally lived mostly in the American Midwest, near the Ohio, Mississippi, or Missouri River, and were more familiar with travel by horse or wagon than those living in the East. Nearly all those going overland reached their jumping-off place by using a steamboat to get there with their animals and supplies. The Chinese arrived primarily by ship. Most, of course, wanted to make their fortune in the 1849-era California Gold Rush. The Chinese did not, however, only come for the Gold Rush in California, but also helped build the Transcontinental Railroad, worked the southern plantations after the Civil War, and participated in setting up California's agriculture and fisheries.[2] They were also fleeing the Taiping Rebellion (a massive civil war in China from 1850 to 1864, against the ruling Manchu-led Qing Dynasty) that eventually led to the deaths of approximately twenty million Chinese. Forced from their own country by war and famine, the Chinese came to America looking for riches, hoping to either stake a claim in the gold country, or find a niche in California's booming economy. Most of their dreams were never realized. Stranded in a new country and ostracized from much of the population, they found themselves working for the railroad, for public projects, or for the mines. From the outset, they were faced with the racism of the settled European immigrant population, which during the 1870s culminated in massacres and forced relocations of Chinese migrants into what became known as Chinatowns. The Chinese, particularly the ones working as miners, were much more badly situated in the United States than most other ethnic minorities. They had to pay special taxes (all foreign miners had to pay a tax of $20 a month), were not allowed to marry white European partners, and could not acquire US citizenship.[3]

Illegal immigration by the Chinese began to be a problem after passage of the Pacific Railroad Act in 1862, and work started on the Transcontinental Railroad. The railroad replaced the wagon trains of previous decades and allowed for the transportation of larger quantities of goods over longer distances, in a shorter amount of time. It was a good idea, but linking up the Central Pacific Railroad and Union Pacific Railroad to create the 1,928 mile "Pacific Railroad" link between Council Bluffs, Iowa, and Omaha, Nebraska, and the San Francisco Bay at Oakland, California, via Ogden, Utah, and Sacramento, California, connecting with the existing railroad network to the East Coast, required a huge source of cheap labor. The Chinese, both legal and illegal immigrants, quickly filled the vacuum. While industrial employers were eager to get this new and (relatively) cheap labor, the white public was stirred

Train Check, El Paso, Texas. © U.S. Border Patrol Museum. Used with permission.

to anger by the presence of this "yellow peril." Desperate to find work and escape a civil war in their home country, the Chinese would take a boat to the western coast of Mexico, then hike to the interior and take the Mexican Central Railroad to Ciudad Juarez just south of El Paso, where Mexican smugglers gladly escorted them across the border to America, for a fee.

A major part of the duty of the early mounted guard officers was searching for the smugglers' trails in Arizona used to bring Chinese immigrants to meeting (and dispersal) points (known as Chinese Farms by the mounted guards) on American soil. The immigrants would then be transported all over the country to meet the increasing demand for cheap labor. Many of these smugglers' trails led directly to Tombstone, Arizona. Per Krauss and Pacheco (2004), almost every legal Chinese immigrant in Tombstone had a basement dug under his house, specifically used to hide the illegal Chinese immigrants until they could be transferred to another location.[4]

Aside from not having more modern technology, such as motion sensors, four-wheel-drive vehicles, airplanes, and boats, the job the Mounted Inspectors did patrolling the border in 1904 is essentially the same as what the Border Patrol agents do today. The early version of the Border Patrol, the Mounted Inspectors, worked out a successful plan to detour and apprehend the human smugglers of the day. The first line of defense was along the river itself. A few of them camped out along the Rio Grande, to seize the smugglers and their human cargo the minute they crossed the river. The border was long, however, and there were too few inspectors to fully protect the border, and the agents missed many of them. To catch the Chinese they missed at the river, other inspectors on horseback would "read sign" or "cut sign" (decipher footprints, horse prints, broken branches and twigs, etc., made by the movement of men over terrain) and track them overland to cut them off before they could reach the relative safety of the Chinese Farms. If the inspectors missed them before they reached the dispersal points, the illegal immigrants were not completely in the clear. More agents were stationed at inspection stations along the rail lines heading north and south of the border. This strategy worked well for a time, but the smart smugglers soon learned to unload their cargo in advance of the "surprise" inspection points, and trek on foot to avoid them. Later, another team of inspectors was stationed further inland to again search for the illegal aliens.

The more elaborate smuggling rings supplied the Chinese with papers, for a cost, so that the immigrants could travel without harassment on the railways. Sometimes deals with railway workers were made by the smuggling rings in advance, to allow the immigrants to stow away in the boxcars. The plan was ingenious, because the border inspectors could not demand to inspect the cars without probable cause, or consent (much like the law enforcement officers of today, after stopping a vehicle on the nation's highways). The border patrol agents soon came up with an even better idea—they would walk along the tracks, holding a bee smoker under the boxcars so that the smoke could filter up through the cracks. If the agents heard any coughing from cars that were only supposed to hold cargo, they then had the probable cause they needed to demand the doors be opened for inspection.[5]

Despite the provisions for equal treatment of Chinese immigrants in the 1868 Burlingame Treaty, political and labor organizations rallied against the immigration of what they regarded as a degraded race and "cheap Chinese labor." Newspapers condemned the policies of employers of Chinese, and even church leaders denounced the entrance of these aliens into what was regarded as a land for whites only. So hostile was the opposition that in 1882 the United States Congress eventually passed the Chinese Exclusion Act, which prohibited immigration from China for the next ten years. The Chinese Exclusion Act was the only US law ever to prevent immigration and naturalization solely based on race.[6]

Although the Chinese Exclusion Act did restrict legal immigration, it permitted those Chinese in the United States as of November 17, 1880, to stay, travel abroad, and return; prohibited the naturalization of Chinese; and created the Section 6 exempt status for teachers, students, merchants, and travelers. These exempt classes could be admitted into this country with the presentation of a certificate from the Chinese government verifying their status.

The next significant exclusionary legislation related to immigration was the Act to Prohibit the Coming of Chinese Persons into the United States of May 1892 (27 Stat. 25). Referred to as the Geary Act, it allowed Chinese laborers to travel to China and reenter the United States but its provisions were somewhat more restrictive than preceding immigration laws. This Act required Chinese immigrants to register with the government and obtain a certificate as proof of their right to be in this country. The penalties for those who failed to have the required papers or witnesses were imprisonment or deportation. Other restrictive immigration acts affecting citizens of Chinese ancestry followed. During World War II, when China and the United States were allies, President Franklin D. Roosevelt signed an Act to Repeal the Chinese Exclusion Acts, to Establish Quotas, and for Other Purposes (57 Stat. 600-1). This Act of December 13, 1943, also lifted restrictions on naturalization. However, until the Immigration Act of October 1965 (79 Stat. 911) numerous laws continued to have a restrictive impact on Chinese immigration.[7]

Certain federal agencies were particularly active in enforcing the exclusion laws. Initially the Customs Service took the lead because of the maritime nature of immigration. In 1900 the Office of the Superintendent of Immigration, which had been established in the Department of the Treasury in 1891, became the chief agency responsible for implementing federal regulations mandated by the Chinese exclusion laws. This agency eventually evolved into the present Immigration and Naturalization Service (INS). Both the Chinese Bureau within the Customs Service and the Chinese Division of the INS employed "Chinese" inspectors, people designated to enforce the Chinese exclusion laws. Immigration-related decisions made by these Federal officials were sometimes appealed to federal courts, which also heard criminal cases involving Chinese alleged to be living in the United States illegally. Many of the records created to implement the Chinese exclusion laws are now in the custody of the National Archives and Records Administration's (NARA) Regional Archives, which are a major resource for the study of Chinese immigration and Chinese-American travel, trade, and social history from the late-19th to mid-20th centuries.

Prohibition and Tighter Immigration Laws

Prohibition began on January 16, 1920, when Congress passed the Eighteenth Amendment to the US Constitution, prohibiting the importation, transport, manufacture, or sale of alcoholic beverages. Much of the American public was outraged, but smugglers north and south of the border were ecstatic. For every legal drinking establishment that closed because of Prohibition, ten "speakeasies" and "line houses" opened, to satisfy Americans' thirst for beer and liquor.

Black market trade in "hooch," or illegal, often homemade, liquor, demanded most of the attention of the Border Patrol effort during the thirteen years of Prohibition. Officers on duty in the North patrolled the Canadian border to stem the liquor traffic between "wet" Canada and the "dry" United States. But the northern border did not have a monopoly on liquor smuggling—whiskey bootleggers operated along the Mexican border, avoiding the bridges and slipping their forbidden cargo across the Rio Grande by way of pack mules. Many illegal liquor distributors near the southern border turned to Mexican cattle thieves who became booze smugglers overnight. Tequila and mescal began to flow north from Mexico in wagons and on the backs of donkeys, and rum, ale, and beer began to flow south from Canada, in boats, cars, and trucks. The alcohol smugglers along the southern border usually protected their shipment by hiring heavily-armed local bandits who had no qualms about shooting Texas Rangers, Marshals, mounted inspectors, or anyone else along the way. The Mounted Inspectors had not had a single death in the ranks since the agency began

Liquor seizure — Rouses Point, New York — 1920s. (Note bullet holes in fenders and gas tank, from attempts to disable the vehicle). © U.S. Border Patrol Museum. Used with permission.

in 1904, but that ended with the beginning of Prohibition. In the first year of Prohibition, half a dozen Border Patrol agents were killed in the line of duty.[8]

Emanuel Wright, a Border Patrolman who joined in 1925, was later quoted in the *El Paso Times* on May 28, 1974, "This was one of the most vicious times in the history of the border. Smugglers had pretty much of a free hand and knew how to handle horses and a gun. They knew the brush country and you were dealing with a man who was equivalent to you. We lost a lot of men — we killed a lot of smugglers."[9]

Liquor smuggling was a major concern because it often accompanied alien smuggling. The majority of the Border Patrol was assigned to the Canadian border during the Prohibition years. The thinking was that since Canada was a "wet" country, and the United States was "dry," most of the illegal liquor would be coming south, from Canada, not north, from Mexico.

In June 1933, President Franklin D. Roosevelt combined the Bureau of Immigration and the Bureau of Naturalization into the Immigration and Naturalization Service (INS). After Prohibition ended on December 5, 1933, Border Patrol agents along the southern border who were accustomed to gun battles with Mexican bootleggers and their hired guns had a new enemy to contend with — policymakers in Washington, D.C. Suddenly, politicians who had never been within five hundred miles of either border knew not only exactly how Border Patrol agents should do their job, but also somehow knew exactly who should do it. Many of the tough, brave Border Patrol

Rouses Point, New York — 1956. © U.S. Border Patrol Museum. Used with permission.

agents who had learned to survive by acting first and asking questions later lost their jobs. The new requirements for Border Patrol required all applicants (and prior agents) to take and pass a detailed Civil Service Examination, which consisted of arithmetic, writing, and knowledge of Spanish. If agents either refused to take the exam, or failed it, they were summarily fired.[10]

If an applicant passed the Civil Service Exam, then he had to be approved by a group of administrators, after an oral exam. If he passed the oral examination, then he was given approval to attend classes at the Border Patrol Academy. The first Border Patrol Academy opened as a training school at Camp Chigas, El Paso, in December 1934. Thirty-four trainees were in the first class and attended classes in marksmanship and horsemanship, as well as classes in immigration and international law. The recruits had to prove their prowess using a gun as well as a horse. After passing a shooting test, the applicants were taken to Mount Cristo Rey, on the outskirts of El Paso, and had to ride up the nearly vertical incline as well as descend, without falling off their horses.[11]

The current problem with illegal immigration across the southern border, involving Mexicans, didn't begin until 1917, and it had more to do with trying to recruit needed laborers from south of the border (twice) than it did with the (continually poor) Mexican economy. After World War I began, the United States experienced a severe

Buslift — Fabens, Texas — 1953. © U.S. Border Patrol Museum. Used with permission.

labor shortage, particularly in agriculture. This shortage was due primarily to the number of able-bodied American men who went overseas to fight, or were working in wartime factories, making bombs and airplanes for the Allied war effort in Europe. Politicians representing wealthy agriculturists and industrialists soon became aware of the problem, by virtue of communication with their constituents and their lobbyists, and with the approval of the Secretary of Labor, a special departmental order was issued, rescinding many of the restrictive immigration laws. Immigrants from south of the border were suddenly no longer required to pay the head tax that had been levied in 1882, or pass the literacy law requirements. Suddenly, the southern border was wide open for Mexican immigrants wanting work. Word quickly spread in Mexico that American farmers would hire anyone who could walk, swim, or crawl across the border. Between 1917 and 1924, more than a hundred thousand Mexicans came to the United States, seeking work (and obtaining it) on farms and in factories.[12] Once the floodgates are opened, for whatever reason, it is always difficult, and sometimes impossible, to completely close them again. The flood of Mexican workers that began in 1917 did not stop, of course, with the end of the First World War in 1918, or with the reinstatement of the immigration laws that had been temporarily lifted during the war. When the Mexican people realized that jobs were available in the country to the north, they simply made their way across the border, regardless of the head tax and literacy law requirements, or the Border Patrol agents attempting to stop them, much as they do today.

Radio room — 1946. © U.S. Border Patrol Museum. Used with permission.

Prior to the Great Depression in 1929, few Americans outside of the Border Patrol cared about the increasing numbers of Mexicans crossing the border illegally. However, things changed after 1929. With thousands of American workers out of work, there was a public outcry not only to stop the illegal immigration across the border, but also to remove the hundreds of thousands of illegal immigrants already in this country. The Deportation Act of 1929 was passed on March 4, authorizing the Immigration Service to round up Mexican workers and ship them back across the border. Between 1929 and 1939, approximately 500,000 Mexicans were repatriated to Mexico.[13]

Although horses remained the transportation of choice for many years, by 1935, the Border Patrol began using motorized equipment, including government surplus Jeeps with radios that used Morse code, to communicate with headquarters. Some of the older Border Patrolmen had some problems trying to learn how to operate the new technology, including using Morse code. A few weeks after they had been installed, half of the new radios mysteriously ended up broken. This was probably just a coincidence.

Rugged terrain and the need for quick, quiet transportation require that horses remain essential transportation to the Border Patrol even to the present day. This is just another example of the fact that the essential job of the Border Patrol, protecting the borders, has not really changed since the days of the Mounted Inspectors in 1904. They began by cutting/reading sign, tracking those crossing the border illegally, and they are doing the same thing today.

Sign Cutting

Those men responsible for protecting the border during the war years of the 1940s were not demonstrably different people than those working as mounted inspectors during 1904. Most of the men in either group were raised in the country on a ranch or farm, and were familiar (long before they began collecting paychecks from Uncle Sam) with primitive tracking skills, used to round up lost cattle or wounded game. Ab Taylor, raised on a farm outside of San Angelo, in the central part of Texas, was representative of those men. Although familiar with basic tracking skills, once hired by the Border Patrol in 1949, he soon realized that tracking humans was much more difficult than tracking animals. Humans are much more difficult to follow, especially those aware of the possibility of their being tracked. They will generally attempt to disguise their movements, and use brush to camouflage their tracks and rocky ground to hide their footprints. They do whatever they can think of to hide from inexperienced trackers.

Reading (or "cutting") sign is simply the art, or science, of learning to spot and interpret correctly any disturbance in the natural terrain related to the passing of human traffic. This can include footprints, broken twigs, displaced rocks or pebbles, and/or vegetation moved or depressed by a passing foot. Among the most difficult parts of tracking is determining the age of the sign. It was (and is) important for an agent to make an accurate reading of how long ago a person

Sign Cut, El Paso, Texas — 1950s. © U.S. Border Patrol Museum. Used with permission.

has passed. If it has been longer than a few hours, or days, then it is (relatively) unimportant, because the person or persons have long since passed a particular point along the border. Natural elements change sign on a real-time basis. Wind, rain, sunlight, and changes in temperature all modify tracks, depending on degree and type of terrain. Wind and rain modify the outline of footprints in sand or snow, and sunlight and changes in temperature alter displaced soil on rocky ground. A tracker who can look at sign and determine accurately when tracks were made and how far ahead the person or persons are has a distinct advantage.

Of course, locating the tracks and deciding how many aliens had passed, their direction, and how long ago they had passed was only part of the process—the point of it was to catch them. If they had an eight- to ten-hour head start, catching them was difficult, if not impossible, so the Patrol agents came up with an ingenious method of making up for lost time. Called "leapfrogging," it worked this way: once an agent decided how many people were in a group, and which direction they were going, another agent or group of agents would drive ahead a mile or so, and look for similar tracks. If the second agent found tracks, he had to determine if they belonged to the original group. Analyzing the tracks, using the print patterns of the original persons' shoes, could do this. If the tracks were similar, then the first agent would be contacted by radio, and go ahead another mile, to see if he could locate similar tracks. This method allowed the Border Patrol to cover large distances in a relatively short amount of time, and apprehend illegal aliens who would otherwise have escaped.

Ab Taylor became so good at tracking that he soon was "promoted" to a teaching position within the agency. "Tracking and sign cutting was something that men gravitated to, but not everyone liked it because the step-by-step procedure was damn tedious. It's a challenge that will either turn you on, or make you so frustrated that you quit. But there were those of us in the Border Patrol that just couldn't go home and sleep at night if some son of a *cabron* bitch had beaten us. It's that kind of competition that makes a good tracker. They had other good trackers in other sectors of the Border Patrol, but those were men who had done it for years. We were producing some good trackers in a short period of time, men who could track over terrain where most people couldn't see anything. In a normal walking pace, they were seeing a clue or evidence with every step they took."[14]

Border Patrol during World War II

During the Depression years, the funding for the Border Patrol was cut as the entire country struggled financially. As the decade grew to a close, interest in the border and border security began to increase, particularly as Hitler and the Nazis gained power in Germany, and the public began to worry about terrorists and spies crossing the borders, much as people worry about terrorists crossing the border today. The workload and manpower of the Patrol remained fairly constant until 1940, when the

1940s International Fence Construction — Calexico, CA — El Centro District.
© U.S. Border Patrol Museum. Used with permission.

Immigration Service was moved from the Department of Labor to the Department of Justice. An additional 712 agents and 57 auxiliary personnel brought the force to 1,531 officers. More than 1,400 people were employed by the Border Patrol in law enforcement and civilian positions by the end of World War II.

During the Second World War, the Patrol provided tighter control of the border, manned alien detention camps, guarded diplomats taken from embassies, and assisted the US Coast Guard in searching for Axis saboteurs. Aircraft proved extremely effective and became an integral part of operations.

The beginning of World War II, in terms of a labor shortage in the United States, was similar to what had happened in 1917, with the First World War. After the onset of World War II, American farm laborers entered the military or found jobs in the expanding war industry, creating an acute labor shortage in agriculture. Food production was critical to winning the war, and immigrant labor was deemed necessary to accomplish it. The leaders of American agriculture and industrial companies complained to the US Government for help in obtaining cheap labor from across the border. And, once again, official appeals were made to Mexico from Washington to provide that labor. President Franklin D. Roosevelt met with Mexican President Manuel Ávila Camacho in Monterrey, Mexico, to discuss Mexico's participation as part of the Allies in World War II and the Bracero Program was begun (named for the Spanish term for "manual laborer"). The Bracero Program was basically a diplomatic agreement between the two countries for the importation of "temporary" contract laborers from Mexico to the United States. The agreement with Mexico, effective August 4, 1942, provided for the importation of Mexican nationals to work in America's agriculture industry. Once again, the flood of legal (and illegal) Mexican immigration did not end with the end of the war. What happened was that Mexicans returned to Mexico from the United States driving nice cars, and telling friends and relatives how much money they earned in America, which resulted in entire Mexican towns wanting to relocate to the United States.

Kennedy Alien Camp — 1942.
© U.S. Border Patrol Museum. Used with permission.

Between 1942 and 1956, the American agricultural industry imported Mexican laborers, some British West Indians, and a few Canadian woodsmen under a variety of provisions. The Bracero Program officially began slowly, with the US Government bringing in a few hundred experienced Mexican agricultural laborers to harvest sugar beets in the Stockton, California, area. The program soon spread to cover most of the United States and provided workers for the agricultural labor market (with the notable exception being Texas, which initially opted out of the program in preference to an "open border" policy; Texas was denied braceros by the Mexican government until 1947 due to the perceived mistreatment of Mexican laborers). The Bracero railroad program was independently negotiated to supply US railroads initially with

Japanese Internment Camp — Ft. Lincoln, ND — 1942.
© U.S. Border Patrol Museum. Used with permission.

unskilled workers for railroad track maintenance but eventually to cover other unskilled and skilled labor. By 1945, the official quota for the agricultural program was more than 75,000 braceros working in the US railroad system and 50,000 braceros working in US agriculture at any one time. Mexico was initially in favor of the program because it hoped to take advantage of the experienced laborers returning from the United States to boost its own national efforts to industrialize, grow the economy, and eliminate labor shortages. The Bracero railroad program officially ended with the conclusion of World War II in 1945.

At the behest of US growers, who claimed ongoing labor shortages (whether true or not), the agricultural part of the Bracero Program was extended under several acts of Congress until 1948. Between 1948 and 1951, the importation of Mexican agricultural laborers continued under negotiated administrative agreements between American growers and the Mexican government. On July 13, 1951, President Truman signed Public Law 78, a two-year program that embodied formalized protections for Mexican laborers. The program was renewed every two years until 1963 when it was extended for a single year with the understanding it would not be renewed. After the formal end of the agricultural program in 1964, there were agreements covering a much smaller number of contracts until 1967, after which no more braceros were admitted. As part of the program, braceros were supposed to be guaranteed wages, housing, food, and exemption from military service. However, American farm owners sometimes ignored these terms. After this agreement was reached, the Mexican government continued to pressure the United States to strengthen its border security or face the suspension of the legal stream of Mexican laborers going into this country under the Bracero Program.

Deportation back to Mexico — 1950s. © U.S. Border Patrol Museum. Used with permission.

Airlift — McAllen, Texas — 1957. © U.S. Border Patrol Museum. Used with permission.

The emphasis on border security before 1943 offers an interesting perspective on the changing political concerns of the nation. More US Border control officers were posted along the country's northern border with Canada than along the southern one with Mexico. Pressure from angry Mexican land and farm owners frustrated with the inability of the Bracero Program to return agriculture workers to Mexico after their time in the United States expired prompted the Mexican government to call a meeting in Mexico City with representatives from the United States Departments of Justice and State, the INS, and the US Border Patrol. This meeting resulted in increased border patrol along the United States–Mexico border by the United States, yet illegal immigration persisted. One of the main issues was that although the increased pressure by the Mexican government did yield more deportations, the Mexicans being deported would simply reenter the United States by re-crossing the undermanned and under-protected southern border. Combating this issue, the Mexican and American governments developed a strategy in 1945 to deport Mexicans deeper into Mexican territory by utilizing a system of planes, boats, and trains.[15]

Sixty-two Canadian border units were transferred south for a large-scale repatriation effort. In 1952, the government airlifted 52,000 illegal immigrants back to the Mexican interior. Legislation in 1952 codified and carried forward the essential elements of the 1917 and 1924 acts. The same year, Border Patrol agents for the first time were permitted to board and search any conveyance (cars, boats, trains, trucks, etc.) for illegal immigrants anywhere in the United States. For the first time, illegal entrants traveling within the country were subject to arrest, anywhere.

However, in 1954, negotiations surrounding the Bracero Program broke down, prompting the Mexican government to send 5,000 troops to its border with the United

States. Two million Mexican nationals legally participated in the program during its existence, yet the program and its ultimate ineffectiveness in limiting illegal immigration into the United States was one of the primary factors influencing the implementation of Operation Wetback in 1954.[16]

Operation Wetback[17] was a system of tactical control and cooperation within the US Border Patrol and with the approval of the Mexican government. Planning between the INS, led by Gen. Joseph Swing, and the Mexican government began in early 1954, while the program was formally announced in May 1954. On May 17, 1954 command teams of Border Patrol agents, equipped with buses, planes, and temporary processing stations, began locating, processing, and deporting Mexicans who had illegally entered the United States. Seven hundred fifty immigration and Border Patrol officers and investigators, 300 jeeps, cars, and buses, and 7 airplanes were allocated for the operation.[18]

Operation Wetback teams were focused on quick processing and deportation, as planes could coordinate ground efforts more quickly and with increased mobility. Those deported were handed off to Mexican officials, who in turn transported them into central Mexico. While the operation would include the cities of Los Angeles, San Francisco, and Chicago, its main targets were border areas in Texas and California. Overall, there were 1,078,168 apprehensions made in the first year of Operation Wetback, with 170,000 being captured from May to July 1954.[19] As part of the operation, the Border Patrol began expelling adult Mexican males by boatlift from Port Isabel, Texas, to Vera Cruz, Mexico, in September 1954. The project was discontinued two years later after nearly 50,000 illegal aliens had been returned home. In terms of apprehensions, Operation Wetback was considered a success, but it would ultimately fail to limit the number of illegal workers entering the United States from Mexico. The program would also result in a more permanent, strategic border control presence along the United States–Mexico border. The total number of Border Patrol agents more than doubled to 1,692 by 1962, and an additional plane was also added to the force.

Significant numbers of illegal aliens began entering the United States on private aircraft in the late 1950s. In cooperation with other federal services, the Border Patrol began tracking suspect flights. During the Cuban Missile Crisis of the early 1960s, Cuban defectors living in Florida flew aircraft out over the ocean to harass their former homeland. The American government made this harassment illegal, and assigned the Border Patrol to prevent unauthorized flights. The Patrol added 155 officers, but discharged 122 of them when the crisis ended in 1963, generally breaking even.

The early 1960s also witnessed aircraft-hijacking attempts. On August 3, 1961, the first attempted skyjacking to Cuba was thwarted in El Paso, Texas. Leon Bearden and his 17-year-old son, Cody, boarded a Continental jet in Phoenix and demanded to be taken to Cuba. The plane carried 65 passengers. The plane's pilot, Bryon Richards, calmly convinced Bearden that they would need to land in El Paso, Texas, to get enough fuel to fly to Cuba. The FBI was waiting at the airport when the plane touched down. Agents persuaded Bearden to release most of the passengers during

Various other flights, train trips, and bus trips originated along the border and terminated in the Mexican interior. In spite of the major efforts of repatriation, many deportees simply turned around and recrossed the undermanned and under-protected border. Repatriation programs proved extremely expensive and were phased out primarily because of cost. People were smuggled into the United States in all manner of vehicles, hidden inside all types of cargo. Apprehension — Chula Vista, California — 1970s. © U.S. Border Patrol Museum. Used with permission.

Part of the immigration roundup program in the 1950s was the establishment and staffing of detention centers, such as the one located in McAllen, Texas. This picture is an overhead shot taken in 1954 of the McAllen Center. McAllen, Texas.
© U.S. Border Patrol Museum. Used with permission.

Continental Airlines Hijacking, August 3, 1961. El Paso, Texas.
© U.S. Border Patrol Museum. Used with permission.

the refueling, and as the plane was taxiing down the runway, agents disabled it with machine-gun fire. An FBI agent boarded the plane to attempt to end the hijacking, but it was actually one of the remaining hostages who managed to knock out the enraged Bearden. Cody Bearden surrendered without a struggle. Leon Bearden received a life sentence for the hijacking attempt. After the August 1961 hijacking attempt, President John F. Kennedy ordered Border Patrol agents to accompany domestic flights to prevent takeovers.

Continental Airlines Hijacking, August 3, 1961. El Paso, Texas.
© U.S. Border Patrol Museum. Used with permission.

Smuggling — Chula Vista Sector, California — 1969.
© U.S. Border Patrol Museum. Used with permission.

By the late 1960s, the business of alien smuggling began to involve drug smuggling as well. Although it was the primary agency responsible, the Border Patrol assisted other agencies in intercepting illegal drugs and people from Mexico. Items smuggled included everything from the typical illegal drugs, such as heroin, cocaine, and marijuana, to other contraband such as peyote and lobsters. Anything people can make money smuggling across the border, they will. If there was profit in smuggling pencil erasers, then erasers would be transported, hidden in cars, trucks, boats, and planes.

Peyote Seizure, Laredo, Texas — 1975. © U.S. Border Patrol Museum. Used with permission.

Seizure of drugs — Chula Vista, California — 1973.
© U.S. Border Patrol Museum. Used with permission.

Modernizing Strategy

In 1986, the Immigration Reform and Control Act placed renewed emphasis on controlling illegal immigration by going after the employers that hire illegal aliens. Utilizing the theory that jobs were what attracted most illegal aliens to come to the United States, the Border Patrol increased interior enforcement and Form I-9 audits of businesses through an inspection program known as "employer sanctions." These new employer checks were a follow-on to earlier programs to spot-check employment locations for illegal immigrants. These programs, their scope, and the authority of the Border Patrol to carry out its mandate vary with each subsequent administration. For example, with the swearing-in of President Barack Obama in January 2009, and the appointment of Secretary of Homeland Security Napolitano, the Border Patrol and its sister agency, Customs and Border Protection (CBP), as well as Immigration and Customs Enforcement (ICE) were all prohibited from conducting further workplace inspections anywhere in the United States. Additionally, nearly all Border Patrol facilities farther than fifty miles inland from the United States–Mexico border were closed and the remaining agents either forced to retire or moved closer to the border. These changes are not unique to the Obama administration, but routinely occur as any new administration is seated and the political pressures of constituents and lobbyists come to bear.[20] These changed again with the election of Donald Trump as President of the United States (see chapter 1).

Employer/employee ID Check, Miami Sector, Florida — 1969.
© U.S. Border Patrol Museum. Used with permission.

US Government Accounting Office Report on the Border Patrol Employer Sanctions

August 2009

Unfortunately, the Border Patrol's employer sanctions never became nearly as effective as expected by Congress, or the public. Illegal immigration continued to swell after the 1986 amnesty despite efforts by the Border Patrol to check employers for illegal aliens. By 1993, Californians passed Proposition 187, denying benefits to illegal aliens and criminalizing illegal aliens in possession of forged green cards, identification cards, and Social Security numbers. It also authorized law enforcement officers to question non-nationals as to their immigration status and required departments to cooperate and report illegal aliens to the INS. Fortunately or unfortunately, California's Proposition 187 drew nationwide attention to illegal immigration.[21]

Prior to 2003 and the creation of the Department of Homeland Security, the US Border Patrol was part of the Immigration and Naturalization Service (INS), an agency that was initially within the US Department of Justice. The INS was officially decommissioned in March 2003 when its operations were divided between Customs and Border Patrol, United States Citizenship and Immigration Services, and US Immigration and Customs Enforcement as part of the creation of the Department of Homeland Security (DHS).

Prior to the September 11, 2001, terror attacks, the Border Patrol's traditional mission was the deterrence, detection, and apprehension of illegal aliens and individuals (some of whom are involved in the illegal drug trade) who generally enter the United States by routes other than through designated ports of entry. The priority mission changed as a direct result of the September 11th attacks and the Border Patrol's merging into DHS in 2003. Now, the primary mission is to prevent terrorists and terrorist weapons from entering the United States of America. As part of that mission, the Border Patrol also operates 33 permanent interior checkpoints along the southern border of the United States, between Mexico and California, Arizona, and Texas.

Inspection Stations

United States Border Patrol Interior Checkpoints are inspection stations operated by the USBP within 100 miles (160 km) of a national border (with Mexico or Canada) or in the Florida Keys, along major US highways and traffic routes. In the American Southwest, the checkpoints are divided among nine Border Patrol sectors, which include San Diego, El Centro, Yuma, Tucson, El Paso, Marfa, Del Rio, Laredo, and the Rio Grande Valley.

Industry check — Detroit, Michigan — 1965. © U.S. Border Patrol Museum. Used with permission.

El Paso Sector's "Operation Hold the Line"

When Silvestre Reyes was head of the McAllen sector of the Border Patrol in the 1980s, he became aware of a dramatic increase in the number of Central American immigrants crossing the border illegally. Guatemalan residents would cross the Guatemala-Mexico border, come up the east coast, over the Rio Grande, and then up through Texas. Reyes, as head of McAllen Border Patrol, had officially asked the Mexican government to tighten their southern border, to try to reduce the number of Central American illegals entering their country. The Mexican government, however, did not see the problem as a major concern, since the illegals spent their money in Mexico, prior to leaving their country. After that, they all became America's problem, not Mexico's. Reyes was told that he would have to take care of the problem himself. So, he came up with the idea of increasing the number of Border Patrolmen assigned to McAllen and placing them on every trail crossing the Rio Grande. When the immigrants from Guatemala realized they could not cross the border, they simply started backing up, on the Mexican side of the border, which soon began causing problems for the Mexican towns along the border. This situation changed the mind of the Mexican government about increasing security along their southern border. Reyes decided that if it worked in McAllen, then it might work in El Paso.

When he became the Border Patrol Sector Chief in El Paso in 1993, he started a program called "Operation Blockade" along a 25-mile stretch between El Paso and Juarez, using hundreds of "extra" Border Patrolmen specifically assigned to El Paso for that purpose. Later, the name was changed to "Operation Hold the Line," in response to complaints from Mexican officials about the negative connotations of the word "blockade." At midnight, September 19, 1993, four hundred Border Patrolmen spread out, making sure they could see their fellow officers, along a wall of law enforcement 25 miles long. The Border Patrol agents no longer reacted to illegal entries with the resulting apprehensions, but instead were standing on the border, deterring crossing to a more remote location. The idea behind the operation was that it might be easier to capture illegal entrants in the wide-open areas than within the urban alleyways of the city. The good news was that the program significantly reduced illegal entries in the urban part of El Paso; the bad news, however, was that the operation simply shifted the illegal entries to other, more remote areas, where (it was perceived, at least, by those attempting to cross) it was much easier to enter the United States. Operation Hold the Line (or Blockade) was a definite success, by any measure. In fiscal year 1993, apprehensions in the El Paso sector were approximately 285,000—the year following Operation Hold the Line, the number of apprehensions had dropped to 79,000. The Governor of Texas at the time, Ann Richards, came to El Paso to see the program, and was impressed with how well it had worked. Reyes, in describing the effect of Operation Hold the Line on the city of El Paso and its residents, said,

> Those people who I had walked through their neighborhoods now felt safe sitting out there after dark. They could leave their lawn chairs, water hoses,

and sprinklers outside without the fear of them getting stolen. It's working. El Paso likes it. The city has taken on a new feel and look to it, and I think if we stop the operation we're going to have some serious problems and backlash from the community. We [Border Patrol] literally went from being the scourge of the community to being the heroes of the community.[22]

San Diego Sector's "Operation Gatekeeper"

The San Diego sector tried Chief Reyes's approach of deploying agents in other regions to attempt to deter illegal entries to the country. Congress authorized the hiring of thousands of new agents, and many were sent to the San Diego sector. In addition, Congressman Duncan Hunter obtained surplus military landing mats to use as a border fence. Stadium lighting, ground sensors, and infrared cameras were also placed in the area. Eventually the primitive landing mat fence was replaced with a modern triple fence line that begins more than one hundred yards into the Pacific Ocean at Imperial Beach, California, and ends more than 13 miles (19 km) inland on Otay Mesa where the mountains begin. Apprehensions decreased dramatically in that area as illegal migrants moved further inland to find crossing points (like the result in El Paso).[23]

Tucson Sector's "Operation Safeguard"

Because of the fence and the increased Border Patrol presence in California, it was no longer the hotbed of illegal entry and the traffic shifted to Arizona, primarily in Nogales (currently the largest Border Patrol station in the United States). The Border Patrol then used in Arizona the same deterrent strategy it had used in San Diego.[24] According to the INS,

> Operation Safeguard redirected illegal border crossings away from urban areas near the Nogales port-of-entry to comparatively open areas that the Border Patrol could more effectively control. By moving potential crossers away from urban areas where they were able to disappear into local communities, the Border Patrol has taken advantage of new equipment and technology and increased staffing to make apprehensions.[25]

Operation Safeguard resulted in the movement of illegal migrants away from controlled areas, just as did Operation Gatekeeper and Operation Hold the Line. However, unlike the previous two operations, those intent on crossing into the United States from Mexico in the Tucson sector found themselves paying smugglers, or abandoned and wandering in "some of the most dangerous areas known to man within the United States," according to Chief Aguilar.[26] Many illegal migrants died in the expansive desert due to heat exhaustion, heatstroke, or dehydration. Clearly, the combination of strong enforcement efforts and natural barriers to human movement were successful in reducing the numbers of illegal migrants interdicted in the Tucson sector. Civil rights activists argue that such efforts are inhumane and immoral.[27]

Border Patrol Station POE Lynden, Washington — 1957.
© U.S. Border Patrol Museum. Used with permission.

Northern Border

Northern border staffing had been increased by 1,128 agents to 1,470 agents by the end of fiscal year 2008, and was projected to expand to 1,845 by the end of fiscal year 2009, a six-fold increase. Resources that directly support Border Patrol agents on the northern border include the use of new technology and a more focused application of air and marine assets.

The northern border sectors are Blaine (Washington), Buffalo (New York), Rochester (New York), Malone (New York), Detroit (Selfridge ANGB, Michigan), Grand Forks (North Dakota), Havre (Montana), Houlton (Maine), Spokane (Washington), and Swanton (Vermont).

Moving Away from Interior Security

In the 1990s, due most likely to public pressure and controversy surrounding the increasing number of illegal aliens crossing the border and in the United States illegally, Congress mandated that the Border Patrol shift agents away from the interior and focus them on the borders. After the September 11 attacks, the Department of Homeland Security created two immigration enforcement agencies out of the old Immigration and Naturalization Service: US Immigration and Customs Enforcement

 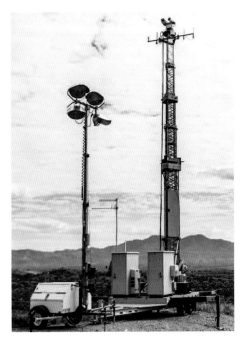

Left: El Paso Sector Tower #2 — 1950s. © U.S. Border Patrol Museum. Used with permission.
Right: Modern light and camera tower. The border fence can be seen in the background. CBP, n.d.

(ICE) and the US Customs and Border Protection (CBP). ICE was tasked with investigations, detention, and removal of illegal aliens, and interior enforcement. Customs and Border Protection was tasked with inspections at US ports of entry and with preventing illegal entries between the port of entry, transportation check, and entries on US coastal borders. Homeland Security management decided to align the Border Patrol with CBP, since both agencies had similar functions and responsibilities. CBP's Office of Field Operations is solely responsible for America's ports of entry, while Border Patrol maintains jurisdiction over all locations between ports of entry, giving Border Patrol agents federal arrest authority nationwide.

In July 2004, the Livermore sector of the United States Border Patrol was closed. Livermore sector served Northern California and included stations at Dublin (Parks Reserve Forces Training Area), Sacramento, Stockton, Fresno, and Bakersfield. The Border Patrol also closed other stations in the interior of the United States including Roseburg, Oregon, and Little Rock, Arkansas. The Border Patrol functions in these areas consisted largely of local jail and transportation terminal checks for illegal aliens. These functions were turned over to US Immigration and Customs Enforcement.

The (Two) New Strategies

According to the 2012–16 Border Patrol Strategic Plan, there are two primary strategies: securing America's borders, and strengthening the Border Patrol. In terms of securing America's borders, the measurable objectives of this goal are to:

- Manage risk through the introduction and expansion of sophisticated tactics, techniques, and procedures. These include methods of detecting illegal entries such as using "change detection" techniques, increased mobile-response capabilities, and expanded use of specially trained personnel with "force-multiplying" skills and abilities;
- Disrupt and degrade Transnational Criminal Organizations by targeting enforcement efforts against the highest priority threats and expanding programs that reduce smuggling and crimes associated with smuggling;
- Expand CBP's situational awareness at and between the POEs and employ a comprehensive and integrated "whole-of-government" approach; and
- Increase community engagement by participating in community programs and engaging the public to assist the US Border Patrol.[28]

In terms of strengthening the Border Patrol, the measurable objectives are:

- Reinforcing employee-support initiatives and programs that continue the tradition of the US Border Patrol;
- Addressing threats to organizational integrity and remaining vigilant in training and promoting initiatives to combat corruption;
- Improving organizational processes, systems, and doctrine by standardizing reporting and planning processes;

A CBP Air Unit UH-60 Blackhawk helicopter intimidates two vehicles on a remote airstrip in America's southwest border region. James Tourtelotte. CBP.gov.

The techniques used to avoid detection have not changed since the 1960s.
Sign Cutting — Yuma Sector — 1960s. © U.S. Border Patrol Museum. Used with permission.

- Introducing improved tools to collect and analyze data to develop measures for the improvement of organizational outcomes; and
- Enhancing overall efficiency by improving planning, resource allocation, and acquisition processes.[29]

Capabilities

The border is a (usually) barely discernible line in uninhabited deserts, canyons, or mountains. The Border Patrol utilizes a variety of equipment and methods, such as electronic sensors placed at strategic locations along the border, to detect people or vehicles entering the country illegally. Video monitors and night vision scopes are also used to detect illegal entries. In most areas along the border, agents patrol in vehicles, boats, aircraft, and afoot. In some more remote areas, agents employ horses, all-terrain motorcycles, bicycles, and snowmobiles. Air surveillance capabilities are provided by unmanned aerial vehicles, such as the MQ-9 Reaper.

The primary activity of a Border Patrol agent is "line watch," which involves the detection, prevention, and apprehension of terrorists, undocumented aliens, and smugglers of aliens at or near the land border by maintaining surveillance from a covert position; following up on leads; responding to electronic sensor, television systems, and aircraft sightings; and interpreting and following tracks, marks, and other physical evidence. Line watch is essentially what the Mounted Inspectors did in 1904. They just didn't have the modern monitoring equipment. The basic mission is the same; only the process is different.

The major activities of the modern Border Patrol include traffic check, traffic observation, city patrol, transportation check, administrative, intelligence, and anti-smuggling activities. Traffic checks are conducted on major highways leading away from the border to detect and apprehend illegal aliens attempting to travel farther into the interior of the United States after evading detection at the border, and to detect illegal narcotics. Transportation checks are inspections of interior-bound conveyances, which include buses, commercial aircraft, passenger and freight trains, and marine craft.

A CBP "Midnight Express" high speed boat patrols the waterways in around the northern border of the United States. Gerald Nino. CBP.gov.

Marine patrols are conducted along the coastal waterways of the United States, primarily along the Pacific coast, the Caribbean, the tip of Florida, and Puerto Rico, and interior waterways common to the United States and Canada. Border Patrol conducts border con-

Border Patrol boat Jeff Milton — Miami Sector, 1944. © U.S. Border Patrol Museum. Used with permission.

trol activities from 130 marine craft of various sizes. The Border Patrol maintains watercraft ranging from blue-water craft to inflatable-hull craft, in 16 sectors, in addition to headquarters special operations components. Border Patrol marine operations are nothing new. They assisted the US Coast Guard with coastal security during World War II and before the war participated in efforts to interdict rum runners from Cuba and whiskey boats from Canada.

Horse and bike patrols are used to augment regular vehicle and foot patrols. Horse units patrol remote areas along the international boundary that are inaccessible to standard all-terrain vehicles. Snowmobiles are used to patrol remote areas along the northern border in the winter.

Expansion

In 1992 the Border Patrol had approximately 4,139 Patrol Agents on the job. Attrition in the Border Patrol was normally at 5 percent. Attrition spiked to more than 10

A Border Patrol Special Response Team searches room-by-room a hotel in
New Orleans in response to Hurricane Katrina. CBP.gov.

percent between 1995 and 2001, which was a period when the Border Patrol was undergoing extensive hiring. In 2002 the attrition rate climbed to 18 percent. The 18 percent attrition was largely attributed to agents transferring to the Federal Air Marshals, which hired significant numbers of people after the September 11 attacks. Since that time the attrition problem has decreased significantly; this is at least indirectly related to the fact that Congress has increased the average Border Patrol agent pay from GS-9 to GS-11. The Border Patrol Marine Position (BPA-M) was created in 2009.

The Intelligence Reform and Terrorism Prevention Act of 2004 (signed by President Bush on December 17, 2004) authorized hiring an additional 10,000 agents, "subject to appropriation." This authorization nearly doubled the Border Patrol manpower from 11,000 to 20,000 agents by 2010. During that time, the number of illegals caught dropped from 1.2 million in 2005 to 415,816 in 2016.[30] The number of apprehensions in 2016 was an increase over the number arrested in the previous year, but lower than either fiscal year 2014 or 2013, and much lower than the average number observed from the 1980s through 2008.

Special Operations Group

The US Border Patrol maintains several special operations groups with dedicated focus. These include:

- Border Patrol Tactical Unit (BORTAC)
- Border Patrol Search, Trauma, and Rescue (BORSTAR)

- Air Mobile Unit (SDC/SOG/AMU)
- Mobile Response Team (MRT)

BORTAC

The Border Patrol Tactical Unit provides an immediate response capability to emergency and high-risk incidents requiring specialized skills and tactics. BORTAC has a group of full-time team members headquartered in El Paso, Texas. and non-full-time members dispersed throughout the United States who can be called upon when needed, 24 hours a day, seven days a week, 365 days a year. The team is unique in that it conducts training and operations both within the United States and in other countries in furtherance of the Border Patrol's mission. BORTAC also trains and equips Sector Special Response Teams that provide Sector Chief Patrol Agents with the same specialized rapid-response capability within their respective areas of responsibility. The unit was created in 1984, initially in response to rioting at INS agencies. Originally created to fulfill this civil disturbance function, the unit quickly evolved and acquired additional skill sets in high-risk warrant service, intelligence/reconnaissance and surveillance, foreign internal defense training, airmobile operations, maritime operations, and precision marksman/observer.

Applicants for BORTAC have to not only be in extremely good physical shape, they cannot be afraid of heights, rappelling from helicopters, or be concerned about being detailed away from home and family for up to 120 consecutive days. The BORTAC agents may be assigned to "breaking up riots in INS detention centers, as well as on the streets ... drug interdiction missions along the southwest border—camping out on remote trails for days on end, monitoring smuggling activity, then making arrests.... serve some high-risk warrants. And there's always the possibility that you'll be called to go to countries like Guatemala or Honduras to train their drug police."[31]

BORSTAR

BORSTAR, or Border Patrol Search, Trauma, and Rescue, is comprised of Border Patrol agents who volunteer to go beyond their regular duties and perform search and rescue missions on an as-needed basis. After serving two years in the Border Patrol, agents must apply for and pass a selection process to attend a five-week BORSTAR Academy. During the extreme physically and mentally demanding BORSTAR Academy, candidates learn various search and rescue techniques and other skills, including tactical medicine, technical rescue, land navigation, communication, swift-water rescue, air operations, and, possibly the most important, teamwork. Following the basic academy, BORSTAR agents will attend an emergency medical technician course to be certified as Basic Emergency Medical Technicians. BORSTAR agents may receive additional specialized training after the Academy, including paramedic, police safety diver, rescue watercraft/boat operator, and cold-weather operations training.

BORSTAR national headquarters is in El Paso, Texas, but there are local BORSTAR teams at each Southwest Border sector, primarily to cut down the amount of time it takes to put Border Patrol Search and Rescue teams on the ground in a needed situation. BORSTAR works closely with the Border Patrol Tactical Unit and Special Response Teams by providing medical and other support during training and operations. All Border Patrol Special Operations Group members, including BORSTAR trained agents, perform these functions in addition to their primary law enforcement duties as Border Patrol agents. Search and rescue operations are conducted throughout the year in varying climates and topographies. BORSTAR agents have responded to rescue operations lasting from a few hours to Federal Emergency Management Agency–supported natural disaster operations for weeks at a time. These situations vary in difficulty from simply locating victims and providing them with water to complex rescues requiring agents to rappel into remote canyons to assist victims and extract them by helicopter.

The response to a surprise storm that hit southern California during the weekend of April 1, 2001, is typical. After responding to a call from several Border Patrol agents a little after midnight about some missing Mexicans lost in the mountains near Interstate 8, the San Diego BORSTAR team located five individuals, all borderline hypothermic, who told the agents that there were others not far down the trail. The BORSTAR agents took the first group to safety and then redeployed to find the others, in the now-blinding snowstorm. After locating three more individuals, they were told there were still others, in the mountains, lost in the storm. At about this time, the BORSTAR unit realized they were going to need some help in locating all the lost individuals, so they contacted both San Diego County Search and Rescue, and the Coast Guard. A Coast Guard helicopter arrived, and with the help of BORSTAR agents on the ground, located the individuals who had been reported by the earlier immigrants. En route to the hospital, the Coast Guard pilot noticed thirteen more people stranded by the storm. BORSTAR agents immediately redeployed to that group. "We started at two o'clock in the morning, and I don't think we pulled out of there until late in the evening the following day," said Keith Jones, a member of the San Diego BORSTAR unit. Jones continues,

> There was one guy—his feet were so frostbitten that they started a fire sometime during the night, and he had put his feet up against the fire and actually melted his shoes to his feet. You just do what you have to do—it's no different than firefighters and police officers. When you have a crisis, you've just got to suck it up and do it. All in all, it was about thirty-one people, plus or minus, that we ended up pulling out. And I believe there were nine dead.[32]

Other Specialized Border Patrol Programs

In 2007, the Border Patrol created the Special Operations Group (SOG), headquartered in El Paso, Texas, to coordinate the special operations units of the agency. The Border Patrol has several other specialized programs and details. Marine Patrol—in the riverine environments of the northern and southwestern borders of the United States, the Border Patrol conducts border control activities from the decks of marine craft of various sizes. Since 2006, the Border Patrol has relinquished its law enforcement missions in the Great Lakes and territorial seas to the Office of Air and Marine. The Border Patrol maintains more than 130 vessels, ranging from blue-water craft to inflatable-hull craft, in 16 sectors. Other specialized Border Patrol units include: K9 Units, Mounted Patrol, Bike Patrol, Sign-cutting (tracking), Snowmobile units, Infrared scope units, Intelligence, Anti-smuggling Investigations Unit (ASU/DISRUPT), Border Criminal Alien Program, Multi-agency Anti-Gang Task Forces (regional and local units), Honor Guard, Pipes and Drums, Chaplain, Peer Support, and the Mobile Surveillance Unit.

Border Patrol Organization Today

Training

All new Border Patrol agents spend a minimum of 55 basic training days (eight weeks) at the Border Patrol Academy in Artesia, New Mexico, which is one of the components of the Federal Law Enforcement Training Center (FLETC). At the conclusion of the 55 days of training, the recruits are given a language competency exam; those who do not attain a Spanish benchmark score established by Academy subject matter experts are assigned a Spanish class that begins after successful completion of the 55-day basic training program. The Task-Based language program is focused on Border Patrol-specific operations. Border Patrol agent trainees are instructed in courses including: criminal law, nationality law, and administrative immigration law, police operations, self-defense and arrest techniques, firearms training with pistol, shotgun, and rifle, police vehicle driving, and other Border Patrol/federal law enforcement subjects.

Once they arrive back at their duty station, Trainees then must graduate from the Field Training Officer (FTO) program, an on-the-job training program, which varies in length from 12 weeks to more than 16 weeks, depending on the practical demands of the duty station and local management. They must also successfully complete the Post Academy Training Program, an extension of the Border Patrol Academy where Trainees complete additional classroom-based training over the course of their first nine months back at their duty station.

Uniforms

The Border Patrol currently wears the following types of uniforms:

- Dress uniform—The dress uniform consists of olive-green trousers with a blue stripe, and an olive-green shirt, which may or may not have blue shoulder straps. The campaign hat is worn with the dress uniform.
- Ceremonial uniform—When required, the following items are added to the dress uniform to complete the ceremonial uniform: olive-green Ike jacket or tunic with blue accents (shoulder straps and cuffs), blue tie, brass tie tack, white gloves, and olive-green felt campaign hat with leather hat band.

- Rough duty uniform — The rough duty uniform consists of green cargo trousers and work shirt (in short or long sleeves). Usually worn with green baseball cap or tan Stetson.
- Accessories, footwear, and outerwear — Additional items are worn in matching blue or black colors as appropriate.
- Organization patches — The Border Patrol wears two:
- The CBP patch is worn on the right sleeve of the uniform. It contains the DHS seal against a black background with a "keystone" shape. A "keystone" is the central, wedge-shaped stone in an arch, which holds all the other stones in place.
- Border Patrol agents wear the circular legacy Border Patrol patch, which is worn on the left sleeve.

Ronald Vitiello entered duty as Chief of the United States Border Patrol on February 1, 2017. DHS, USBP, Official Photo.

The Border Patrol uniform is getting its first makeover since the 1950s to appear more like military fatigues and less like a police officer's duty garb. Leather belts with brass buckles are being replaced by nylon belts with quick-release plastic buckles, slacks are being replaced by lightweight cargo pants, and shiny badges and nameplates are being replaced by cloth patches.

Weapons

Border Patrol agents are issued the H&K P2000 double action LEM (Law Enforcement Modification) pistol in .40 S&W caliber. It can contain as many as 13 rounds of ammunition (12 in the magazine and one in the chamber). The Border Patrol adopted the Beretta Model 96D, a .40 S&W caliber semiautomatic pistol (modified for Double-Action only) (with a 12-round capacity magazine) as its duty issue sidearm in 1995. The .40 S&W caliber jacketed hollow-point cartridge was adopted because of its excellent "stopping" power and its superior ballistic characteristics over the 9mm cartridge. In late 2006 the H&K P2000 pistol was adopted as the Border Patrol's primary duty sidearm. The H&K Model USP Compact pistol, H&K Model P2000SK (sub-compact) and Beretta M96D .40 S&W caliber pistols are authorized as secondary sidearms.

The 12-gauge Remington Model 870 is the standard pump-action shotgun. The Border Patrol issue Model 870 has been modified by Scattergun Technologies to Border Patrol specifications including: a 14-inch barrel, a five-shot capacity magazine, a composite stock with pistol grip, and night sights with a tactical "ghost-ring" rear sight. Border Patrol agents also commonly carry the .223 caliber M4 Carbine and the H&K UMP .40 caliber submachine gun. The .308 caliber M14 rifle is used primarily for ceremonial events.

As a less than lethal option, the Border Patrol uses the FN303. The Border Patrol also uses compressed-air cartridge powered guns that fire plastic pellet balls containing OC (Oleoresin Capsicum) pepper dust. The plastic pellet balls burst on impact spraying the suspect with OC pepper dust. This dust stings the eyes, skin, nose, and throat and causes the eyes to water severely, thus temporarily disabling a suspect. The Border Patrol also issues its agents OC pepper spray canisters, Tasers, and a collapsible, telescoping steel police baton.

Transportation

The Border Patrol currently operates more than 10,000 SUVs and pickup trucks, which have individual revolving lights (strobes or LEDs) and/or light bars and sirens. These vehicles are equipped with wireless radios in contact with a central control room. Border Patrol vehicles also carry emergency first aid kits. The border patrol uses approximately 2,000 sedans. The Border Patrol also operates ATVs, motorcycles, snowmobiles, and small boats in river environments.

In 2005, all Border Patrol and ICE aircraft operations were combined under CBP's Office of Air and Marine. All CBP vessel operations within the Customs Waters and on the high seas are conducted by Marine Interdiction Agents of the Office of Air and Marine.

The Border Patrol also uses horses for remote-area patrols. Most are employed along the Mexico–United States border. In Arizona, these animals are fed special processed feed pellets so that their wastes do not spread non-native plants in the national parks and wildlife areas they patrol.

Killed in the Line of Duty

The Border Patrol has suffered more losses in line of duty deaths than any other federal law enforcement agency since the patrolling of the border began by the Mounted Inspectors in 1904. Daily Patrol Agents often work alone in remote wilderness areas along the United States international border in areas notorious for alien smuggling, narcotics and contraband smuggling, human trafficking, and banditry.

Line of Duty Deaths

As of February 17, 2017, total Border Patrol line of duty deaths (since 1924):[33]

- Aircraft accident: 14
- Assault: 2
- Automobile accident: 36
- Drowned: 4
- Duty related illness: 2
- Fall: 4
- Gunfire: 32
- Gunfire (Accidental): 4

- Heart attack: 7
- Heat exhaustion: 2
- Motorcycle accident: 2
- Stabbed: 2
- Struck by train: 3
- Struck by vehicle: 4
- Vehicle pursuit: 2
- Vehicular assault: 4

Javier Vega, Jr.

Entered on Duty: 2008-02-11

End of Watch: 2014-08-03

On Sunday, August 3, 2014, Border Patrol Agent Javier Vega, Jr. was shot and killed near Santa Monica, Texas, as he attempted to take a law enforcement action during a robbery while he was fishing with his wife, children, and parents. Two illegal aliens approached them and attempted to rob them. Agent Vega was shot in the chest when he attempted to draw his weapon. His father was also shot and wounded as he returned fire at the men.

Both men fled the scene but were arrested a short time later. They were charged with capital murder, attempted capital murder, and other crimes. It is believed the same subjects had committed numerous similar robberies at the direction of a Mexican cartel. Both men had been previously deported numerous times.

On September 20, 2016, it was determined that, in light of information identified during the intensive investigation completed by the Willacy County Sheriff's Department, Agent Vega's actions were indicative of his law enforcement training and that he instinctively reacted, placing himself in harm's way to stop a criminal act and protect the lives of others. His death was re-determined to have been in the line of duty.

Agent Vega, who was 36 years old, entered on duty with the US Border Patrol on February 11, 2008, as a member of Academy Class 745.

Agent Vega was a US Marine Corps veteran and had served with the United States Border Patrol for six years. He is survived by his wife, three children, parents, and brother.[34]

Armed Incursions

There have been so many armed incursions on the American side of the border, by Mexican troops (at least 118, according to Krauss and Pacheco, 2004), that Border

Patrol agents reporting for duty at the Ajo office are given index cards with the word "SALUTE" on them. The SALUTE acronym, per the card, stands for:

S—Size of the unit (Number of [Mexican Military] Personnel)
A—Activity
L—Location and direction of travel
U—Unit (identify, if possible)
T—Time (if reporting an earlier encounter)
E—Equipment of the Personnel

The above is on the front side of the card. On the back of the card, it reads:

- Remember: Mexican military are trained to escape, evade, and counter-ambush if it will effect their escape.
- Secure detainees and pat down immediately.
- Separate leaders from the group.
- Remove all personnel from the proximity of the border.
- Once scene is secure, search for documents.
- Keep a low profile.
- Use cover and concealment.
- Don't move excessively or abruptly.
- Use shadows and camouflage to conceal yourself.
- Stay as quiet as possible but communicate.
- Hiding near landmarks makes you easier to locate.

The clear implication of a card like this is that armed incursions by Mexican troops happen so often that warnings must be constantly given to our federal agents along the border, to stay alert for the possibility. Of course, there are obvious contradictions, including "Secure detainees and pat down immediately," and "Use shadows and camouflage to conceal yourself," as well as "Don't move excessively or abruptly." It is a little difficult for anyone, including a federal agent, to physically "secure" someone at the same time they are "staying as quiet as possible."

As one example of the multiple incursions, on August 7, 2008, Mexican troops crossed the border into Arizona near Menagers Dam, approximately thirty miles south of the Ajo Border Patrol office, using two Humvee-style vehicles, at approximately 3 a.m. There were two federal agents waiting at the border crossing, quietly, in their SUVs. After crossing the clearly marked border, and after the Border Patrol vehicle had turned on their overhead lights, from twenty feet away, to unmistakably and clearly identify to the Mexican soldiers who they were, the four Mexican soldiers in the lead vehicle opened fire on the clearly marked CBP truck, and its two agents. Per one of the agents,

> Out of my peripheral vision, I saw the sagebrush to the left of my vehicle being ripped apart. Sand kicked up by the bullets showered my windshield. Under normal circumstances, I wouldn't have hesitated to answer the assault with gunfire of my own, but these were not what I considered normal circumstances. The men before me, trying to the best of their abilities to end my life, were not your run-of-the-mill drug runners or a group of desperate

immigrants willing to risk it all for entrance into the Promised Land. They were soldiers of a neighboring country, one that was supposed to be friends with the United States. According to the flashcard tucked into my pocket, I had a choice to make—separate leaders from the group, or use shadows to camouflage and conceal myself. At the moment, both options seemed preposterous. Just as I began raising my sidearm to take aim, the second Humvee appeared—it also had four soldiers, all armed with assault rifles. I had seen the damage such guns could inflict. My partner and I were outmanned and outgunned, and if we exchanged fire, the battle would only end up with two more border patrolmen in the grave. With a burst of bullets slipping into the earth all around me, I watched my partner throw his vehicle into reverse, and then I did the same. Using the driver's training we received both in the academy and in the field, we maneuvered across the rocky terrain and made a desperate escape to the north. Some distance from the border, as I looked into the rearview mirror and saw the taillights of the Humvees disappear back into Mexico, a swirl of emotions hit me, the most prominent of which were relief and anger. I felt relief because by God's grace my partner and I were still alive and well. I felt anger because, once again, the Mexican military had driven north of the border, fired on two federal officers, and then retreated back into Mexico, free to accomplish their mission at a later date, which could have had something to do with the delivery of a large shipment of narcotics. I would file a memorandum and an Assault on a Federal Officer Charge the moment I got back to the station, but the chances were good that it would receive no more attention than the 118 Mexican military incursions before it. No preventive measures would be taken, and I felt anger because situations such as these, ones that occurred in America's backyard, were some of the country's best-kept secrets. Just as I expected, news of my little encounter did not garner the attention it deserved, and just a few weeks later, three Mexican soldiers in a military Humvee jumped the line and fired on another Border Patrol agent who was patrolling near Menagers Dam. One bullet shattered the rear window of the agent's vehicle, and then deflected off the prisoner's partition located directly behind his seat. Not surprisingly, earlier that day twenty-two hundred pounds of narcotics had been confiscated in the immediate vicinity. The agent was lucky, just as my partner and I had been lucky, but along the borders luck only goes so far. In August 2002, Chris Eggle, a park ranger assigned to Organ Pipe Cactus National Park in Ajo, attempted to assist Border Patrol agents in the apprehension of two suspects who had illegally crossed the border. During the pursuit, he was shot and killed. All three of the incidents occurred along a thirty-mile stretch of border between Lukeville Port of Entry and Menagers Dam.[35]

Death Threats

On numerous occasions Patrol Agents have been fired upon from the Mexican side of the international border. Intelligence gathering has discovered bounties being placed on Patrol Agents to be paid by drug cartels and smuggling organizations upon the confirmed murder or kidnapping of a US Border Patrol agent. In 2008, intelligence learned of a two-million-dollar contract for the murder of a Border Patrol agent.[36] In 2009 Border Patrol Agent Rosas was murdered in an ambush while on patrol; it is likely that a bounty may have been paid to the assassins.[37] A group of five armed men had traveled in Mexico to the United States–Mexico border with the intent of robbing a Border Patrol agent. Three of the five men crossed into the United States while the other two remained as lookouts on the Mexico side of the border. The three men who crossed into the United States set up an ambush and lured Agent Rosas out of his vehicle. He was shot multiple times and then robbed of his gear bag, handcuffs, firearm, and night vision goggles. Four of the five suspects, including the 17-year-old who shot Agent Rosas, were subsequently apprehended. The suspect who shot him was sentenced to 40 years in prison.[38]

Criticisms

Ramos and Compean

In February 2005, Border Patrol Agents Ignacio Ramos and Jose Compean were involved in an incident while pursuing a van in Fabens, Texas. The driver, later identified as Aldrete Davila, was shot by Agent Ramos during a scuffle. Davila escaped back into Mexico, and the agents discovered that the van contained approximately a million dollars' worth of marijuana (about 750 pounds). None of the agents at the scene reported the shooting, including two supervisors. The Department of Homeland Security later opened an internal affairs investigation into the incident.[39] The two Border Patrol agents were charged with multiple crimes. Ramos was convicted of causing serious bodily injury, assault with a deadly weapon, discharge of a firearm in relation to a crime of violence, and a civil rights violation.[40] Compean was found guilty on 11 counts, including discharging a firearm during the commission of a violent crime, which by itself carries a federally mandated 10-year minimum sentence. Ramos was sentenced to 11 years and a day in prison and Compean to 12 years.[41] On January 19, 2009, President Bush commuted the sentences of both Ramos and Compean, effectively ending their prison term on March 20, 2009, and they were released on February 17, 2009.[42]

Death of Sergio Hernandez

Sergio Adrian Hernandez was a teenager who was shot once and killed on June 7, 2010, by Border Patrol agents under a bridge crossing between El Paso, Texas, and Juarez, Mexico.[43] Border Patrol agents claimed that the shooting was in retaliation for a mob that was throwing stones at them. On June 10, 2010, Mexican president

Felipe Calderón called on the United States to launch a "thorough, impartial" probe into the deaths of two Mexican nationals, including the 14-year-old Hernandez, at the hands of US border police.[44]

Allegations of Abuse

Various civil society and human rights organizations have alleged that abuses of migrants by Border Patrol agents occur frequently:

- A PBS report, *Crossing the Line at the Border*, released in April 2012, profiled the case of Anastasio Hernandez-Rojas, who died after allegedly being beaten and then shocked by a Taser by a group of Border Patrol officers at the San Ysidro port of entry near San Diego in May 2010.[45] In 2012, in a letter to President Obama posted on the website of the Washington Office on Latin America, 118 civil society organizations criticized the Border Patrol for failing to thoroughly investigate the crime and stated that the Border Patrol "is operating with very little transparency and virtual impunity, especially in the southern border region where Border Patrol and other CBP agents regularly violate the human and civil rights of those who call the border region home."[46]
- The Arizona organization No More Deaths interviewed nearly 13,000 migrants between 2008 and 2011 who had been in Border Patrol custody, in the Arizona border towns of Naco, Nogales, and Agua Prieta. Their report, *A Culture of Cruelty*, documents abuses including denial of or insufficient water and food; failure to provide medical treatment; verbal, physical, and psychological abuse; separation of family members and dangerous repatriation practices. In February 2012, Border Patrol Chief Michael Fisher stated in congressional testimony that the Border Patrol takes allegations of abuse seriously.[47]
- There are allegations of abuse by the United States Border Patrol such as the ones reported by Jesus A. Trevino. An article published in the Houston Journal of International Law (2006) concludes with a request to create an independent review commission to oversee the actions of the Border Patrol, and that creating such review board will make the American public aware of the "serious problem of abuse that exists at the border by making this review process public" and that "illegal immigrants deserve the same constitutionally-mandated humane treatment of citizens and legal residents."[48]

In 1998, Amnesty International investigated allegations of ill treatment and brutality by officers of the Immigration and Naturalization Service, and particularly the Border Patrol. Their report said they found indications of human rights violations during 1996, 1997, and early 1998.[49]

- An article in *Social Justice* by Michael Huspek, Leticia Jimenez, and Roberto Martinez (1998) cites that in December 1997, John Case, head of the INS Office of Internal Audit, announced at a press conference that public complaints to the INS had risen 29 percent from 1996, with the "vast majority" of complaints emanating from the southwest border region, but that of the 2,300 cases, the 243 cases of serious allegations of abuse were down in 1997. These serious cases are considered to be distinct from less serious complaints, such as "verbal abuse, discrimination, extended detention without cause."[50]

• Former Border Patrol agents Raul Villareal, 42, and Fidel Villareal, 44, were found guilty in August of 2012 of conspiracy to bring in illegal immigrants for financial gain, multiple counts of bringing in illegal immigrants for financial gain and conspiracy to launder money, and receiving bribes by public officials. According to prosecutors, the brothers started a smuggling ring that brought Mexican immigrants into the United States illegally using Border Patrol vehicles between 2005 and 2006. The former Border Patrol agents were arrested on October 18, 2008, in Tijuana, Mexico.[51]

US Customs

The First United States Congress passed and President George Washington signed the Tariff Act of July 4, 1789, which authorized the collection of duties on imported goods. Four weeks later, on July 31, the United States Customs Service was created. As part of this new government agency, the position of "Customs Collector" was created. The Customs Collector had the responsibility to supervise the collection of customs duties in a city or region. The US Customs Service was the primary source of funds for the entire government, and paid for the nation's early growth and infrastructure for the next one hundred years. Purchases include the Louisiana and Oregon territories; Florida and Alaska; funding the National Road and the Transcontinental Railroad; building many of the nation's lighthouses; the US Military and Naval academies, and the building of Washington, DC.

In the 20th century the Customs Service transitioned from an administrative bureau to a federal law enforcement agency (which allowed some of them to carry firearms). Inspectors still inspected goods and took customs declarations from travelers at ports of entry, but customs agents used modern police methods—often together with other federal agencies, such as the Federal Bureau of Investigation, US Postal Inspection Service, US Immigration and Naturalization Service and/or US Border Patrol—to investigate cases often far from international airports, bridges, and land crossings.

In March 2003, it was rolled into the US Department of Homeland Security as the Bureau of Customs and Border Protection and Immigration and Customs Enforcement. The United States Customs Service had three major missions: collecting tariff revenue, protecting the US economy from smuggling and illegal goods, and processing people and goods at ports of entry.

Examples of illegal items:

• All Cuban products without a specific license for their importation, such as cigars
• Child pornography
• Counterfeit merchandise (e.g., cellphones, perfume, and other consumer products)
• Excessive quantities of textiles

- Items Violating Intellectual Property Rights
- Illegal drugs
- Stolen property
- Tobacco products over allowable limits
- Undeclared firearms and weapons
- Undeclared liquor over allowable limits
- Undeclared money or monetary instruments over $10,000
- Unscreened fruits and meats

Immigration Services

Shortly after the US Civil War, some states started to pass their own immigration laws, which prompted the US Supreme Court to rule in 1875 that immigration was a federal responsibility. The Immigration Act of 1891 established an Office of the Superintendent of Immigration within the Treasury Department. This office was responsible for admitting, or rejecting, and processing all immigrants seeking admission to the United States, and for implementing national immigration policy. 'Immigrant Inspectors,' as they were called then, were stationed at major US ports of entry collecting manifests of arriving passengers. Its largest station was located on Ellis Island in New York Harbor. A "head tax" of fifty cents was collected on each immigrant.

Paralleling some current immigration concerns, in the early 1900s Congress's primary interest in immigration was to protect American workers and wages. The federal government considered immigration more a matter of commerce than revenue. In 1903, Congress transferred the Bureau of Immigration to the newly created (now-defunct) Department of Commerce and Labor. There were several predecessor agencies to INS between 1891 and 1933. The Immigration and Naturalization Service (INS) on June 10, 1933, to administer matters related to established immigration and naturalization policy by the merger of the Bureau of Immigration and the Bureau of Naturalization. Both those bureaus, as well as the newly created INS, were controlled by the Department of Labor. President Franklin Roosevelt moved the INS from the Department of Labor to the Department of Justice in 1940.

After World War I, Congress attempted to stem the flow of immigrants, still mainly coming from Europe, by passing a law in 1921 and the Immigration Act of 1924 limiting the number of newcomers by assigning a quota to each nationality based upon its representation in previous US Census figures. Each year, the US State Department issued a limited number of visas; only those immigrants who could present valid visas were permitted entry.

The (old) United States Immigration and Naturalization Service (INS), (now referred to as Legacy INS), ceased to exist under that name on March 1, 2003, when most of its functions were transferred from the Department of Justice to three new entities—US Citizenship and Immigration Services (USCIS), US Immigration and Customs Enforcement (ICE), and US Customs and Border Protection (CBP)—within the newly created Department of Homeland Security, as part of a major government reorganization which occurred after the September 11 attacks of 2001.

In 2003 the administration of immigration services, including permanent residence, naturalization, asylum, and other functions became the responsibility of the Bureau of Citizenship and Immigration Services (BCIS), which existed only for a short time before changing to its current name, US Citizenship and Immigration Services (USCIS). The investigative and enforcement functions (including investigations, deportation, and intelligence) were combined with INS and US Customs investigators, the Federal Protective Service, and the Federal Air Marshal Service, to create US Immigration and Customs Enforcement (ICE). The border security functions of the INS, which included the Border Patrol along with INS Inspectors, were combined with US Customs Inspectors into the newly created US Customs and Border Protection (CBP).

Mission

The primary mission of INS (Immigration and Naturalization Service) was to protect and enforce the laws of naturalization, the process by which a foreign-born person becomes a citizen. The INS also was responsible for any illegal entrants to the United States, preventing receipt of benefits such as social security or unemployment by those ineligible to receive them, and investigating, detaining, and deporting those illegally living in the United States.

Structure

The organizational head of the Immigration and Naturalization Service was a commissioner directly appointed by the President. The commissioner reported to the Attorney General. The commissioner worked closely with the United Nations, the Department of State, and the Department of Health and Human Services to coordinate all immigration within the country. The INS was a very large and complex organization that had four main divisions—Programs, Field Operations, Policy and Planning, and Management—that were responsible for operations and management.

The operational functions of the INS included the Programs and Field Operations divisions. The Programs division was responsible for handling all the functions involved with enforcement and examinations, including the arrest, detaining, and deportation of illegal immigrants as well as controlling illegal and legal entry.

The Field Operations division was directly responsible for overseeing various Immigration and Naturalization offices operating throughout the country and the world. The Field Operations division specifically implemented policies and handled tasks for its three regional offices, which in turn oversaw 33 districts and 21 border areas throughout the country. Internationally, the Field Operations division oversaw the Headquarters Office of International Affairs, which in turn oversaw 16 offices outside of the United States.

Managerial functions of the Immigration and Naturalization Service included the Policy and Planning and Management divisions, which coordinated all information for the INS and communicated directly with other cooperating government agencies and the public. The office was divided into three areas: the Policy Division; the Planning Division; and the Evaluation and Research Center. The second managerial division, called the Management division, was responsible for maintaining the overall mission of the INS throughout its many offices and providing administrative services to these offices. These duties were handled by the offices of Information Resources Management, Finance, Human Resources and Administration, and Equal Employment Opportunity.

US Border Security Agencies after the Advent of Homeland Security

"Our border patrol and immigration agents are doing a fine job, but we still have a problem, ... Too many illegal immigrants are coming in, and we're capturing many more non-Mexican illegal immigrants than we can send home."

— *George W. Bush, President*

Ports of Entry

Ports of entry are responsible for daily port-specific operations. As of October 2017, there were 328 official ports of entry in the United States and 15 pre-clearance offices in 6 countries. Port personnel are the face of border security, and the face of Border Patrol, for most visitors entering the United States. Here Customs and Border Protection enforces the import and export laws and regulations of the United States federal government and conducts immigration policy and programs. Ports also perform agriculture inspections to protect the country from potential carriers of animal and plant pests or diseases that could cause serious damage to America's crops, livestock, pets, or the environment.

CBP's Fiscal Year 2015 Drug Control Summary Report in Review

(January 27, 2016)

Washington — US Customs and Border Protection (CBP) released a summary of fiscal year (FY) 2015 Drug Control Performance efforts toward disrupting domestic drug trafficking.

Office of Field Operations: Amount of currency seized on exit from the United States

The "Amount of currency seized on exit from the United States" is the total dollar amount, in millions, seized during an inspection of exiting passengers and vehicles, including both privately owned and commercial, on all ports of entry on both the southwest and northern borders, and including all types of transportation (air, land, and sea). This measure is one method of evaluating the success of CBP's Outbound Enforcement Program in disrupting domestic drug trafficking at the land borders by stemming the flow of narcotics-related proceeds possibly destined for transnational criminal groups. In FY 2015 the total currency seized on exit from the United States was $37.6 million, $7.6 million above the target figure of $30.0 million.

Air and Marine Operations

CBP's Air and Marine Operations (AMO) deploys assets in support of extended border operations in the designated source (Bolivia, Columbia, and Peru) and transit zones (Central America, Mexico, the Caribbean Sea, Gulf of Mexico, and the eastern Pacific Ocean) through liaison with other US agencies and international partners. AMO coordinates with other agencies through a partnership with the Joint Interagency Task Force–South (JIATF-S). AMO typically supports JIATF-S requests with P-3 Airborne Early Warning (AEW) and P-3 Long-Range Tracker (LRT), DHC-8, and C-12M fixed-wing aircraft, Black Hawk rotary-wing aircraft, and unmanned aerial systems (UAS). AMO aircraft flew a total of 7,299 hours in FY 2015 with its P-3 (6,069 hours) and King Air B-350 Multi-Role Enforcement aircraft (1 hour), AS350 aircraft (2 hours), DHC-8 aircraft (318 hours), and 909 hours with UAS.

Automation Modernization — Office of Information Technology

The TECS system is an updated version of the former Treasury Enforcement Communications network. TECS, owned by the CBP, is both an information-sharing platform as well as the name of a system of records relevant to the antiterrorism and law enforcement mission of CBP and other agencies that it supports. It is considered to be a mission-critical law enforcement software application system designed to identify individuals and businesses suspected of being in violation of federal law. The measure, "Percent of time TECS is available to end users" quantifies the availability of the system to all users based on an ideal level of 24X7 service. During FY 2015, TECS had an availability of 99.9%.[52]

Operations

Customs and Border Protection

On July 31, 1789, the US Congress passed its fifth act establishing 59 custom collection districts in the 11 states that had ratified the Constitution, and this began a tradition of service that has grown with the nation. Throughout these 220 years, the work of the men and women of the US Customs Service and US Customs and Border Protection has evolved to meet the changing needs of a growing nation.

Immigration and Customs Enforcement

US Immigration and Customs Enforcement is the principal investigative arm of the US Department of Homeland Security (DHS) and the second largest investigative agency in the federal government. Created in 2003 through a merger of the investigative and interior enforcement elements of the US Customs Service and the Immigration and Naturalization Service, as of Oct. 2017 ICE has more than 20,000 employees in offices in all 50 states and 50 countries.

Homeland Security Investigations

The ICE Homeland Security Investigations (HSI) directorate is a critical asset in the ICE mission, responsible for investigating a wide range of domestic and international activities arising from the illegal movement of people and goods into, within, and out of the United States.

HSI investigates immigration crime, human rights violations, human smuggling, smuggling of narcotics, weapons, and other types of contraband, financial crimes, cybercrime, and export enforcement issues. ICE special agents conduct investigations aimed at protecting critical infrastructure industries that are vulnerable to sabotage, attack, or exploitation.

In addition to ICE criminal investigations, HSI oversees the agency's international affairs, operations, and intelligence functions. HSI consists of more than 20,000 employees, consisting of 6,700 special agents, who are assigned from 26 field offices to more than 400 cities throughout the United States and 50 countries.

Enforcement and Removal Operations

The Enforcement and Removal Operations (ERO) department has the job of enforcing the nation's immigration laws in as fair and effective manner as possible. The agency identifies and apprehends illegal aliens who either entered illegally or stayed past their allowable visa time, detains these individuals when necessary, and removes those illegal aliens from the United States. This unit prioritizes the apprehension, arrest, and removal of convicted criminals, those who pose a threat to national security, fugitives, and recent border entrants who entered the country illegally. Individuals seeking asylum also work with ERO.

ERO transports removable aliens from point to point, manages aliens in custody or in an alternative to detention program, provides access to legal resources and representatives of advocacy groups, and removes individuals from the United States ordered deported.

US Citizenship and Immigration Service

US Citizenship and Immigration Services (USCIS) is the government agency that oversees lawful immigration to the United States. USCIS' strategic goals include:

- Strengthening the security and integrity of the immigration system.
- Providing effective customer-oriented immigration benefit and information services.

- Supporting immigrants' integration and participation in American civic culture.
- Promoting flexible and sound immigration policies and programs.
- Strengthening the infrastructure supporting the USCIS mission.
- Operating as a high-performance organization that promotes a highly talented workforce and a dynamic work culture.

Other Border Security Agencies around the World

Border Security Zone of Russia

The country of Russia, approximately 1.8 times the size of the United States, has 12,577.5 miles (20,241.5 km) of border with other countries and 23,396.5 miles (37,653 km) of coastline. With 14 neighboring countries, Russia faces a similar problem as the United States when it comes to border security. How they manage their border security problems when faced with the most populous nation in the world to their southeast and Muslim terrorists to their south is instructive.[53]

The Border Security Zone in Russia is the designation of a strip of land (usually, though not always, along a Russian state border) where economic activity and access are restricted. To visit the zone, a permit issued by the local FSB (Federal Border Service) department is required. The restricted access zone (of 7.5 km width generally, but sometimes running as much as 90 km deep along the Estonian border) was established in the Soviet Union in 1934.

During the dissolution of the Soviet Union in 1991, the state borders changed dramatically but the zone was not corrected accordingly and hence effectively ceased to exist. In 1993 the Law on the State Border was adopted and reestablished a border strip with restricted access, which usually does not exceed 5 km (although in fact it became much wider in some places). In 2004 the law was amended, the 5-km restriction was excluded, and FSB was legally authorized to draw the zone's limits on its own without coordination with local authorities. In 2006 FSB Director Nikolay Patrushev and his deputy Sergei Smirnov issued decrees delimiting the zone, which was expanded and included many large settlements, important transport routes, and resort areas, especially in the Republic of Karelia, Leningrad Oblast, and Primorsky Krai. In 2007, pressured by the public, the FSB decreased the zone in some places.

Imperial Russia

The origin of the Russian border service can be traced to the 16th century. In 1782 Catherine II of Russia created Border Customs Guards originally manned by Russian Cossacks as well as low-ranking cavalry troops. In 1810, General Mikhail Barklay de Tolly organized various border posts consisting of 11 regiments of Cossacks along the Western Russian border. The Russian Border Guards were among the first to fight Napoleon's invasion of Russia. In 1832 armed customs officials subordinate to the ministry of finance replaced Cossacks and cavalry in peacetime (in wartime the border guards were automatically transferred to the army). In the same year, the coast guard was created, originally to serve Black Sea and Azov seacoasts. In 1893 Count Sergei Witte, Russian minister of finance in Alexander III's government, reformed the service into the Border Guards. In 1906 about 40,000 soldiers and officers served in the Separate Corps of Border Guards responsible for the defense of the vast Imperial border.

Modern Period

Following the collapse of the Soviet Union, the Federal Border Guard Service of Russia was created on December 30, 1993, and given a status of a separate ministry. This organization retained some old traditions, most notably the dark green-colored uniform and "Border Guarder's Day" (an official holiday commemorated by celebrations of ex-servicemen). The first minister of FBS (Federal Border Service) was Andrei Nikolayev, a young and outspoken general who later became deputy of the State Duma. Russian Border Guards were also stationed outside of Russia most notably in southern Tajikistan, to guard the border with Afghanistan, until summer 2005. On the Afghan-Tajik border on many occasions they were engaged in heavy fighting with drug-traffickers and Islamic extremists. The Russians also still guard Armenia's border with Turkey and Iran. On March 11, 2003, Russian president Vladimir Putin changed the status of Border Guard Service from a separate ministry into a branch of Russian Federal Security Service. The current head of Border Guard Service of Russia is General Vladimir Pronichev. Border Guard Service of Russia is still tasked with the defense of the longest national border in the world.

Russia has recently increased its military activity in the Arctic. Putin has created a new Arctic command with 14 new operational airfields, 40 icebreakers, and 4 new brigade combat teams.[54]

Mission

Responsibilities of Border Guard Service of Russia include:

- Defense of the Russian national border, including prevention of illegal crossing of the land and sea border by people and goods (smuggling).
- Protection of economic interests of the Russian Federation and its natural resources within land and sea border areas, territorial waters, and internal seas, including prevention of poaching and illegal fishing.
- Combatting any threats to national security in the border area, including terrorism and foreign infiltration.

Republic of South Africa

Just slightly less than twice the size of Texas, lying at the southern tip of the African continent is the country of South Africa. The country has 3,021 miles (4,862 km) of land borders and 1,738.6 miles (2,798 km) of coastline.[55] With many African countries in some state of civil war, invasion, or economic collapse, the country of South Africa's approach to border security offers an interesting comparison to that of the United States, particularly when it comes to refugees. Another major issue South Africa must deal with is the poaching and smuggling of endangered species—much like the United States has to identify and interdict unauthorized export shipments of illicit cash and firearms.

South Africa has a separate organization to coordinate security of their land and maritime borders. The Border Control Operational Coordinating Committee (BCOCC) is affiliated with the Justice, Crime Prevention and Security Structure and was created in 2005 to manage the South African border environment. The BCOCC works with and coordinates the activities of several other government institutions including National Intelligence, Department of Home Affairs, Transport, Public Works, Agriculture, Health, and Defense, as well as the South African Police Service and the South African Revenue Service.[56] A unique aspect of South Africa is that when it comes to border security, the country surrounds another nation: Lesotho. Additionally, it borders five other countries and two oceans.

Strategic Vision

The BCOCC's vision for Integrated Border Management is to deliver excellent border management outcomes for South Africa by planning and acting within one framework while retaining agency-specific accountabilities.

Mission

The mission of the BCOCC, as the country's principal integrated border management structure, is to facilitate interagency cooperation and coordination; smooth and easy transit across the ports of entry for legitimate traffic; concurrently deterring, detecting, preventing, and interdicting without prejudice or favor and in accordance with the law, individuals and organizations engaged in illegal cross-border activity.

Culture and Behaviors

The BCOCC, in accordance with the provisions of Chapter 3 of the Constitution of the Republic of South Africa, read with Section 4 of the Intergovernmental Relations Framework Act, fosters a shared common culture amongst border management agencies. This will include the skills and competencies to work collaboratively and at a minimum, over time, institutionalize the following shared values:

- Service to our country—Defend and uphold the Constitution and contribute to Government's developmental agenda;
- Vigilance—Deter, detect, and prevent threats to our economy and society;

- Assertiveness — Act decisively, with courage and knowledge;
- Integrity — Act honestly, fairly, and with dependability;
- Professionalism — Act with professional pride, efficiency and effectiveness, commitment to doing a good job, and leading by example;
- Discipline — Respect and obedience to the chain of command and organizational policies and procedures.

Border Control Stakeholders

Currently, several state departments and agencies are directly involved in South African border management through their respective enabling legislation. Border management activities are coordinated on a non-statutory basis by the BCOCC, established under the principles of Cooperative Government in Chapter 3 of the Constitution. The South African Revenue Service (SARS) is the current lead agency and chairs the BCOCC. The various agencies involved in border control include:

- Department of Home Affairs (DHA): regulates and facilitates the legal entry and exit movement of persons across South Africa's borders and the sojourn of foreigners in the RSA;
- South African Revenue Service (SARS) — Customs: controls the movement of goods across borders;
- South African Police Service (SAPS): prevents, combats, and investigates crime; maintains public order; protects and secures the inhabitants of the country and their property; and upholds and enforces the law;
- The Department of Health (DOH): controls and regulates cross-border movement of medicaments and other health care products; prevents and controls cross-border transmission of contagious communicable diseases; and mitigates any health risks associated with cross-border movement;
- The Department of Agriculture, Forestry and Fisheries (DAFF): regulates the importation of animals, plants, their products and other regulated articles that can carry pests, diseases, and other biosecurity threats that could harm South African agricultural industries, the environment, and society;
- The Department of Transport (DOT): regulates the movement of vessels, craft, and vehicles in and out of the country;
- The Department of Trade and Industry (DTI): formulates import and export policy that is administered by SARS — Customs;
- The State Security Agency (SSA): collects, collates, and analyzes information on security threats posed by movement of people and goods across international borders;
- The Department of Public Works (DPW): manages the provision and maintenance of accommodation (operational and residential) and required infrastructure to support the border control operations;
- The Department of Environmental Affairs (DEA): regulates and monitors cross-border movement of tourists within the Trans-Frontier Conservation

Areas (TFCAs); indigenous plants and animals; and hazardous and dangerous materials;
- Parastatals and regulatory bodies with an interest in border management are:
  - Airports Company of South Africa (ACSA): is responsible for managing all commercial airport infrastructure and security
  - Air Traffic and Navigation Services (ATNS): is responsible for regulating the airspace
  - Transnet Group: is responsible for managing infrastructure and security at sea ports.

South African Border Security Issues

South Africa has placed military units to assist police operations along the borders with Lesotho, Zimbabwe, and Mozambique to control smuggling, poaching, and illegal migrations. The country has become a transshipment center for heroin, hashish, and cocaine, as well as a major cultivator of marijuana. There is a rising consumption of heroin and cocaine in the country and it is the world's largest market for methaqualone, usually imported illegally from India through east African countries.[57] The problems facing the country of South Africa are very like those facing the United States and yet their approach to border security is different.

Conclusion

This chapter has detailed the operations of the United States Customs and Border Protection agency, beginning with the Mounted Inspectors in 1904, and continuing today with the CBP operations safeguarding the borders of America, on the ground, in American coastal waters, and in the air. Controlling the borders is key to mitigating the risk due to the possibility of allowing dangerous people (in all senses of the word) into the country. No modern nation can long survive the unlimited access to their country by anyone who simply wishes to enter, for whatever reason.

In 1904, the Mounted Inspectors were the first representatives of our country's border security forces, and did an admirable job of protecting our southern border against an influx of determined Chinese immigrants. The Border Patrol, as a federal agency, was created in 1924 with the specific purpose of protecting the nation's borders. At least in part the creation of the Border Patrol was due to the continued flood of Mexican immigrants into America, following the end of WWI.

Prohibition, from 1920 to 1933, was a particularly bad time for the Border Patrol agents. The fact that most of the country preferred their alcohol, in various forms, despite the new federal law, made things much worse for the fledgling agency. Prior to 1920, the mounted patrol, the predecessor to the Border Patrol, had not lost a single man due to enemy gunfire. That changed quickly with Prohibition. As one Border Patrol agent described it later, "This was one of the most vicious times in the

Immigration officers collect information for processing of illegal immigrants for return to Mexico. Bus lift — Fabens, Texas — 1950s. © US Border Patrol Museum. Used with permission.

history of the border. Smugglers had pretty much of a free hand and knew how to handle horses and a gun. They knew the brush country and you were dealing with a man who was equivalent to you. We lost a lot of men — we killed a lot of smugglers."

The Bracero Program, begun in 1942, was started due to a shortage of cheap labor primarily because of the war effort. Most of the American able-bodied men (and some of the women) were called up to either fight or assist in the factories, making weapons and bombs for the war effort. That left a severe shortage of workers in the agriculture industry. So the appeal went out to our southern neighbor for help. The Bracero Program supplied workers from 1942 to 1956. (The railroad version of Bracero ended with the end of the war, in 1945, but the agriculture version of Bracero went on for a while longer.) Of course, when the program(s) officially ended, the flood of Mexicans who wanted to earn more money in the Promised Land to the north didn't stop. They kept coming, as they do today. Repatriation efforts began with Operation Wetback in 1954, and continue to the present day.

Border security operations are a universal function of every country, as is the enforcement of immigration laws and customs. No single country has the best answer to the varied issues of border security, but as can be seen by a comparison with Russia and South Africa, the United States is not alone in facing terrorism, refugees, mass migration, drug and other contraband smuggling, or the maintenance of sovereign borders against incursion.

Questions for Further Consideration

1. Since the consolidation under the Department of Homeland Security there have been several calls to restore the US Border Patrol and US Customs and Immigration Enforcement back to their pre-DHS organization and function. Based on what you know about current border security issues, would you agree or disagree with these proposals?
2. The techniques and tactics of identifying, tracking, capturing, and processing illegal border crossers has remained largely unchanged for the past 150 years. Are there modern technologies that could be used to improve the operations of the USBP and CBP?
3. Compared with other countries, how do you think the United States fares in border security?

Chapter 3 Endnotes

1. "California Gold Rush, 1848–1864," Retrieved 05-12-2013. http://www.learn california.org/doc.asp?id=118.

2. "Chinese Fisheries in California," Chamber's Journal, Vol. L (Jan. 21, 1954), 48.

3. Chinn, Thomas W. Ed. *A History of the Chinese in California: A Syllabus* (San Francisco: Chinese Historical Society of America, 1969), 72.

4. Krauss, Erich and Alex Pacheco, *On the Line: Inside the U.S. Border Patrol* (New York: Citadel Press, 2004).

5. Myers, John, *The Border Wardens* (New Jersey: Prentice Hall, Inc., 1971), 15.

6. Chin, Gabriel J., *UCLA Law Review*, Vol. 46, No. 1 (1998); "Segregation's Last Stronghold: Race Discrimination and the Constitutional Law of Immigration."

7. Ibid.

8. Krauss and Pacheco (2004).

9. Ibid.

10. Myers (1971).

11. Metz, Leon, "United States Border Patrol," Handbook of Texas Online, https://tshaonline.org/handbook/online/articles/ncujh.

12. "The Bracero Program," www.farmworkers.org/bracerop.html, 36.

13. Johnson, Kevin (Fall 2005). "The Forgotten 'Repatriation' of Persons of Mexican Ancestry and Lessons for the 'War on Terror,'" Davis, California: *Pace Law Review*.

14. Krauss and Pacheco (2004).

15. Ngai, Mae M., *Impossible Subjects: Illegal Aliens and the Making of Modern America*. (Princeton: Princeton University Press, 2004).

16. Hernandez, Kelly L. "The Crimes and Consequences of Illegal Immigration: A Cross Border Examination of Operation Wetback, 1943–1954." *Western Historical Quarterly* 37 (2006): 421–44.

17. It is not the authors' intent to offend readers by using the term "Wetback." That is the actual name of the operation when it was implemented.

18. Ngai (2004).

19. Ibid, 156–57.

20. Consolidated from personal communications with several senior Border Patrol command officers over several years. They have requested to remain anonymous to protect their jobs.

21. August 2009 U.S. Government Accounting Office Report on the Border Patrol.

22. Reyes, quoted in Krauss and Pacheco, 93.

23. Department of Justice, background to the Office of the Inspector General Investigation, Available at: http://www.justice.gov/oig/special/9807/gkp01.htm.

24. Web-Vignery, June, Chairperson et al., Arizona Advisory Committee to the U.S. Commission on Civil Rights. (April 2003). Tragedy Along the Arizona-Mexico Border: Undocumented Immigrants Face the Desert. Available at: http://www.law.umaryland.edu/marshall/usccr/documents/cr182t67b.pdf.

25. Ibid., 2.

26. Ibid., 3.

27. Ibid.

28. 2012–2016 Border Patrol Strategic Plan, https://nemo.cbp.gov/obp/bp_strategic_plan.pdf

29. Ibid.

30. CBP Border Security Report, Fiscal Year 2016. Available at: https://www.cbp.gov/sites/default/files/assets/documents/2016-Dec/CBP-fy2016-border-security-report.pdf

31. Krauss and Pacheco (2004), 120.

32. Ibid., 99.

33. "United States Department of Homeland Security — Customs and Border Protection — Border Patrol." The Officer Down Memorial Page. Last accessed 17 February 2017. Available at: http://www.odmp.org/agency/4830-united-states-department-of-homeland-security-customs-and-border-protection-united-states-border-patrol-us-government. Updated based on statistics from: https://www.cbp.gov/in-memoriam-obp

34. U.S. Customs and Border Protection: About CBP: In Memoriam: Javier Vega, Jr. (05 January 2017). Available at: https://www.cbp.gov/about/in-memoriam/javier-vega-jr

35. Krauss and Pacheco (2004), xvii–xix.

36. Dvorak, Kimberly. https://www.liveleak.com/view?i=a44_1271589956 "Mexican drug cartels threaten U.S. Border Patrol Agents — place a bounty on their lives — San Diego County Political Buzz Examiner." Retrieved 30 March 2012.

37. ODMP. Border Patrol Agent Robert Wimer Rosas, Jr. Available at: http://www.odmp.org/officer/20005-border-patrol-agent-robert-wimer-rosas-jr.

38. Ibid.

39. "Glenn Beck: Ramos & Compean — the whole story." The Glenn Beck Program. Premiere Radio Networks. 2008-07-29. Available at: http://www.glennbeck.com/content/articles/article/196/13098/

40. Seper, Jerry (2006-08-23). "Lawmakers seek review of border agent case," *The Washington Times.* Retrieved 2006-12-14.

41. Gilot, Louis (2006-10-20). "Sentence handed to border agents; free until Jan. 17," *El Paso Times.* Retrieved 2006-12-14.

42. Riechmann, Deb. "Bush commutes prison sentences of 2 former U.S. border agents," Associated Press, January 19, 2009.

43. "U.S. border agent kills Mexican teen," *Toronto Sun.* 2010-06-09. Retrieved 2010-07-01.

44. "Mexico urges U.S. probe of border deaths," *Sydney Morning Herald.* 2010-06-11. Retrieved 2010-07-01.

45. Epstein, Brian. "Crossing the Line at the Border," PBS. Retrieved April 20, 2012. Available at: http://www.pbs.org/wnet/need-to-know/security/video-first-look-crossing-the-line/13597/

46. "A Culture of Cruelty," No More Deaths. Retrieved April 24, 2012. Available at: http://forms.nomoredeaths.org/abuse-documentation/a-culture-of-cruelty/

47. Fisher, Michael, "Testimony of Chief Michael Fisher." Transcript of House Appropriations Subcommittee on Homeland Security Hearing on the Proposed Fiscal 2013 Appropriations for the U.S. Customs and Border Protection, House Appropriations Subcommittee on Homeland Security. Retrieved August 23, 2012.

48. Jesus A. Trevino (1998). "Border violence against illegal immigrants and the need to change the border patrol's current complaint review process" (PDF). *Houston Journal of International Law* 21 (1): 85–114. Retrieved 2009-06-01.

49. *United States of America: Human rights concerns in the border region with Mexico,* Amnesty International. 1998-05-19. Archived from the original on October 21, 2007. Retrieved 2009-06-01.

50. Huspek, Michael; Roberto Martinez, and Leticia Jimenez (1998). "Violations of human and civil rights on the U.S.-Mexico border, 1995 to 1997: a report" (reprint). *Social Justice* 25 (2). ISSN 1043-1578. Retrieved 2009-06-01.

51. Garske, Monica, 10 Aug 2012, Former BP Agents Convicted of Smuggling Illegal Immigrants. San Diego. Available at: http://www.nbcsandiego.com/news/local/Border-Patrol-Agents-Convicted-of-Smuggling-Illegal-Immigrants-Villareal-Brothers-165815146.html#ixzz2X4fmhv00.

52. Customs and Border Protection's Fiscal Year 2015 Drug Summary Report, 27 Jan 2016.

53. CIA World Factbook. Russia. Available at: https://www.cia.gov/library/publications/the-world-factbook/geos/rs.html.

54. Gramer, Robbie. "Here's What Russia's Military Build-Up in the Arctic Looks Like," The Cable. Available at: http://foreignpolicy.com/2017/01/25/heres-what-russias-military-build-up-in-the-arctic-looks-like-trump-oil-military-high-north-infographic-map/. Retrieved 2017-7-7.

55. CIA World Factbook, South Africa. Available at: https://www.cia.gov/library/publications/the-world-factbook/geos/sf.html.

56. BCOCC Website. Available at: http://www.saborders.gov.za/index.html.

57. CIA World Factbook, South Africa. Available at: https://www.cia.gov/library/publications/the-world-factbook/geos/sf.html.

Chapter 4

Physical Border Security

"Our number one defense against terror involves the perimeter, keeping dangerous enemies from entering the United States of America."

—Michael Chertoff, Secretary of DHS, September 11, 2006

Key Words and Concepts

Compliance Enforcement Unit
Hart-Cellar Act
IIRIRA
Immigration Act (1990)
Office of Air and Marine

Secure Fence Act (2006)
SEVIS/SEP
Unmanned Aerial Vehicle
Unmanned Aerial System

Border fence between El Paso, Texas, and Ciudad Juarez, Mexico, on the US side of the Rio Grande (Rio Bravo). The river and Mexico are to the right. James Phelps. 2012.

Introduction

Prior to the twentieth century, immigration into the United States was only of one kind: legal. Anyone who wanted to better himself or herself, or anyone wanting religious freedom, or freedom from other forms of persecution, including legal (for alleged crimes), could get passage into America by stowing aboard a ship or crossing a land border from either Mexico or Canada. Once here, the person was an American, since we were, in general, a nation of people coming from somewhere else, all starting a new life. Things changed in the early 1900s in this country, with a distinction being made between "legal" and "illegal" immigration. At that point there were two kinds of immigration, a situation that continues to this day. Most Americans favor some form of legal immigration, with differences of opinion only on the degree or number of immigrants allowed. According to the Pew Research Center, 72% of Americans indicated in a survey May 2015 that they approved allowing undocumented immigrants to stay in this country legally if they met certain requirements.[1]

The increasing number of terrorist attacks worldwide, along with the attacks on the World Trade Center in February 1993, the *USS Cole* in October 2000, and the Twin Towers in September 2001, forced the US Government to analyze weaknesses in border security as well as shortcomings in its domestic security policies. Establishing a monolithic organization such as the Department of Homeland Security was one possible reaction to the increased concern over physical border security. A political move by Congress to attempt to reduce the interference between intelligence organizations to enable them to operate more efficiently was another. How effective that was is still to be determined, although the fact that 9/11 has not been repeated (at the time of this writing) is evidence in the positive category.

Physical Borders

The United States has two extensive land borders with two other countries: Mexico and Canada. The border with Mexico is 3,145 kilometers (1,954 miles) long, and extends from Imperial Beach, California, and Tijuana, Baja California, in the west to Matamoros, Tamaulipas, and Brownsville, Texas, in the east. The border with Canada extends from Maine to Washington State and between Canada and Alaska. The Canadian border extends for 8,893 kilometers (5,526 miles) and is the longest international border shared by two countries.

Control of the United States' borders is a major component of national security, and is one of the five stated goals of the Department of Homeland Security (the others being: preventing terrorism and enhancing security; enforcing and administering the immigration laws; safeguarding and securing cyberspace; and ensuring resilience to disasters). The 7,500-mile length of the land borders of the United States poses a significant security challenge. Drug and people smugglers, illegal immigrants, terrorists, fugitives, and other criminals benefit from the porous nature of the southern and northern US borders. Each year an estimated 500,000 immigrants attempt to enter the country illegally, according to the Migration Policy Institute, adding to the approximately 11.1 million illegal aliens currently in America.

The US Border Patrol is directly responsible for securing the nation's land and water borders. The Border Patrol's general mission is to prevent terrorists, their weapons, narcotics, agricultural pests, and smuggled goods from entering the country, while also identifying and arresting those with outstanding arrest warrants. Border protection, immigration, and visa matters have long been a discussion of concern since well before the attacks of 9/11. The Border Patrol was formed in 1924 and manned by uniformed squads and Texas Rangers as needed. The chief objective was to prevent the entry of illegal alcohol and drugs along the southwestern border of the United States. Now the Border Patrol has been incorporated into the Department of Homeland Security, ICE and other Department of Justice entities, and consolidated into the sub-department known as US Customs and Border Protection (CBP). The US CBP's primary strategies are to secure the borders of America, by combatting the smuggling of drugs, weapons, terrorists, and illegal immigrants into the United States, and strengthening the Border Patrol.[2] Among the challenges CBP faces is the vast terrain across which illegal activity occurs. There are 327 air, land, and sea ports of entry, along with 7,500 miles of land border and 95,000 miles of shoreline. This is the primary reason why the CBP has joined forces with the Border Patrol, US Coast Guard, and the Naval and Air commands. However, when there is a strong desire there is a way, and while the current system may stop a percentage of illegal border activity, it is unable to stop it all.

History of US Immigration

Legal immigration rose quickly following the 1965 passage of the Immigration and Nationality Act, which allowed permanent residents and naturalized citizens of America to petition for relatives in Mexico to join them. The Act, also known as the Hart-Cellar Act, effectively abolished the national origins immigration formula that had been in place since the passage of the Immigration Act of 1924. Hart-Cellar replaced the quota system with immigration requirements for job skills or familial relationships with citizens or naturalized residents. The numbers of legal immigrants rose sharply in the 1970s, primarily due to Hart-Cellar.

Coupled with an increasing number of legal immigrants was a (seemingly) tacit approval of an increased number of illegal immigrants crossing the border, particularly from Mexico. The increasing pressure from the border states (Texas, Arizona, New Mexico, and California) to "do something" about the illegal immigrants by the federal government was more than matched by the pressure from economic interests (such as the hotel and agriculture industries) to turn a blind eye on the increasing numbers of people coming over the border, looking for work. The illegal immigration supplied (and continues to supply) cheap and honest labor (albeit generally unskilled), which apparently does have some negative economic effects. According to an article in the New York Times and a University of California economist named Giovanni Peri, although undocumented workers do in fact lower the wages of U.S. adults without a high-school diploma by somewhere between .4 and 7.4 percent, they actually "complement" skilled workers, allowing them to make more money, and work longer hours, increasing their pay by as much as ten percent.[3]

The continuing controversy between control of the borders and economic interests increased after passage of the 1986 Immigration Reform and Control Act (IRCA), also known as the Simpson-Mazzoli Act. Simpson-Mazzoli basically made it unlawful for any person to hire, either directly or through a subcontractor, any alien, knowing that person is unable to work legally, or to fail to verify that any person hired can work legally, or continue to employ an alien knowing that he is in the country illegally. Simpson-Mazzoli also established a worker verification system, which required that: the employer attest that the employee's work status has been verified through an examination of a passport, birth certificate, social security card, alien documentation papers, or other proof; the worker was required by the Act to attest that he or she is a legal resident of the United States, and is therefore able to work; and, that the employer keep records for at least three years, verifying the above.

In addition, the Simpson-Mazzoli Act also granted amnesty and resident status to certain seasonal agricultural illegal immigrants, as well as to illegal immigrants who had entered the country prior to January 1, 1982, and who had resided in the United States continuously since that time. Essentially, a Dream Act prior to the Dream Act, which attempted to couple legalization for 3 million illegal immigrants with a semi-promise to enact workplace enforcement to discourage additional illegal immigration.

Illegal immigration jumped tremendously in the 1980s and 1990s based primarily on three factors: One was the economic crisis in Mexico in the 1980s that slowed economic growth, and limited the number of jobs, particularly for young people. The second factor was the impact of NAFTA, the North American Free Trade Agreement, which restructured Mexican agriculture. The number of Border Patrol apprehensions grew from only a few hundred in the 1960s to more than one million per year during the 1980s to almost two million by the end of the 1990s.[4] The problem of illegal immigration changed from what Washington (and the public) considered a minor nuisance to what was publicly perceived to be an issue of national security, and state welfare in the border states of California, Arizona, and Texas. As daily border crossings (to work and school in this country) became more difficult, more migrant workers opted to simply remain in the United States, and bring their spouses and children with them, which put more pressure on American hospitals, schools, and other state social service organizations. The third factor related to the immigration increase in the 1990s was the Immigration Act of 1990, which increased the limits on legal immigration, and revised grounds for deportation and exclusion. After passage of the 1990 law, 700,000 immigrants could enter the country legally, an increase of 200,000 people annually.[5]

The terrorist attacks of September 11, 2001, forever changed the concept of border control, from what was considered (prior to that date) to be a matter of public order to a matter of the highest level of security. All the hijackers had entered the United States legally, on either tourist or student visas, and some had simply overstayed the limits on the visas, to complete their mission.[6] After the attacks of 9/11, stopping any future attacks became the highest national priority, and increased border control became a foundation for that strategy. It concomitantly increased both awareness and concern for more than just the southern border of the country; people became concerned with any air and sea entry into the United States, along with any entry through the northern border with Canada.

People can enter the United States legally in many ways. They can enter the country as tourists, as students, as business travelers, or as workers on short-term work visas. Or, they can immigrate permanently, sponsored by a family member already in this country, or based on employment skills. During 2016, for example, more than 11 million people applied for immigrant or non-immigrant visas to enter the United States (617,752 immigrant visas, and 10,891,745 non-immigrant visas).[7] And, an unknown number of those people simply stayed in this country after their legal visas had expired.

Over the past twenty years, the US Government has begun a series of measures aimed at reducing the flow of illegal immigrants into this country. The first (and largest) was an increase in the number of Border Patrol agents at the borders. An active border patrol function has existed in the United States since the start of the twentieth century. Horse-mounted US Immigration Service watchmen conducted the first border patrols in 1904. At that time the border patrols were called the Mounted Guards. Border patrols were irregular, and conducted based on the availability of men (and horses). The Border Patrol was based in El Paso, Texas, and consisted of 75 men. At that time in US history, the primary concern was illegal immigration of Chinese, not Hispanics, and the Mounted Guards were looking for Chinese crossing the Mexican border, not Mexicans.

Today, Customs and Border Protection is the largest law enforcement agency in the United States. When it comes to borders with economic disparity between adjoining countries, the border between the United States and Mexico is the longest in the world. As long as a significant economic disparity exists between the two countries, some people will risk coming into the United States illegally. There are indications, however, that the increased law enforcement along the border has been having its intended effect.

During the mid-1990s, the Border Patrol was apprehending approximately 600,000 people annually attempting to cross the border from Mexico in both Texas and California, and apprehending about 300,000 people attempting to cross the border into Arizona. Illegal immigration seemingly responded to the tougher enforcement in Texas and California in the mid-1990s by changing to the harsher crossing routes in Arizona. Arizona apprehensions rose to more than 700,000, and fell in the other two states. The number of apprehensions during fiscal year 2016 nationwide was 415,816, which was an increase over FY 2015, but lower than either FY 2014 or 2013, and a fraction of the average between the 1980s through 2008 (more than 1.1 million).[8] Of course, attempting to correlate arrest data with the total number of illegal border crossings is simply indirect evidence, not scientific proof, but the data shows a decline.

Enacted Border Patrol Program Budget by Fiscal Year
(Dollars in Thousands)

Fiscal Year	Budget Amount	Fiscal Year	Budget Amount
1990	262,647	2004	1,409,480**
1991	298,718	2005	1,524,960***
1992	326,234	2006	2,115,268
1993	362,659	2007	2,277,510****
1994	399,995	2008	2,245,261
1995	451,535	2009	2,656,055
1996	568,012	2010	2,958,108
1997	717,389	2011	3,549,295*****
1998	877,092	2012	3,530,994
1999	916,780	2013	3,466,880
2000	1,055,444	2014	3,634,855
2001	1,146,463	2015	3,797,821
2002	1,416,251	2016	3,642,820
2003	1,515,080*		

* Includes carryover counter-terrorism funds from Fiscal Year 2002
** New funding structure related to the transfer of the Border Patrol Program to DHS.CBP
*** Includes Fiscal Year 2005 Emergency Supplemental
**** Includes Fiscal Year 2006 War Supplemental carryover funds
***** Includes Fiscal Years 2010/2011 Border Security Supplemental

U.S. Border Patrol Budget by FY, 1990–2016. Available at: https://www.cbp.gov/sites/default/files/assets/documents/2016-Oct/BP%20Budget%20History%201990-2016.pdf]]

Whether the declining number is due to increased enforcement along the border, a weakened US economy, or some other reason is open to debate.

A drop in the number of arrests of illegal aliens attempting to cross the Mexican border may be due to a number of different factors, which may or may not include a "catch and release" policy followed by immigration enforcement agencies. Essentially this was the unofficial name for a protocol followed by US Immigration and Customs Enforcement and US Customs and Border Patrol, prior to 2006, where people caught for being in unlawful immigration status were released while awaiting a hearing before an immigration judge. Due to a lack of resources available to Immigration and Customs Enforcement to detain people (at least, in 2005), in addition to the lengthy time between apprehension and the appearance before the federal immigration court (89 days, in 2005, according to the National Center for Policy Analysis), catch and release was the de facto policy used by ICE and USBP. Those believed to be in violation of immigration status were released and given a date when they were to appear before an immigration judge. However, of those ordered to appear before the federal immigration court in Harlingen, Texas, approximately 98 percent never showed up.[9] Which begs the question: did the 2 percent who actually showed up simply not receive the memo, or did they get lost, and appear in court by accident?

In 2005, Michael Chertoff, at that point Secretary of the Department of Homeland Security, told a Senate hearing that DHS planned on ending the catch and release policy very soon, with the hope that it would reduce illegal immigration to the United States. Chertoff reported in July of 2006 that the catch and release program had ended, and that a new influx of money for border security purposes had been helpful in implementing the "new" policy, which was to detain those caught in immigration violation until their hearing, with the exception of Mexicans who had recently arrived, who would be subject to expedited removal.[10]

During the eight years Obama was in office, he generally and gradually restricted who ICE agents could apprehend. For example, on November 20, 2014, the Secretary of DHS, C. J. Johnson, sent a memo to the heads of both ICE and CBP, describing new priorities regarding illegal immigration. He ordered agents to concentrate on illegal aliens who posed a threat to national security, or who were "misdemeanants," and not waste resources on illegal immigrants who were in neither category. A new Priority Enforcement Program resulted from this memo. A reporter writing for Breitbart.com, Brandon Darby, wrote in January 2015 that training documents supplied by an anonymous USBP agent basically instructed workers to "only arrest someone who they directly see cross the border, if they are a wanted criminal, a convicted felon, have an extensive or a violent criminal history, or otherwise pose a national security or public safety threat."[11] Although characterized as Catch and Release-2.0, reporter Dara Lind noted that ICE agents disputed that anything had changed—the guidance they received had always been similar, and the original catch and release policies had never actually ended in 2006.

Other possible factors that may have affected illegal immigration into this country include the DREAM Act (Development, Relief, and Education for Alien Minors), a legislative proposal introduced into Congress in August 2001, and several times since, but has so far failed to pass; the DACA (Deferred Action for Childhood Arrivals), and DAPA (Deferred Action for Parents of Americans) programs. The DREAM Act intended to first grant conditional legal residency, and permanent residency if certain qualifications were then met. Although the bill failed several times, the "Dreamers" were given executive amnesty in 2012, by then-President Obama. DACA, begun by the President in 2012, is an immigration policy that allows undocumented immigrants who entered the country as minors to receive a renewable two-year period of deferred action from deportation, and eligibility for a work permit. DAPA was announced by President Obama in 2014 and grants an exemption from deportation and a renewable three-year work permit to certain undocumented immigrants who have lived in this country since 2010 and have children who are either American citizens or lawful permanent residents. At the time of this publication, there is a lawsuit in the Supreme

Court brought by 26 states against DAPA and a widening of DACA eligibility. Whatever the Supreme Court ruling, it is logical to assume that the three policy decisions have helped to fuel an increase of illegal immigration to this country.

Recently elected President Trump has apparently decided to modify the former president's immigration policies. According to a recent article in the Washington Post, DHS Secretary John Kelly ordered federal immigration agents to begin arresting and deporting more illegal immigrants.[12] He also, according to the reporter, exempted the "Dreamers" (those participating in former President Obama's "Dream Act" executive order), but told the agents that there were no longer any other "special" classes of people who should be considered "off-limits" for purposes of possible deportation. The reporter also mentioned that the President wants to hire 5,000 new Border Patrol agents, 10,000 more Immigration and Customs people, and 500 more officers for Air and Marine CBP operations.[13]

Another factor that may affect illegal immigration numbers and apprehensions along the border are raids, targeting illegal immigrants. The first illegal immigrant raid by DHS officers under the new President Trump did not exactly agree with his promise to utilize Immigration and Customs Enforcement (ICE) officers to concentrate on "murderers, rapists, and other bad hombres" who pose a serious threat to America's public safety. During a raid the week of February 6, 2017, 678 people were apprehended in 12 states; 74 percent had been convicted of a crime, down from 92 percent of illegal immigrants detained under the prior president in 2016, according to a USA Today analysis.[14] In fact, according to the USA Today, the percentages of non-criminals targeted and deported with a previous criminal conviction went up gradually, from a "low" of 67 percent in 2011 to a "high" of 92 percent in 2016.[15]

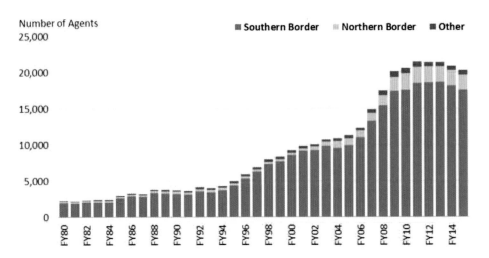

U.S. Border Patrol Agents, Total and by Region, FY 1980–FY2015. Available at: http://www.cbp.gov/sites/default/files/documents/BP%20Staffing%20FY1992-FY2015.pdf.

Statement of Subcommittee Chairwoman Martha McSally (R-AZ)
Border and Maritime Security Subcommittee

Overstaying Their Welcome: National Security Risks Posed by Visa Overstays

June 14, 2016

Border security naturally evokes images of the hot Arizona desert, dusty border roads, agents in green, fencing and camera towers. But a broader view of border security recognizes that there is more than just security along the southwest border to consider. Time and time again, terrorists have exploited the visa system by legally entering America. The 9/11 Commission put it this way: "For terrorists, travel documents are as important as weapons." The Commission's focus on travel documents is not surprising. Since the 1993 World Trade Center bombing, terrorists have abused the hospitality of the American people to conduct attacks here at home. Mahmud Abouhalima, an Egyptian convicted of the 1993 World Trade Center bombing, worked illegally in the US as a cab driver after his tourist visa had expired. At least four of the 9/11 hijackers overstayed their visas, or were out of status—a missed opportunity to disrupt the attacks that killed nearly 3,000 of our fellow Americans. And among the most important weaknesses the attackers exploited was the porous "outer ring of border security." The hijackers passed through U.S. border security a combined total of 68 times without arousing suspicion. More recently, Amine el-Khalifi attempted to conduct a suicide attack on the U.S. Capitol in 2012. He had been in the country since 1999 on a tourist visa, but never left. Another man, arrested in the aftermath of Boston Marathon bombing who helped destroy evidence, was able to return to the United States despite being out of status on his student visa. Clearly, visa security is an important element of keeping the homeland secure. To put the national security risks in perspective, a widely cited 2006 Pew Hispanic Center Study, indicated as many as 40% of all illegal aliens who come into our country do not cross the desert in Arizona, but come in through the "front door" at our land, sea, and air ports of entry, with permission, and then overstay their welcome. Earlier this year, the Department of Homeland Security released a visa overstay report demonstrating the visa overstay problem may be much worse than previously thought. In fiscal year 2015, fewer people were apprehended by the US Border Patrol, than overstayed their visas and are suspected of still being in the country, making the estimate closer to 60% of those illegally in the United States. I am concerned that there are unidentified national security and public safety risks in a population that large, which has historically been the primary means for terrorist entry into the United States. In order to tackle the challenge, the Department has to first identify those who overstay their visa in the first place. A mandate to electronically track entries and exits from the country has been in place for more than 20 years, and a mandate for a biometrically-based entry-exit system has been a requirement for 12 years. Since 2003, we made substantial progress adding biometrics to the entry process and we now take fingerprints and photographs of most visitors entering on a visa. But CBP has made, in fits and starts, only marginal progress when it comes to biometric exit. There have been a series of exit pilot projects at the nation's air, land and sea ports over the last 10 years, but no plan to ever implement a biometric exit capability was seriously considered by CBP and the Department. CBP is now engaged in a series of operational experiments, such as the use of mobile devices with biometric readers, designed to support a future biometric exit system. In fact, until very recently, the political will to make biometric exit a priority was missing from Department and CBP leadership. Thankfully, it appears that the Department has finally turned a corner. Secretary Johnson has now committed to a 2018 roll out of an operational biometric exit system at the nation's highest volume airports   an ambitious timeline, but long overdue. And Congress has recently provided a steady funding stream, in the form of new fees that will enable CBP to make investments to bring the system online. Putting a biometric exit system in place is, as the 9/11 Commission noted, "an essential investment in our national security," because without a viable biometric exit system, visa holders can overstay their visa, and disappear into the United States; just as four of the 9/11 hijackers were able to do. And once we identify overstays, especially those who present national security and public safety threats, we must dedicate the resources necessary to promptly remove those in the country illegally—otherwise we put our citizens at risk unnecessarily. Yet, even as we dedicate scarce resources to pursue this small sub-set of overstays, up to 25% of this group was found to have already departed the United States after ICE Special Agents conducted full field investigations. We are spending too much time chasing our tails. Adding a reliable exit system will be an immediate force multiplier that allows national security professionals to focus their efforts on preventing terrorist attacks. Doing so mitigates the chance that visitors can stay in the country beyond their period of admission—and reduces the terrorist threat in the process. The American people need to know answers to these simple questions: How many more overstays are out there who pose a serious threat to the security of the homeland? Can Immigration and Customs Enforcement quickly identify and remove visa overstays to mitigate the substantial national security risks? I look forward to receiving answers to these important questions.[16]

Fences

A separation barrier, or fence, is simply a physical means of preventing the free movement of people and vehicles across a border. The US Border Patrol utilizes both physical fencing, which is placed to impede the illegal entry of individuals, and vehicle barriers, which aim to impede the illegal entry of vehicles into the country. Both fences and vehicle barriers can be either temporary or permanent.

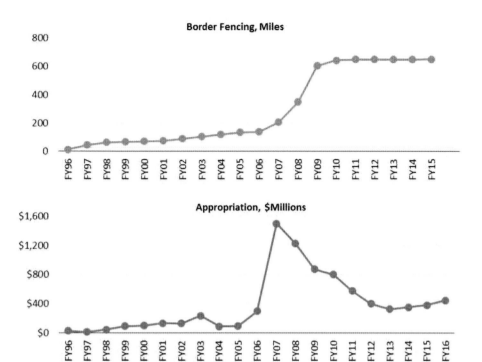

Tactical Infrastructure Appropriations and Miles of Border Fencing, FY1996–2016. Created from multiple sources. From Carl Argueta, Border Security: Immigration Enforcement Between Ports of Entry, Congressional Research Service, 19 April 2016, p. 15.

The San Diego Border Primary Fence. Wikicommons, n.d.

The San Diego Border Primary Fence

The USBP's San Diego sector extends along the first 66 miles, from the Pacific Ocean, of the international border with Mexico, and covers approximately 7,000 square miles of territory. Located north of Tijuana and Tecate, Mexican cities with a combined population of more than two million people, the sector features no natural barriers to entry by unauthorized migrants and smugglers. As a result of this geographical reality and in response to the large numbers of unauthorized aliens crossing the border in the area, in 1990 the US Border Patrol began erecting a physical barrier to deter illegal entries and drug smuggling. The ensuing "primary" fence covered the first 14 miles of the border, starting from the Pacific Ocean, and was constructed of 10-foot-high welded steel.

Barriers Along the U.S. Borders: Key Authorities and Requirements

Michael John Garcia
Acting Section Research Manager
November 18, 2016

Securing the borders is an issue of perennial concern to Congress. Federal law authorizes the Department of Homeland Security (DHS) to construct barriers along the U.S. borders to deter illegal crossings. DHS is also required to construct reinforced fencing along at least 700 miles of the land border with Mexico (a border that stretches 1,933 miles), though Congress has not provided a deadline for its completion. Nor has Congress provided specific guidelines about the characteristics of such fencing (e.g., the height or material composition of the fencing) or other barriers that DHS may deploy. At this time, fence construction has largely been halted, though DHS still needs to deploy fencing along nearly 50 additional miles of the southwest border to satisfy the 700-mile requirement. The primary statute authorizing DHS to deploy barriers along the international borders is Section 102 of the Illegal Immigration Reform and Immigrant Responsibility Act of 1996 (IIRIRA; P.L. 104-208, div. C). Congress made significant amendments to IIRIRA Section 102 through three enactments — the REAL ID Act of 2005 (P.L. 109-13, div. B), the Secure Fence Act of 2006 (P.L. 109-367), and the Consolidated Appropriations Act, 2008 (P.L. 110-161, div. E). These amendments required that DHS construct hundreds of miles of new fencing along the border, and they also provided the Secretary of DHS with broad authority to waive "all legal requirements" that may impede construction of barriers and roads under IIRIRA Section 102. These statutory modifications, along with increased funding for border projects, resulted in the deployment of several hundred miles of new barriers along the southwest border between 2005 and 2011. In recent years, DHS has largely stopped deploying additional fencing along the border, as the agency has altered its enforcement strategy in a manner that places less priority upon barrier construction. Both during and immediately following the 2016 presidential campaign, President-elect Donald Trump stated that the construction of additional barriers along the U.S.-Mexico border would be a top priority for his Administration. Although interest in the framework governing the deployment of barriers along the international border during the Obama Administration typically focused on the stringency of the statutory mandate to deploy fencing along at least 700 miles of the southern border, attention may shift to those provisions in current law that allow, but do not require, the deployment of fencing or other physical barriers along additional mileage of the border. IIRIRA Section 102 authorizes DHS to construct additional fencing or other barriers along the U.S. land borders beyond the 700 miles specified in statute. Indeed, nothing in current statute would appear to bar DHS from potentially installing hundreds of miles of additional fencing or other barriers along the border, at least so long as the action was determined appropriate to deter illegal crossings in areas of high illegal entry. Moreover, IIRIRA Section 102 grants DHS authority to waive any legal requirement that would impede the expeditious construction of additional barriers and roads. DHS's current policy not to deploy a substantial amount of additional fencing, beyond what is expressly required by law, appears primarily premised on policy considerations and funding constraints, rather than significant legal impediments. This report discusses the statutory framework governing the deployment of fencing and other barriers along the U.S. international borders. For more extensive discussion of ongoing activities and operations along the border between ports of entry, see CRS Report R42138, Border Security: Immigration Enforcement Between Ports of Entry, by Carla N. Argueta.[17]

In addition to border fencing, the Border Patrol deploys both permanent and temporary vehicle barriers at the border. Vehicle barriers are meant to stop the entry of vehicles, but not people, into the United States. Temporary vehicle barriers are typically chained together and can be moved to different locations at the USBP's discretion. Permanent vehicle barriers are embedded in the ground and are meant to remain in one location.

Border Security: Immigration Enforcement Between Ports of Entry

Carla N. Argueta, Analyst in Immigration Policy
April 19, 2016

Border enforcement is a core element of the Department of Homeland Security's effort to control unauthorized migration, with the U.S. Border Patrol (USBP) within the U.S. Customs and Border Protection (CBP) as the lead agency along most of the border. Border enforcement has been an ongoing subject of congressional interest since the 1970s, when unauthorized immigration to the United States first registered as a serious national problem; and border security has received additional attention in the years since the terrorist attacks of 2001. Since the 1990s, migration control at the border has been guided by a strategy of "prevention through deterrence"—the idea that the concentration of personnel, infrastructure, and surveillance technology along heavily trafficked regions of the border will discourage unauthorized migrants from attempting to enter the United States. Since 2005, CBP has attempted to discourage repeat unauthorized migrant entries and disrupt migrant smuggling networks by imposing tougher penalties against certain unauthorized migrants, a set of policies eventually described as "enforcement with consequences." Most people apprehended at the Southwest border are now subject to "high consequence" enforcement outcomes. Across a variety of indicators, the United States has substantially expanded border enforcement resources over the last three decades. Particularly since 2001, such increases include border security appropriations, personnel, fencing and infrastructure, and surveillance technology. In addition to increased resources, the USBP has implemented several strategies over the past several decades in an attempt to thwart unauthorized migration. In 2014, the Obama Administration announced executive actions to "fix" the immigration system. These actions address several issues, including a revised security plan at the southern border. The Border Patrol collects data on several different border enforcement outcomes; this report describes trends in border apprehensions, recidivism, and estimated "got aways" and "turn backs." Yet none of these existing data are designed to measure unauthorized border flows or the degree to which the border is secured. Thus, the report also describes methods for estimating border security at the strategic and operational levels. Drawing on multiple data sources, the report reviews the state of border security. Robust investments at the border were not associated with reduced unauthorized inflows during the 1980s and 1990s, but a range of evidence suggests a substantial drop in unauthorized inflows from 2007 to 2011, followed by a rise from 2012 to 2014 and a decrease in 2015. Enforcement, along with the 2007 economic downturn in the United States, likely contributed to the drop in unauthorized migration, though the precise share of the decline attributable to enforcement is unknown. Enhanced border enforcement also may have contributed to a number of secondary costs and benefits. To the extent that border enforcement successfully deters unauthorized entries, such enforcement may reduce border-area violence and migrant deaths, protect fragile border ecosystems, and improve the quality of life in border communities. But to the extent that migrants are not deterred, the concentration of enforcement resources on the border may increase border-area violence and migrant deaths, encourage unauthorized migrants to find new ways to enter and to remain in the United States for longer periods of time, damage border ecosystems, harm border-area businesses and the quality of life in border communities, and strain U.S. relations with Canada and Mexico.[18]

Operation Gatekeeper

The primary fence, by itself, did not have a discernible impact on the influx of unauthorized aliens coming across the border in San Diego. Because of this, Operation Gatekeeper was officially announced in the San Diego sector on October 1, 1994. The chief elements of the operation were large increases in the overall manpower of the sector, and the deployment of USBP personnel directly along the border to deter illegal entry. The strategic plan called for three tiers of agent deployment. The first tier of agents was deployed to fixed positions on the border. The agents in this first tier were charged with preventing illegal entry, apprehending those who attempted to enter, and generally observing the border. A second tier of agents was deployed north of the border in the corridors that were heavily used by illegal aliens.

The second tier of agents had more freedom of movement than the first tier and was charged with containing and apprehending those aliens who made it past the first tier. The third tier of agents was typically assigned to man vehicle checkpoints further inland to apprehend the traffic that eluded the first two tiers. Operation Gatekeeper resulted in significant increases in the manpower and other resources deployed to the San Diego sector. Agents received additional night vision goggles, portable radios, and four-wheel drive vehicles, and light towers and seismic sensors were also deployed.

Sandia National Laboratory Study

Per the Customs and Border Patrol, the primary fence, in combination with various other USBP enforcement initiatives along the San Diego border region (i.e., Operation Gatekeeper), proved to be successful but fiscally and environmentally costly. For example, as unauthorized aliens and smugglers breached the primary fence and attempted to evade detection, USBP agents were often forced to pursue the suspects through environmentally sensitive areas. It soon became apparent to immigration officials and lawmakers that the USBP needed, among other things, a "rigid" enforcement system that could integrate infrastructure (i.e., a multi-tiered fence and roads), manpower, and new technologies to further control the border region.

The concept of a three-tiered fence system was first recommended by a 1993 Sandia National Laboratory study commissioned by the former Immigration and Naturalization Service (INS). According to the Sandia study, the use of multiple barriers in urban areas would increase the USBP's ability to discourage a significant number of illegal border crossers, to detect intruders early and delay them as long as possible, and to channel a reduced number of illegal border crossers to geographic locations where the USBP was better prepared to deal with them. The Sandia study further noted that segments of the border could not be controlled at the immediate border due to the ruggedness of the terrain, and recommended the use of highway checkpoints in those areas to contain aliens after they had entered the country illegally. The study concluded that aliens attempting to enter the United States from Mexico had shown remarkable resiliency in bypassing or destroying obstacles in their path, including the existing primary fence, and postulated that "[a] three-fence barrier system with vehicle patrol roads between the fences and lights will provide the necessary discouragement."[19]

Congressional Border Barrier Legislation

As previously mentioned, the INS constructed the primary fencing in San Diego using the broad authority granted to the Attorney General to guard and control the US border by the Immigration and Nationality Act (INA). In 1996, Congress expressly authorized the AG to construct barriers at the border for the first time in the Illegal Immigration Reform and Immigrant Responsibility Act (IIRIRA). Congress has subsequently amended this legislation on several occasions.

Section 102 of IIRIRA — Improvement of Barriers at the Border

Section 102 of the IIRIRA concerned the improvement and construction of barriers at the international borders. As originally enacted, Section 102(a) appeared to give the Attorney General broad authority to install additional physical barriers and roads "in the vicinity of the United States border to deter illegal crossings in areas of high illegal entry into the United States." The phrase "vicinity of the United States border" *was not* defined in the INA or in immigration regulations. This section also *did not* stipulate what specific characteristics would designate an area as one of "high illegal entry."

As originally enacted, Section 102(b) mandated that the Attorney General construct a barrier in the border area near San Diego, California. Specifically, the barrier consists of three tiers along the 14 miles of the international land border of the United States, starting at the Pacific Ocean and extending eastward. The Secure Fence Act of 2006 (P.L. 109-367) amended IIRIRA Section 102(b) by removing the specific provisions authorizing construction of the San Diego fence (though not the provisions concerning fence safety features, easements, or appropriations) and adding provisions authorizing five stretches of two-layered reinforced fencing, totaling roughly 850 miles, along the southwest border. Section 102(b) was again amended in 2008, with the passage of the Consolidated Appropriations Act (P.L. 110-161). This Act requires the Secretary of Homeland Security to construct reinforced fencing along not less than 700 miles of the southwest border, in locations where fencing is deemed most practical and effective. The Consolidated Appropriations Act also amended the IIRIRA Section 102(b) to authorize the appropriation of "sums as may be necessary to carry out this subsection."

As originally enacted, IIRIRA's Section 102(c) waived the Endangered Species Act (ESA) of 1973 and the National Environmental Policy Act (NEPA) of 1969 to the extent the AG determined necessary, to ensure expeditious construction of the barriers authorized to be completed under Section 102. The waiver authority in this provision

Border fence in Del Rio, Texas. James Phelps, 2013.

appeared to apply both to barriers that may be constructed near the border and to the barrier that was to be constructed near the San Diego area. The INS (and CBP after 2003) never exercised this original waiver authority, instead choosing to comply with the NEPA and the ESA. The INS published a Final Environmental Impact Study pursuant to NEPA and received non-jeopardy Biological Opinion from the US Fish and Wildlife Service under the ESA. This waiver authority was expanded in the 109th Congress by the REAL ID Act, and DHS has exercised this expanded waiver authority in order to continue construction of the San Diego border fence, as well as physical barriers and roads alongside the southwest border.

Section 102(d) also provided the Attorney General with various land acquisition authorities. In 2002, Congress authorized the AG to use INS funds to purchase land for enforcement fences and to construct the fences.

The scope of the waiver authority is substantial. Whereas IIRIRA had previously authorized the waiver of both NEPA and ESA requirements, the REAL ID Act authorizes the waiver of all legal requirements determined necessary by the Secretary of DHS for the expeditious construction of authorized barriers, and only allows judicial review for constitutional claims. This waiver authority appears to apply to all barriers that may be constructed under IIRIRA—that is, both to barriers constructed near the border in areas of high illegal entry and to the barrier that is to be constructed in the San Diego area. Furthermore, these claims can only be appealed to the Supreme Court, whose review is discretionary.

The Secure Fence Act was signed into law on October 26, 2006. The Act directed DHS to construct two-layered reinforced fencing and additional physical barriers, roads, lighting, cameras, and sensors along five stretches of the southwest border. CBP has estimated that these stretches of fencing total 850 miles of the southern border. The five stretches of the border that DHS was required by law to fence were the 20 miles around Tecate, California; from Calexico, California, to Douglas, Arizona; from Columbus, New Mexico, to El Paso, Texas; from Del Rio, Texas, to Eagle Pass,

Texas; and from Laredo, Texas, to Brownsville, Texas. The Act designated the roughly 370-mile portion of the fence between Calexico and Douglas a priority area and directed DHS to ensure that "an interlocking surveillance camera system" was installed along this area by May 30, 2007, and that the fence was completed in this area by May 30, 2008. The Act also designated a 30-mile stretch around Laredo as a priority area and directed DHS to complete this fencing by December 31, 2008.

Congress modified the requirements of the Secure Fence Act by the Consolidated Appropriations Act, FY 2008 (P.L. 110-161), on December 26, 2007. The Act makes several modifications to Section 102 of IIRIRA, significantly increasing the Secretary's discretion as to where to construct fencing along the southwest border. Whereas the Secretary was previously required to install roughly 850 miles of reinforced fencing along five stretches of the southwest border, a more general requirement has now been imposed on the Secretary to construct reinforced fencing:

> Along not less than 700 miles of the southwest border where fencing would be more practical and effective and provide for the installation of additional physical barriers, roads, lighting, cameras, and sensors to gain operational control of the southwest border.

The Act further specifies that the Secretary of Homeland Security *is not* required to install:

> Fencing, physical barriers, roads, lighting, cameras, and sensors in a particular location along an international border of the United States, if the Secretary determines that the use or placement of such resources *is not* the most appropriate means to achieve and maintain operational control over the international border at that location.

Deploying additional fencing along the Southwest border has been a subject of heated debate among policymakers in recent years, particularly regarding cost versus perceived effectiveness. Largely due to changes in prioritization in the Department of Homeland Security's border enforcement strategy, the construction of additional fencing along the land border with Mexico has been halted. DHS said in October 2014 that it had constructed a total of 352.7 miles of pedestrian fencing and 299 miles of vehicular fencing along the southwest border.[20]

As noted in Chapter One, President Trump, in one of his first acts as President, issued an Executive Order directing that a border wall be constructed between the United States and Mexico. When, how, and where that wall will be constructed, and of what material, has yet to be determined.

The San Diego Fence and USBP Apprehensions

Apprehension statistics have long been used as a performance measure by the USBP. However, the number of apprehensions may be a misleading statistic, for several reasons, including the data's focus on events rather than people, and the fact that there are no reliable estimates for how many aliens successfully evade capture, either along the border, or inland. This makes it difficult to establish a firm correlation between the number of apprehensions in each sector and the number of people attempting to enter through that sector. While caution should be taken when attempting to draw conclusions about the efficacy of policy initiatives based solely on apprehension statistics, they remain perhaps the most reliable way to identify trends in illegal immigration along the border.

CBP Tower in El Paso, Texas. Note the cameras and lights. James Phelps, 2012.

The San Diego fence spans two Border Patrol stations within the San Diego sector: Imperial Beach and Chula Vista. As previously noted, the primary fence was constructed at those two stations beginning in FY 1990; the secondary fence was constructed beginning in FY 1996. Customs and Border Patrol data related to apprehensions at the two locations indicate the stark decrease in apprehensions at the Imperial Beach station from FY 1992 to FY 2004 (from 202,173 to 9,112).[21] Most of the decrease occurred in the four-year period from FY 1995 through FY 1998 and coincided with Operation Gatekeeper, which as previously noted combined the construction of fencing along the border *with an increase in agents and other resources* deployed directly along the border. One can draw the conclusion, based on evidence from the Imperial Beach station, that focused efforts work to reduce apprehensions along the border.

Office of Air and Marine Operations

The mission of the US Customs and Border Protection, Office of Air and Marine Operations (AMO), is to protect American citizens and the nation's critical infrastructure through the coordinated use of integrated air and marine forces to detect, interdict, and prevent acts of terrorism and the unlawful movement of people, drugs, and other contraband across United States borders. This includes direct support to CBP's anti-terrorism mission at the US borders, to include air-to-ground interception of people and contraband illegally crossing land borders, air-to-air interception of aircraft, and air-to-water interception of transportation vessels.

Excerpts from the Fact Sheet: U.S. Customs and Border Protection

2015

With approximately 1,660 federal employees, 240 aircraft and 300 marine vessels operating from 74 locations throughout the continental United States, Puerto Rico, and U.S. Virgin Islands, AMO serves as the nation's experts in airborne and maritime law enforcement. AMO operates beyond the nation's borders in drug source and transit zones, between ports of entry, in our coastal waters, and within the nation's interior.

AMO Accomplishments during Fiscal Year 2015

AMO enforcement actions resulted in the seizure or disruption of 230,579 pounds of cocaine; 719,549 pounds of marijuana; 1,427 weapons and $49.3 million; 4,485 arrests and 51,130 apprehensions.

- Unmanned aircraft system (UAS) missions resulted in the detection of more than 9,300 persons of interest at or near the border. UAS missions also led to the seizure or disruption of 5,552 pounds of cocaine and 68,721 pounds of marijuana.
- National Air Security Operations (NASO) aircrews flew 6,600 hours of counternarcotic missions in the drug source and transit zones between South America and the U.S. and participated in 198 interdiction events. NASO missions led to the seizure or disruption of 206,844 pounds of cocaine.

Air and Marine Operations Mission

- AMO's missions fall into four broad categories that reflect our core competencies: interdiction, investigation, domain awareness, and contingency operations and national tasking missions.
- Interdiction encompasses our efforts to intercept, apprehend, or disrupt threats in the land, sea, and air domains as they move toward or across the United States borders.
- AMO leverages the expertise of our agents in the air and maritime domains to conduct investigations to defeat criminal networks.
- Domain awareness is the observation of the operating environment (air, land, and water) and the information gathered through the network of sensors deployed on aircraft, vessels, and land-based persistent wide-area surveillance.[22]

Unmanned Aerial Vehicle (UAV) Systems

The US Customs and Border Protection (CBP), Office of Air and Marine Operations (AMO), operates the highly capable and proven Predator B unmanned aircraft system (UAS) in support of law enforcement and homeland security missions

MQ-9 Reaper drone operated by United States Customs and Border Protection.

at the nation's borders. AMO selected the Predator B unmanned aircraft, manufactured by General Atomics Aeronautical Systems, for its unique combination of operational capabilities, payload capacity, mission flexibility, potential to accommodate new sensor packages, and its safety and performance record with other federal agencies.

The CBP UAS program focuses operations on the CBP priority mission of anti-terrorism by helping to identify and intercept potential terrorists and illegal cross-border activity. The system also supports disaster relief efforts of its Department of Homeland Security partners, including the Federal Emergency Management Agency and the US Coast Guard. The remotely piloted Predator B allows AMO personnel to safely conduct missions in areas that are difficult to access or otherwise too high-risk for manned aircraft or CBP ground personnel.

AMO first employed the Predator B to enhance law enforcement operations on the southwest border in 2005 and along the northern border in 2009. AMO has operated Predator Bs from Libby Army Airfield in Sierra Vista, Arizona, and along the Texas border since 2011.

MQ -9 Predator B Performance and Weight:
- Maximum Speed 240 knots (276 mph)
- Service Ceiling Altitude 50,000 feet
- Endurance Up to 20 hours
- Maximum Gross Weight 10,500 pounds Other System Components
- Fixed and mobile ground control stations
- Electro-optical/infrared sensors, which allow for crewmembers to maintain awareness of targets in all environments
- Surface search radar/ground moving target indicator to conduct missions within the maritime border areas.[23]

AMO expects to employ the Predator B throughout the border regions with command and control from a network of ground control stations across the country. The Predator B's capability to provide high-quality streaming video to first responders, and to assess critical infrastructure before and after events, makes it an ideal aircraft to aid in emergency preparations and recovery operations. The UAS has provided emergency support for multiple hurricanes and floods since 2008. Video recorders document suspect activities for evidentiary use.

AMO also operates a maritime variant UAS called the Guardian. AMO's Guardian aircraft fly from Naval Air Station Corpus Christi in Texas and along the Northern Region. The Guardian can be operated from any designated UAS location. The Guardian was modified from a standard Predator B with structural, avionics, and communications enhancements, as well as the addition of a Raytheon SeaVue Marine Search Radar and an electro-optical/infrared sensor that is optimized for maritime operations.

AMO uses the Guardian to conduct long-range surveillance in support of joint counter-narcotics operations in the southeast coastal and Gulf of Mexico border regions and drug source and transit zones, where maritime radar is necessary to detect a variety of threats.

CBP Guardian UAS Operations

Aircrews operate the Guardian to enhance law enforcement missions in the Southwest, Southeast, and Northern Regions, and Joint Interagency Task Force South, to include the Eastern Pacific and Caribbean Transit Zones.

Performance and Weight:

- Maximum Speed 240 knots (276 mph)
- Service Ceiling Altitude 50,000 feet
- Endurance Up to 20 hours
- Maximum Gross Weight 10,500 pounds Other System Components
- Fixed and mobile ground control stations
- Electro-optical/infrared sensors, which allow for crewmembers to maintain awareness of targets in all environments.[24]

Conclusion

This chapter has considered the history of immigration, along with other factors that have impacted that immigration, both legal and illegal. The United States shares 5,525 miles of border with Canada and 1,933 miles with Mexico, and the maritime border includes 95,000 miles of shoreline and a 3.4-million-square-mile exclusive economic zone. Border entry points also include airports and seaports, all of which have become exponentially more important in terms of national security since 9/11. Legal immigration into America was the only type of immigration that existed prior to 1882 and the passage of the Chinese Exclusion Act. We examined changing immigration laws that have affected legal (and illegal) immigration, and the physical impediments such as fences and vehicle barriers. The border "problem" and its relation to national security is going to exist if economic disparity continues to exist between between America and its bordering countries, and as long as people are willing to risk their lives to get to the United States.

Questions for Further Consideration

1. Immigration control began as a racial issue, moved into an employment issue, and today is a combination of racial, cultural, economic, and security issues. Considering that the United States would be a population in decline were it not for immigration, how should we address the issue of migrant (seasonal) workers as an integral and necessary part of the American workforce?
2. A great deal has been made about the 700+ miles of fencing along the southern border of the United States. Yet illegal immigration and drug smuggling still happen, even in fenced areas. Are there alternatives to physical barriers that would better address the issue of maintaining national sovereignty than fences?
3. In every instance where the US Border Patrol instituted massive personnel deployment across a region, the level of attempted illegal border crossings has significantly decreased. Installation of multilayered fencing has also reduced illegal border crossings. What combination of the two would best protect the United States?
4. Technology is an important part of securing the border. After 9-11 more than $1 billion was expended in contracts to General Electric and General Dynamics to develop and install a "virtual fence" that would detect illegal border crossings along the southern border. Not a single section of the virtual fence was ever made to function and the technology was never delivered. What types of virtual fencing would you recommend installing and how would it operate to restrict illegal crossings?

Chapter 4 Endnotes

1. Goo, Sara K. "What Americans Want to do About Illegal Immigration," Pew Research Center, 24 August 2015. Available at: http://www.pewresearch.org/fact-tank/2015/08/24/what-americans-want-to-do-about-illegal-immigration/

2. "5 Facts about Illegal Immigration in the U.S.," Pew Research Center, 3 November 2016, http://www.pewresearch.org/fact-tank/2016/11/03/5-facts-about-illegal-immigration-in-the-u-s/

3. 2012-2016 Border Patrol Strategic Plan. https://nemo.cbp.gov/obp/bp_strategic_plan.pdf

4. Davidson, Adam. "Do Illegal Immigrants Actually Hurt the U.S. Economy?" February 12, 2013. The New York Times Magazine. Available at: http://www.nytimes.com/2013/02/17/magazine/do-illegal-immigrants-actually-hurt-the-us-economy.html

5. Cato Journal, Vol. 32, No. 1 (Winter 2012). Copyright Cato Institute. All rights reserved.

6. Eldridge, T., et al. (2004). 9/11 and Terrorist Travel: Staff Report of the National Commission

on Terrorist Attacks upon the United States. Washington: National Commission on Terrorist Attacks.

7. Report of the Visa Office 2016, Department of State; available at: https://travel.state.gov/content/visas/en/law-and-policy/statistics/annual-reports/report-of-the-visa-office-2016.html

8. CBP Border Security Report, Fiscal Year 2016. Available at: https://www.cbp.gov/sites/default/files/assets/documents/2016-Dec/CBP-fy2016-border-security-report.pdf

9. "The Catch and Release Immigration Enforcement Policy," National Center for Policy Analysis. July 14, 2005. Available at: http://www.ncpa.org/sub/dpd/index.php?Article_ID=1966

10. "U.S. Announces End of Catch and Release. Chertoff says new Detain Policy Means all non-Mexicans would be returned home," World Net Daily. August 23, 2006. Available at: http://www.wnd.com/2006/08/37593/

11. Darby, Brandon (January 11, 2015). "Exclusive: Catch and Release 2.0 — Leaks Highlight Teardown of Immigration Enforcement." Available at: http://www.breitbart.com/big-government/2015/01/11/exclusive-catch-and-release-2-0-leaks-highlight-teardown-of-immigration-enforcement/

12. Dinan, Stephen (February 21, 2017). "DHS Cancels Obama policies, orders agents to expand deportations." Available at: http://www.washingtontimes.com/news/2017/feb/21/dhs-cancels-obama-policies-released-agents-to-expa/

13. Ibid.

14. "Democrats Concerned about new Immigrant Order." Available at: http://www.usatoday.com/videos/news/nation/2017/02/16/democrats-concerned-new-immigrant-order/98009362/

15. Ibid.

16. McSally, Martha (R-AZ), "Overstaying Their Welcome: National Security Risks Posed by Visa Overstays," Border and Maritime Security Subcommittee. June 14, 2016.

17. Garcia, Michael John. "Barriers Along the U.S. Borders: Key Authorities and Requirements." Congressional Research Service 7-5700 www.crs.gov R43975 November 18, 2016.

18. Argueta, Carla. "Immigration Enforcement Between Ports of Entry." Congressional Research Service 7-5700 www.crs.gov R42138

19. Andreas, P. (1998). "The Escalation of U.S. Immigration Control in the Post-NAFTA Era," *Political Science Quarterly*, vol 113, no. 4, (Winter 1998), 595.

20. Argueta, Carla. "Immigration Enforcement Between Ports of Entry." Congressional Research Service 7-5700 www.crs.gov R42138

21. Haddal, Kim, & Garcia. (2009). Border Security: Barriers Along the U.S. International Border, Congressional Research Service (March 16).

22. U.S. Customs and Border Protection Fact Sheet 2015: Air and Marine Operations.

23. U.S. Customs and Border Protection. Unmanned Aircraft System MQ-9 Predator B Fact Sheet 2015.

24. 24. U.S. Customs and Border Protection. Guardian UAS Maritime Variant Predator B Fact Sheet 2015.

Chapter 5

Maritime Border Security

"The origin of navies is to be looked for in the necessity for national protection of commerce to the advantage of the state and its citizens, both in peace and in war."

— Vice Admiral William Ledyard Rodgers[1]

Key Words and Concepts

Coastline
International Maritime Organizations
International Outreach and Coordination
 Strategy
Maritime Commerce Security Plan
Maritime Domain Awareness
Maritime Interception Operations
Maritime Transportation System

National AIS Project
National Strategy for Maritime Security
Naval Operations Concept 2010
Sea Power
US Coast Guard
US Navy
Maritime Operational Threat Response
Maritime Security Force Assistance

Introduction

Maritime Security is such an important component of National Security that it has been addressed with its own Homeland Security Presidential Directive (HSPD-13). More so, the overall Maritime Security plan for the United States is one of the most extensive collections of Homeland Security documents dealing with a single issue. The United States is dependent upon its sea lines of communication and attachment to a global market for its economic survival. Protecting that commerce has been the focus of nations throughout history.

We think of Border Security as an issue dealing primarily with the protection of national borders with other countries. Our paradigm is one where we think of land borders and designated crossing points between countries. Today, 90 percent of all commodities marketed worldwide are moved across the maritime realm. Protecting the border between the United States and China is just as essential as protecting the border between the United States and Mexico. That raises the question, "Where are the borders between the United States and China?"

USCG Cutter Bertholf, WMSL 750. USCG Photo.

The answer is, arguably, the sea. The same could be said for all US commerce originating or terminating outside of North and Central America. Defining the point where national interests terminate becomes problematic when our focus shifts away from the land borders with Canada and Mexico. The United States has gone to extremes when it comes to securing our maritime lifelines to expedite commerce, and provide a level of security. The Customs and Border Protection Agency maintains offices worldwide through which shipping containers bound for the United States are identified, inspected, loaded, and shipped. Goods are inspected for contraband, prohibited items, illegal immigrants, dangerous insects, produce that exceeds tariff restrictions, etc. Documentation is pre-screened and the process put in place to expedite the delivery of goods to US ports and the end users.

The ongoing effort to secure maritime commerce and maintain access to world markets is not a new concern. In fact, it is one of the oldest issues the United States has dealt with. In fact, every country today is essentially tied to maritime commerce and all countries that have coastlines have long been concerned with securing their access to the ocean while concurrently ensuring that illegal commerce was prevented.

The Problem of Coastline

The fundamental problem with coastline is that of permeability. If the island nations in Table 5.1 are eliminated, we see that the United States has the fourth longest coastline, behind Canada, Russia, and Norway. If Indonesia (a nation

Table 5.1 Longest Coastline Countries with Corresponding Land Borders

Country	Coastline		Land Border	
	Miles	KM	Miles	KM
Antarctica	11,164.8	17,968.0	0.0	0.0
Australia	16,006.5	25,760.0	0.0	0.0
Canada	125,566.7	202,080.0	55,297.7	88,993.0
China	9,009.9	14,500.0	14,115.7	22,717.0
Greenland	27,394.4	44,087.0	0.0	0.0
Indonesia	33,999.0	54,716.0	1,759.5	2,830.0
Japan	18,486.4	29,751.0	0.0	0.0
Mexico	5,797.4	9,330.0	2,704.8	4,353.0
New Zealand	9,403.8	15,134.0	0.0	0.0
Norway	15,626.2	25,148.0	1,579.5	2,542.0
Philippines	22,554.5	36,289.0	0.0	0.0
Russia	23,396.5	37,653.0	12,566.5	20,241.5
United Kingdom	7,723.0	12,429.0	223.7	360.0
United States	12,380.2	19,924.0	7,477.6	12,034.0
Turkey	4,473.9	7,200.0	1,645.4	2,648.0

Data derived from CIA World Factbook, 2/2012.

combined of islands and peninsular land mass) is included, then the U.S. is fifth. When the Canadian and Russian coastlines are examined, it becomes clear that the majority of their coast resides in Arctic regions and are therefore not continuously open to maritime traffic.

The United States maintains land borders with Mexico and Canada totaling 7,477.6 miles (12,034 km). The United States-Canada border is a combination of land, lake, and ocean boundaries that are mostly unguarded and open along their length to nearly free transit. If the open land border with Canada is removed from this total, there are only 1,969 miles (3,169 km) of land border with Mexico that require focused protective efforts. However, there are 12,380.2 miles (19,924 km) of US coastline that require security. **Coastline** and **shoreline** are two different measures. The "coast" is determined by a "smoothed" line running across inlets, bays, channels, harbors, etc. The "shore" is an actual point where land meets ocean saltwater. The difference is a fundamental matter of measurement. While the United States has 12,380.2 miles of "coastline" it has over 95,000 miles of "shoreline."

Along the Texas coast, which is nearly 1,000 miles (1,600 km) in total length, there are about 1,150 seaports. In addition to actual ports, small craft can make landings along virtually any stretch of beach to load or unload cargo of all types. Even with armed guards placed every half-mile, working continuous shifts 24/7 to provide security, people and goods would still slip through and make it into a port or onto a beach. The cost of staffing such an effort would be astronomical.

The Texas Gulf Coast is emblematic of the problem facing all nations with ocean access. What is the probability of contraband or illegal immigrants coming ashore at any given point and how much effort is necessary to minimize the likelihood of those goods or people entering the economy? At some point, the cost of security becomes prohibitive. Therefore, other means of securing the maritime realm must be implemented. Historically this task of securing the sea lanes has fallen to the navies of the world.

Maritime Security in History

The United States has always been dependent upon the sea lines of communication. It was through trade with France and other nations that we succeeded in defeating the British during the Revolutionary War. Our first international conflict after becoming a nation was with the pirates of the Barbary Coast (along North Africa). This history of dependence upon the sea for access to trade partners continues today. Understanding the origins of maritime security across the historical expanse is a key component of comprehending our perspective and policies in the modern era.

The Navy traces its origins to the Continental Navy, which was established during the American Revolutionary War and was essentially disbanded as a separate entity shortly thereafter. The United States Constitution provided the legal basis for a military force by giving Congress the power "to provide and maintain a navy." Depredations against US shipping by Barbary Coast pirates in the Mediterranean Sea spurred Congress to employ this power by passing the Naval Act of 1794 ordering the construction and manning of six frigates. These ships were used to end most pirate activity off the Barbary Coast.

Until the Declaration of Independence in 1776 British treaties with the North African states protected American ships from the Barbary corsairs. Morocco, which in 1777 was the first independent nation to publicly recognize the United States, became in 1784 the first Barbary power to seize an American vessel after independence. While

Lieutenant Decatur boarding the Tripolitan gunboat, Library of Congress.

the United States managed to secure peace treaties with the pirates, these obliged it to pay tribute for protection from attack. Payments in ransom and tribute to the

Barbary States amounted to 20 percent of United States Government annual expenditures in 1800.

The Barbary threat led directly to the creation of the United States Navy in March 1794. In 1802 the Congress passed "An act for the Protection of Commerce and seamen of the United States against the Tripolitan cruisers" authorizing President Thomas Jefferson to send naval vessels to the Mediterranean. This led to the first of two wars fought with the Northwest African Berber Muslim states, collectively known as the Barbary States. Some of the earliest military heroes in US history arose during this effort to ensure safe maritime commerce including Commodore Edward Preble and Lieutenant Stephen Decatur (of the US Marine Corps). Today, these battles are memorialized in the US Marine Corps anthem with the words, " ... to the shores of Tripoli." Algiers broke the 1805 peace treaty after only two years, and subsequently refused to implement the 1815 treaty until compelled to do so by Britain in 1816. Since this time the United States has always maintained an active naval fleet to secure its coasts and protect its trading interests worldwide.

Modern US Naval Policy

Modern naval policy and the establishment of a world class navy can be dated to the 1890 publication of *The Influence of Sea Power Upon History, 1660–1783*, by Captain Alfred Thayer Mahan. This pivotal text is considered by most military scholars as the single most influential book in naval strategy ever published. The theory developed by Mahan was readily accepted by all major nations in the naval arms race leading up to the First World War and was significantly influential throughout the twentieth century and the rise of the United States as the dominant naval power of most of the twentieth and early twenty-first centuries.

Mahan (1890) notes, "The unresting progress of mankind causes continual change in the weapons; and with that must come a continual change in the manner of fighting,— in the handling and disposition of troops or ships on the battlefield."[2] Comprehending the impact of maritime commerce, and the accompanying need to provide security for the continued movement of merchant ships, is

Alfred Thayer Mahan, US Navy.

essential to understanding the process currently in place to secure the maritime realm. Joint operations between the French, British, and Americans were conducted off the North African coast in the early 1800s to put an end to pirate attacks on merchant shipping. Two hundred years later, joint operations involving many different nations are ongoing along the West African Coast and in the Red Sea to protect merchant shipping from Somali pirates. Today's efforts are part of a concerted international effort to implement a maritime security strategy that involves defense in depth, the same concept that gave rise to the US Navy in the late 1700s.

The United States Navy still conducts operations in accordance with Mahan's treatise on sea power. Of course, politics directs who may be a threat and therefore the focus of naval deployments, but the theory of a defense in depth used today derives from a book written more than 120 years past.

PIRACY INCIDENTS ATTRIBUTED TO SOMALI PIRATES, 2008-2009

Piracy incidents attributed to Somali pirates, 2008–2009.

The Influence of Sea Power upon History, 1660–1783

Alfred Thayer Mahan (1890)

The history of Sea Power is largely, though by no means solely, a narrative of contests between nations, of mutual rivalries, of violence frequently culminating in war. The profound influence of sea commerce upon the wealth and strength of countries was clearly seen long before the true principles which governed its growth and prosperity were detected. To secure to one's own people a disproportionate share of such benefits, every effort was made to exclude others, either by the peaceful legislative methods of monopoly or prohibitory regulations, or, when these failed, by direct violence. The clash of interests, the angry feelings roused by conflicting attempts thus to appropriate the larger share, if not the whole, of the advantages of commerce, and of distant unsettled commercial regions, led to wars. On the other hand, wars arising from other causes have been greatly modified in their conduct and issue by the control of the sea (p. 1).

The first and most obvious light in which the sea presents itself from the political and social point of view is that of a great highway; or better, perhaps, of a wide common, over which men may pass in all directions, but on which some well-worn paths show that controlling reasons have led them to choose certain lines of travel rather than others. These lines of travel are called trade routes; and the reasons which have determined them are to be sought in the history of the world.

Notwithstanding all the familiar and unfamiliar dangers of the sea, both travel and traffic by water have always been easier and cheaper than by land.... This advantage of carriage by water over that by land was yet more marked in a period when roads were few and very bad, wars frequent and society unsettled, as was the case two hundred years ago. Sea traffic then went in peril of robbers, but was nevertheless safer and quicker than that by land (p. 25).

Under modern conditions, however, home trade is but a part of the business of a country bordering on the sea. Foreign necessaries or luxuries must be brought to its ports, either in its own or in foreign ships, which will return, bearing in exchange the products of the country, whether they be the fruits of the earth or the works of men's hands.... The ships that thus sail to and fro must have secure ports to which to return, and must, as far as possible, be followed by the protection of their country throughout the voyage (p. 26).

In the present day friendly, though foreign, ports are to be found all over the world; and their shelter is enough while peace prevails. It was not always so, nor does peace always endure, though the United States have been favored by so long a continuance of it. In earlier times the merchant seaman, seeking for trade in new and unexplored regions, made his gains at risk of life and liberty from suspicious or hostile nations, and was under great delays in collecting a full and profitable freight. He therefore intuitively sought at the far end of his trade route one or more stations, to be given to him by force or favor, where he could fix himself or his agents in reasonable security, where his ships could lie in safety, and where the merchantable products of the land could be continually collecting, awaiting the arrival of the home fleet, which should carry them to the mother-country. As there was immense gain, as well as much risk, in these early voyages, such establishments naturally multiplied and grew until they became colonies; whose ultimate development and success depended upon the genius and policy of the nation from which they sprang, and form a very great part of the history, and particularly of the sea history, of the world (p. 27).

In these three things—production, with the necessity of exchanging products, shipping, whereby the exchange is carried on, and colonies, which facilitate and enlarge the operations of shipping and tend to protect it by multiplying points of safety—is to be found the key to much of the history, as well as of the policy, of nations bordering upon the sea. The policy has varied both with the spirit of the age and with the character and clear-sightedness of the rulers; but the history of the seaboard nations has been less determined by the shrewdness and foresight of governments than by conditions of position, extent, configuration, number and character of their people,—by what are called, in a word, natural conditions (p. 28).

The principal conditions affecting the sea power of nations may be enumerated as follows: I. Geographical Position. II. Physical Conformation, including, as connected therewith, (p. 29) natural productions and climate. III. Extent of Territory. IV. Number of Population. V. Character of the People. VI. Character of the Government, including therein the national institutions (p. 30).

The US Coast Guard

After the US Navy completes the outside layer of the defense in depth strategy of the United States, the US Coast Guard (USCG) provides the next layer. Recently moved to the Department of Homeland Security, the USCG carries out extensive functions with what has traditionally been a very limited capacity. Dating back to 1790, today's USCG came into being when the first Congress authorized the construction of ten vessels to enforce federal tariff and trade laws and to prevent smuggling. Known variously through the nineteenth and early twentieth centuries as the Revenue Marine and the Revenue Cutter Service, the agency expanded in size and responsibilities as the nation grew.

The USCG received its present name in 1915 under an act of Congress that merged the Revenue Cutter Service with the Life-Saving Service, thereby providing the nation with a single maritime service dedicated to saving life at sea and enforcing the nation's maritime laws. The Coast Guard began to maintain the country's aids to maritime navigation, including operating the nation's lighthouses, when President Franklin Roosevelt ordered the transfer of the Lighthouse Service to the Coast Guard in 1939.

In 1946 Congress permanently transferred the Commerce Department's Bureau of Marine Inspection and Navigation to the Coast Guard, thereby placing merchant marine licensing and merchant vessel safety under USCG purview.

The Coast Guard is one of the oldest organizations of the federal government and until Congress established the Navy Department in 1798 served as the nation's only armed force afloat. They have protected the nation throughout its long history and served proudly in every one of the nation's conflicts.[3]

Following the terrorist attacks of September 11, 2001, the United States moved to consolidate and better organize the agencies associated with the defense of the United States. Part of the efforts was the move of the Coast Guard from the Department of Transportation to the newly formed Department of Homeland Security. This was accomplished in law by a major revision to Title 14 of the US Code and the Ports and Waterways Safety Act of 1972.

The USCG is a military service and *always* a branch of the armed forces of the United States. It is a component of the Department of Homeland Security, except when operating as a service in the Navy. Essentially, the USCG is the military arm of the Department of Homeland Security. Unlike the US Navy, the officers, warrant officers, and petty officers of the USCG are also federal *law enforcement* officers with the authority to carry out the duties and functions of any other federal law enforcement agency. The primary duties of the USCG can be found in Chapter 1 paragraph 2 of Title 14 of the United States Code.

14 USC 1 § 2. Primary Duties

The Coast Guard shall enforce or assist in the enforcement of all applicable Federal laws on, under, and over the high seas and waters subject to the jurisdiction of the United States; shall engage in maritime air surveillance or interdiction to enforce or assist in the enforcement of the laws of the United States; shall administer laws and promulgate and enforce regulations for the promotion of safety of life and property on and under the high seas and waters subject to the jurisdiction of the United States covering all matters not specifically delegated by law to some other executive department; shall develop, establish, maintain, and operate, with due regard to the requirements of national defense, aids to maritime navigation, ice-breaking facilities, and rescue facilities for the promotion of safety on, under, and over the high seas and waters subject to the jurisdiction of the United States; shall, pursuant to international agreements, develop, establish, maintain, and operate icebreaking facilities on, under, and over waters other than the high seas and waters subject to the jurisdiction of the United States; shall engage in oceanographic research of the high seas and in waters subject to the jurisdiction of the United States; and shall maintain a state of readiness to function as a specialized service in the Navy in time of war, including the fulfillment of Maritime Defense Zone command responsibilities.

Maritime Security in the Post-9/11 Era

Following the terrorist attacks of September 11, 2001, the United Stated recognized maritime security as an area of significant vulnerability. Action was taken to address the issue with the issuance of Homeland Security Presidential Directive 13, the National Strategy for Maritime Security (NSMS).

As noted in the opening matter of the NSMS, "The safety and economic security of the United States depends upon the secure use of the world's oceans" (p. ii). This hearkens directly to A. T. Mahan's 1890 treatise on sea power. The United States is "dependent" upon open oceans for its economic survival. Economics implies a joint relationship between the corporate world and the Government when it comes to maritime security. The NSMS identifies five threats to maritime security. They are:

Nation-State Threats: In the absence of inter-state conflict, individual state actions represent a significant challenge to global security. In particular, those states providing safe havens for criminals and terrorists.

Terrorist Threats: Successful attacks by non-state terrorist groups that exploit open borders provide opportunities to cause significant disruption to regional and global economies. Terrorists have also taken advantage of criminal smuggling networks to circumvent border security measures. Terrorists can also develop effective attack capabilities relatively quickly using suicide boats and light aircraft; merchant and cruise ships as kinetic weapons; commercial vessels as launch platforms for missile attacks; underwater swimmers to infiltrate ports; and unmanned underwater explosive delivery vehicles. Terrorists can also take advantage of a vessel's legitimate cargo, such as chemicals, petroleum, or liquefied natural gas, as the explosive component of an attack.

US Coast Guard icebreaker escorts a Russian supply freighter to Barrow, Alaska, 2011, USCG.

Transnational Criminal and Piracy Threats: The smuggling of people, drugs, weapons, and other contraband, as well as piracy and armed robbery against vessels, pose a threat to maritime security. Piracy and incidents of maritime crime tend to be concentrated in areas of heavy commercial maritime activity, especially where there is significant political and economic instability, or in regions with little or no maritime law enforcement capacity. Maritime drug trafficking generates vast amounts of money for international organized crime syndicates and terrorist organizations. Those funds can then be used to bribe government officials, bypass established financial controls, and fund additional illegal activities, including arms trafficking, migrant smuggling, and terrorist operations.

Environmental Destruction: Intentional and unintentional acts can have far-reaching, negative effects on the economic viability and political stability of a region.

Illegal Seaborne Immigration: This is a long-standing issue that remains a major challenge to regional stability because of the strain migrants and refugees place on fragile economies and political systems. In some countries the collapse of political and social order prompts maritime mass migrations. The potential for terrorists to take advantage of human smuggling networks in attempts to circumvent border security measures cannot be ignored.

USS New Jersey (BB-62) fires a salvo from her 16″/50 guns during a deployment off the coast of Beirut, Lebanon, January 9, 1984. Photographed by PH1 Ron Garrison. US Navy.

Excerpts from the *National Strategy for Maritime Security*[4]

The United States has a vital national interest in maritime security. We must be prepared to stop terrorists and rogue states before they can threaten or use weapons of mass destruction or engage in other attacks against the United States and our allies and friends. Toward that end, the United States must take full advantage of strengthened alliances and other international cooperative arrangements, innovations in the use of law enforcement personnel and military forces, advances in technology, and strengthened intelligence collection, analysis, and dissemination.

Salt water covers more than two-thirds of the Earth's surface. These waters are a single, great ocean, an immense maritime domain[5] that affects life everywhere. Although its four principal geographical divisions—Atlantic, Arctic, Indian, and Pacific—have different names, this continuous body of water is the Earth's greatest defining geographic feature.

The oceans, much of which are global commons under no State's jurisdiction, offer all nations, even landlocked States, a network of sea-lanes or highways that is of enormous importance to their security and prosperity. They are likewise a source of food, mineral resources, and recreation, and they support commerce among nations. They also act as both a barrier to and a conduit for threats to the security of people everywhere. Like all other countries, the United States is highly dependent on the oceans for its security and the welfare of its people and economy.

In today's economy, the oceans have increased importance, allowing all countries to participate in the global marketplace. More than 80 percent of the world's trade travels by water and forges a global maritime link. About half the world's trade by value, and 90 percent of the general cargo, are transported in containers. Shipping is the heart of the global economy, but it is vulnerable to attack in two key areas. Spread across Asia, North America, and Europe are 30 megaports/cities that constitute the world's primary, interdependent trading web. Through a handful of international straits and canals pass 75 percent of the world's maritime trade and half its daily oil consumption. International commerce is at risk in the major trading hubs as well as at a handful of strategic chokepoints.

The infrastructure and systems that span the maritime domain, owned largely by the private sector, have increasingly become both targets of and potential conveyances for dangerous and illicit activities. Moreover, much of what occurs in the maritime domain with respect to vessel movements, activities, cargoes, intentions, or ownership is often difficult to discern. The oceans are increasingly threatened by illegal exploitation of living marine resources and increased competition over nonliving marine resources. Although the global economy continues to increase the value of the oceans' role as highways for commerce and providers of resources, technology and the forces of globalization have lessened their role as barriers. Thus, this continuous domain serves as a vast, ready, and largely unsecured medium for an array of threats by nations, terrorists, and criminals.

Defeating this array of threats to maritime security—including the threat or use of weapons of mass destruction (WMD)—requires a common understanding and a joint effort for action on a global scale. Because the economic well-being of people in the United States and across the globe depends heavily upon the trade and commerce that traverses the oceans, maritime security must be a top priority. Maritime security is required to ensure freedom of the seas; facilitate freedom of navigation and commerce; advance prosperity and freedom; and protect the resources of the ocean. Nations have a common interest in achieving two complementary objectives: to facilitate the vibrant maritime commerce that underpins economic security, and to protect against ocean-related terrorist, hostile, criminal, and dangerous acts. Since all nations benefit from this collective security, all nations must share in the responsibility for maintaining maritime security by countering the threats in this domain.

Today's transnational threats have the potential to inflict great harm on many nations. Thus, the security of the maritime domain requires comprehensive and cohesive efforts among the United States and many cooperating nations to protect the common interest in global maritime security. This Strategy describes how the United States Government will promote an international maritime security effort that will effectively and efficiently enhance the security of the maritime domain while preserving the freedom of the domain for legitimate pursuits.[6]

This approach does not negate the United States' inherent right to self-defense or its right to act to protect its essential national security interests. **Defending against enemies is the first and most fundamental commitment of the United States Government. Preeminent among our national security priorities is to take all necessary steps to prevent WMD from entering the country and to avert an attack on the homeland.** This course of action must be undertaken while respecting the constitutional principles upon which the United States was founded.

Three broad principles provide overarching guidance to this Strategy. First, *preserving the freedom of the seas* is a top national priority. The right of vessels to travel freely in international waters, engage in innocent and transit passage, and have access to ports is an essential element of national security. The free, continuing, unthreatened intercourse of nations is an essential global freedom and helps ensure the smooth operation of the world's economy.

Second, the United States Government must *facilitate and defend commerce* to ensure this uninterrupted flow of shipping. The United States is a major trading nation, and its economy, environment, and social fabric are inextricably linked with the oceans and their resources. The adoption of a just-in-time delivery approach to shipping by most industries, rather than stockpiling or maintaining operating reserves of energy, raw materials, and key components, means that a disruption or slowing of the flow of almost any item can have widespread implications for the overall market, as well as upon the national economy.

Third, the United States Government must *facilitate the movement of desirable goods and people across our borders, while screening out dangerous people and material.* There need not be an inherent conflict between the demand for security and the need for facilitating the travel and trade essential to continued economic growth. This Strategy redefines our fundamental task as one of good border management rather than one that pits security against economic wellbeing. Accomplishing that goal is more manageable to the extent that screening can occur before goods and people arrive at our physical borders.

In keeping with these guiding principles, the deep-seated values enshrined in the US Constitution, and applicable domestic and international law, the following objectives will guide the Nation's maritime security activities:
- Prevent Terrorist Attacks and Criminal or Hostile Acts
- Protect Maritime-Related Population Centers and Critical Infrastructures
- Minimize Damage and Expedite Recovery
- Safeguard the Ocean and Its Resources

The United States recognizes that, because of the extensive global connectivity among businesses and governments, its maritime security policies affect other nations, and that significant local and regional incidents will have global effects. Success in securing the maritime domain will not come from the United States acting alone, but through a powerful coalition of nations maintaining a strong, united, international front. The need for a strong and effective coalition is reinforced by the fact that most of the maritime domain is under no single nation's sovereignty or jurisdiction. Additionally, increased economic interdependency and globalization, largely made possible by maritime shipping, underscores the need for a coordinated international approach. Less than 3 percent of the international waterborne trade of the United States is carried on vessels owned, operated, and crewed by US citizens. The United States also recognizes that the vast majority of actors and activities within the maritime domain are legitimate. Security of the maritime domain can be accomplished only by seamlessly employing all instruments of national power in a fully coordinated manner in concert with other nation-states consistent with international law.

Bringing about security of the maritime domain makes it necessary to employ all the instruments of national power in conjunction with other nation-states and consistent with international law. Achieving these national objectives, a partnership between public and private entities is necessary along with the development of scalable layers of security and implementation of strategic actions by all concerned. These strategic actions are:

1. Enhance International Cooperation
2. Maximize Domain Awareness
3. Embed Security into Commercial Practices
4. Deploy Layered Security
5. Assure Continuity of the Marine Transportation System

Perhaps the most important of these strategies, from the perspective of this chapter, is the idea of layered security. This is the fundamental focus of the deployment of national assets, from naval forces, to Coast Guard, to local port security, to the security of shipments and cargos. In support of the concept of layered security the NSMS directs the development of eight other support plans of varying lengths that address the need for interoperability between the private and public sectors at federal, State, and local levels as well as cooperation with other nations. These supplemental plans are:

1. **National Plan to Achieve Maritime Domain Awareness** lays the foundation for an effective understanding of anything associated with the maritime domain that could impact the security, safety, economy, or environment of the United States, and identifying threats as early and as distant from our shores as possible.

2. **Global Maritime Intelligence Integration Plan** uses existing capabilities to integrate all available intelligence regarding potential threats to US interests in the maritime domain.

3. **Maritime Operational Threat Response Plan** aims for coordinated United States Government response to threats against the United States and its interests in the maritime domain by establishing roles and responsibilities that enable the Government to respond quickly and decisively.

4. **International Outreach and Coordination Strategy** provides a framework to coordinate all maritime security initiatives undertaken with foreign governments and international organizations, and solicits international support for enhanced maritime security.

5. **Maritime Infrastructure Recovery Plan** recommends procedures and standards for the recovery of the maritime infrastructure following attack or similar disruption.

6. **Maritime Transportation System Security Plan** responds to the President's call for recommendations to improve the national and international regulatory framework regarding the maritime domain.

7. **Maritime Commerce Security Plan** establishes a comprehensive plan to secure the maritime supply chain.

8. **Domestic Outreach Plan** engages non-federal input to assist with the development and implementation of maritime security policies resulting from NSPD-41/HSPD-13.

Excerpts from the *National Plan to Achieve Maritime Domain Awareness*[7]

October 2005

PURPOSE OF THE PLAN

The *National Plan to Achieve Maritime Domain Awareness* is a cornerstone for successful execution of the security plans tasked in NSPD-41/HSPD-13. This Plan serves to unify United States Government and support international efforts to achieve MDA across the federal government, with the private sector and civil authorities within the United States, and with our allies and partners. It directs close coordination of a broad range of federal departments and agencies for this lasting endeavor. Implementation of this Plan will be conducted under the oversight of an interagency implementation team.

KEY DEFINITIONS

Maritime Domain is all areas and things of, on, under, relating to, adjacent to, or bordering on a sea, ocean, or other navigable waterway, including all maritime-related activities, infrastructure, people, cargo, and vessels and other conveyances.

Maritime Domain Awareness is the effective understanding of anything associated with the maritime domain that could impact the security, safety, economy, or environment of the United States.

Global Maritime Community of Interest (GMCOI) includes, among other interests, the federal, state, and local departments and agencies with responsibilities in the maritime domain. Because certain risks and interests are common to government, business, and citizen alike, community membership also includes public, private, and commercial stakeholders, as well as foreign governments and international stakeholders.

STRATEGIC ENVIRONMENT

There are few areas of greater strategic importance than the maritime domain. The oceans are global thoroughfares that sustain our national prosperity and are vital for our national security. Distinct from other domains (e.g., air and space), the maritime domain provides an expansive pathway through the global commons. Terrorist organizations recognize this, and also realize the importance of exploiting the maritime domain for financial gain and movement of equipment and personnel, as well as a medium for launching attacks. The maritime domain presents a broad array of potential targets that fit terrorists' operational objectives of achieving mass casualties and inflicting economic harm.

The basis for effective prevention measures is awareness and threat knowledge, along with credible deterrent and interdiction capabilities. Without effective understanding of maritime domain activities, gained through persistent awareness, vital opportunities for an early response can be lost. Awareness grants time and distance to detect, deter, interdict, and defeat adversaries. The maritime threat environment of the twenty-first century requires broader scope and a more comprehensive vision. We must look beyond traditional surveillance of ports, waterways, and oceans, and continuously adapt to new challenges and opportunities. We must set priorities for existing and developing capabilities to efficiently minimize risks while contending with an uncertain future. Our understanding of the maritime domain must incorporate intelligence originally acquired in overseas land areas and domestic law enforcement and intelligence information. MDA provides operational maritime commanders a near-real-time ability to defeat hostile nation and transnational terrorist threats.

MDA Goals

MDA supports core national defense and security priorities over the next decade. MDA serves to simplify today's complex and ambiguous security environment by meeting the following strategic goals:

- Enhance transparency in the maritime domain to detect, deter and defeat threats as early and distant from U.S. interests as possible;
- Enable accurate, dynamic, and confident decisions and responses to the full spectrum of maritime threats; and
- Sustain the full application of the law to ensure freedom of navigation and the efficient flow of commerce.

MDA Objectives

Achieving MDA depends on the ability to monitor activities in such a way that trends can be identified and anomalies differentiated. Data alone are insufficient. Data must be collected, fused, and analyzed, preferably with the assistance of computer data integration and analysis algorithms to assist in handling vast, disparate data streams, so that operational decision makers can anticipate threats and take the initiative to defeat them. The following objectives constitute the MDA Essential Task List, which will guide the development of capabilities that the United States Government will pursue and when executed will provide the GMCOI an effective understanding of the maritime domain.

- Persistently monitor in the global maritime domain:
  - Vessels and craft
  - Cargo
  - Vessel crews and passengers
  - All identified areas of interest
- Access and maintain data on vessels, facilities, and infrastructure.
- Collect, fuse, analyze, and disseminate information to decision makers to facilitate effective understanding.
- Access, develop and maintain data on MDA-related mission performance.
- Achieving the essential tasks will make MDA the critical enabler for national maritime security and enable effective decision-making for United States Government maritime operational threat responses. The pursuit of the goals and objectives outlined above will be guided by the following principles and assumptions.

GUIDING PRINCIPLES

The first step towards meeting these principles is to ensure GMCOI stakeholders, at all levels, know what they can do to help, how they can do it and, most importantly why Maritime Domain Awareness is in their collective best interest. The openness of American society and the structure of our traditional governance argue against centralizing all aspects of MDA within an expanded federal infrastructure. However, it will demand a common purpose and agreed upon procedures.

Unity of Effort. MDA requires a coordinated effort within and among the GMCOI, including public and private sector organizations, and international partners. The need for security is a mutual interest requiring the cooperation of industry and government.

Information Sharing and Integration. MDA depends upon unparalleled information sharing. MDA must have protocols to protect private sector proprietary information. Bilateral or multilateral information sharing agreements and international conventions and treaties will be MDA enablers. The primary method for information sharing is the national maritime common operational picture (COP). The COP is a near-time, dynamically tailorable, network-centric virtual information grid shared by all U.S. Federal, state, and local agencies with maritime interests and responsibilities. COP data will be accessible to all users, except when limited by security, policy, or regulations. The COP also contains decision-maker toolsets fed by one or more distributed and exchanged object and track databases to facilitate collaborative planning and assist all echelons in achieving situational awareness. Each user can filter and contribute to these databases according to his or her information needs, responsibilities, and level of access.

Safe and Efficient Flow of Commerce. Public safety and economic security are mutually reinforcing. All members of the GMCOI must recognize that the safe and efficient flow of commerce is enhanced and harmonized by an effective understanding of the maritime domain. The converse is also true, that MDA is enhanced by responsible participation in an accountable system of commerce. The two concepts are mutually reinforcing.

The purpose of MDA is to **facilitate timely, accurate decision making.** MDA does not direct actions, but enables them to be done more quickly and with precision. MDA is achieved by (1) collecting, analyzing and disseminating data, information and intelligence to decision makers, and (2) applying functional and operational knowledge in the context of known and potential threats. A United States Government MDA capability that is integrated, interoperable, and efficient, coupled with continually improving knowledge is required to meet today's mission requirements.

The global maritime domain includes a wide variety of interlocking and connected systems operating within, adjacent to and beyond the physical oceans and waterways that must be brought into better focus. Detecting and interdicting threats within a system that crosses domestic and international jurisdictions requires a persistent awareness.

Intelligence, Surveillance and Reconnaissance (ISR) capabilities are required in a layered approach that provides more comprehensive awareness of threats and illegal activities as they approach the United States.

Achieving MDA requires integration of data, information and intelligence from a broad range of sources, categorized as follows:

- **Vessels** — characteristics such as flag, type, tonnage, maximum speed, origin, and track

- **Cargo** — from a vessel's manifest, shipment origin, human intelligence (HUMINT), or as input from chemical/biological/nuclear/radiation/explosive detection sensors
- **Vessel crews and passengers** — to include crew, dockworkers, and passengers
- **Maritime Areas of Interest** — a focusing of surveillance capabilities to particular geographic points such as sea lanes or oceanic regions
- **Ports, waterways, and facilities** — port terminals, piers, cranes, petrol facilities, and other characteristics
- **The Environment** — weather, currents, natural resources, fish stocks
- **Maritime Critical Infrastructure** — nuclear power plants, rail heads, transportation nodes, bridges, and undersea fiber optic cables and pipelines
- **Threats and Activities** — identified threats and inherently dangerous activities such as illegal migration, drug smuggling, or offshore drilling
- **Friendly Forces** — operational information on military, federal, state, local, and/or allied assets operating in the maritime domain
- **Financial Transactions** — illegal money trails, hidden vessel or cargo ownership

Of the above categories, priority is placed on the data, information, and intelligence associated with **people, cargo, and vessels engaged in maritime activities. The potential for exploitation in these areas makes them the most critical priorities of information and intelligence collection.**

To meet emerging threats, MDA may be required to support the entire spectrum of national security events — from the Global War on Terrorism and stability operations to disaster response and recovery. These requirements may call for a surge or sustained capability to provide MDA where strategically, operationally, or tactically most important. In these cases, capabilities supporting MDA will be focused toward identified maritime areas of interest, such as military vessels or formations, the center of a maritime operating area or a geographic area of interest (e.g., choke point, special security events, sea lines of communication, strategic port, high threat area, etc.).

The United States faces a complex, dynamic strategic environment. We are engaged in a global war on terrorism with stateless actors while confronted with traditional state threats as well. These challenges to our security and economic livelihood require a new mindset — one that sees the total threat and takes all necessary actions through an active, layered defense-in-depth.

The extraordinary value of the maritime domain to global prosperity makes it an attractive medium for use by nation-states, terrorists, and other illicit elements. To achieve an active layered defense, the nation must harness or develop the means to detect illicit activities, deter our enemies from taking advantage of the maritime domain, defend United States interests at home and abroad, and defeat threats that seek to exploit our vulnerabilities as far from our shores as possible. To defeat these threats, we must achieve a more comprehensive and effective understanding of the maritime domain.

MDA is the critical enabler that allows leaders at all levels to make effective decisions and act early against a vast array of threats to the security of the United States, its interests, allies, and friends.

The implementation of this plan will necessarily be continuous. This *National Plan to Achieve Maritime Domain Awareness* sets forth the path toward achieving understanding of the maritime domain and ensuring its effectiveness in meeting national requirements. Achieving the capabilities called for in this plan requires the continued investment of our Nation's intellectual, technological, human and financial resources as well as a partnership with other nations.

The second major supporting document for the *National Strategy for Maritime Security* is the *Global Maritime Intelligence Integration Plan*. The United States has more than 95,000 miles of shoreline and 3.4 million squares miles of water within its exclusive economic zone (EEZ), so it is particularly open to attack from the maritime domain. The openness that makes the maritime domain so important to international commerce also represents a great vulnerability. The vastness of the oceans, as well as the great length of shorelines, provides both concealment and numerous access points to land. Capitalizing on the relative ease and anonymity of movement by commercial ship or small, private vessels through the maritime domain, terrorists, criminal organizations, and rogue nations are smuggling or attempting to smuggle contraband and weapons, money, narcotics, and human beings. Where possible, they use legitimate maritime business or apparent recreational activities as fronts for these attempts. With 80 percent of the world's population living within 200 miles of the shoreline, large numbers of people are potentially subject to threats from these groups.

Recognizing that the maritime domain requires a comprehensive and robust layered security posture, the NSMS assumes dependency on globally networked and collaborative operations with information and maritime domain awareness developed from many intelligence and other sources. Although the United States, with its allies and international partners, has

A rescue swimmer from Coast Guard Air Station Los Angeles is lowered into the water to rescue three fishermen, Dec. 18, 2011. USCG photo.

historically maintained a loosely connected maritime surveillance system that enhanced maritime domain awareness, promoted maritime security, maintained freedom of the sea, and facilitated legitimate global commerce under relatively low-threat conditions, the increasing maritime threat environment demands a more integrated and robust maritime intelligence enterprise that can identify, track, and transfer maritime threat information to operational or law enforcement responders at a maximum time and distance from the United States, its allies, and international partners. The gathering and dissemination of this intelligence is the function of the *Global Maritime Intelligence Integration Plan* (GMIIP).

Through use of legacy intelligence capabilities, existing policy and operational relationships to integrate all available data, information and intelligence and support maritime security planning and operations, the Department of Homeland Security, Department of Defense, Department of State, the Intelligence Community, Department of Justice, Department of Energy, and other US Government departments with responsibility for international maritime trade, and foreign security and intelligence services work together to identify, locate, and track potential threats to US maritime interests and subsequently transfer accurate, relevant, and collaborated information to those operational entities. The guiding philosophy is community information access and integration rather than organizational consolidation of maritime intelligence activities. Helping consolidate this intelligence, a Director of Global Maritime Intelligence Integration along with a Deputy Director and associated support staff were established by the GMIIP. The US Government loves to use acronyms and has designated more than a few new ones in the development of the NSMS. In the GMIIP there are several different designations for similar activities and functions that are carried out by the Director and subordinates. The conglomeration is difficult, if not nearly impossible, to differentiate. In case the reader of this text determines to read further in the various documents concerning National, Homeland, and Maritime Security, some of the acronyms you may see are:

GMCOI: Global Maritime Community of Interest
MSPCC: Maritime Security Policy Coordinating Committee
USCG ICC: US Coast Guard Intelligence Coordination Center
NM-COP: National Maritime Common Operating Picture
MOTR: Maritime Operational Threat Response
JIOCs: Combatant Commander's Joint Intelligence Operations Centers
JIATFs: Joint Interagency Task Forces
USCG MIFCs: US Coast Guard Maritime Intelligence Fusion Centers
TTPs: Tactics, Techniques and Procedures
SILO: Single-integrated Lookout
NGA: National Geospatial-Intelligence Agency
BTS: Bureau of Transportation Security

Working under the Director of National Intelligence, the GMCOI Director and associated intelligence enterprise are based at the National Maritime Intelligence Center in Suitland, Maryland. There, they leverage the existing civil maritime intelligence elements of the Office of Naval Intelligence and the USCG ICC.

Additionally, representatives of the NSA, NGA, DHS, BTS, DOJ, and Departments of Transportation and the Treasury are available to round out the analytic and information-sharing capabilities of the GMCOI core element.

The GMIIP is intended to be a flexible effort that evolves with changing or improved capabilities, operational relationships, and changes in strategy or policy. A major aspect of the plan, establishing improved access to maritime information, data, and intelligence for all those requiring such access, is difficult. The shared common awareness between the intelligence, law enforcement, and operational communities is complex and has many policy and legal implications that must be overcome to accomplish this necessary task. It is the task of the leadership of the maritime intelligence enterprise to identify and seek to resolve these issues.

The *Maritime Operational Threat Response Plan* (MOTR) is the third component of supporting documents for the *National Strategy for Maritime Security*. A classified document, the MOTR is available only to those with a SECRET security clearance and the associated "need to know." Fundamentally, the MOTR coordinates agencies across the range of maritime response activities, including the deployment capabilities and use of force required to intercept, apprehend, exploit, and, when necessary, defeat maritime threats. Using the integrated network of existing national-level maritime command centers, a coordinated, unified, timely, and effective planning and operational response protocol addresses a full range of global maritime security threats.

Excerpts from the
International Outreach and Coordination Strategy

November 2005

STRATEGIC GOALS

To safeguard the maritime domain, the United States must forge cooperative partnerships and alliances with other nations, as well as with public and private stakeholders in the international community. We cannot and should not attempt to patrol every coastline, inspect every ship, screen every passenger, or peer into every container crossing the world's oceans. To foster stronger partnerships within the international community, the United States must have a coordinated and consistent approach to building international support and cooperation to reinforce global maritime security. We will propose ideas, and encourage others to do the same. We will speak frankly. We will also listen carefully. We will work together. Security must be a team effort.

Consistent with National Security Presidential Directive NSPD-41 and Homeland Security Presidential Directive HSPD-13, this *Strategy* establishes the following Strategic Goals:

- **A *coordinated policy* for United States government maritime security activities with foreign governments, international and regional organizations, and the private sector.**

- *Enhanced outreach* to foreign governments, international and regional organizations, private sector partners, and the public abroad to solicit support for improved global maritime security.

The United States recognizes the inherent right of every nation, including our own, to defend itself, to protect its legitimate national interests, and to prevent unlawful exploitation of the maritime domain. The United States will foster cooperation within the international community through diplomacy and mutual assistance. The United States will also, when necessary, take all appropriate actions, consistent with U.S. and international law, to defend ourselves, our allies, and our national interests around the world.

STRATEGIC EXECUTION AND OBJECTIVES

The Department of State, in close coordination with other Departments and Agencies in the United States Government with responsibilities and authorities for security of the maritime domain, will lead active international outreach and engagement to enhance global maritime security. These efforts will be aligned with domestic outreach efforts and activities to ensure the development of consistent messages and materials. Comprehensive security of the maritime domain must be approached in partnership not only with foreign governments and international organizations, but also with the international business community that relies upon security and efficiency in the movement of vessels, people, and goods. The United States will continue to explore new avenues and opportunities for outreach and cooperation both domestically and internationally, as well as support and expand upon the work that has already begun in this critical area of our national security efforts.

The United States will seek early dialogue with international partners when developing maritime security policy initiatives, and will maintain regular contact to discuss implementation and ensure effectiveness. The goal is mutually supportive policies, focused on keeping maritime systems secure and recognizing that a variety of approaches, based on different physical circumstances as well as different political, legal, and economic institutions, may foster security of the maritime domain. We will work continuously in the United States and abroad to identify best practices and to communicate them to others, reflecting the priorities of the United States and our partners.

Foreign governments and industry officials will be provided clear and consistent United States government positions on programs and initiatives related to maritime security, as coordinated through the Maritime Security Policy Coordinating Committee. Appendix B lists ongoing United States Government maritime security initiatives. This annex will be updated regularly, to reflect the latest United States maritime security policies and initiatives. Appendix C lists international, regional and industry organizations that support efforts to enhance maritime security in the international community and with which the United States will continue to work closely in advancing global maritime security.

In order to achieve the Strategic Goals of this *International Outreach and Coordination Strategy*, the Department of State (through the Office of Transportation Policy in the Bureau of Economic and Business Affairs and the Office of Oceans Affairs in the Bureau of Oceans and International Environmental and Scientific Affairs), in close coordination with all U.S. government components with equities in securing the maritime domain, will pursue the following Strategic Objectives:

Strategic Goal: A *coordinated policy* for United States government maritime security activities with foreign governments, international and regional organizations, and the private sector.

- **Strategic Objective:** Establish unified, consistent U.S. positions on maritime security programs and initiatives for U.S. bilateral and multilateral exchanges.
- **Strategic Objective:** Emphasize the importance of maritime security as a key priority in U.S. international policy.
- **Strategic Objective:** Ensure the full integration of international law in the advancement of global maritime security at international meetings and exchanges.
- **Strategic Objective:** Optimize the use of meetings and other exchanges with countries, international and regional organizations, and private sector groups to advance maritime security.

Goal: *Enhanced outreach* to foreign governments, international and regional organizations, private sector partners, and the public abroad to solicit support for improved global maritime security.

- **Strategic Objective:** Build partnerships with other countries and the maritime community to identify and reach out to regional and international organizations in order to advance global maritime security.
- **Strategic Objective:** Coordinate U.S. and international technical assistance to promote effective maritime security in developing nations and critical regions.
- **Strategic Objective:** Coordinate a unified message on maritime security for public diplomacy.
- **Strategic Objective:** Provide U.S. missions abroad with guidance to enable them to build support for U.S. maritime security initiatives with host governments, key private-sector partners, and the general public abroad.

The security of the maritime domain is a global issue. The United States is committed to working closely with our allies and partners around the world to ensure that lawful private and public activities in the maritime domain are protected against attack and criminal or otherwise unlawful or hostile exploitation. Our allies and trading partners recognize the importance the United States places on maritime security, and we will work closely with them to develop effective international maritime security programs. The United States will continue to expand our working partnerships with all who share the goal of a secure and prosperous international trading community. Many Departments and Agencies of the United States government share the challenge of engaging our allies and partners, as well as working with appropriate international and regional organizations and private sector groups in order to secure United States maritime interests around the globe. The Department of State will coordinate with and support other Departments and Agencies in developing and communicating to foreign partners a unified and consistent message regarding global maritime security and United States maritime security programs and initiatives.

The fifth, sixth, and seventh component plans of the *National Strategy for Maritime Security* are the *Maritime Infrastructure Recovery Plan* of April 2006, the *Maritime Transportation System Security Plan*, and the *Maritime Commerce Security Plan* of October 2005. These three supplementary plans are so interrelated that it is necessary to discuss them as if they were a single composite plan.

According to the American Association of Port Authorities, the Marine Transportation System (MTS) moved more than $1.434 trillion in imports and exports through US ports in 2010. In 2016 the MTS moved over 1.285 trillion metric tons valued in excess of $1.477 trillion.[8] The MTS makes it possible for goods from other countries to be delivered to our front doorstep. It enables the United States to project military presence around the globe, creates jobs that support local economies, and provides a source of recreation for all Americans. Fundamentally, the Nation's economic and military security are closely linked to the health and functionality of the MTS.[9]

National Strategy for Maritime Security Policy Action Working Groups, DHS

Taken from the Maritime Infrastructure Recovery Plan, April 2006, page 1.

The 2010 Vessel Calls Snapshot report contains data on calls by oceangoing vessels at US ports. In 2010, 7,579 oceangoing vessels made 62,747 calls at US ports. Of the 2010 calls,

- 35 percent were by tankers carrying oil and gas used to power our cars and heat our homes,
- 31 percent were by container ships carrying general export and import cargo for markets around the United States and the world,
- 17 percent were by dry bulk vessels carrying iron, coal, and grain for export,
- 9 percent were by roll-on/roll-off vessels carrying vehicles for import and export, and
- 6 percent were by general cargo ships.

In addition, the report shows that tanker operators are replacing single-hull vessels with new, greener double-hull ships. In 2010, 97 percent of the tanker calls were by double-hull vessels, up from 78 percent five years earlier. Note that Port Calls data is published 5 years late. The most recent data is dated 2012 and is incomplete.

US seaports are responsible for moving nearly all of the country's overseas cargo volume ... 99.4 percent by weight and 64.1 percent by value. Each of our 50 states relies on at least 15 seaports to handle its imports and exports, which total some $3.8 billion worth of goods moving in and out of US seaports each day. Seaports also support the employment of more than 13 million people in the United States, which accounts for $650 billion in personal income. Additionally, for every $1 billion in exports shipped though seaports, 15,000 US jobs are created.[10]

A complex system, the MTS is geographically diverse and composed of many types of assets, operations, and infrastructure that are operated and influenced by a diverse set of stakeholders, all of which play an important role in the system. In addition, the MTS is an open system that enables many users to benefit from it at minimal cost. The complexity and openness of the MTS make it efficient, however these characteristics also present many challenges to those trying to improve system security.

Overcoming these challenges, the cooperation of all stakeholders is paramount and is central to improving security. Envision Maritime Transportation System Security as:

> A systems-oriented security regime built upon layers of protection and defense in-depth that effectively mitigates critical system security risks, while preserving the functionality and efficiency of the MTS. Understanding the most effective security risk management strategies involves cooperation and participation of both domestic and international stakeholders acting at strategic points in the system, the U.S. seeks to improve security through a cooperative and cohesive effort involving all stakeholders.[11]

This vision can further be thought of as a series of security nets providing layers of protection that are actualized through a series of strategic recommendations. These strategic recommendations were developed in consultation with a wide spectrum of MTS stakeholders, including federal agencies, state and local governments, and industry representatives. The Department of Homeland Security is responsible for overseeing the development and implementation of these eight recommendations:

1. Risk Management—Improve security management through the development and consistent application of risk assessment methodologies to prioritize and track the outcomes of security improvement efforts.

2. Security Information Management—Develop an interagency security data management plan to improve the quality, transparency, sharing, and protection of critical security information among all appropriate MTS stakeholders, including federal, state, and local government agencies as well as MTS operators.

3. International & National Regulatory Framework—Continually improve the international and national regulatory framework established by the International Ship and Port Facility Security Code (ISPS Code) and Maritime Transportation Security Act 2002 (MTSA 2002).

4. Stakeholder Responsibility & Coordination—Create and manage a coordinated network of stakeholders who:

> (1) understand and accept their roles/responsibilities for ensuring maritime security; and,
>
> (2) are actively engaged in collaborative efforts to reduce security risks in the maritime domain.

5. Credentialing—Develop the ability for US authorities to identify with confidence:

> (1) individuals working aboard commercial vessels and operating recreational boats, foreign or domestic, in the US Maritime Domain, and,
>
> (2) workers at land-based MTSA-regulated facilities and critical infrastructure components within the US MTS.

6. Leverage Safety Frameworks—Examine international, national, and industry transportation safety frameworks with respect to potential terrorist attack scenarios and determine if reasonable safety enhancements can significantly improve the inherent security of the MTS.

7. Security Technology—Promote the development of technologies to address security gaps and improve the current Maritime Transportation System Security Network. Identify and support MTS changes needed to incorporate these technologies effectively into the security network.

8. Security Training—Ensure that port and maritime personnel both domestically and internationally are properly trained in maritime security in accordance with their function within the MTS.

It is interesting to note that in the Maritime Transportation System Security Recommendations, the very first formal recommendation proposed is the need to effectively improve risk management through the development and consistent application of risk assessment methodologies to prioritize and track how well security improvement efforts work. Another critical issue is the need to address information security as it relates to critical security information. The Maritime Commerce Security Plan also takes a risk management and security information approach to the issue of maritime security.

Coast Guard, INS, FBI, and other agency investigators move into position to open a cargo container suspected of housing Chinese migrants smuggled into the United States. USCG.

Implementing a five-part framework, the MCS proposes:

1. Accurate data in the form of advance electronic information to support the risk assessment of the cargo. This assessment identifies cargo that may present a threat and thus may require some type of intervention. This information is needed early in the process to identify high-risk cargo before it enters the maritime domain.

2. Secure cargo requires that cargo to be loaded on the vessel conforms to the cargo information electronically transmitted to the authorities. This process connects firsthand knowledge of the cargo with the validation of the cargo information. This process also ensures that safeguards are in place to prevent unlawful materials (or persons) from being combined with the legitimate cargo. As an example, this process would involve security procedures to prevent unauthorized cargo and stowaways from being added to a container while it is being packed (stuffed) at a factory. This part also includes a risk management process that includes the inspection (physical inspection and/or the use of non-intrusive inspection equipment) of cargo identified as high-risk prior to loading at foreign ports and, in some cases, after arrival at the US port.

3. Secure vessels and ports protect the security of the cargo while it is in the maritime domain. The MCS does not focus on this element of maritime commerce security. The security of vessels and foreign and domestic ports is supported by the security requirements of the Maritime Transportation Security Act, the International Ship

and Port Facility Security Code, and other requirements such as the advance notice of arrival regulations. The Maritime Transportation Security Act regulations specifically address the cargo handling security requirements for vessels and maritime facilities (33 CFR 104-105). Improvements to the national and international regulatory framework are covered in the Maritime Transportation System Security Plan.

4. Secure transit is the procedure to ensure that the secure cargo remains in that status as it enters and moves through the maritime domain. Successful implementation of a method to detect that security has been compromised during transit and a response protocol to determine if the cargo has remained secure is essential.

5. Improvements to security within the first four parts of the framework are addressed in a way that ensures consistency and substantive improvements across the supply chain. An important way this goal is achieved is through engagement of appropriate international organizations (e.g., the World Customs Organization, the International Maritime Organization, and the International Organization for Standardization) in the development of standards. Standards are the only meaningful way that the government can ensure that a certain level of security across the supply chain can be expected and achieved. Accurate data, secure cargo, and secure transit goals are all areas where internationally accepted standards substantially improve the system. Secure vessels/ports is one area that is already subject to consistent international standards through the International Ship and Port Facility Security Code and associated domestic regulations.

The Maritime Infrastructure Recovery Plan (MIRP) is fundamentally a FEMA document that addresses the process by which infrastructure is recovered following a Transportation Security Incident (TSI) that occurs under, in, on, or adjacent to waters subject to the jurisdiction of the United States.[12] If a TSI is of such a significance as to require the implementation of the National Response Framework and mobilization of personnel in accordance with HSPD-5, then it becomes a "national TSI." This triggers the implementation of the MIRP, which becomes guidance for the designees of the Secretary of Homeland Security in the decision-making process to maintain the nation's MTS operational capabilities, and if compromised, to restore transportation capabilities.

The MIRP recognizes that the MTS is a system and as such must be dealt with as if it were a living organism that will adapt to problems as they develop, provided there is sufficient information available to inform those controlling the overall movement of vessels in the maritime domain. It also recognizes that most ocean traffic is commercial in nature and that cooperation with businesses is the best way to redirect the delivery and shipment of goods rather than a top-down government assumption of control in the event of a national TSI. With more than 2,100 possible threat scenarios in hundreds of ports, the MIRP is necessarily general in nature to provide flexibility for recovery management.

The primary objective of the MIRP is to provide guidance for federal decision makers to use in restoring maritime transportation capabilities if compromised, specifically the restoration of cargo flow and passenger vessel activity after a national TSI. This guidance includes recommended recovery management procedures to assist in the development of viable strategies or Courses of Action (COA). Assuming the effect of a national TSI (or other similarly disruptive incident) impairs the loading/offloading or movement of vessels, this plan provides a framework with clearly defined roles to facilitate restoration of cargo flow, as well as passenger vessel activity. Restoration of cargo flow and passenger vessel activity may include the redirecting/diverting of vessels to ports with reserve or excess capacity. To assist with the recovery/restoration of maritime transportation capabilities, the MIRP accomplishes or considers the following:

1. Provides recovery management procedures for the Secretary of Homeland Security and designated representatives (e.g., the Interagency Incident Management Group (IIMG)) to make decisions affecting national maritime recovery efforts;

2. Provides recovery management procedures for those making decisions at the incident site and at non-incident sites that provide support;

3. Recognizes that, based on the nature and circumstances of the incident, a transition in focus from homeland defense operations to recovery management may occur between the Secretary of Defense and the Secretary of Homeland Security;

4. Takes into consideration initial post-incident decisions made by senior officials from the US Coast Guard (USCG) and the US Customs and Border Protection (CBP) regarding short-term, targeted operational actions to help maintain flow of commerce through non-incident sites;

5. Lists roles and responsibilities of federal, state, local, and tribal governments, and the private sector. The listing is specific to the functional responsibilities related to recovery of maritime transportation capabilities;

6. To evaluate the effectiveness of the plan, the MIRP subscribes to an exercise program that includes periodic validation of the concepts of this recovery plan; and

7. Identifies next steps and makes recommendations to improve recovery management.[13]

To accomplish these objectives, the goals of decision makers utilizing the MIRP are:

- Facilitate achieving the optimum balance between ports and waterways security and the recovery of maritime transportation capabilities,
- Maximize the Maritime Transportation System's (MTS) continued operational equilibrium,
- Minimize disruption to the US economy from unnecessarily constrained cargo flow.[14]

The remainder of the MIRP is a detailed assignment of duties and responsibilities to those agencies that would respond to a national TSI. This takes us to the final component of the NSMS, the Domestic Outreach Plan.

In a three-stage process the domestic outreach working group strategically selected individuals and organizations that represent large groups of stakeholders in the MTS. Approximately 2,700 individuals, representing more than 4 million private-sector organizations and state, local, tribal, and territorial governments, were given the opportunity to comment on initial drafts of the implementation plans. Gathering the input from such a wide-ranging group enhanced the final development and implementation of the National Strategy for Maritime Security.

The final components of the National Strategy for Maritime Security are three additional documents not listed in HSPD-13: *The US Coast Guard Strategy for Maritime Safety, Security, and Stewardship;* the joint US Navy, US Marine Corps, and US Coast Guard publications *A Cooperative Strategy for 21st Century Seapower;* and the *Naval Operations Concept, 2010: Implementing the Maritime Strategy.* Of these three, the last is the most important.

> *Naval Operations Concept 2010* (NOC 10) describes when, where, and how US naval forces will contribute to enhancing security, preventing conflict, and prevailing in war. NOC 10 is not designed for a cursory reading; it is a publication intended for serious study by professionals. Readers will quickly discern several themes that collectively embody the essence of naval service to our Nation. Implicit in these themes is that Sailors, Marines, and Coast Guardsmen should expect to be engaged in both preventing and winning wars. These themes reflect the content of CS-21 as well as the guidance provided by the Secretary of Defense in the *National Defense Strategy* (NDS) and the 2010 Quadrennial Defense Review (QDR).
>
> The sea services have a long history of accomplishing diverse missions, from protecting American merchantmen during an undeclared naval war in the late 18th century, to establishing our naval prowess in the War of 1812, to suppressing the African slave trade and West Indian piracy in the 19th century, to fighting the major wars and confronting the irregular challenges of the twentieth century. As the twenty-first century unfolds, we must continue to be effective warriors as well as informed and articulate ambassadors, serving our Nation's interests and facilitating free global interaction from the sea.[15]

US Coast Guard Cutter Legare (WMEC 912) patrols alongside the Senegalese Navy vessel, Poponquine, during joint operations as part of the Africa Partnership Station mission Saturday, Aug. 8, 2009. US Coast Guard photo/Petty Officer 2nd Class Thomas M. Blue.

Excerpts from the *Naval Operations Concept 2010: Implementing the Maritime Strategy*

Purpose

Naval Operations Concept 2010 (NOC 10) describes when, where and how US naval forces will contribute to enhancing security, preventing conflict and prevailing in war in order to guide Maritime Strategy implementation in a manner consistent with national strategy. NOC 10 describes the *ways* with which the sea services will achieve the *ends* articulated in *A Cooperative Strategy for 21st Century Seapower* (CS-21). (Page 1)

Scope

The integration of naval capabilities to achieve specific joint mission objectives is the responsibility of commanders, who formulate their concepts of operations to achieve advantage and decision. In contrast, Service operational concepts are designed to describe the capabilities that operational commanders can expect the Services to provide, and indicate selected ways these capabilities can be integrated to achieve mission success. Consequently, NOC 10 is designed to inform development of joint concepts, plans and experimentation. The term "naval" and "the Naval Service" are used throughout this publication to encompass Navy, Marine Corps, and Coast Guard personnel and organizations.

NOC 10 articulates the ways naval forces are employed to achieve the strategy conveyed in CS-21. Published in 2007, CS-21 described a set of core capabilities that added maritime security and humanitarian assistance and disaster response (HA/DR) to the traditional forward presence, deterrence, sea control, and power projection. Not to be viewed as discrete missions or functions, these core capabilities are intrinsically linked and mutually supporting enablers for achieving the Naval Service's strategic imperatives:

Regionally concentrated, credible combat power to:
- Limit regional conflict with deployed, decisive maritime power
- Deter major power war
- Win our Nation's wars

Globally distributed, mission-tailored maritime forces to:
- Contribute to homeland defense in depth
- Foster and sustain cooperative relationships with more international partners
- Prevent or contain local disruptions before they impact the global system

NOC 10 does not prescribe Naval Service *tactics*, nor is it *doctrine*. Rather, it serves as a *precursor to the development of both*. It describes how the Navy, Marine Corps, and Coast Guard operate together, and will be complemented by Service-specific concepts. Collectively, the ideas put forth are to be applied, tested, analyzed and refined through war games, exercises, experiments, and operational lessons learned. This innovation will ultimately inform future revisions of the NOC, as it is updated to remain relevant in the evolving security environment.

In an increasingly complex world, naval forces provide the Nation with the global presence and the freedom of maneuver needed to influence world events. Persistently postured forward, naval forces are continuously engaged with global partners in cooperative security activities aimed at reducing instability and providing another arm of national diplomacy. Their expeditionary capabilities enable and support the joint force effort to combat both conventional and irregular challenges. NOC 10 describes how naval forces will blend "soft" and "hard" power in support of the approach, objectives and enduring national interests articulated in the National Defense Strategy (NDS). These enduring interests include "protecting the nation and our allies from attack or coercion, promoting international security to reduce conflict and foster economic growth, and securing the global commons and with them access to world markets and resources." NOC 10 also expounds upon CS-21's core capabilities: forward presence, maritime security, HA/DR, sea control, power projection and deterrence. (Pages 2–3)

Maritime Security
Naval power is the natural defense of the United States.
—President John Adams, 1796,
2nd President of the United States

Maritime security is a non-doctrinal term defined as those tasks and operations conducted to protect sovereignty and maritime resources, support free and open seaborne commerce, and to counter maritime related terrorism, weapons proliferation, transnational crime, piracy, environmental destruction, and illegal seaborne immigration. Effective maritime security requires a comprehensive effort to promote global economic stability and protect legitimate ocean-borne activities from hostile or illegal acts in the maritime domain. In addition to security operations along the US coastline, globally-distributed naval forces conducting maritime security operations contribute to homeland defense in depth.

Maritime security may be divided into *individual* or *collective* categories. *Individual* maritime security operations involve actions taken by a single nation-state to provide for its safety and security, consistent with its rights. While the responsibility and capacity of individual nations to secure their territorial waters is the foundation upon which global maritime security is built, *A Cooperative Strategy for 21st Century Seapower* (CS-21) notes that unilateral action by a single nation cannot ensure the security of the global maritime commons: *collective* maritime security operations are required to unite actions of like-minded nation-states to promote mutual safety and security at sea.

Opportunity and Challenge
The size and complexity of the maritime commons create unique security challenges for the international community as terrorists and criminals leverage the

easily accessible, largely unregulated expanse of the maritime domain to mask and facilitate their illicit activities. Threats to safety and security include piracy, narcotics smuggling, human trafficking, weapons proliferation, environmental destruction, and the pilfering of natural resources. Identifying, tracking, and neutralizing these threats is essential to US national security and the global economy.

The sea is vast, the littorals extensive, and the threats to US interests are varied, determined, and persistent. These conditions cannot be sufficiently shaped by the Naval Service alone, and demand that America partner with nations that share its interest in global maritime security and the prosperity it underpins.

Central Idea

Global maritime security can only be achieved through the integration of national and regional maritime cooperation, awareness and response initiatives. To this end, unprecedented coordination among governments, the private sector, and multinational organizations including naval and maritime security forces, law enforcement agencies, customs and immigration officials, masters of vessels and other merchant mariners, shipping companies, and port operators is required. The Naval Service plays a critical role in facilitating this coordination, and is uniquely manned, trained and equipped to help allies and partners develop the maritime professionals, infrastructure, awareness and response capabilities that are a prerequisite for maritime security. The Nation's *globally distributed, mission-tailored naval forces* not only conduct the full range of related operations — from unilateral assistance at sea, law enforcement and maritime interception operations to multinational counter-piracy operations — they help willing allies and partners build the capacity, proficiency and interoperability to do the same.

Increased Cooperation

The United States has numerous maritime law enforcement treaties and security arrangements to address various maritime security challenges, including drug interdiction, migrant interdiction, counter-piracy, fisheries enforcement, and proliferation security. Each agreement is unique and tailored to requirements, diplomatic and political relationships, and the domestic laws and policies of the participating nations. These agreements expand US maritime authority and eliminate border seams that are exploited by illicit actors. As transnational maritime threats evolve, the Naval Service will continue to collaborate with the requisite US authorities to develop any additional arrangements with foreign partners that are required to achieve maritime security. The Naval Service also supports mechanisms that underpin maritime security, including organizations such as the International Maritime Organization (IMO) that has instituted vessel tracking, vessel and port security measures, and strengthened the Convention on Suppression of Unlawful Acts at Sea (SUA); international law including the U.N. Convention on the Law of the Sea; regional, multinational, and bilateral agreements; domestic laws and regulations; and private-sector practices and procedures.

Within the US Government, the Naval Service is a key stakeholder in the Maritime Operational Threat Response (MOTR) plan, which establishes protocols that facilitate coordinated, unified, timely, and effective planning and execution by the various agencies that have maritime responsibilities. Lead and supporting agencies are based on the location of the threat, existing law, desired outcome, magnitude of the hazard, response capabilities required, asset availability and authority to act. This interagency approach builds upon the unique contributions of each entity to respond to a full range of maritime security threats, including terrorism, and establishes the procedures to coordinate actions that frequently support a tactical response by the Naval Service. The Navy and Coast Guard, in accordance with the *National Fleet* policy, integrate their multi-mission platforms, infrastructure, and personnel to generate force packages tailored for specific maritime security responses and missions. This practice allows each Service to leverage the unique capabilities of the other, as part of a joint task force thousands of miles from the United States, or in response to operational tasking close to home in support of civil authorities. The increasing commonality between Navy and Coast Guard systems, including radars, antennas, deck guns, airframes and unmanned systems, has improved both interoperability and sustainability during joint maritime security operations.

The responsibility of individual nations to maintain maritime security within their waters is the foundation upon which global maritime security is built. US allies and partners possess capabilities that range from limited port or coastal maritime security forces to major navies with potent sea control and power projection capabilities. US naval forces, in accordance with combatant commander theater security cooperation (TSC) plans, collaborate with allies and partners alike to develop the expertise, infrastructure, awareness, and capacity to respond to the full range of maritime security threats and irregular challenges.

Maritime Security Force Assistance (MSFA)

MSFA comprises efforts to strengthen security burden-sharing with foreign military and civilian maritime security forces and government institutions, as well as multinational and regional maritime security entities. These activities assist partner naval forces to become more proficient at providing security to their populations. In the context of the global maritime commons, MSFA promotes stability by developing partner nation capabilities to govern, control, and protect their harbors, inland and coastal waters, natural resources, commercial concerns, and national and regional maritime security interests. MSFA activities are conducted across the range of military operations (ROMO) and during all phases of military operations, in coordination with US government agencies and in support of larger US policy goals. Many of the Coast Guard's statutory missions align with foreign partner emerging demand to proactively deal with increasing threats to their sovereignty and resources. Geographic combatant commanders' (GCC) theater campaign plans and security cooperation initiatives are evolving to encompass combined Navy and Coast Guard capabilities tailored to develop competencies of host nation maritime security forces. Often these nations do not possess the requisite assets and tactics to self-police. Navy ships, Coast Guard cutters coupled with complementary law enforcement detachments (LEDETs) and training teams are ideal instruments of soft power to effect national objectives.

MSFA initiatives foster trust and interoperability with allies and enduring partners, increase capabilities and capacities to address conventional and irregular threats, reduce the ungoverned areas within the maritime domain, promote regional stability, and set conditions that dissuade disruptive acts through cooperative actions. Expeditionary operations, enduring partnership missions, as well as bilateral and multi-lateral exercises involving nearly every Naval Service capability comprise the most common MSFA initiatives.

Fleet and Expeditionary Operations

Naval forces will often conduct MSFA concurrent with other forward operations. For example, while conducting security patrols around the Iraqi off-shore oil platforms, Navy and Coast Guard maritime security forces integrated Iraqi military personnel into the operation to improve their expertise and proficiency. Similarly, while maintaining port and waterway security, Coast Guard port security unit (PSU) and Navy maritime expeditionary security squadron members trained Iraqi naval forces on point and perimeter security defense operations under the supervision of the Iraq Training and Advisory Mission. As general purpose forces embarked on naval vessels, Marines also conducted MSFA with coalition and partner nation naval forces. In these cases, Naval Service personnel benefited from the MSFA activities as well, gaining a greater understanding of local customs and conditions, which enhanced their effectiveness.

Likewise, Coast Guard cutters and LEDETs—active duty Coast Guard personnel employed on partner nation naval vessels in order to provide expanded law enforcement authority, expertise and capability to carry out interdiction and apprehension operations—frequently provide technical assistance to foreign law enforcement partners. Cutter boarding teams and LEDETs instruct, demonstrate and assist with searches, and evidence testing and processing. MSFA, in the form of advanced boarding procedure training, is increasingly requested by coalition partners and has reduced the risk associated with counter-piracy operations off Somalia. Additionally, the Coast Guard's International Port Security (IPS) program assesses the effectiveness of anti-terrorism measures in the ports of US trading partners pursuant to a US statutory requirement. This form of MSFA evaluates countries' implementation of the International Ship and Port Facility Security (ISPS) Code, shares maritime security "best practices," and makes recommendations for improvement.

Enduring, Rotational Maritime Partnership Missions

The global fleet station concept has given rise to a variety of enduring capacity-building activities that are supported by mission-tailored rotational forces. The Africa Partnership Station (APS) initiative exemplifies the rigorous, holistic approach to enhancing maritime security that the Naval Service employs around the world. Beginning with a specific maritime security condition to be achieved, for example "trafficking is stopped through western Africa," individual *country action plans* are collaboratively developed with the littoral countries to build the cadre of maritime professionals, maritime security infrastructure, maritime domain awareness, and maritime security force response capability necessary to achieve the objective condition. The country action plans integrate and synchronize supporting activities by other US government entities, as well as those of allies, other partners, international organizations, and non-governmental organizations that share a common interest in achieving the maritime security condition. The detailed planning that is the foundation of this approach facilitates resourcing the initiative, avoids duplication of effort among international stakeholders, and drives the long-term scheduling of rotational forces to maximize progress by the partner. Moreover, the synchronization of related country action plans through a *regional action plan* that establishes enabling capabilities such as *regional coordination centers*, serves to establish a regional capacity that is invariably required to achieve measurable improvements in maritime security. To this end, Naval Service capabilities are employed in both supported and supporting roles, and typically conduct training events, exercises, and combined operations with numerous partners during a single deployment. For example, a subset of APS includes the African Maritime Law Enforcement Partnership (AMLEP), in which Navy warships, Coast Guard cutters, and partner vessels with embarked Coast Guard LEDETs and mobile training teams (MTTs) conduct operations and professional exchanges to advance maritime security and law enforcement competencies. The character of such activities and required capabilities vary depending on the security enhancement sought—from protection of ports, off-shore infrastructure, undersea resources or the environment to the interdiction of illegal fishing, piracy, narcotics smuggling, human trafficking, and weapons proliferation—but the first principle for successful maritime partnership missions is a steadfast focus on planned activities that make progress toward the specific maritime security condition to be achieved.

Fleet and Regional Exercises and Training

Bilateral and multi-lateral exercises serve to increase the proficiency, interoperability and confidence of US naval forces and those of its allies and partners across the entire ROMO. Such exercises incorporate tailored training objectives to address the needs of the maritime security forces involved, from fundamental competencies such as basic naval seamanship to the most technically complex aspects of naval warfare such as ballistic missile defense, amphibious assault and undersea warfare. Exercises also bring together nations that otherwise would not conduct combined operations. Major maritime exercises include: Rim of the Pacific (RIMPAC), the largest combined exercise in the Pacific; Cooperation Afloat Readiness and Training (CARAT); Southeast Asia Cooperation Against Terrorism (SEACAT); Annual Exercise (ANNUALEX) with Japan; FOAL EAGLE in Korea; Baltic Operations Exercise (BALTOPS); and UNITAS, PANAMAX, and TRADEWINDS in the Western Hemisphere. All of these exercises involve ships, aircraft, and personnel ashore to conduct MSFA, ultimately improving the ability of US naval forces to respond effectively to regional security threats in concert with its allies and partners.

Enhanced Awareness

Comprehensive maritime domain awareness (MDA) is the foundation of global maritime security. MDA requires an architecture that collects, fuses, analyzes and disseminates enormous quantities of classified and unclassified information regarding vessels, people, cargo, infrastructure, maritime areas of interest, and ongoing maritime security operations. The contributions of forward postured, persistent and culturally aware naval forces are critical, but not sufficient, to achieve comprehensive MDA. In fact, the combined efforts of the world's naval forces — if they could be aligned through military-to-military relationships — would still be insufficient. Comprehensive MDA can only be achieved through the seamless collaboration of the entire maritime community — naval forces, maritime-related organizations, the shipping industry, insurance companies, and mariners of every ilk. The Naval Service is responsible for facilitating such collaboration among the naval forces of allies and partners as a matter of first priority, and among the balance of the maritime community secondarily.

The basic objective of MDA initiatives is to discern who owns, operates, and controls a vessel; what activity is being conducted by the vessel; when will the activity be conducted; where will the activity be conducted; why the activity is being conducted; and how illegal activities are being concealed. To this end, collaboration correctly begins with the sharing of information available from existing systems, such as shore-based, shipborne, and airborne radar systems, to build a common operating picture (COP). A comprehensive, real-time COP is considered as important for safe, effective maritime operations as clearly defined command and control relationships. Additional information to augment the basic radar COP can be gleaned from a variety of public databases and systems such as the Automatic Identification System (AIS). Similar to aircraft identification transponders, AIS is a protocol adopted by the International Maritime Organization to automatically share unclassified ship identification, safety of navigation and voyage information between AIS users operating in proximity to each other. This data is collected and fused with geospatial and oceanographic data to create increasingly comprehensive maritime domain awareness that can be shared with other US agencies, allies and partners. The US Coast Guard's National AIS (NAIS) project, which collects data from AIS-equipped surface vessels in the Nation's territorial waters and adjacent seas out to 2,000 nautical miles, is a conduit for maritime domain information that supports both Naval Service and international operations.

Response Operations

US naval forces, often in concert with joint general purpose and special operations forces, other government agencies, and international partners, actively respond to conventional and irregular maritime threats. Naval Service response operations include:

- *Increased Surveillance and Tracking.* Vessels of interest are subject to increased surveillance and tracking, using a wide variety of military and commercial space-based systems, as well as air, surface, and underwater sensors. These actions facilitate more efficient, effective interdiction operations and are increasingly conducted by long-range, extended-endurance unmanned platforms with multi-spectral sensors.
- *Combined Task Force (CTF) Operations.* US naval forces, in conjunction with allies and partners, will continue to conduct combined operations to counter specific maritime security threats such as piracy, smuggling and weapons trafficking. For example, the multinational task force CTF 151 was established in January 2009 to conduct counter-piracy operations in the Gulf of Aden and Somali basin.
- *Maritime Interception Operations (MIO).* MIO monitor, query, and board merchant vessels to enforce sanctions against other nations such as those embodied in United Nations Security Council Resolutions and prevent the transport of restricted goods. Boarding teams comprised of Sailors, Marines, Coast Guardsmen and other law enforcement personnel are trained in visit, board, search, and seizure techniques and conduct specific missions in accordance with relevant authorities, laws, jurisdictions and capabilities.
- *Law Enforcement Operations.* Law enforcement operations (LEO) are a form of interception operations distinct from MIO. Coast Guard cutters frequently conduct independent LEO while exercising Title 14 authority in deep water and littoral environments. US Navy and foreign naval vessels routinely embark Coast Guard LEDETs and shift tactical control to the Coast Guard while conducting LEO.
- *Expanded Maritime Interception Operations.* Expanded MIO (EMIO) are authorized by the President and directed by the Secretary of Defense to intercept vessels identified to be transporting terrorists and/or terrorist-related materiel that pose an imminent threat to the United States and its allies.

Summary

Global maritime security can only be achieved through the coordinated activities of governments, the private sector, and multinational organizations including naval and maritime security forces, law enforcement agencies, customs and immigration officials, and the maritime community writ large. The Naval Service plays a critical role in facilitating this coordination, and is uniquely manned, trained and equipped to help allies and partners develop the maritime professionals, infrastructure, awareness and response capabilities that are a prerequisite for maritime security. US *globally distributed, mission-tailored naval forces* effectively conduct the full range of maritime security operations and are instrumental in building the capacity, proficiency and interoperability of partners and allies that share our aspiration to achieve security throughout the maritime commons. (Pages 35–43)

The 2010 Naval Operations Concept makes reference to the Automatic Identification System (AIS). This is an international tracking system installed on every commercial vessel, tracking in real time every ship's movement and current location, and transmitting that information to central data collection centers. Through the AIS system it is possible to identify and follow every commercial ship anywhere in the world.

AIS is a fusion of technologies that allows the layered overlay of different data on common platforms, such as Google Earth. The data has been adapted to allow the real-time position of all AIS vessels to be displayed on a Google Earth background. By layering the data, it becomes possible to simply mouse over any given icon and get quick information on the vessel, including name, speed, and course. The display also provides the vessel length, breadth, draft, destination, and estimated time of arrival. There is even a photograph of the vessel. All of this allows for the maritime security apparatus to rapidly identify any vessel, its origin and destination, and a variety of other data that helps to indicate which ships or cargos may require closer observation, or attention.

A person is transferred from a Navy helicopter to an Ohio Class ballistic missile submarine. US Navy photo.

The technological advances in port security are also significant. Most of the world's goods are shipped in containers that are easily stacked, loaded, unloaded, moved to trucks or rail

Cargo is removed from an incoming ship newly arrived at the Port of Los Angeles/Long Beach. The trucks moving the unloaded containers pass through a portable x-ray machine before leaving the terminal. US Customs and Border Protection, 11/03/2006.

cars, and delivered to the end user. This containerization allows for shippers to load a diverse selection of products into a single metal box and have that container moved to anyplace on the globe in a matter of days. These containers also meet certain international standards for portability. A container loading facility in Suez, Egypt, functions the same as the one in Long Beach, California. This allows a shipping company in Egypt to purchase bulk dates, cotton cloth, olive oil, spices, and any other marketable commodities and load them into a single container. That locked metal box is identified by a serial number and with a breakable metal seal that is unique to that container. It is loaded on a truck and delivered to Suez where it is loaded on a freighter bound for Singapore and then the United States. The invoice for the goods loaded in Egypt is electronically transmitted to the shipping company, and to US Customs and Border Protection, before the box ever leaves Egypt. When the ship arrives in Long Beach and the containers are unloaded, the Customs Inspector checks the container number to see if the lock and seal are intact. Any indication that the box has been tampered with or opened in route triggers the need for a secondary inspection, which can be conducted in a variety of manners, including x-ray, and physical inventory.

The entire process is essentially seamless and provided there is no indication of tampering or contraband in the container, it will be delivered to the importer within a day or two—perhaps even transshipped across the United States by train in the process. This is the ultimate benefit of a modern transportation system in a globalized economy when the maritime security system functions as intended.

Conclusion

Throughout history a major concern of empires and countries with ocean borders has been the safety and security of their maritime commerce. No security system, no matter how technologically advanced, is perfect. As long as there are people involved in the supply chain, the potential for human error, corruption, and compromise exists. This opens the maritime domain to an unlimited number of potential threats. More than two hundred years after the days of the Tripolitan pirates, navies continue to conduct joint operations to contain piracy in many locations throughout the world.

The complex nature of the Maritime Transportation System is apparent, and the critical balance of security and commerce cannot be achieved without the cooperation and participation of both domestic and international stakeholders involved in the operation of the system. Recognition of the joint responsibility for maritime security held by the private sector and government entities is clearly stated in the National Strategy for Maritime Security: "Maritime security is best achieved by blending public and private maritime security activities on a global scale into an integrated effort that addresses all maritime threats."[16] An expansive network of cooperation has developed between government and the private sector, to accomplish the objective to secure the maritime domain while maintaining the smooth flow of international commerce. Through use of the latest technology, goods and cargo are tracked from their origin to the customer in a modern supply chain to minimize the potential impact to the MTS of a maritime transportation security incident. In an era of Global Positioning Satellites, Automatic Identification Systems, and RFID tracking, every effort is being made to secure the maritime domain and ensure maritime commerce moves unimpeded.

Questions for Further Consideration

1. Where are the borders between the United States and China?
2. Along the Texas coast, which is nearly 1,000 miles (1,600 km) in total length, there are about 1,150 seaports. In addition to actual ports, small craft can make landings along virtually any stretch of beach to load or unload cargo of all types. The Texas Gulf Coast is emblematic of the problem facing all nations with ocean access. What is the probability of contraband or illegal immigrants coming ashore at any given point and how much effort is necessary to minimize the likelihood of those goods or people entering the economy?
3. A great deal of time and effort has been expended on detailing the cooperative nature of layered maritime defense. Considering all the components of this defense in depth — where is there the greatest vulnerability?

Chapter 5 Endnotes

1. Rodgers, W. L. (1937, 1964). *Greek and Roman naval warfare: A study of strategy, tactics, and ship design from Salamis (480 B.C.) to Actium (31 B.C.)*. Annapolis, MD: Naval Institute Press.

2. Mahan, A. T. (1890). *The Influence of Sea Power Upon History, 1660–1783*. Boston: Little, Brown, and Company, 9.

3. The United States Coast Guard maintains an extensive collection of historical documents readily available on its website. Among these documents are extensive histories. More on the USCG can be found at: http://www.uscg.mil/history/.

4. The *National Strategy for Maritime Security*, 2005. Washington, D.C.

5. The maritime domain is defined as all areas and things of, on, under, relating to, adjacent to, or bordering on a sea, ocean, or other navigable waterway, including all maritime-related activities, infrastructure, people, cargo, and vessels and other conveyances. Note: The maritime domain for the United States includes the Great Lakes and all navigable inland waterways such as the Mississippi River and the Intracoastal Waterway.

6. The National Strategy for Maritime Security is guided by the objectives and goals contained in the National Security Strategy and the National Strategy for Homeland Security. This strategy also draws upon the National Strategy for Combating Terrorism, the National Strategy to Combat Weapons of Mass Destruction, the National Strategy for the Physical Protection of Critical Infrastructure and Key Assets, the National Defense Strategy, the National Military Strategy, and the National Drug Control Strategy.

7. The *National Plan to Achieve Maritime Domain Awareness for the National Strategy for Maritime Security*, October 2005.

8. American Association of Port Authorities, Port Industry Statistics. Available: http://www.aapa-ports.org/Industry/content.cfm?ItemNumber=900&navItemNumber=551, Last accessed: July 16, 2017. 2016 information acquired from: http://aapa.files.cms-plus.com/Statistics/U.S.%20WATER-BORNE%20FOREIGN%20TRADE%202016%20BY%20U.S.%20CUSTOMS%20DISTRICT.xlsx. Last accessed: Oct. 21, 2017.

9. Interagency Task Force on Coast Guard Roles and Missions. A Coast Guard for the Twenty First Century: Report of the Interagency Task Force on U.S. Coast Guard Roles and Missions. December 1999. National Strategy for Maritime Security—Maritime Transportation System Security Recommendations, ii.

10. American Association of Port Authorities, U.S. Port Industry. Available: http://www.aapa-ports.org/Industry/content.cfm?ItemNumber=1022&navItemNumber=901, Last accessed: July 16, 2017.

11. National Strategy for Maritime Security—Maritime Transportation System Security Recommendations, October 2005, ii.

12. 33 CFR 101.105.

13. National Strategy for Maritime Security—The Maritime Infrastructure Recovery Plan, April 2006, 4.

14. National Strategy for Maritime Security—The Maritime Infrastructure Recovery Plan, April 2006, 8.

15. *Naval Operations Concept, 2010: Implementing the Maritime Strategy*, Preface.

16. The *National Strategy for Maritime Security*, 2005, ii.

Part Two

Border Security and Transnational Crime

"While organized crime is not a new phenomenon today, some governments find their authority besieged at home and their foreign policy interests imperiled abroad. Drug trafficking, links between drug traffickers and terrorists, smuggling of illegal aliens, massive financial and bank fraud, arms smuggling, potential involvement in the theft and sale of nuclear material, political intimidation, and corruption all constitute a poisonous brew—a mixture potentially as deadly as what we faced during the cold war."

—R. James Woolsey, Former Director of Central Intelligence

Every border crossing between the United States and Mexico has signs warning travelers to Mexico that carrying firearms or ammunition into Mexico is a crime punishable by imprisonment. Border security is a two-way street, with each country having its own primary concerns about what crosses into its country. James Phelps, 2013.

Chapter 6

Trafficking: Contraband, Smuggling, and the Law

"Forbid a man to think for himself or to act for himself and you may add the joy of piracy and the zest of smuggling to his life."

—Elbert Hubbard[1]

Key Words and Concepts

Antidumping
Contraband
Countervailing Duties
Fast and Furious

Poaching
Smuggling
Dumping

Introduction

Borders establish the point where one nation's laws end, and another's begin. This creates a boundary where what is legal on one side may be illegal on the other, where customary and religious practices by one group may be abhorrent to those living on the other side, where the benefits of an industrialized economy may not be equally shared with a neighbor. These conditions and others drive countries to establish laws and regulations that function to protect their existing cultural, political, economic, and religious interests from external influence. Those who want to profit or benefit from the differences between countries may try to work within the law, or, when faced with a cumbersome, coercive, corrupt, or simply

Elbert Hubbard (1856–1915).

inflexible system, find ways to circumvent the existing laws and regulations. Smuggling contraband is the process of circumventing these legal and regulatory barriers.

Contraband

Contraband is anything prohibited by law from being imported or exported. In a globalized world where virtually everything comes from somewhere else, or is assembled elsewhere, or is comprised of parts that originate in many different countries, how do you identify any particular item as being illegal or legal? What particular items should any given country determine to be contraband and under what conditions? The answers to these questions are economic and political.

> **Contraband:** Its most extensive sense means all commerce that is carried on contrary to the laws of the state. This term is also used to designate all kinds of merchandise that are used, or transported, against the interdictions published by a ban or solemn cry.[2]
>
> **Smuggling:** *The criminal offense of bringing into, or removing from, a country those items that are prohibited or upon which customs or excise duties have not been paid.* Smuggling is the secret movement of goods across national borders to avoid Customs Duties or import or export estrictions.[3]
>
> **Antidumping (AD) and Countervailing Duties (CVD):** Additional duties that may be assessed on imported goods intended for sale in the United States at abnormally low prices. These low prices are the result of unfair foreign trade practices that give some imports an unearned advantage over competing U.S. goods.[4]

If the country you live in has a manufacturing base, or is known for the high quality of the products it produces, then protecting those industries by limiting competition becomes important from both economic and political perspectives. Competing products or lower quality products produced at a lower price will undercut the foundation of your economic base as people will naturally tend to buy the less expensive item, even if it is known to be of some lower quality. This will reduce the demand for your existing production and subsequently reduce manufacturing output, or force a decrease in product quality to reduce cost and maintain competitiveness. Or companies may close due to an inability to compete. Any of these cases is a problem for your country.

If the importation of too many tires from China results in the closure of tire manufacturing plants in South Carolina, then lawmakers will restrict or prohibit the competing products. Not doing so will result in lowering the output of your manufacturing base. This results in a need for fewer employees, which leads to layoffs, increased unemployment, and a greater welfare burden on the state, which then must be carried by the still employed through payment of higher taxes. This process also

CBP K-9 officer runs a car selected for secondary exam. Photo by Gerald L Nino/CBP.gov.

affects the political system, as elected representatives who fail to protect their constituents' employment from competition will soon find themselves in the same category of being unemployed.

These are the fundamental reasons for lawmakers determining that importation of certain products and goods should be prohibited or restricted. An additional reason is the issue of morals. This is where societal standards and religious influence will impact the issue of prohibition and regulation of certain products and goods. If the consumption of narcotics is bad for individuals and society, then to protect society the importation of narcotics becomes a point of interest for lawmakers. If the sexual exploitation of children is considered anathema in a country, then the importation of child pornography should be made illegal. People who subsequently determine that the profit potential of smuggling narcotics or child pornography into a country is greater than the perceived risk associated with being caught will continue to transport such items across international boundaries.

Smuggling

When a person unintentionally has possession of goods the state has determined to be illegal or prohibited, and cannot adequately explain their presence, the person can be convicted of smuggling. Any person who is guilty of knowingly smuggling any goods that are prohibited by law or that should have come through customs, or who receives, buys, sells, transports, or aids in the commission of one of these acts can be charged with smuggling (a felony in the United States), and be assessed civil penalties. Not only can the government seize the merchandise, any vessel or vehicle used to transport the contraband can also be taken under forfeiture proceedings.

In circumventing the prohibitions against importing contraband into a country the smuggler has traditionally used two methods. One is to simply avoid entering a country at a regular border crossing. The other is to conceal the contraband in a conveyance and hope it remains undetected when passing through a regulated port of entry.

The History of Smuggling

Before the modern era of drug smuggling and human trafficking, smuggling had acquired a romanticism, if not heroism, among those locals who benefited from the act. Those who willfully worked to circumvent the high duties and taxes levied on imports and exports reaped not only high profits, but also the respect and admiration of their fellow smugglers and the communities that benefited from the trade. During the pre-drug smuggling and human trafficking days the purpose of smuggling was to circumvent the established trade policies of governments. Whether this stemmed from a rejection of the imposition of central taxation or from differences in religious beliefs between smugglers and the monarch was immaterial. The fundamental outcome was profit for the smuggler and loss of revenue for the government.

Smuggling is simply an illegal form of the import/export business. All countries have experienced smuggling of one kind or another throughout history. A Roman ship, dating to the third century CE, was discovered by Italian archaeologists at the entry of

the river Birgi, near the shore of Marausa Lido. The official cargo consisted of assorted jars filled with walnuts, figs, olives, wine, and oil. However, the archaeologists also discovered several small terracotta tubes with one pointed end. Roman builders used these tubes to support the vaulting then used in construction. Apparently, it was less expensive to purchase these terracotta tubes in Africa than to manufacture them in Italy and the poorly paid sailors were smuggling them into the Roman Empire as a means of supplementing their meager incomes.[5]

Smuggling is not just a Western phenomenon, but has a truly global flavor. In Southeast

Smugglers, Wikicommons, n.d.

Asia, the early civilizations did not have clear borders and boundaries but instead existed as a core of strong authority (mandalas), which then radiated outward in progressively weaker fashion until it simply stopped having authoritative control over peoples and populations. In addition to the larger empires, petty kingdoms often arose at the mouths of rivers where they exercised authority to tax products and goods that moved up and down the waterways. Both governmental structures led to smuggler activities to circumvent local control and taxation of profit.[6]

The narrow waters of the Straits of Malacca offered local governments the opportunity to establish numerous outposts on both the Sumatran and Malay Peninsula sides of the Straits, forcing shipping to submit to coercive taxation. By the seventh to the twelfth centuries, during the time of the Srivijaya Empire, merchant vessels attempted to circumvent such taxation. Similarly, the Malacca Sultanate, which succeeded Srivijaya, tried to lower customs to encourage higher trade volumes, yet due to the nature of the cargos transiting the area the smugglers continued to avoid taxation.[7] Eric Tagliacozzo notes:

> With the appearance of the Dutch on the scene in the seventeenth century, however, some of these patterns began to change. The V.O.C., or *Vereenigde Oost-ndische Compagnie* (Dutch East Indies Company), tried to ensure profits in its conquest of parts of the East Indies by enacting draconian policies of enforced monopoly, especially on the production and transit of spices. In Eastern Indonesia, particularly in Maluku (what used to be called the Moluccas, or Spice Islands), these policies included wholesale murder of the inhabitants of certain clove and nutmeg-producing islands, deportation, and armed surveillance over spice gardens, to ensure that the commodities were not smuggled out to the financial detriment of the Dutch monopoly. In Western Indonesia during the eighteenth and nineteenth centuries, repressive measures were also taken against the free trade of tin from Bangka and Belitung islands, which induced the inhabitants to try to sell their ores to passing English merchantmen and Chinese junks on the sly. Certain inlets and creeks outside Batavia, the Dutch Indies capital (modern-day Jakarta) were famed in Eastern waters as rendezvous points for smugglers. Some of the primary actors in these midnight liaisons, of course, were underpaid V.O.C. men themselves, bargaining within sight of the capital. The role of the state—or agents of the state—in defining and controlling contrabanding [sic], therefore, was always ambiguous at best. Corruption seems to be at least as old as smuggling or "states" in the region, and was entwined with the pursuit of power and wealth from a very early date.[8]

Smuggling in Southeast Asia was not limited to the Straits of Malacca, but also occurred in the Spanish Philippines, a vast island archipelago that was almost impossible to patrol, where Chinese junks conducted an extensive unregulated trade between mainland Asia and the surrounding islands. Additionally, the British colony in Burma found that smugglers moved great quantities of jade, serpentine, rubies, and emeralds to China rather than selling them to the Brits.[9]

In the west, the islands of Great Britain saw much smuggling to and from mainland Europe between 1300 CE and the twentieth century. The eighteenth century saw a prodigious increase in the amount of smuggling across England's coasts, growing into a sizable industry that syphoned money abroad and channeled huge volumes of contraband into southern England. A typical smuggling trip would bring upwards of three thousand gallons of spirits. In some areas, such as the Isles of Scilly, the population was totally dependent upon smugglers for survival. In other areas, such as Shetland and Falmouth, there was no available cash or coin because every available penny had been collected to fund a smuggling venture. There are even reported cases of whole communities rising and taking it upon themselves to recover contraband seized by government revenue agents.[10]

The increase in smuggling activities in Great Britain during the eighteenth and nineteenth centuries was the direct result of punitive taxation implemented to pay for a series of costly wars on the Continent and in the Americas. In 1809 the Preventive Waterguard [sic] was established using cutters and small rowing boats of the customs service. This provided more central control, and in conjunction with the establishment of coastal watchtowers, brought about greater anti-smuggling coordination. However, it was not until after the battle of Waterloo that a significant smuggling prevention effort was set up along the British coast. The Coast Blockade was instituted between North and South Foreland on the east Kent coast and accompanied by a land force commanded by Captain "Flogging" Joe McCulloch. However, the members of the Blockade were poorly paid and not very enthusiastic in their work and often took bribes in cash or contraband to simply be nonobservant. By 1831 the British Coast Guard established a blockade all the way around the coast and laid the foundations for the modern service in place today.[11]

In North America, there was also an ongoing smuggling venture. The Treaty of Utrecht in 1713 supposedly settled the boundaries of France and Great Britain. Unfortunately, the treaty failed to address several issues of boundaries with Spain. The result was that while, by treaty, the British could supply Spain's American empire with slaves and one annual shipload of goods, the British South Seas Company shamefully abused the privilege by constantly restocking its vessel with fresh goods and sending it back to Spain's new world possessions. Smuggling also was carried out by colonial interests and abetted by the Spanish Creoles, who needed colonial imports to survive. Spanish officials took umbrage to the blatant smuggling and enforced Spain's mercantilist system through the *guarda costa*. In the process of capturing and detaining smugglers, several were abused. In one case, Captain Jenkins, a British mariner, allegedly had his ear cut off.[12]

This led the British to dispatch an expedition under Admiral Vernon to capture the Spanish port of Porto Bello, followed by a more ambitious attack against Cartagena accompanied by members of the colonial militia. The War of Jenkins' Ear continued until 1742. Thus, a war between England and Spain in the Americas directly resulted over an issue of smuggling.[13]

After American independence in 1783, smuggling developed at the edges of the United States at places like Passamaquoddy Bay in New Brunswick and Maine, St. Mary's in Georgia, Lake Champlain in New York, Vermont, and Quebec, and Louisiana.

During Thomas Jefferson's embargo of 1807–9, these same places became the primary locations where goods were smuggled out of the nation in defiance of the law. Like Britain, a gradual liberalization of trade laws as part of the free trade movement meant less smuggling. In 1907 President Theodore Roosevelt tried to cut down on smuggling by establishing the Roosevelt Reservation along the United States–Mexico border.[14] The Prohibition Era saw a revival in smuggling, and following the repeal of the Eighteenth Amendment to the Constitution by the Twenty-First Amendment on December 5, 1933, smugglers turned to drug smuggling, which developed into a major issue for the United States by 1970.

The United States, United Nations, and other individual and groups of countries have attempted to use economic sanctions to influence politics and wars. Of course, anytime a restriction is placed on import or export of goods to or from a certain country, smugglers will take advantage of the situation. In the 1990s, when the United States and the UN imposed economic sanctions on Serbia, a large percentage of the Serbian population lived off smuggling petrol and consumer goods from neighboring countries. The Serb government unofficially allowed this to continue or otherwise the entire economy would have collapsed. Similarly, as sanctions were placed and tightened on Iran to drive the country into a situation where it would give up a perceived quest for nuclear weapons, a massive (and ignored) trucking industry has arisen in Iraq, shipping both bulk oil and refined gasoline into Iran on a scale dwarfing the Allied supply chains of the Second World War.

In modern times, as many first-world countries have struggled to contain a rising influx of immigrants, the smuggling of people across national borders has become a lucrative extra-legal activity. The dark side, human trafficking, has become concerning for the world community, especially the trafficking of women who may be enslaved, typically as prostitutes.

Baggage Surprises

If cicadas, the inch-long winged insects with red, beady eyes, recently invading the Eastern seaboard, give you the willies, or if your reaction to tripe is Eeeuuw, then don't read any further. U.S. Customs and Border Protection officers and agriculture specialists are trained to look for goods that are prohibited from entering the United States. But they also need traits that aren't listed as job requirements, like an unflappable nature and a strong stomach.

It is almost impossible to imagine the assortment of things, and the methods travelers' employ to bring in their special brand of contraband. As CBP officers and agriculture specialists look through baggage, they expect to find the usual: swimsuits, sweaters, snakes, pants, parrots, and toiletries. Wait a minute—snakes and parrots?

Wildlife, dead or alive, is popular contraband and is brought into the United States for any number of reasons. Birds, lizards and snakes top the list, but bats, snails and anteaters are not uncommon. While the U.S. Department of Agriculture's

(USDA), Veterinarian Services; U.S. Fish and Wildlife Service; and the Public Health Service have responsibilities for establishing policy regarding wildlife or meat importation, CBP officers and agricultural specialists may be the first to find these illegal imports.

Though the prestige of having a unique pet or specimen drives some, money is the ultimate force behind the wildlife trade on the black market. Importing wildlife is extremely lucrative, and many believe it ranks second in profits only to illegal drug traffic. For example, a bird caught in the rain forest and sold there is worth $20, but that same bird sells for $2,000 to $4,000 in the United States.

Why Regulate?

Regulating the importation of wildlife isn't just an effort to stymie hobbyists. It's intended to keep our livestock and crops safe from contamination by non-indigenous diseases or pests, protect endangered species, and prevent invasive species from entering our country. Controls also exist to preserve the public health.

Wild birds can bring in diseases that are unknown to our geographic area. Exotic Newcastle disease, a highly contagious virus, can spread quickly to poultry and caged birds. Because of their vulnerability to this virus, one infected bird can spread the disease rapidly to others in proximity and then from location to location. From 1971 to 1974, there was an outbreak of exotic Newcastle disease in southern California, which resulted in the destruction of 12 million birds and cost U.S. taxpayers $56 million to eradicate. USDA epidemiologists studying the disease traced these outbreaks directly to smuggled birds.

Outbreaks of monkey pox and severe acute respiratory syndrome (SARS), both of which can be transmitted from animals to humans, have focused public attention on the health issues that can result from illegal importations. In addition, uncontrolled harvesting of wildlife can have an environmental impact—trees are cut down and nesting areas destroyed resulting in permanent destruction of the habitats.

Ants in Your Pants? Or Is It Monkeys?

Take the case of Californian Robert Cusack. While undergoing a routine inspection at Los Angeles International Airport, a CBP officer opened Cusack's suitcase. Imagine the surprise when a bird of paradise flew out. Careful examination found three more birds slipped inside nylon stockings and 50 orchids of an endangered species.

When asked if there was anything else, he volunteered, "Yes, I've got monkeys in my pants." And indeed, Cusack had a pair of pygmy monkeys inside his pant legs. Cusack defended his actions by saying he was a concerned environmentalist who had purchased the animals in Jakarta, Indonesia and was taking them to a Costa Rican wildlife sanctuary. Nonetheless, he was arrested for smuggling.

Smugglers try every trick in the book to bring in their illicit cargo. Airport x-ray systems have made it harder to smuggle birds and reptiles in baggage or cargo, so smugglers use couriers to move their contraband traffic. Eggs of rare macaws, the largest breed of parrot, can be hidden in a vest or a pocket. Once these eggs, worth several thousand dollars each, reach their destination, it is impossible to tell if they came from a legal captive bird or a wild one.

Stories abound. Fish smuggled in gas tanks of vehicles, reptiles wrapped and taped around a person, birds drugged with their beaks and feet taped in PVC pipes in a suitcase, and the list goes on. Craig Hoover, the Deputy Director of the North America office of TRAFFIC, an organization that monitors trade in wild animals and animal products, says, "I've seen everything ... birds stuffed in tennis ball cans, inserted into false compartments in vehicles. I had someone try to smuggle a live toucan taped to the small of his back. There have been examples of primates—small monkeys—smuggled inside hand luggage."

Grandpa's Family Sausage Recipe

Contraband may also be food (bush meat) or animal parts used for religious rituals or medicinal purposes. Travelers carrying the head of an anteater, a tiger, lizard, or rodents in their luggage may be bringing in for friends and family what is considered a delicacy in their country. In fact, non-English-speaking travelers may go to great lengths to show that something they are carrying is food. Jose Estrada, a CBP officer in Baltimore, says, "Travelers who bring in smoked bats will eat them right in front of you to make the point that they are food and thus will not harm anything." Animals and animal parts are also used as medicines— tiger and rhino skeletons are ground up and used in traditional Chinese medicines, and animal parts hold a place in rituals for many cults and religions practiced around the world.

CBP officers and agriculture specialists must use diplomacy and sensitivity in their interaction with the traveling public. James M. Armstrong, a 13-year veteran of the USDA and now a CBP port canine coordinator for agriculture detector dogs at JFK International Airport, says, "Most passengers bringing in food or meat products are not smugglers and have innocent motives. In our interaction with passengers, we have to be sensitive to the value of food. We confiscate a sausage because it could bring in the organism that causes hog cholera, but for the passenger, it is more than just a sausage. That sausage is granddad's recipe and uses apples from a generations old family orchard. It represents culture and tradition, areas charged with emotion."

Whether it is a monkey peeping out from a passenger's coat, a suitcase full of sheep entrails, or a couple of oranges from the family orchard, CBP officers and agriculture specialists must be steadfast as they protect our agriculture, our livestock and our health from purposeful or inadvertent contamination.

From Customs and Border Protection TODAY, July/August 2004[15]

The Law

Countries have established many regulatory agencies to address virtually every type of commodity as importable, prohibited, or importable with a permit (or following quarantine). The same system is instituted for exported items. Listing the items that are regulated or prohibited would take several volumes of books this size and once listed, would change before the publisher could get the print copies distributed. In today's world, even listing the various international conventions that regulate commerce would be a daunting task and both are beyond the scope of this chapter. Besides, with every session of Congress, and every change in which nations are considered "friendly" versus "nonfriendly" to a country, the list of acceptable products and their quantitative limitations changes.

Importing to the United States: A Guide for Commercial Importers[16] provides a 211-page reference of materials and conventions that importers must comply with should they desire to bring items to the United States. When consulting this list, it becomes obvious why some people simply choose not to go through the paperwork necessary to legally import their products. For many manufacturers, it would be less costly to lose a load or two of product than to comply with the legal requirements for importation. The Guide also provides a list and contact information of thirty-seven federal agencies and subagencies with regulatory or criminal jurisdiction over the various imports that are restricted or prohibited.

You may think that it can't be that difficult to comply with the law and legally bring into the United States relatively common items that you use every day. Consider the following requirements for information that must be provided on the invoice for Cotton Fabrics and Yarns imported to the United States:

> **Cotton fabrics** classifiable under the following HTSUS headings: 5208, 5209, 5210, 5211, and 5212 — (1) Marks on shipping packages; (2) Numbers on shipping packages; (3) Customer's call number, if any; (4) Exact width of the merchandise; (5) Detailed description of the merchandise; trade name, if any; whether bleached, unbleached, printed, composed of yarns of different color, or dyed; if composed of cotton and other materials, state the percentage of each component material by weight; (6) Number of single threads per square centimeter (All ply yarns must be counted in accordance with the number of single threads contained in the yarn; to illustrate: a cloth containing 100 two-ply yarns in one square centimeter must be reported as 200 single thread); (7) Exact weight per square meter in grams; (8) Average yarn number use this formula:
>
> $$\frac{100 \times (\text{total single yarns per square centimeter})}{(\text{number of grams per square meter})}$$
>
> (9) Yarn size or sizes in the warp; (10) Yarn size or sizes in the filling; (11) Specify whether the yarns are combed or carded; (12) Number of colors or kinds (different yarn sizes or materials) in the filling; (13) Specify whether the fabric is napped or not napped; and (14) Specify the type of weave, for example, plain, twill, sateen, oxford, etc., and (15) Specify the type of machine on which woven: if with Jacquard (Jacq), if with Swivel (Swiv), if with Lappet (Lpt.), if with Dobby (Dobby).[17]
>
> **Yarns** — (1) All yarn invoices should show: (a) fiber content by weight; (b) whether single or plied; (c) whether or not put up for retail sale (See Section Xl, Note 4, HTSUS); (d) whether or not intended for use as sewing thread.
>
> (2) If chief weight of silk, show whether spun or filament.

   (3) If chief weight of cotton, show:
      (a) whether combed or uncombed
      (b) metric number (mn)
      (c) whether bleached and/or mercerized.
   (4) If chief weight of manmade fiber, show:
      (a) whether filament, or spun, or a combination of filament and spun
      (b) If a combination of filament and spun — give percentage of filament and spun by weight.
   (5) If chief weight of filament manmade fiber, show:
      (a) whether high tenacity (See Section Xl, note 6 HTSUS)
      (b) whether monofilament, multifilament, or strip
      (c) whether texturized
      (d) yarn number in decitex
      (e) number of turns per meter
      (f) for monofilaments — show cross-sectional dimension in millimeters
      (g) for strips, show the width of the strip in millimeters (measure in folded or twisted condition if so imported)[18]

What if the product being imported comes from a country that is part of an international trade organization, convention, or free trade agreement? Then each of the various regulations and statutes associated with the product being imported must also comply with the mandates of those agreements and treaties. A short list of common agreements and free trade agreements as of the 2014 CBP publication *Importing to the United States: A Guide for Commercial Importers* includes:[19]

- North American Free Trade Agreement (NAFTA)
- Generalized System of Preferences (GSP)
- Caribbean Basin Initiative (CBI)
- Caribbean Basin Economic Recovery Act (CBERA)
- Andean Trade Preference Act (ATPA)
- Andean Trade Promotion and Drug Eradication Act (ATPDEA)
- U.S.-Israel Free Trade Area Agreement
- U.S.-Jordan Free Trade Area Agreement
- Compact of Free Association (FAS)
- African Growth and Opportunity Act (AGOA)
- U.S.-Caribbean Basin Trade Partnership Act (CBTPA)
- U.S.-Chile Free Trade Agreement (US-CFTA)
- U.S.-Singapore Free Trade Agreement

However, it should be obvious that the system in place to allow import and export of various products has been streamlined. In El Paso, Texas, on average 1,800 truckloads of goods enter the United States from Mexico each day. This is in addition to the eight or more trains carrying goods that also cross the border. Lest we forget, there are hundreds of thousands of people who cross between Ciudad Juarez and El Paso each day. While the laws on importation and exportation may be exacting, once an importer or exporter establishes a system to comply with the various regulations and reporting requirements, the system does tend to function in a relatively smooth manner. The primary concern of customs inspectors then becomes the issue of contraband items being secreted within an otherwise legal shipment. The major concerns are narcotics, insects and other biological threats to agriculture, weapons of mass destruction, trafficked humans, and the dumping of regulated merchandise.

Dumping and Antidumping

Dumping is the practice of trying to sell products in the United States at lower prices than those same products would bring in the producer's home market. Dumping also includes trying to sell a product in the United States at a price lower than it cost to manufacture that item. Subsidizing is the practice by some governments of providing financial assistance to reduce manufacturers' costs in producing, manufacturing, or exporting specific commodities. Countervailing duties may be assessed to "level the playing field" between domestic and subsidized imported goods. However, to meet the criteria for assessing antidumping or countervailing duties, the imported merchandise must, in addition to being subsidized or sold at less than fair value, also injure a US industry.[20] The Department of Commerce, the International Trade Commission (ITC), and US Customs and Border Protection each have a role in administering and enforcing antidumping and countervailing duty laws.

The Commerce Department is responsible for the general administration of these laws. Commerce determines whether the merchandise is being sold at less than fair value, whether it has been subsidized, and what percentage rate of duty will be assessed. The ITC determines whether the product poses an injury[21] to a specific US industry. CBP assesses the actual duties — the amount — based upon the rate set by the Commerce Department once the ITC has determined that the import injures a certain industry.

In general, the following processes must be completed before antidumping or countervailing duties are established. Antidumping and countervailing duty investigations are usually initiated by the Commerce Department through the petition process. A domestic industry or another interested party such as a trade union or industry association petitions the department, although occasionally the Commerce Department may also initiate an investigation. If the party seeking the investigation also wants the ITC to test for injury, that party must simultaneously — on the same day — file the petition with both the Commerce Department and with the ITC.

If the petition contains the necessary elements, the Commerce Department and the ITC will initiate separate investigations that yield preliminary and final determinations. If appropriate, the Department of Commerce issues either an antidumping or countervailing duty order and assesses whatever antidumping or countervailing duties the investigation determines are appropriate.

If a test is required for injury to a domestic industry, the ITC makes the first, preliminary determination concerning the likelihood of injury. If that determination is negative, there will be no further investigation or action by the ITC. If it is affirmative, however, the Commerce Department issues its preliminary determination regarding sales (antidumping) or subsidy (countervailing duties) issues.

After additional review by the Commerce Department and analysis of public comments received in the case, Commerce issues its final duty determinations. If either determination (antidumping or countervailing duties) is affirmative, Commerce directs CBP to suspend liquidation of entries for the merchandise subject to the investigation and to require cash deposits or bonds equal to the amount of the estimated dumping margin (the differential between the fair market value and the US price) or the net subsidy.

After this step, the ITC follows with its final injury determination. If this determination is also affirmative, Commerce issues an antidumping or countervailing duty order. At that time, Commerce directs CBP to collect, with a very limited exception for new shippers, cash deposits of estimated duties.

A negative final determination either by Commerce or the ITC would terminate the investigations, and that termination would remain final for this inquiry. Both agencies announce their determinations, including orders and the results of the administration reviews (described below), in the Federal Register.

Each year during the anniversary month of the antidumping or countervailing duties order, interested parties may review the order with respect to the individual producers or resellers it covers. This review generally looks at the twelve months preceding the anniversary month, but the first review can also include any period for which the suspension of liquidations was directed prior to the normal twelve-month period.

If no annual review is requested, Commerce directs CBP to continue collecting deposits and assessing duties on the subject merchandise at the cash or bond rate in effect on the date of entry, and to continue requiring deposits at that rate for future entries of such merchandise. If a review is requested, Commerce conducts a review comparable to its original investigation, issues revised rates for duty assessment and deposits, and instructs CBP to collect duties and liquidate entries per the results of its latest review.

At this point, you should be totally lost! That's okay, because the overall process also confuses the chapter's author. What is important to remember is that there are processes in place to address the issue of "dumping" products on a market by foreign competition. There are experts who deal with these issues every day from the manufacturing and agricultural industries as well as within the Government. As with most issues dealing with the law, it is often best to let lawyers and accountants handle the issue.

Smuggling Today

Smuggling is big business and the profits are considerable. Throughout history one problem with measuring smuggling has been that the only accurate numbers governments must work with are the people who are caught. If you catch one hundred

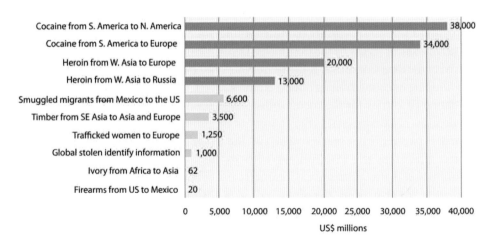

Cocaine from S. America to N. America	38,000
Cocaine from S. America to Europe	34,000
Heroin from W. Asia to Europe	20,000
Heroin from W. Asia to Russia	13,000
Smuggled migrants from Mexico to the US	6,600
Timber from SE Asia to Asia and Europe	3,500
Trafficked women to Europe	1,250
Global stolen identify information	1,000
Ivory from Africa to Asia	62
Firearms from US to Mexico	20

US$ millions

Estimated values of selected transnational trafficking flows, 2008. Source: UNODC.

cocaine shipments, and the street price does not increase, then have you made any real impact on the supply of product to the consumers? Probably not. However, if the street price of cocaine begins to rise, then the interdiction efforts may have had an impact. The same can be said for any contraband.

There is one major change being experienced in the smuggling of contraband that has become problematic in the United States. Illegal migrants are now being coerced by the Mexican drug cartels into being drug mules in partial payment for being allowed to cross certain areas of Mexico, or for coyotes (paid cartel guides) to guide them across remote areas of the Southwest. This creates a situation where the illegal migrant is now no longer considered a person returnable to their country of origin, but drug traffickers subject to long prison sentences if caught.

As always, smugglers will shift their efforts from one location to another based on the interdiction efforts of the violated country. The numbers of migrants apprehended at the US borders between 1999 and 2016 demonstrates that in addition to responding to changes in interdiction efforts, the illegal movement of humans across national boundaries is also dependent upon the demand for labor, economic conditions in the receiving country, economic conditions in the country of origin, and perceived chances of being released, if detained at the border. According to the American Immigration Lawyers Association, "With the end of 'catch and release,' the past decade has seen record-high levels in immigration detention. In 2006, when 'catch and release' was formally ended by the Bush Administration, DHS detained, on average, 21,450 migrants daily. The *daily number of detainees has grown steadily* under the Obama Administration, and in July 2016 the average number of people *detained for immigration purposes* reached a high of 37,350—an increase of 74 percent since the end of 'catch and release.'" This is a typical political statement and not based in fact. Over the fiscal year periods 2010 to 2015 the US Border Patrol apprehended more than one million illegal migrants. With the exception of a few thousand, all were provided with an I-9 immigration document and approval to seek work permits under an Obama executive policy, and released to the interior of the United States. Less than 10 percent of these illegal migrants could be contacted for their federal immigration hearings and even fewer showed up for their court dates. Therefore, while 37,000 plus may have been detained as criminal aliens, illegal re-entries, or known gang/cartel members, the release of more than one million unknown persons to the interior of the United States is a much more significant number that the government didn't report.

Lobsters smuggled from Mexico. Seized by U.S. Border Patrol in the Chula Vista Sector, California. © US Border Patrol Museum. Used with permission.

Another change between ancient and modern smuggling is the contraband. Today, with recognition of the number of nearly extinct plants and animals being on the rise, the world's nations have come together to restrict the harvesting of sensitive species. This requires an expanded presence of investigators with specific training in identifying unique items such as sperm whale teeth, elephant ivory, and wildlife parts. One example is Charles Manghis, age 54, of Nantucket, Massachusetts, who was convicted in January 2010 for "one count of conspiracy to smuggle wildlife, six substantive counts of smuggling wildlife and two counts of making false statements to federal agents." Manghis, a commercial scrimshaw artist—artistically etching ivory pieces—was using eBay to purchase raw materials from suppliers outside of the United States. His case was investigated by NOAA, Office of Law Enforcement, US Fish and Wildlife Service, Office of Law Enforcement, and Immigration and Customs Enforcement in conjunction with the Nantucket Police Department and the Massachusetts Environmental Police in what Acting US Attorney Jack Pirrozolo commented was "a fine example of multi-agency cooperation focused on the reduction and elimination of this illegal trafficking."[22]

Other recent cases of unique smuggling include the illegal importation of spiny lobster and queen conch from the Bahamas, avian influenza virus, lobster tails from Honduras, farm raised Asian catfish, Lake Victoria perch, foreign farm-raised shrimp, baby leopard sharks, and stony corals. The US Customs and Border Protection office maintains a Know Before You Go website that lists common items sold to US tourists that are prohibited from importation into the country. The list is extensive and includes items specified under the following categories:[23]

Absinthe (Alcohol)	Dog and Cat Fur
Alcoholic Beverages	Drug Paraphernalia
Automobiles	Firearms
Biologicals	Fish and Wildlife
Ceramic Tableware	Food Products (Prepared)
Cultural Artifacts and Cultural Property	Prior Notice for Food Importation
Defense Articles or Items with Military	Fruits and Vegetables
or Proliferation Applications	Game and Hunting Trophies

Gold	Pets
Haitian Animal Hide Drums	Plants and Seeds
Meats, Livestock and Poultry	Soil
Medication	Textiles and Clothing
Merchandise from Embargoed Countries	Trademarked and Copyrighted Articles

The products CBP officers prevent from entering the United States are those that would injure community health, public safety, American workers, children, or domestic plant and animal life, or those that would defeat national interests. Sometimes the products that cause injury, or have the potential to do so, may seem innocent. As is identified in the descriptive information on the CBP website, appearances can be deceiving.

On an international scale, there are other major smuggling concerns. The trafficking of endangered species is of particular importance, particularly elephant ivory and rhinoceros horn. Traditional Chinese medicine touts rhinoceros horn as a cure for fevers and seizures (both unproven). This has created a situation where poachers kill rhinos for their horns. Law and convention in all countries prohibit the trafficking of rhino horn, and yet, the continued demand for the item has driven every species of rhinoceros to the brink of extinction. As of August 31, 2016, a total of 414 rhino poachers had been arrested in South Africa since January 1, 2016. This indicates that rhino poaching is on track to match previous years. In 2014, 1,215 rhinos were killed, an increase from the 1,004 poached in 2013.

Department of Environmental Affairs

Republic of South Africa
11 September 2016
Media Release

Between January and the end of August 2016, a total number of 458 poached rhino carcasses were found in the KNP, compared to 557 in the same period last year. This represents a 17.8% decline in the number of rhino carcasses.

Poaching rates, i.e., the number of carcasses as a percentage of the number of live rhinos estimated the previous September for each year, reduced by 15.5% compared between the same periods in 2015 (9.6% poaching rate) and 2016 (7.9% poaching rate).

These figures come amidst a 27.87 % increase in the number of illegal incursions into the KNP—a staggering 2,115 for the first eight months of 2016.

Nationally, 702 rhino were poached since the beginning of 2016 whereas between January and July 2015, a total of 796 rhinos were poached.

There may be indications however that the success of anti-poaching efforts in the KNP has led to poaching syndicates shifting operations to other provinces.

In the period under review, the number of rhino poached has increased in a number of other provinces in comparison to the same period in 2015, such as Kwa-Zulu/Natal, Free State and the Northern Cape.

However, despite these increases there is still a downward trend in the number of rhino poached.

It is also of concern that we have also begun experiencing an increase in elephant poaching, despite the vigorous and determined efforts by our rangers, the police and soldiers on the ground. Since January 36 elephants have been poached in the KNP.

"We are utilising our experience and expertise gained through our efforts to combat rhino poaching to end elephant poaching as well," the Minister said.

"What is evident, is that these successes can be attributed to the work being done on the ground by our people, our hardworking law-enforcement teams and our rangers in particular," says Minister Molewa.

The combined efforts of DEA, law-enforcement and the conservation agencies—with the support of international partners and donors, are slowly but steadily making a dent in the rhino poaching numbers.[24]

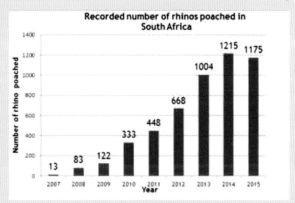

Graph showing South African rhino poaching statistics using data published by South African Department of Environmental Affairs (2016).

Another animal nearly driven to extinction is the African Elephant. Elephant tusks are ivory, and are highly prized as decorative pieces. The primary demand is in China, where artisans create some of the most beautiful carved works. The demand for these carved works has resulted in an increase in elephant poaching, which has decimated many of the herds throughout Africa. According to the World Wildlife Foundation, in the 1980s an estimated 100,000 elephants were being killed per year. In 1989 the Convention on International Trade in Endangered Species of Wild Fauna and Flora placed an international ban on trade in elephant ivory. This has not stopped poachers from killing elephants across Africa. At the beginning of 2017 there are only 400,000 elephants remaining in all of sub-Saharan Africa. From 2006 to 2011 there was a steady increase in the numbers of elephants poached. That number is now on a slow decline. From 2003 to 2015 there were 14,606 poached elephant carcasses identified in 29 African states. While some wildlife protection groups estimate poachers have killed as many as 36,000 elephants in  2009 alone, such numbers are uncorroborated and cannot be supported by wildlife managers. As with all smuggling operations, we can only estimate the amount of smuggling based on what is seized in shipment, and, in the case of rhinos and elephants, the numbers of dead animals identified by wildlife managers as non-natural deaths.

Smuggling is also a major concern for the countries of the European Union. In the economic downturn from 2008 to 2012 there was a significant increase in the smuggling of cigarettes and other tobacco products into the EU. Law enforcement agencies in the EU seized 4.7 billion illicit cigarettes in 2009.[25] Sources of the illegal cigarettes are Moldova, Ukraine, Belarus, and Russia and many of the cigarettes are counterfeits of branded products. In 2010, Phillip Morris International Management S.A., a major cigarette manufacturer, commissioned KPMG LLC to conduct a study of the cigarette smuggling problem in the EU. The KPMG report, issued in August 2011, reported that 64.2 billion counterfeit and contraband cigarettes were imported to the EU in 2010. Non-EU countries accounted for 60.8 percent of the counterfeit and contraband cigarettes, up 4.7 percent from 2009.[26] In Slovakia the police discovered a 2,300-foot long tunnel under the border with neighboring Ukraine. The tunnel had its own rail system and was quite sophisticated in construction. The tunnel contributed to the loss of upwards of 50 million euros ($60 million) in tobacco taxes.[27] The KPMG 2015 report, issued in 2016, showed additional changes to tobacco smuggling in the EU. This most recent study showed that about 10% total cigarette consumption in the EU, or about 53 billion cigarettes, consisted of counterfeit and contraband cigarettes. This resulted in about €11.3 billion in tax revenues.[28]

Counterfeit cigarettes are not the only problem in the European Union. The magnitude of the smuggling and counterfeiting problem faced by the EU can be clearly seen in the following charts and graphs generated from the United Nations Office of Drug Control, United States Border Patrol, the United States Department of State, and other data sources.

COUNTERFIT SEIZURES MADE AT THE EUROPEAN BORDERS BY PRODUCT TYPE (NUMBER OF INCIDENTS), 2008

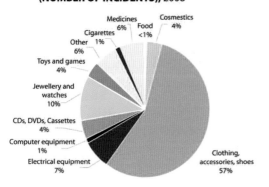

COUNTERFIT ITEMS SEIZED ENTERING THE EU BY MEANS OF CONVEYANCE, 2008

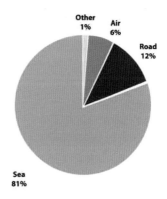

ORIGIN OF COUNTERFIT GOODS SEIZED AT THE EUROPEAN CUSTOMS UNION BORDER, 2008

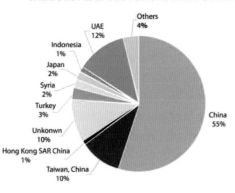

Source: UNODC & European Commission.

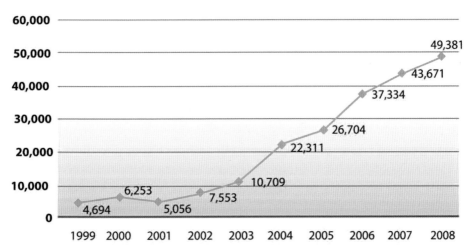

Attempts to import counterfeit goods detected at the European customs union border, 1999–2008. Source: UNODC & European Commission.

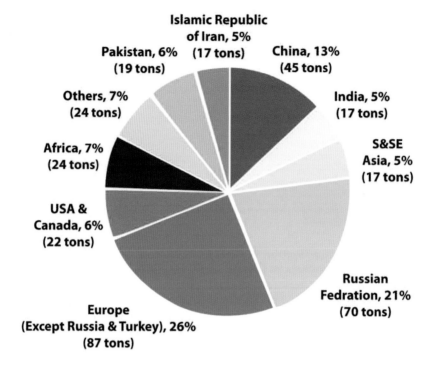

Global heroin consumption (340 tons), 2008 (share of countries/regions). Source: UNODC.

High taxation is the fundamental issue driving smuggling into the European Union. Member countries are required to tax certain products at rates so high that purchasing the same product in a non-member country offers not only a cost savings to the purchaser, but the opportunity to sell that product in the EU country for a considerable profit as part of the underground economy, or "black market." A clear example is the issue of gasoline smuggling in the EU countries of Latvia and Estonia, which border Russia. Per Urmas Koidu, head of Estonian customs, approximately 12 million liters of cheap Russian gasoline is smuggled into Estonia every year, resulting in a loss of 5.8 million euros in tax revenue annually.[29] The economic impact on Estonia is so great that a major anti-smuggling effort has been undertaken to stop gasoline smuggling.

Estonia and the other Baltic nations are now facing an even more dangerous threat from their neighbor than the smuggling of gasoline. Apparently, per European sources, Russia kidnapped Eston Kohver, a security officer, from Estonian territory in August 2014 and subsequently tried him for espionage.[30] Facing additional concerns about the nearly unguarded borders with Russia, Estonia and Latvia are clearing forest land and opening border regions so they can construct fences, some significant, others more to prevent the bypassing of border control stations. Additionally, Poland is constructing improved, high-tech watchtowers on its border with Russia's Kaliningrad, to the tune of 3.5 million Euros.[31]

Due to interior economic problems, Russia has been cracking down on what are called Black Workers—those non-Russians who are working in the country without documentation, much like the illegal workers the United States encounters. Thus, large numbers of Vietnamese are finding themselves without work and are paying smugglers to get them into EU countries. In the first eight months of 2015, "Latvian border guards detained 220 Vietnamese nationals ... [71] requested asylum and 147"[32] were expelled. Ninety-eight had been detained in 2014. The expulsions have cost Latvia more than 1,000 Euros per person to expel as they had expended their funds from the European Commission's European Return Fund.[33]

Another modern smuggling issue is the one of guns into Mexico. The Mexican government requested United States Bureau of Alcohol, Tobacco, Firearms, and Explosives (BATFE) traces on 99,691 firearms between January 1, 2007, and December 31, 2011. Of those that could be traced, 69.72 percent originate in the United States. Interestingly, between January 2007 and December 2011, only 27,825 (27.9 percent) of the requested traces could be traced to private sales in the United States. The rest came from unknown sources or other countries.[34] Mexico's CESOP governmental research service estimates 2,000 weapons illegally entered Mexico from the United States every day in 2015. The report also states that some 40 percent of firearms used by drug traffickers in Mexico come from Texas. While the report accuses the United States as the primary source for illegal firearms in Mexico, it neglects to report on Mexican security forces, which InSight Crime found in their 2011 study to be the primary source of black market weapons. Additionally, the CESOP report provides no basis for its claim that 2,000 illegal firearms enter Mexico daily from the United States.[35] According to narco-blogs, about half the firearms they acquire are "diverted" from official shipments to the Mexican government by corrupt officials and cartel members. From earlier reports, those firearms seized in 2004 that are traceable to private sales within the United States have been mapped to a variety of locations. It is important to note that the BATFE offers a disclaimer at the beginning of their statistical report noting that "Not all firearms used in crime are traced and not all firearms traced are used in crime."[36]

It was these earlier tracing efforts that led to the *Fast and Furious* program by the BATFE to allow the sale of firearms to persons prohibited from owing firearms in an attempt to trace the guns to the cartel leadership. Not only was *Fast and Furious* a failure, not a single cartel leader has ever been tied to one of the sold firearms, but several of the firearms have shown up on crime scenes where US federal law enforcement agents were killed. Part of the fallout over *Fast and Furious* was the US House of Representatives holding US Attorney General Eric Holder in contempt of Congress on June 28, 2012, for his failure to turn over documents requested by a Congressional committee. This was the first ever move by Congress against a sitting Cabinet official.[37] The vote to hold Attorney General Eric Holder in contempt was 255–67 and forced President Barack Obama to invoke Executive Privilege to block compliance with a Congressional subpoena.[38]

Narcotics smuggling is another highly profitable enterprise. The specifics on smuggling of drugs are beyond the scope of this text and there are many very good books on the subject. Drug smuggling has an impact on every country involved, from point of origin to the end consumer. The UNODC reported that in 2008 the worldwide

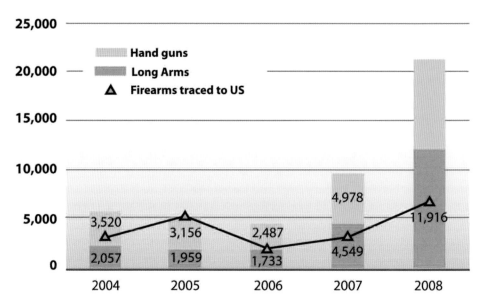

Number of firearms seized in Mexico by federal authorities versus firearms traced to the United States from all sources, 2004–2008. Source: UNODC & Attorney General of Mexico.

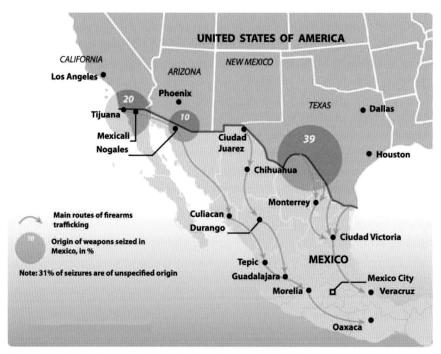

Firearms trafficking from the USA to Mexico. Source: UNODC & Attorney General of Mexico, United States Accountability Office.

consumption of heroin reached 340 tons. Heroin, a derivative of opium, has its primary origins in Afghanistan, the "Golden Triangle" of Myanmar, Thailand, and Cambodia, and in Mexico. When the countries and regions that consume heroin are evaluated, the smuggling routes are easy to imagine.

Another major issue associated with smuggling is the trafficking of humans. Worldwide humans are trafficked for labor, as forced brides, and for sex. The traffickers do not discriminate by age, gender, or race and virtually every country has some form of modern slavery. This topic is of such a concern that we have dedicated an entire chapter to it.

Conclusion

Smuggling has been occurring since humans established import and export restrictions or taxed goods sold in any city or state, from the most ancient of times. Smugglers take advantage of the profit potential that results when countries try to restrict the free exchange of commodities based on market values. Laws and other regulations are instituted to protect domestic manufacturing interests, safety of the population, and for reasons of political policy to help or hinder economics in other countries. Much of the worldwide smuggling effort is tied to attempts to circumvent high taxes on certain commodities or to supply a demand for illicit products, such as narcotics. Smuggling affects every country. Wherever there is a border, there is smuggling. Whether the attempt is to transport rhino horn to a Chinese traditional medicine shop, or to deliver young girls and boys to brothels in South East Asia for use in the international sex trade, it is all smuggling.

Anything of value can be declared contraband by a country for any number of reasons. Throughout history, all manner of items have been illegal to import, export, or possess, from narcotics to French cheese to English wool to Chinese tires to exotic and endangered species of animals and plants. In many cases, the only reason certain animals such as sea turtles, rhinoceros, African elephants, cheetahs, Siberian tigers, panda bears, and coral reefs have not been driven to extinction is because of the concerted and focused efforts of the international community to fight smuggling of tortoise shell, ivory, animal skins, and corals. It is through this continuing effort of the world's customs inspectors that smuggling is detected and prevented.

A wide variety of organizations, governmental and nongovernmental alike, report statistics on smuggling. It is important to note that a great deal of local, national, and international politics determine which sources are reported, estimated, and the origins of the data used to develop statistics on smuggling. Not all information, claims, and shocking reports are based in reality, and statistics have been used throughout history to support or deny particular political goals or the motivations of a nongovernment agency. We do not know the extent of smuggling of any given product anywhere in the world. It is only possible to ESTIMATE the quantities of smuggled goods and persons based on what is seized in transit, and the corresponding changes in price for the goods that do get through the gauntlet of agencies working to prevent smuggling. Clearly, this is a very imprecise system of measurement leaving much open to interpretation.

Questions for Further Consideration

1. In a globalized world where virtually everything comes from somewhere else, or is assembled elsewhere, or is composed of parts that originate in many different countries, how do you identify any particular item as being illegal or legal? What particular items should any given country determine to be contraband and under what conditions?

2. If you catch one hundred cocaine shipments, and the street price does not increase, then have you made any real impact on the supply of product to the consumers?

3. RFID tagging is used in almost everything today. If you could insert an RFID tag into the stock of an AK-47 type rifle, then you could use electronic detection equipment to follow that RFID tag where ever it went — thereby allowing you to track the rifle. Fast and Furious was a major mistake by the BATFE primarily because they didn't use technology, they depended on tracking the humans who were straw buyers of the guns. If the BATFE had been using RFID technology instead would the program have had better results?

Chapter 6 Endnotes

1. The Project Gutenberg eBook of Little Journeys to the Homes of the Great, Volume 6, by Elbert Hubbard. Page 51 of PDF-generated version.

2. The Free Dictionary. Accessed 9/21/2012. http://legal-dictionary.thefreedictionary.com/contraband.

3. The Free Dictionary. Accessed 9/21/2012. http://legal-dictionary.thefreedictionary.com/Smuggling.

4. Importing into the United States: A Guide for Commercial Importers, 77. CBP Publication No. 0000-0504, revised November 2006. Available at: http://www.cbp.gov/linkhandler/cgov/newsroom/publications/trade/iius.ctt/iius.pdf.

5. Lorenzi, Rossella. Smuggled Cargo Found on Ancient Roman Ship. *Discovery News*. April 25, 2012. Accessed at: http://news.discovery.com/history/roman-shipwreck-smuggling-120425.html.

6. Tagliacozzo, Eric. Smuggling in Southeast Asia: History and its contemporary vectors in an unbounded region. *Critical Asian Studies* 34:2 (2002), 193–220.

7. Ibid., 196.

8. Ibid., 196–97.

9. Ibid., 197.

10. *Smugglers' Britain.* Britain's Smuggling History. Accessed at: www.smuggling.co.uk/history.html.

11. HM Waterguard: A website dedicated to the memory of the Preventive Service of HM Customs & Excise. Accessed at: http://www.hm-waterguard.org.uk/index.htm.

12. Middleton, Richard. Colonial America: A history, 1565–1776, 3rd ed. (Malden, MA: Blackwell, 2002).

13. Ibid.

14. Spangle, Steven L. "Biological Opinion for the Proposed Installation of 5.2 Miles of Primary Fence near Lukeville, Arizona" (PDF) (U.S. Fish and Wildlife Service, 2008-02-11), 3. Retrieved 2012-09-23.

Nuñez-Neto, Blas and Yule Kim. "Border Security: Barriers Along the U.S. International Border" (PDF). *Federation of American Scientists,* 2008-05-14, 24. Retrieved 2012-09-23.

15. Kane, Linda (Public Affairs Specialist, CBP Office of Public Affairs). "Baggage Surprises," *Customs and Border Protection TODAY.* July/August 2004. Accessed at: http://www.cbp.gov/xp/CustomsToday/2004/Aug/baggage_surprises.xml.

16. U.S. Customs and Border Protection, "Importing into the United States: A Guide for Commercial Importers." 2006. Important is that this was the latest print publication on this topic. The web page maintained by CBP was last updated on March 1, 2014, and no longer included access or links to this earlier publication: https://www.cbp.gov/trade/quota/guide-import-goods As of July 16, 2017, there is no single page with commercial importation information, however the associated webpages and links provide similar information to that in the original 2006 publication, amended by law where appropriate.

17. Ibid., 159.

18. Ibid., 169–70.

19. Ibid., 3.

20. CVD cases apply only if the foreign country is a signatory to the World Trade Organization's Agreement on Subsidies and Countervailing Measures.

21. Section 771(7) (a) of the Tariff Act of 1930 defines material injury to a US industry as "harm [that] is not inconsequential, immaterial, or unimportant."

22. Diiorio-Sterling, Christina, Department of Justice, "Nantucket Scrimshaw Artist Guilty of Smuggling Sperm Whale and Elephant Ivory, Conspiracy, and Lying to Federal Agents," NOAA Office of Law Enforcement new release, 2010-01-28. Accessed July 16, 2017, at https://www.fws.gov/northeast/PDF/MANGHISverdictPR.pdf

23. CBP.gov, "Prohibited and Restricted Items," 2012-04-05. Accessed July 16, 2017, at: https://www.cbp.gov/travel/us-citizens/know-before-you-go/prohibited-and-restricted-items

24. Environmental Affairs; Republic of South Africa. Media Release. 11 Sept 2016. Available at: https://www.environment.gov.za/mediarelease/molewa_highlightsprogress_onrhinopoaching2016

25. "Tobacco Tactics: Tobacco Smuggling in the EU." Accessed July 16, 2017, at: http://www.tobaccotactics.org/index.php/Tobacco_Smuggling_in_the_EU

26. KPMG. Project Sun 2010 Results, 22 August 2011, 37. Accessed December 24, 2012, at: http://www.tobaccotactics.org/index.php/Tobacco_Smuggling_in_the_EU

27. Business Insider, "Underground smuggling tunnel discovered between Ukraine and the EU," July 25, 2012. Accessed July 16, 2017, at: http://www.businessinsider.com/underground-smuggling-tunnel-discovered-between-ukraine-and-the-eu-2012-7.

28. KPMG. Project Sun: A study of the illicit cigarette market in the European Union, Norway and Switzerland, 2015 Results. 2016: UK (no city). Accessed July 16, 2017 at: https://assets.kpmg.com/content/dam/kpmg/pdf/2016/06/project-sun-report.pdf

29. EU Business, "Estonia's petrol smuggling crackdown slashes border traffic," July 21, 2012. Accessed July 16, 2017, at: http://www.eubusiness.com/news-eu/estonia-latvia.htj.

30. Rettman, Andrew. "Security fears prompt fences on EU-Russia border." (Belgium: EUobserver, 28 August 2015). Accessed February 17, 2017, at: https://euobserver.com/justice/130037

31. Ibid.

32. Ibid.

33. Ibid.

34. Department of Justice, Bureau of Alcohol, Tobacco, Firearms and Explosives Office of Strategic Intelligence and Information, *ATF Mexico: Calendar Years 2007–2011*. Accessed December 28, 2012, at: http://www.atf.gov/statistics/download/trace-data/international/2007-2011-Mexico-trace-data.pdf. The original report has disappeared from the web. Current ATF reports can be found at: https://www.atf.gov/about/firearms-trace-data-2015 The information has not been updated since 2015. The authors expect the data will be updated now that a new Presidential Administration is in the Executive Office. However, data from earlier periods may no longer be available due to government records purges and transfers to the Obama Presidential Library at the end of the Obama Administration.

35. Gagne, David, "2000 Illegal Weapons Cross US-Mexico Border Per Day: Report," *Insight Crime*. Accessed July 16, 2017, at: http://www.insightcrime.org/news-analysis/2000-illegal-weapons-cross-us-mexico-border-every-day

36. Ibid., 2.

37. Silverleib, Alan. "House Holds Holder in contempt," *CNN*. (29 June 2012). Accessed July 16, 2017, at: http://www.cnn.com/2012/06/28/politics/holder-contempt/index.html The original Politico report on 28 June 2012, cited in the first edition of this text, has disappeared from the web.

38. Weisman, J. and C. Savage, "House finds Holder in contempt over inquiry on guns," *New York Times*, 28 June 2012. Accessed July 16, 2017, at: http://www.nytimes.com/2012/06/29/us/politics/fast-and-furious-holder-contempt-citation-battle.html?pagewanted=all&_r=0

Chapter 7

People Movers: Human Trafficking and Population Migrations

"Ending this crime so monstrous is not a political issue; it is an American imperative, and a human responsibility. This is why there are still modern-day abolitionists. And this is why the rest of us should join them."

—Richard Holbrooke, 2008

Key Words and Concepts

Child Soldier Prevention Act
Child Soldiers
Debt Bondage
Domestic Servitude
Forced Labor

Human Trafficking
Palermo Protocol
Sex Trafficking
Slavery Trafficking Victims Protection Act

Introduction

This chapter distinguishes between various types of human trafficking; provides an overview of the history of human trafficking and counterstrategies; discusses the causes and consequences of human trafficking; and critically assesses the policies developed to counter human trafficking by governments, international organizations, and private actors. In all its forms, trafficking amounts to a human rights violation, since it includes the (involuntary and voluntary, in some situations) manipulation and exploitation of men, women, and children by others.

Human trafficking exists simply because it is profitable. Whether for sexual purposes, a source of labor, for use as child soldiers, or some other reason, the profit is there, and where there is a demand, there is a ready supply, whether it is illicit drugs, stolen goods, or people. The increasing influence of globalization has affected nations and transnational criminal organizations. According to Shelley (2010), "Human smuggling and trafficking have been among the fastest growing forms of transnational crime because current world conditions have created increased demand and supply."[1] A huge economic disparity has always existed between developed and undeveloped

Billboard used in Houston, Texas.

nations, and globalization has furthered this inequality. The economic disparity affects the migration of people, and the increased smuggling and trafficking is hidden within the increased migration.

Human trafficking and human smuggling are two of the fastest growing areas of international crime, according to the US Department of Justice. Each can involve a number of different crimes, and span several countries.

Even though there are significant differences between human trafficking and human smuggling, the underlying issues that give rise to these illegal activities are often similar. Generally, extreme poverty, mobility (either voluntary or involuntary), lack of economic opportunities, low societal status of women and girls, lax border checks, and the collusion of law enforcement contribute to an environment that encourages human smuggling and trafficking in persons.[2]

Human Trafficking Defined

The Trafficking Victims Protection Act (2000) defines "severe forms of trafficking in persons" as:

a. Sex trafficking in which a commercial sex act is induced by force, fraud, or coercion; or in which the person induced to perform such an act has not attained 18 years of age; or,

b. The recruitment, harboring, transportation, provision, or obtaining of a person for labor or services, through the use of force, fraud, or coercion for the purpose of subjection to involuntary servitude, peonage, debt bondage, or slavery.

A victim need not be physically transported from one location to another in order for the crime to fall within these definitions. Although the TVPA was allowed by Congress to expire in September of 2011, the Senate re-authorized the Act in February of 2013. Senator Patrick Leahy (D-VT) offered the TVPA reauthorization as an amendment to the reauthorization of the Violence Against Women Act (VAWA).[3]

Causes of Human Trafficking

According to the International Labor Organization (2008), the root causes of human trafficking include poverty, lack of employment, and an inefficient system of labor migration. People move, in general, from one place to another in an attempt to find a better life. This applies whether the persons involved are from a third-world country or a developed one and usually involves some type of labor. Sometimes the move is voluntary, sometimes not. According to the ILO, "Some of them are coerced into work they have not chosen voluntarily. They have been deceived about the nature of their work or [the] conditions of their employment contract, they work under threat, are subjected to violence, confined to their workplace or do not receive the wage that was promised to them."[4] According to a May 2014 report from the International Labor Organization, summarized by Human Rights First (2017), "An estimated 21 million victims are trapped in modern-day slavery. Of these, 14.2 million (68%) were exploited for labor, 4.5 million (22%) were sexually exploited, and 2.2 million (10%) were exploited in state-imposed forced labor."[5]

The United Nations Report on Trafficking in Persons 2016 notes that most trafficking cases follow a similar pattern: people (usually women and children) are abducted or recruited in their home country of origin, and then transferred either voluntarily or

The U.S. Department of State estimates between 600,000 and 800,000 people are trafficked across international borders each year. Millions more are enslaved within national borders. Human trafficking is truly a world-wide phenomenon — paradoxically hidden in the shadows and out in the open for all to see. Kay Chernush. U.S. State Department.

This sign, outside a Hong Kong club, reads: "Young, fresh Hong Kong girls; White, clean Malaysian girls; Beijing women; Luxurious ghost girls from Russia." According to U.S. Government statistics, the majority of victims of human trafficking moved across international borders — about 65% — are trafficked for the purpose of sexual exploitation. Kay Chernush. U.S. State Department.

involuntarily through various intermediate countries to the destination country. In some cases, it is possible to interrupt the exploitation process and rescue the victims at which point they could receive aid and assistance either in the country of interruption, or the destination country. Theoretically, some victims could be repatriated to their country of origin at some point. Unfortunately, too often they are simply deported from either the destination or transit countries, as illegal immigrants. This is much more likely to happen if the victims do not speak the language of either the transit or destination country.[6]

At the global level, human trafficking for sexual exploitation is reported more frequently than trafficking for forced labor. Depending upon the subregion, reported trafficking varies, with sexual exploitation reported by many sources in relation to Central and South Eastern Europe and by relatively fewer to Africa. Where sources expressly report exploitation of boys, this tends to be in the labor market, while sexual exploitation is reported more frequently among female children.

For several decades, the primary discussion around human trafficking has concerned itself with the issue of trafficking for sexual exploitation. In most cases, the issue of trafficking for labor has simply not been viewed as a significant issue in many countries, and is therefore, of less concern to global powers.

Traffickers

In many countries the largest number of traffickers arrested for that crime consist of nationals of the country. This suggests that, where statistics are available, the criminal groups exploiting trafficking victims have strong national connections to the destination country. In addition, traffickers and their victims usually come from the same nationality, or ethnicity, and speak the same language. These similar characteristics help the traffickers establish a false sense of security, or trust, which enables them to carry out the trafficking crime. Traffickers do not usually travel abroad to generate victims, but they do travel to the destination countries. Traffickers in origin countries are generally nationals, and traffickers in destination countries are generally either citizens or the same nationality as those trafficked.[7]

In terms of attempting to explain (or understand) the motivation of traffickers, one possible theory comes to mind (aside, of course, from the obvious one of economic gain): Milgram's obedience to authority. Obedience to authority is a simple, straightforward concept, and readily understandable: all of us, probably, have been asked to work late on a Friday afternoon, for example, and unless we have a good reason not to agree, we usually end up postponing dinner, to satisfy the supervisory request. Stanley Milgram (1963), a psychologist at Yale University, devised a series of experiments which focused on the possible conflict between obedience to authority figures and individual conscience. He was attempting to determine how far individuals would go in obeying instructions if they involved harming another person. The conclusion that he found was that "ordinary people are likely to follow orders given by an authority figure, even to the extent of killing an innocent human being. Obedience to authority is ingrained in us all from the way we are brought up."[8]

The full extent of the global trafficking problems is complex and difficult to describe. The problem has gotten worse, and it is now reported to be worse than at any other time in human history. A review of recent reports such as the 2016 US State Department Report, Trafficking in Persons, reveals how more than 120 of the world's countries have embarked on a journey to legislate human rights issues to control trafficking and all its manifestations. The primary problem with human trafficking is that to this point the efforts to control it have been relatively ineffective and inefficient. Only by attempting to understand the depth and scope of the problem can we begin to design effective policies to control it.

Although many countries are now attempting to report the extent of the trafficking problems, at least within their own geographic borders, much more is known about how it has become firmly entrenched in social, cultural, political, economic, and legal systems of countries throughout the world. Human trafficking is reportedly more prevalent than most crimes and falls behind only drugs and weapons trafficking in significance.[9]

Slavery

The history of slavery presents one with a foundation upon which to view the mistreatment and exploitation of human beings. Whether viewing the use of humans to accomplish unusual feats of architecture, or gaining an understanding of the efforts of American colonists and eighteenth or nineteenth century landowners and politicians, the effect has been the same. People have been marginalized and oppressed for thousands of years and many nations have not progressed beyond these imperialistic aims. Many oppressed people remain under the control of authoritarian governments, powerful businesses and landowners, wealthy groups, and in the arms of transnational organized crime groups.

According to Bales (2004), slavery has long existed in the city of New York and continues to exist today. In reference to the African Burial Ground Project in New York, and the more than four hundred slaves buried in Lower Manhattan, Bales says that "The slaves of Lower Manhattan and the slaves of today share many forms of suffering,

Left: Thai and Burmese fishermen are detained behind bars in the compound of a fishing company in Benjina, Indonesia. The imprisoned men were considered slaves who might run away. They said they lived on a few bites of rice and curry a day and were confined to a space barely big enough to lie down until the next trawler came and the traffickers forced them back to sea.

Right: This desperate mother traveled from her village in Nepal to Mumbai, India, hoping to find and rescue her teenage daughter who was trafficked into an Indian brothel. Nepalese girls are prized for their fair skin and are lured with promises of a "good" job and the chance to improve their lives. "I will stay in Mumbai," said the mother, "until I find my daughter or die. I am not leaving here without her." Kay Chernush. US State Department.

among them the abuse and death of their children, the damage to their bodies through trauma and untreated disease, the theft of their lives and work, the destruction of their dignity, and the fat profits others make from their sweat. Slavery still exists in New York and around the world. Today it is often hard to see, but it is there. And like the slaves of the African Burial Ground in New York, the slaves all around us today have waited a long time for us and our governments to come awake to their existence."[10] The invisible chains of economic disparity which hold the bar girls in Latin America are just as strong as the iron ones which held African Americans taken involuntarily from their tribes and sold on the streets of Charleston, South Carolina, in the 1800s.

Laws

There are several types of legislation that specifically refer to human trafficking. These include (but are not limited to) the Trafficking Victims Protection Act (TVPA)[11] of 2000, 2003, 2005, 2007, and 2013, the Child Soldiers Prevention Act (CSPA)[12] of 2008, and the Protocol to Prevent, Suppress and Punish Trafficking in Persons, Especially Women and Children[13] (also referred to as the Trafficking Protocol, the Palermo Protocol, or the UN TIP Protocol, adopted by the United Nations in Palermo, Italy, in 2000). The TVPA and CSPA are both United States laws.

This woman in her early 20s was trafficked into a blue jean sweatshop, where she and other young women were locked in and made to work 20 hours a day, sleeping on the floor, with little to eat and no pay. She managed to escape and was brought to the government-run Baan Kredtrakarn shelter in Bangkok. After a few days, when she felt safe enough to tell her story to the director, the police were informed and they raided the sweatshop, freeing 38 girls, ages 14–26. Kay Chernush. US State Department.

Excerpts from the Trafficking Victims Protection Act (TVPA) 114 STAT. 1467

PUBLIC LAW 106–386 — OCT. 28, 2000

The purposes of this Act are to combat trafficking in persons, a contemporary manifestation of slavery whose victims are predominantly women and children, to ensure just and effective punishment of traffickers, and to protect their victims.

Congress finds that:

(1) As the 21st century begins, the degrading institution of slavery continues throughout the world. Trafficking in persons is a modern form of slavery, and it is the largest manifestation of slavery today. At least 700,000 persons annually, primarily women and children, are trafficked within or across international borders. Approximately 50,000 women and children are trafficked into the United States each year.

(2) Many of these persons are trafficked into the international sex trade, often by force, fraud, or coercion. The sex industry has rapidly expanded over the past several decades. It involves sexual exploitation of persons, predominantly women and girls, involving activities related to prostitution, pornography, sex tourism, and other commercial sexual services. The low status of women in many parts of the world has contributed to a burgeoning of the trafficking industry.

(3) Trafficking in persons is not limited to the sex industry. This growing transnational crime also includes forced labor and involves significant violations of labor, public health, and human rights standards worldwide.

(4) Traffickers primarily target women and girls, who are disproportionately affected by poverty, the lack of access to education, chronic unemployment, discrimination, and the lack of economic opportunities in countries of origin. Traffickers lure women and girls into their networks through false promises of decent working conditions at relatively good pay as nannies, maids, dancers, factory workers, restaurant workers, sales clerks, or models. Traffickers also buy children from poor families and sell them into prostitution or into various types of forced or bonded labor.

(5) Traffickers often transport victims from their home communities to unfamiliar destinations, including foreign countries away from family and friends, religious institutions, and other sources of protection and support, leaving the victims defenseless and vulnerable.

(6) Victims are often forced through physical violence to engage in sex acts or perform slavery-like labor. Such force includes rape and other forms of sexual abuse, torture, starvation, imprisonment, threats, psychological abuse, and coercion.

(7) Traffickers often make representations to their victims that physical harm may occur to them or others should the victim escape or attempt to escape. Such representations can have the same coercive effects on victims as direct threats to inflict such harm.

(8) Trafficking in persons is increasingly perpetrated by organized, sophisticated criminal enterprises. Such trafficking is the fastest growing source of profits for organized criminal enterprises worldwide. Profits from the trafficking industry contribute to the expansion of organized crime in the United States and worldwide. Trafficking in persons is often aided by official corruption in countries of origin, transit, and destination, thereby threatening the rule of law.

(9) Trafficking includes all the elements of the crime of forcible rape when it involves the involuntary participation of another person in sex acts by means of fraud, force, or coercion.

(10) Trafficking also involves violations of other laws, including labor and immigration codes and laws against kidnapping, slavery, false imprisonment, assault, battery, pandering, fraud, and extortion.

(11) Trafficking exposes victims to serious health risks. Women and children trafficked in the sex industry are exposed to deadly diseases, including HIV and AIDS. Trafficking victims are sometimes worked or physically brutalized to death.

(12) Trafficking in persons substantially affects interstate and foreign commerce. Trafficking for such purposes as involuntary servitude, peonage, and other forms of forced labor has an impact on the nationwide employment network and labor market. Within the context of slavery, servitude, and labor or services which are obtained or maintained through coercive conduct that amounts to a condition of servitude, victims are subjected to a range of violations.

(13) Involuntary servitude statutes are intended to reach cases in which persons are held in a condition of servitude through nonviolent coercion. In *United States v. Kozminski*, 487 U.S. 931 (1988), the Supreme Court found that section 1584 of title 18, United States Code, should be narrowly interpreted, absent a definition of involuntary servitude by Congress. As a result, that section was interpreted to criminalize only servitude that is brought about through use or threatened use of physical or legal coercion, and to exclude other conduct that can have the same purpose and effect.

(14) Existing legislation and law enforcement in the United States and other countries are inadequate to deter trafficking and bring traffickers to justice, failing to reflect the gravity of the offenses involved. No comprehensive law exists in the United States that penalizes the range of offenses involved in the trafficking scheme. Instead, even the most brutal instances of trafficking in the sex industry are often punished under laws that also apply to lesser offenses, so that traffickers typically escape deserved punishment.

(15) In the United States, the seriousness of this crime and its components is not reflected in current sentencing guidelines, resulting in weak penalties for convicted traffickers.

(16) In some countries, enforcement against traffickers is also hindered by official indifference, by corruption, and sometimes even by official participation in trafficking.

(17) Existing laws often fail to protect victims of trafficking, and because victims are often illegal immigrants in the destination country, they are repeatedly punished more harshly than the traffickers themselves.

(18) Additionally, adequate services and facilities do not currently exist to meet victims' needs regarding health care, housing, education, and legal assistance, which safely reintegrate trafficking victims into their home countries.

(19) Victims of severe forms of trafficking should not be inappropriately incarcerated, fined, or otherwise penalized solely for unlawful acts committed as a direct result of being trafficked, such as using false documents, entering the country without documentation, or working without documentation.

(20) Because victims of trafficking are frequently unfamiliar with the laws, cultures, and languages of the countries into which they have been trafficked, because they are often subjected to coercion and intimidation including physical detention and debt bondage, and because they often fear retribution and forcible removal to countries in which they will face retribution or other hardship, these victims often find it difficult or impossible to report the crimes committed against them or to assist in the investigation and prosecution of such crimes.

(21) Trafficking of persons is an evil requiring concerted and vigorous action by countries of origin, transit or destination, and by international organizations.

(22) One of the founding documents of the United States, the Declaration of Independence, recognizes the inherent dignity and worth of all people. It states that all men are created equal and that they are endowed by their Creator with certain unalienable rights. The right to be free from slavery and involuntary servitude is among those unalienable rights. Acknowledging this fact, the United States outlawed slavery and involuntary servitude in 1865, recognizing them as evil institutions that must be abolished. Current practices of sexual slavery and trafficking of women and children are similarly abhorrent to the principles upon which the United States was founded.

(23) The United States and the international community agree that trafficking in persons involves grave violations of human rights and is a matter of pressing international concern. The international community has repeatedly condemned slavery and involuntary servitude, violence against women, and other elements of trafficking, through declarations, treaties, and United Nations resolutions and reports, including the Universal Declaration of Human Rights; the 1956 Supplementary Convention on the Abolition of Slavery, the Slave Trade, and Institutions and Practices Similar to Slavery; the 1948 American Declaration on the Rights and Duties of Man; the 1957 Abolition of Forced Labor Convention; the International Covenant on Civil and Political Rights; the Convention Against Torture and Other Cruel, Inhuman or Degrading Treatment or Punishment; United Nations General Assembly Resolutions 50/167, 51/66, and 52/98; the Final Report of the World Congress against Sexual Exploitation of Children (Stockholm, 1996); the Fourth World Conference on Women (Beijing, 1995); and the 1991 Moscow Document of the Organization for Security and Cooperation in Europe.

(24) Trafficking in persons is a transnational crime with national implications. To deter international trafficking and bring its perpetrators to justice, nations including the United States must recognize that trafficking is a serious offense. This is done by prescribing appropriate punishment, giving priority to the prosecution of trafficking offenses, and protecting rather than punishing the victims of such offenses. The United States must work bilaterally and multilaterally to abolish the trafficking industry by taking steps to promote cooperation among countries linked together by international trafficking routes. The United States must also urge the international community to take strong action in multilateral fora to engage recalcitrant countries in serious and sustained efforts to eliminate trafficking and protect trafficking victims.[14]

The 2016 Trafficking in Persons (TIP) Report notes that globalization has impacted not only economics transnationally, but also human trafficking. The end of the Cold War resulted in a rise in the number of refugees, including those victims of trafficking. An umbrella term, "trafficking in persons" implies activities involved when one person obtains or holds another person in compelled service. The "compelled service" can be defined in several ways, including involuntary servitude, slavery, debt bondage, and forced labor.

Escaping desperate conditions of forced labor and political repression at home, these Burmese laborers look to commercial fishing in Thailand as a way to a better life. Like illegal or marginalized immigrants everywhere, they are prey to unscrupulous traffickers who, for a fee, sell them to greedy ship captains and exploiters. Kay Chernush. U.S. State Department.

Left: Burmese migrants who are often trafficked onto fishing ships are kept at sea for months and even years at a time. If they protest and ask to be put ashore, they may be threatened at gunpoint and locked in containers, or fired and not paid for their work. Kay Chernush. U.S. State Department.

Right: A 9-year-old girl toils under the hot sun, making bricks from morning to night, seven days a week. She was trafficked with her entire family from Bihar, one of the poorest and most underdeveloped states in India, and sold to the owner of a brick-making factory. With no means of escape, and unable to speak the local language, the family is isolated and lives in terrible conditions. Kay Chernush. U.S. State Department.

Human trafficking involves the use of force, fraud, or coercion to enslave a person. Sometimes traffickers use a bond, or debt, to keep a person trapped. Many workers around the world fall victim to debt bondage when they assume a debt as part of their employment, or inherit debt in more traditional systems of bonded labor. Especially in South Asia, people can be trapped in debt bondage from generation to generation. Kay Chernush. U.S. State Department.

Forced Labor

Also known as "involuntary servitude," forced labor results when unscrupulous employers exploit workers made more vulnerable by high rates of unemployment, poverty, crime, discrimination, corruption, political conflict, or cultural acceptance of the practice. Immigrants are particularly vulnerable, but individuals also may be forced into labor in their own countries. Female victims of forced or bonded labor, especially women and girls in domestic servitude, are often sexually exploited as well.

Sex Trafficking

When an adult is coerced, forced, or deceived into prostitution—or maintained in prostitution through coercion—that person is a victim of trafficking. All of those involved in recruiting, transporting, harboring, receiving, or obtaining the person for that purpose are committing a trafficking crime. This includes those who purchase the "services" of the victim. Sex trafficking can occur within debt bondage, as women and girls are forced to continue in prostitution through the use of unlawful "debt" purportedly incurred through their transportation, recruitment, or even their crude "sale"—which exploiters insist they must pay off before they can be free. It is critical to understand that a person's initial consent to participate in prostitution is not legally determinative. If thereafter they are held in service through psychological manipulation or physical force, they are trafficking victims and should receive benefits outlined in the Palermo Protocol and applicable domestic laws.

Debt Bondage

Often referred to as "bonded labor" or "debt bondage," the practice has long been prohibited under United States law by the term *peonage*, and the Palermo Protocol requires its criminalization as a form of trafficking in persons. Workers around the world fall victim to debt bondage when traffickers or recruiters unlawfully exploit an initial debt the worker assumed as part of the terms of employment. Workers may also inherit debt in more traditional systems of bonded labor. The UN estimates that in South Asia there are millions of trafficking victims working to pay off their ancestors' debts.

Debt Bondage among Migrant Laborers

Abuses of contracts and hazardous conditions of employment for migrant laborers do not necessarily constitute human trafficking. However, the **imposition** of illegal costs and debts on these laborers in the source country, often with the support of labor agencies and employers in the destination country, can contribute to a situation

Carpet weavers, like this family, are usually Dalits or "Untouchables," the lowest caste in South Asian society. In many instances, the children are helping a family member, or someone else in their village who has fallen into debt. An offer is made to place a loom in their hut so they can pay off their debt, but this only ensures their enslavement, sometimes for generations. Kay Chernush. US State Department.

of debt bondage. This is the case even when the worker's status in the country is tied to the employer in the context of employment-based temporary work programs. Often seen in Middle Eastern countries dependent upon imported/migrant labor for basic services, construction, resource exploitation, etc., this has become a major cause of population unrest in countries such as Bahrain, Kuwait, the United Arab Emirates, and Saudi Arabia.

Domestic Servitude

A unique form of forced labor is the involuntary servitude of domestic workers, whose workplaces are informal, connected to their off-duty living quarters, and not often shared with other workers. Such an environment, which often socially isolates domestic workers, is conducive to nonconsensual exploitation since authorities cannot inspect private property as easily as they can inspect formal workplaces. Investigators and service providers report many cases of untreated illnesses and, tragically, widespread sexual abuse, which in some cases may be symptoms of a situation of involuntary servitude.

The problem of forced domestic servitude, a form of modern slavery, is a major issue within the United States. In 2007, Varsha and Mahender Sabhnani, two naturalized US citizens (from India), were tried in a Long Island federal court for keeping two women enslaved. In 2006 the wife of a Saudi prince was convicted in Boston for keeping two house servants in virtual slavery. In 2005 two Wisconsin doctors were convicted of keeping a Filipina woman as an indentured servant for more than twenty years. In 2003 a Maryland couple were convicted in federal court for keeping a Brazilian woman in their home as a domestic servant, without pay, for fifteen years. In the Long Island case the two women "were forced to work day and night, threatened, tortured, beaten with rolling pins and brooms, deprived of adequate food and never allowed out of the house except to take out the garbage," according to court testimony.[15] According to a UNWomen.Org report, of the 67.1 million domestic workers worldwide, 11.5 million are migrant domestic workers.[16] Almost all are uneducated women (and some are children) from the poorest countries in the world.

Children such as this young girl are prized in the carpet industry for their small, fast fingers. Defenseless, they do what they're told, toiling in cramped, dark, airless village huts from sunrise until well into the night. Kay Chernush. US State Department.

Forced Child Labor

While many international organizations and national laws recognize children may legally engage in certain forms of work, the growing consensus is that the worst forms of child labor, including bonded and forced labor of children, should be eradicated. A child can be a victim of human trafficking regardless of the location of that non-consensual exploitation. Indicators of possible forced labor of a child include situations in which the child appears to be in the custody of a non-family member who has the child perform work that financially benefits someone outside the child's family and does not offer the child the option of leaving.

The Fair Labor Standards Act (FLSA) "sets a minimum age of 14 for most employment in non-hazardous, non-agricultural industries," but it limits the times of day and the number of hours that 14- and 15-year-olds may work and the tasks that they may perform. The FLSA establishes an 18-year-old minimum age for non-agricultural occupations that the Secretary of Labor declares to be particularly hazardous or detrimental to children's health or well-being. There are currently 17 Hazardous Occupation Orders (HOs), which include a partial or total ban on work for minors in the occupations or industries they cover. Despite these restrictions and limitations, in 2014, there were 14 fatal occupational injuries among youth ages 16–17, and 8 fatal occupational injuries among children below age 16 in the United States; in 2015, there were 12 fatal occupational injuries among children between the ages of 16 and 17, and 12 fatalities among children below age 16."[17]

The Bureau of Labor, Wage and Health Division (WHD), carries out investigations, including "monitoring for violations of the FLSA's child labor provisions. Complaints from the public about child labor, although not numerous, are given the highest priority within the agency. In Fiscal Year 2011, WHD concluded over 700 cases where child labor violations were cited, more than half of which involved violations of the referenced [Hazardous Occupation Orders]. In this same fiscal year, WHD assessed over $2 million in civil money penalties for violations of FLSA child labor laws, $78,557 of which were in the agriculture industry."[18]

Child Soldiers

Child soldiering is a manifestation of human trafficking when it involves the unlawful recruitment or use of children—through force, fraud, or coercion—as combatants or for labor or sexual exploitation by armed forces. Perpetrators may be government forces, paramilitary organizations, or rebel groups. Many children are forcibly abducted and used as combatants. Others are unlawfully made to work as porters, cooks, guards, servants, messengers, or spies. Young girls can be forced to marry or have sex with male combatants. Both male and female child soldiers are often sexually abused and are at high risk of contracting sexually transmitted diseases. See the break-out box for more information on child soldiers.

Child Soldiers

The Child Soldiers Prevention Act of 2008 (CSPA)[19] was signed into law on December 23, 2008 (Title IV of Pub. L. 110-457), and became effective on June 21, 2009. The CSPA requires publication in the annual TIP Report of a list of foreign governments identified during the previous year as having governmental armed forces

Child soldier, Afghanistan, n.d.

or government supported armed forces or groups that recruit and use child soldiers, as defined in the Act. According to the CSPA, and generally consistent with the provisions of the Optional Protocol to the Convention on the Rights of the Child on the Involvement of Children in Armed Conflict (adopted by the United Nations in May 2000), the term "child soldier" means:

(i) Any person under 18 years of age who takes a direct part in hostilities as a member of governmental armed forces;

(ii) Any person under 18 years of age who has been compulsorily recruited into governmental armed forces;

(iii) Any person under 15 years of age who has been voluntarily recruited into governmental armed forces; or

(iv) Any person under 18 years of age who has been recruited or used in hostilities by armed forces distinct from the armed forces of a state.

The term "child soldier" includes any person described in clauses (ii), (iii), or (iv) "who is serving in any capacity, including in a support role such as a cook, porter, messenger, medic, guard, or sex slave."

In the 2014 TIP Report, the US Department of State listed nine states not meeting the CSPA standards: the Central African Republic (CAR), the Democratic Republic of Congo (DRC), Myanmar (Burma), Rwanda, Somalia, South Sudan, Sudan, Syria and Yemen.[20]

Young men sew beads and sequins in intricate patterns onto saris and shawls at a "zari" workshop in Mumbai, India. The boys, who arrive by train from impoverished villages across India, often work from six in the morning until two in the morning the next day. Some sleep on the floor of the workshop. If they make the smallest mistake, they might be beaten. All say they work to send money back to their families, but some employers are known to withhold their meager pay. Kay Chernush. US State Department.

Street kids, runaways, or children living in poverty can fall under the control of traffickers who force them into begging rings. Children are sometimes intentionally disfigured to attract more money from passersby. Victims of organized begging rings are often beaten or injured if they don't bring in enough money. They are also vulnerable to sexual abuse. Kay Chernush. US State Department.

Child Sex Trafficking

UNICEF reports that as many as two million children each year are subjected to prostitution in the global commercial sex trade. International covenants and protocols obligate criminalization of the commercial sexual exploitation of children. The use of children in the commercial sex trade is prohibited under both the Palermo Protocol and Unites States law as well as by legislation in other countries around the world. There can be no exceptions and no cultural or socioeconomic rationalizations preventing the rescue of children from sexual servitude. Sex trafficking has devastating consequences for minors, including long-lasting physical and psychological trauma, disease (including HIV/AIDS), drug addiction, unwanted pregnancy, malnutrition, social ostracism, and possible death.[21]

Sex trafficking networks are woven together with invisible threads of desperation, greed, and poverty. Experts, prosecutors, and academics generally say the same thing: that the crime is difficult to detect, and even more difficult to measure accurately. Kevin Bales, author of the book *Disposable People: New Slavery in the Global Economy,* says there are important things that distinguish it from a traditional means of slavery: there is no paperwork to prove ownership of the slave; there is a low cost of acquisitions relative to a high rate of returns; and a constant turnover of victims. After drug and arms trafficking, human trafficking may be the most lucrative illicit business in the world. According to Bales, there are up to 27 million sex slaves in the world, and the United Nations Office on Drugs and Crime (UNODC) says the business generates up to $32 billion in annual profits.[22] Assuming the above figures are accurate, that means that two million children are trafficked each year to produce income related to the global sex trade, for a profit of approximately 2.48 billion dollars U.S.

Excerpts from the US State Department 2016 TIP Report

Since the last Global Report on Trafficking in Persons in 2014 there have been a number of significant developments that reinforce this report's importance, and place it at the heart of international efforts undertaken to combat human trafficking. Perhaps the most worrying development is that the movement of refugees and migrants, the largest seen since World War II, has arguably intensified since 2014. As this crisis has unfolded, and climbed up the global agenda, there has been a corresponding recognition that, within these massive migratory movements, are vulnerable children, women and men who can be easily exploited by smugglers and traffickers. Other changes are more positive. In September 2015, the world adopted the 2030 Sustainable Development Agenda and embraced goals and targets on trafficking in persons. These goals call for an end to trafficking and violence against children; as well as the need for measures against human trafficking, and they strive for the elimination of all forms of violence against and exploitation of women and girls. Thanks to the 2030 Agenda, we now have an underpinning for the action needed under the provisions of the UN Convention against Transnational Organized Crime, and its protocols on trafficking in persons and migrant smuggling. Another important development is the UN Summit for Refugees and Migrants, which produced the groundbreaking New York Declaration. Of the nineteen commitments adopted by countries in the Declaration, three are dedicated to concrete action against the crimes of human trafficking and migrant smuggling. UNODC's report is also the last before the world gathers in 2017 at the UN General Assembly for the essential evaluation of the Global Plan of Action to Combat Trafficking in Persons. These decisive steps forward are helping to unite the world and produce much needed international cooperation against trafficking in persons. But, to have tangible success against the criminals, to sever the money supplies, to entertain joint operations and mutual legal assistance, we must first understand the texture and the shape of this global challenge. The Global Report on Trafficking in Persons does exactly this. It provides a detailed picture of the situation through solid analysis and research. The findings are disturbing. Traffickers may target anyone who can be exploited in their own countries or abroad. When foreigners are trafficked, we know that human trafficking flows broadly follow the migratory patterns. We know from the report that some migrants are more vulnerable than others, such as those from countries with a high level of organized crime or from countries affected by conflicts. Just as tragically, 79 per cent of all detected trafficking victims are women and children. From 2012-2014, more than 500 different trafficking flows were detected and countries in Western and Southern Europe detected victims of 137 different citizenships. These figures recount a worrying story of human trafficking occurring almost everywhere. In terms of the different types of trafficking, sexual exploitation and forced labour are the most prominent. But the report shows that trafficking can have numerous other forms including: victims compelled to act as beggars, forced into sham marriages, benefit fraud, pornography production, organ removal, among others. In response, many countries have criminalized most forms of trafficking as set out in the UN Trafficking in Persons Protocol. The number of countries doing this has increased from 33 in 2003 to 158 in 2016. Such an exponential increase is welcomed and it has helped to assist the victims and to prosecute the traffickers. Unfortunately, the average number of convictions remains low. UNODC's findings show that there is a close correlation between the length of time the trafficking law has been on the statute books and the conviction rate. This is a sign that it takes time, as well as resources, and expertise to chase down the criminals. Perhaps the 2016 Report's main message is that inroads have been made into this horrendous crime. We must, however, continue to generate much needed cooperation and collaboration at the international level, and the necessary law enforcement skills at the national and regional levels to detect, investigate and successfully prosecute cases of trafficking in persons. The 2016 report has done a fine job of setting out the situation, but there is more to be done.[23]

The problem of human trafficking is sometimes said to exist, at least in part, to accommodate the needs of a country's economic system. One example of this is the (relatively) blind eye turned toward the millions of illegal immigrants in this country. Many of them do work that other Americans do not want, or are not willing to perform. If there is work of any kind to be done, and a profit to be made from human trafficking, there will be manipulation and exploitation of workers. This is in no way limited by geopolitical boundaries.

Trafficking in Europe

European countries are examples of places that have many more jobs than workers, while the economies of other countries cannot function without slave labor. Unique social and political as well as economic systems in Europe contribute to the trafficking and migration problem. The end of the Cold War and the collapse of the former Soviet Union both contributed to the human trafficking problem in Europe.

According to Shelley (2010), "The end of the Cold War had its greatest impact in the former Soviet Union and the former socialist bloc of Eastern Europe. Human trafficking proliferated in the final years of the Soviet period, in the 1980s. At first, trafficking victims were primarily women, but after the dissolution of the USSR, diverse forms of trafficking developed, facilitated by the rise of organized crime, the decline of borders, high levels of corruption, and the incapacity of the transitional states to protect their citizens. Also, contributing to human susceptibility to traffickers were the social and economic collapse, discrimination against women and minorities, and the conflicts that accompanied the demise of the socialist system. Millions were unemployed, disoriented, displaced, and vulnerable to exploitation."[24]

This woman used in prostitution in Western Europe is forced through threats and intimidation to give all earnings to her trafficker. The amount varies between 200 and 400 Euro ($250–$500 USD) per month. These fees come on top of a huge bogus "debt" typically about 35,000 Euro (44,000 USD) owed by the woman to the trafficker who brought her, usually from Africa or Eastern Europe. Wealthy European countries are magnets for sex trafficking. Kay Chernush. U.S. State Department.

The problem of human trafficking is one form of transnational crime. All forms of transnational crime, including human trafficking, seem to increase in proportion to the economic disparity and political unrest of a country or region. Eastern Europe, particularly after the fall of the USSR, is no exception to that general rule. "This region, which spans Europe and Asia, is characterized by enormous cultural, political, economic, and religious diversity. Parts of the former Soviet Union such as the Baltic States have standards of living approximately 40 percent of the level of long-time members of the EU, whereas income levels in the impoverished countries of Central Asia and Moldova in the worst periods averaged as little as $50 monthly. These economic differences are accompanied by equally significant political differences."[25]

Although many resources have been applied to the problem of human trafficking for many years, the problem persists. The problem continues to exist because the underlying conditions that promote it continue to exist.

The sociological and cultural problems associated with the integration of former East German immigrants into what was West Germany (after the Fall of the Berlin Wall in 1989) is symptomatic of a more general problem in Europe—the transition of immigrants *into* a country, as opposed to those leaving, to more prosperous areas of the world. As Shelley notes, "the increased number of illegal migrants and trafficking victims compound the challenge that already exists in Western Europe of absorbing the diverse migrants and political refugees with different cultural, educational, and life experiences than western Europeans who have grown up in prosperous democratic societies. These problems of assimilation are compounded by the fact that those who are being smuggled and trafficked often are racially different from Europeans and have different religions."[26]

Excerpts from 2016 TIP Report

WESTERN AND SOUTHERN EUROPE

Key findings:
Most frequently detected victim profile: Women, 56%
Most frequently detected form of exploitation: Sexual exploitation, 67%
Gender profile of convicted offenders: 78% males
Share of national citizens among offenders: 40%
Summary profile of trafficking flows: Destination; particularly for medium-distance trafficking.
Emerging trend: Increasing significance of trafficking for forced labour.
A clear majority of the approximately 15,200 victims detected, with gender and age reported, in Western and Southern Europe between 2012 and 2014 were women (56%). Men and girls were detected in near-equal numbers (19% and 18%, respectively).

Between 2012 and 2014, Austria, Denmark, Germany, Greece, Norway and the United Kingdom all registered clearly increasing shares of adult male victims, compared to two years before. Other countries reported stable shares; the Netherlands, for example, around 10 per cent, and Turkey, less than 1 per cent. Considering data from the last seven years, detections of men and children have fluctuated year-on-year, but clearly increased over the period. The shares of detected women, on the other hand, have decreased consistently and significantly.

Trafficking for the purpose of sexual exploitation is the most commonly reported form in this part of the world. Out of the 12,775 victims detected between 2012 and 2014 whose form of exploitation was reported, some 67 per cent were exploited for sexual purposes and 30 per cent for forced labour. Trafficking for forced labour includes exploitation in a range of sectors, such as agriculture, construction, commercial cleaning and domestic servitude. Nearly 4 per cent of the victims were trafficked for 'other' purposes, including about 0.7 per cent for begging, and another 0.7 per cent for the commission of crime. In addition, victims were trafficked for sham and forced marriages and for mixed forms of exploitation (usually involving a combination of sexual exploitation and some type of forced labour). About 85 per cent of the victims trafficked for other purposes were females, especially girls.[27]

Trafficking in Asia

If human trafficking can be compared to an atomic bomb, then Asia is ground zero. According to remarks by Roger Plant, the head of the Special Action Program to Combat Forced Labor to the US Congressional Committee Meeting on China on March 6, 2006, by May of 2005 there were 12.3 million victims of forced labor, and of those 9.5 million were in the region of Asia. "Most people are trafficked into forced labor for commercial sexual exploitation, but at least one third are also trafficked for other forms of economic exploitation. We also observed that four out of every five cases of forced labor today involve exploitation by private agents rather than the State."[28]

Per Shelley (2010), both large and small Asian crime organizations specialize in human trafficking, as opposed to their counterparts in other regions of the world, which profit more significantly from drug trafficking. "Crime groups became key actors in both domestic and transnational trafficking earlier and on a larger scale than their criminal counterparts in other parts of the world. Crime groups alone are not the sole facilitators. Governmental officials in most regions of Asia assume important roles in perpetuating the trafficking."[29] It is difficult, if not completely impossible, for human trafficking to thrive in a region without either the covert or overt support of local officials. "Corruption is not confined to border areas but also involves police in the cities and officials in ports, airports, and many other parts of state bureaucracies. In some parts of Asia, such as the Philippines, elites are also traffickers."[30]

Bar girls, like these young women in Southeast Asia, are typically trafficked from impoverished rural communities and neighboring countries. They are required by the bar's owner or "mama-san" to entice male patrons to buy drinks for them. If they do not meet their monthly quota, they may be beaten or brutalized. Other girls work in discos and massage parlors where sex is for sale. Kay Chernush. US State Department.

Excerpts from 2016 TIP Report

EASTERN EUROPE AND CENTRAL ASIA

Key findings:

Most frequently detected victim profile: Men, 53%

Most frequently detected form of exploitation: Forced labour, 64%

Gender profile of convicted offenders: 55% females

Share of national citizens among offenders: 98%

Summary profile of trafficking flows: Destination for intraregional and origin for transregional trafficking.

Emerging trend: Trafficking from poorer to richer countries within the region.

A total of 27,800 victims of trafficking whose age and gender profiles were known were detected in this region between 2012 and 2014. More than 90 per cent were adults and a majority were men. Even though men comprise the majority of detected victims, there are marked geographical differences within the region. Eastern European countries detected a larger number of women, and Central

Customers/exploiters come from all over the world. Legalized or tolerated prostitution is a magnet for sex trafficking. The US Government considers prostitution to be "inherently demeaning and dehumanizing," and opposes efforts to legalize it. The PROTECT Act makes it illegal for an American to sexually abuse a minor in another country. Perpetrators can receive up to 30 years in jail. Kay Chernush. US State Department.

Asian countries detected more men. Countries across the region, however, reported increased shares of adult male victims over the last few years, which is related to the increasing share of detected victims of trafficking for forced labour. Forms of exploitation: The increasing prevalence of men among trafficking victims across the region is also reflected in the detection of cases of trafficking for forced labour. Considering the 10,950 victims detected during the reporting period whose form of exploitation was known, trafficking for forced labour accounted for more than twice as many victims as trafficking for sexual exploitation. Although the available information is scattered, covering different years and countries, an increasing trend in the detection of trafficking for forced labour can be observed in different countries of Eastern Europe and Central Asia.

Geographic variations can also be observed for forms of exploitation, even among countries that are very close or share a border. In Eastern Europe, victims of trafficking for sexual exploitation were more frequently detected in most countries, whereas Ukraine reported more victims of trafficking for forced labour. In Central Asia, Kazakhstan and Uzbekistan detected more victims for forced labour while in Tajikistan, sexual exploitation was more frequently detected.[31]

Like slaves on an auction block waiting to be selected, victims of human trafficking have to perform as they are told or risk being beaten. Sex buyers often claim they had no idea that most women and girls abused in prostitution are desperate to escape, or are there as a result of force, fraud, or coercion. Kay Chernush. US State Department.

Excerpts from 2016 TIP Report

NORTH AND CENTRAL AMERICA AND THE CARIBBEAN

Key findings: North America
Most frequently detected victim profile: Women, 60%
Most frequently detected form of exploitation: Sexual exploitation, 55%
Gender profile of convicted offenders: 61% males
Summary profile of trafficking flows: Mostly local trafficking, but also a significant destination for long-distance flows.
Emerging trend: Many women and girls trafficked for forced labour.

Key findings: Central America and the Caribbean
Most frequently detected victim profile: Girls, 46%
Most frequently detected form of exploitation: Sexual exploitation, 57%
Gender profile of convicted offenders: 51% males
Share of national citizens among offenders: 88%
Summary profile of trafficking flows: Mainly domestic and intraregional flows.
Emerging trend: Many children among the detected victims.

Both North America and Central America and the Caribbean detect many female victims. About 70 per cent of the approximately 8,900 victims detected across the region whose age and sex profiles were reported were females. However, while girls are more frequently detected in Central America and the Caribbean, in North America, women predominate.

Forms of exploitation: Trafficking for sexual exploitation is the most frequently detected form in Central America and the Caribbean, with about 57 per cent of the victims detected in 2014 (or most recent). The share in North America is similar; about 55 per cent. The two areas differ in terms of the second most common form of exploitation, however. In Central America and the Caribbean, trafficking for 'other' purposes is frequently reported, accounting for about 27 per cent of the victims detected there. Many of these victims were trafficked for begging, and some, for illegal adoption. The share of victims who were trafficked for forced labour is small in a global perspective. In North America, on the other hand, the level of forced labour is quite high, accounting for about 40 per cent of the approximately 6,800 victims detected between 2012 and 2014 for whom the form of exploitation was reported. Few victims were trafficked for 'other' purposes; most of the 6 per cent of victims in this category were subjected to mixed exploitation.[32]

Trafficking in the United States

The United States, per Shelley (2010), is unique among developed nations, regarding its human trafficking problem, and more closely approximates a developing country than a developed one: "Its sex trafficking victims are younger, more often native born, and more mobile. The United States, like many developing countries, is a major source country for sex trafficking victims, has sex tourism on its territory, and its native-born sex trafficking victims have Hobbesian lives that are 'brutish and short.' Yet many other forms of trafficking occur among the massive illegal migrant population. Despite the absence of widespread corruption and close links between traffickers and state officials, patterns of American trafficking more closely resemble those of a developing than a developed country."[33] Shelley gives several reasons for this, including the idea of American exceptionalism, which produces marked differences in social organization, culture, and society from other developed countries. "According to American exceptionalism, the United States emphasizes individual achievement rather than support for an extensive social welfare system similar to that which characterizes many industrialized countries. Consequently, in contrast to Western Europe, Australia, or Japan, there is greater economic and social differentiation, and many citizens remain with only the bare minimum of a social safety net."[34]

HSI, FBI Dismantle Sex Trafficking Ring in Atlanta

May 22, 2013
Atlanta, GA

ATLANTA—Three Mexican citizens are in federal custody on sex trafficking charges in Atlanta following a joint investigation by US Immigration and Customs Enforcement's (ICE), Homeland Security Investigations (HSI), and the FBI.

Arturo Rojas-Coyotl, Odilon Martinez-Rojas and Severiano Martinez-Rojas, all of Tenancingo in the State of Tlaxcala, Mexico, have been indicted on charges of sex trafficking and alien harboring. A fourth man, Daniel Garcia-Tepal, also of Tlaxcala, Mexico, is charged with encouraging and inducing aliens to enter and reside in the United States unlawfully.

"Sex trafficking is a malicious crime whether the victims are American citizens or foreign nationals," said United States Attorney Sally Quillian Yates. "The defendants are charged with preying on young women from Mexico and Guatemala, smuggling them into the United States under false pretenses, and forcing them into prostitution. US laws protect all trafficking victims, and we will prosecute those who engage in this practice."

"The enslavement of women forced into prostitution is a heinous crime that occurs all too frequently in our communities," said Brock D. Nicholson, special agent in charge of HSI Atlanta. "Across the country, law enforcement agencies from the federal to the local level are teaming up to identify, arrest and prosecute those who seek to profit at the expense of the suffering of others. This case could not have happened without the excellent relationships we have with the FBI and the US Attorney for the Northern District of Georgia."

Mark F. Giuliano, special agent in charge of the FBI Atlanta Field Office, stated: "Today's indictments and subsequent arrests are a continuation of the federal law enforcement effort to stem the international trafficking of individuals to fuel the commercial sex industry here in the United States and in particular in Atlanta. The FBI asks anyone with information regarding this type of activity to contact their nearest FBI field office immediately."

According to Yates, the charges and other information presented in court: Rojas-Coyotl and his uncles Odilon Martinez-Rojas and Severiano Martinez-Rojas used force, fraud and coercion to compel three women to engage in prostitution in Atlanta and Norcross at various times between 2006 and 2008. Daniel Garcia-Tepal and Arturo Rojas-Coyotl are also charged with encouraging and inducing a fourth woman to unlawfully enter and remain in the United States between 2010 and 2013.

Special agents from the FBI and HSI arrested Arturuo Rojas-Coyotl, Odilon Martinez-Rojas, and Daniel Garcia-Tepal in a highly coordinated law enforcement sweep Tuesday. Severiano Martinez-Rojas remains a fugitive and is believed to be in Mexico. The FBI will coordinate with its legal attaché in Mexico City to effect his arrest and subsequent extradition back to the United States. Four search warrants were also executed today in Atlanta and Norcross in conjunction with the arrests.

Each sex trafficking charge carries a maximum sentence of life in prison while each alien harboring charge has a maximum sentence of 10 years in prison, with all counts carrying a fine of up to $250,000 each. In determining the actual sentence, the Court will consider the United States Sentencing Guidelines, which are not binding but provide appropriate sentencing ranges for most offenders.

Assistant United States Attorney Susan Coppedge and Trial Attorney Benjamin Hawk of the Civil Rights Division's Human Trafficking Prosecution Unit are prosecuting the case.[35]

A disproportionate number of trafficking victims, including children, come from native-born black and Hispanic victims. This is not so much an American problem as a North American problem. For example, Canada has a similar problem among First Nation members. The First Nation are native Canadians, similar to America's native Indians. The Royal Canadian Mounted Police has identified trafficked girls as young as 13 from the First Nation group in Canada.[36]

The problem of human trafficking truly is worldwide. Shelley (2010) contends that "trafficking exists in every state of the United States. Victims of trafficking are exploited in rural, urban, and suburban communities and along the nation's highways. American trafficking victims originate from all regions of the world — Latin America, Asia, Africa, Europe, and Eurasia. Almost all identified forms of human trafficking, except for child soldiers, exist in the United States."[37]

Poverty, ignorance, superstition, social customs, greed, government corruption, and human cruelty combine to put families — particularly women and children — at risk. Too often traffickers are known to their victims as family members or neighbors. Kay Chernush. U.S. State Department.

Left: A social worker from a Catholic religious order goes daily to Mumbai's central train station to help young boys like this one who arrive from rural India thinking they will find work in order to send money home. Sometimes he convinces them to come to the shelter, where they are given a bed, schooling, medical attention, and guidance. But the boys often fall prey to unscrupulous traffickers and corrupt officials. Kay Chernush. U.S. State Department.

Right: Children of Burmese migrants working in Thailand's commercial fisheries industry lead particularly precarious lives. They are subject to economic hardship, discrimination, entrapment into child labor and deportation back into the very conditions their parents fled. Burma is a Tier 3 country in the 2005 Trafficking in Persons Report. Kay Chernush. U.S. State Department.

Trafficking in Sex in Latin America
of Slaves and Serfs: Guatemala's Sex Trade

Sexual exploitation has long been a crime in Guatemala, but innumerable bars and "night clubs," and the clients that frequent them, normally escape official scrutiny and/or a law enforcement response. Both society and the Guatemalan legal system give them a pass. The women are the focus, but the fact they are forced to be there seems to be overlooked, both unofficially and officially.

The National Commission for Adolescents and Children estimated in 2009 that some 15,000 children and adolescents were victims of human trafficking in the country. In Guatemala, sexual exploitation of women — including brokering or "pimping" sex — is against the law. This does not stop it, however. The process of laundering money from this business is easy in places like Guatemala, because the Treasury cannot legally verify whether declared income matches the amount deposited into bank accounts.

In urban areas and businesses throughout the country, this is how the system usually works: captors seek women in small villages, lying to them about the promise of work to get them to leave; or paying their families for their "services." The men in charge bring the women to bars where they live in poor conditions under the "care" of fellow females, who are in charge of helping to run the criminal network.

Somewhat surprisingly, not all the women are physically coerced into working in the sex trade. Some desperate women enter the business out of sheer necessity after reaching the point of having no other options, in order to support themselves and their families. These same women later recruit others like them, and the vicious cycle continues.

Eventually, most of these women end up working in low-scale bars — nicknamed "cevicheria." Some of them eventually find their way to relatively "fancier" businesses, which advertise as "night clubs." Regardless of where the women end up, all of them are sexually exploited.

According to Sandra Gularte, of the Guatemalan ombudsman's office, there exists a diverse range of organizations that take advantage of the market for sex trafficking. She defines three types of traffickers: the lone trafficker who is a relative or acquaintance of the victim; the small or "medium" network, and the big network. The lone trafficker simply sells his victim to the buyer. There is no relation to organized crime, though the consequences are similar for the victim.

The second type of organization, according to Gularte, are the small networks of three or four people who buy or coerce women — including those who feign romantic relationships in order to convince them. These groups trick women by offering them work as maids or waitresses and then selling them in bars. These "medium" networks, as Gularte defines them, supply women to businesses with a "lower and middle class market." The Guatemalan victims are often taken from a poor region and transferred to a less poor one. There are many "poor" and "less poor" areas in Guatemala.

Finally, Gularte says there are the big networks that coordinate with networks in other countries. "Mafiosos, politicians, military men, businessmen, industrialists, religious leaders, bankers, police, judges, assassins, and average men make up an enormous chain in the international map of organized crime that has existed throughout centuries," asserts journalist Lydia Cacho in the investigation "Esclavas del Poder" (Slaves of Power). For this large machine to function, the gears have to be oiled. The "oil" in the machine are the nameless officials who profit from the sex trade, either directly or indirectly.[38]

Conclusion

Human trafficking is modern-day slavery, and a crime against humanity. Whether voluntarily or involuntarily, people are being taken advantage of, in heinous ways. The pain and suffering enacted on these people is simply incalculable, and takes place within the boundaries (and with the full knowledge) of every nation on earth. Whether the victim is being used as slave labor in India, as a child soldier in Africa, or as a prostitute in Alabama, makes no ethical difference. Only the amount of suffering of each victim differs, and the rationalizations for the abuse on the part of those taking advantage of the ones being trafficked.

The International Labor Organization estimates that about 20.9 million people are enslaved globally—an overwhelming number. One-and-a-half million of these people are in developed economies and the European Union. The National Center for Missing and Exploited Children estimates that 100,000 of these people are children within the United States. Trafficking is not just a foreign problem. It's an American problem.

Potential victims are taken from their home communities to unfamiliar destinations, including foreign countries, away from family and friends, religious institutions, and other sources of protection and support, leaving the victims defenseless and vulnerable. People are lied to and forced into debt bondage for months, years, and lifetimes. Children are forced to work under unbelievably bad conditions, for pennies a day, seven days a week, robbed of a normal childhood. Crimes the authors consider should be capital offenses are committed daily by monsters who continue to escape justice. The fact that most trafficking occurs in poor nations and regions is not an excuse, nor a reason, for the inhumanity to continue. The truth is that it also occurs in the richest nations on earth. It is not a function of wealth; it is simply a lack of conscience.

Additional Closing Note: Human Trafficking of a Different Sort

"Today, we continue the long journey toward an America and a world where liberty and equality are not reserved for some, but extended to all. Across the globe, including right here at home, millions of men, women, and children are victims of human trafficking and modern-day slavery. We remain committed to abolishing slavery in all its forms and draw strength from the courage and resolve of generations past."

—President Barack Obama[39]

As this chapter was going to print an event occurred where one of the authors became involved. The authors have determined that providing too much specificity about the victim would be life threatening, so we are intentionally choosing to be vague.

A faculty member from an American University in an Arab country was told her father was ill and she should visit. Her father lives in Riyadh, the capital of the Kingdom of Saudi Arabia. The faculty member is a 40-year-old, never married, Saudi-born Iraqi with US citizenship. She is also Muslim.

Upon arrival in Riyadh just before Christmas 2016, she cleared immigration control and her US passport was handed to a male relative that met her at the airport, as is customary in the country. Almost immediately she was out of contact by phone, social media, and e-mail from her coworkers and friends. Over the next month there were no responses to social media contacts and only two, cryptic responses to e-mail that were obviously not written by an English speaker.

The author and their American co-workers and friends contacted the US embassy and appropriate consulates in the Arab country where they reside to report a missing US citizen in an Islamic country. No responses or even acknowledgments from the US embassy or consulates were ever received. About one week later, an e-mail written by the missing faculty member (we compared it to prior valid e-mails and social media communications) arrived in one of their inboxes. The two lines important to this chapter are: "It seems that I will be in Saudi for a while … My dad is going to marry me off to a nice gentleman with similar age." One following message was received that said, "I have been to the marital office and signed the contract. Now I have to practice all the rules about contact with unrelated men and wear a heejab (hijab)." No subsequent communications have been received by her co-workers.

A US citizen, traveling on a US passport, employed as a faculty member at an American University, is being married off by her father to an unknown male in Saudi Arabia? Hard to believe that is possible in the twenty-first century.

Per the International Business Times, there are more than 4 million virgin spinsters in Saudi Arabia. The groom, under Islamic law, pays a dowry to his bride that often exceeds $1 million. Dowries don't actually go to the bride, but to her family, as compensation should the marriage not work out, and to pay for the loss of a female family worker within the home. In many cases, a woman who is returned to her family by her husband is found at fault for bringing disrespect on the family and killed by her male family members (honor killing). The family keeps the dowry. Recently the tribal leaders in Saudi Arabia agreed to limit the dowry for virgin brides to 50,000 Saudi riyals ($13,000) and 30,000 Saudi riyals ($8,000) for women who have been previously married. The tribes acted because they had seen prices reach a point where Saudi men would marry outsiders because they couldn't pay the bride price for a Saudi woman. In fact, a study conducted by the Islamic University determined that the number of spinsters in Saudi Arabia had increased from 1.5 million in 2010 to 4 million in 2015. Such a decision to limit dowries wouldn't apply to non-Saudi residents.[40]

Questions for Further Consideration

1. Why do you believe human trafficking is known as "modern-day slavery"? Provide at least one example to support your understanding of this perspective.
2. Explain why cultural values in some Latin American countries contribute to the problem of human trafficking. Provide at least one example.
3. Explain why economic or political values in some European countries contribute to the problem of human trafficking.
4. Why does it appear that most of the sex trafficking focus appears to originate from Asian countries? Are most sex trafficking victims from Asia? What contributes to this problem?
5. What can be done to gain compliance with developing laws in control of human trafficking from countries designated as Tier 3 Countries by the US Trafficking in Persons Report?
6. Does the payment of a dowry to the family of a bride, where the male family members are in strict control of arranging marriages for their unmarried daughters, sisters, and nieces, constitute a "sale" under the definitions of slavery? What about under the definition of "sex trafficking"?

Chapter 7 Endnotes

1. Shelley, L., *Human Trafficking: A Global Perspective* (New York: Cambridge University Press, 2010), p. 2.

2. Bureau of International Narcotics and Law Enforcement Affairs, Human Smuggling and Trafficking Center, *Distinctions Between Human Smuggling and Human Trafficking* (Washington, DC: U.S. Department of State, Bureau of International Narcotics and Law Enforcement Affairs, Human Smuggling and Trafficking Center, 2005). Accessed July 18, 2017. Available at: http://www.ojp.usdoj.gov/ovc/pubs/existeayuda/glossaries/humantrafficking/smuggling.html.

3. Trafficking Victims Protection Act, TVPA 114 STAT. 1467 PUBLIC LAW 106–386 — OCT. 28, 2000.

4. International Labour Organization, *ILO Action Against Trafficking in Human Beings.* (Geneva, Switzerland: United Nations, International Labour Organization, 2008).

5. "Human Trafficking by the Numbers," Human Rights First, January 7, 2017. Accessed July 18, 2017. Available at: http://www.humanrightsfirst.org/resource/human-trafficking-numbers

6. United Nations Report, *Global Report on Trafficking in Persons 2016.* Accessed July 18, 2017. Available at: http://www.unodc.org/documents/data-and-analysis/glotip/2016_Global_Report_on_Trafficking_in_Persons.pdf

7. Ibid.

8. McLeod, Saul (2007). "The Milgram Experiment." Accessed July 18, 2017. Available at: http://www.simplypsychology.org/milgram.html

9. Shelley, L. (2010).

10. Bales, K., *Disposable People: New Slavery in the Global Economy.* Berkeley: University of California Press, 2014).

11. Trafficking Victims Protection Act, TVPA 114 STAT. 1467 PUBLIC LAW 106-386- OCT. 28, 2000.

12. Child Soldiers Prevention Act of 2008 (CSPA). Signed into law on December 23, 2008 (Title IV of Pub. L. 110-457).

13. Protocol to Prevent, Suppress, and Punish Trafficking in Persons, Especially Women and Children. Adopted by the United Nations in Palermo, Italy, in 2000.

14. Trafficking Victims Protection Act, TVPA 114 STAT. 1467 PUBLIC LAW 106-386- OCT. 28, 2000.

15. Vitello, Paul, 3 Dec 2007. From Stand in Long Island Slavery Case, a Snapshot of a Hidden U.S. Problem. *The New York Times.* Accessed July 18, 2017. Available at: http://www.nytimes.com/2007/12/03/nyregion/03slavery.html

16. UNWomen.Org, "Infographic: Migrant Domestic Workers: Facts Everyone Should Know," 09 September 2016. Accessed July 18, 2017. Available at: http://www.unwomen.org/en/digital-library/multimedia/2016/9/infographic-migrant-domestic-workers

17. Bureau of Labor Statistics, U.S. Department of Labor, 16 December 2016. Accessed July 18, 2017. Available at: https://www.bls.gov/news.release/pdf/cfoi.pdf

18. Bureau of Labor Statistics. U.S. Department of Labor, 25 April 2012.

19. Child Soldiers Prevention Act of 2008 (CSPA). Signed into law on December 23, 2008 (Title IV of Pub. L. 110-457).

20. Trafficking in Persons Report 2014, June 2014. Accessed July 18, 2017. Available at: https://www.state.gov/documents/organization/226844.pdf

21. United Nations Report, Global Report on Trafficking in Persons 2016.

22. Bales, K. (2004).

23. United Nations Report, Global Report on Trafficking in Persons 2016.

24. Shelley, L. (2010).

25. Ibid.

26. Ibid.

27. United Nations Report, Global Report on Trafficking in Persons 2016.

28. Plant, Roger, Head of the Special Action Program to Combat Forced Labor; speech to the U.S. Congressional Committee Meeting on China on March 6, 2006.

29. Shelley, L. (2010), p. 141.

30. Sidel, J. T. Capital, Coercion, and Crime Bossism in the Philippines. (Stanford, CA: Stanford University Press); quoted in Shelley, 2010. Human Trafficking: A Human Perspective. New York: Cambridge University Press), 142.

31. United Nations Report, Global Report on Trafficking in Persons 2016.

32. Ibid.

33. Shelley, L. (2010), p. 229.

34. Ehrenreich, B..*Nickeled and Dimed: On (not) Getting by in America* (New York: Henry Holt, 2001), quoted in Shelley, 2010, 230.

35. Immigration and Customs Enforcement, News Release, 22 May 2013. Accessed July 18, 2017. Available at: https://www.ice.gov/news/releases/hsi-fbi-dismantle-sex-trafficking-ring-atlanta

36. Van Doren, M., RCMP Human Trafficking Awareness Coordinator, "Human Trafficking—Canada Law Enforcement Perspective." The Commodification of Illicit Flows: Labour Migration, Trafficking, and Business, Centre for Diaspora and Transnational Studies, University of Toronto, October 9-10, 2009; quoted in Shelley, p. 231.

37. Shelley, L. (2010), p. 233.

38. "Of Slaves and Serfs: Guatemala's Sex Trade." Accessed July 18, 2017. Available at: http://www.insightcrime.org/categories/slaves-victims-of-crime-in-guatemala

39. Trafficking in Persons Report, June 2016, 4. Accessed July 18, 2017. Available at: https://www.state.gov/j/tip/rls/tiprpt/2016/

40. Information to support this added section was sourced from this and other confidential sources: International Business Times, India Edition, 19 August 2015, at: http://www.ibtimes.co.in/saudi-arabia-sets-dowry-limit-virgin-brides-combat-rise-spinsters-643419. Last Accessed July 18, 2017.

Chapter 8

Borders, Economic Interdependence, and Internet Crime

"It has been said that arguing against globalization is like arguing against the laws of gravity."

—Kofi Annan[1]

Key Words and Concepts

Council of Europe Convention on
    Cybercrime
Cybercrime
Free Trade Agreements
Globalization
InfraGard

Interdependence
North American Free Trade Agreement
    (NAFTA)
Transnational Organized Crime
United Nations Convention against
    Transnational Organized Crime

Introduction

In many chapters, we discuss the impact of globalization on border security. The impact of modern economic interdependence upon border (and thereby national) security is the focus of this chapter. Understanding what globalization is and how it impacts each country's national security and therefore its border security efforts, is imperative to comprehend the difficulty faced by societies everywhere when attempting to enforce their own laws in defense of their culture, language, environment, and economy. Embedded within the issue of globalization is the issue of energy security. As industrialized nations shifted from locally supplied energy resources to energy resources shipped across vast distances, a change occurred resulting in the alteration of perceived limits on political and economic borders, as did the increasing vulnerability of industrialized nations to efforts by the smallest nation states or criminal enterprises to disrupt the energy supply lines. Along with the rise of the Internet has come an increase in small international businesses conducting trade and sharing information

Ross Perot: "There will be a giant sucking sound going south." — 1992.

across borders. Concurrently there has been a rise in internationally based crime associated with the Internet, from theft of personal identification information to corporate espionage.

All countries are now economically interdependent upon other countries. This interdependence has changed the way we view border security and has become a consideration of national security in the United States and other countries. For more than half a century, every country that has industrialized has found itself dependent on energy sources from other parts of the world, often from the Middle East or North Africa, areas that have seen much political and religious turmoil as their national resources are being drained for the benefit of other countries and a few indigenous wealthy dynasties.

Economic interdependence is fundamental to survival in the globalized world. No country can survive independent of other countries and even the most isolated of countries often find themselves dependent upon aid from their staunch enemies. R. J. Ahearn writes,

> The current wave of globalization is supported by three broad trends. The first is technology, which has sharply reduced the cost of communication and transportation that previously divided markets. The second is a dramatic increase in the world supply of labor engaged in international trade. The third is government policies that have reduced barriers to trade and investment.[2]

The Internet gave rise to information interdependence that has impacted cultural and political beliefs around the world. Restricting the free flow of information across the Internet is virtually impossible, even for totalitarian governments such as China's.

The supply of workers contributing to the world economic marketplace has expanded nearly exponentially in the past half century. Rising industrial nations such as China, India, and Vietnam are simply the tip of the iceberg as we observe rapid manufacturing and agricultural expansion in south and central America, as well as natural resource development across Africa. As Ahearn notes, the expansion of government policies by all nations to reduce trade barriers and expand markets has a significant impact on economic interdependence. One area that Ahearn does not note as having an impact on the US economy is the growing war for access to energy resources brewing around the world; the prime issue driving the upcoming conflict is the question of borders, where they are, and who controls the resources in those disputed areas, particularly beneath the oceans.

Globalization

Globalization is the process of international integration arising from the interchange of worldviews, products, ideas, and other aspects of culture. Simplified, globalization refers to processes that promote worldwide exchanges of national and cultural resources. So, globalization is a contradiction of the fundamental purpose of borders. Several scholars place the origins of globalization in modern times; others trace its history long before the European age of discovery and voyages to the New World. Some even trace the origins to the third millennium BCE. Regardless, since the beginning of the

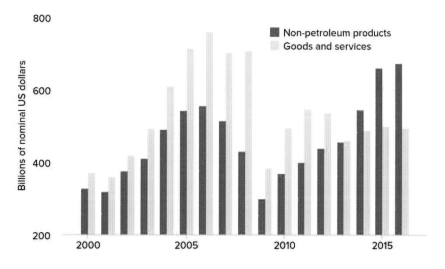

U.S. trade deficits, 2000 – 2016

Source: EPI analysis of US Census Bureau, US International Trade Commission, and Bureau of Labor Statistics data. EPI, Feb. 7, 2017.

twentieth century, the pace of globalization has increased at an exponential rate. Advances in transportation and telecommunications infrastructure, including the rise of the Internet, are major factors in globalization, generating further interdependence of economic and cultural activities.

As the United States entered 2017, of 41 top trading partners, the United States maintained a negative trade balance with all except Australia, Belgium, Egypt, Hong Kong, and four South American countries. The largest negative trade balance was with China at $31,304,000,000. Except for Hong Kong, none of the 8 trade surplus countries came close to reaching $1 billion.[3]

Globalization has given rise to several conventions that impact border and national security. The North American Free Trade Agreement (NAFTA) and many other free trade agreements (FTAs) are of primary concern to Americans, Canadians, and Mexicans, and impact the traffic between these countries. This free movement of goods was critical in the 2016 election of Donald Trump as 45th President of the United States with his calls to cut off Mexico with a wall and return lost jobs to America.

United States participation in FTAs with countries such as Mexico, Chile, and Colombia plays a role in accelerating the integration of global markets. Through a mutual reduction in trade barriers, countries entering an FTA accelerate specialization in production and trade. Opening new opportunities for the export of US goods and services, FTAs support jobs associated with increased exports. At the same time, some US jobs and production shift to FTA partners who can offer lower costs of production, including labor cost.[4]

The United States has FTAs with 20 countries (as of this writing) including: Australia, Bahrain, Canada, Chile, Colombia, Costa Rica, Dominican Republic, El Salvador, Guatemala, Honduras, Israel (including the Palestinian Authority), Jordan, South Korea, Mexico, Morocco, Nicaragua, Oman, Panama, Peru, and Singapore.[5] The first of these FTAs was established with Israel in 1985 and most recently with South Korea in 2011. FTAs have resulted in an increase in trade, particularly in exports with other countries as can be seen in the figure above from Customs and Border Protection (CBP).

The downside to FTAs is the movement of jobs from high-wage-and-benefit countries to low-wage-and-benefit countries. This was graphically predicted by Presidential candidate Ross Perot during the third Clinton-Bush-Perot debate on October 19, 1992, when Perot was asked (in a town hall format) the opening question of the debate: "What will you do as President to open foreign markets to fair competition from American business and to stop unfair competition here at home from foreign countries so that we can bring jobs back to the United States?"[6] His reply has become the classic response to FTAs and the fundamental problem they pose. Perot replied:

> That's right at the top of my agenda. We ship millions of jobs overseas, and uh, we have a strange situation because we have a process in Washington where after you've served for a while you cash in, become a foreign lobbyist,

make $30,000 a month, then take a leave, work on presidential campaigns, make sure you got good contacts and then go back out. Now if you just want to get down to brass tacks the first thing you ought to do is get all these folks who got these one way trade agreements that have been negotiated over the years and say 'fellas we'll take the same deal we gave you' and they'll gridlock right at that point because, for example, we got international competitors who simply could not unload their cars off their ships if they had to comply, ya [sic] see, if it was a two way street, just couldn't do it. We have got to stop sending jobs overseas. To those of you in the audience who are business people it's pretty simple. If you are paying 12 or 13 or 14 dollars an hour for factory workers and you can move your factory south of the border, pay a dollar an hour for labor ... have no health care ... no environmental controls, no pollution controls, and no retirement, and you don't care about anything but making money, there will be a giant sucking sound going south.[7]

He continued with an explanation that the North American Free Trade Agreement (NAFTA) would continue to be disruptive to American business for 12 to 15 years until Mexican wages came up to six dollars an hour and ours came down to six dollars an hour. He predicted that in the meantime FTAs would wreck the American manufacturing base. It turns out that Ross Perot was right. According to data released just as this chapter was going to print, the United States lost more than 5 million manufacturing jobs to Mexico and Canada after the initiation of NAFTA — fully one-third of all manufacturing jobs before NAFTA.

Robert Scott writes in a briefing paper for the Economic Policy Institute, as of 2010, the US trade deficit with Mexico totaled $97.2 billion and had resulted in the displacement of 682,900 jobs. In 1993 President Clinton and economists predicted trade surpluses that never materialized. The year before NAFTA took effect in 1993, the United States had a $1.6 billion trade surplus with Mexico supporting about 29,400 jobs in the United States. Following implementation of NAFTA in 1994 the United States saw a loss of jobs to Mexico with the computer and electronic parts, and motor vehicles and parts sectors equaling nearly 38% of the total job shift. All 50 states, the District of Columbia, and Puerto Rico suffered job losses resulting from NAFTA.[8]

By 2011, US exports to Mexico, under NAFTA, supported about 791,900 jobs in the United States. However, that pales in comparison to the 1.47 million jobs that would exist in the United States had NAFTA never been ratified. More so, the "great sucking sound" predicted by Ross Perot has not stopped. In 2010 alone, the growth of Mexican auto exports to the United States resulted in the addition of 30,400 jobs in Mexico, more than all jobs in the United States auto industry.[9] In 2014, the United States imported 51 percent of its autos and associated parts from Canada and Mexico. This is a 679 percent increase in auto-related imports from Mexico and a 59 percent increase from Canada over the 1993 pre-NAFTA numbers.[10]

NAFTA's Economic Impact

James McBride and Mohammed Aly Sergie
Council on Foreign Relations, 24 January 2017
How has NAFTA affected the US economy?

In the years since NAFTA, US trade with its North American neighbors has more than tripled, growing more rapidly than US trade with the rest of the world. Canada and Mexico are the two largest destinations for US exports, accounting for more than a third of the total. Most estimates conclude that the deal had a modest but positive impact on US GDP of less than 0.5 percent, or a total addition of up to 80 billion dollars to the US economy upon full implementation, or several billion dollars of added growth per year.

Such upsides of trade often escape notice, because while the costs are highly concentrated in specific industries like auto manufacturing, the benefits of a deal like NAFTA are distributed widely across society. Supporters of NAFTA estimate that some fourteen million jobs rely on trade with Canada and Mexico, while the nearly two hundred thousand export-related jobs created annually by the pact pay 15 to 20 percent more on average than the jobs that were lost.

Critics of the deal, however, argue that it is to blame for job losses and wage stagnation in the United States, driven by low-wage competition, companies moving production to Mexico to lower costs, and a widening trade deficit. The United States–Mexico trade balance swung from a $1.7 billion US surplus in 1993 to a $54 billion deficit by 2014. Economists like the Center for Economic and Policy Research's (CEPR) Dean Baker and the Economic Policy Institute argue that this surge of imports caused the loss of up to 600,000 US jobs over two decades, though they admit that some of this import growth would likely have happened even without NAFTA.

Many workers and labor leaders point to these numbers to blame trade, including NAFTA, for the decline in US manufacturing jobs. The US auto sector lost some 350,000 jobs since 1994—a third of the industry—while Mexican auto sector employment spiked from 120,000 to 550,000 workers. CEPR's Baker argues that econometric research shows that increased trade also puts downward pressure on wages for non-college educated workers, who are more likely to face direct competition from low-wage workers in Mexico.

But other economists like Gary Clyde Hufbauer and Cathleen Cimino-Isaacs of the Peterson Institute for International Economics (PIIE) emphasize that increased trade produces gains for the overall US economy. Some jobs are lost due to imports, but others are created, and consumers benefit significantly from the falling prices and often improved quality of goods created by import competition. A 2014 PIIE study of NAFTA's effects found that about 15,000 jobs on net are lost each year due to the pact—but that for each of those jobs lost, the economy gains roughly

$450,000 in the form of higher productivity and lower consumer prices. By contributing to the development of cross-border supply chains, NAFTA lowered costs, increased productivity, and improved US competitiveness.

Many economists also assert that the recent troubles of US manufacturing have little to do with NAFTA, arguing that manufacturing in the United States was under stress decades before the treaty. Research by David Autor, David Dorn, and Gordon Hanson published in January 2016 found that competition with China had a much bigger negative impact on US jobs since 2001, when China joined the WTO. Hanson, an economist and trade expert at the University of California, San Diego, says that the steepest decline in manufacturing jobs, which fell from seventeen million to eleven million between 2000 and 2010, is mostly attributable to trade with China and underlying technological changes. "China is at the top of the list in terms of the employment impacts that we found since 2000, with technology second, and NAFTA far less important," he says.

In fact, says Hanson, NAFTA helped the US auto sector compete with China. By contributing to the development of cross-border supply chains, NAFTA lowered costs, increased productivity, and improved US competitiveness. This meant shedding some jobs in the United States as positions moved to Mexico, he argues, but without the pact, even more would have otherwise been lost. "Because Mexico is so close, you can have a regional industry cluster where goods can go back and forth. The manufacturing industries in the three countries can be very integrated," he says. These sort of linkages, which have given US automakers an advantage in relation to China, would be much more difficult without NAFTA's tariff reductions and protections for intellectual property.

Edward Alden, a senior fellow at the Council on Foreign Relations, says anxiety over trade deals has grown because wages haven't kept pace with labor productivity while income inequality has risen. To some extent, he says, trade deals have hastened the pace of these changes in that they have "reinforced the globalization of the American economy."[11]

The shifting of jobs from one country to another raises the issue of what to do with those unemployed as a result of FTAs. A 2015 article by Robert Scott of the Economic Policy Institute reports, "Although increased exports support US jobs, increased imports cost US jobs. Thus, it is trade balances—the net of exports and imports—that determine the number of jobs created or displaced by trade agreements. Rather than reducing our too-high trade deficit, past trade agreements have actually been followed by larger US trade deficits."[12] Using the trade imbalance with China as an example, Scott writes,

- The growth of US exports to China between 2001 and 2011 supported 538,000 US jobs; on average, jobs in the industries exporting to China paid $872.89 per week in 2009–2011 (the last years for which we have complete wage data).

- The growth of US imports from China between 2001 and 2011 displaced nearly 3.3 million (3,280,200) US jobs; on average, jobs in these import-competing industries paid an average of $1,021.66 per week in 2009–2011.
- Jobs in nontraded industries (industries that do not involve traded goods) paid an average weekly salary of $791.14 per week in 2009–2011.
- Overall, the increase in the US trade deficit with China between 2001 and 2011 eliminated more than 2.7 million US jobs.
- Total wage losses due to trade with China were $37.0 billion in 2011. This assumes that 538,000 of the 3.3 million workers who lost jobs in importing-competing jobs found work in the newly created exporting jobs paying $148 a week less, or $7,736 less per year, and that the remaining 2.7 million workers displaced by growing US imports from China found jobs in industries unaffected by trade paying $230 less per week, or $11,987 less per year.
- The displacement of manufacturing jobs by growing US trade deficits with China has been particularly hard on minority workers: 958,800 were displaced, with wage-related losses in 2011 of $10,485 per worker and $10.1 billion overall.
- The rapidly growing China trade deficit displaced nearly 1.1 million jobs in computer and electronic products between 2001 and 2011, well over a third of all the jobs displaced. Wages in the computer and electronic products sector are high, even higher than average manufacturing wages, and therefore higher than wages in nontraded industries. Nearly three-fourths (74.3 percent) of the workers in this industry sector earn wages in the top half of the income distribution.[13]

If we look at this again we see that in only ten years, the United States lost 2.7 million jobs to China. This has been a major concern for organized labor around the world as well as politicians dependent upon the labor vote for reelection. A 2007 article by Paul Krugman noted that Mexican wages were only 11 percent and Chinese wages only 3 percent of the US level.[14] How can American labor with its high wages and even higher benefit costs begin to compete in the international marketplace when confronted with low wages in competing countries?

The conservative approach to FTAs is that an open marketplace, free enterprise, and limited government interference naturally drive innovation and economic prosperity and provide security for all Americans. The basic idea of this approach is that individuals are best helped not by government intervention but by making their own choices in a free marketplace.[15] This view of globalization provides unprecedented opportunities for the United States to derive large-scale economic benefits through free trade policies, which raises the overall economic standing of all Americans, on average, even if a few must find a way to re-purpose themselves after their jobs have moved to other countries.

The liberal approach to FTAs is that existing employees should receive higher minimum wage, universal health care, a union-friendly workplace, and expanded funding for research and development for new industries, particularly in the area of alternative energy.[16] This approach is based largely on the model of universal unions, high minimum wages, and strong welfare state benefits. Two Scandinavian countries,

Norway and Sweden, which enjoy among the lowest unemployment rates in Europe, are highly open to international trade and to job churning (hiring and firing) in their economies. Firms are not free to compete by undercutting the union rate but must try to keep productivity high if they are to survive.[17] The premise of this high-standards job creation approach is that the foundation of a strong American middle class rests with laws, regulations, and standards developed at home. Instead of worrying about what impact trade with low-wage developing countries has on US wages, this approach maintains that a high-wages domestic economy will have a favorable impact on trade. A high-wage strategy, of course, depends on the ability and willingness of companies to invest in capital and technology to generate high labor productivity to pay for high wages.[18] The problem with this model is that it cannot be universally instituted in the United States or many other nations because the one component that makes it successful in Scandinavia, job churning, is anathema to American politicians and organized labor, resulting in extensive protection of jobs based on any number of justifications, including ethnic, gender, sexual orientation, and simple longevity as bases for lawsuits against employers who increase and decrease their workforce to meet changing production demands.

Both the conservative and liberal approaches to free trade are flawed! Neither approach has resulted in greater benefits or jobs for Americans. In fact, the jobs have bled from the country overseas while the importation of cheap consumer goods has resulted in depressed wages and limited employment opportunities across all US industries—except that of government employment.

The FTAs the United States has with other countries include provisions to protect worker rights and facilitate cooperation among labor ministries. This is an attempt to ensure fair labor practices are enforced in countries that the United States has FTAs with as well as to address issues associated with claims of unfair labor practices in other countries. The Office of Trade and Labor Affairs (OTLA), a component of the US Department of Labor, receives and reviews claims made by US labor and businesses under the North American Agreement on Labor Cooperation (NAALC) and FTAs to ensure other countries follow the FTAs as well as other international agreements and that unfair labor practices are corrected when substantiated. Since July 30, 2010, when the first-ever labor-related consultations under a specific FTA were instituted with Guatemala, the OTLA has conducted additional consultations with Bahrain, Honduras, the Dominican Republic, Mexico, and Peru.[19]

Not all aspects of FTAs are detrimental to the United States. There are components that result in job loss in the countries that otherwise benefit from signing an agreement with the United States. For example, as a result of NAFTA, Mexico lost 1.3 million farm jobs. The 2002 Farm Bill subsidized US agribusiness by as much as 40 percent of net farm income. When NAFTA reached the point of implementation where tariffs on food were removed, corn and other grains were exported to Mexico below cost. Rural Mexican farmers could not compete. At the same time, Mexico reduced its subsidies to farmers from 33.2 percent of total farm income in 1990 to 13.25 in 2001. Most of those subsidies went to Mexico's largest farms.[20] Concurrently, the Mexican government nationalized the farmlands around rural villages and leased or sold these lands to large agribusinesses, resulting in the near complete destruction of village cultures across the country and creating a situation of such destitution that a mass migration to the border region began as the maquiladoras were expanding to provide products to the United States.[21]

Nor do all FTAs get fully implemented. When the component of NAFTA that would allow Mexican truckers to continue carrying loads beyond the 20-mile economic zone along the border to the rest of the United States a cry was raised by professional trucking labor organizations and American trucking businesses that resulted in a proposal by the Department of Transportation to conduct a demonstration project to see if implementing this component of the FTA was feasible.[22] By a vote of 385 to 18 the US House of Representatives passed H.R. 6630 terminating the pilot project and prohibiting the Department from granting new authority to Mexican trucks to operate beyond the 20-mile commercial zone along the border without express permission from Congress.[23] Many argued that implementing NAFTA provisions to allow Mexican truckers access to American roads would result in the reciprocal implementation of US trucks being allowed on Mexican roads. However, this argument failed to take into consideration that Mexican roads and infrastructure are not designed nor constructed to handle the heavier American trucks, so even if reciprocity were implemented, US truckers would not be able to take advantage of the agreement.[24] Although never passed by the Senate, the threat of congressional action was enough to shut down any future attempts to implement this portion of NAFTA.[25]

Other countries have also established FTAs with various partners. The People's Republic of China has FTAs with fourteen countries and is negotiating agreements with nineteen more.[26] The European Union has FTAs or other liberal trade agreements with more than fifty nonmember countries and is in the process of negotiating or implementing agreements with another nine countries as of January 2017.[27] Switzerland has FTAs with more than fifty countries. Clearly economic globalization is here to stay no matter what the pros or cons may be for any country or employment group.

Energy Interdependence

"True energy security can only come from energy independence."[28]

—James Phelps, 2013

Energy security can be described as "the uninterrupted availability of energy sources at an affordable price,"[29] while respecting environment concerns. The need to increase "energy security" was the main objective underpinning the establishment of the International Energy Agency (IEA) in 1973–74. With particular emphasis on oil security, the IEA was created in order to establish effective mechanisms for the implementation of policies on a broad spectrum of energy issues: mechanisms that were workable and reliable, and could be implemented on a cooperative basis.

International Energy Agency Member Countries[30]

Australia	Korea
Austria	Luxembourg
Belgium	The Netherlands
Canada	New Zealand
Czech Republic	Norway
Denmark	Poland
Estonia	Portugal
Finland	Slovak Republic
France	Spain
Germany	Sweden
Greece	Switzerland
Hungary	Turkey
Ireland	United Kingdom
Italy	United States
Japan	

Oil security remains a cornerstone of the IEA, with each IEA member required to hold oil stocks equivalent to at least ninety days of net imports and to maintain emergency measures for responding collectively to sudden disruptions in oil supply. At the same time, the IEA recognizes the broader needs of ensuring energy security and is progressively taking a more comprehensive approach to the security of supplies, including for example natural gas supplies, nuclear, coal, renewables, and power generation.

Energy security has many aspects: long-term energy security is mainly linked to timely investments to supply energy in line with economic developments and environmental needs. Short-term energy security is the ability of the energy system to react promptly to sudden changes in supply and demand. Another way to look at energy security is to study the different energy sources (coal, oil, gas, and renewables), intermediate means (electricity, refineries) and transportation modes (grids, pipelines, ports, ships). These all have risks of supply interruptions or failures, challenging the security of undisturbed energy supply.

The United States is not energy independent, no matter the number of days of petroleum reserves on hand. The United States is an importer of crude oil making a large portion of the industry, energy production, and economy dependent upon supplies from other countries, some of whom are not necessarily friendly or supportive of the country's political positions. The United States is a member of the Organisation for Economic Co-operation and Development (OECD), a group consisting of thirty-five countries intended "to promote policies that will improve the economic and social well-being of people around the world.... The OECD provides a forum in which governments can work together to share experiences and seek solutions to common problems. We work with governments to understand what drives economic, social and environmental change. We measure productivity and global flows of trade and investment. We analyse and compare data to predict future trends. We set international standards on a wide range of things, from agriculture and tax to the safety of chemicals."[31] Using data the OECD collects makes it possible to see the energy dependency of the organization overall, its member states, and nonmember states. Appendix A at the end of this chapter includes specific Sankey diagrams showing OECD and selected country energy balance and final consumption for several member and nonmember states. Current information on any country can be accessed at the OECD website: http://www.oecd.org/.

In 2015 the United States was importing 9.4 million barrels of petroleum products every day. About 78 percent of those imports included 7.33 million barrels of crude oil, up from 6.833 million barrels of crude oil in 2012. Of the 2015 imports, 31 percent were from OPEC with half that coming from Middle East suppliers.[32]

Top sources and amounts of U.S. petroleum imports (percent share of total), respective exports, and net imports, 2015 (million barrels per day)

Import Sources	Gross Imports	Exports	Net Imports
Total, all countries	9.45	4.74	4.71
OPEC countries	2.89	0.24	2.65
Persian Gulf Countries	1.51	0.02	1.49
Top Five Countries*			
Canada	3.76	0.96	2.81
Saudi Arabia	1.06	0.00	1.06
Venezuela	0.83	0.07	0.75
Mexico	0.76	0.69	0.07
Colombia	0.40	0.17	0.22

*Based on gross imports by country of origin

US Oil Imports 2015, US Energy Information Administration, available at: http://www.eia.gov/tools/faqs/faq.cfm?id=727&t=6

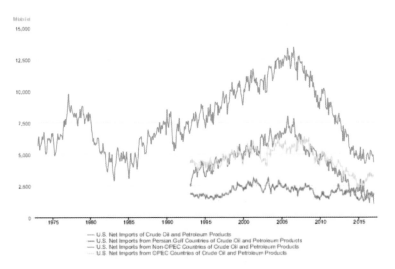

US net imports by country, 1973–2016. Source: US Energy Information Administration.

The continued US dependence on crude oil and other energy sources from such countries as Mexico, Russia, Venezuela, and other OPEC nations creates a dilemma. A single nation can cut off their portion of the oil supply resulting in a temporary disruption in oil deliveries, which can be easily absorbed by the on-hand reserves maintained under IEA guidelines and the reaction of market forces. However, if a group of countries, such as OPEC, were to institute another oil embargo of sufficient duration to significantly impact the on-hand reserves, or even deplete those reserves, then the impact on the economy could be significant, particularly as prices rise due to regional supply and demand vagaries. Several strategies may offset the potential impact of such an event.

Table 8.1 US Energy Information Administration/Monthly Energy Review January 2017 Petroleum Overview (Thousands of Barrels per Day)

Year Average	Field Production	Imports	Exports	Net Imports
1950	5,906	850	305	545
1955	7,578	1,248	368	880
1960	7,965	1,815	202	1613
1965	9,014	2,468	187	2281
1970	11,297	3,419	259	3161
1975	10,007	6,056	209	5846
1980	10,170	6,909	544	6365
1985	10,581	5,067	781	4286
1990	8,914	8,018	857	7161
1995	8,322	8,835	949	7886
2000	7,733	11,459	1,040	10,419
2005	6,901	13,714	1,165	12,549
2006	6,825	13,707	1,317	12,390
2007	6,860	13,468	1,433	12,036
2008	6,784	12,915	1,802	11,114
2009	7,263	11,691	2,024	9,667
2010	7,549	11,793	2,353	9,441
2011	7,862	11,436	2,986	8,450
2012	8,895	10,598	3,205	7,393
2013	10,073	9,859	3,621	6,237
2014	11,778	9,241	4,176	5,065
2015	12,757	9,449	4,738	4,711
2016	17,348	10,054	5,162	4,862

Adapted from: http://www.eia.gov/totalenergy/data/monthly/pdf/sec3_3.pdf

An important aspect to remember about the influence of other countries on the US economy is that since the 2008 economic recession, net imports of petroleum have been steadily declining and the availability of internal reserves has risen. In fact, based on information from the US Energy Information Administration (Table 8.1), total petroleum imports to the United States are now at their lowest level since the 1970s.[33]

In addition to petroleum there are several other energy sources available including renewables such as wind, solar, nuclear, geothermal, tidal, and hydroelectric; coal; and natural gas. How the United States uses these energy sources can be seen in Appendix B at the end of this chapter.

One strategy that has already proved useful in improving energy security is to advance economic interdependencies. As consumer nations get their resources from multiple sources, supplier nations have less ability to use their natural resources as economic weapons.[34] Another strategy is to create the kind of environment that will promote a healthier energy industry. Supplier states like Iraq need to enact laws that will persuade investors that money flowing into the country will not fuel corruption.[35] States like Nigeria need to give their people a stake in industrial development to reduce unrest and increase productivity. The propagation of good business practices as well as state-of-the-art technologies should be encouraged. The oil business, for example, can share knowledge about good field management and engineering, to the benefit of all concerned.[36] Sharing advanced, safe, and "green" technologies with developing nations promises to pay security dividends.[37] The third strategy is to enlarge the energy pie by creating new (alternative) forms of energy, developing new and better ways to exploit older ones, and by promoting efficiency and conservation. There are compelling reasons to rapidly develop alternatives:

- It will help to ensure that more and cheaper fossil fuels can be reserved for use by the military in wartime.
- The spread of alternative energy might allow developing nations to break into new markets.[38]
- Reducing dependence on fossil fuels in the transportation sector will help liberate our foreign policy.

These arguments are especially applicable to renewables. Because the United States has extensive domestic natural gas reserves and because of the security advantages to be derived from reduced dependency on oil, shale gas has its strong supporters. There is also considerable support for the development of new technologies for cleaning coal. Hard carbons like coal, though not a renewable fuel, are abundant. Opponents, however, resist continued reliance on fossil fuels and worry about the environmental damage done by extraction and disposal. Conservation and efficiency are essential parts of any strategy that focuses on the expansion of supply through technology. Improved efficiency can be achieved by a wide variety of means. Many of these carry little risk—such as the use of more energy-efficient building materials in our homes. Others, like recycling waste in breeder reactors, are more problematic.

Another strategy to ensure energy security is the application of military force. The use of military force to protect our energy security is controversial. American military power provides the stability that allows the global oil market to function.[39] At the same time, there are clear limits to what military force can accomplish. It cannot affect growing energy demand. Nor can it prevent "peak oil" demands. Some argue that forward military deployment is not the best answer to politically motivated disruptions of supply. Radical disruptions might result from a variety of scenarios including a major war in the Middle East, or civil wars within an oil-rich nation but intervention in these cases would be counterproductive. Most disruptions are likely to be temporary because market forces naturally compensate for obstructions in the flow of oil. This is good news, because a strategy of military restraint will help the United States in a time of fiscal retrenchment.[40]

The United States is not the only country dependent on other countries for its energy supply. Chile resides along a narrow strip of land between the Andes Mountains and the Pacific Ocean. It borders Argentina, Bolivia, and Peru. Because of its geography and the population distribution, much of the energy production and consumption occurs in the center, near the major population centers of Santiago and Valparaiso. Large portions of the country to the north and south of the population centers are dependent upon electricity and natural gas imports from neighboring Argentina and Bolivia.[41] Chile's major industry, mining, is the major consumer of energy resources outside of the central cities. The Chilean Mining Ministry estimates the country will need an additional capacity of 8,000 megawatts by 2020 to meet the mining sector's rising demand. This represents a 50 percent increase over current production capacity. Until 2010, Argentina supplied 15 percent of the electricity used to supply copper and aluminum mining operations in Chile's Atacama and Antofagasta regions. Copper production alone accounts for 13.5 percent of Chilean GDP so any impact on the industry would impact the country's overall economy. Matching the expected growth in global demand and counterbalancing the rising competition from regional and international producers, the Chilean government has set the goal of producing 7 million metric tons of copper annually by 2020, up from 5.3 million in 2010. However, this goal may prove to be overambitious because of the shortage of cheap energy. The problems of energy interdependence on cross-border suppliers weres exasperated when in August 2012 the country's Supreme Court struck down a proposal to allow German and Brazilian energy companies to construct a large coal-fired power plant and its associated coal import port in northern Chile.[42] Much of the conflict over energy in Chile is the result of political protests over environmental destruction. The protestors often are native peoples who have a special status under the constitution.[43]

Several facts compound Chile's energy problems. Chile relies on thermoelectric plants powered by natural gas, oil, or coal for 60 percent of its domestic electricity production. Natural-gas-fired power plants account for 18 percent of Chile's electricity output, coal-fired plants for 28 percent, and oil-fired for 14 percent. Hydroelectric power also satisfies a relatively high share of Chile's energy needs at 36 percent. Increasing hydroelectric power generation is unfeasible to meet the requirements of the growing mining sector because all of Chile's hydroelectric plants are located in the south, nearly 1,600 kilometers (1,000 miles) away from the nearest mining sites. Chile has considered constructing massive power transmission lines from the hydroelectric power-generating region of Patagonia in the south to the Atacama Desert in the north, but costs and environmental concerns have so far proved prohibitive. High costs have also hampered the development of other potential renewable energy sources like solar and tidal power. Chile's frequent earthquakes are also a major deterrent for the construction of new nuclear power plants, especially since the 2011 Japanese nuclear disaster. Unlike hydroelectric plants, thermoelectric plants can be placed near mining sites, but require a stable supply of oil, natural gas, or coal to produce energy. Chile's indigenous reserves of those hydrocarbons are not nearly sufficient to meet its domestic needs, leading the country to import nearly 75 percent of its energy.[44]

Chile's economic interdependence on energy from other countries does have a simple, inexpensive, and environmentally sound solution. The country could become entirely self-sufficient for its electrical needs by shifting to geothermal electrical generation in the north. Chile sits on the largest source of geothermal energy in South America. Once again, the problem becomes one of bringing the native peoples into an agreement with the government and the mining companies so that the original peoples are satisfied that using geothermal as an energy source will not harm the environment or the tourism income the pristine conditions of Atacama, Patagonia, and Antofagasta bring to the country.[45]

The United States has an energy dependency that makes the entire economy, and therefore US national security, susceptible to market vagaries as well as international disturbances and conflicts. Chile has plenty of internal resources that could be tapped to meet the energy demands of its growing economy and mining industry but the internal politics keep it from doing so, making Chile dependent upon its neighbors. Both countries face problems associated with how to get energy resources across their borders, and in both cases, across oceans and mountains. The same problems exist for many countries. Japan has no petroleum reserves and is dependent upon imports from South East Asia and the Middle East. China is dependent upon oil imports from the Middle East and is undertaking an expanding conflict with its neighbors in South East Asia for access to resources around disputed islands. Europe, in particular, has a major natural gas and heating oil supply problem as virtually all the natural gas and heating oil consumed by the EU comes from Russia, a traditional antagonist. Russia has, in the past, shut off the natural gas supply to EU countries and other neighbors in the middle of winter over political slights and differences of opinion on country membership in NATO.[46]

Countries that are not energy independent are subject to the influence exerted by those countries that control the supply of essential natural resources. As the world becomes more industrialized and economically interdependent, the transmission of information becomes more important. This has created another cross-border threat to national security: the Internet.

The Internet and Transnational Crime

If you have an e-mail account, then you've received spam. You've probably even received notifications that you've won the British or Irish Lottery, or the Nigerian

Finance Minister wants you to accept delivery of several million US dollars that they have determined is yours due to some family relationship with an unknown uncle, or some individual from Cote d' Ivory (Ivory Coast) has a trunk loaded with cash that they need you to claim, for which you will receive a "fee" as recompense for your assistance.

How do you secure borders and thereby prevent crime against your citizens in a world where electronic data flies between countries at nearly the speed of light? The answer to this question depends upon the country in which you live.

Some countries, like China, attempt to control the flow of information and the associated political ideology that comes with it, as they consider political thought that deviates from the "party line" to be criminal. During the "Arab Spring" in 2012, the government of Egypt periodically shut down Internet communications to try to establish control over the communications between crowds gathering in downtown Cairo and other major cities. The governments of Saudi Arabia, Oman, Bahrain, Pakistan, and other countries have occasionally suspended cellular communications across their countries in the attempt to stop the populace from receiving outside political or religious input, as well as internal communications ranging from e-mail to text messages to tweets, so they could maintain or reestablish control of the populace.

The reality is that unless you take down all forms of international communication within a country, from landline telephones, to Internet access, to e-mail, etc. you cannot stop the flow of information across borders. The world has become so technologically connected that the movement of information from person to person has become an endemic part of our lives and economies. If the various forms of communication were to be suddenly isolated from international connectivity, stock markets would crash, business transactions would cease, and communications between employers and employees, as well as customers, would come to a halt.

Try a simple experiment. Without telling anybody, not even your mother, turn off your cell phone (not sleep, OFF). Turn off your e-mail on your computer. Turn off your Internet access. If you have a home phone, unplug it from the wall. If you use any sort of tablet as a communications device, shut it down and set it aside. Now spend a full twenty-four hours away from your communications means. After waiting a full day, how many texts, tweets, e-mails, instant messages, Facebook posts, etc., did you get asking you if everything was okay? How many asking why you weren't responding? Or where you were? Who was most concerned? Who tried to track you down the most aggressively?

Now expand that experiment to all interstate and international communications. Shut down one day (1/365th) all business and personal communications and imagine the impact. This is the only way to effectively protect a country's communications infrastructure from outside assault by hackers, transnational criminals, or foreign governments. If your device, and therefore your data, is connected to any other device, by Wi-Fi, cellular, Bluetooth, or direct-line connection, it is vulnerable to any number of attacks and is most likely being constantly probed for vulnerabilities. The same situation exists for government and business communication devices, and computers are communication devices.

Savvy criminals constantly develop new techniques to target persons, businesses, and interests. Kristin Finklea, a Congressional Research Service specialist in Domestic Security, points out that central to the evolution of modern-day crime are four broad operational realities — geographic borders, criminal turf, cyberspace, and law enforcement jurisdiction.[47] Our concern here is with the latter two realities — cyberspace and law enforcement jurisdiction. Individual criminals as well as broad criminal networks exploit these realities and often leverage the unique characteristics of one against the other to dodge countermeasures and efforts to disrupt illicit activity.

The Internet is a largely borderless, virtual environment where criminals can carry out illicit business. Criminals operate in the cyberworld partly to circumvent more conventional, established constructs such as international borders. In the virtual realm, criminals can rely on relative anonymity and a rather seamless environment to conduct their nefarious business enterprises. Some criminals use electronic banking systems to quickly smuggle cash out of one nation and into another.[48]

US and international law enforcement agents often remain constrained by geographic and legal boundaries or even their own notions of "turf," partly defined in terms of competing agency-level priorities and jurisdictions. Law enforcement officials have suggested that as criminals have evolved their operations, they have relied less on turf to conduct business.[49] Individual law enforcement agencies, even while collaborating through means such as interagency agreements, task forces, and fusion centers, retain investigational jurisdiction over certain categories of crime. Recent reports have suggested that interagency disagreements over organizational boundaries remain.[50]

Local, state, federal, and international law enforcement agencies face hurdles presented by the overlap of any or all the four realities. Policy changes in one reality, both administratively and legislatively, impact criminal activity and law enforcement countermeasures in other realities. Criminal investigations unfold in an environment of geographic borders and law enforcement jurisdictions. The criminal turf is borderless in the realm of cyberspace. Key to effectively spanning jurisdictional restrictions is evaluation of how law enforcement agencies are coordinating their investigations through use of interagency agreements, task forces, and fusion centers.

The relatively clear borders and turf lines that exist within the physical world are not replicated in the virtual realm. Of course, some distinct boundaries separate the physical and the cyberworlds. A keyboard, mouse, screen, and password can all mediate between these physical and virtual realms.[51] Cyberspace, however, has much more nebulous borders. This is because the same geographic borders that exist in the real world do not exist in the cyberworld.[52] High-speed internet communication has not only facilitated the growth of legitimate business but it has bolstered criminals' abilities to operate in an environment where they can broaden their pool of potential targets and rapidly exploit their victims.

Between 2000 and 2016, the estimated number of Internet users grew from almost 361 million to nearly 3.424 billion, an increase of more than 894 percent.[53] Frauds and schemes that were once conducted face-to-face are now carried out remotely from across the country and around the world. The United Nations Office on Drugs and Crime notes that cybercrime has "evolved from the mischievous one-upmanship of cybervandals [sic] to a range of profit-making criminal enterprises in a remarkably short time."[54]

Cyberspace is not completely without borders. It has both technological and jurisdictional boundaries. Some web addresses are country-specific and the administration of those websites is controlled by national governments. For instance, website addresses ending in ".us" indicate that the United States owns the servers controlling the website, while those ending in ".au" indicate Australian control. Another barrier in cyberspace involves subscriptions or fee-based access to website content. Certain businesses such as news sites, journals, file sharing sites, and others require paid access. One example used as a reference when writing this book is STRATFOR, a private, for profit business-intelligence company based in Austin, Texas. Yet even such companies are not immune from cybercriminals. In December 2011 the group Anonymous hacked into the STRATFOR company database and published on the internet the names, addresses, and credit card numbers of subscribers.[55] One of this book's authors was one of the victims of that hacking and experienced months of disruption of financial transactions resulting in a significant blow to their credit rating as well as a need to make major changes to their future online financial transaction practices.

This was not the only time hackers acquired access to our personal information. May 3, 2006, a Veterans Administration analyst lost an external hard drive and laptop when her Maryland home was burglarized. The theft resulted in the loss of an unencrypted national database with names, Social Security numbers, dates of births, and some disability ratings for 26.5 million veterans, active-duty military personal, and spouses.[56] Admittedly, this was a regular crime, but the theft exposed the data to release to anybody and everybody who may have wanted to purchase it from the thief. While the original hardware that was stolen was anonymously returned to the police on June 29, 2006, it was never determined if the data contained on the hardware was compromised. Several subsequent data breaches have occurred at Veteran's Administration facilities, and their employees continue to take home and lose electronic data with sensitive personal information.[57]

From the list of the 15 biggest data breeches posted by CSO on July 12, 2017, some other significant data breeches that may have impacted you or your family include:

Yahoo: 2013-2014, 1.5 billion user accounts. In addition to "names, dates of birth, email addresses and passwords that were not as well protected as those involved in 2014, security questions and answers were also compromised."
eBay: May 2014, 145 million users. "Hackers got into the company network using the credentials of three corporate employees, and had complete inside access for 229 days, during which time they were able to make their way to the user database."
Heartland Payment Systems: March 2008, 134 million credit cards.
Target Stores: December 2013, up to 110 million people compromised.
TJX Companies Inc.: December 2006, 94 million credit cards exposed. Interestingly, the only person convicted of the Target Stores breech in 2013 was working as a paid informant of the U.S. Secret Service at $75,000/year at the

time he was concurrently conducting this breech of TJX. The companies, banks and insurers lost close to $200 million.

JP Morgan Chase: July 2014, 76 million households and 7 million small businesses.

U.S. Office of Personnel Management: 2012-2014, personal and security information of 22 million current and former federal employees including job applicants' information.[58]

Certain traditional crimes such as fraud and identity theft are increasingly being moved to the cyberworld, a world without borders. Many crimes considered cybercrimes could be considered traditional, or "real world," crimes if not for the virtual venue in which they occur. Criminals view the virtual world as a borderless space that provides relative anonymity and a place to operate. Cyberspace can also be a tool that criminals use to subvert borders. Due to the global nature of the Internet and other rapid communication systems, crimes committed on the Internet can quickly impact victims in multiple state and national jurisdictions.[59] Jason Weinstein, from the Criminal Division of the Department of Justice (DOJ), indicated in his congressional testimony that most cybersecurity incidents are transnational in nature.[60] One merely has to subscribe to the FBI, ICE, HSI, CBP, and other related newsfeeds to see weekly reports of arrests, investigations, commissions, and indictments related to cybercrime with suspects being arrested in joint operations involving many countries.

Importantly, laws remain effective primarily within the territorial lines of a given jurisdiction. The reasons for the establishment of these jurisdictional boundaries have been expounded upon at length in previous chapters. When criminal behavior crosses these boundaries, the jurisdiction for law enforcement changes, necessitating involvement and cooperation of multiple agencies. Criminals have long understood this phenomenon and exploited it. In May 2009, four New York residents were arrested in New Hampshire for allegedly stealing hair care products from pharmacies. Authorities reportedly found in the suspects' van maps indicating drugstore locations in several East Coast states.[61] Consider the following traditional crime: A person is kidnapped in Texas, transported to New Mexico, where the victim is ultimately murdered. Who has jurisdiction for the murder, New Mexico or Texas? Or the federal government? Clearly, the transport of the victim across state borders changed the dynamics of the crime as well as the jurisdiction for the investigation, prosecution, court with authority to hear the case, and ultimately the correctional system that would impose punishment of the murderer/kidnapper.

The Texas–New Mexico border changes the dynamics in several other manners as well. Which agency gets credit for solving the crime? Which county carries the burden of the expense of prosecuting a capital murder case? Which state taxpayers carry the burden of funding the correctional system that will house the murderer? The jurisdictional problems for this type of traditional crime have been resolved over many decades such that we now know that the suspect would be extradited to Texas for trial on kidnapping and capital murder, and possibly trial in federal court for the kidnapping and transport across state lines. How this process will work for the non-traditional cybercrime has yet to be determined.

In the United States, jurisdictional battles exist not only between federal and state law enforcement, where these fights may be complicated by federal/state concurrent jurisdiction over a case but also between federal law enforcement agencies. Several agencies have overlapping missions and jurisdictions over the types of cases they may prosecute. For instance, there have been turf disputes between the Federal Bureau of Investigation (FBI) and the Bureau of Alcohol, Tobacco, Firearms, and Explosives (BATFE) over cigarette smuggling and explosives cases, among others;[62] between US Immigration and Customs Enforcement (ICE) and BATFE over transnational firearms trafficking cases and firearms cases involving unauthorized immigrants;[63] and between ICE and the Drug Enforcement Administration (DEA) over transnational drug trafficking and other cases.[64]

Now consider a cybercrime. A hacker in Belarus uses an Internet server in Russia to activate a botnet that attacks thousands of bank accounts associated with US military veterans served by the Department of Veterans Affairs. The hacker purchased the veteran's names, addresses, birthdates, and Social Security numbers from a Chinese hacker who downloaded the data set from a VA analyst's government laptop while it was connected to her home Internet service. An 80-year-old disabled veteran, when picking up medication at the local CVS pharmacy is told his credit card has been canceled. When he tries to write a check, he finds his account is overdrawn. Confused by the financial troubles that have struck out of nowhere, he tries to call his bank only to find that his cell phone has been deactivated. Shocked, dazed, and confused by the sudden changes in his financial stability as well as his inability to acquire needed medicine, as he walks out to his car so he can drive to the bank to find out what is happening he does not pay attention to the cross-traffic and is struck by another CVS patron who is distracted because she is texting while driving. The veteran dies of his injuries. Who is responsible for his death? Who has jurisdiction? The driver who struck him clearly has some culpability. What about the hacker in Belarus who stole his savings and maxed out his credit cards; the hacker in China who initially stole and sold the VA data set; or the VA analyst who attached a government computer to her unsecure home Internet service? This is the problem with crimes committed on the Internet. Traditional borders and the delineation of jurisdiction are tenuous, at best.

Many twenty-first century criminals exploit borders and cyberspace in their illicit activities. Their operational turf is unconstrained by these lines. Criminals also rely on constantly advancing technology and near anonymity in cyberspace to work both within and across borders and jurisdictions. All the while, law enforcement jurisdiction is often constrained by boundaries, established by jurisdictions and otherwise. Even within a given jurisdictional boundary, multiple agencies may have investigative authority, contributing to possible disagreements over case leadership and control. Moisés Naím has noted, "Criminal networks thrive on international mobility and their ability to take advantage of the opportunities that flow from the separation of marketplaces into sovereign states with borders."[65] Criminals are proactive, creative, and flexible. They are not constrained by jurisdiction in the same manner as law enforcement. They carry out their illicit activities despite geographic lines or jurisdictional boundaries, often using the boundaries to their advantage.

Transborder Victimization

Not only do criminals operate and network with one another across borders, criminals (both individuals and organizations) often target victims without regard for borders. According to the Internet Crime Complaint Center (IC3), of those reported scams and frauds from 2010 where the locations of the victim and perpetrator were both known, a minority of cases involved victims and perpetrators in the same state.[66] As expected, the four states with the largest populations in the United States were in the top ten in complainants reporting the perpetrators came from the same state. California, Florida, New York, and Texas reported 39.1, 30.9, 29.4, and 25.4 percent respectively. While most complaints are made against other persons in the United States, a number do come from other countries. These include Canada, United Kingdom, Australia, India, South Africa, Germany, Mexico, France, and the Philippines.[67]

Of course, modern criminals readily leverage technology to victimize targets across borders. They can rely upon botnets to electronically target victims throughout borderless cyberspace. The Coreflood botnet has infected more than 2.3 million computers around the world, almost 1.9 million of which are located in the United States. This botnet is a malicious key-logging program that records users' keystrokes and transmits the data to cyberthieves, who use this data to steal personal and financial information. Compromised US businesses suffering financial losses from the botnet include everything from real estate and investment companies to law firms and defense contractors. The FBI has filed a complaint against 13 "John Doe" defendants believed to have engaged in wire fraud, bank fraud, and illegal interception of electronic communications in connection with the Coreflood botnet.[68] It is unknown whether authorities have determined the exact identities or locations of these alleged criminals. However, they are believed to be foreign nationals.[69] Authorities in the United States and Estonia have seized servers that are believed to have current, or have had previous, control over the Coreflood botnet.[70]

Actual Phishing Email

from: INTERNATIONAL MONETARY FUND (IMF) <INFO@imf.org>
-reply-to: mr.smithmattimfoffice@gmail.com
to:
date: Wed, Mar 6, 2013 at 7:24 PM
subject: INSTRUCTION TO RELEASE YOUR OVERDUE FUND
INTERNATIONAL MONETARY FUND (IMF)
HEAD OFFICE NO: 23 ADEBOYE ST,
APAPA LAGOS.
Tell: +234-8033671343

-REF:-XVGNN8809
INSTRUCTION TO RELEASE YOUR OVERDUE FUND

This is to intimate you of a very important information which will be of a great help to redeem you from all the difficulties you have been experiencing in getting your long overdue payment due to excessive demand for money from you by both corrupt Bank officials and Courier Companies after which your fund remain unpaid to you.

I am mr .Smith Matt a highly placed official of the international Monetary Fund (IMF). It may interest you to know that reports have reached our office by so many correspondences on the uneasy way which people like you are treated by Various Banks and Courier Companies/Diplomat across Europe to Africa and Asia/London Uk and we have decided to put a stop to that and that is why I was appointed to handle your transaction here in Nigeria.

All Governmental and Non-Governmental prostates, NGOs, Finance companies, Banks, Security Companies and Courier companies which have been in contact with you of late have been instructed to back up from your transaction and you have been advised NOT to respond to them anymore since the IMF is now directly in charge of your payment.

You are hereby advised NOT to remit further payment to any institutions with respect to your transaction as your fund will be transferred to you directly from our source. I hope this is clear. Any action contrary to this instruction is at your own risk. you are advise to respond immediately for further details on how your fund will be released into your designated bank account. below is our contact details, we are Expecting your prompt reply thank you.

Direct Hotline: CALL: +234-8033671343
Fax line 234-1-7769964
Reply to; mr.smithmattimfoffice@gmail.com
Sincerely
Mr. Smith Matt
I.M.F OFFICIAL

Advance fee fraud (AFF) schemes have long been used to swindle victims without regard across borders. The Internet has only expanded the scope of the fraudsters. AFF scams often involve criminals sending unsolicited, or spam, e-mails that present an opportunity for a "lucky" individual to come into a large sum of money. The letters promise the money will be disbursed once the victim sends a small cash payment, purportedly used to facilitate the transfer. The large sum of money is never transferred to the victim. In one case from February 2011, the second of two Nigerian nationals was sentenced to nine years in prison for his role in an AFF scheme targeting US, European, and Australian individuals. At least eighteen people were duped out of more than $9.5 million. The fraudsters posed as lawyers, bankers, and government officials who collected the "fees" that were advertised as necessary to secure the transfer of large sums of money to the victims.[71] Of course, the victims never received their promised riches. The perpetrators were eventually arrested in the Netherlands (where they had been residing) and extradited to the United States.

The Internet is also used to perpetuate transborder intellectual property rights (IPR) violations, one of the primary cybercrime concerns voiced by federal law enforcement and the Obama administration. Counterfeit and pirated goods harm legitimate businesses and consumers on several levels. This crime threatens competition and innovation, siphons profits deserved by the rightful manufacturer, and poses health risks to consumers. In June 2011, a Chinese national was sentenced for trafficking in counterfeit versions of the pharmaceutical weight-loss drug, "Alli," an over-the-counter weight-loss drug manufactured by Glaxo-Smith-Klein. The defendant reportedly shipped the products from China to a business partner in Texas for US distribution. The FDA issued public alerts about this as well as other supposed weight-loss products.[72] The warnings indicated that the counterfeit drugs were being imported from China and that the "counterfeit version [of Alli] did not contain orlistat, the active ingredient in its product. Instead, the counterfeit product contained the controlled substance sibutramine." One consumer was even reported to have suffered a mild stroke after consuming the counterfeit product. Over the course of the investigation, law enforcement purchased the counterfeit drug, traced the wired money used in the purchase of the counterfeit drug, located the defendant in China and posing as potential buyers of the drug, agreed to meet the defendant face-to-face. Law enforcement met the defendant in Hawaii, where he was arrested.[73] As you can tell from the process of investigation in this case, it was ultimately necessary for US law enforcement investigators to convince the perpetrator to leave China and come to the United States, where it was then possible to exercise jurisdictional enforcement of the law. Most criminals would not agree to a meeting in a country where they could be seized, charged, or extradited to another country.

Cross-Border Criminal Networks

Criminals routinely move illicit products and proceeds across state and international boundaries. Amid the war on drugs the Mexican drug traffickers utilize underground, cross-border tunnels, which have become increasingly prevalent and sophisticated, to smuggle drugs from Mexico into the United States. They also have used ultra-light aircraft, cannons, catapults, and cars to get their product from one side of the fence to the other, where their US comrades pick up the deliveries and move them to trans-shipment points and customers.

Simple "gopher hole" tunnels are dug on the Mexican side of the border, travel just below the surface, and pop out on the US side as close as 100 feet from the border. Some more advanced tunnels rely on existing infrastructure, such as storm drains or sewage systems. These systems may be shared by neighboring border cities such as the tunnel shared by Nogales, Arizona, in the United States and Nogales, Sonora, in Mexico. Exploiting infrastructure allows smugglers to move drugs further than they could by digging tunnels alone. The most sophisticated tunnels have rail, ventilation, and electrical systems. One of the most extensive tunnels discovered to date was found in January 2006 in Otay Mesa, California. It stretched nearly three-quarters of a mile in length, traveled

Drug tunnel near San Diego, California, equipped with solid flooring, electric lights, and ventilation. CBP

more than 85 feet below the surface, and had lighting, ventilation, and groundwater drainage systems.[74] In November 2010, the San Diego Tunnel Task Force uncovered two similar tunnels running between Tijuana, Mexico, and Otay Mesa, California.[75]

Traffickers also use semisubmersible maritime vessels to move illicit products. Semisubmersible vessels are typically made of fiberglass, can travel up to 2,000 miles with multi-ton shipments of drugs, primarily Colombian cocaine, and are difficult to detect from the air. Rear Admiral Atkins, US Coast Guard, indicated in testimony before the House Subcommittee on Homeland Security that more than 25 percent of the cocaine eventually destined for the United States is moved during part of its journey via semisubmersible vessels.[76]

Cocaine submarine. USCG.

Smugglers and traffickers are constantly innovating means to circumvent borders and supply their products to areas where there is demand. Mexican drug traffickers have increasingly employed ultra-light aircraft to smuggle drugs across the southwest border. These small planes can fly as low as tree level and have such a low metal content they are not easily detected by radar. Some traffickers land the ultra-lights on the US side of the border to pass off drug loads to distributors. Others attach drop baskets to release packages of drugs that will fall to the ground when a lever in the aircraft is activated. These packages are then picked up and distributed by local traffickers or gangs. Richard Marosi of the *Los Angeles Times* reports that in fiscal year 2010, border authorities reported 228 ultra-light incursions from Mexico into the United States. This is nearly double the number reported from fiscal year 2009.[77]

Law Enforcement Efforts to Overcome Barriers

Modern-day criminals take advantage of geographic borders, criminal turf, cyberspace, and law enforcement jurisdictions. This has led law enforcement to transform their crime-fighting efforts. The FBI, for instance, has, particularly since September 11, 2001, relied more heavily on collaboration, information sharing, and technology.

Interagency Cooperation and Information Sharing

Crimes, particularly those considered cybercrimes or that contain a cyber-component, are increasingly transborder and transnational. Further, criminal organizations are becoming less hierarchical and more networked in structure. These evolutions in the nature of crime and criminal organizations require that law enforcement simultaneously become nimbler and networked in order to effectively counter the threats. This poses a problem in the United States as, generally, law enforcement agencies and government entities charged with combating criminal networks are relatively hierarchical, and some experts suggest, "Hierarchies have a difficult time fighting networks."[78] To overcome the inherent crime-fighting difficulty of hierarchal organizations, many law enforcement agencies have adopted networked practices (rather than actual structure) to confront twenty-first century criminals.[79]

Federal law enforcement has already taken steps toward interagency coordination through development of networks with other federal, state, local, and international partners. This model has been used for decades to combat more traditional crime, and it has more recently been used to combat cybercrime. The FBI, to target cyber-criminals, embedded agents with international law enforcement partners in Romania in 2006.[80] FBI collaboration has expanded to countries including Estonia, Ukraine, and the Netherlands. These partnerships have proved beneficial in investigating and prosecuting transnational criminals. For example, when hackers attacked the RBS

WorldPay computer network, law enforcement agencies including the FBI, US Secret Service, Estonian Central Criminal Police, Netherlands Police Agency National Crime Squad High Tech Crime Unit, and the Netherlands National Public Prosecutor's Office, as well as the Hong Kong Police Force, all contributed to investigating a criminal network involved. Five hackers have been indicted in the case. These individuals allegedly defeated the encryption used by RBS WorldPay to protect customer information associated with the payroll card processing system. Using counterfeit payroll debit cards that allow employees to withdraw their regular salaries from ATMs, the hackers and their associates withdrew more than $9 million from more than 2,100 ATMs in at least 280 cities around the globe, including in the United States, Russia, Ukraine, Estonia, Italy, Hong Kong, Japan, and Canada. Notably, the more than $9 million loss occurred in less than twelve hours. In August 2010, Estonia extradited to the United States one of the principal leaders of the hacking ring, who has since been arraigned on charges of conspiracy to commit wire fraud, wire fraud, conspiracy to commit computer fraud, computer fraud, and aggravated identity theft.[81]

In "Operation Fire and Ice," from June 2011, US, Colombian, and Italian law enforcement worked together to investigate "La Oficina de Envigado," a Colombian narcotics trafficking and money laundering network. The organization, a vestige of the notorious Medellín Cartel, is based in Medellín, Colombia, but operates internationally, including in Massachusetts. Authorities seized forty-eight bank accounts in the United States. Additionally, officials estimate that through the course of Fire and Ice they seized more than $200 million in cash, more than 1,100 kilograms of cocaine, and forty-six kilograms of heroin around the world.[82]

Federal law enforcement agencies may work with one another (and with their international counterparts), either informally or through formal agreements, to counter the transnational nature of crimes, both traditional and cyber. The United States as a signatory to the United Nations Convention against Transnational Organized Crime as well as the Council of Europe Convention on Cybercrime, participates in the Group of 8 (G8) High Tech Crime Subgroup.

United Nations Convention against Transnational Organized Crime

The United Nations Convention against Transnational Organized Crime is the primary international tool for combating organized crime. The United States, in 2005, ratified the convention as well as the companion protocols on trafficking in persons and smuggling of migrants. The convention provides for greater law enforcement cooperation and mutual legal assistance across nations where there were no previous agreements for such assistance among other provisions. The convention also requires signatories to criminalize certain offenses such as participation in an organized criminal group, money laundering, corruption, and obstruction of justice. It also requires the enhancement of training and technical assistance to combat transnational organized crime. Ratifying the convention in 2005, Congress took a step in working with foreign governments and law enforcement agencies to combat multinational and multijurisdictional organized crime. Given the increasingly transnational nature of organized crime, this coordination with international organizations is essential.[83]

Council of Europe Convention on Cybercrime

The Council of Europe Convention on Cybercrime was developed in 2001 to address several categories of crimes committed via the Internet and other information networks. It is the first international treaty to address cybercrime, and its primary goal is to "pursue a common criminal policy aimed at the protection of society against cybercrime, especially by adopting appropriate legislation and fostering international co-operation." To date, forty-seven countries are signatories to the convention and thirty-one of these, including the United States, have ratified it.[84]

Not all activities considered crimes in one country are also considered criminal acts in another. Currently, there is not an international standard view on what constitutes cyber-, or computer-related, crime. Signatories to the convention, however, must define criminal offenses and sanctions under their domestic laws for four categories of computer-related crimes: security breaches such as hacking, illegal data interception, and system interferences that compromise network integrity and availability; fraud and forgery; child pornography; and copyright infringements. The convention also requires signatories to establish domestic procedures for detecting, investigating, and prosecuting computer crimes, as well as collecting electronic evidence of any criminal offense. It also requires that signatories engage in international cooperation "to the widest extent possible."

G8 High Tech Crime Subgroup

DOJ is a key player in US participation in the G8 Subgroup on High-Tech Crime. In 1996, the G8 created the Lyon group of experts on transnational organized crime. These experts developed forty recommendations to combat transnational organized crime. Subsequently, the G8 created various subgroups (one of which is a High-Tech Crime subgroup) to address crime-related issues. The High-Tech Crime subgroup created a network for 24-hour points of contact for high-tech crime. It has negotiated an action plan and a set of widely accepted principles to combat high-tech crime. It has also created numerous best practices documents such as guides for securing computer networks, requesting international assistance, drafting legislation, and tracing networked communications across borders. The subgroup assesses threats and the impact on law enforcement from new technology such as encryption, as well as malicious Internet activities such as viruses and worms. It also sponsors training conferences for cybercrime agencies as well as conferences for law enforcement and industry on improved cooperation.

Interagency Agreements

Through interagency agreements and Memoranda of Understanding (MOUs) federal law enforcement agencies have tried to minimize jurisdictional discrepancies and coordinate efforts. In June 2009, the BATFE and ICE signed an MOU, citing a shared jurisdiction in combating criminal organizations engaging in violent crime and drug trafficking. The agencies agreed to involve one another in cases of shared jurisdiction and to enhance information sharing in such cases. The Department of Justice (DOJ) Office of the Inspector General (OIG) found that, despite this MOU, BATFE and ICE do not work together effectively on investigations of firearms trafficking to Mexico, and therefore BATFE's Project Gunrunner cases do not benefit from ICE's intelligence and prosecutorial options.[85] BATFE and ICE rarely conduct joint investigations of firearms trafficking to Mexico, do not consistently notify each other of their firearms trafficking cases, and do not consistently coordinate their investigative work with each other. The OIG attributed this lack of information sharing to both an unawareness of the MOU's existence as well as misunderstanding of its purpose. Clearly, not all MOUs function as intended. Or perhaps it is the ingrained agency-specific hierarchical "stovepipe" mentality that prevents effective implementation of interagency MOUs.

ICE also shares an interagency cooperation agreement with the DEA that has been in effect since June 18, 2009. The agencies agree to share information through the DEA's Special Operations Division, the Organized Crime Drug Enforcement Task Force (OCDETF) program Fusion Center and the El Paso Intelligence Center (EPIC). The agreement also allows ICE to select agents for cross-designation by the DEA Administrator and permits these ICE agents to investigate narcotics smuggling with a clear nexus to the US border. It also provides procedures for deconfliction and operational coordination in domestic and international cases. On August 10, 2009, ICE and DOJ signed two MOUs to enhance information sharing at the OCDETF Fusion Center and the International Organized Crime Intelligence and Operations Center (IOC-2).[86]

Fusion Centers and Task Forces

Intelligence-led policing has resulted in many modern law enforcement operations increasingly relying on fusion centers and task forces. According to DHS, fusion centers and task forces (with specific reference to Joint Terrorism Task Forces, or JTTFs) serve "distinct, but complementary roles."[87] Fusion centers are a "collaborative effort of two or more Federal, state, local, or tribal government agencies that combines resources, expertise, or information with the goal of maximizing the ability of such agencies to detect, prevent, investigate, apprehend, and respond to criminal or terrorist activity."[88] DHS indicates that fusion centers serve as focal points within the state and local environment for the receipt, analysis, gathering, and sharing of threat-related information among federal and state, local, tribal, and territorial (SLTT) partners. They produce actionable intelligence for dissemination, which can aid other law enforcement organizations, including the JTTFs, in their investigative operations.[89]

It is interesting that it only takes the cooperation of two law enforcement agencies to establish a fusion center. While some cooperative intelligence operations are small, others, such as the El Paso Intelligence Center (EPIC) are large and encompass numerous agencies. Generally, intelligence-based fusion centers are intended to share information between agencies. The effectiveness of such intelligence sharing is not known. Nor is it known how well fusion centers can operate to address current, real-time crime events or address violent gangs or online fraud.

Information-Sharing Systems

The push for information sharing has been more visible regarding the investigation of terrorism and related crimes than it has been for the investigation of more traditional crime. In the 2004 Intelligence Reform and Terrorism Prevention Act (P.L. 108-458), Congress mandated the creation of an Information Sharing Environment, commonly known as the "ISE." Through this act, Congress directed that the ISE provide and facilitate the means of sharing terrorism information among all appropriate federal, state, local, and tribal entities as well as the private sector using policy guidelines and technologies.[90] Congress has not directed the creation of an information-sharing environment for the investigation of more traditional crimes in either the real or cyber worlds.

While there is not a sole clearinghouse for information sharing on traditional criminal investigations, there are several databases that contain a given subset of information. These include the FBI's Law Enforcement Online, Automated Fingerprint Identification System, National Crime Information Center, National Data Exchange, and Violent Criminal Apprehension Program; ATF's Arson & Explosives National Repository and Bomb Arson Tracking System; and the High Intensity Drug Trafficking Area Deconfliction, among others. Through a 2006 nationwide survey, the Justice Statistics and Research Association (JSRA) identified 266 information sharing systems (that were either in place or under development) spanning 35 states and Canada.[91] These systems share information about crime at the national, regional, state, and county levels. Of these systems, 10 percent were identified as sharing national-level data. When survey respondents recommended system improvements, the most common suggestion involved including additional agencies in the information-sharing system.

Databases have been established to coordinate information on specific types of crime. The National Identity Crimes Law Enforcement (NICLE) network, for instance, was established to coordinate information on identity theft and related crimes. This network consolidates information from local, state, and federal law enforcement agencies. Data in NICLE is available to nearly 100 law enforcement agencies through the Regional Information Sharing System Intranet (RISSNET).[92]

Another national database used by law enforcement to consolidate information on identity theft is InfraGard, through which the FBI gathers information on cybercrimes and other cases. InfraGard is an FBI partnership with businesses, academic institutions, and other law enforcement agencies. Through this program, the Bureau can collect and disseminate information to private sector entities as well as other law enforcement partners. The InfraGard program began to share cybercrime information, but its mission has expanded to include other crimes and threats, particularly those involving critical infrastructure. As of February 2017, InfraGard had more than 54,000 members across 84 chapters.[93]

The Domestic Security Alliance Council (DSAC) is like InfraGard. DSAC is a security and intelligence-sharing initiative among the FBI, DHS, and the private sector, focusing on crimes impacting interstate commerce. These include computer intrusions, insider threats, fraud, theft of trade secrets, product tampering, and workplace violence. As of 2015, DSAC had 367 US private sector companies and organizations, a jump of 24 percent from 2014.[94]

Another partnership, the Law Enforcement Retail Partnership Network (LERPnet), has been established to combat organized retail crime. In 2006, through the Violence Against Women and Department of Justice Reauthorization Act of 2005, Congress directed the Attorney General and the FBI to establish a clearinghouse within the private sector for information sharing between retailers and law enforcement. The result was LERPnet.[95] It began as a partnership between the FBI, ICE, various local police departments, individual retailers, and retail organizations, including the Food Marketing Institute (FMI), National Retail Federation (NRF), and Retail Industry Leaders Association (RILA). As of January 2010, LERPnet has been linked with the FBI's Law Enforcement Online (LEO) system, providing federal and local law enforcement with a direct link to retail industry crime reports.

Complexity Theory

An extension of the application of organizational theory, complexity theory, deals with the evolving of disparate parts of organizations out of chaos into self-organization (Grobman, 2005). Schwan (2012) discusses the use of complexity theory and a systems perspective to explain that the fragmented approach of various organizations and countries to US borders results in ineffective and dysfunctional attack of the problem. Focusing on breaking down components and then building systemic relationships and strategies cooperatively, Schwann suggests that dysfunctional can evolve into functional and coordinated efforts and that the efficacy of the nascent whole will increase.

Grobman, Gary M. (2005), "Complexity Theory: a new way to look at organizational change," *Public Administration Quarterly*, 29(3).

Schwan, Michael J. (2012), *Border cracks: approaching border security from a complexity theory and systems perspective*, Naval Post Graduate School, Thesis, Monterey, CA.

Technology Implementation

Criminals are constantly evolving their methods to stay ahead of law enforcement. They traverse through and around physical and cyberspace, capitalizing on ever-advancing technology to evade detection. Responding, law enforcement has utilized an array of methods, from human intelligence to advanced technology, to investigate these criminals. Nonetheless, the FBI and others continue to recognize the value of human intelligence and confidential sources/informants.

Even in cyberinvestigations, the FBI and other federal law enforcement agencies rely heavily on confidential sources. It has been estimated that "25% of hackers in the US may have been recruited by the federal authorities to be their eyes and ears."[96] Both the FBI and the US Secret Service have had success in infiltrating the underground world of hackers, and hackers-turned-informants have worked not only with law enforcement, but with the military as well. In 2004 Adrian Lamo, a notorious hacker, pled guilty to hacking into *The New York Times'* internal network containing personally identifiable information of Times contributors. He also reportedly accessed the *Times'* LexisNexis subscription account, creating fictitious usernames and conducting unauthorized searches. In 2010, Bradley Manning, a US Army intelligence analyst who is alleged to have passed classified cables to Wikileaks, purportedly contacted Lamo. After Manning claimed responsibility for the leaks, Lamo turned Manning over to the Army and FBI.[97]

Despite the use of human intelligence coupled with advances in technology, outmoded laws and a lack of resources, training, and personnel keep law enforcement "in the dark" as criminals evade detection. Law enforcement simply does not have the financial resources or personnel to keep pace with the technology available to the criminal, hacktivist, or activist. In response to the January 11, 2013, suicide of Aaron Swartz, who was facing prosecution for hacking the JSTOR website and making freely available hundreds of thousands of published articles, the group Anonymous hacked the US Sentencing Commission website and turned it into a game of Asteroids. They made the claim they had hacked hundreds of government websites and would use the information they downloaded to punish the US government for disproportionately punishing hackers who were not acting for profit, but to make information available for the public good.[98]

Congress has yet to address the myriad issues surrounding law enforcement's inability to effectively address transnational cybercrime, hacking, Internet and information accessibility, Internet security, and the vast privacy issues any such law would violate. A major concern of privacy advocates is that enabling law enforcement to more easily obtain information from communications services providers could jeopardize individuals' privacy. Some have suggested that "[a]lthough massive penetration into criminal communities may help curtail some unlawful activities, the invasive penetration into communities and the absolute control over whatever happens in the digital space amount to disruption of natural rights."[99]

October 2012, Southwest Arizona, a silver Jeep Cherokee tries to
drive over the border fence with Mexico. CBP.

Conclusion

We have discussed the impact of globalization on border security and how the globalized economy has led to the development of communications systems that transcend borders. All countries are now economically interdependent upon other countries. The movement of business information, economic data, and financial transactions has resulted in the development of the Internet, a free flow of information across borders, around the world, and even into space. The movement of goods, provision of services, and even the writing of this book are the results of globalization, the Internet, and the lack of border controls over the ability to communicate thoughts and information across the global marketplace. This has, of course, led to the exploitation of the Internet by criminals and terrorists, threatening the very security that allows these systems to exist for the use of free societies.

Globalization clearly impacts each country's national security, and therefore its border security efforts. How each individual country enforces their own laws in defense of their culture, language, environment, and economy is impossible to address, but hopefully the material presented in this chapter has helped you understand some of the difficulties countries face.

Just as border security is homeland security, so too is energy security. Until relatively recently in human history industrialized nations were entirely dependent upon local sources of energy. In the globalized world where energy resources are shipped across vast distances, a change resulting in the alteration of perceived limits on political and economic borders has resulted in the vulnerability of economies and societies to even slight disruptions in the movement and supply of energy resources. The rise of the Internet has brought an increase in small international businesses conducting trade and sharing information across borders while concurrently there has been a rise in internationally based crime associated with the Internet, from theft of personal identification information to corporate espionage.

This interdependence has changed the way we view border security and has become a consideration of national security in the United States and other countries. Economic interdependence is fundamental to survival in our globalized world. No country can survive independent of other countries and even the most isolated of countries often find themselves dependent upon aid from their staunch enemies. Concurrently, the Internet gave rise to information interdependence that has impacted cultural and political beliefs across the world. Government policies have reduced restrictions on trade and economic investment while concurrently opening the door to a new form of criminal behavior. Restricting the free flow of information across the Internet is virtually impossible, and attempts to do so have resulted in attacks on governments by other governments, and activist groups such as Anonymous.

Questions for Further Consideration

1. How can American labor, with its high wages and even higher benefit costs, begin to compete in the international marketplace when confronted with low wages in competing countries?
2. How do you secure borders, and thereby prevent crime against your citizens in a world where electronic data flies between countries at nearly the speed of light?
3. Consider the following traditional crime: A person is kidnapped in Texas, transported to New Mexico, where the victim is ultimately murdered. Who has jurisdiction for the murder, New Mexico or Texas? Or the federal government?
4. Looking at the changing importation of petroleum products to the United States, has a point been reached where another oil embargo along the lines of those instituted by OPEC in the 1970s be as effective?
5. Should the United States work to achieve energy independence, including independence from Canadian and Mexican sources of energy?
6. The Internet is essentially borderless. Should governments attempt to legislate regulation of the Internet and mandate backdoor access to Internet-based communications, such as e-mail, text messaging, websites, cellular communications, and data exchange?
7. Review the DHS website: https://www.us-cert.gov for the most current updates on cyber issues and known vulnerabilities. Examine how the Equifax breach of July 2017 effected you.

Chapter 8 Endnotes

1. Annan, Kofi, BrainyQuote.com, Xplore Inc., 2013. Accessed January 1, 2013, at http://www.brainyquote. com/quotes/quotes/k/kofiannan130999.html

2. Ahearn, R. J., *Globalization, Worker Insecurity, And Policy Approaches,* Congressional Research Service, 27 February 2012. 7-5700 www.crs.gov RL34091. From the summary.

3. Census.gov., n.d. Exhibit 14. U.S. Trade in Goods by Selected Countries and Areas. Accessed July 18, 2017. Available at: https://www.census.gov/foreign-trade/Press-Release/current_press_release/exh14.pdf

4. Ahearn (2012), 11.

5. International Free Trade Administration, United States Department of Commerce, Free Trade Agreements. Accessed 18 February 2017 at: http://trade.gov/fta/

6. Ross Perot in 1992 on NAFTA and the "Giant Sucking Sound," YouTube. Accessed July 18, 2017, at: http://www.youtube.com/watch?v=xQ7kn2-GEmM

7. Ibid.

8. Scott, R. E., Heading South: U.S.-Mexico trade and job displacement after NAFTA. *EPI Briefing Paper.* Economic Policy Institute. Briefing Paper #308.

9. Strachan, M., *U.S. Economy Lost Nearly 700,000 Jobs Because of NAFTA, EPI Says.* The Huffington Post. 12 May 2011. Accessed July 18, 2017, at: http://www.huffingtonpost.com/2011/05/12/nafta-job-loss-trade-deficit-epi_n_859983.html

10. Villarreal, M. Angeles and Ian F. Fergusson, "The North American Free Trade Agreement (NAFTA)," Congressional Research Service, April 16, 2015. Accessed July 18, 2017. Available at: https://fas.org/sgp/crs/row/R42965.pdf

11. CFR Backgrounders. Accessed July 18, 2017. Available at: http://www.cfr.org/trade/naftas-economic-impact/p15790

12. Scott, R. E. Unfair trade deals lower the wages of U.S. workers. Economic Policy Institute. Fact Sheet, March 13, 2015. Accessed July 18, 2017. Available at: http://www.epi.org/publication/unfair-trade-deals-lower-the-wages-of-u-s-workers/

13. Ibid.

14. Krugman, P., Divided Over Trade. *New York Times*, 14 May 2007, 16.

15. Griswold. D. "Free Trade, Free Markets: Rating the 108th Congress," CATO Institute, Center for Trade Policy Studies, No. 28, March 16, 2005.

16. Drezner, D. W., *"U.S. Trade Strategy: Free Versus Fair,"* Council on Foreign Relations, 2006.

17. Galbraith, J. K. "Why Populists Need to Re-think Trade," *American Prospect,* May 10, 2007.

18. Ahearn (2012), 12.

19. U.S. Department of Labor. Bureau of International Labor Affairs. Office of Trade and Labor Affairs (OTLA). *Free Trade Agreements (FTAs).* Accessed July 18, 2017, at: https://www.dol.gov/agencies/ilab/our-work/trade

20. Carlsen, L., International Forum on Globalization, America's policy report on the Mexican Farmers' movement: Exposing the myths of free trade, 25 February 2003. Accessed July 18, 2017, at: https://www.iatp.org/sites/default/files/Mexican_Farmers_Movement_Exposing_the_Myths_of.htm

21. Amadeo, K., *Disadvantages of NAFTA,* About.com, US Economy. Last accessed July 18, 2017, at: http://useconomy.about.com/od/tradepolicy/p/NAFTA_Problems.htm

22. Ibid.

23. H.R.6630 — To prohibit the Secretary of Transportation from granting authority to a motor carrier domiciled in Mexico to operate beyond United States municipalities and commercial zones on the United States–Mexico border unless expressly authorized by Congress. Accessed July 18, 2017, at: https://www.congress.gov/bill/110th-congress/house-bill/6630?q=%7B%22search%22%3A%5B%22H.R.6630%22%5D%7D&r=2

24. Amadeo (2013).

25. H.R. 6630. Bill Summary & Status. Major Congressional Actions. Accessed July 18, 2017, at: https://www.congress.gov/bill/110th-congress/house-bill/6630?q=%7B%22search%22%3A%5B%22H.R.6630%22%5D%7D&r=2

26. China FTA Network. Updated 18 Feb 2017. Available at: http://fta.mofcom.gov.cn/english/

27. European Commission, Trade. Last updated 03 Feb 2017. Available at: http://ec.europa.eu/trade/policy/countries-and-regions/agreements/#_other-countries

28. Phelps, James. Lead Author of this Book.

29. International Energy Agency, *Energy Security.* Last accessed July 18, 2017, at: http://www.iea.org/topics/energysecurity/

30. As of February 18, 2017, based on the IEA website. Accessed at: https://www.iea.org/countries/membercountries/

31. The Organisation for Economic Co-operation and Development (OECD). About. Available at http://www.oecd.org/about/. Last accessed 18 February 2017.

32. U.S. Energy Information Administration, Frequently Asked Questions. Accessed July 18, 2017. Available at: http://www.eia.gov/tools/faqs/faq.cfm?id=727&t=6

33. Ibid. http://www.eia.gov/totalenergy/data/monthly/pdf/sec3_3.pdf

34. Pumphrey, C. W,. Introduction, *The Energy and Security Nexus: A strategic dilemma*. Carolyn W. Pumphrey, ed. (Carlisle, PA: Strategic Studies Institute, 2012).

35. Korin, A., Oil and Global Security. *The Energy and Security Nexus: A strategic dilemma*. Carolyn W. Pumphrey, ed. (Carlisle, PA: Strategic Studies Institute, 2012).

36. Cekuta, R. F., Unconventional Threats to Energy Supplies, *The Energy and Security Nexus: A strategic dilemma*, Carolyn W. Pumphrey, ed. (Carlisle, PA: Strategic Studies Institute, 2012).

37. Book. K. Coal, Climate Change, and Conflict, *The Energy and Security Nexus: A strategic dilemma*. Carolyn W. Pumphrey, ed. (Carlisle, PA: Strategic Studies Institute, 2012).

38. Korin (2012).

39. Kelanic, R. Fossil Fuels — Commentary, *The Energy and Security Nexus: A strategic dilemma*, Carolyn W. Pumphrey, ed. (Carlisle, PA: Strategic Studies Institute 2012).

40. Gholz, E., Protecting the prize, *The Energy and Security Nexus: A strategic dilemma*, Carolyn W. Pumphrey, ed. (Carlisle, PA: Strategic Studies Institute, 2012).

41. CIA World Factbook — Chile. Accessed July 18, 2017, at: https://www.cia.gov/library/publications/the-world-factbook/geos/ci.html

42. STRATFOR, *Chile's Energy Problems, Part 1: A Mining Sector Starved for Electricity*, 6 September 2012.

43. Pierce, S. A. Presentation given to the Concho Valley Geologic Society and the Angelo State University Geosciences Club, December 2012. See also, ENCOMPASS: Research for Earth-Society Systems, Jackson School of Geosciences, The University of Texas at Austin. http://www.geo.utexas.edu/tatio/default.htm

44. STRATFOR, *Chile's Energy Problems, Part 2: Looking For Alternatives*, 7 September 2012.

45. Pierce (December 2012).

46. STRATFOR, *Dispatch: Russian Energy as Political Leverage*, 20 January 2011.

47. Finklea, K. M., *The Interplay of Borders, Turf, Cyberspace, and Jurisdiction: Issues Confronting U.S. Law Enforcement*, Congressional Research Service, 7-5700 www.crs.gov R41927, 20 July 2012. Accessed July 18, 2017, at: www.fas.org/sgp/crs/misc/R41927.pdf

48. Ibid.

49. U.S. Department of Justice, *FY2012 Performance Budget, Drug Enforcement Administration, U.S. Department of Justice*. Congressional Budget Submission, 11.

50. U.S. Government Accountability Office, *Law Enforcement Coordination: DOJ Could Improve Its Process for Identifying Disagreements Among Agents*, GAO-11-314, April 2011, 2.

See also U.S. Department of Justice, Office of the Inspector General, Audit Division, *The Federal Bureau of Investigation's Ability to Address the National Security Cyber Intrusion Threat*, Audit Report 11–22, April 2011, iv–vii.

51. Johnson, David R. and David Post, "Law and Borders — The Rise of Law in Cyberspace," *Stanford Law Review*, vol. 48 (May 1996), 1379.

52. Ibid., 1370.

53. Internet World Stats, *Internet Usage Statistics, The Internet Big Picture, World Internet Users and Population Stats*, accessed 5 January 2013 at: http://www.internetworldstats.com/stats.htm. And Internet Live Stats, Internet Users, accessed 17 February 2017 at: http://www.internetlivestats.com/internet-users/

54. United Nations Office on Drugs and Crime, *The Globalization of Crime: A Transnational Organized Crime Threat Assessment*, ISBN: 978-92-1-130295-0, 2010, 203, accessed July 17, 2017, at: http://www.unodc.org/documents/data-and-analysis/tocta/TOCTA_Report_2010_low_res.pdf

55. STRATFOR, e-mail to author, 25 December 2012, 3:50 PM MST.

56. Armerding, T., The 15 worst data security breaches of the 21st Century, CSO Data Protection, 15 February 2012. Accessed 6 January 2013 at: http://www.csoonline.com/article/700263/the-15-worst-data-security-breaches-of-the-21st-century This was updated under the same author, title, and website link on July 12, 2017. Accessed July 18, 2017.

57. Navigant, *Information Security and Data Breach Report, June 2012 update*. Accessed at: https://www.privacyassociation.org/media/pdf/knowledge_center/2012_InfoSec_Data_Breach_Report_Navigant.pdf

58. Armerding, 2017.

59. Finklea, K. M., 20 July 2012.

60. Testimony by Jason Weinstein, Criminal Division, U.S. Department of Justice, before U.S. Congress, Senate Committee on the Judiciary, Subcommittee on Crime and Terrorism, *Cybersecurity: Responding to the Threat of Cyber Crime and Terrorism*, 112th Cong., 1st sess. Presented April 12, 2011. Accessed July 18, 2017, at: https://www.justice.gov/sites/default/files/testimonies/witnesses/attachments/04/12/11/04-12-11-crm-weinstein-testimony-re-cybersecurity.pdf

61. "NRF Organized Retail Crime Survey Finds Criminals View Global Recession as Opportunity to Abuse Retailers and Consumers Organized Retail Crime Activity Jumps by 8%, According to NRF Survey," *Business Wire*, June 10, 2009. Accessed July 18, 2017, at: http://www.businesswire.com/news/home/20090609006373/en/NRF-Organized-Retail-Crime-Survey-Finds-Criminals

62. Jerry Markon, "FBI-ATF Turf Battle Hurts Bomb Probes, Official Says," *Washington Post*, August 27, 2010, http://www.washingtonpost.com/wp-dyn/content/article/2010/08/26/AR2010082606631.html See also Jerry Markon, "FBI, ATF Battle for Control of Cases: Cooperation Lags Despite Merger," *Washington Post*, May 10, 2008, http://www.washingtonpost.com/wp-dyn/content/article/2008/05/09/AR2008050903096.html Accessed July 18, 2017.

63. U.S. Department of Justice, Office of the Inspector General, *Review of ATF's Project Gunrunner*, I-2011-001, November 2010, http://www.justice.gov/oig/reports/ATF/e1101.pdf See also U.S. Immigration and Customs Enforcement, "ATF, ICE update partnership agreement to maximize investigative efforts," press release, June 30, 2009, https://www.atf.gov/file/60751/download Accessed July 18, 2017.

64. Joe Palazzolo, "Rival Agencies Agree to Halt Turf Battles," August 10, 2009, cited in Kristin Finklea, The Interplay of Borders, Turf, Cyberspace, and Jurisdiction: Issues Confronting U.S. Law Enforcement, CRS, January 17, 2013. Accessed July 18, 2017, at: https://fas.org/sgp/crs/misc/R41927.pdf

65. Naím, Moisés, *Illicit: How Smugglers, Traffickers, and Copycats are Hijacking the Global Economy* (New York: Anchor Books, 2005), 13.

66. Internet Crime Complaint Center, *2010 Internet Crime Report*, 9. Accessed July 18, 2017, at: https://pdf.ic3.gov/2010_IC3Report.pdf

67. Ibid, 10.

68. Federal Bureau of Investigation, "Department of Justice Takes Action to Disable International Botnet: More Than Two Million Computers Infected with Keylogging Software as Part of Massive Fraud Scheme," press release, April 13, 2011. Accessed 24 February 2013 at: http://newhaven.fbi.gov/dojpressrel/pressrel11/nh041311.htm

69. Ibid.

70. Kim Zetter, "FBI vs. Coreflood Botnet: Round 1 Goes to the Feds," *Wired.com*, April 26, 2011. Accessed July 18, 2017, at: https://www.wired.com/2011/04/coreflood_results/

71. U.S. Department of Justice, "Nigerian National Sentenced in North Carolina to 108 Months in Prison for Role in Advance Fee Fraud Scheme," press release, February 24, 2011. Accessed July 18, 2018, at: https://www.justice.gov/opa/pr/nigerian-national-sentenced-north-carolina-108-months-prison-role-advance-fee-fraud-scheme

72. See Federal Bureau of Investigation, "Gordon M. Snow, Assistant Director, Cyber Division, Federal Bureau of Investigation, Statement Before the Senate Judiciary Committee, Subcommittee on Crime and Terrorism," April 11, 2011. Accessed July 18, 2017, at: http://www.ncpc.org/resources/files/pdf/internet-safety/13020-Cybercrimes-revSPR.pdf See also White House, *International Strategy for Cyberspace: Prosperity, Security, and Openness in a Networked World*, May 2011, 4. Accessed July 18, 2014, at: https://obamawhitehouse.archives.gov/sites/default/files/rss_viewer/international_strategy_for_cyberspace.pdf

73. U.S. Immigration and Customs Enforcement, "Chinese National Sentenced to More Than 7 Years in Federal Prison for Trafficking Counterfeit Pharmaceutical Weight-Loss Drug," press release, June 3, 2011. Accessed July 21, 2017, at: http://www.ice.gov/news/releases/1106/110603denver.htm

74. U.S. Drug Enforcement Administration, "DEA/ICE Uncover 'Massive' Cross-Border Drug Tunnel, Cement lined passage thought to link warehouses in Tijuana and Otay Mesa," press release, January 26, 2006. Accessed July 21, 2017, at: http://www.justice.gov/dea/pubs/pressrel/pr012606.html

75. U.S. Drug Enforcement Administration, "Discovery of 2nd Major San Diego-Area Cross-Border Drug Tunnel Leads to 8 Arrests, Seizure of More Than 20 Tons of Marijuana," press release, November 26, 2010. Accessed July 21, 2017, at: http://www.justice.gov/dea/pubs/states/newsrel/2010/sd112610.html

76. Rear Admiral Vincent Atkins, U.S. Coast Guard, Testimony before the House Subcommittee on Homeland Security, on Department of Homeland Security Air and Marine Operations and Investments, April 19, 2010. Accessed July 21, 2017, at: http://www.dhs.gov/ynews/testimony/testimony_1271690315007.shtm

77. Richard Marosi, "Ultralight Aircraft Now Ferrying Drugs Across U.S.-Mexico Border," *Los Angeles Times*, May 19, 2011. Accessed July 21, 2017, at: http://www.latimes.com/news/local/la-me-border-ultralight-2011 0520, 0, 731 5999.story

78. U.S. Department of Justice, Office of the Inspector General, *A Review of the Department's Anti-Gang Intelligence and Coordination Centers*, I-2010-001, November 2009. Accessed July 21, 2017, at: http://www.justice.gov/oig/reports/FBI/i2010001.pdf

79. Federal Bureau of Investigation, "Richard A. McFeely, Special Agent in Charge, FBI, Statement Before the Senate Judiciary Committee, Wilmington, Delaware," June 20, 2011. Accessed July 21, 2017, at: https://archives.fbi.gov/archives/news/testimony/information-sharing-efforts-with-partners--span-many-fbi-programs

80. "The Advent of Netwar (Revisited)," in *Networks and Netwars: The Future of Terror, Crime, and Militancy*, ed. John Arquilla and David Ronfeldt, 15.

81. RBS WorldPay is an Atlanta, Georgia-based credit card processing company that is part of the Royal Bank of Scotland. For more information on this case, see U.S. Department of Justice, "Alleged International Hacking Ring Caught in $9 Million Fraud," press release, November 10, 2009. Accessed July 21, 2017, at: http://www.justice.gov/opa/pr/2009/November/09-crm-1212.html

82. U.S. Department of Justice, "International Hacker Arraigned After Extradition," press release, August 5, 2010. Accessed July 21, 2017, at: https://www.justice.gov/archive/usao/gan/press/2010/08-06-10.pdf

83. United Nations Office of Drugs and Crime, *United Nations Convention Against Transnational Organized Crime and the Protocols Thereto* (New York: United Nations, 2004).

84. For more information on the Convention, see archived CRS Report RS21208, *Cybercrime: The Council of Europe Convention*, by Kristin Archick. Accessed July 21, 2017, at: http://conventions.coe.int/Treaty/EN/Treaties/html/185.htm

85. Statement of Janice Ayala, Deputy Assistant Director, Office of Investigations, U.S. Immigration and Customs Enforcement, Department of Homeland Security, before the U.S. Congress, House Committee on Homeland Security, Subcommittee on Border, Maritime, and Global Counterterrorism, *Cargo Security at Land Ports of Entry: Are We Meeting the Challenge?*, 111th Cong., 1st sess., October 22, 2009.

86. U.S. Department of Justice, "ICE and DOJ Sign Agreements to Share Information on Drug Trafficking and Organized Crime," press release, August 10, 2009. Accessed July 21, 2017, at: http://www.justice.gov/opa/pr/2009/August/09-crm-784.html

87. Department of Homeland Security, *Fusion Centers and Joint Terrorism Task Forces*, February 28, 2011. Accessed July 21, 2017, at: http://www.dhs.gov/files/programs/gc_1298911926746.shtm

88. 153 P.L. 110-53, Aug. 3, 2007, § 511, 121 STAT. 322. Amends *Homeland Security Act of 2002* by adding § 210A(j).

89. Department of Homeland Security, *Fusion Centers and Joint Terrorism Task Forces*, February 28, 2011.

90. For more information on the ISE, see CRS Report R40901, *Terrorism Information Sharing and the Nationwide Suspicious Activity Report Initiative: Background and Issues for Congress*, by Jerome P. Bjelopera. See also http://www.ise.gov/

91. Justice Research and Statistics Association (JRSA), *Information Sharing Systems: A Survey of Law Enforcement*, July 31, 2006, 14. Accessed July 21, 2017, at: http://www.jrsa.org/pubs/reports/improving-crime-data/Info_Sharing.pdf

92. U.S. Department of Justice, United States Attorney, Eastern District of Pennsylvania, *Launch of the National Identity Crime Law Enforcement Network (NICLE)*. Accessed July 21, 2017, at: http://www.theiacp.org/investigateid/pdf/appendices/Launch-of-the-Natitonal-Identity-Crime-Law-Enforcement-Network-NICLE.pdf

93. The President's Identity Theft Task Force, *Combating Identity Theft: A Strategic Plan*, April 23, 2007, 56. Accessed July 21, 2017, at: https://www.ftc.gov/sites/default/files/documents/reports/combating-identity-theft-strategic-plan/strategicplan.pdf See also: *InfraGard*, February 17, 2017, available at: https://www.infragard.org

94. Federal Bureau of Investigation, *Domestic Security Alliance Council*. Last accessed 17 February 2017 at https://www.dsac.gov

95. For more information on LERPnet, see http://www.lerpnet2.com/

96. Ed Pilkington, "One in four US hackers 'is an FBI informer'," *The Guardian*, June 6, 2011. Accessed July 21, 2017, at: http://www.guardian.co.uk/technology/2011/jun/06/us-hackers-fbi-informer

97. U.S. Department of Justice, "Hacker Pleads Guilty in Manhattan Federal Court to Illegally Accessing New York Times Computer Network," press release, January 8, 2004. Accessed July 21, 2017, at: https://www.justice.gov/archive/criminal/cybercrime/press-releases/2004/lamoPlea.htm

98. Anonymous, 2013, Operation Last Resort. Accessed July 21, 2017, at: https://www.youtube.com/watch?v=nSrDRnqpMCY

99. Jacob, Jijo, "FBI moles run illegal sites that deal in hackers' loot of sensitive data," *International Business Times*, June 7, 2011. Accessed July 21, 2017, at: http://www.ibtimes.com/fbi-moles-run-illegal-sites-deal-hackers-loot-sensitive-data-288939

Appendix A

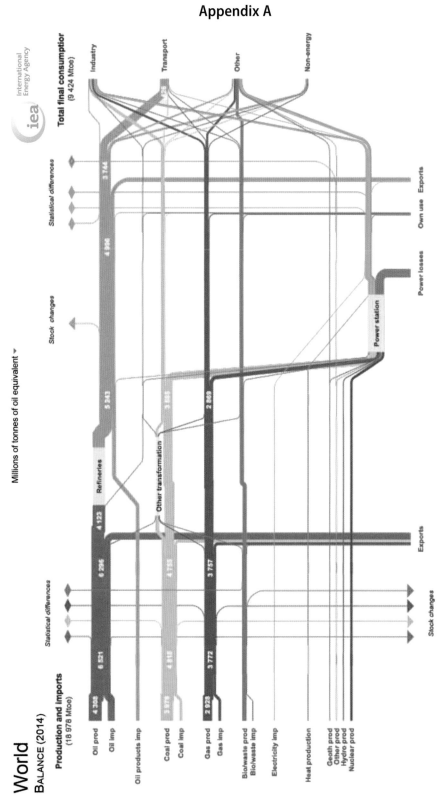

WORLD Energy Balance (2014), from the International Energy Agency Sankey Diagram, 18 February 2017.]

Appendix A

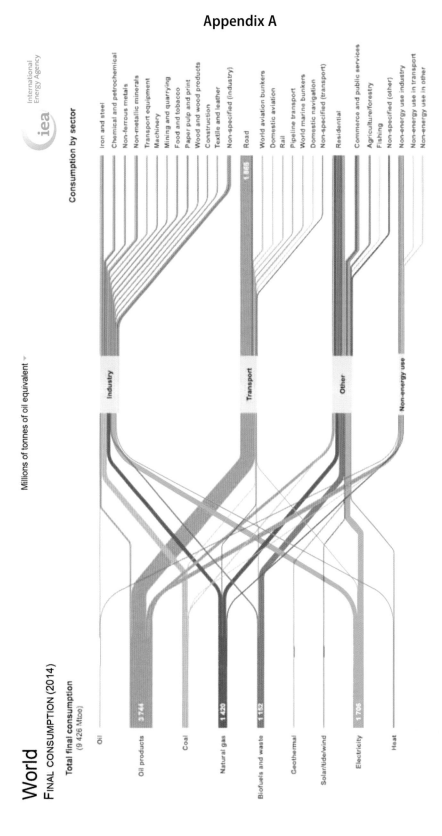

WORLD Final Energy Consumption (2014), from the International Energy Agency Sankey Diagram, 18 February 2017.

Appendix A

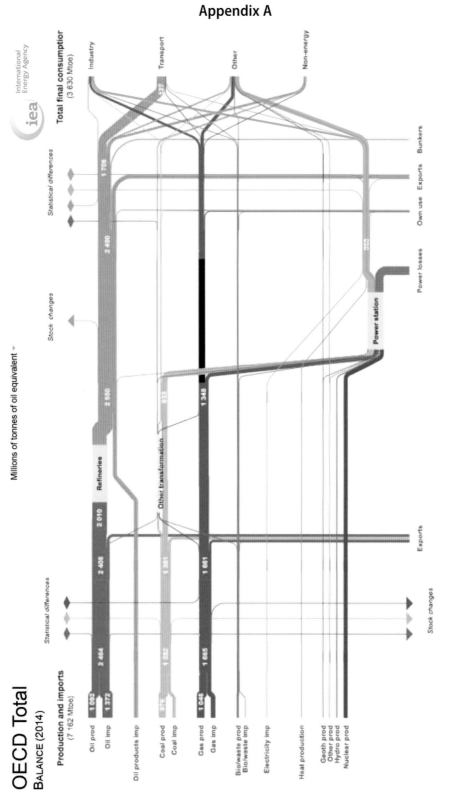

OCED Energy Balance (2014), from the International Energy Agency Sankey Diagram, 18 February 2017.

Appendix A

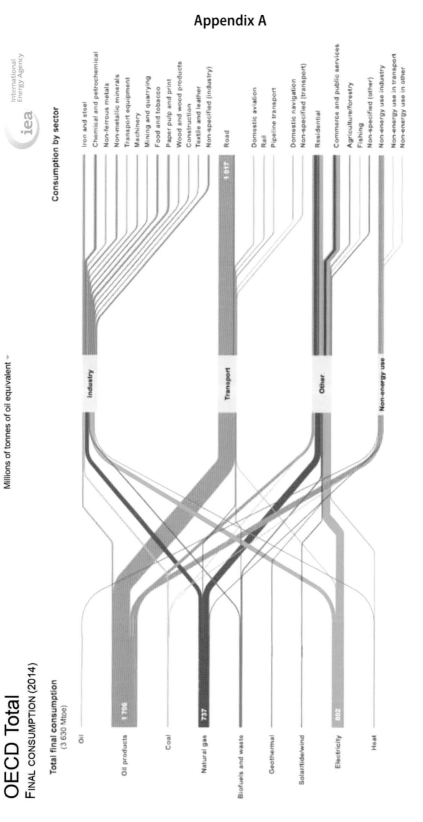

OECD Final Energy Consumption (2014), from the International Energy Agency Sankey Diagram, 18 February 2017.

Appendix A

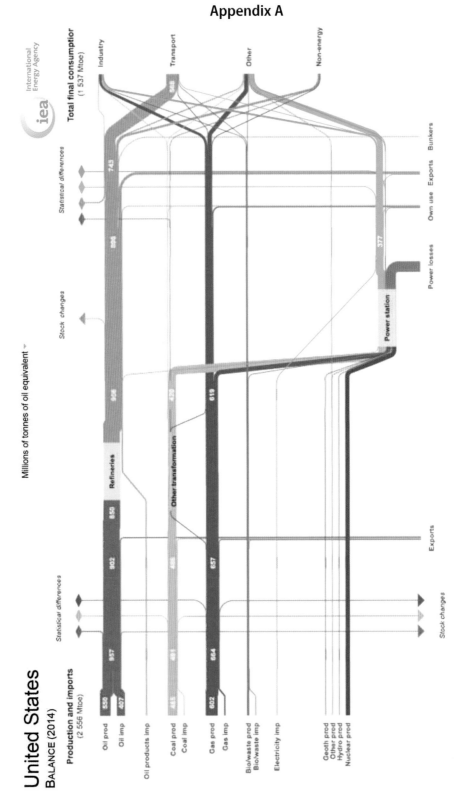

OECD member: United States Energy Balance (2014), from the International Energy Agency Sankey Diagram, 18 February 2017.

Appendix A

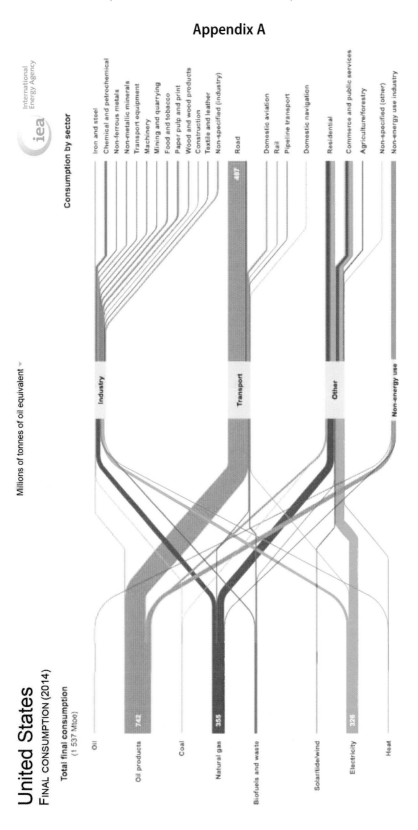

OECD member: United States Final Energy Consumption (2014), from the International Energy Agency Sankey Diagram, 18 February 2017.]

Appendix A

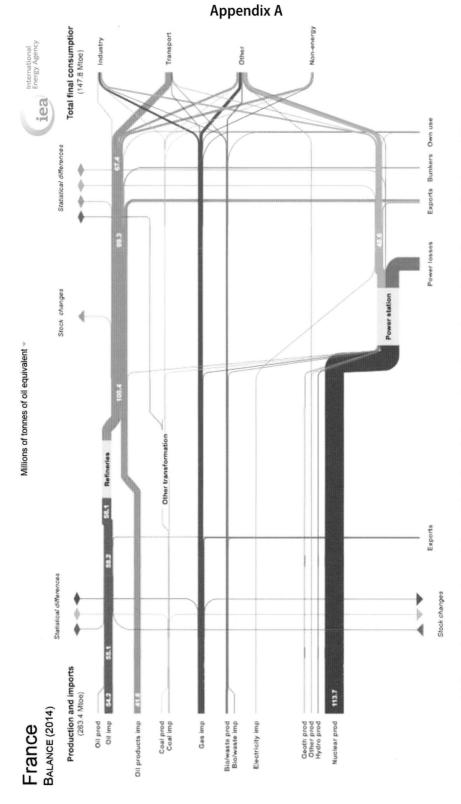

OECD member: France Energy Balance (2014), from the International Energy Agency Sankey Diagram, 18 February 2017.

Appendix A

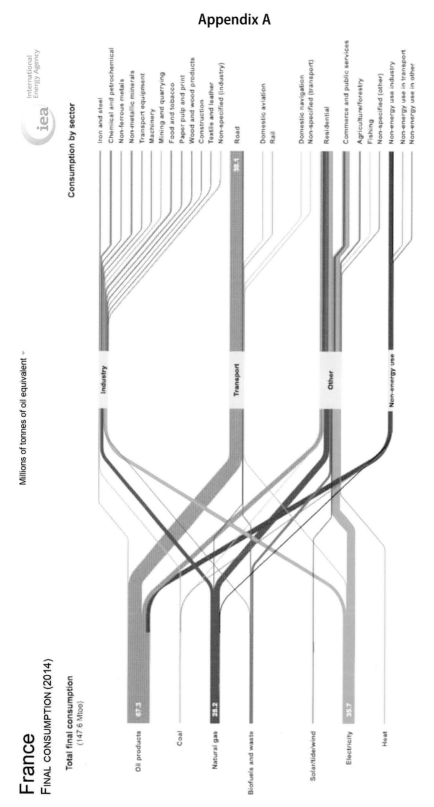

OECD member: France Final Energy Consumption (2014), from the International Energy Agency Sankey Diagram, 18 February 2017.

Appendix A

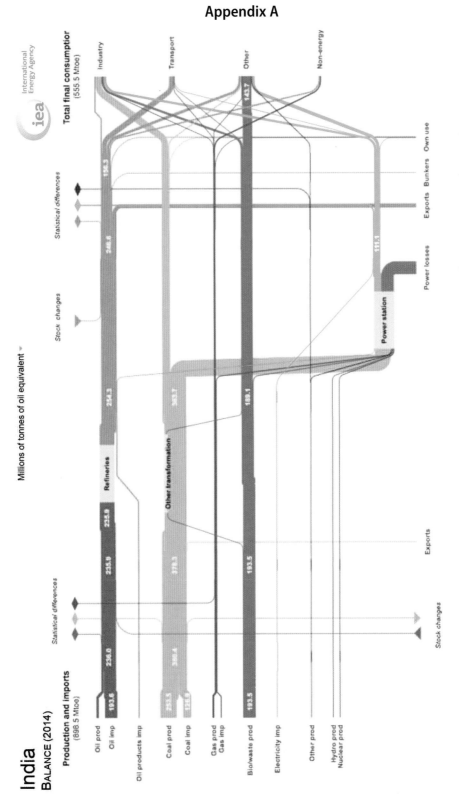

OECD nonmember: India Energy Balance (2014), from the International Energy Agency Sankey Diagram, 18 February 2017.

Appendix A

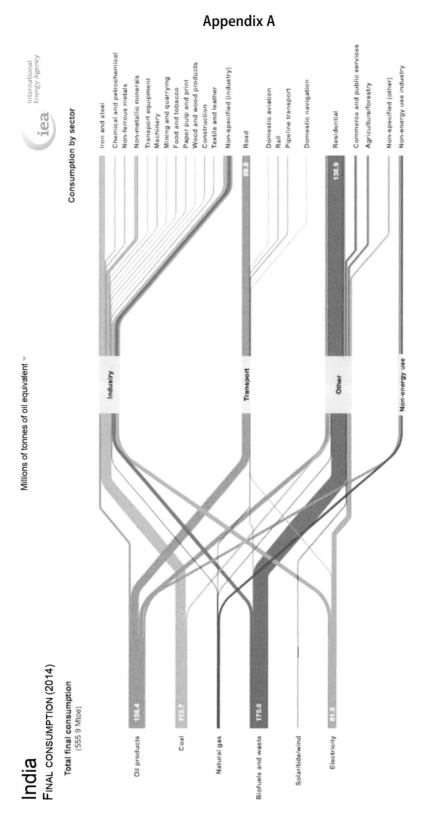

OECD nonmember: India Final Energy Consumption (2014), from the International Energy Agency Sankey Diagram, 18 February 2017.

Appendix A

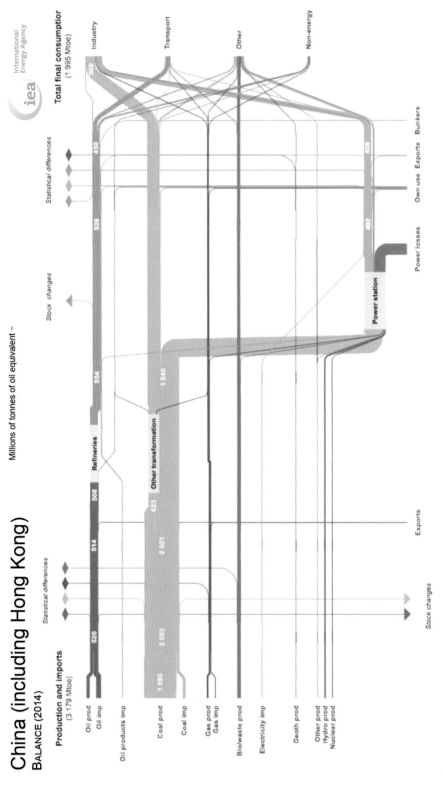

OECD nonmember: China Energy Balance (2014), from the International Energy Agency Sankey Diagram, 18 February 2017.

Appendix A

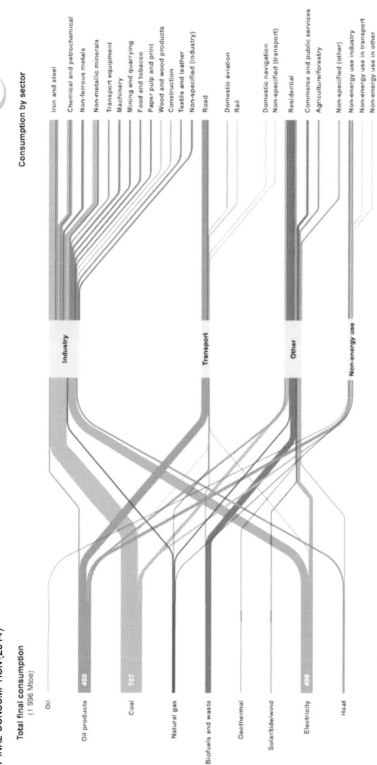

OECD nonmember: China Final Energy Consumption (2014), from the International Energy Agency Sankey Diagram, 18 February 2017.

Appendix B

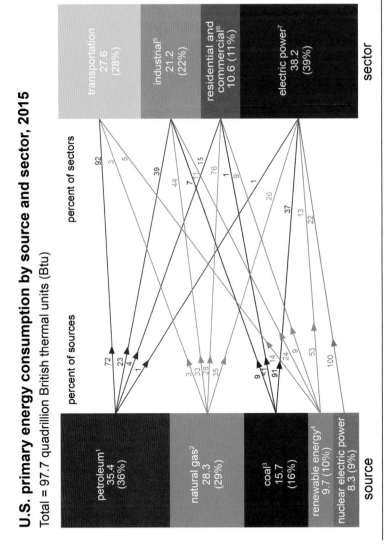

US Primary Energy Consumption by Source and Sector, 2015. US Energy Information Administration, available at: http://www.eia.gov/totalenergy/data/monthly/pdf/flow/css_2015_energy.pdf

Appendix B

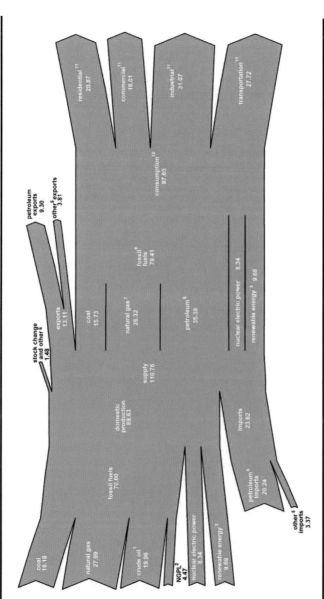

US Energy Flow, 2015. US Energy Information Administration, available at: http://www.eia.gov/

Appendix B

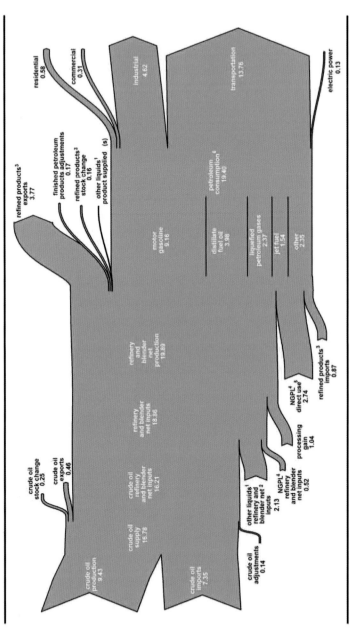

US Petroleum Flow, 2015. US Energy Information Administration, available at: http://www.eia.gov/

Appendix B

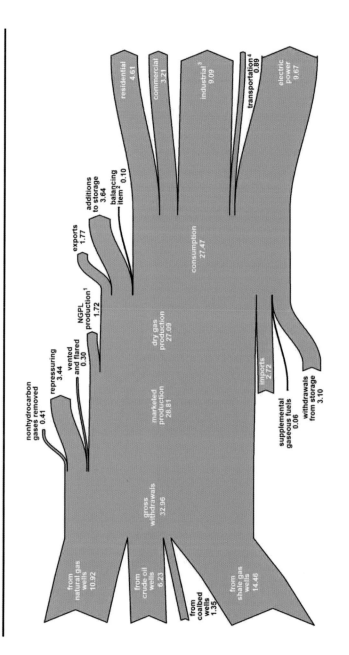

US Natural Gas Flow, 2015. US Energy Information Administration, available at: http://www.eia.gov/

Appendix B

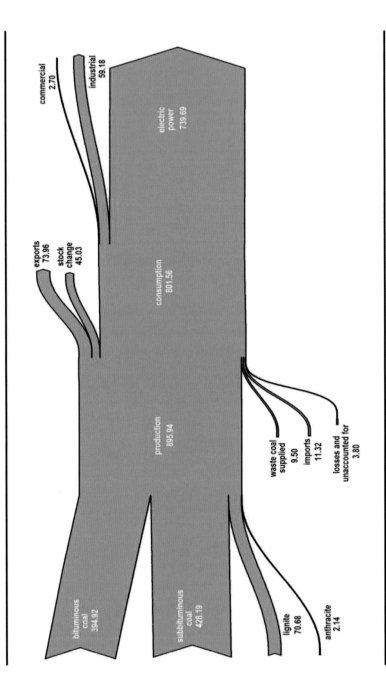

U.S. Coal Flow, 2015
million short tons

bituminous coal 394.92

subbituminous coal 428.19

lignite 70.68

anthracite 2.14

production 895.94

waste coal supplied 9.50

imports 11.32

losses and unaccounted for 3.80

exports 73.96

stock change 45.03

consumption 801.56

commercial 2.70

industrial 59.18

electric power 739.69

Notes: • Production categories are estimated; all data are preliminary. • Values are derived from source data prior to rounding for publication. • Totals may not equal sum of components due to independent rounding.

Sources: U.S. Energy Information Administration (EIA), *Monthly Energy Review* (April 2016), Tables 6.1 and 6.2; and EIA estimates based on U.S. Department of Labor, Mine Safety and Health Administration, Form 7000-2, "Quarterly Mine Employment and Coal Production Report."

US Coal Flow, 2015. US Energy Information Administration, available at: http://www.eia.gov/

Appendix B

U.S. Electricity Flow, 2015
quadrillion Btu

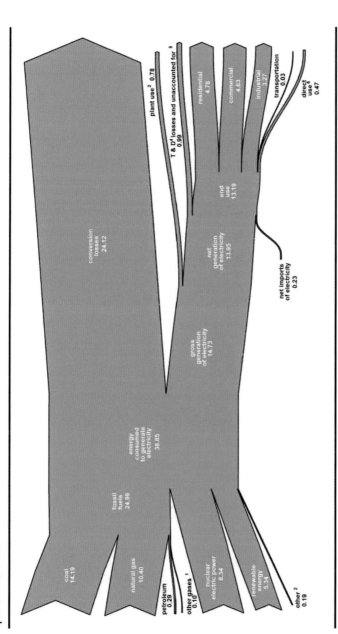

[1] Blast furnace gas and other manufactured and waste gases derived from fossil fuels.
[2] Batteries, chemicals, hydrogen, pitch, purchased steam, sulfur, miscellaneous technologies, and non-renewable waste (municipal solid waste from nonbiogenic sources), and tire-derived fuels).
[3] Electric energy used in the operation of power plants.
[4] Transmission and distribution losses (electricity losses that occur between the point of generation and delivery to the customer).
[5] Data collection frame differences and nonsampling error.
[6] Use of electricity that is 1) self-generated, 2) produced by either the same entity that consumes the power or an affiliate, and 3) used in direct support of a service or industrial

process located within the same facility or group of facilities that house the generating equipment. Direct use is exclusive of station use.
Notes: • Data are preliminary. • See Note 1, "Electrical System Energy Losses," at the end of EIA, Monthly Energy Review (April 2016), Section 2. • Net generation of electricity includes pumped storage facility production minus energy used for pumping. • Values are derived from source data prior to rounding for publication. • Totals may not equal sum of components due to independent rounding.
Sources: U.S. Energy Information Administration, Monthly Energy Review (April 2016), Tables 7.1, 7.2a, 7.3a, 7.6, and A6; and EIA, Form EIA-923, "Power Plant Operations Report."

US Electricity Flow, 2015. US Energy Information Administration, available at: http://www.eia.gov/

Chapter 9

Transportation Security

"The reality about transportation is that it is future-oriented. If we're planning for what we have, we're behind the curve."

— Anthony Fox

Key Words and Concepts

Deterrence Theory

General Systems Theory

Hurricane Rita

Layered Security

Logistics

Maritime Shipping

National Highway System

Social Contract

Stove Piping

Transportation Security Administration

Observe-Orient-Decide Act

Introduction

The security of any transportation system is based on the safe and efficient movement of people, goods, and information utilizing air, land, and sea. This is the fundamental core of Transportation Security. The global economic system is driven by the ability to move raw materials, parts, and finished goods from suppliers to consumers. Interrupting the smooth flow of commerce in any way can have a devastating impact on every aspect of an economy.

Eads Bridge over Mississippi River. William Rosmus. Wikicommons.

Following the 9/11 attacks on New York City and Washington, DC, the government of the United States shut down all commercial air traffic throughout the country. Many aircraft were forced to land at remote Canadian airfields not equipped to handle the traffic. This was the tip of the iceberg as far as impact to our transportation systems, and our nation's economic structure.

More importantly, the normal border crossings were also closed, stopping the delivery of everything from pharmaceutical supplies to fresh foods (the amount that rotted while waiting to be released for delivery has never been calculated) and parts for manufacturing. Just-in-time deliveries for automobile assembly plants were prevented from crossing into the United States from Canada, shutting down virtually every automobile manufacturer within hours of the attacks. This was just a small fraction of the economic impact brought about by the terrorists. Securing transportation from terrorists, natural disaster, or man-made disasters is an essential component of ensuring that national and international commerce continues unabated. Thus, understanding the basics of transportation security in a globalized world is essential to understanding the overall process of Border Security.

Logistics Transformation

The economic problems caused by the terrorist attacks were not (all) intended. Some of them were the result of a transportation system that was locked in a world where "we have always done it this way" was the mantra of logisticians and transportation experts. We have been handcuffed, historically, by a "stovepipe" management approach to transportation that has addressed all components independently from one another, with limited communication technology and organizational coordination. One way to improve this situation is through what is known as *logistics transformation*. Logistics transformation is the process whereby productivity and capability are increased through deliberate application of continuous process improvement and other methods to constantly change and adapt existing paradigms to the demands of an ever-changing world. This application should not only be available at the right time, place, and cost, but also should contribute to the *enterprise value*: it should increase the operational effectiveness and achieve economies necessary for the public good. There are common characteristics of logistics systems' transformation: these include transparency, agility, and robust communications. Improvements in these common characteristics should be reflected in any attempt at improvement in the modern transportation logistics enterprise.

In the security domain, mandates for system change come from disasters, both natural and man-made, terrorism, and political instability. Changes are usually event driven. If economic and physical national security is going to be responsive to the new challenges of the global economy, then logistics transformation is essential.

Nations have a choice: continue to do things the way they've always done them or develop innovative solutions to future transportation and infrastructure needs.

Achieving economic, national, and transportation security can be achieved only through the transformation of the logistics enterprise.

Transportation Systems Theory

In Clifford Bragdon's words, "An integrated intermodal system of transportation involves … a complex system of integrated or holistic transport [which] consists of both physical modes of movement (classically involved with roadways, rail, transit, airports, maritime transportation, utilities, and pipelines) and electronic modes of movement (associated with communication, electronic data exchange, related information technology, satellite and digital and fiber optic connectivity and interoperability)." However, this state of systems compatibility simply doesn't exist. The current system is "a gridlock condition that underoptimizes [sic] our economic potential and social responsiveness and … impairs the total effectiveness of emergency preparedness, response, and recovery."
Bragdon, Clifford, *Transportation Security* (New York: Elsevier, 2008), 36.

Impediments currently exist to an integrated approach to transport movement. These include specific types of transport. Each mode of transport has evolved relatively independently, modified (more or less) by a series of governmental agreements, and patents, reflecting territorial exclusiveness. For instance, in the New York area it began with maritime transportation involving sailing ships, followed by railway systems. Subway systems began in the 1800s in Paris, New York, and London. A national highway system supporting automobiles came next, with the support of the federal government, based primarily on national defense, and known as the Dwight D. Eisenhower National System of Interstate and Defense Highways. A national aviation system came next, with the establishment of the Federal Aviation Administration.

Each of these disparate systems worked independently, with its own core businesses and supporting organizations, such as lobbyists, and others "working" Congress and the federal government. Each protected its own "turf" and each was an insular system with no provision for any linkage to another part. This is just one example of "stovepiping," with individual interests prevailing over the system as a whole.

Virtually all the modal changes in transportation in this country have come because of institutional self-interests. One example of this modal self-interest is the change from a trolley or streetcar system to a bus-oriented one. General Motors, Firestone, and Standard Oil formed a partnership in 1936, National City Lines, which was created to support trolley-based public transportation systems switching their fixed-rail systems to buses powered by General Motors diesel engines. The goal of the National City Line organization was the elimination of the trolley system, replaced by General Motors diesel-powered buses running on Standard Oil gasoline and Firestone tires. The decline of the metropolitan trolley system became a national trend, and the streetcar rail system, used throughout the United States, was abandoned in favor of buses. In 1965, for example, only 5,000 streetcars remained.

Not only is mobility a national and international requirement to both our economic and national security, it can also be a psychological and physiological requirement at the individual level. Bragdon writes,

> Constrained transportation-related conditions involving both drivers and passengers result in health-related impacts ranging from nuisance to hazard potential. Neural-humoral stress response in traffic-related conditions can include elevated blood pressure and cardiovascular and circulatory effects. Performance efficiency can also be impaired, resulting in mental health–related stress outcomes whose by-products are road rage, aggressive behavior, and general annoyance. The transportation management approach to initiate "traffic calming" in surface transport design is recognition of this growing problem and the need for physical design solutions in urban traffic-impacted environments.[1]

The federal government has recognized the need for a more comprehensive plan for transportation, passing the Intermodal Surface Transportation Efficiency Act (ISTEA) in 1991, the Transportation Equity Act in 1998, and the Safe, Accountable, Flexible, and Efficient Transportation Act — A Legacy for Users in 2005. At least part of the reasoning behind pieces of legislation such as these is the realization that response times relative to both natural and man-made disasters as well as emergency preparedness need to be improved. Progress is now being made toward addressing integrated transportation issues, if not resolving them.

Another problem relative to an integrated transportation system outcome is our culturally based concept of "land." We tend to think of property and urban space as having only two dimensions, rather than three, and follow a land use-based model, which diminishes our spatial options. Following a natural or man-made disaster, we tend to think first of surface access routes, and to ignore the air and sea evacuation possibilities. One example of this was egress from New Orleans, following Hurricane Katrina. Everyone, including emergency management planners, thought of Interstate 55, which quickly became gridlocked, and which turned into a long, thin, parking lot. Other examples include I-45 North out of Houston, in preparation for Hurricane Rita, and the egress from Key West, via US-1, in preparation for any of several hurricanes in the 1980s and 1990s. When a disaster hits, people tend to immediately think of things (including modes of transportation) *with which they are most familiar*, and since most of us primarily use our personal vehicles for (almost) all our transportation needs, our cars immediately come to mind when we need to get to somewhere else.

General Systems Theory (GST)

One of the several methodologies (such as operations research, systems analysis, systems dynamics) that employ a system approach to understanding complex phenomena and problems. GST focuses on the system's structure instead of on the system's function. It proposes that complex systems share some basic organizing principles irrespective of their purposes, and that these principles can be modeled mathematically (Mele et al., 2010). The concept was introduced by the Austrian biologist Ludwig von Bertalanffy (1958) and by the UK economist Kenneth Boulding (1958). The Business Dictionary goes on to define the Systems Approach as *Management thinking that emphasizes the interdependence and interactive nature of elements within and external to an organization.*

Mele, Cristina et al. (2010) A Brief Review of Systems Theories and Their Managerial Applications, *Service Science,* Vol. 2, 126–35, INFORMS Online. Retrieved 02/27/17.

Bertalanffy, Ludwig v., (1958) General Systems Theory, *General Systems, Yearbook of the Society for General Systems Research,* Bertanlanffy and Rapoport, eds., Vol. 1, Society for General Systems Research.

Boulding, Kenneth E. (1958) General Systems Theory: The Skeleton of Science, *General Systems, Yearbook of the Society for General Systems Research,* Bertanlanffy and Rapoport, eds., Vol. 1, Society for General Systems Research.

"General Systems Theory," BusinessDictionary.com. Retrieved 02/27/17.

The systems approach has been applied by business schools, biology, ecology, sociology, and virtually every other form of academic study. There are theories of World Systems, Entropy Systems, Complex Systems, Family Systems, etc. It is instructive to examine transportation theory in terms of both a systems approach, and in terms of a "learning organization."

In *The Fifth Discipline*, author Peter Senge details five characteristics that comprise what he calls a "learning organization"—in other words, an organization that cultivates an effective learning environment. According to Senge, the five traits of a learning organization are: Systems Thinking, Personal Mastery, Shared Vision, Team Learning, and developing Mental Models. Senge defines System Thinking as finding the patterns that exist between component parts of the system and the system as a whole. The key to Personal Mastery is to learn to see reality objectively. Shared Vision occurs when a group of individuals collectively develops a vision of the future. Team Learning occurs when people communicate with each other. When this happens, the group's IQ is greater than the sum of its parts. Senge defines Mental Models as the ingrained assumptions and generalizations that we carry around as excess baggage, and that influence how we perceive and interact with the world. Once we understand our biases, then we can change them.[2]

Mobility and Security

Mobility and security concerns are often diametrically opposed. As Charles Nemfakos put it, "There is tension between the needs of a developed nation-state for cheap labor, goods, and materials and the nation's assurance of the safety of its citizens and culture. There is corresponding tension between the needs of developed nation-states and the desires of individuals from developing nations to participate in the economies of developed nation-states, both as producers of goods and as migratory providers of labor."[3]

How a populace responds to notifications of threats is determined by the psychosocial makeup of that population. These behavioral responses to perceived threats determine what the society is willing to accept in the way of losses while simultaneously limiting how much loss of freedom is acceptable in the trade-off for security. One example of the trade-off between mobility and security is the experience of travelers at airports as they attempt to "go through security" to get to the gates prior to boarding their plane. Do you remember when the only items prohibited were weapons, and ammunition? Now, virtually all liquids and gels, including toothpaste and deodorant, are excluded (except for very small versions, which will fit inside a plastic bag). And, of course, shoes, coats, belts, etc. must be removed and scanned separately. The latest in sensor technology is more intrusive than the metal scanning devices, and renders images of everything under one's clothing.

No society can be secure from all threats, all the time. Deviant behavior (crime) has always existed and will always exist; because of this, society accepts a certain amount of threat to its social order, both culturally and individually, daily (various theories are used to "explain" deviance, including both sociological theories, and individual-based theories). Modern democratic societies rely on a constant tradeoff between a practical level of security balanced against a reasonable infringement on mobility. The technology and mechanisms required to provide constant daily security against increasingly dangerous threats by their nature constrain mobility; citizens agree to a certain infringement on their mobility to "feel" safer, to achieve the individual perception that they are "safer" against a threat.

The government of any democratic society works to alert its populace to threats while striving to maintain the members of that society's reasonable expectations of safety through security control mechanisms, which infringe upon those members to a greater or lesser extent. The fine line the government walks is defined by three theories: deterrence theory, terror management theory, and protection motivation theory. Together, these three theories define a population's behavior responses to external threats. The bottom line is, unless a nation is constantly mobilized against a perceived threat, its members tend to become complacent and ignore the threat, whatever it is, and however dangerous it is "perceived" to be. People, as a culture, as well as individually, want to believe that they are invincible, that they are safe, and that the world is ordered, and logical. They want to believe in a world of cause and effect. People usually disable or ignore security measures when they are perceived as intrusive or ineffective, unless and until they perceive an impending threat to be real and/or imminent. People operate daily as if they can set goals and plan activities based on expectations regarding their environment. They act as if their world is orderly, stable, and meaningful. When people act as if their environment is stable, they are less likely to take security precautions, particularly if those precautions affect their planned schedule, or their mobility.[4]

Deterrence Theory

The basis of deterrence theory is the belief that by increasing the perceived punishment for a potential crime (or decreasing its possible benefits), the chances of a criminal committing the crime are less. It was derived from social philosopher Cesare Beccaria's book, *On Crime and Punishment* in 1764 in which he condemned the harsh punishments of the time, including torture and the death penalty. Beccaria said that for punishment to be effective, and act as a deterrent, it should conform to rational principles; it should be swift, certain, and proportionate to the crime committed. According to Beccaria, if any of the three were missing, then the punishment given would not act as a deterrent. Academic disciplines have adopted this as a part of rational conservative political theory, to the detriment of policies favoring rehabilitation, even though in his time, Beccaria was a radical theorist reasoning to lessen the most torturous and harshest punishments and introduce moderation.

This was taken to an entirely new level with the Cold War, and Mutually Assured Destruction (MAD). The premise of MAD was the rational model of human behavior, taken large. This implies the recognition that if either side begins a nuclear war, the end result is the assured, complete destruction of both sides; this recognition and assumed awareness is what prevents either side from starting a war (Kaplan, 2015). This rationale breaks down, unfortunately, when the other side does not fear complete annihilation. After 9/11, Western analysts have come to realize that deterrence does not apply to certain nontraditional foes who are neither geographically identified nor conform to traditional Western rational thinking.

Paolucci, Henry, *On Crime and Punishment* by Cesare Beccaria 1764, Translated, with intro. (Indianapolis: Bobbs-Merrill Online, 1963).

Kaplan, Edward, *To Kill Nations: American Strategy in the Air-Atomic Age & the Rise of Mutually Assured Destruction* (Ithaca, NY: Cornell University, 2015).

It is increasingly difficult (or impossible) to predict nonrational individual behaviors, therefore most Western democratic governments have begun to rely more and more on a deterrence strategy that depends on information gathered through data mining and the identification of patterns based on data collected from the entire population, both pervasively and invasively.

For the populace to approve the spending required for (and acquiesce to) the pervasive and invasive collection of data, the government must mobilize its citizens against perceived threats so that they will relinquish their privacy and (at least) some of their (constitutional) freedoms. This is the basis for terror management theory. A perceived threat is psychological, physical, or sociological, and can be a threat to either oneself or to others, or both. This is the mechanism by which governments mobilize populations, making even remote threats seem imminent, but mitigated due to the government's watchful eye and dutiful care. For example, during the Cold War era, schoolchildren were taught to hide under their desks at school, and close their eyes, in case of a Soviet nuclear attack. This supposedly would protect them from both the nuclear explosion and the blinding flash itself. In more recent times the government has used "threat levels" to alert the population of a possible terrorist attack, related to color codes ("orange" meaning increased vigilance on the part of the population, versus "yellow," which is only "elevated"). The media (and public) have acquiesced, in the face of this perceived terrorist threat, leading to both visible and invisible ramifications in our daily lives. The visible changes include increased security measures at airports, and thousands of new surveillance cameras at street corners and intersections. The invisible changes include many brought about by the Patriot Act, including the government's increased ability to search individuals' e-mail, and medical, financial, and other records.

Protection Motivation Theory

According to protection motivation theory, people act to protect themselves based on four beliefs: the severity of a perceived threat, the likelihood of its occurrence, the probability that performing the recommended behaviors can alleviate the threat, and the likely possibility that the individual can actually perform the recommended actions. Protection motivation is based on both the perceived threat and the coping appraisal (Rogers, 1975). The threat appraisal estimates the threat and how serious and likely the threat is. The coping appraisal gauges how effective the proposed actions would likely be, toward ameliorating the threat, and how likely the chances that the individual can perform the requisite actions, to alleviate the threat. Protection motivation theory essentially translates the sociological-level theories of deterrence and terror management into individual behavior, based on the amount of fear the government appeals can generate. Individuals will then modify their behavior, based on the perceived threat levels, and the effect on the individual. Turner (1989) indicates that providing information on the level of threat and actions required is most effective.

Rogers, R. W, A Protection Motivation Theory of Fear Appeals and Attitude Change, *Journal of Psychology*, Vol. 91, 1975, 93–114.

Turner, John F., Jr., Protection Motivation Theory: An Extension of Fear Appeals Theory in Communication, *Journal of Business Research*, Vol. 19(4), Elsevier, 1989, 267–76.

The Social Contract

The social order is established by what Jean Jacques Rousseau described as the *Social Contract* in 1762. In his book by the same name he describes how social orders work and how governments evolve (or devolve) over time. The theory of the social contract finds its roots with Plato, in his description of Socrates' discourse on the Laws of Athens. In the discourse, Socrates argues that a type of social contract exists between the adult citizens of Athens, and the city-state itself, by virtue of the fact that, as a child, the laws protected Socrates, and nurtured him to adulthood. At that point, every adult Athenian makes the choice, as Socrates did, to either stay in Athens, and modify the existing laws, if desired, or leave the city. If he stays, as Socrates does (until his death, by poison), then he agrees to the laws, and the contract.

The social contract establishes what is and isn't acceptable behavior within a society. It also places limits on governmental behavior, and when it is considered a violation of individual freedom. In times of perceived severe threats, people will often trade their freedom for even the illusion of safety. This process is pervasive in our society and permeates everything we do, particularly when it comes to individual movement.

Not that long ago people could freely walk up to the gate in an airport to greet arrivals or see friends and family off. In the 1970s several terrorist organizations took advantage of this freedom of movement and hijacked airplanes for political purposes. The response of government was to restrict access to airport gates by screening individuals, using metal detectors and x-ray machines. Yet anybody could still move freely through those security measures to greet or say goodbye to travelers.

When the first Boeing 747 landed at Sky Harbor Airport in Phoenix, Arizona, anybody from the city could go on a tour of the aircraft by walking through the airport and across the tarmac to where the plane was parked. Then came the Lockerbie Bombing, also known as the Pan Am Flight 103 disaster, on Wednesday, December 21, 1988. Originally scheduled to fly from London's Heathrow Airport to New York's JFK airport, the plane crashed in Lockerbie, Scotland, after an explosive device detonated inside the plane. The airplane, a Boeing 727, was destroyed, killing all 243 passengers, 16 crewmembers, and 11 innocent bystanders on the ground. At that point, it suddenly became necessary for all electronics to be removed from carry-on bags and x-rayed separately, sometimes even checked for explosive residue.

Shortly after this, security was heightened further. The decision was made that only those traveling could go through security and get to the airplane gates. The public was excluded from anything beyond the ticket-purchase areas of airports.

After September 11, 2001, it became necessary for much more intrusive inspections of people and their carry-on luggage. Then, in December 2001 Richard Reid, a British citizen and self-admitted member of Al-Qaeda, attempted to light a fuse that led to a bomb in his shoe while on American Airlines flight 63. Now everybody had to remove their shoes and send them through an x-ray machine to get on an airplane.

Then in December 2009 the Underwear Bomber, Umar Farouk Abdulmutallab, attempted to detonate plastic explosives he had hidden in his underwear while on Northwest Airlines flight 253. Now travelers must either go through extremely personal pat downs where TSA employees (or their subcontractors) touch you in areas a professional masseur wouldn't, or expose yourself to a whole-body scanner. It should be noted though that due to blow-back from frequent travelers and special interest groups there have been numerous changes to the mandatory screening process since 2009. Persons using

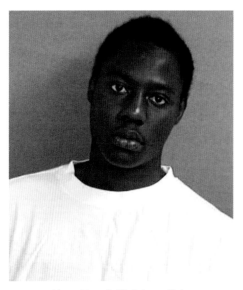

Umar Farouk Abdulmutallab;
US Marshals Office. 2009.

TSAPreCheck or Global Entry can bypass much of the airport security checks and simply walk through a metal detector. Persons who are elderly, or very young, need not remove their jackets or shoes. Other changes come and go with variations based on the airport involved.

The key to the examples used is that in every instance, the response of the government was *reactive*, never *proactive*. The security put in place, and resultant loss of mobility and freedom, *was in response to the anomaly, not the norm.*

At some point the populace of the society may make the determination that the intrusive nature of all these screenings is unacceptable, and has gone too far, and they may revolt against what the government is doing and take back their freedom of movement—accepting the risk that sometimes a terrorist will get through security and either be dealt with by the passengers or Air Marshals, or perhaps even be successful. The trade-off between personal freedom, commerce, and the bounds of the social contract will be redrawn.

The National Highway System

We look at another aspect of the transportation system with roads, which we tend to think of as simply asphalt and concrete. We normally tend to think of the security of this core transportation infrastructure as a function of state police and radar/laser speed-control devices. There is much more to roadways than this, and the security of this part of the fundamental transportation system of any country is of paramount concern.

The experience of September 11, 2001, showed that terrorists, armed with sufficient weapons and determined to harm large numbers of civilians through attacks on highly visible targets, would succeed no matter what defensive systems are in place. The targets were buildings—but in the terrorist's mind, any highly visible target is appropriate to advancement of their cause. Other than high-profile buildings, what is more visible than the iconic American system of roadways?

With more than 3,995,635 miles of roads, it is not possible for America (or any other nation) to provide constant security for this essential component of the transportation system. With major choke points created by natural obstacles such as mountains and rivers, the potential for severe economic disruption because of a targeted terrorist attack is significant. And the information required to effectively drop a bridge into a river is available online, in libraries, and at most gun shows.

For purposes of developing an example, consider the Eads Bridge over the Mississippi River in St. Louis, Missouri. Begun in 1867 and completed in 1874, this structure is now more than 135 years old. This three-span steel structure is supported by massive stone pillars sunk beneath the riverbed all the way to bedrock. It is not likely that the support structures could be easily damaged or destroyed. However, the spans themselves are steel, and recently began carrying foot traffic and light rail

Highway Interchange outside Houston, TX. Dhanix. Wikicommons.

(something the bridge was obviously not designed for). Dropping this bridge into the Mississippi River would stop all river (barge) traffic for an indefinite period. Yet such an effort would require nearly as much planning and manpower as flying a 767 into one of the World Trade Center towers. Not likely or easy.

Additionally, knowing how to look at and identify vulnerabilities is important, particularly when it comes to national assets such as the interstate highway system. Of course, the same analytical process is important on a local scale. If you live in a community that has only one or two main roadways by which disaster responders can access you, then those roads, whether or not they are highways, become critical to your community in the event of a disaster, whether man-made or natural.

Highways are frequently used to evacuate populations from areas where there are expected (hurricane) and unexpected (terrorist) disasters. How these roads are used to move large numbers of people is instructive in explaining the need for effective security in preparation for either a man-made or natural disaster. For instance, let's look at the evacuations of the Florida Keys and Houston, Texas, prior to Hurricane Rita in 2005.

Hurricane Rita

Hurricane Rita was the fourth-most intense Atlantic hurricane ever recorded, with sustained winds over 180 mph. It made landfall between Sabine Pass, Texas, and Johnson Bayou, Louisiana, on September 24, 2005, as a Category 3 Hurricane. It continued through southeast Texas, causing extensive damage to parts of the Louisiana and Texas coasts and Texas coastal towns.

Hurricane Rita hit America a few weeks after Hurricane Katrina devastated New Orleans. The country (and the federal government) was still reeling from the effects of Katrina, as well as the aftereffects of some of the decisions made by state, local, and

Hurricane Rita. NASA/GSFC.

federal officials. Officials at all levels were very much aware of the extreme criticism leveled at New Orleans (and state and federal) administrators following Katrina, and did not want to face any negative press relating to slow or inadequate recommendations to evacuate.

On September 18, 2005, when Rita was declared a tropical storm, phased evacuations began in the Florida Keys. All tourists and other temporary visitors to the area were told to evacuate the Lower Keys immediately and residents in mobile homes were told to prepare to evacuate. Two days later, on September 20, mandatory evacuations were in place for the 85,000 residents of the Keys. The only road into or out of the Keys is US 1, a 110-mile (mostly) two-lane highway going southwest from Miami (or northeast, from Key West). Both lanes on US 1 were directed northbound to speed up evacuations. City buses picked up those who did not have transportation out of the Keys. An estimated 2.3 million people in Miami-Dade County were warned about the possibility of a direct hit on Miami and told to prepare to evacuate. A State of Emergency was declared ahead of Rita later that day by President George W. Bush, which would allow federal assistance to aid the affected areas in the wake of the storm. Throughout Florida, a total of 340,000 people were placed under mandatory or voluntary evacuation orders.

The Texas evacuation was somewhat like Florida's. As part of the preparations for Rita, Texas Governor Rick Perry recalled all emergency personnel, including almost 1,200 Texas National Guard and 1,100 Texas State Guard members from Katrina recovery efforts in Louisiana, and several hundred Texas Game Wardens in anticipation of Hurricane Rita's arrival. In addition, the Federal Government responded by deploying 11 Disaster Medical Assistance Teams (DMATs), mobile field hospitals, to stage across eastern Texas. On September 22, Governor Perry and the Texas Department of Transportation implemented a contraflow lane reversal leaving Houston on Interstate 45 north toward Dallas, on Interstate 10 west toward San Antonio, and on US Highway 290 northwest to Austin.

Some critics of the forced (and suggested) mass evacuations in Texas argued that the effects were worse than the results of the Hurricane. Just three weeks after Hurricane Katrina devastated the northern Gulf Coast, the threat of yet another major hurricane prompted city administrators to order mass evacuations from coastal Texas and to suggest voluntary evacuation from cities as far north as Houston. An estimated 2.5 to 3.7 million people fled prior to Rita's landfall, making it the largest evacuation in United States history.[5]

Officials in Galveston County (which includes the city of Galveston), ordered mandatory evacuations, effective September 21 at 6 p.m., in a staggered sequence. Officials designated geographical zones in the area to facilitate an orderly evacuation. People were scheduled to leave at different times over a 24-hour period depending on the zone in which they were located. The scheduled times were set well in advance of the storm's possible landfall later in the week, but not soon enough to ensure that all residents could evacuate safely in advance of the storm. Nonetheless, many residents remained in the county because they were either unaware of the danger of the storm or believed that it was more important to protect their belongings, particularly in the wake of looting following Hurricane Katrina.

On Wednesday, September 21, Houston mayor Bill White urged residents to immediately evacuate the city, telling residents, "Don't wait; the time for waiting is over," reminding residents of the disaster in New Orleans. Fear related to the media coverage surrounding the deaths caused by the rising water and hurricane winds in New Orleans prompted millions of Houston residents to leave their homes in Houston (most of them at the same time) and attempt to exit the city via I-45 North, causing immediate bumper-to-bumper traffic congestion. After heavy traffic snarled roads leading out of town and gas shortages left numerous vehicles stranded, Mayor White backed off his earlier statement with, "If you're not in the evacuation zone, follow the news," advising people to use common sense, and not add to the congestion related to his

Hurricane Rita Evacuation at Magnolia. Orgullomoore. Wikicommons.

earlier warnings to leave the city immediately. However, by 3 p.m., the freeway system in and around Houston was at a standstill.

During the Rita evacuation, highways in surrounding towns were overwhelmed by the enormous and unprecedented number of people fleeing from the Houston area prior to the departure of locals. By the time Jefferson County began their mandatory evacuation, local roads were already full of Houstonians heading north. Traffic on designated evacuation routes was forced to go far slower than the speeds experienced with any previous hurricane.

By late Thursday (September 22) morning, the contraflow lanes had been ordered opened after officials determined that the state's highway system had become completely gridlocked. Apparently caught by surprise, and completely unprepared for a large-scale evacuation, the Texas DOT took eight to ten hours to coordinate and implement the contraflow plan, as police officers forced all inbound traffic to exit the highways. A minimum number of available state police were stationed at highway interchanges, to try to assist with traffic flow. Evacuees fought traffic Wednesday afternoon through midday Friday, moving only a fraction of the normal distance expected. Average travel times to Dallas were 24 to 36 hours, to Austin were 12 to 18 hours, and to San Antonio were 10 to 16 hours, depending on the point of departure in Houston. Many motorists ran out of gas or experienced breakdowns in temperatures that neared 100°F (38°C). Traffic volumes did not ease for nearly 48 hours as more than three million residents of the Houston area attempted to evacuate the area in advance of the storm. Hopefully city administrators learned something from this experience.

Evacuation Deaths

As an estimated 2.5 to 3.7 million people evacuated the Texas coastline and surrounding cities, a significant heat wave affected the region. The combination of severe gridlock and excessive heat led to between 90 and 118 deaths even before the storm arrived.[6] Reports from the *Houston Chronicle* indicated 107 evacuation-related fatalities. Texas Representative Garnet Coleman criticized the official downplay of the deaths in the evacuation and questioned whether the storm would be deadlier than the preparations.[7] Per local officials, the traffic reached a point where residents felt safer riding out the storm at home than being stuck in traffic when the hurricane hit. Many evacuees periodically turned off their air conditioning to reduce fuel consumption as well as drank less water to limit the number of "restroom stops." According to a post-storm study, which reported 90 evacuation-related deaths, nine people perished solely as a result of hyperthermia.[8]

In addition to the heat-related deaths, 23 nursing home evacuees were killed in a single vehicle after a bus caught fire on Interstate 45 near Wilmer.[9] The bus erupted into flames after the vehicle's rear axle overheated, due to insufficient lubrication, and ignited therapeutic oxygen tanks on board.[10] Many of the passengers were mobility impaired, making escape difficult or impossible. In June 2009, nearly four years after the fire, families of those who died in the accident won an $80 million settlement against the manufacturer of the bus and the company that provided it to the nursing home.[11]

Aviation Security

Security of aviation transportation has long been the purview of aviation corporations themselves and only recently has there been a move toward government management and execution of air transportation security. As Thomas Jensen notes, "Aviation security began as an industry-driven, reactive course of action and evolved into a proactive, government-driven process."[12] Whether the government version of aviation security is proactive is definitely debatable. Yet the concept, whether proactive or simply reactive, is certainly an ongoing evolutionary process.

In securing air transportation, what is our goal? Is it to guarantee that every flight is safe, and arrives without injury or loss of life? Should it include ensuring that air cargo is delivered on time, in the right location, and that only safe materials are transported? Is aviation security, as it is currently applied, a proactive, target-driven process or is it a reactive government bureaucracy that intrudes on citizen privacy, collecting data to be mined by intelligence operatives for future use against a rebellious population? Depending on what you read and where you access your information, the answer to all the above questions may be a resounding *yes!*

According to the Transportation Security Administration website:

> The Transportation Security Administration (TSA) was created in the wake of 9/11 to strengthen the security of the nation's transportation systems while ensuring the freedom of movement for people and commerce. Within a year, TSA assumed responsibility for security at the nation's airports and deployed a Federal workforce to meet congressional deadlines for screening all commercial airline passengers and baggage. In March 2003, TSA transferred from the Department of Transportation to the Department of Homeland Security.[13]

TSA advertises itself as a "risk-based, intelligence-driven counterterrorism agency dedicated to protecting our transportation systems." Part of that intelligence-driven system is the multiple layers of security that are employed by the TSA.

Layers of Aviation Security

From the TSA website:

> We use layers of security to ensure the security of the traveling public and the Nation's transportation system. Because of their visibility to the public, we are most associated with the airport checkpoints that our Transportation Security Officers operate. These checkpoints, however, constitute only one security layer of the many in place to protect aviation. Others include intelligence gathering and analysis, checking passenger manifests against watch lists, random canine team searches at airports, federal air marshals, federal flight deck officers and more security measures both visible and invisible to the public.

Each one of these layers alone is capable of stopping a terrorist attack. In combination their security value is multiplied, creating a much stronger, formidable system. A terrorist who has to overcome multiple security layers in order to carry out an attack is more likely to be pre-empted, deterred, or to fail during the attempt.[14]

One of the components of aviation security that few of us consider daily is the security of air cargo. Consider how that overnight package made it from your home to Sacramento, California. What steps did it go through? How many airplanes did it ride? Who handled it? What security processes were in place to ensure that it wasn't a printer cartridge packed with PETN (pentaerythritol tetranitrate, a powerful explosive) that was being shipped to a synagogue? When the Wright brothers flew at Kitty Hawk they could not imagine the future of aviation, or how their invention would be used on September 11, 2001. They had enough difficulty simply getting airborne with a single passenger. Today, people are still flying single passenger aircraft. However most of us use commercial air transport and fly packed inside an aluminum tube with a couple of hundred other travelers. The world has changed over the past 100 years and will continue to change in the future.

Maritime Shipping

The lifeline of the global economy is the maritime shipping industry. From bulk cargo containers to supertankers, from LNG (liquefied natural gas) floating bombs to containerized cargo freighters, the entire modern world functions primarily through ships and the cargos they carry. Securing ships, their cargo, and the terminals where those loads are assembled and delivered is the topic of this part of the chapter.

There is a great deal of sensationalism in the reports of potential threats to shipping and ports, much of it misguided, or presented by clearly biased "experts" with the goal of selling more copies of their books. What is the reality of the threat against shipping? Of interest is the actual process whereby shipping or ships have been attacked and for what purposes. The 1985 seizure of the *Achille Lauro* was clearly politically motivated.

The 2000 bombing of the *USS Cole* was both a demonstration against American military presence in the Middle East and concurrently a test of naval security protocol and defenses. There may have also been intent to measure the requirements for a floating bomb to effectively damage or sink a ship.

Damaging a ship has the potential of major consequences beyond the immediate sinking of the vessel. Think back to the Exxon Valdez, which ran aground in March 1989. The environmental damage was significant, and although it has been "cleaned up" to a certain extent, the tar balls are still there—under rocks and in coves. A *USS Cole*-type attack on a supertanker like the Valdez would produce a much more severe problem should it occur in a major port or waterway.

Sinking a ship is another potentially economically significant problem, particularly if that ship sinks in a main shipping channel. It would be particularly traumatic were

The Houston Ship Channel. US Army Corps of Engineers.

a waterway like the Houston Ship Channel to become blocked. One of the major concerns for the security forces at Pearl Harbor, Hawaii, was the consideration that one of the frequent commercial tour boats that entered the harbor daily would sink in the narrow and shallow waters off Nevada Point. That would result in the effective maritime closure of the naval base and prevent any warships, supply ships, or submarines from exiting while concurrently forcing any arriving vessels to sail to the West Coast. The logistics behind such a forced rerouting (and the economic impact) would be enormous. The sudden loss of the ability to project a naval presence to hot spots in Asia could be a national political and military disaster.

Regardless of what you may see on television or in the movies, most criminals are not technologically competent, or even of above average intelligence. The truth is somewhat less exciting than what is presented in the numerous CSI, NCIS, Law and Order, or terrorist programs that saturate today's "entertainment media." What is true is that no physical security system is capable of complete, standalone protection of a site; just as attempting to isolate a computer system from outside connectivity does not completely protect that system from viruses and access breaches. Every physical site and computer system is accessible to a truly competent, technologically savvy attacker. The constant challenge and trade-off is between increased security (at a substantially increased cost) and a "reasonable" amount of protection (at a lesser cost).

Global Supply Chain Security

The global supply chain is now dependent upon the ubiquitous "cargo container" that moves 95 percent of all goods. They are seen everywhere, on trucks, trains, at loading docks, and in farmer's fields. Security of intermodal transportation and its cargo is imperative in today's interconnected world.

The *Emma Maersk* is the largest container ship in the world. The vessel has fantastic

Emma Maersk, currently the world's largest container ship. September 2006. Nico-dk/Nils Jepsen. Wikicommons.

measurements, with a length of 397 meters, beam of 56 meters, and a draft of 30 meters. The deadweight of the ship is 156,907 metric tons, without any cargo. The capacity of containers that can be carried by *Emma Maersk* is 11,000 twenty-foot equivalents (TEUs) according to the company and more than 13,800 TEUs according to the International Maritime Organization.[15] This mode of international and internal transport of cargo has become so commonplace that we no longer find amazement in the process by which goods from Singapore get to San Angelo, Texas, in a matter of weeks.

The cargo container is more properly termed an intermodal container, as it can be moved by a wide variety of common carriers.

Pipelines and Power Grids

Some components of transportation infrastructure are not portable or don't move anything. Yet we see them every day and are entirely dependent upon the products they deliver. If you are reading this on an electronic device, like a Kindle or tablet of some sorts, you are using electricity, which was delivered through a grid. If you use natural gas to heat your water, or your home, or as a cooking fuel for your stove, then imagine the impact should the natural gas pipeline be broken or simply shut down. Securing these systems is a key to maintaining modern society.

Trans-Alaska Pipeline. Luca Galuzzi http://www.galuzzi.it Wikicommons.

Have you turned on a faucet and used hot water today? Unless you live on well water, completely off the grid, that simple act of using hot water implies that you have access to both a water supply, and the means to heat it.

Let's analyze that process. First, the water had to be collected and stored. Then it had to be transported from the reservoir to a treatment plant where it was clarified, treated for contamination, and moved to another storage location like a water tank or tower. After that, the system pressure moved it through pipes to your street and into your house, where it entered a hot water tank or heater. The hot water tank or heater needed some sort of power supply to generate the energy necessary to raise the temperature of the water to a level you would find useful.

That power most likely came from either the electrical grid or natural gas. Neither power source is local to your home, but were transported from their origins to your house.

If your system is electric, a generating station produced the electricity and fed the "juice" into high-voltage power lines that spread out across the country, interconnecting with the current produced by other power plants, and fed into what is commonly called the "grid."

The electric grid is broken into regions by the North American Electric Reliability Corporation (NERC). The high voltages necessary to move usable quantities of electricity through the wires we see strung across fields is not usable in your home. Instead, it is stepped down from very high voltages to lower voltages, and finally through the transformer that is either on the pole or set in the ground near your house. At this point the electricity passes through a circuit-breaker box (fuse box if you live in an old home) and is distributed throughout your house at a usable voltage.

If your water heater operates on natural gas, then the process is similar—except instead of wires and transformers the natural gas moves through pipes and compressor stations. Of course, the natural gas comes from wells, while electricity comes from generators.

The US natural gas pipeline network is a highly integrated transmission and distribution grid that can transport natural gas to and from nearly any location in the lower forty-eight states. The natural gas pipeline grid comprises:

- More than 210 natural gas pipeline systems.
- 305,000 miles of interstate and intrastate transmission pipelines.
- More than 1,400 compressor stations that maintain pressure on the natural gas pipeline network and assure continuous forward movement of supplies.
- More than 11,000 delivery points, 5,000 receipt points, and 1,400 interconnection points that provide for the transfer of natural gas throughout the United States.
- 24 hubs or market centers that provide additional interconnections.
- 400 underground natural gas storage facilities.
- 49 locations where natural gas can be imported/exported via pipelines.
- 8 LNG (liquefied natural gas) import facilities and 100 LNG peaking facilities.

The Transmission Grid and Compressor Stations

The natural gas mainline (transmission line) is a wide-diameter, oftentimes long-distance, portion of a natural gas pipeline system, excluding laterals, located between the gathering system (production area), natural gas processing plant, other receipt points, and the principal customer service area(s). The lateral, usually of smaller diameter, branches off the mainline natural gas pipeline to connect with or serve a specific customer or group of customers.

A natural gas mainline system will tend to be designed as either a grid or a trunkline system. The latter is usually a long-distance, wide-diameter pipeline system that generally links a major supply source with a market area or with a large pipeline/local distribution company (LDC) serving a market area. A trunkline tends to have fewer receipt points (usually at the beginning of its route), fewer delivery points,

An electric power transmission line. Wikicommons.

interconnections with other pipelines, and associated lateral lines.

A grid type transmission system is usually characterized by many laterals, or branches, from the mainline, which tend to form a network of integrated receipt, delivery, and pipeline interconnections that operate in, and serve, major market areas. In form, they are similar to a local distribution company (LDC) network configuration, but on a much larger scale.

Between the producing area, or supply source, and the market area, several compressor stations are located along the transmission system. These stations contain one or more compressor units whose purpose is to receive the transmission flow (which has decreased in pressure since the previous compressor station) at an intake point, increase the pressure and rate of flow, and thus, maintain the movement of natural gas along the pipeline.

Compressor units that are used on a natural gas mainline transmission system are usually rated at 1,000 horsepower or more and are of the centrifugal (turbine) or reciprocating (piston) type. The larger compressor stations may have as many as 10 to 16 units with an overall horsepower rating of from 50,000 to 80,000 HP and a throughput capacity exceeding three billion cubic feet of natural gas per day. Most compressor units operate on natural gas (extracted from the pipeline flow); but in recent years, and mainly for environmental reasons, the use of electricity-driven compressor units has been growing.

Many of the larger mainline transmission routes are what is generally referred to as "looped." Looping is when one pipeline is laid parallel to another and is often used as a way to increase capacity along a right-of-way beyond what is possible on one line, or an expansion of an existing pipeline(s). These lines are connected to move a larger flow along a single segment of the pipeline system. Some very large pipeline systems have 5 or 6 large diameter pipes laid along the same right-of-way. Looped pipes may extend the distance between compressor stations, where they can transfer part of their flow, or the looping may be limited to only a portion of the line between stations. In the latter case, the looping often serves as essentially a storage device, where natural gas can be line-packed to increase deliveries to local customers during certain peak periods.

Addressing the potential for pipeline rupture, safety cutoff meters are installed along a mainline transmission system route. Devices located at strategic points are designed to detect a pressure drop that would result from a downstream or upstream pipeline rupture and automatically stop the flow of natural gas beyond its location. Monitoring the pipeline overall are apparatuses known as SCADA (Systems Control and Data Acquisition) systems. SCADA systems provide monitoring staff the ability to direct and control pipeline flows, maintaining pipeline integrity and pressures as natural gas is received and delivered along numerous points on the system, including flows into and out of storage facilities.

The Department of Energy (DOE) has the primary responsibility for ensuring the safety of the national power distribution system in the United States. They deal with security through Emergency Preparedness, Emergency Response, Security of Control Systems, and the national plan to establish a "smart grid" that is redundant and reliable.

One of the most interesting considerations about the DOE is that their interpretation of "security" leans more to the reliability of continued supply of electricity and natural gas. They look at "security" of physical installations as primarily the function (and responsibility) of the owner/operator of the facility (except for nuclear plants). This poses a gap in what is and isn't secured from the standpoint of the potential business loss of income vs. the business value of the infrastructure.

Railroads

Trains haul freight worldwide. Shippers that don't want to pay the fee for their cargo to transit the Suez Canal simply offload their cargo at one end of the canal and pick it up at the other—after it has been moved the length of the canal by rail. Yet, unless you are associated with the business of rail transportation, you probably see the passing of a train as some piece of American nostalgia, or a closed railroad crossing as simply another delay on your way to work. Without a functioning rail system, the US economy would simply collapse overnight. This part of the chapter looks at the security of this strategic infrastructure.

Mexican train engines on the US side of the Rio Grande in Eagle Pass, Texas. These engines are about to enter the screening building prior to picking up rail cars headed to Mexico. James Phelps, 2013.

Unless you ride AMTRAK or a commuter rail line, the likelihood you see much more of the rail industry than a passing train is slim (except for those employed by the rail industry).

Trains move nearly 99 percent of all coal delivered to power plants each year. If rail traffic were disrupted, delivery of coal to power plants would essentially stop, shutting down America's primary source of electricity.

Photograph of Army Boxcar at the Ft. Eustis Army Transportation Museum. William Grimes. Wikicommons.

Another 7 percent of freight moved by rail in 2009 was chemicals. What kind, you may ask? Every kind—from chlorine to anhydrous ammonia to toluene. The amount of toxic chemicals moved through our major cities by rail is absolutely staggering—yet necessary for our economy to survive.

As of this writing, terrorists have yet to target a freight train, but they have targeted passenger trains. On March 11, 2004, a series of coordinated bombings killed 191 and wounded 1,800 commuter rail passengers in Madrid, Spain. On July 7, 2005, four terrorists killed themselves and 52 others, injuring another 700, on the London commuter rail system (and one double-decker bus).

Modern tank cars such as TILX 290344 are designed to carry many liquid or gaseous commodities. Harvey Henkelmann. Wikicommons.

There have been terror plots against the NY–NJ subway system—all disrupted at the date this chapter was written.

What would be the outcome if terrorists or criminal organizations targeted freight rail traffic? The impact would be significantly larger than either attack in Madrid or London. The casualties resulting from a single ruptured chlorine tanker car as a train passed through Colorado Springs, Denver, Tucson, Los Angles, Houston, Chicago, Atlanta, or even a smaller town like Abilene, or Laredo, would easily exceed all the deaths attributed to the terrorist attacks of 9/11.

The same can be said about rail cars carrying LP gas, isobutane, or ammonia hydroxide. Of course, it doesn't take a terrorist attack to cause considerable damage and destruction. Trains derail all the time—sometimes catastrophically.

Situational Awareness

A new type of visual monitoring system has been installed in every major and many smaller cities across the country of Turkey. These observation and control centers utilize a combination of fixed-position cameras and variable-view cameras with day/night capability accompanied by a computer system that constantly monitors and records the input from each camera. The variable-view cameras can be remotely trained to view any area within a 360-degree field. The computer system automatically blocks out camera views that may show interiors of homes or apartments, restricting the viewing capability to publicly accessible areas. Another capability of the computer system, and the image capture system, is the ability to read and immediately identify license plates.

As with most digital video monitoring systems, the ability of the Turkish system to record and playback events is imperative to post-action evaluation, analysis, development of lessons learned, and procedural improvements and feedback to the responsible agencies. This also provides the ability to utilize these recordings for training or demonstration purposes. This is what we would call the Observe-Orient-Decide-Act (OODA) decision-execution cycle. Keep in mind that the loop is iterative. Steps may have to be repeated several times before moving to the following step. After an action is taken, the results should always be observed and analyzed. In the field of Emergency Management (as it applies to Transportation Security) the same type of process applies, but is better referred to as the Prepare/Prevent-Detect-Respond-Recover cycle.

The history of terrorism within Turkey has resulted in the country becoming acutely aware that maintaining constant situational awareness is essential to rapidly responding to incidents and preventing terrorist attacks on their population and infrastructure. Situational awareness is not paranoia! It is knowledge of what is around you, or within the area in which an incident has occurred. Sending firefighters to a warehouse fire—and not knowing that the owner has stored propane cylinders in the building (or 270 tons of ammonium nitrate fertilizer as happened in West, Texas, in 2013)—is a recipe for a deadly disaster. Not knowing where the emergency exits are in an unfamiliar building puts you at a grave disadvantage when the fire alarms are suddenly activated and smoke fills the room and hallways. On a larger scale, you should be aware of alternative routes of travel, rerouting options to move people and cargo around a train derailment or overturned LNG transporter.

Such situations can become logistics and evacuation nightmares relatively quickly. Bridges and culverts on what appears to be the most logical roads may not have the load-carrying capacity for the types of traffic you must reroute. Or, perhaps the alternative route sends trucks carrying hazardous cargo past an elementary school.

Remember that the communication and control systems available to those such as Law Enforcement, First Responders, and Emergency Managers may not be the only assets available to you in case of an actual emergency. Virtually every company that utilizes transportation systems has its own internal communications and dispatch systems. Some of these are much more utilitarian than those available to Emergency Managers because of their ability to contact assets worldwide, nationwide, or in extremely remote locations such as oil and natural gas fields.

The key to any effective and efficient collection of intelligence (usable, timely, and relevant information) is the ability to collate, interpret, and act on that information in an effective and timely manner. Doing so efficiently and responding in a timely manner to rapidly evolving situations is the result of two key items: being able to effectively interface with the information collection and communication systems available to you, and maintaining a level of situational awareness relevant to the surrounding environment. Not getting into a "tunnel vision" mentality is difficult as adrenaline courses through your body—sometimes it is essential to have a second set of dispassionate eyes from a knowledgeable observer who is tasked only with watching the big picture. Input and recommendations from such a person will be invaluable during a disaster. Keep this in mind as you move forward in your studies and your profession.

Twenty years ago, when bar codes were first coming into vogue, this technology was unheard of. Today, it is everywhere. We still use bar codes to identify all sorts of items from books to bananas. Open the driver's door on a new vehicle and you'll find a bar code. Pop the hood on your new truck and you'll find a bar code in addition to the stamped engine block number. The back of your computer probably has some sort of ID tag or manufacturer's bar code, along with an identification number placed there by the organization that bought it (such as a university). They are everywhere, right along with RFID tags.

Automated Identification Technologies can be used to improve and enhance transportation security. Recently, IBM came out with a couple of commercials that highlighted the capabilities of RFID technology. These are not "futuristic" proposals, but already here and in use in a variety of locations. As we move into the future, these technologies will ultimately be replaced, most likely with nanotechnology.

Illegal Immigration and Transportation Security

It is estimated that approximately 500,000 illegal immigrants cross US borders each year in search of the American dream: finding a job, building a home, saving money, and creating a future for their family. This is a real problem today, as there are approximately 12 million illegal aliens in the United States. What the actual annual numbers are, or how many illegal aliens are currently in the country, is unknown. These numbers are estimates, based on guesses, based on services utilization, and/or based on media-generated fears and exaggerations.

We don't know how many people cross into the United States illegally every year or how many are here. We do see the impact those who make it here have on hospital services, public schools, and our criminal justice system. It is the economic impact that is the primary problem of illegal immigration. A secondary problem, and one that could rise to become the primary problem at any moment, is the threat posed by those wishing to do our country harm getting into the country through what are traditionally migrant worker transportation routes.

In the world of transportation security there are two components of human movement across a nation's borders to control. The first is how to effectively move large numbers of legal visitors, international ambassadors, and business and leisure travelers while ensuring that the process of verifying identity and legal authority to cross the border is efficient and effective. The second is much more problematic. How does a country prevent the illegal crossing of international borders, the identification of the individuals they capture, the deportation/repatriation of those captured who are in a country illegally, and the identification and protection of those who are legally asking for asylum?

Passports are required for international travel, but passports are not required for citizens who do not travel outside the country. Are the same International Civil Aviation Organization (ICAO) standards for passports applicable to state-issued IDs? Should they be? This is something for citizens and their legislators to decide. Or should the national government mandate minimum standards of security for state-issued IDs? In a country without guarded interstate borders, where anybody from one state can travel through or to another state, does it make sense that individual states still maintain sovereignty over the means of identification?

As we have reviewed the various components of transportation security, it has probably dawned on you that there is no way the entire transportation infrastructure can be protected against potential man–made and natural disasters. Risk is inherent in the open operation of such massive and interconnected systems. As such, there is always the one primary issue that faces first responders, law enforcement, politicians, businesses, and the citizenry: recovery following a disaster.

The Loma Prieta Earthquake

The 1989 Loma Prieta earthquake, which occurred in the San Francisco Bay Area on October 17, 1989, is one example of a local disaster with national implications for disaster preparedness for local, state, and federal agencies, as well as the public.

The Loma Prieta earthquake, also known as the World Series Earthquake, was a major earthquake that struck the San Francisco Bay Area of California on October 17, 1989, at 5:04 p.m. local time. Caused by a slip along the San Andreas Fault, the quake lasted 10 to 15 seconds and measured 6.9 both on the moment magnitude scale (surface-wave magnitude 7.1) and on the open-ended Richter Scale. The quake killed 63 people throughout northern California.[16]

The earthquake occurred during the pre-game warm-up broadcast for the third game of the 1989 World Series, featuring both Bay Area teams, the Oakland Athletics and the San Francisco Giants. The game-related coverage made this the first major earthquake in the United States to have its initial shockwave broadcast live on television.

The epicenter of the quake was in the Forest of Nisene Marks State Park in Santa Cruz County, an unpopulated area in the Santa Cruz Mountains (geographical coordinates 37.040° N 121.877° W), approximately 2 to 3 miles (3 to 5 km) north of unincorporated Aptos and approximately 10 miles (16 km) northeast of Santa Cruz.[17] The quake was named for the nearby Loma Prieta Peak, which lies 5 miles (8 km) to the northeast in Santa Clara County.

The San Francisco-Oakland Bay Bridge suffered relatively minor damage, as a 76-by-50-foot (23 m × 15 m) section of the upper deck on the eastern side crashed onto the deck below. The quake caused the Oakland side of the bridge to shift 7 inches (18 cm) to the east, and caused the bolts of one section to shear off, sending the 230-ton section of roadbed crashing down like a trapdoor.[18] When that part of the bridge collapsed one car

San Francisco-Oakland Bay Bridge Collapse. Wikicommons. 1989.

Collapsed Cypress Creek Viaduct. USGS: PD-USGOV-INTERIOR-USGS; PD-USGOV-USGS.

drove into the hole, resulting in the death of the driver. Traffic on both decks came to a halt, blocked by the fallen section of roadbed. Police began unsnarling the traffic jam, telling drivers to turn their cars around and drive back the way they had come. Eastbound drivers stuck on the lower deck between the collapse and Yerba Buena Island were routed up to the upper deck and westward back to San Francisco. A miscommunication made by emergency workers at Yerba Buena Island routed some of the drivers the wrong way; they were directed to the upper deck where they drove eastward toward the collapse site. One of these drivers did not see the open gap in time; the car plunged over the edge and smashed onto the collapsed roadbed. The driver died and the passenger was seriously injured. Caltrans removed and replaced the collapsed section, and re-opened the bridge on November 18.

The worst disaster of the earthquake was the collapse of the two-level Cypress Street Viaduct of Interstate 880 in West Oakland. The failure of a 1.25-mile (2.0 km) section of the viaduct, also known as the "Cypress Structure" and the "Cypress Freeway," killed 42 and injured many more.[19]

Built in the late 1950s, the Cypress Street Viaduct, a stretch of Interstate 880, was a double-deck freeway section made of nonductile reinforced concrete that was constructed above and astride Cypress Street in Oakland. Roughly half of the land the Cypress Viaduct was built on was filled marshland, and half was somewhat more stable alluvium. Because of improper rebar placement in the concrete, the columns broke during the earthquake, sending the structure down.

During the earthquake, the support columns on the freeway buckled and sent the upper deck crashing to the lower deck. Forty-one people were instantly crushed to death in their cars. Cars on the upper deck were tossed around violently, some of them flipped sideways and some of them were left dangling at the edge of the highway. Nearby residents and factory workers came to the rescue, climbing onto the wreckage with ladders and forklifts and pulling trapped people out of their mangled cars from under a four-foot gap in some sections. Some 60 members of Oakland's Public Works Agency left the nearby city yard and joined rescue efforts. Employees from Pacific Pipe (a now-closed factory adjoining the freeway) drove heavy lift equipment to the scene and started using it to raise sections of fallen freeway enough to allow further rescue. One person was pulled from the wreckage, alive, but died 24 hours later.

Effects on Transportation

Immediately following the earthquake, San Francisco Bay Area airports closed to conduct visual inspection and damage assessment procedures. San Jose International Airport, Oakland International Airport, and San Francisco International Airport all opened the next morning. Massive cracks in Oakland's runway and taxiway reduced the usable length to two-thirds normal, and damage to the dike required quick re-mediation to avoid flooding the runway with water from the bay. Oakland Airport repair costs were assessed at $30 million.[20]

The San Francisco Municipal Railway lost all power to electric transit systems when the quake hit, but otherwise suffered little damage and no injuries to operators or riders. Cable cars and electric trains and buses were stalled in place—half of the Municipal Railway's transport capability was lost for 12 hours. The railway relied on diesel buses to continue abbreviated service to the public until electric power was restored later that night, and electric units could be inspected and readied for service on the morning of October 18. After 78 hours, 96 percent of the railway services were back in operation, including the cable cars. The earthquake changed the Bay Area's automobile transportation landscape. Not only did the quake force seismic retrofitting of all San Francisco Bay Area bridges, it caused enough damage that some parts of the region's freeway system had to be demolished. Damage to the region's transportation system was estimated at $1.8 billion.[21]

Flying Cars

The future is here—finally! For a century, science fiction writers have been telling us about a future where we will be able to fly our cars to work and simply avoid all the congestion and dangers of the road. Since the 1980s the Sky Car has been available and test flown, but the FAA would never allow it to operate without being tethered to a crane. PAL-V, a Dutch flying car developer, announced on February 14, 2017, that the Liberty, its three-wheel gyrocopter, was for sale, with expected deliveries by

The EHANG 184 is essentially a passenger UAV. Known as an Autonomous Aerial Vehicle (AAV) made of carbon fiber, epoxy, and aircraft aluminum alloy; electric powered; it is eco-friendly, with a flight limit of 3,500m, speed of 60 km/hr and a 25-minute cruising duration for medium-short distance transportation.

December 2018. The gyrocopter developed by PAL-V uses a Rotax engine-based drivetrain, and can supposedly reach speeds of 100 mph on the ground and a maximum altitude of 11,480 feet.[22]

Conclusion

We have examined the various aspects of transportation security, and the ramifications for national and regional security. The various modes of transportation have been discussed, as have the historical improvements in each. The events in California on and after October 17, 1989, are a good example of the severity of a regional transportation disaster, and how the consequences of a local disaster translate to both the region and the nation. The importance of treating the modes of transportation security as a total system has been emphasized. If we do not consider each part of the system as a vulnerable part of the whole, we are ignoring the risk of the collapse of the entire system.

The United States, like all countries, depends on international traffic across its borders to sustain its economy. Any event that disrupts that smooth movement of goods and services impacts the overall functioning of the entire nation. It became clear after 9/11, when the border crossings were closed, that interruption of traffic from Canada would shut down US industry. A similar interruption of traffic from Mexico will result in quantities of produce rotting in the trucks and trains that transport our food supply. Even a strike by union dockworkers will prevent the loading and unloading of cargo and container ships, delaying commerce worldwide! Clearly, maintaining open borders for the transportation of goods and commodities, as well as the movement of people, is essential to a country's lifeblood in this globalized world. However, it must be remembered, that those very transportation systems we depend upon to move food, energy, commodities, and people can also move terrorists, drugs, weapons of mass destruction, and illegal migrants. There is a fine line between maintaining the security of the transportation system and shutting down an economy out of efforts to secure a border.

Questions for Further Consideration

1. In securing air transportation, what is our goal? Is it to guarantee that every flight is safe, and arrives without injury or loss of life? To ensure that air cargo is delivered on time, in the right location, and that only safe materials are transported?
2. Is aviation security, as it is currently applied, a proactive, target-driven process or is it a reactive government bureaucracy that intrudes on citizen privacy, collecting data to be mined by intelligence operatives for future use against a rebellious population?
3. What is the reality of the threat against shipping?
4. What would be the outcome if terrorists or criminal organizations targeted freight rail traffic?
5. Passports are required for international travel, but passports are not required for citizens who do not travel outside the country. Are the same International Civil Aviation Organization (ICAO) standards for passports applicable to state-issued IDs? Should they be?
6. Reflecting on the impact the Loma Prieta earthquake had on local and regional transportation systems, should a similar event occur in your community, how would the transportation systems fair?

Chapter 9 Endnotes

1. Bragdon, Clifford. Transportation Security (New York: Elsevier, 2008).
2. Senge, Peter. *The Fifth Discipline: The Art and Practice of the Learning Organization* (New York: Knopf Doubleday, 2006).
3. Nemfakos, Charles, and S. James, Transportation Security Through Logistics Transformation, In Bragdon, C. (2008) *Transportation Security,* 20.
4. Bragdon, 2008, p. 74.
5. Knabb, Richard D., Daniel P. Brown, and Jamie R. Rhome, "Hurricane Rita Tropical Cyclone Report," National Hurricane Center, March 17, 2006. http://www.nhc.noaa.gov/data/tcr/AL182005_Rita.pdf. Retrieved January 15, 2009.
6. Zachria, Anthony and Bela Patel, "Deaths Related to Hurricane Rita and Mass Evacuation," *University of Texas Health Science Center–Houston,* American College of Chest Physicians, October 24, 2006. http://journal.publications.chestnet.org/article.aspx?articleid=1214984. Retrieved February 25, 2012.
7. Horswell, Cindy and Edward Hegstrom, "Exodus weighs heavily in death toll: 107," *Houston Chronicle,* September 29, 2005. http://www.chron.com/news/hurricanes/article/Exodus-weighs-heavily-in-death-toll-107-1502590.php. Retrieved February 25, 2012.

8. Zachria and Patel (2006).

9. Ibid.

10. Belli, Anne and Lisa Falkenberg, "24 nursing home evacuees die in bus fire." *Houston Chronicle,* September 24, 2005. http://www.chron.com/news/hurricanes/article/24-nursing-home-evacuees-die-in-bus-fire-1946742.php. Retrieved February 25, 2012.

11. Langford, Terri, "Settlement over Hurricane Rita bus fire brings closure," *Houston Chronicle,* June 4, 2009. http://www.chron.com/news/houston-texas/article/Settlement-over-Hurricane-Rita-bus-fire-brings-1736019.php. Retrieved February 25, 2012.

12. Jensen, T. (2008). Aviation Security, in Bragdon, C, *Transportation Security*, p. 125.

13. TSA website. http://www.tsa.gov/

14. Ibid.

15. A.P. Moller-Maersk Group, "Emma Maersk: The Largest Container Ship." www.emma-maersk.com.

16. Eberhart-Phillips J. E., T. M. Saunders, A. L. Robinson, D. L. Hatch, R.G. Parrish, "Profile of mortality from the 1989 Loma Prieta earthquake using coroner and medical examiner reports," *Disasters* 18 (2), June 1994, 160–70.

17. USGS, *San Andreas Fault*, chapter 1, 5. "Comparison of the Bay Area Earthquakes: 1906 and 1989." Retrieved August 31, 2009.

18. "The California Quake: The Bay Bridge; Damage to Link Across Bay Is More Serious Than Thought," *The New York Times,* October 20, 1989. Retrieved September 5, 2009.

19. SFGate.com. *On the Cypress Freeway, Strangers Joined Together for a Snap in Time,* Kevin Fagan, Chronicle Staff Writer, October 12, 1999. Retrieved August 31, 2009.

20. McDonnell, Janet A, Office of History, US Army Corps of Engineers, *Response to the Loma Prieta Earthquake,* 1993. Retrieved September 5, 2009.

21. USGS, Historic Earthquakes, *Santa Cruz Mountains* (Loma Prieta), California. Retrieved September 6, 2009.

22. Carriere, Dave. "PAL-V Flying Cars Now for Sale." Flying. February 14, 2017. Available at: http://www.flyingmag.com/pal-v-flying-cars-now-for-sale#page-2

Part Three

US Border Security Today

"One of the most important missions of DHS is its law enforcement mission. This is a law enforcement agency. For too long, your officers and agents haven't been around to properly do their jobs.... But that's all about to change.... From here on out, I'm asking all of you to enforce the laws of the United States of America. They will be enforced and enforced strongly.... We will work within the existing system and framework. We are going to restore the rule of law in the United States.... We're in the middle of a crisis on our southern border. The unprecedented surge of illegal migrants from Central America is harming both Mexico and the United States. And I believe the steps we will take, starting right now, will improve the safety in both of our countries.... A nation without borders is not a nation. Beginning today, the United States of America gets back control of its borders, gets back its borders.... The Secretary of Homeland Security, working with myself and my staff, will begin immediate construction of a border wall.... This will help Mexico by deterring illegal immigration from Central America and by disrupting violent cartel networks. As I have said repeatedly to the country, we are going to get the bad ones out.... The day is over when they can stay in our country and wreak havoc.... [Our order] ends the policy of catch and release on the border. Requires other countries to take back their criminals.... Cracks down on sanctuary cities. Empowers ICE officers to target and remove those who pose a threat to public safety. Calls for the hiring of another 5,000 Border Patrol officers. Calls for the tripling of the number of ICE officers.... We want safe communities. We demand safe communities for everyone. We want respect.... We want dignity and equality for everyone."

—President Trump at the Department of Homeland Security,
January 25, 2017.

POTUS at DHS, 25 January 2017

Chapter 10

The United States–Mexico Border

Key Words and Concepts

Border Crossing Card
DREAM Act
Gadsden Purchase
"Green Card"
Narcotrafficantes

¿Plata o Plomo?
Treaty of Guadalupe Hidalgo
Road Checks
Ports of Entry

Introduction

The United States–Mexico border is a combination of barriers, boundaries, water, and vast expanses of emptiness. More than half the border is denoted by the centerline of the Rio Grande (Rio Bravo) River. The rest is essentially a long westward reaching tract of desert, from just north of El Paso, Texas, to Imperial Beach, California. At 1,969 miles (3,169 km), it is the most frequently crossed border in the world with

Sometimes the United States Border Patrol utilizes horses in difficult terrain to ensure the safety of the nation's border. James Tourtellote. CBP.gov

The San Diego Tunnel Task Force arrested six individuals and seized more than
32 tons of marijuana after discovering one of the most sophisticated
smuggling tunnels along the United States–Mexico border in recent years.
US Immigration and Customs Enforcement. April 5, 2012.

approximately 350 million people legally transiting the border annually. It is also one
of the most politically debated issues in border security.

The border between the United States and Mexico has a history extending from
the founding of the first English colonies in North America, through the expansion
of the new United States westward, to the acquisition of the Louisiana Territory, to
the war over Texan independence, and the subsequent Mexican-American War. The
history doesn't end with the expansion of the United States from Atlantic to Pacific,
but continues with multiple conflicts over water and land, and raids into the United
States by Pancho Villa during the Mexican Revolution. Telling the story of the border
between the United States and Mexico would fill a book of its own, and there are
several books written about these lands, peoples, and conflicts. It is not the intent of
this book or this chapter to reiterate that history. Instead, we look at the current
border, how it came about, and the present-day issues dealing with concerns over
the security (or perhaps the insecurity) of the borderland region.

In the pre-9/11 era, before the establishment of the Department of Homeland
Security and the incorporation of the US Customs Agency, Immigration and Naturalization Service, and the US Border Patrol into DHS, the primary concerns over
the southern border of the United States were illegal narcotics and illegal immigration.
Today, although border security is supposed to be about the prevention of terrorists
and weapons of mass destruction entering the United States, the focus of border
security in Texas and the Southwest is still on illegal immigration and illegal narcotics,
except we now include the prevention of firearms, ammunition, and undeclared cash
from leaving the United States and entering Mexico. US border security agents no

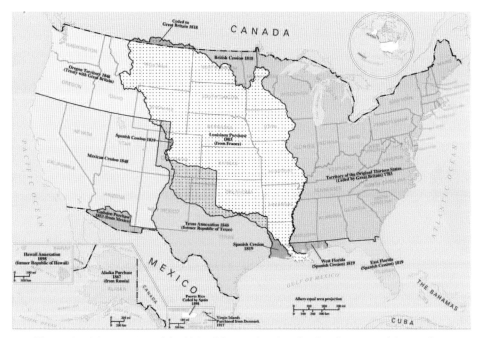

The territorial expansion of the United States showing the development of the modern border between Mexico and the United States. USGS. National Map.

Mexican-American War (without Scott's campaign). Wikipedia Commons.

longer focus solely on keeping the United States safe, but also must conduct operations and work to keep Mexico safe by cutting off the supply of firearms and ammunition that fuel the Mexican drug cartel wars and preventing the illegal proceeds of narcotics sales from funding those wars.

This, then, is the conundrum facing those who secure the southern US border: Commerce and people must continuously move across the border for the benefit of both countries. Illegal commodities and nonauthorized people must be prevented from crossing the border in either direction. This must be accomplished in the most politically charged environment conceivable where competing interests drive changing policies from administration to administration, with long-lasting effects on the processes of border security and the people who implement them.

The Southwest Border Today

Mexico's northern border (the United States southwest border) that we know today came about as the result of two wars and several political maneuvers. When the Texans revolted in 1835 and formally declared their independence from Mexico on March 2, 1836, General Antonio Lopez de Santa Anna marched north from Mexico City and attempted to put down the revolution in battles we remember today as the Alamo and Goliad. Santa Anna was defeated at the battle of San Jacinto on April 21, 1836, and subsequently signed the Treaties of Velasco recognizing the Republic of Texas.[1] Upon his return to Mexico, General Santa Anna was deposed and the Mexican government rejected the independence of Texas. This would lead to several other battles that would not resolve the issue until the United States became involved.

The Mexican-American War

With the Republic of Texas annexation into the United States on December 29, 1845, Mexico declared war on the United States and, of course, the United States responded. Then came the dispute over where the southern border of Texas was, followed by the invasion of Mexico by the United States during the Mexican-American War, from spring 1846 to fall 1847. Guerilla warfare continued until the spring of 1848 when the Treaty of Guadalupe-Hidalgo was signed, bringing an end to the conflict.[2]

The Treaty of Guadalupe Hidalgo does not list the territories to be ceded by Mexico to the United States. Nor did the Treaty deal with the causes of the conflict, the secession of the Republic of Texas, or the annexation of Texas into the United States. Fundamentally, the Treaty simply brings the conflict to an end and describes a new northern border for Mexico as the demarcation between the two countries.[3]

The Treaty of Guadalupe Hidalgo, February 2, 1848

Article V

The boundary line between the two Republics shall commence in the Gulf of Mexico, three leagues from land, opposite the mouth of the Rio Grande, otherwise called Rio Bravo del Norte, or Opposite the mouth of its deepest branch, if it should have more than one branch emptying directly into the sea; from thence up the middle of that river, following the deepest channel, where it has more than one, to the point where it strikes the southern boundary of New Mexico; thence, westwardly, along the whole southern boundary of New Mexico (which runs north of the town called Paso) to its western termination; thence, northward, along the western line of New Mexico, until it intersects the first branch of the river Gila; (or if it should not intersect any branch of that river, then to the point on the said line nearest to such branch, and thence in a direct line to the same); thence down the middle of the said branch and of the said river, until it empties into the Rio Colorado; thence across the Rio Colorado, following the division line between Upper and Lower California, to the Pacific Ocean.

The southern and western limits of New Mexico, mentioned in the article, are those laid down in the map entitled "Map of the United Mexican States, as organized and defined by various acts of the Congress of said republic, and constructed according to the best authorities. Revised edition. Published at New York, in 1847, by J. Disturnell," of which map a copy is added to this treaty, bearing the signatures and seals of the undersigned Plenipotentiaries. And, in order to preclude all difficulty in tracing upon the ground the limit separating Upper from Lower California, it is agreed that the said limit shall consist of a straight line drawn from the middle of the Rio Gila, where it unites with the Colorado, to a point on the coast of the Pacific Ocean, distant one marine league due south of the southernmost point of the port of San Diego, according to the plan of said port made in the year 1782 by Don Juan Pantoja, second sailing-master of the Spanish fleet, and published at Madrid in the year 1802, in the atlas to the voyage of the schooners Sutil and Mexicana; of which plan a copy is hereunto added, signed and sealed by the respective Plenipotentiaries.

In order to designate the boundary line with due precision, upon authoritative maps, and to establish upon the ground land-marks which shall show the limits of both republics, as described in the present article, the two Governments shall each appoint a commissioner and a surveyor, who, before the expiration of one year from the date of the exchange of ratifications of this treaty, shall meet at the port of San Diego, and proceed to run and mark the said boundary in its whole course to the mouth of the Rio Bravo del Norte. They shall keep journals and make out plans of their operations; and the result agreed upon by them shall be deemed a part of this treaty, and shall have the same force as if it were inserted therein. The two Governments will amicably agree regarding what may be necessary to these persons, and also as to their respective escorts, should such be necessary.

The boundary line established by this article shall be religiously respected by each of the two republics, and no change shall ever be made therein, except by the express and free consent of both nations, lawfully given by the General Government of each, in conformity with its own constitution.[4]

Unfortunately, the failure to address the specifics leading to the Mexican-American War, and the failure to deal with the specifics associated with indigenous peoples in the ceded territory, as well as with existing land grants and laws, has resulted in years of continuing legal battles, racism, and discrimination in both countries up to the present day. According to those who work in border security along the United States–Mexico border, they frequently hear the people crossing into the United States from Mexico referring to Texas, New Mexico, Arizona, and California as "los estados ocupados de México del norté" or "the occupied states of North Mexico."

The Gadsden Purchase

The 1854 purchase of 29,670 square miles (76,800 sq. km.) from Mexico essentially rounded out the final continental land acquisition of the United States. Known as the Gadsden Purchase (Venta de La Mesilla in Mexico), this sale of land resulted in moving the southern border of the United States further south in Arizona and New Mexico, to the boundaries we know today. Interestingly, the purpose for the purchase of the land was to build a railroad connecting the Southern States to the Pacific Coast, expanding trade opportunities. To avoid the mountains of central Arizona and western New Mexico, it was determined that moving the proposed rail line further south would ease the cost of construction. The piece of land ultimately purchased and agreed to by the US Senate in a highly contentious pre-Civil War political confrontation was significantly smaller than originally proposed.[5] The schism between North and South led to a major delay in railroad construction. It wasn't until 1881 that the Southern Pacific railroad reached El Paso, Texas, from its start in Los Angeles, California.[6]

Ignacio Ibarra writes, "For Mexico, the sale of the southern strip of Arizona and New Mexico to the United States 150 years ago was a betrayal that eventually toppled its government and continues in many ways to define the United States–Mexico relationship."[7] For Mexicans, the Gadsden Purchase is considered the final humiliation of an embarrassing defeat suffered in their war with the United States over annexation of Texas. The defeat of Mexico in the war was so complete that the United States could have simply annexed all of Mexico.[8] Perhaps it should have. The political, economic, and security issues both countries are experiencing today would not exist if the United States had annexed Mexico.

Ports of Entry

A Port of Entry (POE) is any designated place where a Customs and Border Protection officer is authorized to accept entries of merchandise, to collect duties, and to enforce the various provisions of the customs and navigation laws.[9] According to the CBP website (July 2017), U.S. Customs and Border Protection has a complex mission at ports of entry with broad law enforcement authorities tied to screening all foreign visitors, returning American citizens and imported cargo that enters the U.S. at more than 300 land, air and sea ports.[10]

Each year, more than 11 million maritime containers arrive at our seaports. At land borders, another 11 million arrive by truck and 2.7 million by rail. We are responsible for knowing what is inside, whether it poses a risk to the American people, and ensuring that all proper revenues are collected. Working with the trade community, programs like the Container Security Initiative and the Customs-Trade Partnership Against Terrorism help to increase security and safeguard the world's trade industry.[11]

An officer is responsible for determining the nationality and identity of each applicant for admission and for preventing the entry of ineligible aliens, including criminals, terrorists, and drug traffickers, among others. U.S. citizens are automatically admitted upon verification of citizenship; aliens are questioned and their documents are examined to determine admissibility based on the requirements of the U.S. immigration law. Under the authority granted by the Immigration and Nationality Act (INA), as amended, a CBP officer may question, under oath, any person coming into the United States to determine his or her admissibility. In addition, an inspector has authority

In the 1950s there were 8 lanes of U.S.-bound traffic and two lanes of Mexico-bound traffic at the San Ysidro, California, Port of Entry. Compare this with the traffic in the following photo from 2012.
© U.S. Border Patrol Museum. Used with permission.

Daily traffic lined up to cross into the U.S. from Mexico at San Ysidro, California, Port of Entry, 2012. CBP.gov.

to search without warrant the person and effects of any person seeking admission, when there is reason to believe that grounds of exclusion exist which would be disclosed by such search. The INA is based on the law of presumption: an applicant for admission is presumed to be an alien until he or she shows evidence of citizenship; an alien is presumed to be an immigrant until he or she proves that he or she fits into one of the nonimmigrant classifications. The mission of the inspections program

Train check in the 1950s in California.
© US Border Patrol Museum. Used with permission.

is to control and guard the boundaries and borders of the United States against the illegal entry of aliens.[12]

Millions of pounds of fresh fruits, vegetables, cut flowers, herbs, and other items enter the United States via commercial shipments from other countries every year. Although these items appear to be harmless, there could be hidden threats in that baggage and in those truckloads, trainloads and containers of fresh items that could seriously threaten U.S. agriculture, our natural resources and our economy. The CBP agriculture specialist and the CBP officer at U.S. ports of entry and international mail facilities target, detect, intercept, and thereby prevent the entry of these potential threats before they have a chance to do any harm. Each year, CBP agriculture specialists intercept tens of thousands of "actionable pests" — those identified through scientific risk assessment and study as being dangerous to the health and safety of U.S. agricultural resources.[13]

The San Ysidro Port of Entry is the busiest border crossing in the world with 24 northbound vehicle lanes entering the United States and 6 southbound lanes into Mexico. Over 50,000 northbound vehicles and 25,000 northbound pedestrians cross the border each day. The San Ysidro POE is undergoing a major expansion; of which Phase 1 will be completed about the time this text is printed. Subsequent phases of the expansion will be forthcoming in future years.[14]

San Ysidro is just one of 47 Ports of Entry along the United States–Mexico border (see Table 10.1). The POEs at El Paso and Laredo, Texas, are pushing to overcome San Ysidro's title as busiest border crossing in the world and by some estimates, the Laredo POEs are now the busiest cargo land POE in the world. Below are listed the crossings by state. Each of these crossings requires the presence of a formal Customs and Border Protection outfit, with associated Drug Enforcement Administration, Federal Bureau of Investigation, US Border Patrol, CBP Air and Marine, US Citizenship and Immigration Services, and Homeland Security Investigations representatives, and in many cases offices.

Table 10.1 U.S.–Mexico Border Crossing Locations

Truck, automobile, and foot traffic (47 crossings) by U.S. City	
California	San Ysidro, Otay Mesa, Tecate, Calexico West, Calexico East, Andrade
Arizona	Douglas, Lukeville, Naco, Nogales-Mariposa, Nogales-Grand Avenue, Nogales-Morley Gate, San Luis, San Luis II, Sasabe
New Mexico	Antelope Wells, Columbus, Santa Teresa
Texas	El Paso-PDN, El Paso-Stanton, El Paso-BOTA, El Paso-Ysleta, Fabens, Ft. Hancock, Presidio, Amistad Dam, Del Rio, Eagle Pass, Eagle Pass II, Laredo-Colombia Solidarity, Laredo-World Trade, Laredo Bridge 1, Laredo-Juarez/Lincoln, Falcon Dam, Roma, Rio Grande City, Los Ebanos, Anzalduas, Hidalgo, Pharr, Donna, Progreso, Los Indios, Brownsville-B&M, Brownsville-Gateway, & Brownsville-Veterans
Rail Crossings (8 crossings) by U.S. and Mexico Cities	
California	San Ysidro-Tijuana, Calexico-Mexicali
Arizona	Nogales-Nogales
New Mexico	None
Texas	El Paso-Ciudad Juarez, Presidio-Ojinaga, Eagle Pass-Piedras Negras, Laredo-Nuevo Laredo, Brownsville-Matamoros

In addition to checking the citizenship of those crossing the border at Ports of Entry, the CBP agents also check their visas to determine if they are approved to enter the United States and for what duration. Additionally, all persons, packages, and cargo must be considered for additional screening for contraband, such as narcotics, as well as for agricultural inspections.

CBP agricultural specialists have extensive training and experience in agricultural and biological inspection. Their historic mission of preventing the introduction of harmful pests into the United States provides CBP with the expertise to recognize and prevent the entry of organisms that could be used for biological warfare or terrorism. More likely to be identified and stopped are the non-native insects that may be hidden within foreign cargo, or have hitched a ride with the bananas or asparagus. These insects can be devastating if they establish a foothold in the United States, where they have no natural predators. Since 2005 CBP and Animal and Plant Health Inspection Service (APHIS) have worked to prevent the entrance of invasive species at Ports of Entry. Some get through. Most are stopped. In fiscal year 2015 CBP and APHIS conducted more than 382 million traveler inspections, enrolled more than 965,000 people in the DHS Trusted Traveler Programs bringing total enrollment to more than 4.2 million, processed more than $2.4 TRILLION in imports including more than 33 million cargo inspections, and collected about $46 billion in duties, taxes, and other fees.[15] In FY 2016 APHIS and CBP stopped more than 61,000 thousand dangerous pests from entering the country.[16]

Immigration Inspection at Ports of Entry

Individuals who want to enter the United States are inspected at Ports of Entry by CBP agents to determine admissibility. The inspection process includes identifying the nationality and identity of the person wanting to enter the country; preventing the entry of ineligible aliens, including criminals, terrorists, and drug traffickers, among others. Another function is the verification of documents (passports, visas, etc.) to ensure compliance with US immigration law. CBP agents have the authority to question under oath any person coming into the United States to determine admissibility. CBP agents may also search without a warrant the person and effects of any person seeking admission, provided there is reason to believe that grounds for exclusion that a search would reveal exist.[17]

These searches are conducted under the authority of the Immigration and Nationality Act (INA). This act is based on the law of presumption: an applicant for admission is presumed to be an alien until they show evidence of citizenship. An alien is presumed to be an immigrant until they prove that they fit into one of the nonimmigrant categories. These inspections occur at every POE, including the forty-seven along the border with Mexico.

Infectious Disease

The vast majority of admissions into the United States occur at the land border, where local and regional economies are dependent upon the movement of goods and people across the border to maintain economic viability. From the perspective of the US Customs and Border Protection (CBP), the most significant challenge in screening for infectious diseases comes at the land border. Even without medical screening or other special circumstances, land borders can build up inspection lines that are several hours long due to the high demand for crossings and inadequate infrastructure at most POEs to accommodate such crossings.

The CBP Inspector's Field Manual states that CBP officers are responsible for observing all travelers for obvious signs and symptoms of quarantinable and communicable diseases, such as:

(1) fever, which could be detected by a flushed complexion, shivering, or profuse sweating;

(2) jaundice (unusual yellowing of skin and eyes);

(3) respiratory problems, such as severe cough or difficulty breathing;

(4) bleeding from the eyes, nose, gums, or ears or from wounds; and

(5) unexplained weakness or paralysis. Additionally, a person is considered to be ill in terms of foreign quarantine regulations when symptoms meet the following criteria:

1. Temperature of 100 degrees Fahrenheit or greater which is accompanied by one or more of the following: rash, jaundice, glandular swelling, or which has persisted for 2 days or more.

2. Diarrhea severe enough to interfere with normal activity or work.

However, CBP officers are not medically trained or qualified to physically examine or diagnose illness among arriving travelers.

United States–Mexico Commerce and Border Security

The integration of the United States and Mexican economies has transformed the international border. As the second largest destination for US exports and the third largest source of imports, both countries have a vested interest in seeing the smooth flow of commerce across the border in both directions. One of the components of the United States–Mexico trade is that unlike other countries, more than 40 percent of the content of a product made in Mexico (*Hecho en México*) was produced in the United States. The same cannot be said for any other country, except Canada, where the US content of products made in Canada is as high as 25 percent. Compared with other countries exporting goods to the United States, clearly the country's economy has a direct dependence upon the bilateral manufacturing relationship with Mexico.[18]

Not surprisingly, Texas has the strongest trade relationship with Mexico. About 35 percent of Texas exports head south. Mexico is the number one destination for California exports with about $20 billion in exports annually (as of 2010). Arizona and New Mexico have between 25 and 33 percent of their exports heading to Mexico. Interestingly, Detroit's metropolitan area exports more goods to Mexico than any other city in the United States — as would be expected with the amount of joint automobile manufacturing that occurs in the United States and Mexico.[19]

A key component of the United States–Mexico interdependence in commerce is the production sharing and cross-border investment brought about by NAFTA. According to Christopher Wilson, "Nearly 80 percent of trade with Mexico is land trade, meaning it enters or exits the United States through one of the ports of entry along the Southwest border."[20] In the face of rising concerns about border security, significant steps have been taken to improve the security of transborder shipments by trusted parties, thereby freeing up capacity to inspect potentially dangerous shipments.

Production sharing is also known as vertical specialization. Factories in each country produce the parts and products used by factories in the other country. Ultimately, the parts for any given product that is produced in Mexico and exported to the United States may have crossed the border several times, in different configurations, before becoming the end product the customer purchases. Similarly, the process works for Canada to Mexico, U.S. to Mexico, Mexico to Canada, and Canada to U.S. exports. The entire production stream is interrelated.

Businesses on both sides of the border depend on the crossings. The businesses are linked together in a variety of ways, from management structures to manufacturing. Due to labor costs, many US and Canadian companies have relocated their manufacturing factories to Mexico. These are called maquiladoras. When NAFTA went into effect in 1994, one of the key provisions was the establishment of a commercial zone along the US-Mexico border. Mexican trucks are permitted to operate on the US side of the border within this commercial zone to facilitate efficient cross-border freight movement. This is where efficient border security is essential. Many companies contract their freight movements to drayage operators. These short-haul dray trucks are hired to transport loaded trailers across the border to staging locations where long-haul truckers pick them up for further movement inland in either country. With factories and distribution systems on both sides of the border, moving commerce around in a timely manner is essential to maintain profitability. The typical dray truck can make "four to six individual crossings (two to three round trips, otherwise known as 'turns') per day, often using more than one crossing on inbound and outbound trips."[21] Concurrently, it is essential that the security of the process be maintained. It is simply impossible to physically inspect every truck that crosses in either direction. Even if enough technology and personnel were put in place to inspect every truck, the expense to do so would be prohibitive as would be the delays by trucks on either side of the border waiting to clear the inspection process.

Maquiladoras practice "just-in-time" inventory management, making timely deliveries essential. Whenever inventory sits idly at a border crossing, the cost can ultimately be stopping of production. When the numbers of maquiladoras in Mexico are considered, the closure of a single bridge across the Rio Grande, or the blocking of traffic in a single Mexican city by a Cartel, can wreak havoc on entire companies

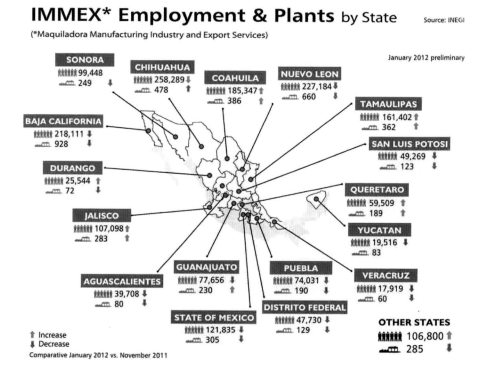

Number of IMMEX manufacturing establishments for the states of Mexico. Source: MexicoNow Magazine (June 2012 Edition). Available at: http://www.elpasoredco.org/regional-data/ciudad-juarez/twin-plant/employment.

on both sides of the border. Therefore, every effort must be made to ensure that cargos are prescreened, approved for entry in advance, and appropriate security seals attached at the point of origin to ensure that the vehicle clears customs and immigration inspections expeditiously.

There are significant political interests in ensuring that a perceived climate of security exists in Mexico and the US border states. This results in the intentional failure to focus on or even report security issues related to international commerce. Finding statistical data that is reliable and not politically manipulated is difficult to impossible. However, there have been three consecutive studies by the American Chamber Mexico and Kroll (the world's leading risk consulting company).

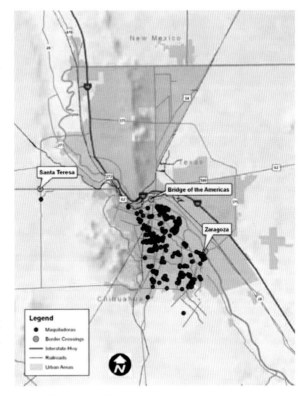

Maquiladoras in Ciudad Juárez. El Paso Regional Ports of Entry Operations Plan. Final Report. Texas Department of Transportation. June 2011.

The most recent study (2011) showed that most multinational firms reported a deteriorating security situation in Mexico. Overall, 45 percent of the company executives surveyed reported their companies at greater risk than during the previous year. As many as 8 percent of the companies surveyed said they were looking at moving operations to another country due to the security situation in Mexico.[22] The largest concern facing companies with business in Mexico was the issue of employee security. While efforts to protect facilities and executives have improved over the past several years, their employees have stated that they are threatened both inside the company and outside the business (going to and from work). With daily executions, running gun battles in the streets, cartel sicarios (hitmen) attacking and killing entire families in their homes, all being reported daily in Mexico, it is not surprising that those same cartels are targeting maquiladora employees.[23]

The companies that the American Chamber Mexico and Kroll surveyed reported that the Mexican states with the most insecurity were Chihuahua, Nuevo León, Tamaulipas, Federal District (Mexico City), the State of Mexico, and to a lesser extent Baja California, Coahuila, Jalisco, and Michoacán. Those company executives who participated in the 2011 survey said they felt a growing sense of insecurity. Of those surveyed, 92 percent felt there had been no improvement in security and 67 percent felt less secure than the previous year. The primary reason (58 percent) for this increasing feeling of insecurity for their companies and employees in Mexico was the increasing strength of organized crime.[24]

The principal cause of corporate insecurity in Mexico was extortion by organized crime (nearly 40 percent). Corruption of government officials was a close second followed by impunity in the Mexican judicial processes. More than 20 percent of the companies reported that inadequate access control, kidnapping, information theft, and internal frauds contributed to their increased insecurity concerns. Overall, the number one threat to their security was aggression against their employees. More than half of the logistics companies and 60 percent of the service and manufacturing sectors saw this as their major problem. Almost 33 percent of the companies reported a breech in their supply chains, the second most common occurrence reported. According to the study, "As a result of the situation facing those surveyed, more than one third of the companies have limited visits to Mexico because of the present insecurity."[25]

Simply stated, the problem is that employees of maquiladoras are threatened and extorted by organized crime, sometimes from within the company itself. This leads to a vulnerability of the supply chain, and as much as one third or more of the commercial traffic crossing the border may have been compromised at some point in the movement of commodities. From a border security perspective, the failure to utilize this data to implement improved security methods and screening of commercial vehicles crossing from Mexico into the United States is a form of politically created porosity in the border. In a May 2013 meeting with Mexican President Pena Nieto, President Obama stated, "Our shared border is more secure than it's been in years."[26] It is difficult to believe such a statement when the American Chamber Mexico-Kroll statistical data is evaluated.

The line that divides the United States and Mexico on maps is less a barrier than a method of economic control. More than half a million people and about a billion dollars in goods cross the border each day. Made up of four US states and six Mexican states, the tightly integrated economies have a combined GDP greater than $3.5 trillion. Nearly 80 percent of all goods traded with Mexico by all fifty US states cross land POEs along the southern border.[27] Therefore efficient operation of border crossings by officials in both countries is key to keeping both countries economically competitive in a globalized world. Anything that disrupts the movement of commodities across the border, be it weather, failing infrastructure, or cartel extortion and corruption has the potential to be devastating to the economy of both countries.

As Christopher Wilson (2011) notes, "Unfortunately, in the past decade increased attention to border security appears to have come at a cost. Analysts have identified what they describe as a 'thickening' of the border since the terrorists attacks of September 11, 2001."[28] Yet, overall, commercial truck and train traffic is up. Demand on the system is growing.[29]

Security between the Ports of Entry

Between the Ports of Entry border security falls to the US Border Patrol and local and state law enforcement. The area that must be monitored and patrolled along the southern border is significant. Much of it is unfenced. In Texas, New Mexico, and Arizona the Border Patrol frequently must cross private lands to reach potential illegal aliens, while maintaining the security of private property such as gates, buildings, and private roads. Of course, they also should remember to shut gates so that horses, cattle, and wild game cannot escape—all while in pursuit of illegal aliens whose primary concern is evading capture.

The US-Mexico border region is an enormous geographical space, with much of it in extremely remote and mountainous terrain. Managing the area between ports of entry (POE) is challenging. While numerous US federal agencies have a say in border security affairs, historically it has been up to the US Border Patrol to secure the regions between POEs. Between 1992 and 2011 the Border Patrol saw a significant increase in staffing in an effort to address border security issues, particularly on the southern border. Having had fewer than 5,000 agents in 1992, today the number of Border Patrol agents stands at 19,828, as of FY 2016.[30]

However, as Border Patrol staffing has increased, apprehensions of illegal migrants have decreased. There are several reasons for this. Among them is that increased Border Patrol visibility has resulted in fewer attempts to come to the United States. Concurrently, a bad economy coupled with high unemployment since the recession of 2008 has resulted in fewer job opportunities for illegal migrants, while a stronger Mexican economy has resulted in improved opportunities within the country.[31] The political policies implemented by the Obama administration have also contributed to fewer apprehensions, in particular, the cessation of workplace ID checks, the prohibition of Border Patrol conducting operations farther than 50 miles from the border, effective efforts at forcing border crossings into more hostile terrain, the cartel control

Anti-vehicle barriers (fences) along the southwest border. Unknown date. CBP.gov.

and increasing costs for being smuggled into the United States across that hostile terrain, and the focus of ICE on only identifying and deporting criminal illegal aliens, have all contributed to lower apprehension numbers. No single effort to implement better border security can be credited for the lower apprehension numbers. While the government estimates its interdiction effectiveness rate at 84 percent, a study by the Council on Foreign Relations rates actual apprehension rates along the border with Mexico to be more likely only 40 to 55 percent, at best![32]

Building of infrastructure between POEs has also contributed to improved border security. Beginning in 2008 there was a massive increase in the construction of border fencing, with more than 450 miles of new fencing being installed.[33] The border fencing project varies by political administration, as does the counting of the miles of fencing installed. For example, if the fence is three layers deep along a single mile of border, that would, in some reports, count as three miles of fencing, versus a single mile of border being fenced. Additionally, some fencing is more effective than other fencing. Vehicle barriers do not stop pedestrian traffic. Pedestrian fence is not all that effective in stopping vehicle traffic when the persons trying to cross are intent on success, and highly innovative.

Fencing has resulted in the diversion of illegal migrants from easy crossing locations to much more difficult terrain. Thus, the inhospitable terrain has resulted in an increase in the number of people dying while attempting to enter the United States. According to a March 2013 report by the National Foundation for American Policy, 477 persons died while trying to enter the United States in 2012, a number of deaths eclipsed only by the 492 deaths reported in 2005. Since 1998 nearly 5,600 people have died trying to enter the United States illegally across the southern border.[34] Stuart Andersons notes, "This tragic loss of life is a direct result of the absence of legal avenues for foreign nationals to work at jobs in hotel, restaurants, construction and other industries. The current visa categories for agriculture (H-2A) and nonagricultural work (H-2B) are considered cumbersome and are only for seasonal work, not the type of year-round jobs filled by most illegal immigrants in the United States."[35] The problems with visas for visitors, guest workers, and immigrants are discussed in detail below. See tables 10.2 and 10.3 for selected visa fees to come to the United States.

Road Checks Interior to the Southern Border

Any person who travels east or west on Interstate 10, between San Diego, California, and Sierra Blanca, Texas, or north on any road leading away from the US-Mexico border, has encountered a Border Patrol checkpoint. These traffic check locations are sometimes mobile, other times fixed. All are intended to interdict potential human and contraband smugglers before they get far enough inland as to be outside of the operations areas of CBP and the Border Patrol.

A CBP flier with information on these interior checkpoints states,

A Border Patrol road checkpoint in 1941. Note that while one officer is checking the driver and passenger identification, the other is standing by their radio-equipped car holding a Thompson submachine gun. Temporary road checks by Border Patrol agents have always been a component of border security enforcement along the southern border of the United States. © US Border Patrol Museum. Used with permission.

Border Patrol checkpoints are a critical enforcement tool for securing the Nation's borders against all threats to our homeland.

Checkpoints restrict the ability of criminal organizations to exploit roadways and routes of egress away from the border. Checkpoints provide an additional layer in our Defense in Depth strategy. Our enforcement presence along these strategic routes reduce the ability of criminals and potential terrorists to easily travel away from the border.

All Border Patrol checkpoints operate in accordance with the Constitution of the United States and governing judicial rulings.

Border Patrol is committed to operating checkpoints in a safe, efficient, and cost-effective manner and will continue to ensure that new technologies, as they become available, are deployed at checkpoints to improve inspections and facilitate legitimate traffic and commerce.[36]

An August 2009 General Accounting Office (GAO) report noted that interior checkpoints took 4 percent of available Border Patrol officers to accomplish operations, but only accounted for 2.4 percent of all interdictions.[37] Beyond just the effectiveness of the interior (aka nonborder) checkpoints is the question of civil liberties and the rights of citizens to travel throughout the country without government interference.

Eastbound traffic on Interstate 10 is diverted off the freeway for interior inspection at a Border Patrol permanent checkpoint outside of Sierra Blanca, Texas. Google Earth, 2013.

Several people are video recording their interactions with Border Patrol agents at these interior checkpoints, and those videos are going viral online. Any search of YouTube or Vimeo for "border checkpoint" will result in numerous options for people to view these interactions.[38] The American Civil Liberties Union of Arizona produced a publication titled *Know Your Rights at Border Checkpoints.* Under the section titled "What You Need to Know" they state,

> US Customs and Border Protection (CBP) can stop, detain, or search any person or vehicle at border checkpoints in the United States — even those located inland and far away from the border — if they suspect there are un-documented persons in the vehicle and even if they suspect other types of criminal activity. At checkpoints located within 100 miles of an "external boundary" of the United States, CBP officers have powers that far exceed traditional law enforcement authority permitted by the US Constitution.
> *CBP officers at border checkpoints can stop you and search your vehicle even if you are a US citizen.*
> At these checkpoints, officers may stop and search people based on minimal suspicion and may use race as a factor in deciding whether to stop and question an individual.
> In some instances, federal CBP agents may act under the authority of state and local law enforcement to issue citations for criminal offenses under Arizona law, for example, for drug possession. They may also call state and local law enforcement to the scene.

Remember, **you always have the right to remain silent.** Anything you say to a CBP officer can be used against you. You do not have to answer questions about your immigration or citizenship status or any suspected criminal activity. However, you should know that, for the officer, your refusal to answer questions may justify continued detention. It is ultimately your decision how to respond to questions asked by officers at border checkpoints.

If you are the driver of a car and a law enforcement officer demands to see your driver's license, vehicle registration or proof of insurance, you must show these.

Remember, fleeing a checkpoint is a *felony* and punishable by a fine and/ or imprisonment up to five years under federal law.[39]

The US Supreme Court has determined that these interior (nonborder) checkpoints are constitutional. In the case *United States v. Martinez-Fuerte*, 428 U.S. 543, July 1976, the Court determined that the stops were consistent with the Fourth Amendment and that the stops at fixed checkpoints need not be pre-authorized by a judicial warrant. The agents at the interior checkpoints do not need any articulable suspicion to conduct the stop nor to conduct a secondary inspection. The fixed checkpoints do not need probable cause to conduct a stop and investigation of the occupants' citizen/resident status.[40] Of course, this can change with a future finding by the Court.

Narcotrafficantes

Perhaps the major issue facing the United States is that of drug trafficking. Illegal drugs coming into the United States are nearly all carried across the southern border. The ongoing warfare between drug cartels in Mexico has overflowed into the United States. According to Robert Bunker, "Much of the concern relating to the Mexican cartels focuses on acts of violence such as homicides, assaults, and torture along with the illicit economic activities of narcotics trafficking, kidnapping, extortion, bulk thefts, and human smuggling."[41] While this is one indication that transnational criminal organizations (TCOs) and the problems in Mexico have crossed the border, there are many other indications that violence has also crossed the border. For example, Hidalgo County (Texas) Sheriff Lupe Treviño has been the subject of numerous death threats by cartels and associated gangs.[42] The cartel violence is not limited to border states. In Oregon there have been three bomb deaths and seven shooting deaths tied to Mexican cartels.[43] Then there is the case of 19-year-old Carina Saunders, who was tortured, beheaded, and dismembered by a cartel-related gang in Oklahoma in December 2011. Saunders was killed to intimidate victims of a human trafficking ring associated with a drug trafficking ring. On June 30, 2008, a little girl, who had resisted being raped, was brought to Florida from Mexico and beheaded in front of other girls who were being held and used for sex by a Mexican drug trafficking organization (DTO). In

Chandler, Arizona, Martin Ale-
jandro Cota Monroy was killed
and beheaded in October 2010
in his apartment by a member
of the Sinaloa DTO in retaliation
for stealing 400 pounds of marijuana from the cartel.[44]

Cartel-related violence is not
isolated to Mexico. It can be
found across the United States
either as direct violence by
DTOs or as violence by their
associated gangs. The ongoing
battle in Mexico over control
of drug trafficking routes and
the plazas in border communities is becoming a growing
problem for the United States.
Appendix A reviews a highly
disturbing trend in the ongoing
drug wars in Mexico.

Drugs hidden in a vehicle in 1958. The drugs were discovered at a Border Patrol checkpoint in Oceanside, California.
© US Border Patrol Museum. Used with permission.

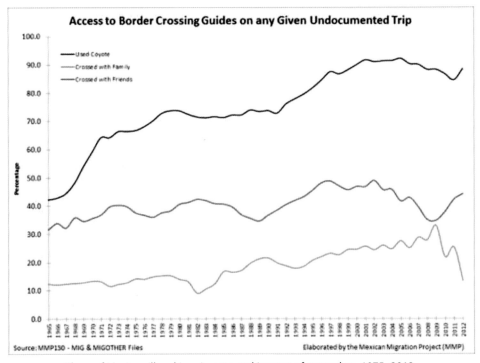

Share of Mexican illegal immigrants making use of smugglers, 1975–2012.

Drugs, Mules, and Migrants

Drugs have been trafficked into the United States since the Chinese brought opium with them when they arrived to work the gold mines of California. Smuggling drugs into the United States has been a profitable, large-scale business since Prohibition was ended. At first a small-scale operation, drugs as contraband has become the major threat to the United States and in particular to the security of the southern border.

In the 1970s and 1980s the Colombian cartels flew cocaine to remote airfields in Florida and Texas. With the United States joining the Colombian government to bring an end to these original cartels, cocaine production was moved into underground economies and the drugs were transshipped to the United States via Mexican cartels that were already bringing tons of marijuana and Mexican black tar heroin into the country on well-established routes. With a change in focus that targeted illegal immigrants as well as drug trafficking, the United States began building fences along the border with Mexico, and diverting foot traffic from easy points of entry to much more difficult terrain. One consequence of this was that illegal immigrants who wanted to get to the United States found themselves having to either pay cartels to guide them into the country through the rough terrain, or work for the cartels as payment for being guided into the country. Cartels have monopolized this business, adding human trafficking and smuggling to their existing business model.

Not only has the cost of being smuggled into the United States gone up, but also the percentage of illegal immigrants being forced into using cartels to get into the United States is now more than 90 percent. Additionally, the cartels no longer take money from the immigrants (although many are robbed somewhere along their route of travel). Instead, carrying loads of drugs across deserts and mountains makes payment. Should a drug mule lose their load to United States border security agents, the mule is held accountable by the cartel for the loss. This has created a very dangerous situation for border security forces who are now facing heavily armed cartel guides leading, and protecting, the illegal immigrants who are carrying their drug loads into the United States.

The cartels are extremely innovative in getting their drug shipments across borders. In addition to simply carrying backpacks of marijuana, they have used boats, submarines, cars, trucks, rail cars, cattle, turkeys, and even dead bodies as containers to ship drugs. They launch drugs over the fences by catapult and cannon. Tunnels are dug under the border, some of them very heavily engineered with electric power, rail systems, ventilation, and elevators. One of the newer means of getting drugs into the United States is the ultra-light. With a cargo net sling under the nearly invisible aircraft, they fly across the border at night to a GPS location in the United States, drop their load where a waiting vehicle is pre-stationed, and return to Mexico without ever having landed.

The cartels have also put to use for their benefit US law and policy. Knowing that the United States will not prosecute a minor for illegally bringing drugs across the border, cartels are using more 16- and 17-year-olds, and younger kids, to bring across drug shipments. If caught, the United States will simply return the underage drug mule to Mexico instead of arresting and prosecuting them for a drug crime. As minors, they would only serve a sentence until they were 18 and be released—making prosecution not cost effective.

Green Cards, Guest Workers, and Undocumented Immigrants

One interesting aspect of border security is that Mexico is treated differently than Canada when it comes to entering the United States. First, it is important to understand that there are a large number of visas under which a traveler to the United States can enter the country.

Table 10.2 Non-Petition-Based Nonimmigrant Visas

B	Visitor Visa: Business, Tourism, Medical treatment	$160.00
C-1	Transiting the U.S.	$160.00
D	Crewmembers—Airline, Ship	$160.00
E	Treaty Trader/Investor, Australian Professional Specialty	$205.00
F	Student, Academic	$160.00
I	Media and Journalists	$160.00
J	Exchange Visitors	$160.00
M	Students, Vocational	$160.00
TN/TD	NAFTA Professionals	$160.00
T	Victim of Trafficking in Persons	$160.00
U	Victim of Criminal Activity	$160.00

Adapted from US State Department (2017), https://travel.state.gov/content/visas/en/fees/fees-visa-services.html

Table 10.3 Petition-Based Visa Categories

H	Temporary Workers/Employment or Trainees	$190.00
L	Intracompany Transferees	$190.00 each +$5,000 additional fees
O	Persons with Extraordinary Ability	$190.00
P	Athletes, Artists & Entertainers	$190.00
Q	International Cultural Exchange	$190.00
R	Religious Worker	$190.00
K	Fiancé(e) or Spouse of U.S. citizen	$265.00

Adapted from US State Department (2017), https://travel.state.gov/content/visas/en/fees/fees-visa-services.html

What these fees and visas mean to the poor Mexican farm worker who wants to come to the United States to earn income picking strawberries (or other farm labor, construction work, etc.) is that it is less expensive to pay a cartel member to guide them across the Sonora Desert and into the United States. To legally come to the United States to work they must acquire a Mexican passport, spend days completing applications (which

Mexican women and children are loaded on a bus in McAllen, Texas, for return to Mexico in the 1950s. © US Border Patrol Museum. Used with permission.

require access to a computer, the Internet, a photo studio that can take a passport photo and digitize it for uploading), processing, traveling to a city with a US Consulate for a scheduled interview and screening, and then waiting to be awarded an "H" visa so that they can temporarily enter the United States and legally work. All to perform backbreaking labor so they can send some money back to their village (provided they are awarded a visa at all). Faced with such a process it is obvious why people choose to cross into the United States illegally. The visa system is simply not conducive to support a guest worker not supported by a corporation or sponsored by a family member.

What these visa fees mean to a family of four, with two teenage kids, who want to visit relatives in the United States, or simply tour the country and enjoy its natural beauty, is that each parent must pay $160 for a "B" visa, along with $15 for each child under 15, and $160 for each child when they turn 15. This gets each of them a Border Crossing Card ("B" visa) provided they pass the interview and screening process at a US Consulate or Embassy.[45]

In comparison, a person traveling with a US passport only pays $20 for a 90-day tourist visa in Turkey or Bahrain, no visa or entry fee in Japan or Canada, and no visa needed to enter Mexico along the border region for 72 hours or less. To stay longer in Mexico or to travel deeper into the country than the border area costs about $20 US for an FMM/FMT tourist card (depending on the exchange rate).

US Department of State Bureau of Consular Affairs

Frequently Asked Questions—Immigrant Visa Interview Medical Examination

Under current law, foreign nationals not already legally residing in the United States who wish to come to the United States generally must obtain a visa and submit to an inspection to be admitted. They must first meet a set of criteria specified in the Immigration and Nationality Act (INA) that determine whether they are eligible for admission. Moreover, they must also not be deemed inadmissible according to specified grounds in the INA. One of the reasons why a foreign national might be deemed inadmissible is on health-related grounds. The diseases that trigger inadmissibility in the INA are those communicable diseases of public health significance as determined by the Secretary of Health and Human Services (HHS). Currently there are seven diseases deemed communicable disease of public health significance: chancroid, gonorrhea, granuloma inguinale, infectious leprosy, lymphogranuloma venereum, active tuberculosis, and infectious syphilis. Other diseases incorporated by reference are cholera; diphtheria; infectious tuberculosis; plague; smallpox; yellow fever; viral hemorrhagic fevers (Lassa, Marburg, Ebola, Crimean-Congo, South American, and others not yet isolated or named); severe acute respiratory syndrome (SARS); and "[i]nfluenza caused by novel or reemergent influenza viruses that are causing, or have the potential to cause, a pandemic." The INA also renders inadmissible foreign nationals who are not vaccinated against vaccine-preventable diseases. Vaccinations are statutorily required for mumps, measles, rubella, polio, tetanus, diphtheria, pertussis, influenza type B and hepatitis B. Vaccinations against other diseases may also be required if recommended by the Advisory Committee for Immunization Practices (ACIP).

Waivers of the Health Grounds

The INA gives the [Secretary of Homeland Security]* the discretionary authority to waive some of the health-related grounds for inadmissibility under certain circumstances. For example, foreign nationals infected with a communicable disease of public health significance can still be issued a waiver and admitted into the country if they are the spouse, unmarried son, unmarried daughter, minor unmarried lawfully adopted child, father or mother of a US citizen, alien lawfully admitted for permanent residence, or an alien issued an immigrant visa, or is a VAWA self-petitioner. Waivers are also available, under certain circumstances, for those inadmissible for lacking proper vaccination and for those who have a physical or mental disorder. The Secretary may also waive the application of any of the health-related grounds for inadmissibility if she finds it in "the national interest" to do so.**

* The text actually names the Attorney General, but the passage of the Homeland Security Act of 2002 transferred the waiver power to the Secretary of Homeland Security.

** References for this section are: INA § 212(g), 8 U.S.C. § 1182(g); INA § 212(g)(1), 8 U.S.C. § 1182(g)(1); INA § 212(g)(2), 8 U.S.C. § 1182(g)(2); (4) INA § 212(g)(3). 8 U.S.C. § 1182(g)(3); and INA, § 212(d)(13)(B)(i).

Border Crossing Card

The Border Crossing Card (BCC) is both a BCC and a B1/B2 visitor's visa. A BCC is issued as a laminated card, which has enhanced graphics and technology, similar in size to a credit card. It is valid for travel until the expiration date on the front of the card, usually ten years after issuance. For children under the age of 15, the BCC is good for 10 years or until they reach the age of 15, whichever comes first. The BCC is only issued to applicants who are citizens and residents of Mexico. The applicants must meet the eligibility standards for a B1/B2 visa.[46]

B-1 (Business Visa) is issued so that the holder may consult with business associates; attend a scientific, educational, professional, or business convention or conference; settle an estate; or negotiate a contract. The B-2 (Tourism and Visit Visa) is issued for tourism; vacation; visit with friends or relatives; to receive medical treatment; participate in social events hosted by fraternal, social, or service organizations; participate in amateur musical, sports, or similar events or contests (cannot be a paid participant); and for enrollment in a short recreational course of study, not for credit toward a degree. What a BCC holder cannot do in the United States is study; work for pay; perform in any professional capacity such as music, dance, athletics before a paying audience; arrive as a crewmember on a ship or aircraft; work as a member of the press for any radio, film, journalists, or other information media; or permanently remain in the United States.[47]

For a Mexican to acquire a BCC they must complete several steps. They must complete an online Nonimmigrant Visa Application, Form DS-160, for each person. A copy of the completed form must be printed and brought to the interview. While completing the DS-160, they must upload a photo that meets the requirements of the State Department. For those between the ages of 14 and 79 they must undergo an interview with a consular officer. The interviews must be scheduled in advance at a US Embassy or Consulate and there can be significant wait times to get an interview. They must pay the nonrefundable visa application fee. They must have a Mexican passport. And they must bring these to the interview. In addition, they must be prepared to provide additional documents showing the purpose of their trip, their intent to depart the United States after their trip; and/or the ability to pay all the costs of their trip. Evidence of their employment and/or family ties may be sufficient to show purpose of trip and intent to return to Mexico. The applicant leaves their passport with the interviewing officer, who takes digital fingerprints of each person. After this, the visa processing begins, along with any further administrative processing. Once processed, the BCC is either delivered by courier to the individuals, or picked up at the Consulate/Embassy.[48]

With a BCC the holder can travel internally in the United States up to 25 miles from the border in California and Texas, 75 miles of the border in Arizona—provided they entered the United States from a Mexico-Arizona border crossing, and as of June 12, 2013, up to 55 miles into New Mexico.[49] The person holding a BCC is exempt from the completion of a form I-94 and the accompanying secondary inspection of luggage, packages, and associated legal paperwork.

Per CBP, the currently issued BCC "is a laminated, credit card style document with many security features, a ten-year validity period and vicinity-read Radio Frequency

Identification (RFID) technology and a machine-readable zone. Using these features, CBP is able to electronically authenticate the BCC against the Department of State (DOS) issuance records."[50]

Green Card

A green card holder is someone who has been granted authorization to live and work in the United States on a permanent basis. As proof of that status, a person is granted a permanent resident card, commonly called a "green card." There are many ways a person can become a permanent resident. Most people with green cards are individuals sponsored by a family member or employer in the United States. Other individuals may become permanent residents through refugee or asylee status or other humanitarian programs. There are some cases where people may be eligible to apply for themselves.[51]

Many people get green cards (become permanent residents) through family members. According to the US Citizenship and Immigration Services (USCIS), people may be eligible to get a green card as:

- an immediate relative of a US citizen; this includes spouses, unmarried children under the age of 21, and parents of US citizen petitioners 21 or older
- a family member of a US citizen fitting into a preference category; this includes unmarried sons or daughters over the age of 21, married children of any age, and brothers and sisters of US citizen petitioners 21 or older
- a family member of a green card holder; this includes spouses and unmarried children of the sponsoring green card holder
- a member of a special category; this can include battered spouse or child (VAWA), a K nonimmigrant, a person born to a foreign diplomat in the United States, a V nonimmigrant or a widow(er) of a US citizen.[52]

USCIS also provides several humanitarian programs and protection to assist individuals in need of shelter or aid from disasters, oppression, emergency medical issues and other urgent circumstances. These include:

- Refugee Status or Asylum may be granted to people who have been persecuted or fear they will be persecuted because of race, religion, nationality, and/or membership in a particular social group or political opinion.
- Battered Spouse, Children and Parents of US citizens or permanent residents may file for immigration benefits without the abuser's knowledge.
- Victims of Human Trafficking and Other Crimes may receive immigration status in certain circumstances.
- Humanitarian Parole is sparingly used to bring someone otherwise inadmissible into the United States for a temporary period due to compelling emergencies.
- Temporary Protected Status is granted to qualified people in the United States who are temporarily unable to return safely to their home country because of an extraordinary condition.
- Deferred Action Process for Young People Who Are Low Enforcement Priorities is for certain young people who were brought to the United States through no

fault of their own as young children and meet several key criteria. They will
be considered for relief from removal from the country or entered removal
proceedings.

- Special Situations occur where assistance may be available to people whose
immigration application or status has been affected by natural catastrophes
and other extreme circumstances.
- Special Immigrant is a person who qualifies for a green card (permanent
residence) under a particular special immigrant program.[53]

Special immigrants include a wide variety of individuals from numerous categories.
For example, a foreigner who is serving in the US Armed Forces may be granted a
green card.

Currently, the most contentious of issues dealing with persons crossing the southern
border of the United States is the issue of citizenship by birth. According to Section
1 of the 14th Amendment to the US Constitution, all persons born in the United
States are citizens of the United States and the State where they reside. This provision
was upheld by the US Supreme Court in *United States v. Wong Kim Ark*, 169 U.S. 649
(1898).[54] However, the parents of Wong Kim Ark were legally in the United States at
the time of his birth. This raises the question: what if Wong Kim Ark's parents were
not legally in the United States when he was born? This question has never been
addressed by the Court and poses a significant problem for those providing border
security between the United States and Mexico.

The Politics of Pregnancy

Any person born in the United States is a citizen and afforded all the rights, responsibilities, and protections associated with citizenship. What if the mother of a
newborn is in the United States illegally? Is that child still a US citizen? If so, can the
mother be deported and separated from the child? These questions have not been addressed by the legislature or the courts and have created an issue appropriate to
discussion in this chapter.

Based on the International Monetary Fund measure of developed versus developing
nations, of the developed nations, only Canada and the United States award automatic
citizenship to children born within their borders or territories.[55] No country in Europe
or Asia allows such a benefit as citizenship to automatically accrue to a person born
within their national borders. In fact, the benefit of *jus soli* (Latin for "right of the
soil") is restricted almost entirely to the Western Hemisphere countries.

Apart from the rising industry of birthright tourism, there is a major issue arising
along the border with Mexico. Absent any formal, or written guidance, each individual
port of entry has to deal with the arrival of a woman in labor in the manner established
by their local administration. In interviews with CBP officers who staff the entry points
for both foot and vehicular traffic, the issue of pregnancy is a problem. An example:

A woman arrives at my entry kiosk, holding her swollen abdomen, grunting
with labor pains and asking for help. She has no documents. She walked

right past the free Social Security Hospital in Juarez and across the Free Bridge to get to El Paso and tell me she's having the baby. My supervisor tells me to let her in and call an ambulance, which picks her up in the parking lot and takes her to University Medical Center a few blocks away. I could have simply sent her back across the bridge, which she just walked across, to the Mexican hospital, but if anything happens to her or the baby in route, then the United States and I could be liable when she brings a lawsuit against me for denying her medical care. My supervisor doesn't want to have to deal with it, so he tells us to let them in. Now El Paso picks up the ambulance transportation costs. The University Medical Center picks up the delivery costs. The baby is a newborn American. The mother is qualified for WIC. The baby is qualified for food stamps, free medical care, and a free education. The kid and mother get more benefits and freebees than taxpayers get. It isn't right![56]

Events like this one happen every day along the border with Mexico. The business is so lucrative doctors have billboards in Mexico advertising their services and asking, "Do you want to have your baby in the US?"[57] Hospitals even advertise their excellent medical treatment facilities in Mexico and offer "birthing packages" to expectant mothers. Wealthy Mexican families routinely take advantage of the opportunity to not only use these facilities but to afford their children the added benefit of dual citizenship.[58]

There is no formal legal benefit to the mother of the newborn American citizen. In fact, the law precludes the child from sponsoring family, including the birth mother, for immigration to the United States until after the child's twenty-first birthday. However few immigration judges will deport the mother of an infant who is a US citizen. A Pew Research Center study in 2009 reported that 73 percent of illegal Mexican immigrants had children born in the United States.[59] The report indicates there are about 4 million US-born children with at least one illegal alien parent living in the United States as of 2008.

The DREAM Act

The DREAM Act (Development, Relief, and Education for Alien Minors) is a legislative proposal that has been bouncing around Congress in a variety of forms for more than a decade. Fundamentally, it is intended to address an issue that is highly politically charged. The problem is, if a mother or father brings their minor child into the United States illegally, and that child is raised in the United States as if they were Americans, what should be done with that child when they ultimately reach the age of majority? Should they be allowed to remain in the only country they have ever known? Or should they be deported to their country of origin, a place they have no familiarity with and where they may not even know the language? This issue is so contentious that it has resulted in numerous political debates. Many of those debates are directly related to state and federally incurred expenses associated with education, medical care, military service, employment eligibility, etc. The proponents and opponents of the DREAM Act raise pros and cons that range from financial costs to legalization of an illegal act.

Of course, the primary concern is one of morality. What choice did the child of an illegal border crosser have in deciding to enter the United States? More so, how can the only country a child has ever known automatically deport that person to a place they have no experience with? Which is the worse of two evils: allowing somebody who is technically in the country illegally to stay; send a person from the only country they have ever known into an environment in which they have no experience and will most likely not be able to survive? This issue was resolved by Congress through the rejection of the DREAM Act. However, President Obama followed this failure of the program to achieve legal status by issuing a Presidential Memo known as the Deferred Action for Childhood Arrivals (DACA) in June 2012. As a result, those people who arrived in the United States before their sixteenth birthday, and before June 2007, who were currently in school and/or had served in the US military, and were under the age of 31 as of June 15, 2012, and met certain legal and conviction limitations, were allowed to apply for permission to remain in the United States indefinitely, and receive a work permit and permission to attend school. Under DACA 750,000 people received permission to remain in the United States—in direct contravention to the law.[60]

President Obama followed this up with several other policies and directives that were subsequently implemented by the DHS to expand the reach and scope of the published programs far beyond their original intent. Essentially, President Obama established a priorities list that protected almost all illegal immigrants from deportation. Border Patrol agents interviewed by the authors reported that for the last five years of the Obama administration they had essentially become processors whose only function, besides narcotics interdiction, was to process illegal migrants, provide them with papers allowing them to remain indefinitely in the United States, and release them into the US interior—where many, more than 90 percent, would never appear for any immigration hearings—and let these people disappear into the underground cash economies around the country.

As noted at the close of chapter 1, President Trump issued Executive Order: BORDER SECURITY AND IMMIGRATION ENFORCEMENT IMPROVEMENTS on January 25, 2017, bringing the Obama immigration policies to an end and empowering federal agents to return to their legislatively authorized functions. On the same day President Trump also issued the Executive Order: ENHANCING PUBLIC SAFETY IN THE INTERIOR OF THE UNITED STATES, allowing "direct executive departments and agencies to employ all lawful means to enforce the immigration laws of the United States." A full copy of this Executive Order is appended at the end of this chapter.

President Trump additionally "called for adding 5,000 more US Border Patrol agents and 10,000 more US Immigration and Customs Enforcement agents to the payroll—his promised 'deportation force'—and released his own set of priorities that put many more illegal immigrants in danger of being kicked out and gave plenty of discretion to agents to decide how to handle the cases. He also proposed a weekly name-and-shame list of sanctuary cities and the criminals they are releasing, saying communities deserve to see who is being let back onto their streets because their local leaders refuse to cooperate with immigration agents."[61] Appendix B examines recent government movement on DACA.

A Border Patrol Agent's Perspectives on the End of the Obama Presidency

Anonymous
January 25, 2017

From what I hear around the station, the Agents are looking forward to this new administration. They seem to be a little too overjoyed, with talk of getting our pay restored and the hopes of interior enforcement among the more popular ideas. I think that might be too optimistic. I also do not see how we as a nation can afford to pay for everything that needs to be done to restore any type of national security. I think Trump will follow through with many of his campaign promises regarding immigration, but I see him as more populist than truly conservative; i.e., more willing to do what the people want than what might be Constitutionally allowed, especially if it is immediately economically beneficial.

Once Trump was elected, the agents began to actively question management regarding current enforcement (or lack thereof) and the basic catch-and-release procedures. There was more talk of how to reinforce the Wall, and how to extend it. From what I have heard from agents, management (HQ) started to loosen the pace of work and not be quite so adamant about enforcing the [Obama] executive orders. The agents were extremely frustrated at how we were releasing illegals without properly or legally verifying their identities or stories.

I see from immigration and USBP sites on FaceBook that there are many, many supporters of Trump, with most posting of increased expectations for greater enforcement. I can tell you that officials and policies from the Obama and Clinton administrations are almost uniformly denigrated and derided. If you have not seen them, or they are restricted, they are [at] the "I'm 10-15" and the legacy Immigration and Naturalization Services sites.

The DEA agents are also eagerly anticipating Trump's actions and administration. They see a new release to enforce the laws, with fewer obstructions by AUSAs [Assistant United States Attorneys]. Their judicial concerns are very similar to those of the BP—the liberal judges appointed by Obama have a very lax view of enforcement and a great sense of "social justice" that excuses criminal behavior. Lax sentences and probations are the order of the day from these judges.[62]

Undocumented Immigrants/Illegal Aliens[63]

Without a doubt, border security is a question of porosity. How porous a country's borders are can be determined in several ways, but most easily by the numbers of people who have illegally crossed into a country. The land borders of the United States are as porous, if not more porous, than those of most countries. In a Pew Research Center study, it was determined that there are about 8.3 million undocumented (illegal) aliens in the United States. Of those, 76 percent are Hispanic with 59 percent (7 million) coming from Mexico, as of March 2008.[64] While the number grew rapidly from 1990 to 2008, it has since stabilized and even dropped some from a peak of 11.9 million. How much of the stabilization can be attributed to the recession of 2008–12 as compared with improved border security efforts is questionable, depending on the political objectives of the speaker. Correlation does not imply causation. The probability of apprehension while illegally entering the United States varies by year, political administration, numbers of available border security agents in a given region, available technology, and the number of people attempting to enter illegally.

A great deal is known about those who reside in the United States illegally. According to the Pew Research Center study[65] on unauthorized immigrants:

- Adult unauthorized immigrants are disproportionately likely to be poorly educated. Among unauthorized immigrants ages 25 to 64, 47 percent have less than a high school education. By contrast, only 8 percent of US-born residents ages 25–64 have not graduated high school.
- An analysis of college attendance finds that among unauthorized immigrants ages 18 to 24 who have graduated from high school, half (49 percent) are in college or have attended college. The comparable figure for US-born residents is 71 percent.
- The 2007 median household income of unauthorized immigrants was $36,000, well below the $50,000 median household income for US-born residents. In contrast to other immigrants, undocumented immigrants do not attain markedly higher incomes the longer they live in the United States.
- A third of the children of unauthorized immigrants and a fifth of adult unauthorized immigrants live in poverty. This is nearly double the poverty rate for children of US-born parents (18 percent) or for US-born adults (10 percent).
- More than half of adult unauthorized immigrants (59 percent) had no health insurance during all of 2007. Among their children, nearly half of those who are unauthorized immigrants (45 percent) were uninsured and 25 percent of those who were born in the United States were uninsured.

Much of the decrease in illegal immigration has to do with a poor economy and very high unemployment in the United States. Some has to do with improved border fencing, and increased defense in depth. More has to do with the continuing violence in Mexico and the cartel control of the overland routes favored by those attempting to cross into the United States illegally. With these changes comes a change in cost to be smuggled into the United States.

Prior to the implementation of DACA those interdicted by either CBP or the Border Patrol were placed into processing for removal. Mexican nationals frequently returned to the nearest POE where they walked back into Mexico. Those from other countries were held in detention facilities until they were processed for deportation, or appear at an immigration hearing before an immigration judge. Some were identified as repeat offenders and receive prison sentences followed by deportation. Others were identified as coming from a distant country and were released to the U.S. general population pending a formal hearing. Some estimate that as many as 59 percent of those released pending an immigration or removal hearing abscond,[66] and simply disappear into the world of illegal immigrants somewhere in the country. The relaxation of immigration enforcement under President Obama's DACA executive order changed the way CBP and USBP addressed those crossing into the U.S. via the border with Mexico, essentially being forced to operate contradictory to Federal Law as of the result of an Executive Policy Statement. Morale of the USBP and CBP plummeted and is only beginning to recover during the first six months of the Trump Administration which implemented a policy of Law Enforcement by Law Enforcement Agents and Officers of the Federal Government.

As with nearly all border security concerns, the process of interdicting, detaining, and removing illegal immigrants is nothing new. This has been happening at the southern border for more than a century. With the consolidation under the Department of Homeland Security, the Immigration Enforcement and Removal Operations were shifted to the subdepartment of Immigration and Customs Enforcement.

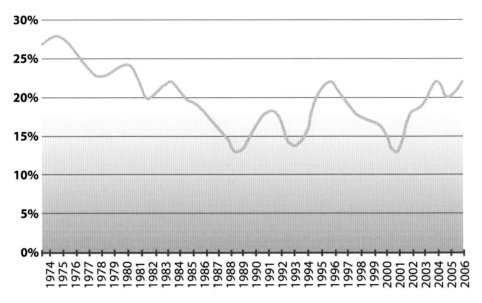

Probability of apprehension during an undocumented border crossing, 1974–2006.
Source: UNODC & Mexican Migration Project.

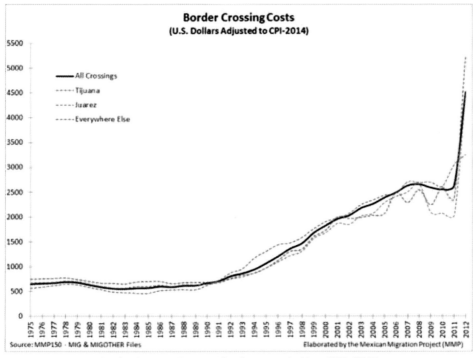

Border Crossing Costs paid to be smuggled into USA. MMP.

Enforcement and Removal Operations (ERO) "transports removable aliens from point to point, manages aliens in custody or in an alternative-to-detention program, provides access to legal resources and representatives of advocacy groups, and removes individuals from the United States who have been ordered to be deported."[67] With a focus on those aliens who have a criminal record, either in the United States or in their country of origin, the primary focus of ERO is to arrest and remove those who pose a threat to national security. On the southern border, most of those apprehended for illegally crossing the border are turned over to private corporations for transportation and housing in contract detention facilities before processing for removal. This has created a massive for-profit industry dependent upon the continued apprehension and removal of illegal immigrants.

Politics in Enforcement

In April 2012 ICE supervisor David Venturella sent an e-mail to ICE Field Officers stating, "The only performance measure that will count this fiscal year is the criminal alien removal target."[68] In a presidential election year such action to "pad" the numbers of deported illegal aliens, thereby demonstrating that the "borders are more secure than they have ever been," has the potential of being borderline criminal and clearly reflects poorly on the aforementioned focus of ERO. It is interesting to note that Mr.

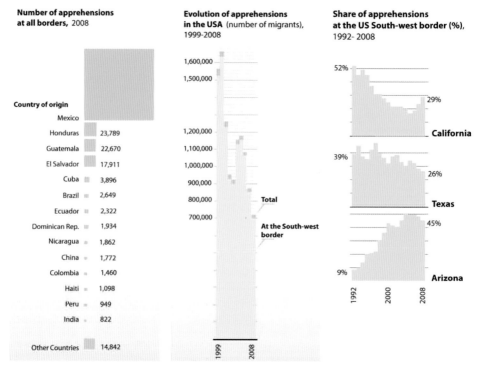

Number of apprehensions at all borders, 2008

Country of origin

Mexico	
Honduras	23,789
Guatemala	22,670
El Salvador	17,911
Cuba	3,896
Brazil	2,649
Ecuador	2,322
Dominican Rep.	1,934
Nicaragua	1,862
China	1,772
Colombia	1,460
Haiti	1,098
Peru	949
India	822
Other Countries	14,842

Evolution of apprehensions in the USA (number of migrants), 1999-2008

1,600,000
1,500,000
1,200,000
1,100,000
1,000,000
900,000
800,000   **Total**
700,000
         At the South-west border

1999   2008

Share of apprehensions at the US South-west border (%), 1992- 2008

52%   29%
                  California
39%   26%
                  Texas
                       45%
9%   **Arizona**

1992   2000   2008

Left: Apprehensions of irregular migrants at the US borders.
Source: UNODC & US Department of Homeland Security.

Right: Trends in apprehensions at the US south-west border, 1992–2008.
Source: UNODC & US Congressional Research Service (CRS) presentation of data from the
US Customs and Border Protection (CBP) and Center for Immigration Research (CIR).

The McAllen, Texas, detention camp in 1954. © US Border Patrol Museum. Used with permission.

Venturella changed jobs in July 2012, becoming the Executive Vice President of Corporate Development at the GEO Group, the second largest private prison company in the United States and a major contractor with DHS for transportation and detention of illegal aliens.[69]

Today, half of the nearly half-million administratively detained undocumented immigrants are held in private facilities. GEO Group earned $216 million and Corrections Corporation of America (CCA) earned $208 million from immigration detention in 2012 alone. As of 2014, CCA earned $195,022,000, and GEO Group $143,840,000 (as quoted in Grassroots Leadership.org).[70]

GEO Group maintains fifty-six facilities in the United States with all but eleven in border states (only three in states along the Canadian border). CCA has more facilities in more states, with about an equal distribution between those housing state and federal inmates and those housing immigrants awaiting detention. Clearly, housing those awaiting removal is big business — particularly along the border with Mexico.

¿Plata o Plomo?

On June 21, 2013, US District Court Judge John Houston sentenced two Border Patrol agents to long prison terms for running a smuggling ring that brought more than 500 illegal immigrants (prosecutors estimated as many as 1,000) into the United States. Raul Villarreal received a 35-year sentence for being the ring leader and his brother, Fidel Villarreal, received 30 years for managing the operation. The two were working with a corrupt Tijuana, Mexico, police officer and a network of others who

Those detained for removal were held without regard for age or gender as demonstrated by this photo of the McAllen, Texas, detention camp in 1954. Note that the "matrons" are dressed in nursing uniforms of the era. © US Border Patrol Museum. Used with permission.

arranged pickups and dropoffs. The Villarreal brothers would pick up and drop off the illegal immigrants using their Border Patrol vehicles, sometimes making multiple trips each day. Each immigrant was charged about $10,000 for the trip and the brothers made more than $700,000 overall while conducting the smuggling operation.[71]

The Villarreal brothers are not alone. Since 2004 more than 150 Border Patrol and CBP agents have been charged with some form of corruption. Mexicans toss bales of marijuana over the fence and Border Patrol agents pick up the bales and deliver them in their government vehicles.[72] Illegal immigrants, such as Oscar Ortiz, using false documents, apply to be Border Patrol or CBP agents, and then use their positions to allow relatives and others to pass freely through their inspection lanes.[73] Relatives who are drug smugglers convince their cousins of the relative safety of the lucrative business smuggling illegals, simply by clearing the way for their passage into the United States as in the case of Eric Balderas; or agents succumbing to the lure of sex with beautiful women, who can legally cross the border with a BCC. Then there are those, like Supervisory Border Patrol Agent Samuel McClaren, who help spring captured smugglers from ICE detention facilities—for a fee.[74]

When people are placed in positions of authority, the opportunity for corruption is great. When those same individuals are placed in close proximity with organized crime on a daily basis, the potential for corruption increases. However, a few bad apples do not imply that all of the forces protecting the border with Mexico are corrupt. In fact, the number of agents adjudicated by the court system for corruption is less than 1 percent of the total number of agents. Contributing to this low number of convictions is an understaffed and overburdened Office of the Inspector General in both the Border Patrol and CBP. The result is that, according to an unclassified report, most OIG investigators spend their time investigating minor misconduct cases rather than potential corruption complaints.[75]

The majority of CBP and Border Patrol allegations of misconduct and corruption occur along the southwest border. This is expected as there are more than 21,400 Border Patrol agents patrolling between POEs (18,000 assigned to the southwestern border), the vast majority assigned to the four states bordering Mexico. When coupled with CBP agents, the total number of agents along the southwest border exceeds 24,000 as of 2011. Since 2005 more than 65 percent (103 of the 144) of the agents arrested or indicted for corruption-related activities, including the smuggling of aliens or drugs, accepting bribes, or allowing illegal cargo into the United States, were stationed along the southwest border. According to CBP Internal Affairs (IA), the other 41 were arrested or indicted for less severe corruption-related activities such as theft of government property and querying personally associates in a government database for purposes other than official business. The acting commissioner of CBP testified,

> [T]hat no act of corruption within the agency can or will be tolerated and that acts of corruption compromise CBP's ability to achieve its mission to secure America's borders against all threats while facilitating and expediting legal travel and trade. In particular, there have been a number of cases in which individuals, known as infiltrators, pursued employment at CBP solely to engage in mis-

sion-compromising activity. For example, in 2007, a CBPO in El Paso, Texas, was arrested at her duty station at the Paso Del Norte Bridge for conspiracy to import marijuana into the United States from June 2003 to July 2007, and was later convicted and sentenced to 20 years in prison. OFO [Office of Field Operations] reported that she may have sought employment with CBP to facilitate drug smuggling. CBP officials view this case as an example of the potential impact of corruption—if the officer had succeeded in facilitating the importation of 5,000 pounds of marijuana per month, this would amount to a total of 240,000 pounds over four years with a retail value of $288 million dollars. In another case, a former BPA previously stationed in Comstock, Texas, was arrested in 2008 for conspiracy to possess, with intent to distribute, more than 1,000 kilograms of marijuana. The agent was convicted in 2009 and sentenced to fifteen years in prison and ordered to pay a $10,000 fine. CBP is also concerned about employees who may not be infiltrators, but began engaging in corruption-related activities after joining the agency. For example, CBP IA officials stated that some employees may have experienced personal hardships after being hired, such as financial challenges, which made them vulnerable to accepting bribes to engage in corrupt activity. In addition, some employees arrested for corruption had no prior disciplinary actions at the time of their arrests.[76]

All new hires in Customs and Border Protection undergo a polygraph examination as part of the pre-employment screening. From 2008 through August 7, 2012, 46 percent of the total applicants failed their polygraph, another 14 percent were inconclusive. Only 40 percent of those applying for employment with CBP, including Border Patrol, passed their polygraph examinations.[77] According to a recent (Jan 13, 2017) article in the *LA Times,* two out of three CBP applicants fail the polygraph examination. This is one of the big reasons that more than 2,000 jobs at the agency go unfilled, and the reason that total employment at the agency has dropped below 20,000, for the first time since 2009.[78]

It's not just new hires who have to undergo background checks and polygraphs. Current employees also have to undergo a reinvestigation under Public Law 111-376, § 3, 124 Stat. 4104, 4104-05 (2011). According to the GAO analysis of the reinvestigations, as of September 2012, 15,027 had been completed. Of the 62 percent of those favorably adjudicated reinvestigations showed that the employee was involved in some form of issue requiring disciplinary action, including criminal or dishonest conduct or illegal drug use.[79]

While the number of crimes specifically related to border security has dropped in cities located near the US side of the border with Mexico, the number of officials charged for corruption in different US security agencies has increased. The fundamental result of this information is that transnational criminal organizations in Mexico have moved into the United States through corruption and co-option of authorities instead of implementation of violence.[80]

Corruption occurs on both sides of the southern border. Bribery is endemic as a form of normal operations within Mexican law enforcement and judicial systems. This isn't new, or unexpected, as the practice originated with the first Spanish alcaldes in the seventeenth century and has become an expected part of conducting business in many of the former Spanish colonies.[81] What is new is that instead of asking for or requiring payment to be allowed to conduct business,[82] it is now the cartels that force the issue with a simple question, silver or lead (¿Plata o plomo?). The cartels, flush with money and guns, are forcing a choice on politicians and law enforcement. A simple offer is made. Accept a bribe or accept a bullet. Those who refuse the cartels are killed.[83] Cartel techniques are often very brutal, including beheadings, dismemberment, castration, and emasculation while the victim is still alive, hangings, and crucifixions. The cartels now go after family members as well as the targeted individual.

Per Robert Bunker (2013),

> A large component of Mexican cartel operations is derived from the targeted corruption of public officials within their areas of operation. The initial intent is to achieve impunity and freedom of action. This represents the 'insurgency' element of the criminal insurgencies taking place in Mexico, Central America, and now over the US southern border, an element, according to John Sullivan, that is still not recognized by many individuals. Essentially, the public agency (be it local, state or federal) being targeted is compromised one official at a time. When combined with the threat (and subsequent use) of violence the well-known cartel technique of offering the choice of silver or lead (¿Plata O Plomo?) is achieved. This is akin to the environmental modification of a street, barrio, or plaza controlled by a cartel or gang with the imposition of a new set of values (narcocultura) and rules (cartel political authority)—though, in this instance, it is directed at the public entity in order to compromise and co-opt it (representing the aggregate of all of the individuals corrupted). What has worked so successfully in Mexico and Central America is now being incrementally utilized by the cartels against the United States' ports of entry—and, we can also assume, much deeper into the US homeland.[84]

Twenty-first century reality is that over the last eleven years in Mexico and Central America the drug war strategy has been ineffective. At best, TCOs are now heavily influencing government politics and becoming allied with government forces, from the local police, to the national army, and the judiciary, in the process of carrying out their business. As Robert Bunker notes, the cartels draw upon both illicit and licit businesses to sustain themselves and pay considerable attention to the necessity of maintaining good relations with the residents in areas under their control as well as driving the electoral processes in those areas.[85] As the cartels vie with each other over control of specific plazas and shipping routes, the violence has exploded across Mexico. This process will ultimately settle down as the new Mexican government under Enrique Peña Nieto pulls back from the Calderon aggressive war on narcotraficante organizations and allows the current cartel structure to once again settle into old patterns that existed thirteen years earlier when the PRI party was last in power. Already, there has been significant pullback from cooperation with US federal anti-drug law enforcement agencies. Mexican authorities have moved toward a strategy of reestablishing safety and a sense of calm on the city streets instead continuing the strategy of going after the cartel leadership.[86] US DEA agents, retired military contractors, and other federal agents have already been asked to leave Mexico, in particular the joint fusion centers built by the two countries to prosecute the war on drugs over the past thirteen years. Now, all intelligence gathered by US sources will be funneled through Mexico's Interior Ministry, which will determine which Mexican law enforcement agency it will be shared with — essentially eliminating all the personal relationships and trust developed over thirteen years of joint operations.[87]

Conclusion

For nearly 200 years the United States and Mexico have been competitors, antagonists, opponents in war, and economic partners. The more than 1,900-mile-long border between the two countries extends an additional 200 nautical miles into the Gulf of Mexico and into the Pacific Ocean as part of each country's exclusive economic zone. The US's insatiable demand for drugs has made Mexico the natural supplier of America's illicit habit. The US habit in return contributes nearly 10 percent of Mexico's GDP — although illegally and without generating any tax revenue for either country. Hundreds of billions of narcodollars flow south across the border annually, contributing to an economy that fuels intense competition between rival cartels. That competition has resulted in more than 180,000 deaths in Mexico from 2004 to 2016. By the cartel's own estimates as reported on their blogs, that number may only be half of the actual deaths in the battle over who controls the smuggling routes into the United States.

The United States has countered what appears to be an unending flow of drugs and humans northward with fences, technology, and people. Along with the increase in staffing in the border security agencies has come an increase in corruption.

Not everybody sees the fortification of the US-Mexico border as either an effective or efficient policy. Michael Dear, of the University of California, Berkeley, in his book *Why Walls Won't Work: Repairing the US-Mexico Divide,* reports on the detrimental effects the border fence has on communities. Dear identifies the growing Border Security–Industrial Complex is nearing the level President Eisenhower feared the Military-Industrial Complex would achieve, becoming a political power in itself. The expansion of the current fences will only create a system of fortifications reminiscent of the Great Wall of China, the Berlin Wall, or Hadrian's Wall. All of them ultimately fell and became useless monuments to the folly of fixed fortifications. While the statistics show that fences are effective — as a great author once wrote, there are lies, damn lies, and statistics — those statistics are questionable. However it appears that with the election of President Trump a significant effort will be made to implement construction of a fixed barrier along the border with Mexico.

Like the United States, Mexican efforts to stem the violence and establish political and legal and judicial control over large swaths of Mexico (by some accounts as high as 60 percent of Mexico is controlled by the cartels), vary with changing administrations.

In the twentieth century, the ruling political PRI political party in Mexico maintained a state of peace with the cartels, allowing them to operate at will for the occasional bribe, so long as violence was contained and public embarrassment of the government was minimized. With the election of Vincente Fox, and his successor Felipe Calderon (of the PAN party), and pressure by the United States, a war was launched against the cartels using methods like those in the war on terror—targeting the leaders in an attempt to disrupt the organization and end the drug trafficking. This effort not only failed, but led to the extensive violence in Mexico as lower lever cartel members and plaza bosses vied for leadership of the very lucrative business. The 2012 election of President Enrique Peña Nieto (of the PRI) portends a change in Mexican policy that will significantly alter border security efforts. These changes, coupled with efforts by the US Congress to improve the security of the southern border as part of an attempt to address the presence of eleven million illegal immigrants in the country indicate a renewed focus on securing the US-Mexico border over the next several years.

With the election of Donald Trump to the US presidency, policy concerning the application and implementation of immigration law drastically changed from that of his predecessor. With the institution of new executive orders, nearly all the policies of the Obama administration were wiped away, returning the border and immigration enforcement agencies of the United States to their core purpose—securing the nation.

Security along the US-Mexico border is going to continue to be a hot topic.

Questions for Further Consideration

1. Considering that the United States has defeated Mexico in war, and seized nearly the entire country at one point, should the United States have simply annexed the country and made it into a portion of the United States?
2. For several years the battle for control of the plazas in Mexico's border cities has used the tactic of simply blocking roads with buses and trucks, essentially shutting down all traffic routes to US POEs. Should there be some sort of consideration implemented by CBP to expedite the restoration of cross-border traffic when these roadblocks are cleared—up to and including the expedited screening of cargo shipments that were delayed?
3. President Obama implemented several of the key provisions of the DREAM Act by Executive Order when the original bill failed to pass Congress. A politically divided Congress then failed to pass a bill overriding the EO. This created a de facto situation where the president implemented changes to immigration law without congressional approval—a direct violation of the separation of powers doctrine. Outside of the constitutional issue, is it morally right to deport adults brought to the United States as children who have spent nearly their entire lives in the United States through no fault of their own? What choice did the child of an illegal border crosser have in deciding to enter the United States? More so, how can a country that is the only country a child has ever known automatically deport

that person to a place they have no experience with? Which is the worse of two evils: allowing somebody who is technically in the country illegally to stay; or sending a person from the only country they have ever known into an environment in which they have no experience and will most likely not be able to survive?

4. The policy of targeting the leadership of Mexico's drug cartels resulted in the cartels battling within and among themselves to reestablish supremacy. More than 180,000 have been killed in the cartel fighting (many of them civilians, police, politicians, and media) over the past twelve years. Is it more appropriate to address the drug problem of the United States from a public health perspective than from a law enforcement perspective? Should we simply end the war on drugs, recognize we have a problem with drug abuse, treat it as a disease, and allow the Mexican supply system to stabilize under new leadership—thereby bringing to an end the major war (hidden from public view by American media) on our southern border?

Chapter 10 Endnotes

1. Todish, Timothy J., Terry Todish, & Ted Spring, *Alamo Sourcebook, 1836: A Comprehensive Guide to the Battle of the Alamo and the Texas Revolution* (Austin, TX: Eakin Press, 1998). See also: Vazquez, Josefina Zoraida, *The Colonization and Loss of Texas: A Mexican Perspective*, in O., Rodriguez, Jaime E., & Kathryn Vincent, *Myths, Misdeeds, and Misunderstandings: The Roots of Conflict in U.S.-Mexican Relations* (Wilmington, DE: Scholarly Resources Inc., 1997).

2. Eisenhower, John S.D., *So Far from God: The U.S. War with Mexico, 1846–1848*. New York: Random House, 1989).

3. *Treaty of Guadalupe Hidalgo*; February 2, 1848. Available at The Avalon Project, Yale Law School. Accessed July 21, 2017, at: http://avalon.law.yale.edu/19th_century/guadhida.asp

4. *Treaty of Guadalupe Hidalgo*; February 2, 1848; Article V.

5. Garber, Paul, *Gadsden Treaty,* (Peter Smith Pub. Inc., 1959).

6. Blaszak, Michael W., "Southern Pacific: a chronology," *Pacific RailNews* (Pasadena, California: Interurban Press, November 1996) (396): 25–31.

7. Ibarra, Ignacio, Land sale still thorn to Mexico: Historians say U.S. imperialism behind treaty. *Arizona Daily Star,* 12 Feb. 2004, Available online at: http://web.archive.org/web/20070503064503/http://www.azstarnet.com/sn/gadsden/9331

8. Ibid.

9. 19 CFR 101.1

10. U.S. CBP: Accessed July 21, 2017 at: https://www.cbp.gov/border-security/ports-entry

11. U.S. CBP: Accessed July 21, 2017, at: https://www.cbp.gov/border-security/ports-entry/cargo-security

12. U.S. CBP: Accessed July 21, 2017, at: https://www.cbp.gov/border-security/ports-entry/overview

13. U.S. CBP: Accessed July 21, 2017, at: https://www.cbp.gov/border-security/protecting-agriculture

14. Government Services Administration. *San Ysidro Land Port of Entry Project Overview.* Accessed July 21, 2017, at: http://www.gsa.gov/portal/content/104872?utm_source=R9&utm_medium=print-radio&utm_term= sanysidro& utm_campaign=shortcuts

15. U.S. CBP, CBP Releases Fiscal Year 2015 Trade and Travel Numbers, March 4, 2016. Accessed July 21, 2017, at: https://www.cbp.gov/newsroom/national-media-release/cbp-releases-fiscal-year-2015-trade-and-travel-numbers# We expect that this material will probably be archived in the near future as this statement appears at the top of the page: Archived Content.

In an effort to keep CBP.gov current, the archive contains content from a previous administration or is otherwise outdated.

16. U.S. CBP, Agriculture Factsheet, January 2017. Accessed January 11, 2017, at: https://www.cbp.gov/sites/default/files/assets/documents/2017-Jan/700897%20-%20FY%202016%20Agriculture%20Fact%20Sheet%20Update_OFO.pdf

17. U.S. CBP: Accessed July 21, 2017, at: https://www.cbp.gov/border-security/ports-entry/overview

18. Wilson, Christopher E., *Working Together: Economic Ties Between the United States and Mexico* (Washington, DC: Mexico Institute: Woodrow Wilson International Center for Scholars, Nov. 2011.

19. Ibid.

20. Ibid., 7.

21. Cambridge Systematics, Inc., *El Paso Regional Posts of Entry Operations Plan.* (Austin, TX: June 2011), 2–18.

22. *Tendencias,* (Mexico City: American Chamber & Kroll, July 2011). Accessed July 21, 2017, at: http://krolltendencias.com/site/browse-archives/general-interest-and-trends/211-report-card-2011mexico-corporate-security.html

23. *The Impact of Security in Mexico on the Private Sector: For a Culture of Prevention*, 3rd ed. (Mexico City: American Chamber-Kroll, July 2011).

24. Ibid.

25. Ibid., 13.

26. Trade Highlighted Over Security for U.S., Mexico, HispanicBusiness.com, 3 May 2013. Available at: http://www.hispanicbusiness.com/2013/5/3/trade_highlighted_over_security_for_us.htm

27. Wilson (2011).

28. Ibid., 30.

29. Cambridge Systematics, Inc. (June 2011).

30. CBP.Gov Accessed July 21, 2017, at: https://www.cbp.gov/sites/default/files/assets/documents/2016-Oct/BP%20Staffing%20FY1992-FY2016.pdf

31. Lee, Erik & Eric Olson, Chapter 3: The State of Security in the U.S.-Mexico Border Region, May 2013. In *The State of the Border Report: A Comprehensive Analysis of the U.S.-Mexico Border* (Washington, D.C.: Wilson Center, Mexico Institute).

32. Plumer, Brad, Study: The U.S. Stops About Half of Illegal Border Crossings From Mexico, Washington Post, 13 May 2013.

33. Lee & Olson (May 2013).

34. Anderson, Stuart, *How Many More Deaths? The Moral Case for a Temporary Worker Program,* NFAP Policy Brief, March 2013.

35. Ibid., 1.

36. U.S. Customs and Border Protection, DHS, *Border Patrol Checkpoints,* CBP Publication 0000-0710, August 2009. Available at: http://www.cbp.gov/linkhandler/cgov/newsroom/fact_sheets/border/border_patrol/bp_checkpoints. ctt/bp_checkpoints.pdf The authors attempted to find updated information on this topic and appropriate links, however the flier used in 2009, at the beginning of the Obama Presidency, has disappeared from the web and the DHS and CBP websites. We expect that the interior checkpoints and work-site employment checks will be restored by the Trump Administration, leading to new information to replace this earlier information.

37. Border Patrol: Checkpoints Contribute to Border Patrol's Mission, but More Consistent Data Collection and Performance Measurement Could Improve Effectiveness, GAO Report: GAO-09-824.

38. Top DHS Checkpoint Refusals. Accessed July 21, 2017, at: https://www.youtube.com/watch?v=6_3dDNPwJTU

39. ACLU, Know Your Rights With Border Patrol. Accessed July 21, 2017, at: https://www.acluaz.org/sites/default/files/field_documents/aclu_border_rights.pdf

40. *United States v. Martinez-Fuerte,* 428 U.S. 543, July 1976.

41. Bunker, Robert, *Mexican Cartel Essays and Notes: Strategic, Operational, and Tactical,* A Small Wars Journal — El Centro Anthology (Bloomington, IL: iUniverse, August 2009), 191.

42. Ortiz, Ildefonso, Sheriff Treviño: Not fazed by death threats, *The Monitor,* 9 Oct 2012. Accessed July 21, 2017, at: http://www.themonitor.com/news/local/article_0521a5d2-128e-11e2-b280-001a4bcf6878.html

43. Zaita, Les, Drug Cartels in Oregon: Violence in the Northwest. Originally published in *The Oregonian,* 24 June 2013. Republished and accessed July 21, 2017, at: http://www.borderlandbeat.com/2013/06/drug-cartels-in-oregon-violence-in.html

44. Bunker, Robert, Teen Tortured, Dismembered, Beheaded by Trafficking Gang in Bethany, Oklahoma, 3 Jan 2012. Republished in Bunker, Robert (2013).

45. Department of State: U.S. Visas. Accessed July 21, 2017, at: https://travel.state.gov/content/visas/en/fees/fees-visa-services.html

46. Ibid.

47. Ibid.

48. Ibid.

49. Federal Register, 35103. Vol. 78, No. 113. Wednesday, June 12, 2013. DHS USCBP, 8 CFR Part 235, RIN 1651-AS95. Extension of Border Zone in the State of New Mexico.

50. Ibid.

51. USCIS. Accessed July 21, 2017, at: https://www.uscis.gov/greencard/eligibility-categories

52. Ibid.

53. Ibid.

54. *United States v. Wong Kim Ark*, 169 U.S. 649 (1898).

55. Nations Granting Birthright Citizenship. NumbersUSA. Accessed July 21, 2017, at: https://www.numbersusa.com/content/learn/issues/birthright-citizenship/nations-granting-birthright-citizenship.html

56. This lamentation from a senior CBP agent was repeated by several agents who staff POEs in Laredo, Del Rio, El Paso, and Nogales. They are all actively employed by DHS and asked that their names be kept out of the book to protect their jobs.

57. Lacy, Marc, Birthright Citizenship Looms as Next Immigration Battle, *The New York Times*, 4 Jan 2011. Accessed July 21, 2017, at: http://www.nytimes.com/2011/01/05/us/politics/05babies.html?_r=2&

58. Alvarado, Mariana, Citizenship for sale? *The Arizona Star,* 21 Jun 2009. Accessed July 21, 2017, at: http://tucson.com/news/local/citizenship-for-sale/article_9dd9a46b-a189-5629-835b-03029d25bbe7.html

59. Passel, Jeffrey, & D'Vera Cohn, A Portrait of Unauthorized Immigrants in the United States, PewResearch Hispanic Center, 14 Apr 2009. Accessed July 21, 2017, at: http://www.pewhispanic.org/2009/04/14/a-portrait-of-unauthorized-immigrants-in-the-united-states/

60. de Vogue, Ariane, Madison Park, Artemis Moshtaghian, and Mary Kay Mallonee, *Immigrant protected under Obama's 'Dreamer' program is detained*, CNN, February 15, 2017. Retrieved February 15, 2017, from: http://edition.cnn.com/2017/02/14/politics/daniel-ramirez-medina-daca-detention/index.html

61. Dinan, Stephen, "Trump eviscerates Obama's immigration policy in two executive orders," *The Washington Times,* January 25, 2017. Available at: http://www.washingtontimes.com/news/2017/jan/25/trump-eviscerates-obamas-immigration-policy/

62. Excerpted from an e-mail received by the author from a senior USBP Agent who requested to remain anonymous.

63. The term undocumented immigrant and illegal alien are used interchangeably in this chapter. It is not our intent to denigrate people who come to the United States without legal basis. Both terms are frequently utilized by political groups and individuals depending upon their political orientation and their target audience.

64. Passel, Jeffrey, & D'Vera Cohn.

65. Ibid.

66. Center for Immigration Studies. Accessed July 21, 2017, at: http://www.cis.org/deportation-basics

67. ICE website, Enforcement and Removal Operations. Accessed July 21, 2017, at: https://www.ice.gov/ero

68. Jones, Andrea, The For-Profit Immigration Imprisonment Racket, *Rolling Stone Magazine,* 22 Feb 2013.

69. Ibid.

70. Grassroots Leadership, "Payoff: How Congress Ensures Private Prison Profit with an Immigrant Detention Quota." Available at: http://grassrootsleadership.org/reports/payoff-how-congress-ensures-private-prison-profit-immigrant-detention-quota CCA 10-K SEC filing, Feb 2015. GEO 10-K SEC filing, Feb. 2015.

71. Watson, Julie, Former Border Patrol Agents Sentenced to 30 Years in Immigrant Smuggling Case, Associated Press, 21 June 2013. Accessed July 21, 2017, at: http://usnews.nbcnews.com/_news/2013/06/21/19081188-former-border-patrol-agents-sentenced-to-30-years-in-immigrant-smuggling-case?lite

72. Hendley, Matthew, Border Patrol Agent Who Said He Was "F***ed" After Being Caught Smuggling Weed Was Right, Will Go to Prison, *Phoenix New Times*, 10 April 2013. Accessed July 21, 2017, at: http://blogs.phoenixnewtimes.com/valleyfever/2013/04/border_patrol_agent_who_said_h.php

73. Becker, Andrew, *Corrupted Gatekeepers,* In Mexico: Crimes at the Border, PBS Frontline, 10 April 2013. Accessed July 21, 2017, at: http://www.pbs.org/frontlineworld/stories/mexico704/history/

gatekeepers_vid3.html

74. Ibid.

75. Ibid.

76. GAO, Border Security: Additional Actions Needed to Strengthen CBP Efforts to Mitigate Risk of Employee Corruption and Misconduct, December 2012, 11. Accessed July 21, 2017, at: https://s3.amazonaws.com/s3.documentcloud.org/documents/551713/gao-13-59.pdf

77. Ibid., 17.

78. "Two out of three Border Patrol job applicants fail polygraph test, making hiring difficult," *Los Angeles Times*, Jan. 13, 2017. Accessed July 21, 2017, at: http://www.latimes.com/local/lanow/la-me-border-patrol-lies-20170113-story.html

79. Ibid., 20.

80. Salcedo-Albarán, Eduardo & Luis Jorge Garay-Salamanca, How Corruption Affects National Security of the United States, 6 Oct 2011. Republished in Bunker, Robert (2013).

81. Miller, Robert Ryal, *Mexico: A History* (Norman, OK: University of Oklahoma Press, 6 Oct. 2011).

82. Aridjis, Homero, The Sun, the Moon and Walmart, *The New York Times*. 30 April 2012. Accessed July 21, 2017, at: http://www.nytimes.com/2012/05/01/opinion/the-sun-the-moon-and-walmart.html?r=0

83. Pitts, Byron, "Silver or Lead" in Mexico: Bribes or Death, Borderland Beat, 10 Jan. 2011). Accessed July 21, 2017, at: http://www.borderlandbeat.com/2011/01/silver-or-lead-in-mexico-bribes-or.html

84. Bunker, Robert (2013), 191.

85. Ibid., 184.

86. Priest, Dana, U.S. Role at a Crossroads in Mexico's Intelligence War on the Cartels, *The Washington Post*, 27 April 2013. Accessed July 21, 2017, at: https://www.washingtonpost.com/investigations/us-role-at-a-crossroads-in-mexicos-intelligence-war-on-the-cartels/2013/04/27/b578b3ba-a3b3-11e2-be47-b44febada3a8_story.html

87. Miroff, Nick, In Mexico, Restrictions on U.S. Agents Signal Drug War Shift, *The Washington Post*, 14 May 2013. Accessed July 21, 2017, at: https://www.washingtonpost.com/world/the_americas/in-mexico-restrictions-on-us-drug-agents-seen-as-overdue/2013/05/14/a86bd394-b9ae-11e2-b568-6917f6ac6d9d_story.html

The White House

Office of the Press Secretary
For Immediate Release
January 25, 2017
Executive Order: Enhancing Public Safety in the Interior of the United States
EXECUTIVE ORDER

ENHANCING PUBLIC SAFETY IN THE INTERIOR OF THE UNITED STATES

By the authority vested in me as President by the Constitution and the laws of the United States of America, including the Immigration and Nationality Act (INA) (8 U.S.C. 1101 et seq.), and in order to ensure the public safety of the American people in communities across the United States as well as to ensure that our Nation's immigration laws are faithfully executed, I hereby declare the policy of the executive branch to be, and order, as follows:

Section 1. Purpose. Interior enforcement of our Nation's immigration laws is critically important to the national security and public safety of the United States. Many aliens who illegally enter the United States and those who overstay or otherwise violate the terms of their visas present a significant threat to national security and public safety. This is particularly so for aliens who engage in criminal conduct in the United States.

Sanctuary jurisdictions across the United States willfully violate Federal law in an attempt to shield aliens from removal from the United States. These jurisdictions have caused immeasurable harm to the American people and to the very fabric of our Republic.

Tens of thousands of removable aliens have been released into communities across the country, solely because their home countries refuse to accept their repatriation. Many of these aliens are criminals who have served time in our Federal, State, and local jails. The presence of such individuals in the United States, and the practices of foreign nations that refuse the repatriation of their nationals, are contrary to the national interest.

Although Federal immigration law provides a framework for Federal-State partnerships in enforcing our immigration laws to ensure the removal of aliens who have no right to be in the United States, the Federal Government has failed to discharge this basic sovereign responsibility. We cannot faithfully execute the immigration laws of the United States if we exempt classes or categories of removable aliens from potential enforcement. The purpose of this order is to direct executive departments and agencies (agencies) to employ all lawful means to enforce the immigration laws of the United States.

Sec. 2. Policy. It is the policy of the executive branch to:

(a) Ensure the faithful execution of the immigration laws of the United States, including the INA, against all removable aliens, consistent with Article II, Section 3 of the United States Constitution and section 3331 of title 5, United States Code;

(b) Make use of all available systems and resources to ensure the efficient and faithful execution of the immigration laws of the United States;

(c) Ensure that jurisdictions that fail to comply with applicable Federal law do not receive Federal funds, except as mandated by law;

(d) Ensure that aliens ordered removed from the United States are promptly removed; and

(e) Support victims, and the families of victims, of crimes committed by removable aliens.

Sec. 3. Definitions. The terms of this order, where applicable, shall have the meaning provided by section 1101 of title 8, United States Code.

Sec. 4. Enforcement of the Immigration Laws in the Interior of the United States. In furtherance of the policy described in section 2 of this order, I hereby direct agencies to employ all lawful means to ensure the faithful execution of the immigration laws of the United States against all removable aliens.

Sec. 5. Enforcement Priorities. In executing faithfully the immigration laws of the United States, the Secretary of Homeland Security (Secretary) shall prioritize for removal those aliens described by the Congress in sections 212(a)(2), (a)(3), and (a)(6)(C), 235, and 237(a)(2) and (4) of the INA (8 U.S.C. 1182(a)(2), (a)(3), and (a)(6)(C), 1225, and 1227(a)(2) and (4)), as well as removable aliens who:

(a) Have been convicted of any criminal offense;

(b) Have been charged with any criminal offense, where such charge has not been resolved;

(c) Have committed acts that constitute a chargeable criminal offense;

(d) Have engaged in fraud or willful misrepresentation in connection with any official matter or application before a governmental agency;

(e) Have abused any program related to receipt of public benefits;

(f) Are subject to a final order of removal, but who have not complied with their legal obligation to depart the United States; or

(g) In the judgment of an immigration officer, otherwise pose a risk to public safety or national security.

Sec. 6. Civil Fines and Penalties. As soon as practicable, and by no later than one year after the date of this order, the Secretary shall issue guidance and promulgate regulations, where required by law, to ensure the assessment and collection of all fines and penalties that the Secretary is authorized under the law to assess and collect from aliens unlawfully present in the United States and from those who facilitate their presence in the United States.

Sec. 7. Additional Enforcement and Removal Officers. The Secretary, through the Director of US Immigration and Customs Enforcement, shall, to the extent permitted by law and subject to the availability of appropriations, take all appropriate action to hire 10,000 additional immigration officers, who shall complete relevant training and be authorized to perform the law enforcement functions described in section 287 of the INA (8 U.S.C. 1357).

Sec. 8. Federal-State Agreements. It is the policy of the executive branch to empower State and local law enforcement agencies across the country to perform the functions of an immigration officer in the interior of the United States to the maximum extent permitted by law.

(a) In furtherance of this policy, the Secretary shall immediately take appropriate action to engage with the Governors of the States, as well as local officials, for the purpose of preparing to enter into agreements under section 287(g) of the INA (8 U.S.C. 1357(g)).

(b) To the extent permitted by law and with the consent of State or local officials, as appropriate, the Secretary shall take appropriate action, through agreements under section 287(g) of the INA, or otherwise, to authorize State and local law enforcement officials, as the Secretary determines are qualified and appropriate, to perform the functions of immigration officers in relation to the investigation, apprehension, or detention of aliens in the United States under the direction and the supervision of the Secretary. Such authorization shall be in addition to, rather than in place of, Federal performance of these duties.

(c) To the extent permitted by law, the Secretary may structure each agreement under section 287(g) of the INA in a manner that provides the most effective model for enforcing Federal immigration laws for that jurisdiction.

Sec. 9. Sanctuary Jurisdictions. It is the policy of the executive branch to ensure, to the fullest extent of the law, that a State, or a political subdivision of a State, shall comply with 8 U.S.C. 1373.

(a) In furtherance of this policy, the Attorney General and the Secretary, in their discretion and to the extent consistent with law, shall ensure that jurisdictions that willfully refuse to comply with 8 U.S.C. 1373 (sanctuary jurisdictions) are not eligible to receive Federal grants, except as deemed necessary for law enforcement purposes by the Attorney General or the Secretary. The Secretary has the authority to designate, in his discretion and to the extent consistent with law, a jurisdiction as a sanctuary jurisdiction. The Attorney General shall take appropriate enforcement action against any entity that violates 8 U.S.C. 1373, or which has in effect a statute, policy, or practice that prevents or hinders the enforcement of Federal law.

(b) To better inform the public regarding the public safety threats associated with sanctuary jurisdictions, the Secretary shall utilize the Declined Detainer Outcome Report or its equivalent and, on a weekly basis, make public a comprehensive list of criminal actions committed by aliens and any jurisdiction that ignored or otherwise failed to honor any detainers with respect to such aliens.

(c) The Director of the Office of Management and Budget is directed to obtain and provide relevant and responsive information on all Federal grant money that currently is received by any sanctuary jurisdiction.

Sec. 10. Review of Previous Immigration Actions and Policies.

(a) The Secretary shall immediately take all appropriate action to terminate the Priority Enforcement Program (PEP) described in the memorandum issued

by the Secretary on November 20, 2014, and to reinstitute the immigration program known as "Secure Communities" referenced in that memorandum.
(b) The Secretary shall review agency regulations, policies, and procedures for consistency with this order and, if required, publish for notice and comment proposed regulations rescinding or revising any regulations inconsistent with this order and shall consider whether to withdraw or modify any inconsistent policies and procedures, as appropriate and consistent with the law.
(c) To protect our communities and better facilitate the identification, detention, and removal of criminal aliens within constitutional and statutory parameters, the Secretary shall consolidate and revise any applicable forms to more effectively communicate with recipient law enforcement agencies.

Sec. 11. Department of Justice Prosecutions of Immigration Violators. The Attorney General and the Secretary shall work together to develop and implement a program that ensures that adequate resources are devoted to the prosecution of criminal immigration offenses in the United States, and to develop cooperative strategies to reduce violent crime and the reach of transnational criminal organizations into the United States.

Sec. 12. Recalcitrant Countries. The Secretary of Homeland Security and the Secretary of State shall cooperate to effectively implement the sanctions provided by section 243(d) of the INA (8 U.S.C. 1253(d)), as appropriate. The Secretary of State shall, to the maximum extent permitted by law, ensure that diplomatic efforts and negotiations with foreign states include as a condition precedent the acceptance by those foreign states of their nationals who are subject to removal from the United States.

Sec. 13. Office for Victims of Crimes Committed by Removable Aliens. The Secretary shall direct the Director of US Immigration and Customs Enforcement to take all appropriate and lawful action to establish within US Immigration and Customs Enforcement an office to provide proactive, timely, adequate, and professional services to victims of crimes committed by removable aliens and the family members of such victims. This office shall provide quarterly reports studying the effects of the victimization by criminal aliens present in the United States.

Sec. 14. Privacy Act. Agencies shall, to the extent consistent with applicable law, ensure that their privacy policies exclude persons who are not United States citizens or lawful permanent residents from the protections of the Privacy Act regarding personally identifiable information.

Sec. 15. Reporting. Except as otherwise provided in this order, the Secretary and the Attorney General shall each submit to the President a report on the progress of the directives contained in this order within 90 days of the date of this order and again within 180 days of the date of this order.

Sec. 16. Transparency. To promote the transparency and situational awareness of criminal aliens in the United States, the Secretary and the Attorney General are hereby directed to collect relevant data and provide quarterly reports on the following:

(a) the immigration status of all aliens incarcerated under the supervision of the Federal Bureau of Prisons;

(b) the immigration status of all aliens incarcerated as Federal pretrial detainees under the supervision of the United States Marshals Service; and

(c) the immigration status of all convicted aliens incarcerated in State prisons and local detention centers throughout the United States.

Sec. 17. Personnel Actions. The Office of Personnel Management shall take appropriate and lawful action to facilitate hiring personnel to implement this order.

Sec. 18. General Provisions. (a) Nothing in this order shall be construed to impair or otherwise affect:

(i) the authority granted by law to an executive department or agency, or the head thereof; or

(ii) the functions of the Director of the Office of Management and Budget relating to budgetary, administrative, or legislative proposals.

(b) This order shall be implemented consistent with applicable law and subject to the availability of appropriations.

(c) This order is not intended to, and does not, create any right or benefit, substantive or procedural, enforceable at law or in equity by any party against the United States, its departments, agencies, or entities, its officers, employees, or agents, or any other person.

DONALD J. TRUMP
THE WHITE HOUSE,
January 25, 2017.

Appendix A

On 20 October 2017, during a Mexican Federal Police/Policía Federal traffic stop in Guanajuato in Central Mexico, a wholly new weapon was discovered in the possession of Narcotraficante group Cártel Jalisco Nueva Generación (CJNG). According to a Small War's Journal report by Robert Bunker and John Sullivan, "In the back of the stolen vehicle inside the hatchback/rear cargo area, a 3DR Solo Quadcopter in an open case with an IED ('Papa Bomba') attached to it with a sling rope and a remote RF detonator was seized."*

This represents a significant technological and tactics change by CJNG and a major addition to the ongoing drug trafficking across the U.S.–Mexico border. The IED demonstrates that the cartels have fused multiple technologies to create a remotely operated explosive delivery and detonation system. The 'Papa Bomba' is composed of "a sphere-like mass of explosives tightly taped together with the inclusion of nuts and nails for shrapnel effect."* There have been at least four identified uses of these devises across Mexico since February 2017.

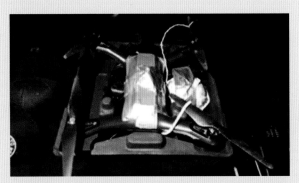

3DR Solo Quadcopter with IED and Remote Detonation Switch (front View)
Source: @On_Point_Skillz, "Maybe @AbraxasSpa might look interesting." Twitter. 20 October 2017, https://twitter.com/On_Point_Skillz/status/921521786768056321

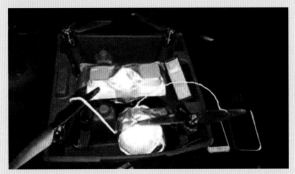

3DR Solo Quadcopter with IED and Remote Detonation Switch (Side View)
Source: "Intercept dron pump!" WRITING. Am . 20 October 2017,
https://www.am.com.mx/2017/10/20/leon/sucesos/interceptan-dron-bomba-385781

"An image analysis of the IED drone recovered in Valtierrilla, Guanajuato suggests that it is a 3DR Solo Quadcopter. Such drones which first appeared in about 2015 can be presently purchased for less than $250.00 USD (less than 5,000 MXN) online. This drone has a flight time of about 20 minutes while carrying a payload of up to 420 g (0.926 pounds). It can achieve a top speed of 55 mph (89 km/h) with a range of about .5 miles (.8 km)."

"The above images of the recovered drone suggest that it is in operational condition. The IED ('Papa Bomba') payload is secured to the drone by means of a white rope slung underneath it. No evidence of metal fragmentation components can be seen on the surface of the IED, however, they may have been formed into an outer shell of the IED with additional binding and taping layers built up over them."*

Mexico is on track in 2017 to have its deadliest year ever with over 2,500 homicides in September and over 21,200 homicides in the first 9 months of 2017.

---

* All quotes and references in this appendix are taken from Bunker, R., and Sullivan, J. (23 Oct 2017), Mexican Cartel Tactical Note #35, Small Wars Journal, available at: http://small-warsjournal.com/jrnl/art/mexican-cartel-tactical-note-35

Appendix B

On September 5, 2017, Attorney General Sessions declared the Obama administration's Deferred Action for Childhood Arrivals Program (DACA) as "an unconstitutional exercise of authority" and the Trump administration's plan to revoke it. Sessions stated, "I'm here today to announce that the program known as DACA that was effectuated under the Obama administration is being rescinded."

It is not known, however, whether President Trump is actually planning on revoking DACA, at least anytime soon. Later on the same day, the President tweeted that "Congress now has 6 months to legalize DACA (something the Obama administration was unable to do). If they can't, I will revisit this issue." In 2010 all Republicans voted against the DREAM Act. Although no one can know the future, it seems that Trump may fulfill a campaign promise to end DACA in six months, while giving Congress the opportunity to "fix" it before that happens, in 2018.

The full text of AG Sessions' remarks:

Attorney General Sessions Delivers Remarks on DACA

Washington, DC
Tuesday, September 5, 2017
Remarks as prepared for delivery

Good morning. I am here today to announce that the program known as DACA that was effectuated under the Obama Administration is being rescinded.

The DACA program was implemented in 2012 and essentially provided a legal status for recipients for a renewable two-year term, work authorization and other benefits, including participation in the social security program, to 800,000 mostly-adult illegal aliens.

This policy was implemented unilaterally to great controversy and legal concern after Congress rejected legislative proposals to extend similar benefits on numerous occasions to this same group of illegal aliens.

In other words, the executive branch, through DACA, deliberately sought to achieve what the legislative branch specifically refused to authorize on multiple occasions. Such an open-ended circumvention of immigration laws was an unconstitutional exercise of authority by the Executive Branch.

The effect of this unilateral executive amnesty, among other things, contributed to a surge of unaccompanied minors on the southern border that yielded terrible humanitarian consequences. It also denied jobs to hundreds of thousands of Americans by allowing those same jobs to go to illegal aliens.

We inherited from our Founders—and have advanced—an unsurpassed legal heritage, which is the foundation of our freedom, safety, and prosperity.

As the Attorney General, it is my duty to ensure that the laws of the United States are enforced and that the Constitutional order is upheld.

No greater good can be done for the overall health and well-being of our Republic, than preserving and strengthening the impartial rule of law. Societies where the rule of law is treasured are societies that tend to flourish and succeed.

Societies where the rule of law is subject to political whims and personal biases tend to become societies afflicted by corruption, poverty, and human suffering.

To have a lawful system of immigration that serves the national interest, we cannot admit everyone who would like to come here. That is an open border policy and the American people have rightly rejected it.

Therefore, the nation must set and enforce a limit on how many immigrants we admit each year and that means all can not be accepted.

This does not mean they are bad people or that our nation disrespects or demeans them in any way. It means we are properly enforcing our laws as Congress has passed them.

It is with these principles and duties in mind, and in light of imminent litigation, that we reviewed the Obama Administration's DACA policy.

Our collective wisdom is that the policy is vulnerable to the same legal and constitutional challenges that the courts recognized with respect to the DAPA program, which was enjoined on a nationwide basis in a decision affirmed by the Fifth Circuit.

The Fifth Circuit specifically concluded that DACA had not been implemented in a fashion that allowed sufficient discretion, and that DAPA was "foreclosed by Congress's careful plan."

In other words, it was inconsistent with the Constitution's separation of powers. That decision was affirmed by the Supreme Court by an equally divided vote.

If we were to keep the Obama Administration's executive amnesty policy, the likeliest outcome is that it would be enjoined just as was DAPA. The Department of Justice has advised the President and the Department of Homeland Security that DHS should begin an orderly, lawful wind down, including the cancellation of the memo that authorized this program.

Acting Secretary Duke has chosen, appropriately, to initiate a wind down process. This will enable DHS to conduct an orderly change and fulfill the desire of this administration to create a time period for Congress to act—should it so choose. We firmly believe this is the responsible path.

Simply put, if we are to further our goal of strengthening the constitutional order and the rule of law in America, the Department of Justice cannot defend this type of overreach.

George Washington University Law School Professor Jonathan Turley in testimony before the House Judiciary Committee was clear about the enormous constitutional infirmities raised by these policies.

He said: "In ordering this blanket exception, President Obama was nullifying part of a law that he simply disagreed with…. If a president can claim sweeping discretion to suspend key federal laws, the entire legislative process becomes little more than a pretense.... The circumvention of the legislative process not only undermines the authority of this branch but destabilizes the tripartite system as a whole."

Ending the previous Administration's disrespect for the legislative process is an important first step. All immigration policies should serve the interests of the people of the United States—lawful immigrant and native born alike.

Congress should carefully and thoughtfully pursue the types of reforms that are right for the American people. Our nation is comprised of good and decent people who want their government's leaders to fulfill their promises and advance an immigration policy that serves the national interest.

We are a people of compassion and we are a people of law. But there is nothing compassionate about the failure to enforce immigration laws.

Enforcing the law saves lives, protects communities and taxpayers, and prevents human suffering. Failure to enforce the laws in the past has put our nation at risk of crime, violence and even terrorism.

The compassionate thing is to end the lawlessness, enforce our laws, and, if Congress chooses to make changes to those laws, to do so through the process set forth by our Founders in a way that advances the interest of the nation.

That is what the President has promised to do and has delivered to the American people.

Under President Trump's leadership, this administration has made great progress in the last few months toward establishing a lawful and constitutional immigration system. This makes us safer and more secure.

It will further economically the lives of millions who are struggling. And it will enable our country to more effectively teach new immigrants about our system of government and assimilate them to the cultural understandings that support it.

The substantial progress in reducing illegal immigration at our border seen in recent months is almost entirely the product of the leadership of President Trump and his inspired federal immigration officers. But the problem is not solved. And without more action, we could see illegality rise again rather than be eliminated.

As a candidate, and now in office, President Trump has offered specific ideas and legislative solutions that will protect American workers, increase wages and salaries, defend our national security, ensure the public safety, and increase the general well-being of the American people.

He has worked closely with many members of Congress, including in the introduction of the RAISE Act, which would produce enormous benefits for our country. This is how our democratic process works.

There are many powerful interest groups in this country and every one of them has a constitutional right to advocate their views and represent whomever they choose.

But the Department of Justice does not represent any narrow interest or any subset of the American people. We represent all of the American people and protect the integrity of our Constitution. That is our charge.

We at Department of Justice are proud and honored to work to advance this vision for America and to do our best each day to ensure the safety and security of the American people.

Thank you.

Chapter 11

The US–Canadian Border

"Our ties are deep and long-standing. We are dependent on each other. And no matter what the issue of the day, whether it be softwood lumber, whether it be a war in Iraq, we need to continue to work together."

—Paul Cellucci[1]

Key Words and Concepts

Border Enforcement Security Taskforces
Canadian Border Security Agency
Critical Infrastructure Protection
Integrated Border Enforcement Teams
International Boundary Commission

North American Aerospace Defense
   Command
Northwest Passage
Royal Canadian Mounted Police
ShipRider pilot program

Introduction

Canada and the United States share the longest border between two countries in the world. It is almost entirely unguarded. It is also one of the few borders where houses, businesses, and even airports are divided by the international border. Since Canada became a country independent of Great Britain the relationship between Canada and the United States has been (mostly) amicable, with an occasional political disagreement. Since 1940 the two countries have shared military defense efforts and in 1957 jointly established the North American Air Defense Command (NORAD) to establish a common defense against the Soviet nuclear threat of the Cold War.

Canada and the United States are the world's largest trading partners. Although there have been trading disputes between the countries, including disputes over the environment, oil exports and imports, firearm smuggling, and illegal immigration, trade between the countries has expanded over the past two hundred years, culminating with the North American Free Trade Agreement (NAFTA) in 1994.

Politically, the two countries have been closely aligned over most issues. They diverged over some American policies, including the Vietnam War, the isolation of Cuba, the 2003 invasion of Iraq, and the way the United States has prosecuted

The US-Canada Border

the War on Terror. Currently, the two countries disagree over the status of the Northwest Passage.

The cultural ties between the countries are very close. Both countries share a common language except for French-speaking Quebec. Yet the cooperation between the countries and their shared cultural heritage has led to efforts to establish joint border security inspection agencies, placement of shared agricultural and food inspectors in each other's countries, joint cooperation, and sharing of intelligence and law enforcement efforts during investigations.

Economically, the two countries are tied closely together through trade and shared energy resources. In 1930 and 1971 the two countries almost ended their economic relationships but recovered from the politically related disputes and became even closer after each event.

With a shared border of 5,525 miles (8,891 km), it would be expected that the two countries would either have a close and cooperative approach to common concerns and shared economic development, or would have developed a significant animosity and moved to erect massive security structures. As the United States moves to expand and enhance the security infrastructure along its border with Mexico, it is instructive to examine the much more open borders with its neighbor to the north for contradictory approaches to border security.

Left: The 49th parallel north, as a border between Canada and the US, Wikicommons, 2012.

Right: The 45th parallel north, defining part of the border between
Canada and the US, Wikicommons, 2012.

Early Canadian–US Relations

Canada–US Border Evolves

Today's border between Canada and the United States is the result of a series of disputes and minor military conflicts that occurred over a span of 120 years. The Treaty of Paris established the original boundary between the former British colonies along the Atlantic seaboard and the British Canadian provinces in 1783. The 45th parallel was established as the boundary between Quebec and New York State. The initial border included the St. Lawrence River and the Great Lakes as part of the combined dividing line. In 1794 the Jay Treaty established the International Boundary Commission to survey and map the border between the two countries.

British Canada and the United States continued their separate westward expansions to the Pacific Ocean over several years. Addressing the border between the countries as they moved westward was essential to maintaining peace between the former adversaries. Initially the westward boundary was established as the 49th parallel west from the Northwest Angle at Lake of the Woods in Minnesota to the Rocky Mountains by the Convention of 1818. This established a smooth line between the countries that would become the basis for determining the outcome of future disputes over the Oregon territories.

One of the biggest territorial mishaps made by the United States was the construction of what would become known as Fort Blunder. Officially known today as Fort Montgomery, the military installation was constructed in 1816 based on the original survey line determined by the International Boundary Commission following the signing of the Jay Treaty. Subsequent improvements in determining longitude and latitude determined that the original border markings were three-quarters of a mile too far to the north. The US military post had been built in Canada! The Webster-Ashburton Treaty of 1842 resolved this issue, along with several other disputes related to the

Fort Montgomery in Rouse's Point, NY. This view is from a fishing access parking lot on the north side of the Rouse's Point Bridge in Vermont. Mfwllls. Wikicommons, 2011.

boundary between British territories and Maine. Webster-Ashburton, in addition to allowing the United States to retain the additional three-quarters of a mile inside Canada that resulted from the earlier surveying errors, also clarified the boundary between Minnesota and Ontario and Lake Superior.

The next major boundary issue came in 1844. The Lewis and Clark expedition to explore and map the Louisiana Purchase had claimed lands along the Columbia River to the Pacific Ocean that Great Britain considered to be theirs. Russia had claimed the Alaska region south to the latitude of 54 degrees 40 minutes north along the Pacific Coast. Resolving this dispute over the Oregon territories, an agreement was reached between Great Britain and the United States to simply extend the current border along the 49th parallel westward from the Rocky Mountains to the Pacific coast. The Oregon Treaty of 1846 formalized this boundary and the Northwest Boundary Survey of 1857–61 set the land boundaries between the countries. The Oregon Treaty did not determine which of the islands in Puget Sound fell on which side of the border, leading to a long-running dispute that would not be resolved until 1872 over control of the San Juan Islands.

The remaining border between Canada and the United States runs north, along the state of Alaska. This

Monument Check — RCMP and Border Patrol — Sweetgrass, Montana — Havre Sector — 1960s.
© US Border Patrol Museum. Used with permission.

territory (twice as large as Texas) was acquired from Russia in March 1867 for $7.2 million, or about 2 cents per acre. At the time of the purchase there were only 23 Russian trading posts and two towns (New Archangel, now named Sitka, and St. Paul). The formal transfer from Russia to the United States took place on October 18, 1867, and is still celebrated as Alaska Day in the state.[2] Russia and the British Empire had an ongoing dispute over the location of the southern and eastern borders of their North American territories. This dispute transferred to the United States upon purchase of the Alaska territory. It was not until 1903 that, through arbitration, the current border was established when the only British member on the six-person committee sided with the three American members over where to locate the border. Canadian judges refused to sign the agreement, leading to widespread anti-British emotions across Canada, leading to the country separating from Great Britain and becoming a self-governing entity at the end of the First World War.[3]

The International Boundary Commission (IBC) became a permanent organization responsible for surveying and mapping the boundary, maintaining boundary monuments (and buoys where applicable), as well as keeping the boundary clear of brush and vegetation for 10 feet (about 3 meters) on each side of the line. The international boundary between Canada and the United States measures 5,525 miles (8,891 km), from the St. Croix River on the Atlantic Ocean to the Strait of Juan de Fuca on the Pacific and from Dixon Entrance on the Pacific to the Arctic Ocean. The border between the countries traverses four of the Great Lakes. Westward from Lake of the Woods in Ontario to the Pacific Ocean, the border is the world's longest, continuous straight international boundary. Canada's only land border is with the United States.[4]

International Boundary Commission

The International Boundary Commission (IBC) has cooperatively maintained the common border between Canada and the United States for more than 100 years. "The boundary defines the limits of national sovereignty, state and provincial rights, local government jurisdiction, and parcels of private land. It allows airspace and mineral rights to be precisely defined. Without the boundary, it would be difficult for adjacent communities to administer everything from law enforcement to school tax assessment to speed limits."[5] The IBC was created by treaty on June 4, 1908, when the United Kingdom (representing Canada) and the United States agreed to each appoint a commissioner to address the marking and maintaining of the boundary. Formalized by treaty in 1925, the IBC was assigned the responsibility to inspect, repair, and rebuild boundary markers and monuments, to keep the terrain on either side of the boundary clear to maintain sight lines, and to provide annual reports to their respective governments. Providing crab fishers in Boundary Bay the information to know which country's laws to abide by and informing moose hunters in Maine when they have entered another country, the boundary is an effective and clear demarcation between two countries.[6]

International Boundary Commission/
Commission de la frontier international

The Commission

The Commission is made up of two commissioners, one appointed in the United States and one in Canada, each chief of his own staff, equipment, and budget. The US Commissioner is appointed by the president and reports to the Secretary of State. The Canadian Commissioner is appointed by Order-in-Council, and reports to the Minister for Foreign Affairs. For administrative purposes, the Canadian Section of the Boundary Commission is located within the Department of Natural Resources of Canada as a section of the Surveyor General Branch.

The two current Commissioners for the United States and Canada are Kyle Hipsley (Acting) and Peter Sullivan. Each country's section operates proprietary offices and field crews …

Officially, the Commission's work is described as maintaining the boundary in an effective state of demarcation. This is done by inspecting it regularly; repairing, relocating, or rebuilding damaged monuments or buoys; keeping the vista cleared, and erecting new boundary markers at such locations as new road crossings.

The Commission also regulates, under the provisions of the 1960 International Boundary Commission Act, all construction within 3 meters, or 10 feet, of the boundary and is responsible for defining the boundary location in any legal situation involving the border. The commissioners report annually on the work done during the year and provide to both governments the latest data on the boundary monuments.

All monuments along the boundary are located so that they tie in with the survey networks of both the United States and Canada through 1,000 survey control stations established for this purpose near the border. The position of any monument may be redetermined at any time by the survey crews of the Commission, which are called on constantly to perform assorted survey duties along the boundary. These duties include improving survey connections to the control stations and establishing new monuments.[7]

Normally the IBC is a very sedate and unobtrusive body. However, in 2007 they determined that Herbert (aka Henry) and Shirley-Ann Leu of Blaine, Washington, built a four-foot-high and 85-foot-long concrete wall 3 feet inside the 10 feet clear site line on the US side of the boundary vista. The Leus said they were protecting their property rights. In July 2007, the Bush administration fired US IBC Commissioner Dennis Schornack because he sided with the IBC and Canada over the issue.[8] The Leus' wall continued to be a problem, the issue was tied up in court for nearly two years. Finally, in January 2009 the Leus signed an agreement in federal district court in Seattle that allows them to keep their wall so long as they do not plant or build anything additional taller than 30 inches within ten feet of the international boundary.[9]

Canada Today

Today, comprising ten North American provinces and three territories, Canada measures 9,984,670 square kilometers, about 160,000 square kilometers larger than the United States. Canada has only one-tenth the population of the United States at 35,568,211, making it one of the least densely populated countries in the world.[10] The two official languages consist of French and English. Eighty-one percent of the Canadian population lives in urbanized areas. About 90 percent of the entire Canadian population lives within 100 miles of the US border. The borders of Canada include the North Atlantic, North Pacific, and Arctic Oceans and the International Boundary with the United States of America. Canada borders only one country and is the largest country in the world to do so.

Facts about the US–Canada Border[11]

Here are a few statistics about the Canada–US border, the longest nonmilitarized border in the world.

8,891: Kilometers the border stretches across land and water.

2,477: Kilometers of border shared with Alaska alone.

1783: Year the Treaty of Paris was signed. Its description of the border running from the Atlantic Ocean to the Prairies between British North America and the American states would become the basis for today's border.

$576 billion: Approximate worth of goods crossing the border annually (2009 numbers).

Over $1 million: Amount of trade between Canada and the United States every minute (2009 numbers).

10 to 20: Minutes people typically wait at land border crossings.

45 and 49: The border follows the 49th parallel from the Strait of Juan de Fuca on the West Coast to Lake of the Woods in Ontario/Minnesota and the 45th parallel between New England and Quebec.

24.2 million: Number of Canadians who made a same-day car trip to the United States in 2007.

11.2 million: Number of Americans who made a same-day car trip to Canada.

10.6 million: Number of Canadians who took overnight car trips to the United States.

13.5 million: Number of trucks crossing the border each year.

90: Percent of Canadians who live within 160 kilometers (100 miles) of the US border.

Fewer than 1 percent: Proportion of travelers who cross the border and are considered high risk.

119: Land-border crossings managed by Canada Border Services Agency.

61: Land-border crossings operating 24/7.

6,400: The number of uniformed border services officers working at about 1,200 points across Canada in 2007–8.

65 per cent: Percentage of trucks arriving in Canada daily by passing through southwestern Ontario border crossings.

6 million: The number of passenger vehicles crossing annually at the Ambassador Bridge in Windsor, Ont., the busiest land crossing.

Current Boundary Disputes

There are five ongoing disputes between the United States and Canada over border issues. The disputes may or may not be resolved before this book goes to print, however it is instructive to note that after 110 years of established borders between the two countries, there are still questions to be resolved about what is and is not the actual, final border. These are:

- Machias Seal Island 44° 30′ 10″ N 67° 06′ 10″ W and North Rock 44.53795° N 67.08805° W (Maine/New Brunswick), also known as the "Grey Zone," is on the United States' side of the boundary but administered by Canada.
- Strait of Juan de Fuca 48° 17′ 58″ N 124° 02′ 58″ W (Washington/British Columbia). The middle-water line is the boundary, but the governments of both Canada and British Columbia disagree and support two differing boundary definitions that would extend the line into the Pacific Ocean to provide a more definite Exclusive Economic Zone (EEZ) boundary.
- Dixon Entrance 54° 22′ N 132° 20′ W (Alaska/British Columbia) is wholly administered by Canada as part of its territorial waters, but the United States supports a middle-water line boundary, thereby providing the United States more maritime waters. Canada claims that a 1903 treaty demarcation is the international maritime boundary, while the United States holds that the maritime boundary is an equidistant line between the islands that form the Dixon Entrance, extending as far east as the middle-water line with Hecate Strait to the south and Clarence Strait to the north.
- Yukon-Alaska dispute, Beaufort Sea 72° 01′ 40″ N 137° 02′ 30″ W (Alaska/Yukon). Canada supports an extension into the sea of the land boundary between Yukon and Alaska. The United States does not, but instead supports an extended sea boundary into the Canadian portion of the Beaufort Sea. Such a demarcation means that a minor portion of Northwest Territories EEZ in the polar region is claimed by Alaska, because the EEZ boundary between Northwest Territories and Yukon follows a straight north-south line into the sea. US claims would create a triangular-shaped EEZ for Yukon/Canada.
- Northwest Passage; Canada claims the passage as part of its "internal waters" belonging to Canada, while the United States regards it as an "international strait" (a strait accommodating open international traffic).[12]

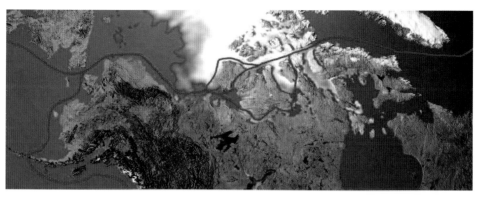

Proposed Northwest Passage shipping routes, Wikimedia commons, 2008.

The most important of these disputes is the issue of the Northwest Passage. With warming arctic temperatures, the sea ice melts earlier and opens a navigable passage from the Atlantic to the Pacific around the top of North America. Additionally, there is intense international interest in mining the natural resources of this newly opened ocean and the associated seabed. The problem is that Canada sees it as part of their internal territory and as an exclusive economic zone while other countries dispute that claim. According to the Canadian Parliament,

> Other countries, including the United States, Russia, Denmark, Japan, and Norway, as well as the European Union, have expressed increasing interest in the region and differing claims in relation to international law. In particular, many observers believe that the Northwest Passage, the shipping route through Canada's Arctic waters, will be open to increased shipping activity in the coming decades as the ice melts. Canada's assertion that the Northwest Passage represents internal (territorial) waters has been challenged by other countries, including the United States, which argue that these waters constitute an international strait (international waters). Interest in the region's economic potential has resulted in discussions of increased resource exploration and disputed sub-surface resources, as well as concerns over environmental degradation, control and regulation of shipping activities, and protection of northern inhabitants. It is important to note that the Arctic is a vast and remote territory that presents many difficulties in terms of surveillance, regulation, and infrastructure development.[13]

Canada–US Border Security Agencies

Securing the northern border is the responsibility of the various Department of Homeland Security (DHS) components in collaboration with other federal, state, local, tribal, and Canadian law enforcement agencies. Within DHS, US Customs and

Border Protection, including the US Border Patrol, is the frontline agency responsible for interdiction of persons and contraband crossing the border illegally. US Immigration and Customs Enforcement (ICE) is responsible for investigating the source of cross-border crimes and dismantling illegal operations. Other federal, state, local, tribal, and Canadian law enforcement agencies also have responsibilities to detect, interdict, and investigate different types of illegal activity within certain geographic boundaries. The US Department of Agriculture, and its subordinate agency the US Forest Service is responsible for protecting natural resources along about 400 miles of contiguous border area. The Department of Justice, and its subordinate agency the Drug Enforcement Administration (DEA) conduct investigations of drug trafficking organizations including those smuggling drugs across the International Boundary or through ports of entry.[14]

Canadian Border Security Agency

On the Canadian side of the border, security responsibility lies with Canadian Border Security Agency (CBSA) and the Royal Canadian Mounted Police (RCMP). The CBSA's mandate is to ensure the free flow of persons and goods across Canada's borders all while ensuring Canada's national security and public safety priorities. They also enforce Canada's Immigration and Refugee Protection Act, the Customs Act, and more than ninety other laws and acts of Parliament. CBSA carries out many of the same functions as CBP and ICE in the United States.

For the 2012 calendar year, CBSA seized 153 non-restricted firearms, 166 restricted firearms, 228 prohibited firearms, and 24,243 other weapons. Canada has a drug

US Border Patrol Horse Patrol near Glacier National Park — Whitefish Area — Havre Sector. 1957.
© US Border Patrol Museum. Used with permission.

problem proportionate to its population. During the same period, CBSA made 11,017 drug seizures with a total street value more than $305 million (Canadian dollars). Seized drugs included, in order of value from highest to lowest, cocaine, ketamine, heroin, opium, marijuana, Catha Edulis (Khat), steroids, other controlled drugs, crack cocaine, and GHB. Tobacco is also an issue since both the United States and Canada have different tax structures on the legal sale of cigarettes and other tobacco products. In 2012 the CBSA seized 2,375 tobacco shipments with a value more than $3 million (Canadian dollars). They also made 93 child pornography seizures and more than 1,000 currency seizures.[15]

As with CBP and ICE in the United States, the CBSA has the responsibility to deny people entry into Canada, and remove those who have entered or remain in the country illegally. In 2012 CBSA removed 18,762 persons, denied entry to nearly 51,000 persons, and recovered 12 missing children.[16]

CBSA also facilitates the legal cross-border movement of people, aircraft, ships, and vehicles to ensure the efficient processing of visitors, returning citizens, and commercial traffic. In 2012 they processed more than 100 million travelers through ports of entry, more than 37 million cars, trucks, and buses, 359,263 aircraft, and 153,582 vessels. They also landed 257,288 permanent residents, issued more than 12,000 temporary resident permits, issued more than 420,000 work permits, and processed more than 20,000 refugee claims.[17]

Royal Canadian Mounted Police

Unlike the United States, Canada has a single national police force. The Royal Canadian Mounted Police (RCMP) is one of the most professional, dedicated, law enforcement agencies in the world. Their mission is to preserve the peace, uphold the law, and provide quality service in partnership with Canadian communities. The RCMP is a world-renowned organization whose "scope of operations includes organized crime, terrorism, illicit drugs, economic crimes, and offences that threaten the integrity of Canada's national borders. The RCMP also protects VIPs, with jurisdiction in eight provinces and three territories."[18]

RCMP has been securing Canada's border for more than 135 years. One of their earliest mandates was to patrol the frontier and to suppress the whiskey trade. American traders were entering Canada to sell whiskey to natives, which is a crime in Canada. During the Alaska gold rush the RCMP operated customs checkpoints for people and goods crossing the Alaska-Canada border on their way overland to the Klondike.[19]

Today, as part of the Integrated Border Enforcement Team (IBET), the RCMP works alongside the US Border Patrol, ICE, the US Coast Guard, and the CBSA to secure Canada's borders between ports of entry. There are 24 IBET units, joint operations agencies that combine investigators from each of the five agencies to work as a single law enforcement and investigative unit, while respecting the laws and jurisdiction of each nation. The RCMP and CBSA are essential to ensuring the national security of Canada, as the US Border Patrol, ICE, and USCG are to US national security.[20]

The RCMP recognizes that the "greatest threat to Canada's national security is the threat of terrorist criminal activity in Canada and abroad."[21] RCMP works to prevent, detect, deny, and respond to terrorist criminal activity.

Stopping Terrorists

A component of the RCMP mission is to protect Canada from terrorism and terrorists. Their efforts in this arena were aptly demonstrated in Project Smooth, when on April 22, 2013, Chiheb Esseghaier and Raed Jaser were arrested for planning to derail a passenger train in the Greater Toronto Area. Canada's VIA Rail system operates passenger trains across the country and connects with AMTRAK passenger trains in the United States.[22] The surveillance operations leading to the arrests of Esseghaier and Jaser included support and information provided by the FBI. The same day, Ahmed Abassi was arrested in connection with the incident while he was in New York's John F. Kennedy Airport. Abassi had been attending school in Canada but had moved to the United States in March 2013.[23]

US–Canada Law Enforcement Cooperation

The United States and Canada enjoy a collaborative law enforcement relationship. Through joint threat assessment, investigations, operations, and support for prosecutions, consistent with each country's domestic laws, both countries are more secure. There are three ongoing partnerships that are key to facilitating cross-border law enforcement collaboration:

- ShipRider pilot program[24] — Officially known as Integrated Cross-border Maritime Law Enforcement Operations (ICMLEO), cross-designated officers perform joint patrols in the maritime areas between our countries, removing the maritime border as an impediment to law enforcement operations. The US Coast Guard (USCG) and the Royal Canadian Mounted Police (RCMP) are the primary ShipRider participants.
- Integrated Border Enforcement Teams (IBETs)[25] — IBETs enhance border in-tegrity and security between designated ports of entry along the US-Canada border by identifying, investigating, and interdicting persons, organizations, and goods that threaten the national security of one or both countries or that are involved in organized criminal activity. The five core IBET agencies are: RCMP; the Canada Border Services Agency (CBSA); US Customs and Border Protection (CBP); US Immigration and Customs Enforcement (ICE); and the USCG.
- Border Enforcement Security Taskforces (BESTs)[26] — BESTs are multiagency teams that identify, investigate, disrupt, and dismantle criminal organizations posing significant threats to border security. BESTs, which are ICE-led, utilize co-located and cross-designated investigative assets of federal, state/provincial,

local, and tribal law enforcement partners on both sides of the border to investigate transnational crime.

In February 2011 President Obama and Prime Minister Harper declared a shared vision for perimeter security and economic competitiveness, commonly referred to as the Beyond the Border agreement. Recognizing that it is the result of shared common values, deep links between the citizens of both countries, and deeply rooted ties that make the Canada–US economic and military partnerships strong, the agreement establishes that both countries are going to pursue a perimeter approach to security, working jointly within, at, and away from the borders to enhance security while improving the legitimate flow of people, goods, and services. Building on the existing efforts of many different partnerships at the local, provincial, state, and federal level, the two leaders recognized that,

> Cooperation across air, land, and maritime domains, as well as in space and cyberspace, our enduring bi-national defense relationship, and military support for civilian authorities engaged in disaster response efforts and critical infrastructure protection, have all contributed significantly to the security of our populations.... We intend to work together to engage with all levels of government and with communities, nongovernmental organizations, and the private sector, as well as with our citizens, on innovative approaches to security and competitiveness.[27]

Reading through the remainder of President Obama's and Prime Minister Harper's shared vision, it is apparent that the intent is to move toward a common North American Union not all that different from the European Union when it comes to open interior borders between the countries.[28]

In addition to identifying and addressing key threats early, implementing a comprehensive cross-border approach to strengthening critical infrastructure and cyber-security, the two countries plan on building the next generation of integrated cross-border law enforcement operations. It is from this agreement that the Integrated Border Enforcement Teams (IBETs) and the Border Enforcement Security Taskforces (BESTs) evolved. The process of developing and implementing these joint law enforcement efforts will continue to evolve over a long time as the two countries move toward establishment of what will ultimately become a North American Union.

Canadian Border Services Agency News Release: Canada and the United States Announce Phase I Pilot Project to Enhance Border Security at Land Ports of Entry

Ottawa, Ontario, September 28, 2012—The Canada Border Services Agency (CBSA) and the Department of Homeland Security (DHS) announced today that, effective September 30, 2012, both agencies will begin the Phase I pilot of the Entry/Exit initiative as outlined in the Beyond the Border Action Plan.

The Phase I pilot project will allow Canada and the United States to test the IT capacity to exchange and reconcile biographic information on the entry of travelers that are not Canadian citizens or US citizens, such that a record of entry into one country could be considered as a record of exit from the other.

Under the pilot project, the CBSA and DHS will exchange data currently collected on third-country nationals (those who are neither citizens of Canada nor of the United States), permanent residents of Canada, and lawful permanent residents of the United States at the following four ports of entry:

- Pacific Highway, Surrey, British Columbia/Pacific Highway, Blaine, Washington;
- Douglas (Peace Arch), Surrey, British Columbia/Peace Arch, Blaine, Washington;
- Queenston-Lewiston Bridge, Niagara-on-the Lake, Ontario/Lewiston-Queenston Bridge, Lewiston, New York; and
- Niagara Falls Rainbow Bridge, Niagara Falls, Ontario/Rainbow Bridge, Niagara Falls, New York.

Beginning October 15, 2012, routine biographic information, collected between September 30, 2012, and January 31, 2013, will be exchanged by both countries. This exchange means that record of entry into one country becomes a record of exit from the other country. This pilot program will not share information regarding Canadian or US citizens. It will not affect regular operations.

"As outlined in the Beyond the Border Action Plan, our governments are committed to maintaining the integrity of our shared border," said Vic Toews, Minister of Public Safety. "This sharing of entry and exit information will play a key part in bolstering border security."

"The sharing of entry and exit information will facilitate the legitimate flow of traffic between the United States and Canada while strengthening border security," said US Customs and Border Protection Deputy Commissioner, David V. Aguilar. "This pilot is an important step forward in the shared perimeter vision."

A coordinated entry/exit system will help the United States and Canada identify persons who potentially overstay their lawful period of admission; track the departure of persons subject to removal orders; and verify that residency requirements are being met by applicants for continued eligibility in immigration programs. The process of collecting and sharing personal information will be done in accordance with each country's privacy laws and policies....

Currently collected data elements being shared are: first name, last name, middle name, date of birth, nationality, gender, document type, document number, work location code/US port of entry codes, date of entry, time of entry, and document country of issuance. In addition to what Canada and the United States currently collect on travelers at ports of entry, the date and time of entry as well as the port through which the traveler entered will also be collected and exchanged.

On February 4, 2011, Prime Minister Harper and President Obama released the Beyond the Border Action Plan, articulating a shared vision in which our countries work together to address threats at the earliest point possible while facilitating the legitimate movement of people, goods and services across our shared border. The Action Plan, released in December 2011, outlines the specific steps our countries intend to take to achieve the security and economic competitiveness goals outlined in the Beyond the Border Declaration.[29]

Guarding the Kitchen

The US-Canada border is one of the few international borders that pass through homes and businesses. Located between the Canadian and US customs buildings on Quebec Route 132 and New York Water Street is the Halfway House, a tavern that was once known as Taillon's International Hotel. The building was built in 1820 before the border was surveyed. For years it was where John B. Taillon (b. 1842) ran a tavern that was known far and wide. The bar room was partly in Fort Covington, New York, United States, and partly in Dundee, Quebec, Canada, which was probably a boon to business during prohibition.[30] The Haskell Free Library and Opera House also straddles the International Boundary. In Stanstead, Quebec, and Derby Line, Vermont, this 1904 building has a thick black line through the opera house and the library's reading room marking the international boundary.[31] There are also several private houses that straddle the International Boundary in Vermont, Maine, and Quebec.

Security Measures

Residents of both nations who own property adjacent to the border are required to report construction of any physical border crossing on their land to their respective governments. The International Boundary Commission enforces this. Where required, fences or vehicle blockades are used. All persons crossing the border are required to report to the respective customs and immigration agencies in each country. This raises a question that doesn't seem to be addressed in the various rules and regulations regulating border crossing between the United States and Canada. If your house straddles the

US Border Patrol near Bonner's Ferry, Idaho. 1957. © US Border Patrol Museum. Used with permission.

border, do you have to report yourself to US CBP and Canadian CBSA every time you walk from your living room to your kitchen?

Remote areas exist where staffed border crossings are unavailable and there are hidden sensors on roads and scattered in wooded areas near crossing points and on many trails and railways, but there are not enough border personnel on either side to verify and stop coordinated incursions. Drug smugglers routinely haul high quality British Columbian marijuana across the border into Washington, as well as into Idaho and Montana. The terrain and weather make interdiction a near impossibility.

Smuggling

The opening of Chapter 10 includes a photo of a Mexican drug smuggling tunnel under the southern border. As expansive as the border is with Canada, it seems that using tunnels to cross the international boundary would be unnecessary. However, that logic does not apply in the drug smuggling business. Three men from British Columbia were arrested on July 20, 2005, for smuggling drugs into the United States. They had built a 360-foot long tunnel from under a Quonset hut on the Canadian side of the border to the living room of a house in Lynden, Washington. The sophisticated tunnel was reinforced with wooden beams and steel bars. CBSA reported that it was not difficult to determine a tunnel was being constructed, with lumber and construction materials going into the hut and earth being hauled out of it. The tunnel was between 3 and 10 feet deep. Although the tunnel originated in British Columbia, the individuals were arrested in the United States and tried in the United States because no drugs had been smuggled into Canada.[32]

Marijuana is the drug most imported from Canada to the United States. Frequently gangs, rather than Mexican cartels, coordinate the drug trafficking from Canada and back into Canada. In May of 2013, James Postlethwaite of North Vancouver, British Columbia, was convicted in US federal court for drug smuggling. The 60-year-old Postlethwaite received a 12-year sentence for transporting 95 drug loads across the border, including thousands of pounds of British Columbian marijuana (600 pounds at a time) into the United States and cocaine (130 pounds at a time) into Canada. His truck was equipped with a sophisticated secret compartment in the floor of the bed with a separate power system to open and close automated panels. The drugs apparently belonged to the Hell's Angels motorcycle gang.[33]

Drug smuggling goes both ways at the international boundary. Cocaine is the primary drug of concern in Canada and it has traditionally been imported by ship. More recently, there has been a shift in how cocaine is getting into Canada. It is now being trucked across the border through ports of entry. In 2009–13 more than a dozen truck drivers were arrested and prosecuted in the Greater Toronto Area for smuggling drugs.[34]

It is not just drugs that are smuggled. A carton of cigarettes in Canada will cost between $75 and $90 (Canadian dollars). That same carton only costs $2 to manufacture. The result—smuggling cigarettes into Canada is big business. There are now at least 12 cigarette factories on the US side of the Akwesasne Indian Reservation (a branch of the Mohawk Tribe). The tobacco is brought from New York to the island reservation by boat. Cigarettes are made and packaged on the reservation, then smuggled into Canada. Because the tribe has special status in both countries and there are more than 13 different law enforcement agencies on either side of the border with varying, limited levels of jurisdiction, this leads to a prosecutorial nightmare in both the United States and Canada.[35] 'What's the big deal? It's just cigarettes!' Remember from Chapter 1 that smuggling is about circumventing government control of licit or illicit commodities. When a country institutes prohibitive taxes or tariffs on any product to control the sale of that item, people will smuggle to circumvent those restrictions and meet the public demand, while reaping significant profit. More than 253,000 cartons of illegal cigarettes were seized in 2007 around Cornwall, Canada, coming from the Akwesasne Reservation. Forty-two different organizations are involved in the smuggling operations, from small family groups to traditional organized crime. That amount of smuggling accounts for more than $19 million, in one year, in lost tax revenues for Canada. The smuggling is in a single location and that number is based strictly on the cigarettes that were seized!

Firearms are also a problem for CBSA and RMCP. Handguns are illegal in Canada. Bringing a handgun into the country is criminal smuggling, and there is a big business associated with the smuggling of handguns. For example, Hi-Point, an Ohio manufacturer of semi-automatic handguns, is the preferred handgun of gangs in Toronto. A Hi-Point that can be purchased in the United States for $150 sells for $1500 in Canada (where they are illegal).[36] With such a profit margin, the smuggling of handguns into Canada has become a major issue for both US and Canadian law enforcement. As with drugs, guns go both ways across the international boundary. In August 2012 a Canadian soldier was arrested for importing and exporting firearms parts, including silencers, templates to manufacture illegal parts (in Canada), and components to make semi-automatic weapons into fully automatic machine guns. A joint operation occurred between the Ontario Provincial Police and the Bureau of Alcohol, Tobacco, Firearms, and Explosives. Search warrants were executed in several Ontario and Quebec locations, including at the base where the soldier was stationed. This resulted in the seizure of hundreds of firearms and enhancement parts. The soldier now faces charges in both Canada and the United States.[37]

Of course, it is not just the for-profit gun smuggler that has to be concerned with CBSA or RCMP catching them crossing into Canada. Every American crossing into Canada is asked if they have firearms of any kind with them. Bringing a firearm into Canada, even a legal one, must be declared, and a fee paid. In December 2011 two elderly Texans, Danny Cross (age 64) and Hugh Barr (age 70) were arrested by CBSA because they told the border agents they had no weapons in their motor home. Unfortunately for them, a subsequent search turned up five pistols (all loaded) and a shotgun. The two elderly Americans spent five days in jail while their wives raised money to post a $50,000 bail. Ultimately they each paid a $10,000 fine after a court hearing.[38] Cross and Barr are not alone. American travelers carry most guns seized by CBSA at the border—they either do not understand Canadian gun laws or they believe that they will not be prosecuted for failure to report or illegally transport guns. Driving from Texas to Alaska can be a wonderful adventure. People in the United

States may choose to carry guns that are perfectly legal in every state they cross, and in their destination in Alaska. When they enter Canada with those same guns, they have violated the law and it can be quite an expensive experience.

Unique US-Canada Airports

Six airports transect the International Boundary. All six were constructed during the Lend-Lease period prior to the US entry into the Second World War. While attempting to maintain neutrality in the ongoing European war, the United States committed to supply England with ships and aircraft, among other weapons, as part of the Lend-Lease program established between President Franklin Roosevelt and Prime Minister Winston Churchill. Canada, as a member of the British Commonwealth, was already involved in the war in defense of England. To transport American-built aircraft to England, without putting American pilots into combat situations that would force an end to US neutrality, airports were built along the International Boundary that actually transect both countries. Essentially, US-built airplanes would be flown from the factories to the border airports and parked on the US side. Overnight, the aircraft would be towed by vehicle or horse, or pushed across the International Boundary to the Canadian side, where the next day, Canadian pilots would fly them to staging points for transshipment to England. All six of these unique airports were built in western states and provinces and are still in use today:

- Piney Pinecreek Border Airport is located in Manitoba and Minnesota. The northwest/southeast-oriented runway straddles the border, and there are two ramps; one in Canada and one in the US. The Minnesota Department of Transportation and the local government of Piney, Manitoba, jointly own the airport. The same airport is assigned the American identifier 48Y and Canadian identifier JX2.[39]
- International Peace Garden Airport is located in Manitoba and North Dakota, adjacent to the International Peace Garden. The runway is entirely within North Dakota, but a ramp extends across the border to allow aircraft to access Canadian customs. While not jointly owned, it is operated as an international facility for Customs clearance as part of the International Peace Garden.[40]
- Coronach/Scobey Border Station Airport is located in Saskatchewan and Montana. The east-west runway is sited exactly on the border. The airport is jointly owned by the Canadian and US governments and is assigned an American identifier of 8U3 and a Canadian identifier of CKK3.[41]
- Coutts/Ross International Airport is located in Alberta and Montana. Like Coronach/Scobey, the east-west runway is sited exactly on the border. It is owned entirely by the Montana Aeronautics Division. It is assigned US identifier 7S8 and Canadian identifier CEP4.[42]
- Del Bonita/Whetstone International Airport is located in Alberta and Montana, and similarly has an east-west runway sited exactly on the border. It is assigned the American identifier H28 and Canadian identifier CEQ4.

- Avey Field State Airport is located in Washington and British Columbia. The privately owned airfield is mostly in the US, but several hundred feet of the north-south runway extend into Canada and both Canadian and US customs are available. It is assigned US identifier 69S but does not have a Canadian identifier.[43]

These unique airports raise additional questions about border security and the requirement to clear customs and immigration. If a private pilot departs from a US airport and subsequently lands at the Piney Pinecreek Border Airport, the aircraft will land in both the United States and Canada, then taxi back into the United States. Do the pilot and passengers have to clear Canadian customs and immigration for having landed in Canada? Do they also have to clear US customs and immigration because they departed the United States upon landing and then returned to the United States from Canada when they taxied back to the US side of the airport? If you were the pilot, how would you know? The information available for these airports indicates that the US CBP and CBSA only have limited operating hours at the facilities. Pilots are advised to contact the local offices by phone before arrival.

Border Crossing and Privacy

Not everybody who crosses the International Boundary has a quick trip through the customs and immigration inspection. Many people find themselves selected for *enhanced* inspection that may include the seizure and searching of their personal electronic devices, from laptops to cell phones, iPads to digital camera flash drives, and any other electronic data storage devices. Because 8 USC § 1357 and 19 USC §§ 1499, 1581, and 1582, authorize such searches and detention, CBP agents may seize any electronic device, access the data on that device, require the person carrying the device to provide passwords so that the data can be accessed, and copy the data for future analysis. The individual gets a written receipt (Form 6051-D) detailing the items being detained and listing the point of contact at CBP to facilitate the return of their property.[44] It is important to note that there are zero restrictions on the collection, retention, and analysis of this data.

What about private business information; intellectual property; scientific, political, or other research; personal data about the individual or those communicated with; inventions; or other sensitive data? Sorry! There are no privacy rights to this information when you cross into the United States if it is on your electronic device. The same policy applies to information that is protected from disclosure within the United States by physician-client or attorney-client privilege. If your physician or attorney has that information on their electronic device when they enter the United States, it can all be taken, copied, and analyzed by CBP. The information collected by CBP may be made available to other investigative agencies.

Normally the requirement of probable cause and/or the production of a valid search warrant would accompany a similar search by local, state, or federal law enforcement agents before they could collect either the devices or the data. CBP and other border security agencies can now carry out such searches without probable cause or the production of a valid search warrant; they can do so as far as 100 miles interior to the US borders.

Government Data about Searches of International Travelers' Laptops and Personal Electronic Devices

August 25, 2010

In response to the ACLU's Freedom of Information Act lawsuit seeking documents about the government's policy of searching travelers' laptops and cell phones at US border crossings without suspicion of wrongdoing, the government has released thousands of pages of documents about the policy. The records reveal new information about how many devices have been searched, what happens to travelers' files once they are in the government's possession, and travelers' complaints about how they are treated by border officials.

The ACLU's analysis of the documents reveals:
- Between October 2008 and June 2010, more than 6,500 people traveling to and from the United States had their electronic devices searched at the border. Nearly half of these people were US citizens.
- The devices the government searched included laptops, cell phones, cameras, hard drives, flash drives, and even DVDs.
- Between October 2008 and June 2009, cell phones were the most commonly searched electronic devices, followed by laptops and digital cameras.
- Between July 2008 and June 2009, border agents transferred data found on travelers' electronic devices to other federal agencies more than 280 times. Half of the time, these unnamed agencies asserted an independent basis for retaining or seizing the data.
- The ACLU provides an index with links to the documents provided by CBP in response to their Laptop Search FOIA request as well as data spreadsheets at: http://www.aclu.org/national-security/government-data-about-searches-international-travelers-laptops-and-personal-electr.[45]

Critical Infrastructure Protection

The United States and Canada established a joint Action Plan for critical infrastructure in 2010.[46] This was based on a December 2008 *Agreement Between the Government of Canada and the Government of the United States on Emergency Management Cooperation* (the Agreement).[47] The Agreement set forth a framework for federal-level, Canada–US collaboration on emergency management issues as well as the integration of federal response and relief efforts for cross-border incidents.

Additionally, the Agreement set the stage for the provision of supplies/equipment, emergency responders, and expert support in the event of a cross-border emergency. In June 2012 the two countries created a Compendium of US-Canada Emergency Management Assistance Mechanisms.[48] There are currently twenty-two different co-operative assistance mechanisms, dating as far back as 1961, between the countries to address issues related to emergency management and critical infrastructure.

These agreements to protect and improve the resiliency of critical infrastructure became particularly important during the worst rail disaster since 1989. The morning of July 6, 2013, a section of rail cars were decoupled from the engine, and rolled seven miles downhill into the small Canadian community of Lac-Mégantic, Quebec. All but one of the train's seventy-three cars were carrying oil. At least five of the cars exploded when they derailed. Others spilled their contents (27,000 gallons of light crude oil) into nearby waters. The explosions and intense fires destroyed more than buildings in the small town and resulted in more than 2,000 persons being forced to evacuate.[49]

First responders from the State of Maine immediately responded to assist the Canadian responders in fighting the fires.[50] Additionally, Maine's Department of Environmental Protection responded to assist with isolation and cleanup of the associated oil spill that had entered international waters between Maine and Quebec.

One of the reasons for quick, interoperable response between the two countries during the Lac-Mégantic disaster was the concerted effort between Canada and the United States to improve interoperable communications across borders. A recent joint operation held in Maine and New Brunswick, including officials from the Maine Emergency Management Agency (MEMA), the Province of New Brunswick Emergency Measures Organization, Department of Homeland Security's (DHS) Science and Technology Directorate (S&T), Federal Emergency Management Agency (FEMA), the Defense Research and Development Canada's Centre for Security Science of the Canadian Department of National Defense, and Public Safety Canada, indicated that even across borders, any immediate confusion or lack of information following an incident may not greatly affect overall rescue efforts.[51] The Lac-Mégantic response and combined practice exercises are indicative that the efforts to jointly improve critical infrastructure resilience and emergency management response are working.

Military Joint Defenses

Perhaps the single most enduring and important relationship between Canada and the United States has been the North American Aerospace Defense Command (NORAD). This military relationship has its origins in the fundamental concept of border security as national security. NORAD is a US–Canada organization charged with the missions of aerospace warning and aerospace control for North America. Aerospace warning includes the monitoring of man-made objects in space, and the detection, validation, and warning of attack against North America whether by aircraft, missiles, or space vehicles, through mutual support arrangements with other commands.

Aerospace control includes ensuring air sovereignty and air defense of the airspace of Canada and the United States. The May 2006 NORAD Agreement renewal added a maritime warning mission, which entails a shared awareness and understanding of the activities conducted in US and Canadian maritime approaches, maritime areas, and inland waterways.[52]

NORAD dates back to the beginnings of the Cold War when the primary threat to North America was the aviation forces of the Soviet Union. These aircraft would have attacked targets in the United States by overflying the Arctic Ocean and Canada. To ensure that these threats were identified and the available combat actions taken to repel any attack by the Soviet Union before bombers reached their targets, Canada and the United States joined forces to establish an early warning system of radar stations along the Arctic Sea, with a centralized command-and-control structure to identify, analyze, and respond to incursions. May 12, 1958, the two countries announced they had formalized a cooperative air defense arrangement as a government-to-government bilateral defense agreement—the NORAD Agreement.[53]

Within one year of announcing the NORAD Agreement, the focus of the joint operation expanded to include the threats posed by intercontinental ballistic and submarine-launched missiles armed with nuclear warheads. The resultant modernization of strategic nuclear forces on both sides of the Cold War resulted in NORAD shifting away from an "Air Defense" function to an "Aerospace" warning and tracking function. After the end of the Cold War, NORAD underwent a strategic review that determined the necessity of continued functions of the agency and its extensive space tracking assets. Additionally, NORAD planners envisioned terrorists using cruise missiles or similar weapons capable of flying over long distances while avoiding radar coverage as a potential threat to North America. They did not foresee that those missiles would include hijacked airliners.[54]

In the immediate aftermath of the September 11, 2001, terrorist attacks, and through June 2006, NORAD assets have responded to more than 2,100 potential airborne threats in the continental United States, Canada, and Alaska. Recognizing the changing threat environment, the US Department of defense created the US Northern Command as a joint service to direct all military homeland defense missions.[55]

With NORAD now more than fifty years old, the agreement between the United States and Canada is no longer renewed every five years. Instead, the two nations simply review the nature of the accord for potential changes. This joint military operations organization has expanded in the post-9/11 world to include representatives from both countries' law enforcement agencies. An excellent example of the intergovernmental, military, and law enforcement cooperation was the air security provided during the 2010 Winter Olympics in Vancouver, British Columbia.[56] Along with NORAD providing the surveillance of the air, maritime, and space realm for potential threats, CBP Air and Marine assets, US Coast Guard, RCMP, and Canadian Navy components worked side-by-side to ensure the safety of the Games.

Conclusion

Canadians and Americans are two peoples united by a mostly common language and heritage. Excepting the French origins of Quebec, Canadians and Americans were birthed from British colonization of North America and the subsequent advance of British fur-trading corporations and the recently independent United States of America westward movement. The inexorable move of both groups toward the Pacific Ocean brought occasions for both conflict and cooperation. Today, that cooperation is rapidly moving toward what appears to be the establishment of a North American Union.

One of the longest-established international commissions in history maintains the International Boundary between Canada and the United States. The very term "International Boundary" implies that the division between Canada and the United States is less a border than a line of demarcation where laws and jurisprudence change. As 90 percent of Canadians live within 100 miles of the US border, there exists more commonality between the two peoples than differences. Canadians do not appear to understand American gun culture but then they did not become an independent country as the result of an armed revolt against their colonial masters.

Both countries approach border security from a similar perspective: preventing smuggling and protecting national sovereignty against foreign aggressors. Possessing the longest land border between two countries, nearly all unguarded, has resulted in the recognition that fencing or militarizing the border, beyond the needs or capabilities of either country, would be economically counterproductive to the world's largest trading partnership. Instead, through the establishment of combined asset ShipRiders, Integrated Border Enforcement Teams, and Border Enforcement Security Taskforces, the two countries enhance their individual border security efforts while maintaining their individual sovereignty. The individual smuggler, and lone wolf terrorist, is almost impossible to identify or interdict. However, through the cooperative efforts of both countries, there has been significant im-

US Border Patrol looks across the St. Lawrence Seaway to Canada. Buffalo Sector. 1960s. © US Border Patrol Museum. Used with permission.

provement in the targeting and dismantling of organized smuggling, drug trafficking, and terrorist groups.

The long-term cooperative efforts at national defense, as demonstrated by NORAD, are continuing with the cooperation between agencies associated with environmental disaster response, critical infrastructure resilience and protection, and emergency management. Recent efforts to combat wildfires across western Canada are indicative of the International Boundary being less a border and more a mere political dividing line. Twenty feet of open space delineating an international border does not stop a raging forest fire from jumping across international boundaries.

The United States and Canada are partners in maintaining international security for each other and will continue to do so for years to come.

Questions for Further Consideration

1. If your house straddles the US and Canada border, do you have to report yourself to US CBP and Canadian CBSA every time you walk from your living room to your kitchen?

2. If a private pilot departs from a US airport and subsequently lands at the Piney Pinecreek Border Airport, the aircraft will land in both the United States and Canada, then taxi back into the United States. Do the pilot and passengers have to clear Canadian customs and immigration for having landed in Canada? Do they also have to clear US customs and immigration because they departed the United States upon landing and then returned to the United States from Canada when they taxied back to the US side of the airport? If you were the pilot, how would you know?

3. Some of the greatest points of contention with the expanding police authority of CBP and other DHS agencies are 8 USC § 1357 and 19 USC §§ 1499, 1581, and 1582, which authorize searches and detention, allowing CBP agents to seize any electronic device, access the data on that device, require the person carrying the device to provide passwords so that the data can be accessed, and copy the data for future analysis. In light of the Fourth Amendment to the Constitution and the prohibitions on unreasonable search and seizure, should this law be changed? Would you answer differently if you knew that the search and seizure applied to anybody within 100 miles of the US borders, even if they had not crossed an international boundary and were just going about their daily lives?

Chapter 11 Endnotes

1. Paul Cellucci, US Ambassador to Canada and former Massachusetts governor. Accessed July 21, 2017, at: http://www.brainyquote.com/quotes/quotes/p/paulcelluc262942.html

2. Naske, Claus, and Herman Slotnick, *Alaska: A History* (Oklahoma City: University of Oklahoma Press, 2011).

3. Gibson, F. W. The Alaskan boundary dispute, *Canadian Historical Association Report*, 1945, 25–40.

4. International Boundary Commission (IBC). Accessed July 21, 2017, at: http://www.internationalboundarycommission.org/en/about/history.php

5. Ibid.

6. Ibid.

7. Ibid.

8. McDonald, Colin, Bush Fires US Representative to International Boundary Commission, *Seattle Post Intelligencer,* 10 July 2007. Accessed July 21, 2017, at: http://blog.seattlepi.com/seattlepolitics/2007/07/10/bush-fires-u-s-representative-to-international-boundary-commission/ See also: Schiff, Stacy, Politics Starts at the Border, *The New York Times,* 22 Jul 2007. Accessed July 21, 2017, at: http://www.nytimes.com/2007/07/22/opinion/22schiff.html?pagewanted=print&_r=0

9. U.S.-Canada Commission Will Halt Drive To Tear Down a Retired Washington State Couple's Backyard Wall: PLF Attorneys Win Settlement Protecting the Property Rights of Herbert and Shirley-Ann Leu, 15 Jan 2009. Accessed July 21, 2017, at: https://www.pacificlegal.org/page.aspx?pid=3952

10. CIA Factbook, Canada, March 15, 2013.

11. Facts About the US-Canada Border, accessed July 21, 2017, at: http://www.cbc.ca/news/canada/story/2009/05/11/f-border-by-the-numbers.html

12. Wikipedia. List of Areas Disputed by Canada and the United States. Last accessed July 21, 2017, at: http://en.wikipedia.org/wiki/List_of_areas_disputed_by_the_United_States_and_Canada

13. Carnaghan, Matthew, and Allison Goody, Canadian Arctic Sovereignty, Political and Social Affairs Division, Parliament of Canada, 26 Jan 2006. Accessed July 21, 2017, at: http://www.parl.gc.ca/Content/LOP/researchpublications/prb0561-e.htm

14. GAO. December 2010. Enhanced DHS Oversight and Assessment of Interagency Coordination is Needed for the Northern Border. Border Security. GAO-11-97.

15. Canadian Border Services Agency, National Statistics—January 1, 2012, to December 31, 2012. This document is now archived by the Canadian Library. It is no longer available on the web and the new version of CBS statistical data page no longer reports these statistics as part of a public, open government venue.Available at: http://www.cbsa-asfc.gc.ca/agency-agence/stats/2012/2012-ann-eng.html#mtab1

16. Ibid. Available at: http://www.cbsa-asfc.gc.ca/agency-agence/stats/2012/2012-ann-eng. html#mtab2

17. Ibid. Available at: http://www.cbsa-asfc.gc.ca/agency-agence/stats/2012/2012-ann-eng.html#mtab3

18. Royal Canadian Mounted Police, The RCMP's History. Accessed July 21, 2017, at: http://www.rcmp.gc.ca/hist/index-eng.htm

19. Ibid., Border Integrity. Available at: http://www.rcmp.gc.ca/bi-if/index-eng.htm

20. Ibid.

21. Ibid., Strategic Priority: National Security. Accessed July 21, 2017, at: http://www.rcmp.gc.ca/terr/index-eng.htm

22. BBC News, Canada Foils 'al-Qaeda linked' Terror Attack on Train, 23 Apr 2013. Accessed July 21, 2017, at: http://www.bbc.co.uk/news/world-us-canada-22258191

23. Bell, Stewart, and Hamilton Graeme, Third Suspect Related to Alleged VIA Rail Terror Plan Discussed Bacteria Plot to Kill '100,000 people': Documents, *National Post,* 9 May 2013. Accessed July 21, 2017, at: http://news.nationalpost.com/2013/05/09/fbi-arrested-third-suspect-related-to-alleged-via-rail-terror-plot/

24. Framework Agreement on Integrated Cross-border Maritime Law Enforcement Operations Between the Government of the United States of America and the Government of Canada, 26 May 2009. Accessed July 21, 2017, at: http://www.dhs.gov/xlibrary/assets/shiprider_agreement.pdf

25. United States-Canada Beyond the Border: A Shared Vision for Perimeter Security and Economic Competitiveness. Action Plan. Hereafter referred to as Beyond the Border. December 2011. Accessed July 21, 2017, at: http://www.whitehouse.gov/the-press-office/2011/02/04/declaration-president-obama-and-prime-minister-harper-canada-beyond-bord

26. H.R. 915 (112th): Jaime Zapata Border Enforcement Security Task Force Act. (1 Jan 2012). Accessed July 21, 2017, at: http://www.govtrack.us/congress/bills/112/hr915/text

27. Beyond the Border, ii.

28. Koslowski, Rey, *The Evolution of Border Controls as a Mechanism to Prevent Illegal Immigration.* Migration Policy Institute, February 2011.

29. CBSA, News Release, Canada and the United States Announce Phase I Pilot Project to Enhance

Border Security at Land Ports of Entry, 28 Sep 2012. Accessed July 21, 2017, at: https://www.yahoo.com/news/canada-united-states-announce-phase-050721511.html

30. Weird Story Locations. Halfway House between Dundee Quebec and Fort Covington NY. Accessed July 21, 2017, at: http://www.waymarking.com/waymarks/WMBY8A_Half_way_House_between_Dundee_Quebec_and_Fort_Covington_NY

31. Haskell Free Library and Opera House National Historic Site of Canada, Canada's Historic Places. Accessed July 21, 2017, at: http://www.historicplaces.ca/en/rep-reg/place-lieu.aspx?id=7322&pid=0

32. Frieden, Terry, Drug Tunnel Found Under Canada Border, CNN, 22 Jul 2005. Accessed July 21, 2017, at: http://www.cnn.com/2005/US/07/21/border.tunnel/

33. ICE News Release, Canadian Trucker Sentenced to 12 Years for Cross Border Drug Smuggling, 7 May 2013. Accessed July 21, 2017, at: http://www.ice.gov/news/releases/1305/130507seattle.htm

34. Lancaster, John, Drugs Increasingly Being Smuggled Into Canada by Truckers: Cocaine Moving via Land From Mexico on Trucks Bound for Canada, CBC News 26 Mar 2013. Accessed July 21, 2017, at: http://www.cbc.ca/news/canada/toronto/story/2013/03/26/greater-toronto-area-truckers-smuggling-charges-cocaine.html

35. Cocburn, Neco, Smuggling's Price: Death of US Couple Focuses Spotlight on Stopping Cigarette 'Runners'. *Ottawa Citizen,* 21 Nov 2008. Accessed July 21, 2017, at: http://archive.tobacco.org/news/275014.html

36. Bruser, David, and Jayme Poisson, The Gun Pipeline: Popular Hi-Point guns 'Cheap and they Work', *Toronto Star,* 21 Apr 2013. Accessed July 21, 2017, at: http://www.thestar.com/news/investigations/2013/04/21/the_gun_pipeline_popular_hipoint_guns_cheap_and_they_work.html

37. Weinreb, Arthur, Canadian Soldier Faces Numerous Bun-trafficking Charges, *Digital Journal,* 24 Apr 2013. Accessed July 21, 2017, at: http://digitaljournal.com/article/348711

38. Bellett, Gerry, Two Pistol-packing Seniors Fined $20,000 After Border Gun Bust. *Vancouver Sun,* 8 Dec 2011. Accessed July 21, 2017, at: http://www.vancouversun.com/news/pistol+packing+seniors+fined+after+border+bust/5827447/story.html

39. Federal Aviation Administration, Airport IQ, Piney Pinecreek Border, 8 Dec 2011. Accessed July 21, 2017, at: http://www.gcr1.com/5010web/airport.cfm?Site=48Y&AptSecNum=0 See also: Minnesota Department of Transportation, Airport Directory and Travel Guide. Pinecreek-48Y. Accessed July 21, 2017, at: http://www.dot.state.mn.us/aero/operations/minnesotaairports.html

40. COPA National, Dunseity/International Peace Garden. Accessed July 21, 2017, at: http://archive.copanational.org/PlacesToFly/airport_view.php?pr_id=4&ap_id=1065

41. SkyVector, Coronach/Scobey Border Station Airport. Accessed July 21, 2017, at: http://skyvector.com/airport/CKK3/Coronach-Scobey-Border-Station-Airport

42. SkyVector, Coutts/Ross International Airport. Accessed July 21, 2017, at: http://skyvector.com/airport/CEP4/Coutts-Ross-International-Airport

43. Washington State Department of Transportation, Avey Field State Airport. Accessed July 21, 2017, at: https://www.wsdot.wa.gov/aviation/AllStateAirports/Laurier_AveyField.htm

44. US CBP Information Card, Inspection of Electronic Devices. Accessed July 21, 2017, at: http://www.aclu.org/files/pdfs/natsec/cbp_20100114_000011-000012.pdf See also, 8 USC § 1357 and 19 USC §§ 1499, 1581, & 1582.

45. ACLU: American Civil Liberties Union, Government Data About Searches of International Travelers' Laptops and Personal Electronic Devices, 25 Aug 2010. Accessed July 21, 2017, at: http://www.aclu.org/national-security/government-data-about-searches-international-travelers-laptops-and-personal-electr

46. Public Safety Canada, Canada-United States Action Plan for Critical Infrastructure. Accessed July 21, 2017, at: https://www.dhs.gov/xlibrary/assets/ip_canada_us_action_plan.pdf Originally published and sourced from Public Safety Canada, this document is now available as a joint publication with DHS.

47. Canada Treaty Information, Agreement between the Government of Canada and the Government of the United States of America on Emergency Management Cooperation. Accessed July 21, 2017, at: http://www.treaty-accord.gc.ca/text-texte.aspx?id=105173

48. DHS, Compendium of US-Canada Emergency Management Assistance Mechanisms, June 2012. Accessed July 21, 2017, at: http://www.dhs.gov/xlibrary/assets/policy/btb-compendium-of-us-canada-emergency-management-assistance-mechanisms.pdf

49. CBS News, Canada Train Derailment Probe Focuses on Fire Hours Before Quebec Disaster, Tankers With History of Puncturing, 9 Jul 2013. Accessed July 21, 2017, at: http://www.cbsnews.com/8301-202_162-57592781/canada-train-derailment-probe-focuses-on-fire-hours-before-quebec-disa-

ster-tankers-with-history-of-puncturing/

50. Maine Emergency Management Agency, State Provides Coordinated Efforts in Response to Lac-Mégantic, Quebec Train Derailment, 8 Jul 2013. The original document is no longer available on the Maine State website. It is hosted by a news aggregator. Accessed July 21, 2017, at: https://www.highbeam.com/doc/1G1-336182788.html

51. DHS, Interoperable Communications Across Borders, n.d. Accessed July 21, 2017, at: http://www.dhs.gov/interoperable-communications-across-borders

52. North American Aerospace Defense Command, NORAD History. Last accessed July 21, 2017, at: http://www.norad.mil/AboutNORAD/NORADHistory.aspx

53. North American Aerospace Defense Command, Office of History, A Brief History of NORAD. As of 31 December 2012. Accessed July 21, 2017, at: http://www.norad.mil/Portals/29/Documents/A%20Brief%20History%20of%20NORAD%20(current%20as%20of%20March%202014).pdf

54. Ibid.

55. Ibid.

56. Ibid.

Chapter 12

The Future of Borders and Boundaries in the Modern World

Key Words and Concepts

Agroterrorism	Korean Demilitarized Zone
Birth Tourism	National Security
Border Crossing Card	Schengen Convention
Border Security	Transnational Criminal Organizations
Globalization	US Department of Homeland Security
Jus Soli	

Introduction

This book opened with the history of borders, boundaries, and barriers. Each was defined and examples were provided. Tactics and techniques used by border security agencies were followed with efforts to secure maritime borders in a globalized world. Border security professionals must deal with many of the same problems today as have been dealt with throughout history, from the trafficking of contraband, to the protection of the national economic base from efforts to undermine it, to identifying and stopping those who traffic in human beings.

Securing borders in the modern world goes beyond efforts at the actual lines that delineate national boundaries, to providing a secure means to move commodities throughout a country as well as across international borders. Any interruption in the smooth movement of commerce in our globalized world would result in reverberating economic impacts both within the immediately affected country and throughout the supply chain, around the world. Whether the interruption occurred at a maritime port, or a port of entry on the United States border with either Mexico or Canada, the impact is the same.

So important are our neighbors to our livelihoods, we wrote extensively about borders between the United States and its immediate neighbors to the north and south. There is a long, and sometimes contentious history between Mexico, the United States, and Canada. The United States and Canada can be considered two peoples separated by a common language. The same cannot be said for the United States and Mexico. There the issues that arise between the countries are much more intense, involving a history of wars, racism, religious discrimination, Spanish monarchal control over colonies versus American individualism and independence and, of course, the issue of different languages.

Borders and boundaries in the modern world have evolved from wooden palisades and stone walls to electronics, biometrics, facial recognition, and RFID threads embedded in passports. Commodities shipped worldwide require screening and tracking from originator to end user. Containers, trucks, and trains are scanned with giant x-ray machines, and the sensitive noses of canines. Every day hundreds of thousands of border security professionals go to work on both sides of every border in the world. They are faced with a conundrum: the expeditious movement of commodities and people versus preventing the importation of contraband and the interdiction of those smuggling goods ranging from African blood diamonds to bales of marijuana and kilos of heroin.

Politics also drive border security actions, initiatives, and statistical reports. Much of the numbers expressed by politicians are simply wrong. Others are intentionally calculated to mislead. As an example, under the Obama administration the statistics supporting the contention that the southern US border is safer than ever before are drawn primarily on apprehension data associated with illegal immigrants. These numbers are manipulated by political policy and departmental and executive branch

The second largest flag in Mexico flies over the Port of Entry in Piedras Negras, Coahuila, Mexico, across the Rio Grande from Eagle Pass, Texas. James Phelps. 2013.

directives that reduce the ability of those charged with securing the border from carrying out their assigned duties. Therefore, fewer illegal immigrants are stopped and the statistics show that fewer are crossing over. That fewer are stopped by border security agencies reflects many different components associated with the issue of illegal immigration, not just the level of border security.

This is nothing new! Every political administration around the world has and will continue to use the issue of border security to accomplish political agendas. This leads to a situation where true border security will always be elusive for every country, except the most totalitarian and reclusive governments.

Border Security Policy Statements Under the Obama Administration

"Protecting our borders from the illegal movement of weapons, drugs, contraband, and people, while promoting lawful entry and exit, is essential to homeland security, economic prosperity, and national sovereignty."

—DHS Website (2013/2017)[1]

"The Department of Homeland Security secures the nation's air, land, and sea borders to prevent illegal activity while facilitating lawful travel and trade. The Department's border security and management efforts focus on three interrelated goals: 1. Effectively secure US air, land and sea points of entry; 2. Safeguard and streamline lawful trade and travel; and 3. Disrupt and dismantle transnational criminal and terrorist organizations."

—DHS Website (2013/2017)[2]

"The Department of Homeland Security prevents and investigates illegal movements across our borders, including the smuggling of people, drugs, cash, and weapons. The Department is working to strengthen security on the southwest border to disrupt the drug, cash and weapon smuggling that fuels cartel violence in Mexico by adding manpower and technology to the southwest border. We support smart security on the northern border and to facilitate international travel and trade."

—DHS Website (2013)[3]

"Keeping our borders secure from potential terrorists, illegal immigrants, and illicit contraband, is vital to the safety and security of the United States. The Committee on Homeland Security supports efforts to gain and maintain operational control of the entire border as well as vigorously enforce our nation's immigration laws."

—Committee on Homeland Security Website,
House of Representatives (2013)[4]

"The potential for terrorists to cross our borders without detection and the extreme violence at the southern border with Mexico have compelled the Committee to keep close watch over the agencies and employees of border, immigration, and customs agencies."

—Committee on Homeland Security and Governmental
Affairs Website, US Senate (2013)[5]

Whether the words come from the US Senate, US House of Representatives, the Department of Homeland Security, or private business entities, they all recognize that effective Homeland Security is integrally tied to and dependent upon Border Security. If the above quotations are boiled down to their basic components, Homeland Security is primarily concerned with human trafficking, illegal immigrants, and the movement of illicit (drug) contraband, at and between ports of entry, primarily along the southwest border. All while facilitating international trade and legal travel. Homeland security is border security!

This has not always been the case. In the early days of Homeland Security the focus was entirely on terrorism. As President Bush noted in *Securing the Homeland: Strengthening the Nation*, "the need for homeland security is tied to the underlying vulnerability of American society and the fact that we can never be sure when or where the next terrorist conspiracy against us will emerge" and "America's vulnerability to terrorism will persist long after we bring justice to those responsible for the events of September 11."[6] President Bush also wrote, "The Government of the United States has no more important mission than fighting terrorism overseas and securing the homeland from future terrorist attacks."[7] Initially, Homeland Security was about preventing terrorist attacks against the homeland and recovering from attacks that did occur. Shortly after Barack Obama was sworn in as president in 2009 there was a concerted move away from using the words "terrorist" and "terrorism." Four years later, as his second term began, we could see that virtually all references to terrorism in official discourse had been eliminated.

For the first edition of this book we conducted a quick check of the **Department of Homeland Security official website** (July 1, 2013) and showed the word "terrorist" was nonexistent and the word "terrorism" only appeared twice: once at the very end of the five-part flash images and in the logo of the **National Terrorism Advisory System (NTAS)**. Instead, the primary concerns as indicated by the flash presentation and other links and images were Hurricane Preparedness, Progress Report on the President's Executive Actions to Reduce Gun Violence, Announcing the New and Improved Blue Campaign (to stop human trafficking), A Day in the Life of DHS, If You See Something campaign, How to Avoid Email Scams, and Active Shooter Preparedness. On the **About DHS** page of the website the opening text provided what was the mission of DHS:

The Department of Homeland Security has a vital mission: to secure the nation from the many threats we face. This requires the dedication of more than 240,000 employees in jobs that range from aviation and border security to emergency response, from cybersecurity analyst to chemical facility inspector. Our duties are wide-ranging, but our goal is clear — keeping America safe.[8] (emphasis in original)

Four pages into the official DHS website (2013 version) we found that there were five core missions in Homeland Security:

1. Prevent terrorism and enhance security;
2. Secure and manage our borders;
3. Enforce and administer our immigration laws;
4. Safeguard and secure cyberspace;
5. Ensure resilience to disasters.[9]

They also had an additional mission listed: "We must specifically focus on maturing and strengthening the homeland security enterprise itself."[10] Three concepts form the foundation of the national homeland security strategy, security, resilience, and customs and exchange. Clearly, terrorism was no longer a focus or concern for DHS under the Obama presidency. How this resolves as the administration of President Donald Trump gets up and running will make for an interesting study.

All of the missions of the border security apparatus were tied directly to the mission of homeland security, from controlling legal cross-border movement of commodities and people, to interdicting illegal immigrants and drug traffickers, from identifying and stopping human traffickers, to examining incoming produce and other commodities for agricultural threats and invasive species, from verifying and issuing visas to visitors, to stopping the movement of guns and bulk cash smuggling into Mexico, to ensuring the effective and efficient movement of goods through the customs and exchange processes. With the move away from the DHS being an agency focused on counterterrorism under the George W. Bush presidency, and instead being an agency focused on border security functions and resiliency to disasters, DHS evolved.

We repeated our check of the DHS website on February 24, 2017, just a month into Donald Trump's presidency. The flash on the main page included the DHS actions on implementing the Trump Executive Orders on protecting the homeland, how DHS protects the homeland, cybersecurity training, the see something/say something program, winter weather preparedness, information on the people of DHS, the National Terrorist Advisory System (NTAS) current bulletin, and ended with a statement about honor and integrity. Immediately under the flash presentation were links to countering violent extremism, active shooter preparedness, and other quick links. A short distance lower on the page were overseas travel alerts and another link to NTAS. Beneath the news briefs was a widget link to NTAS to put on your personal website.[11]

On the Our Mission Web page, which is linked in the About tab, the words "terrorism" and "terrorist" appear five times; with preventing terrorism taking precedence over other missions and even natural disasters.[12]

Checking the NTAS link, we found that the last NTAS bulletin was issued in November, 2016—during the Obama administration—and wasn't scheduled to be changed until May 2017.[13] Going to the Countering Violent Extremism link we see that it still talks about DHS Secretary Jeh Johnson, and nowhere on the page does the term "terrorism" or "terrorist" appear.[14] So, while the Trump administration gets rolling, and begins to implement its vision of America, the websites of the DHS are not keeping pace. However, they now are returning to the original purpose of DHS—protecting the homeland and combating terrorism, at least on the main page.

Border Security is essential to National Security. As was identified in Chapter 1, how well border integrity and security are maintained directly affects all citizens and legal residents of a country. How a country addresses issues of border security and approaches problems such as mass migrations is indicative of national will and perceptions of national sovereignty. Any country that fails to secure its borders cannot expect to be safe within those borders. Nor can that country successfully implement or maintain the existing legal and judicial systems in the face of the corruption that porous borders and the money that transnational crime brings.

When Is a Border Secure?

It is common to assign metrics to measure the level of border security. Those metrics often include the number of illegal immigrants stopped from entering a country, the number of criminal aliens who have been arrested and deported, or the tonnage of illegal drugs confiscated by border security agencies. These are all useful measures for political purposes, but do they accurately measure border security?

The most secure border in the world today is the demilitarized zone between North and South Korea. Only 160 miles (250 km) long and 2.5 miles (4 km) wide, this is the most heavily militarized border in the world. A military demarcation line runs down the center of the DMZ. On either side are extensive mine fields (over 1.2 million land mines), heavily fortified observation posts, pillboxes, and machine-gun nests, and massive electronic technology to sense even the slightest disturbance that may be the incursion of military forces from the opposing side. Should there be an incursion by either side, a war that has never ended could suddenly reignite.

Yet even the DMZ between North and South Korea is not completely closed. Occasionally a North Korean soldier will defect to the South. The South has discovered four tunnels under the DMZ built specifically to support the movement of invasion forces. There could be a number of other tunnels that remain undiscovered, as they have not been finished, simply waiting for the day they need to be punched through.

Nobody knows what it costs to maintain the DMZ. Too many agencies and governments are involved. It is clearly an expensive effort by all parties. Yet it is not even one-tenth the length of the US-Mexico border. There is already nearly seven times as much fence between the United States and Mexico as there is along the entire

A South Korean sentry near the demilitarized zone (Imjingang).
Johannes Barre. August 2005. Wikicommons.

Korean peninsula, coupled with observation towers, technological surveillance systems, and armed patrols. Occasionally the National Guard is mobilized and sent to assist in securing the US southern border, usually to demonstrate the political will of the associated administration and not to actually do anything that is effective in deterring cross-border violations. As in Korea, the Mexicans dig tunnels to invade the United States except instead of invading with tanks and soldiers, the invasion is with illegal immigrants and tons of illegal drugs. When these tunnels are discovered they are filled with concrete at the point where they cross the border. But they are not destroyed, as the government to the south does not fear that the United States will begin using the tunnels to smuggle contraband into Mexico.

Herein lies one of the major problems with establishing effective border security: it takes the concerted effort by the governments and personnel on both sides of a border to establish effective security. One party cannot do it alone, particularly when the other party is encouraging their people to violate their neighbor's sovereign borders.

Measuring Border Security

In her June 27, 2013, testimony before Congress, Rebecca Gambler, then Director of Homeland Security and Justice for the GAO, told the Committee on Oversight and

Government Reform's Subcommittee on National Security, Homeland Defense and Foreign Operations that the Department of Homeland Security "is using the number of apprehensions on the southwest border, between ports of entry, as its goal and measure for border security."[15] Director Gambler said that this is an incomplete method because the Border Patrol is "not able to assess the effectiveness of its efforts because it doesn't compare apprehensions to estimated entrants."[16] This move to using apprehensions of illegal immigrants as a measure of border security by sector was only introduced in 2011. When DHS initially moved away from using "operational control" as a metric for border security, Congress directed DHS to establish a new set of specific metrics for effectively measuring border security. As of March 2016, five years after receiving this directive from Congress, DHS and, in particular CBP, have not yet established new performance goals and measures, nor have they identified milestones and time frames for developing and implementing them. Border Patrol officials reported to the GAO in 2013 that development of metrics to use apprehensions as a measure of border security was contingent on the development of key elements of a new strategic plan, such as a risk-assessment tool.[17] Three years later CBP Operations Assistant Commissioner Randolph Alles and CBP US Border Patrol Acting Chief Ronald Vitiello testified before the House Committee on Homeland Security that,

> CBP recognizes the need for relevant performance measures to verify the effectiveness of our operations and assets. However, due to the sheer size of the air, land, and sea borders, and the motivation of individuals to illegally enter the United States, challenges still exist to measure our success. Furthermore, as border security operations become increasingly integrated, the ability to quantify individual contributions to shared outcomes becomes increasingly complex. AMO and USBP will continue to collaborate with internal and external partners to enhance current metrics, and develop new metrics, that provide meaningful outcome-focused measurements of illegal activity, trends, and effectiveness. We look forward to sharing these efforts with this Subcommittee in the future.[18]

Prior to 2011 DHS used a different metric to measure border security—operational control. As described by then Director Gambler,

> DHS used operational control as its goal and outcome measure for border security and to assess resource needs to accomplish this goal. Operational control—also referred to as effective control—was defined as the number of border miles where Border Patrol had the capability to detect, respond to, and interdict cross-border illegal activity. DHS last reported its progress and status in achieving operational control of the borders in fiscal year 2010. At that time, DHS reported achieving operational control for 1,107 (13 percent) of 8,607 miles across US northern, southwest, and coastal borders. Along the southwest border, DHS reported achieving operational control for 873 (44 percent) of the about 2,000 border miles. At the beginning of fiscal year 2011, DHS transitioned from using operational control as its goal and outcome measure for border security.... The interim goal and measure of number of

apprehensions on the southwest border between POEs provides information on activity levels but does not inform program results or resource identification and allocation decisions, and therefore … DHS and Congress could experience reduced oversight and DHS accountability. Further, studies commissioned by CBP have found that the number of apprehensions bears little relationship to effectiveness because agency officials do not compare these numbers with the amount of cross-border illegal activity.[19]

In 2010 the GAO determined that DHS had less than 50 percent "operational control" of the border, which resulted in then-DHS Secretary Napolitano directing that the means of measuring border security would be changed.[20] Measuring the effectiveness of border security is essential if the country is going to know whether or not the efforts, staffing, operations, and policies that are increasingly expensive are also cost effective. This fundamental information is necessary not only for the benefit of CBP and the Border Patrol administrators, but also for the congressional budgeting process. While representatives and senators were calling for effective measures of border security, "Obama administrations officials said [March 21, 2013] … that they had resisted producing a single measure to assess the border because the president did not want any hurdles placed on the pathway to eventual citizenship for immigrants in the country illegally."[21]

In their testimony before Congress on March 1, 2016, Alles and Vitiello still used the old numbers of apprehensions, drug seizures, and the reduction in captured recidivists as measures of performance. Essentially, since 2011, for six years, DHS has had no way to measure or report the effectiveness of their border security efforts. Even after directives from Congress to create metrics.

A Better Measure of Border Security

Perhaps the best way to determine the effectiveness of border security is through an economic analysis. According to economic theory of "supply and demand": if the supply of any item is high and the demand is low, the price will be low. If the supply of any item is low and the demand is high, the price will be high. If the demand for an item remains relatively constant across 300 million potential consumers, then the price will vary depending on the supply. You see this in the grocery store with changes in seasonally available fruits and vegetables, as well as in the meat market. If we apply this practice to border security, then the better the border security, the greater amount of contraband will be interdicted. Therefore, if the demand is relatively constant, the price should increase at a greater rate than inflation for a given item of contraband. Since illegal drugs must enter the country illegally, avoiding detection and interdiction by border security agents, they are a form of contraband that could easily be used to measure border security effectiveness.

The Office of National Drug Control Policy (ONDCP—an executive branch agency) maintains and analyzes data concerning cost and purity of illicit drugs. The most recent report on price and purity of drugs is from October 2008 and covers the period 1981–

2007.[22] From 2003 to the beginning of 2008 the price of powdered cocaine drifted slightly downward (about 14 percent) while the purity of the street product increased.[23] With the exception of some local price peaks in 1990, the price of a pure gram of heroin steadily decreased, with the possible exception of small increases in 2004 and 2006. From 1997 to the beginning of 2008 the price for heroin dropped about 30 percent for all quality levels.[24] The ONDCP report specifically notes that illicit drug availability and price follows a supply and demand model. The report also provides specific data analysis of d-methamphetamine, marijuana, and crack cocaine. However, these drugs were concurrently produced within the United States (or exclusively inside the United States) as well as Mexico during the study period, making them poor measures of border security effectiveness. Powdered cocaine and heroin were either produced or transshipped into the United States via Mexico (primarily) during this period, making them good examples of contraband that crosses the southern border in response to customer demand.

With the price of powdered cocaine dropping about 14 percent from January 2003 to December 2007, and the price of heroin dropping about 30 percent over the same timeframe, it is instructive to look at the amounts seized during this timeframe as well as the inflation rate. From the beginning of 2003 to the end of 2007 inflation in the United States was 33.1 percent, meaning that for a set price in January of 2003, the same item should have cost 33.1 percent more in December 2017.[25] Yet from the third quarter 2003 to the fourth quarter 2007 over 153,559 kilograms of cocaine was seized as it crossed the US borders; and more than 4,000 kilograms of heroin was seized during the same time frame,[26] and the price of both drugs decreased!

There are several possible reasons for this decrease in drug price and increase in purity while such a large amount was being seized at the border. Americans could have simply stopped using cocaine and heroin, resulting in lower demand for the products. Demand could have remained constant, or increased, while border security became less effective. Narcotraficantes may have found alternative methods of getting cocaine and heroin into the United States without having to cross the southern border. Any or all of these are possible causes to the decreased prices and increased quality of cocaine and heroin between 2003 and 2008 in the face of what, by all measures, are massive seizures. In updating this chapter we looked for new government reports on price and purity of drugs in America and couldn't find anything newer than the October 2008 ONDCP report. Not once during the eight years of the Obama administration did the government submit a report on the price and purity of illegal narcotics flooding into the country.

If these statistics are any measure of border security effectiveness, then the question that must be asked is: How much cocaine and heroin must be making it past border security for this quantity of seizure to have no effect on price, and for the market to experience a decrease in price in a supply-and-demand drug economy?

Clearly, if current border security efforts were effective, the price of imported illicit drugs would be going up, not down.

"Los Estados Ocupados de México del Norté"

Canadians do not look at the states of Montana, Idaho, Washington, and Oregon as the occupied states of southern Canada, even though this significant portion of the former British colony was ceded to the United States as part of post-war treaties. Russians do not view Alaska as a state occupied by Americans, although Alaska was originally part of Imperial Russia.

There is a continuing military conflict over whether Kashmir belongs to India or Pakistan. But that was the result of British government officials drawing lines on maps without consideration as to the ethnicity or religion of the people who lived in their former colonies. Similarly, the ongoing conflict between Turkey and the terrorist group PKK is over ethnic self-governance versus political ownership of land based on the drawing of lines on maps as part of various peace treaties.[27]

Colombians do not view Panama as part of their country, even though it once was, until the United States got involved and brought about a political separation as part of being able to gain exclusive control over the building and operating of the Panama Canal. When President Jimmy Carter signed a treaty giving the Canal to Panama, many Americans were upset with both the president and the loss of what has been considered a strategic resource but we don't look at the Canal Zone as a part of the United States being occupied by another country.

What is it about the relationship between Mexico and the United States that has Mexicans who cross the border talking about visiting the occupied states of North Mexico? This is not a joke to these visitors and business executives from Mexico, but a reality. Understanding the basis for this perspective is essential to understanding what is happening in the Southwest and how it will ultimately affect US economics, politics, and culture. The critical analysis of the attitude that the Southwest United States are the occupied states of North Mexico can be understood through the perspective of experienced CBP professionals (each with more than twenty years in the field), from Brownsville to San Diego, which we have consolidated into the following paragraphs:[28]

Author's Note: We fully understand that some readers may be offended by some of the following paragraphs, or see overgeneralization in some of the statements. It is not our intent to offend or overgeneralize. Our intent is to summarize the perspectives of U.S. Border Patrol and CBP personnel we have interviewed along the southern U.S. border. These experienced and highly perceptive officers/agents have dealt with these issues for many decades, and often are third and fourth generation of border region law enforcement whose ancestors watched the changes that occurred over the past 60+ years. Additionally, as authors we have hunted for and found references to support the analysis of these officers/agents. These references are not all inclusive and there are a number of additional readings that might be appropriate for professors and students to look to when reading this chapter. We reference some in footnote 29.[29]

The political force is theirs: Latinos, the majority of whom are Mexican nationals and Mexican ethnics, are a major political force in the US Southwest. There is an active effort by the Mexican government to organize Mexicans living in the United States to demand political rights and to influence their activities toward furthering the political objectives of Mexico. Mexico has undertaken to convince local governments throughout the United States to recognize the Mexican consulate-issued matricula consular identity document for official purposes in this country—even though the document has value only to Mexicans without legal status in the United States and has no validity in Mexico as an identity document. Mexico has a financial interest in promoting the illegal immigration of its citizens to the United States since they send "remittance" money back to relatives and family in Mexico and other countries. The standards for issuing matricula consular cards are so lax that the cards have no legitimate security function.[30] No major bank in Mexico will accept the card as a form of ID when someone opens a simple bank account, and two-thirds of the states of Mexico will not recognize it as valid.[31]

The United States Southwest is rightfully theirs: There is a substantial majority of Mexican citizens who believe that the southwestern United States of America is rightfully the territory of Mexico and that Mexicans do not need US permission to enter.[32] Mexicans in El Paso are increasingly learning the Mexican interpretation of the Treaty of Guadalupe Hidalgo, and, if they go to El Paso public high schools, El Paso Community College, or the University of Texas at El Paso, they are indoctrinated about the Latino "Aztlán" heritage. Aztlán is a myth started in 1969 that calls for the renewal of Aztlán and recovering the lost Mexican territory.[33] It is at the heart of the Chicano movement and the student organization Movimiento Estudiantil Chicano de Aztlán, or MEChA. Included in this plan is the idea of "reclaiming the land of their birth," or the land annexed to the United States in the 1848 Treaty of Guadalupe Hidalgo.[34]

Jobs: The influx into the labor market of unskilled Mexican immigrants depresses wages and working conditions of native, low-skilled workers (who are often young, minorities, or other recent immigrants). It blocks our native poor from entry-level opportunities, contributes to the widening gap between rich and poor in our society, and increases business' dependency on cheap labor instead of innovation and modernization. This reflects a contribution to poverty that breeds crime. More immigration is not better; America is much different today than it was a century ago and so America's need for massive immigration is ended. This constant northward migration of poor Mexicans to attempt to find potential employment in the United States causes harm to both countries.

Border-crossing students: Students, who live in Mexico and attend public schools (to include the El Paso Community College and the University of Texas at El Paso) in the United States, are not able to carry a full-time student academic load and a full-time job. Therefore, during the extra years of study the local economy suffers an absence of contribution from the Mexican border-crossing students. The local resident property school tax does not adequately cover the cost of the inflated border-crossing students in the public community schools; therefore, there is an additional taxpayer subsidy that is expended on the Mexican border-crossing student pursuing a United States public education.[35]

Traffic standards: Mexican nationals who cross into the United States operating their privately owned vehicles do not need to show proof of vehicle insurance (required for US citizens to operate their vehicles on Texas roadways) nor a driver's license to enter the United States, nor does the vehicle need to display a vehicle license plate. The Mexican vehicle does not have to meet EPA or DOT standards. Yet, if a US citizen drives their vehicle into Mexico with an expired US vehicle registration the US citizen is subject to arrest and/or fine and the vehicle confiscated (see breakout box KFOX14 for more information).

Jealousy: The impoverished of Mexico need only look north of the Rio del Norte to see the horn of plenty beckoning. Jealousy of the material riches the United States has amassed, and the resources that have originated on land that was formerly claimed by Mexico contribute to a sense of "reconquista" (reconquest). The Latin American press exacerbates the problem by reporting only what will sell newspapers, without fact checking. This is evidenced by the aliens crossing the border and turning themselves in, then requesting the "amnesty that [your] president promised." An egregious example is the alien who turned himself in, to register for food stamps and Medicare. He was quite honest about his intentions, and very unhappy when we informed him that he was being arrested and sent to jail before being removed back to Mexico, without his welfare.

Medical care: I have personally encountered many illegal aliens who have told me they came across and deliberately turned themselves in to the Border Patrol in order to receive free food or medical care. Some have actually demanded they be taken to the hospital for follow-up treatment to previous medical care. When questioned as to why they did not go to the local free hospital in Mexico, they have given me tales of "too long a wait" or "they don't help." When I looked at their bandages or medicines, I noted the obviously "Third World" medical care. I once worked with a paramedic who was a licensed physician in Mexico. He would collect outdated supplies and equipment to use in the Mexican hospital. He also had a large collection of stories, verified by anyone who visited the hospitals, of reusing urinary catheters, intravenous needles, or tubing for fluid resuscitation, endotracheal tubes, etc.

Disease: Public health is a major concern for border security. Along the Mexican border, tuberculosis is the primary enemy. I researched the TB rate among arrested aliens for FY 2002 versus the projected rate among those aliens who escaped detection/arrest or were released without being diagnosed as an infectious carrier of TB. Approximately 10 percent of the national TB rate for FY 2002 may be traced to the South Texas area from Roma to Victoria. Texas Department of Health/Emergency Medical Division has conducted scenario training, focusing on the influx of communicable diseases from illegal immigrants.

KFOX14: Thursday 30 May 2013, Woman Thrown in Jail, Car Impounded in Mexico for Expired American Vehicle Registration

By Gina Benitez

EL PASO, Texas—A woman crossing into Juarez for a quick trip to bring back her husband's impounded car had her own car seized, but according to her, that was just the beginning of her two-day ordeal.

The woman told KFOX14 about two weeks ago, at around 9 a.m. she drove over the Stanton Bridge into Juarez, but didn't make it far.

The woman, who wants to remain anonymous, said she was crossing to deal with her husband's car issues, when she ran into car issues of her own—her registration was expired. As soon as a Mexican customs agent realized it, everything went south. They allegedly told her it was illegal to have an expired plate and she was being charged with $20,000 worth of contraband—what her car was worth. Around this time last year, the Texas Department of Motor Vehicles put out a warning to drivers after they'd received reports of similar incidents—the first were reported in El Paso. But this woman said it didn't stop with the seizure of her car. She said she was thrown in jail for almost two days and threatened with being taken to a maximum security prison in Nayarit. "I could not sleep because I was thinking they were going grab me and throw me in a helicopter and I was never going to see my family again. I have three boys that are my life," said the alleged victim. The woman said she was bailed out a day and a half later but said she was told by [Mexican] customs officials she was never getting her car back. In these cases, the DMV will write letters for victims who report these incidents and provide them with the proper documentation, whether it be proof of ownership of a vehicle or an up-to-date registration. In some cases, Mexican officials have turned over the impounded vehicles back to their rightful owners.[36]

According to the 2010 Census, Hispanics account for 16.3 percent of the US population, the single largest minority. This is not equally distributed across the country, as those states in the Southwest have much larger legal Hispanic populations: Texas—37.6 percent, New Mexico—46.3 percent, Arizona—29.6 percent, California—37.6 percent, and Nevada—26.5 percent.[37] These numbers are up considerably from the

2000 (12.5 percent nationally) and 1990 (9 percent nationally) Census figures. In Texas border counties along the lower Rio Grande, from Maverick County to Cameron County on the Gulf of Mexico, Hispanics account for 88 percent or more of the population, in some cases as high as 95.7 percent.[38] In many of these counties English is no longer the language of businesses, government, or education as the population now speaks Spanish, nearly exclusively.

In the 1950s, 1960s, and 1970s people spoke of a phenomenon known as "White Flight" from cities such as Detroit and Cleveland because of racial tensions with a rising African-American population. Today, in many border counties in Texas, New Mexico, Arizona, and California, and in some cases, several counties deep into the states, there is "White Abandonment" occurring. The land, businesses, schools, and governments are being ceded to what some, like (former) Fox News political newscaster Bill O'Reilly,[39] are calling a concerted and coordinated invasion consisting of more than 11 million illegal immigrants and armed cartel forces supported by corrupt Mexican politicians, police, and military forces. According to the nonpartisan Center for Immigration Studies,

> Between 300,000 and 400,000 children are born to illegal immigrants in the United States every year. Put another way, as many as one out of 10 births in the United States is to an illegal immigrant mother. All of these children are considered ... to be US citizens who enjoy the same rights and are entitled to the same benefits as the children of US citizens.
>
> The population of US-born children with illegal alien parents has expanded rapidly in recent years.... The two citizenship benefits that have drawn the most attention in the birthright citizenship debate are, first, food assistance and other welfare benefits to which a family of illegal aliens would not otherwise have access, and second, the ability of the child when he grows up to legalize his parents, and also to bring into the United States his foreign-born spouse and any foreign-born siblings. The sponsored spouse can, in turn, sponsor her own foreign-born parents and siblings, and the siblings can, in turn, sponsor their own foreign-born spouses, and so on, generating a virtually never-ending and always-expanding migration chain.
>
> Because having a child on US soil can cement an immigrant's presence in the United States, provide access to welfare benefits, and ultimately initiate chain migration of the child's extended family and in-laws, children born to illegal aliens and legal temporary visitors are sometimes referred to as "anchor babies." These benefits have contributed to the growth of a "birth tourism" industry.
>
> Eminent legal scholars and jurists, including Professor Peter Schuck of Yale Law School and US Court of Appeals Judge Richard Posner, have questioned whether the Fourteenth Amendment should be read to mandate such a permissive citizenship policy. Nevertheless, the practice has become the de facto law of the land without any input from Congress or the American public.
>
> Advocates of maintaining this citizenship policy argue that the plain language of the Citizenship Clause of the 14th Amendment protects automatic

birthright citizenship for all children born to illegal and temporary aliens. However, several legal scholars and political scientists who have delved into the history of the 14th Amendment have concluded that "subject to the jurisdiction thereof" has no plain meaning and that the executive branch's current, broad application of the Citizenship Clause may not be warranted.

The overwhelming majority of the world's countries do not offer automatic citizenship to everyone born within their borders. Over the past few decades, many countries that once did so—including Australia, Ireland, India, New Zealand, the United Kingdom, Malta, and the Dominican Republic—have repealed those policies.[40]

In 2013 we noted this sentiment was leading to a major political, economic, cultural, and security issue that will continue to develop over the next several decades. After eight years of Obama policies and the appearance of a lack of attention to border security; the seemingly open-door policy for illegal immigrants; the surge in OTM illegals from Central America in the last three years of the administration; and the stagnant economy, with more people on food stamps than ever before and so many unemployed that (while the official rate reported was about 5 percent unemployment) nearly 95 million working-age adults had dropped from the labor force, change was on its way.[41]

The failure of the United States to deal with this phenomenon helped determine who would be elected president in November 2016. Now, with President Trump in the White House we are watching relations with Mexico evolve and the level of border security necessary to re-establish national sovereignty be altered and implemented daily. How this change plays out over the next four years will offer an interesting study in border security and homeland security.

Critical Infrastructure

A secret State Department memo sent in February 2009 identified a comprehensive inventory of critical infrastructure and key resources located outside of the US borders "whose loss could critically impact the public health, economic security, and/or national and homeland security of the United States."[42] The cable lists every border crossing, Port of Entry, hydroelectric and flood control dam, pipeline, transmission line, communications cable, rail crossing, and ferry landing between the United States and Mexico and the United States and Canada as Critical Foreign Dependencies in 2008, all of which, "if destroyed, disrupted or exploited, would likely have an immediate and deleterious effect on the United States."[43] Who protects this critical infrastructure is dependent upon which country you are in. It is the task of several agencies to provide protection for this critical infrastructure within the border of the United States. However, it is the responsibility of many agencies in Canada and Mexico to protect their end of the infrastructure. Managing this cooperative protection of critical infrastructure is essential to ensuring effective border security. This is not a U.S.-unique concept, but a critical issue for every country.

In 2010, Israel consumed 5.3 billion cubic meters of natural gas and about 90 percent went to electricity generation. While offshore gas rigs supplied about 60 percent of Israel's needs, the remainder came from Egyptian gas company EMG. Following the Egyptian revolution during the Arab Spring, and the subsequent election of Muslim Brotherhood Party Candidate Mohamed Morsi as president of Egypt, a series of attacks on natural gas pipelines by rebels/terrorists in the Sinai resulted in disruption of the natural gas supplied to Israel and Jordan. The attacks caused shortages of natural gas in both countries.[44] This is a case where political disruptions in one country have critically impacted power supplies and economics in neighboring countries.

Ethiopia, where 85 percent of the water feeding the Nile River originates, has begun diverting water from the Blue Nile River as part of a construction project on a 6,000-megawatt hydroelectric plant known as the Grand Renaissance project. What does the construction of a hydroelectric plant in Ethiopia have to do with border security or critical infrastructure? The Nile River is the lifeblood of Egypt. It has no other source of fresh water to support its agriculture, industrial, or population needs. The Nile River produces about 85 billion cubic meters a year. Egypt uses about 47 billion cubic meters of that water for irrigation and agriculture. That need is expected to increase an additional 21 billion cubic meters of water by 2050 to support its growing population. Sudan is allotted 18.5 billion cubic meters each year.[45] The result is that a hydroelectric dam in Ethiopia will strangle Egypt's water supply and their single most important key resource. Egypt's very existence is dependent upon a river that originates more than 1,000 miles away in another country. If border security includes the protection of critical infrastructure and key resources critical to the survival of the nation, where does Egypt's border security effort begin and end?

In May 2010 *Los Zetas* apparently acquired the necessary material and planned to blow up Falcon Dam along the Rio Grande. Falcon Dam is one of the critical infrastructure and key resource items listed in the State Department memo. The planned attack was apparently thwarted by increased Mexican military presence and US federal and local law enforcement presence.[46] Had *Los Zetas* succeeded in damaging the dam or causing a major failure, the water rushing out of the dam would have washed away bridges, towns, and villages all the way from Rio Grande City to the Gulf of Mexico. This would have had a significant impact on cross-border drug and human trafficking by the *Cartel Golfo*, *Los Zetas* main competition east of Laredo.

Protecting a country's critical infrastructure and key resources is essential to maintaining a vibrant and stable economy. The energy and agriculture sectors in Mexico and Canada are interrelated with those in the United States. The United States exports natural gas to Mexico. The Mexican economy is so dependent upon their northern natural gas supply they are jointly building, with American companies, four new natural gas pipelines. The United States imports oil from Canada and Mexico and is looking to import more. Ninety percent of Canada's population lives within 100 miles of the US border. Nearly the entire Canadian electrical power grid is tied to the US power grid. All three countries are tied together in such a manner that events affecting critical infrastructure or key resources in Egypt, Ethiopia, or Israel would, should they happen in North America, cause massive disruptions in the economies of the United States, Canada, and Mexico. It has happened before and will happen again, particularly as current economic growth in Mexico exceeds the ability of the infrastructure to support it and as US infrastructure continues its inexorable disintegration.[47]

Perhaps the most sensitive, and unsecured, critical infrastructure component that crosses national borders is the United States and Canadian power grid. Shortly after 4 p.m. Eastern Standard Time on August 14, 2003, in a matter of seconds, the power went out across large portions of Ohio, Michigan, Pennsylvania, Massachusetts, New York, Connecticut, New Jersey, and Ontario. The loss of the electrical grid not only turned out the lights inside buildings, but shutdown airports, subways, trains, and tunnels. No automatic doors or elevators worked. Public utilities that processed water for drinking, as well as removed sewage for treatment, suddenly stopped operating. Hospitals shifted to backup generators. People in New York City were forced to walk home. The massive northeastern blackout of 2003 was brought about when a coal generation plant in Eastlake, Ohio, tripped offline. The subsequent load on the transmission lines exceeded the carrying capacity of the electrical grid and a series of domino trips soon followed, resulting in the loss of power across the most populous regions of the United States and Canada, including the forced shutdown of nine nuclear power plants in both countries.[48]

This was not the first and will not be the last massive blackout that crosses international borders. In November 1964 a faulty relay at a Canadian nuclear power plant sent thirty million Americans and Canadians into darkness. July and August of

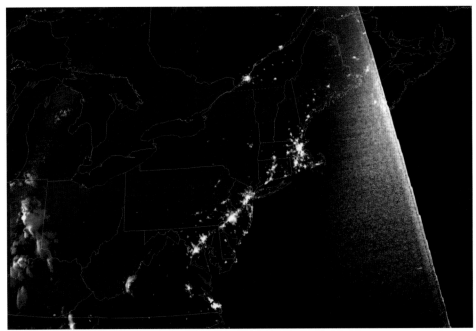

August 14, 2003. NOAA and Defense Meteorological Satellite Program images of the Northeast Blackout, at 9:03 p.m. EDT. High-resolution image available at: http://www.noaanews.noaa.gov/stories2003/images/nightlights-081503-0103z-hires.jpg.

1996 there were two major blackouts, which spanned the western United States and Canada. This was caused when extreme temperatures caused power lines to sag into untrimmed trees.[49]

Protecting a nation's critical infrastructure and key resources is essential to national sovereignty and economic security. Where does national sovereignty begin and end if power grids cross international boundaries in our globalized world? Major sections of Canada have suffered blackouts because of problems with power plants and transmission systems inside the United States. The United States has suffered blackouts that affected our largest city as a result of faulty relays in Canadian power plants. When energy systems become globalized and countries become interdependent on each other's energy infrastructure, then border security becomes a problem. Where does the border begin and end when it comes to power distribution systems?

BCC for Rent

In the early days of the US Border Patrol one focus was on the identification and removal of illegal aliens from the country. The focus was never on Hispanics, but on all people who may be in the country illegally. All sorts of people crossed the borders without permission. There were the Chinese, Central Americans and people from the Caribbean, Europeans, and Mexicans. Many people used forged documents, or papers stolen from those already legally in the United States. Many were rounded up

In this 1927 photo of Border Patrol Agents and illegal immigrants, you can clearly see that all manner of people, white, black, Hispanic, Chinese are gathered together in San Diego for a trip back across the southern border. © US Border Patrol Museum. Used with permission.

and processed for return across the border. Today, with the advent of improved identification and documentation of visitors and immigrants, it is much more difficult
to forge documents. Instead, a whole new industry has arisen to provide appropriate
documents to those without legal access to the United States.

"So, you want to visit the United States? It will cost you $25." So says the purveyor
of Border Crossing Cards (BCC) in a bar/restaurant just across the Bridge of the
Americas from downtown El Paso. Around him are a small group of about 20 women
and men who want to cross into the United States. As he takes their money, he looks
through a thick binder with hundreds of pages of see-though plastic pouches, each
one containing a valid BCC that was "lost" or "stolen" by/from a person with official
approval to cross into the United States. When he finds one with a photo that closely
resembles the person in front of him, he pulls it out and gives it to them with the ad-
monishment that upon clearing customs and immigration they will have to return it
to his "man" who will accompany them across the bridge.

When the group has paid the "rental fee" and each individual received a BCC that
looks a lot like them, they are gathered together and walk across the Bridge of the
Americas, flooding the CBP clearance facility along with valid travelers. Faced with
constant pressure from their administrators and supervisors to keep the wait time to
a minimum, CBP agents allow nearly all those who approach their kiosk with a valid
BCC to enter the United States, even though some of them may be questionable. It
is easier to let them pass than to direct them for secondary inspection and further
evaluation and to suffer the wrath of supervisory and administrative personnel who
see the delays as affecting performance measures predicated on minimizing wait times.

Bridge of the Americas, El Paso, Texas. James Phelps. 2013.

Once the individuals are through the inspection station, the renter's "man" (who actually has a valid BCC of his own) meets the people in the parking lot, collects their rented BCCs, and returns to Mexico. He will make four or five trips a day, seven days a week, with as many as 15–20 people in each trip.

Few, if any of the BCC renters are a threat to the United States. Almost none will be caught, although on occasion some will be directed to secondary inspection, their ID confiscated and the individual turned around and returned to Mexico. Most will simply head to Wal-Mart or some other major shopping center, visit a son or daughter, or perhaps remain a few days or weeks visiting relatives. Then they will walk back across the Bridge of the Americas and head home. This is a normal routine for them, less expensive than the formal process of getting a Mexican passport and applying for a BCC. If they have been barred from entry into the United States because they have previously been caught, or have been deported in the past, this is their only way of getting around a system that punishes illegal immigrants.

Birth Tourism

The Fourteenth Amendment to the United States Constitution guarantees US citizenship to those born on its territory, provided that the person is subject to the jurisdiction of the United States. This exempts the children of diplomats. Recently, there has arisen a new form of tourism to the United States; tourists visit specifically to have children born in the country. Barbara Demick reported on this exploding tourism in a Los Angeles Times article in May 2002. According to Demick, who interviewed pregnant women from Korea, most of them come to the United States and pay cash for the medical procedures, guaranteeing they are not in violation of US laws on tourist visas while guaranteeing their children US citizenship and a US passport.[50]

We often forget that the United States has several outlying territories and protectorates, including Guam and the Mariana Islands. Children born in these territories and protectorates are US citizens. This has created a situation where, without ever having to come to the US proper, a foreign national can simply board a charter flight to Saipan as a tourist and stay long enough to give birth in this remote and outlying territory and their child will get all the benefits of US citizenship. According to the Commonwealth Healthcare Corp's vital statistics department, in 2012 more Chinese women gave birth in the Northern Mariana Islands than all other races, including the indigenous Chamorro peoples. Entire medical facilities served by Mandarin-speaking physicians and staff caters to these "birth tourists." With eight weekly flights from Shanghai and Beijing to the Northern Mariana Islands, upwards of 8,000 tourists a month arrive in the islands. "Most tourism watchers believe the trend of giving birth to what some call 'anchor babies' by Chinese nationals will continue to rise rapidly."[51] For those who are pregnant, the cost is only $6,000 to $8,000 for the pre-natal-through-delivery medical care and about $150 per month in rent.[52] From January 2015 to September 2016, 715 US citizens were born to foreign nationals "visiting" the Marianas Islands. These included 692

Chinese, 15 Koreans, 5 Filipinos, 2 Japanese, and 1 Russian. It's interesting that those practicing "birth tourism" to Saipan are now Chinese. This resulted from the lifting of visa waivers for Chinese and Russian tourists in 2009. In 2009, there were only 2 babies born to Chinese nationals visiting Saipan. In 2012 that number had jumped to 282 and in 2016 to 692.[53] This problem is so significant it has altered the very nature of health care on Saipan — to the point the health care system is asking for federal assistance to cover the costs of births that are simply left unpaid by new mothers once they receive their US birth certificates for their new babies and return to China. In the two and a half years from January 2014 to October 2016, 32.92 percent of births on Saipan were to Chinese parents.[54]

This is not just an issue for remote and outlying territories. According to a January 2013 ABC News broadcast segment, Senator Lindsay Graham informed ABC News that of 4 million births annually in the United States, 7,670 are the result of "birth tourism," children born to mothers who do not live in the United States. The Chinese-language website AsiamChild.com advertises to Chinese women that for between $5,000 and $15,000 they can pre purchase a birthing package that covers all expenses, just outside of Los Angles, California. [**Note:** this website was originally available on the public web. As awareness of the illegal nature of these activities spread, the website, and most others like it, have moved to the dark web and are no longer available via Google, Yahoo, or Bing search engines. We strongly advise students NOT to search for these services without advice from faculty members.] The website includes tips for expectant mothers on how to hide their pregnancies from US customs officers so they can receive a tourist visa.[55] According to Jay Chang, a consultant for nine maternity homes in Los Angles, the trend in "birth tourism"[56] is on the rise, with "more than 40 maternity operations that host 1,000 women in the Los Angeles area alone."[57] For $3,000 to $6,000 a month "the maternity homes provide three meals a day, transportation, and child care.... They even make arrangements with Chinese doctors in the United States who charge $7,000 for a birth."[58]

"Jus Soli"

The doctrine of *jus soli* (Latin: right of the soil) implies that everyone born in a country is a citizen of that country. This differs from the doctrine of *jus sanguinis* (Latin: right of blood) that awards citizenship based on the citizenship of the parents. The United States practices both doctrines. Under the Fourteenth Amendment to the US Constitution, citizenship is granted automatically to all persons born within the territory of the United States. Additionally, all children born to US citizens who are outside of the territory of the United States at the time of that birth are also granted US citizenship. Therefore, a person serving overseas in the US military, for the State Department, or on a business assignment or trip to visit relatives knows that if they give birth while outside of the United States that child will still have US citizenship.

Of the advanced economies of the world, as identified by the International Monetary Fund, only Canada and the United States still practice *jus soli*. Twenty-eight other countries also hold to the doctrine, nearly all of them in North and South America.

A number of the advanced economies of the world have recently withdrawn from the practice of *jus soli* to discourage illegal immigration. By imposing additional requirements, such as at least one of the parents being a citizen of the country before the birth or having resided in the country for a specified period of time as a legal permanent resident, these countries have erected a barrier to the former practice and brought an end to the practice of "birth tourism" within their borders. Among these countries are Australia (1986), Germany (2000), Ireland (2005), New Zealand (2006), South Africa (1995), and the United Kingdom — England, Wales, and Scotland (1983).

Asian birth tourism is just part of the overall industry. Eastern Europeans, wealthy Arabs, Indians, wealthy Mexicans, and others all participate in the birth tourism traffic. Some hospitals actively advertise their quality maternity services in foreign countries to draw in business. According to Selin Burcuog Lu, a Turkish woman who traveled to the United States to give birth last year, the process was easy: "We found a company on the Internet and decided to go to Austin for our child's birth. It was incredibly professional. They organized everything for me. I had no problem adjusting and I had an excellent birth. I don't want her to deal with visa issues, American citizenship has so many advantages."[59] Turkish doctors, hotel owners, and immigrant families in the United States have assembled what amounts to a birth-tourism assembly line, reportedly arranging the US birth of 14,000 Turkish children since 2003. The Turkish-owned Marmara Hotel group offers a "birth tourism package" that includes accommodations at their Manhattan branch. "We hosted 15 families last year [2009]," said Nur Ercan Mag den, head manager of The Marmara Manhattan, adding that the cost was $45,000 each. In other New York hotels the cost runs between $25,000 and $40,000.[60]

This raises the question of the intent of the law versus the letter of the law. All of the above is perfectly legal based on the Fourteenth Amendment to the Constitution and current immigration law. But was that the intent of the Constitution and immigration law? More importantly, the question to be asked in about twenty years will be what the impact of "birth tourism" is on visas for legal immigrant aliens and their spouses and children who have extraordinary ability in the sciences, arts, education, business, etc.? With citizenship by birth to tourist offspring, in about 20 years the United States can expect to see a significant rise in children sponsoring their parents and siblings (and associated spouses and their children) to join them in the United States. This has the potential to significantly impact the numbers of visas available for those truly skilled persons our businesses and economy are dependent upon recruiting from other countries as the US native population continues to see a degradation in science, technology, engineering, and math (STEM) graduates from college.

More importantly, what will the impact be on public health services, social welfare programs, politics, education, infrastructure, etc. as all these "citizens" born in the United States but never residing in the country suddenly decide to exercise their rights, come to the United States, and sponsor all their family members?

Border Security and Globalization

Throughout this book the topic of globalization has been discussed. Globalization is the process of international integration arising from the interchange of worldviews, products, ideas, and other aspects of culture. Advances in transportation and telecommunications have resulted in interdependence of economic and cultural activities. This is demonstrated by "birth tourism," the presence of Kentucky Fried Chicken and McDonald's franchise restaurants in China, Hong Kong, Dubai, and Moscow, and the acceptance of the US dollar as the common currency of international business and exchange. Border security is fundamentally tied to the globalized economy. Globalized trade, outsourcing, supply-chaining, and political forces that have permanently changed the world were brought to American's attention by Thomas L. Friedman's *The Dell Theory of Conflict Prevention*.[61] Many "American" brands are now multinational corporations. You would be familiar with some, such as Coca-Cola, General Motors, Ford, Exxon-Mobil, Shell, and General Electric. Through the exchange of capital, goods, and services across international borders these multinational corporations have a major impact on world trade. The growth of international trade is a fundamental component of globalization and has expanded significantly with the establishment of special economic zones and free trade agreements. Having already discussed the impact of NAFTA, international smuggling, and cybercrime in previous chapters, our concern with globalization in this chapter is the impact it has on border security, in particular the food supply chain and transnational organized crime.

Globalized Agriculture

"Much of US plant and animal agriculture will be a part of industrialized food systems by the year 2020."

—Michael Boehlje, Purdue University[62]

Nearly everybody reading this book will have bought his or her food at a local grocery store or restaurant. Most of the readers will not have access to a local farmer's market nor will they be growers of their own produce. Globalization has directly impacted the everyday life of everybody in the industrialized world, particularly the manner in which people eat. One in five food items is imported. We can eat fresh strawberries when it is 20 degrees outside. American consumers demand fresh limes, blueberries, apples, lettuce, etc., all year round. In the winter, nearly 80 percent of our fresh food comes from other countries.[63]

A case in point: at your local grocery store, look at the bananas. They are certainly not a product of Canada, the United States, Great Britain, Germany, Korea, or South Africa. Depending on the brand, if you are in the United States you will find that your bananas come from Mexico, Guatemala, Honduras, Nicaragua, Panama, Colombia, and Ecuador. Unless you purchase some unique variety of bananas, the ones that are on the shelf in your local grocery came from a tropical country within 20 degrees on either side of the equator and most likely from Central American countries. The largest producer of bananas in the world is India, with nearly 30 million metric tons produced in 2011.[64] There are even "banana" websites just to provide information to consumers. According to the Chiquita Brand banana website, "the average American eats 27 pounds of bananas each year!"[65]

Bread is a staple food product around the world. Bread is made from wheat. China and India are the largest producers of wheat in the world, with the United States the third largest. According to United Nation statistics, in 2009 the United States produced more than 60 million metric tons of wheat and exported more than 23 million metric tons of the wheat produced. The country consumed about 25 million metric tons of the wheat as food. When it comes to wheat (and other cereal grains) the United States has achieved food security and is a net exporter of grains (except for rye and oats).[66] The United States also grows more potatoes, sweet potatoes, sugar, beans, peas, soybeans, vegetables, and grapefruits than it can consume, exporting the remainder. When it comes to bananas, the United States imports more than 3.5 metric tons each year. The United States also does not produce sufficient vegetable oils, apples, oranges, lemons and limes, grapes, coffee, tea, or beef to meet consumer demand. The United States also consumes significantly more freshwater and saltwater fish, crab, and shrimp than is produced.[67]

Looking at another industrialized nation, Great Britain (England, Wales, and Scotland), we see a country that imports one third of all the potatoes, all the rice, sweet potatoes, more than half of the sugar, all of the beans and soybeans, two thirds of the vegetable oil, over half of all vegetables, nearly all of its fruit and citrus, all of the coffee and tea, and, most importantly, more than half of the meat it consumes.[68]

According to Michael Boehlje of Purdue University, "Dramatic changes are occurring in the agricultural sector today. These changes provide opportunities for some, but threats for others. Twenty-first century agriculture is likely to be characterized by: more global competition; expansion of industrialized agriculture; production of differentiated products; precision (information-intensive) production; emergence of ecological agriculture; formation of food supply chains; increasing risk; and more diversity."[69] Industrialized agriculture means the movement away from small farms to large-scale production that operates with standardized technology and management systems. Food produced on an industrial scale. Consider the bag of carrots you buy in the local grocery. They are all the same length, diameter, and uniform color. This is not how carrots grow in a family plot. At a local farmer's market you will find that the carrots, when in season, are different sizes, shapes, and vary in color. But when you bite into a locally grown or homegrown carrot, the flavor is significantly better than that of the mass-produced product.

Boehlje has accurately predicted that, "smaller operations not associated with an industrialized system will have increasing difficulty gaining the economies of size and the access to technology required to be competitive."[70] Yet there is, in response to the globalized and industrialized agriculture system a backlash of local producers and advertising to "buy local." The local producer, who sells eggs for $4 a dozen, competes with the industrial producer that sells eggs for 89 cents a dozen. "Industrialized food systems are those that are holistic in production-processing-marketing and organized to deliver specific-attribute consumer products by development of optimized delivery systems or through differentiation by science or branding."[71]

Return to our Chiquita banana. The entire system in place for selling bananas to American customers is a self-contained food system, from the farms in Central America, to the transportation and processing of the bananas, to the advertisements seen on TV. According to the US Department of Agriculture,

> The structure of the global food industry is continually changing and evolving as food suppliers, manufacturers, and retailers adjust to meet the needs of consumers, who are increasingly demanding a wider variety of higher quality products. Having firsthand knowledge of consumer preferences and purchase habits, food retailers are positioned to transmit this information upstream to other segments of the supply chain. In the quest to meet consumer demands for variety, affordability, safety, and quality, the food retail sector is constantly evolving and generating innovative sale formats. In addition to the popular supermarket format, hypermarkets, discounters, convenience stores, and combined gasoline and grocery outlets have emerged in numerous countries in recent years. Global food retail sales are about $4 trillion annually, with supermarkets/hypermarkets accounting for the largest share of sales. Most of the leading global retailers are US and European firms, as large multinational retailers expand their presence in developing countries and small retail firms increasingly account for a smaller share of total food sales. The top 15 global supermarket companies account for more than 30 percent of world supermarket sales. With improved technologies and economies of size, these retailers enjoy operating cost advantages over smaller local retailers.[72]

The FAO (Food and Agriculture Organization of the UN) Food Security Program defines food security thusly: "Food security exists when all people, at all times, have physical and economic access to sufficient safe and nutritious food that meets their dietary needs and food preferences for an active and healthy life."[73] The World Health Organization defines three facets of food security: food availability, food access, and food use. Food availability is having available sufficient quantities of food on a consistent basis. Food access is having sufficient resources, both economic and physical, to obtain appropriate foods for a nutritious diet. Food use is the appropriate use based on knowledge of basic nutrition and care, as well as adequate water and sanitation.

What does food security have to do with border security? The less secure a country's borders are, the more vulnerable the food supply. Additionally, even countries with high food security, such as Great Britain, face a significant problem in that their sovereignty as a country is vulnerable as they are dependent upon imports to feed their population. Cut off from imports, Great Britain would find itself suffering from famine within a week or two. The United States, because of its size and geography could be cut off from food imports and still provide for the survival needs of its population. However, should an invasive species find its way across the borders and into the wheat belt, the entire country would face a major problem. This is where the US Customs and Border Protection Agriculture Protection Program becomes an essential component of border security.

Agroterrorism

Agro-terrorism is terrorism targeting some component of agriculture or the food supply. Examples include the intentional introduction of a plant or animal pest or disease or contamination of food materials with a toxic substance. Agricultural inspections have traditionally focused on unintentional introduction of pests or diseases—those unnoticed in someone's luggage or hitchhiking on the walls of a container.[74]

With millions of pounds of fresh fruits, vegetables, cut flowers, herbs, and other items entering the United States every year, the CBP Agriculture Specialists work to identify, detect, target, intercept, and ultimately prevent harmful species from entering the country. Every year these border security specialists intercept tens of thousands of pests that are a threat to US agriculture. They use specialized x-ray machines that detect organic materials. They utilize agricultural canines specifically trained to sniff out meat and plant materials in international airport passenger areas. They find the most interesting items, from roasted bat to uncooked yak sausage to destructive insects.

In addition to food and agriculture products, there are a number of other ways that harmful pests can be introduced into a country. With thousands of trucks passing through ports of entry daily, and hundreds of cargo container ships docking in ports, the potential that a single, long-horned beetle will get into the country is pretty high. What's one beetle? In this case, the beetle is a threat to forests of all kinds. Its larvae are woodborers and will destroy trees, untreated lumber, and can cause significant damage to wood frame structures. They have no natural enemies in North America and would wreak havoc on the US forestry industry. It is the responsibility of CBP agricultural inspectors to check incoming cargo from areas where long-horned beetles are native to ensure that none hopped a free ride to the United States.

There are any numbers of invasive species that are detrimental to a country's national ecosystem. Invasive species compete so successfully when introduced into a new ecosystem that they displace native species and disrupt important ecological

Left: Pests that enter the United States via imported flowers could cause extensive damage, so here a CBP agriculture specialist at Miami International Airport performs a thorough examination. CBP.gov. 2013.

Center: A long-horned beetle, *Rhytidodera bowningii*, discovered in a container of granite countertops. William Tang. CBP.gov. 2013.

Right: May 2013: US Customs and Border Protection officers intercepted and seized nearly half a pound of elephant meat and a dead primate at the International Mail Facility. They also seized 387 snake, lizard, and crocodile skin handbags from a passenger arriving from Nigeria at the Los Angeles International Airport (LAX). Jamie Ruiz. CBP Photography.

processes. Plants, fish, insects, mammals, birds, and diseases can all be invasive. So concerning is the issue of invasive species that President Clinton wrote an Executive Order (EO 13112) establishing the National Invasive Species Council to ensure that federal programs and activities were coordinated, effective, and efficient in addressing the problem. The secretaries and Administrators of 13 federal departments and agencies now coordinate their activities to prevent and control invasive species. EO 13112 defines invasive species as "[A]lien (or non-native) species whose introduction does, or is likely to cause, economic or environmental harm or harm to human health."[75] To determine what invasive species are in each state, the US Department of Agriculture maintains a website: www.invasivespeciesinfo.gov. A quick check of listings for Colorado found that there are 157 different nonindigenous aquatic species,[76] including the northern cricket frog, freshwater jellyfish, American eel, rock bass, green sunfish, neon tetra, brown watersnake, snapping turtle, coho salmon, cutbow trout, and many other species that are considered invasive. There are also noxious weeds, invasive plants, and pests. There are 98 invasive threats to Colorado's forests, among them 4 species of beetle.[77] Stopping invasive species from getting into the United States or moving through the United States after establishing themselves is essential to ensuring the country maintains a significant defense against the ecological and economic damage such species bring.

It was previously stated that Border Security is Homeland Security. It can also be said that Border Security is Food and Agricultural Security.

Dealing with Transnational Crime

Transnational Organized Crime of all sorts is recognized as a threat to National Security. According to the president's Strategy to Combat Transnational Organized Crime:

> Transnational organized crime refers to those self-perpetuating associations of individuals who operate transnationally for the purpose of obtaining power, influence, monetary and/or commercial gains, wholly or in part by illegal means, while protecting their activities through a pattern of corruption and/or violence, or while protecting their illegal activities through a transnational organizational structure and the exploitation of transnational commerce or communication mechanisms. There is no single structure under which transnational organized criminals operate; they vary from hierarchies to clans, networks, and cells, and may evolve to other structures. The crimes they commit also vary. Transnational organized criminals act conspiratorially in their criminal activities and possess certain characteristics that may include, but are not limited to:
> - In at least part of their activities they commit violence or other acts which are likely to intimidate, or make actual or implicit threats to do so;
> - They exploit differences between countries to further their objectives, enriching their organization, expanding its power, and/or avoiding detection/apprehension;
> - They attempt to gain influence in government, politics, and commerce through corrupt as well as legitimate means;
> - They have economic gain as their primary goal, not only from patently illegal activities but also from investment in legitimate businesses; and
> - They attempt to insulate both their leadership and membership from detection, sanction, and/or prosecution through their organizational structure.[78]

According to the president's strategy, transnational criminal organizations pose a significant and growing threat to national and international security. TCOs pose a dire threat to public safety, health, democracy, and economic stability worldwide. Not only are TCOs expanding, they are diversifying their activities. TCOs use corruption of public officials, disrupt the global supply chain, threaten the existence of a free press, and suborn the democratic system in countries. There is even a coordination of efforts between TCOs and terrorist organizations, such as Hezbollah and FARC, to exchange training in military and terrorist skills for illicitly received cash.[79]

Whether it is drug cartels and international gangs importing and selling drugs across the United States and Europe, e-mail SPAM originating in Nigeria, or Russian Organized Crime computer hackers, the criminals are taking advantage of borders to protect themselves from prosecution. To address this international criminal behavior effectively, the legal system that constrains law enforcement agencies to specified jurisdictions has to undergo evolutionary change. The beginnings of this can be seen in the cooperative operations between some countries to address this type of globalized crime. Much more needs to be done.

The fundamental problem with addressing this issue is that the very concept of sovereign territory fails in the face of organized international criminal cartels. The criminal laws that states and countries operate under originated in an era when all crime was local. Today, virtually all crime has some sort of international tie. Ranging from humans trafficked in prostitution in Europe, to the child sex trade in Southeast Asia, the organizations involved, and their customers, are international in nature.

Not too long ago US criminal laws stopped at the border. A US citizen who participated in prostitution (as a customer) when outside of the country had not violated any US criminal laws, even if they had sex with a child. Today, a US citizen who knowingly purchases sex from a person who is under age, or forced to work as a prostitute, or who has been trafficked, will find themselves subject to arrest and prosecution upon their return to the United States. The United States has taken a first step toward recognizing that much misery around the world is the result of citizen participation in what would be considered criminal behavior within the national boundaries, and the United States is addressing such significant issues as human trafficking and child sex trafficking by holding its citizens accountable upon return to the United States.

> [T]he American citizen or national may be subject to prosecution under 18 U.S.C. § 2423(c). Even if the person did not have the intent to engage in sex with a minor at the time he or she left the United States, such intent at the time of travel is not necessary. For example, an American citizen or national who travels to a foreign country without any such intent, but who engages in a commercial sex act with a person under 18 at some point during his stay in that foreign country, may be subject to prosecution.[80]

Russians, Ukrainians, Greeks, French, Japanese, Chinese, Colombians, Brazilians, Nigerians, South Africans, and many other peoples are not subject to similar enforcement of national law on acts committed outside of their national jurisdiction. Until laws such as the ones US citizens are subject to are instituted in every country in the world, making all of their citizens subject to prosecution and conviction for crimes committed outside of their national borders, the international trade in humans for sex will continue.

The same situation applies to issues of cybercrime and intellectual property theft. It is not illegal in Nigeria to send SPAM e-mail messages to hundreds of thousands of Americans and attempt (and sometimes succeed) in defrauding the victims of their money. It might be a crime to commit such an act within Nigeria against Nigerians but their legal code and system of enforcement is difficult to interpret. If a person within the United States defrauds another person within the United States the legal system will come into play to address the crime and attempt to rectify the victim's loss. Recently, the Justice Department has taken on the investigation and prosecution of international criminals who have defrauded Americans, including the conviction of a Nigerian national who defrauded victims of $1.5 million, and eleven residents of Israel who ran an illegal lottery that targeted Americans.[81] It is important to note that these were huge scams, costing victims millions of dollars.

We have already discussed at length the issue of expanding power and violence of drug cartels. These are also TCOs that are targeted by the president's *Strategy to*

Combat Transnational Organized Crime. One of the more recent successes was the disruption of a money-laundering operation in Oklahoma, New Mexico, California, and Texas that was sending money to Mexico to support the TCO *Los Zetas.* Each of the four men was found guilty of one count of conspiracy to commit money laundering. One of the men convicted, Jose Trevino Morales is the brother of *Los Zetas* leaders Miguel Trevino Morales and Oscar Omar Trevino Morales. Beginning in 2008, Miguel and Oscar Trevino Morales funneled cash from illegal drug sales to Jose Trevino Morales and his wife to buy, train, breed and race the horses, using front companies to hide the cartel's ownership. During the trial evidence was presented by the government prosecutors of millions of dollars in financial transactions.[82]

The presidential strategy for dealing with TCOs sets out five overarching policy objectives:

1. Protect Americans and our partners from the harm, violence, and exploitation of transnational criminal networks.
2. Help partner countries strengthen governance and transparency, break the corruptive power of transnational criminal networks, and sever state-crime alliances.
3. Break the economic power of transnational criminal networks and protect strategic markets and the US financial system from … penetration and abuse.
4. Defeat transnational criminal networks that pose the greatest threat to national security, by targeting their infrastructures, depriving them of their enabling means, and preventing criminal facilitation of terrorist activities.
5. Build international consensus, multilateral cooperation, and public-private partnerships to defeat transnational organized crime.[83]

The major TCOs of concern are the narcotraficantes in Mexico, and the organizations that deal in human trafficking.

Alternatives to Fixed Fortifications

"We need to see borders not as barriers, but as avenues of opportunity. We need to see the advantages inherent in closer cooperation…. The phenomenon we call globalization—the massive movement of goods, services, ideas, money, and people—has dramatically undermined the ability of national governments to manage their economies and protect societies without significant collaboration with other governments. National governments strain to deal with the social and political consequences of this."

—Stephen Zamora, Director of the Center for US and Mexican Law,
University of Houston Law Center, 2013[84]

Voices in the United States have been rising to a crescendo, calling for politicians to do something about the unsecure borders, in particular the southern US border.

These calls are being heard. State legislatures are taking action, such as the passage of Arizona HB 1070, in an attempt to carry out the immigration control functions the federal government has apparently abandoned. The federal government has brought lawsuits against several states in an attempt to drive the federal courts to decisions that will reinforce federal supremacy over the states, and is succeeding. However, as courts overturn parts of state legislation and leave other parts standing, there is a need for a concerted effort at the federal level to address the issue of illegal immigration, invading Mexican military forces, and the sacrifice of large sections of the southern border to the control of narcotraficante organizations.

Donald Trump was elected the 45th President of the United States on a platform advocating building a wall between Mexico and the U.S., having Mexico pay for that wall, renegotiating NAFTA, and bring industrial jobs back to America. His America First speech at his inauguration on January 20, 2017, clearly brought home these points.[85] Yet, in the first six months of the Trump presidency, state and federal courts, democrat Governors, and democrats in congress are aggressively acting to prevent the implementation of executive orders and confirmation of appointments to federal departments that would address issues of national sovereignty. How this plays out in the courts over the next several years will make for another interesting study by students and faculty using this book.

According to former Pinal County (Arizona) Sheriff Paul Babeu, whose county lies at the center of major drug and alien smuggling routes to Phoenix and cities east and west,

> [H]is deputies are outmanned and outgunned by drug traffickers in the rough-hewn desert stretches of his own county. "Mexican drug cartels literally do control parts of Arizona," he said. "They literally have scouts on the high points in the mountains and in the hills and they literally control movement. They have radios, they have optics, they have night-vision goggles as good as anything law enforcement has". "This is going on here in Arizona," he said. "This is 70 to 80 miles from the border—30 miles from the fifth-largest city in the United States." He said he asked the Obama administration for 3,000 National Guard soldiers to patrol the border, but what he got were 15 signs.[86]

Those signs warned the public that travel was not recommended. That they would be entering an active drug and human smuggling area where they may encounter armed criminals and smuggling vehicles traveling at high rates of speed. Visitors were warned to stay away from trash, clothing, backpacks, and abandoned vehicles and if they encountered suspicious activity, to call 911. The Bureau of Land Management signs encouraged visitors to use public lands north of Interstate 8, essentially ceding to the drug and human traffickers all the lands south of Interstate 8.

As this book goes to print, President Trump has directed the Department of Homeland Security to build a wall along the border with Mexico; the DHS has been ordered to enforce America's immigration laws and move to arrest and deport illegal migrants; and on March 18, 2017, at a news conference in the White House with German Chancellor Merkel the President said, "Immigration security is national security [and] … Immigration is a privilege and not a right, and the safety of our citizens must always come first." Nice statement and a strongly felt political position of many Americans, but clearly not one the activist federal courts and Democrat-controlled states will allow to pass without challenge.

There are those who feel fixed fortifications and increased staffing won't create a secure border. According to Dr. Zamora, of the University of Houston Law Center, the solution is an expansion of investment in the security and stability of Mexico, to enhance the productivity of Mexican labor, thereby reducing the likelihood of illegal Mexican migration to the United States out of economic need.[87] Dr. Zamora is not alone. In 2010, *Forbes Magazine*, a leading business publication, called for the United States to open its borders to anyone who wanted to immigrate:

> America should open its borders. Anyone who wants to immigrate to the U.S. should be allowed to, with the bare minimum of bureaucracy. Those already here illegally should be legalized. Open borders would make this country richer, more entrepreneurial — and more secure. Critics object that lawbreaking [sic] illegals should not be rewarded. Yet for the most part these people's only crime is wanting to work hard to earn a better life for themselves and their children — the epitome of the American Dream. They do the jobs that most people spurn: pick fruit, wash dishes, pack meat. Without them America would grind to a halt. Government efforts to stop migration have mainly driven it underground — at huge financial and human cost. Billions of dollars are wasted annually in a futile effort to seal an inherently unsealable [sic] border. More people have died trying to cross over from Mexico in the past decade than were killed on Sept. 11. Ever tougher measures won't work: Documents can be forged or stolen, people smuggled, officials bribed. Even with a shoot-to-kill policy, people got across the Berlin Wall. Ending this senseless and unwinnable war would make America more secure, not less — instead of chasing harmless migrants, federal agents could concentrate on identifying and neutralizing homegrown and foreign terrorists. Above all, opening the border would bring huge economic benefits.[88]

Andrew Filipowski reminds us that the United States is a nation built on the blood, sweat, and tears of waves of immigrants. With a disproportionate number of companies being started by immigrants, particularly in the technology arena, immigration is an imperative to maintaining the technological and economic viability of the country. Filipowski calls on the United States to open its doors and incentivize talented technology and engineering students to remain in the country when they graduate from school. Instead, the United States maintains an immigration policy that, with current delays in processing work visas, results in the skilled and motivated Indian immigrant having to wait 70 years to get a work visa.[89] For a Mexican it is over 130 years. Thus the tremendous efforts people exercise to circumvent existing immigration processes.

To some the call to secure the borders is a call to secure them against nannies, engineers, carpenters, and waiters. What about the fear of terrorists coming into the country? They can get into the country through open borders but they are more likely already in the United States and other countries as terrorism moves away from an international Al Qaeda-like organization to a much more distributed, lone-wolf, and independent type of terrorist.

Terrorism Today

Dzhokhar Tsarnaev (born 1993) and his brother Tamerlan (1986–2013) came to the United States legally. Dzhokar arrived with his parents in 2002 on a 90-day tourist visa. His parents applied for and received asylum, with their four children being awarded derivative asylum. On April 15, 2013, Dzhokar and his brother Tamerlan (are believed to have) perpetrated the Boston Marathon bombings, killing of a police officer at MIT, and a carjacking, resulting in four deaths and more than 260 injuries including more than 34 people having to undergo amputations due to the effect of the two explosives the brothers (are accused of having) planted. Both brothers were in the United States legally. Tamerlan, the older brother, had traveled multiple times to Russia and Dagestan, was identified by the Russian Federal Police (FSB) as a potential radical Islamist with terroristic tendencies, and placed on a CIA watchlist. However, he was not prevented from returning to the United States and even made application to become a naturalized US citizen in September 2012. The younger brother, Dzhokhar, became a naturalized citizen on September 11, 2012, eleven years after the 9/11 terrorist attacks. Both brothers were in the United States legally, one a naturalized citizen and the other with an application pending. The older of the two was married to an American citizen. Yet they became radicalized and carried out terrorist attacks against the United States because they were angry about the US wars in Afghanistan and Iraq and the killing of Muslims there.[90] The note left by Dzhokar in his hiding place, just prior to his capture, says, "The bombings were in retribution for the US crimes in places like Iraq and Afghanistan [and] that the victims of the Boston bombing were collateral damage, in the same way innocent victims have been collateral damage in US wars around the world."[91]

Faisal Shahzad, a 30-year-old Pakistan-born resident of Connecticut, who became a US citizen in April 2009, attempted to set off a vehicle-borne improvised explosive device in New York City's Time's Square on May 1, 2010. Although he succeeded in lighting the bomb and exiting the area, the bomb was poorly designed and did not detonate. Shahzad had received training in a Pakistani terrorist training camp in the same region that is the home of Al Qaeda and the Pakistani Taliban.[92] Shahzad had come to the United States on an F-1 student visa in 1999, was granted a 3-year H1-B skilled worker visa in 2002, received an M.B.A. in 2005, a green card in 2006, and became a US citizen in April 2009 through his marriage to an American citizen. As early as his arrival in 1999 the US Customs Service (now DHS-ICE) had placed him on a travel watch list.[93]

US-born Nidal Malik Hasan, a major in the US Army Medical Corps, carried out an instance of "workplace violence" at Fort Hood, Texas, on November 5, 2009, when just prior to being deployed to Afghanistan he walked into the Soldier Readiness Processing Center shouting "*Allahu Akbar!*" and shot 42 people, killing 13. At the time of this writing,

Major Hasan's court martial has yet to begin, having been delayed for nearly four years by political wrangling, including whether the shooting was an instance of terrorism or workplace violence (as the US Army and Department of Justice have classified it).[94]

On July 7, 2005, three bombs were detonated on the London Underground and a fourth on an above-ground bus, resulting in 52 killed (not including the 4 bombers) and more than 700 injured. Of the four bombers, three were British-born sons of Pakistani immigrants and the fourth was a convert to Islam born in Jamaica (a British island).[95]

British soldier Lee Rigby (age 25) was run down with a car, stabbed, and hacked to death in broad daylight on a London street, not far from his military barracks. The men who killed him on May 23, 2013, were two British citizens of African descent.[96] The two suspected murderers, who were caught at the scene covered in blood and holding the knives and cleavers used to kill Rigby, were scheduled to go on trial in November 2013.[97]

There is an ongoing shift toward local, lone-wolf terrorists. Building fences and securing borders does not stop these individuals. A better approach to countering this shift in terrorism will have to be addressed through revisions to immigration and naturalization laws, counterterrorism laws, and the systems used to identify and track potential threats. In all of the cases above, except Hasan's, the perpetrators were identified as potential threats by the authorities before they carried out their terrorist attacks. Hasan should have been identified in advance and would have been except for political correctness and a desire not to express anti-Muslim sentiment in military performance evaluations, even though Hasan's contacts with radical Islam were known.

Even if we reach back to the terrorist attacks of September 11, 2001, we find that all those involved in hijacking the planes had initially entered the United States legally. Some had overstayed their visas, or misused them, but they initially entered the country legally.

Defense in Depth

Looking back at Chapters 2, 4, and 5, we see that the best defense is a defense in depth. From the earliest forms of border security, to modern day physical security, the key to effectively protecting sovereign territory, whether it is a country or a nuclear power plant, comes down to instituting and maintaining effective layers of protection. Consider that a nuclear power plant has exterior fencing, motion sensors, cameras, lights, and roving patrols. People who want to enter the facility have to undergo background and security examinations before they can even get to the entry gate. Once through the initial processing, they can only access areas approved by their clearance and level of responsibility. To get into the plant's control room is a whole additional level of security. To actually get into the nuclear containment is virtually impossible. The most important parts of the nuclear power plant, the control room and the actual reactor, are protected by steel-reinforced concrete to ensure that even an aircraft crashing into the building will not damage critical components. The nuclear power plant company could have expended the money to completely enclose the entire facility in impenetrable concrete but that would have been a complete waste of money and added little to the essential security of the facility.

A country is much like a nuclear power facility. There are very important places that need to be completely enclosed and protected, the critical infrastructure and key resources essential to cultural, economic, and political survival. Outside of these areas, there are the places where people who have the right to be there can easily move around to carry out their lives, go to and from work and school, and pursue happiness with a level of liberty unencumbered by excessive rules and regulations, or checkpoints. Outside of this area are the people who should not be granted, or haven't been granted access to the country. They should go through the proper vetting procedures to gain access, and become members of the country when access is granted, assimilating into the "culture" as much as they bring their "culture" with them.

Nuclear power plants do not operate without external supplies, equipment, parts, food, water, and fuel shipments. These have to have a way to get into the plant facility from outside the fence. The plant does not want bombs or terrorists entering the facility any more than a country wants to see a weapon of mass destruction or an invasive agricultural species allowed in along with all the food, fuel, and parts necessary to keep an economy and country functioning.

Experts, engineers, scientists, and skilled labor are needed to operate and maintain a nuclear power plant. They are also needed to ensure a vibrant and innovative country. How many are needed is a question of planned or expected growth, replacement of retiring workers, and sudden changes in demands for certain skills. Just as migrant farm workers are necessary to harvest apples, grapes, lettuce, and operate poultry processing plants, a nuclear power plant needs to bring in migrant workers when it is time to conduct annual shutdowns and maintenance. These temporary workers are examined and cleared to work at the power plant for a specified period of time. So too should the temporary agricultural and construction workers necessary to harvest crops, supply labor during construction booms, etc. The process of admitting them should not be so burdensome that they cannot get in or will not leave after being admitted. Such a process would be a disaster to a nuclear power plant, just as it is with countries. There is an essential need for flexibility in the temporary worker and the immigrant worker processes that cannot be excessively expensive or burdensome.

Maritime security doesn't start at the port or beach, it starts overseas and at the location where the product is produced and initially containerized for shipment. The system of maritime security involves a defense in depth that includes pre-shipping screening, paperwork review and approval, defense of the maritime realm from piracy and terrorism, and screening as the materials are unloaded and prepared to enter the country. This applies to every country, not just the United States. Some countries are better than others at this defense in depth across the maritime realm but all countries have some form of system in place to ensure that not only do the commodities essential to their economic survival arrive on time, and in good condition, but that dangerous people and pests don't come with them. So too does a nuclear power facility; they do not want to see problem people coming into the plant just as they don't want to have somebody infect the computer control systems with a STUXNET-type virus.

Designing an effective defense in depth to effect border security is neither difficult nor expensive. Humans have been doing this for millennia, sometimes successfully, sometimes unsuccessfully. In the cases where a successful system failed, it is almost always because of inflexibility or because the scope of the protective barrier was too narrow.

In Chapters 1 and 2 we referred to the Berlin Wall, a wall to keep people in. The Iron Curtain that fell across Europe in May 1945 was an example of defense in depth before a truly globalized world existed. The wall separating East and West Germany was only part of the defense in depth the Soviet Union created to ensure they would not be invaded a third time in the twentieth century by either Germans or the Western Allies. In addition to the Iron Curtain, they created the Warsaw Pact as a military alliance to confront the North Atlantic Treaty Organization. They established like-minded and friendly political systems in the countries between Russia and the West as a physical buffer to potential invasion. The Soviets also maintained strict control and oversight of their allied governments' communications, militaries, and police apparatuses. This system worked for more than fifty years, keeping most people in and preventing the West from being a military threat in the European theater. Unfortunately for the Soviet Union, their system was inflexible in the face of technological advances in communications and the ultimate economic failure of their centralized, noncapitalist system. Their entire system of government and economics collapsed nearly overnight.

Earlier in this chapter we discussed the security provided to both North and South Korea by the militarized 2.5 mile wide and 160 mile long DMZ. That fortified "wall" is only part of the defense system in place for South Korea. Driving up to the DMZ you cannot see the defense in depth the South Koreans have created. However, driving south from the DMZ the system of layered defenses become readily obvious to a trained observer. In addition to tank traps and fortifications across the width of the country, there are engineered terrain systems that force any invader from the north to funnel forces into choke points. Bridges have been constructed so they can be destructively dropped into chasms to stop southern movement. Tunnels are equipped with north-facing emplacements for heavy artillery and anti-tank weapons, and roads and rail systems designed to preclude rapid movement of military forces southward, while concurrently enhancing deployment of troops northward to key strategic points. South Korea has developed a flexible defense in depth to preclude a successful invasion by North Korea. This makes the DMZ an even better defense than it initially appears.

Border security and a defense in depth are not simply about walls, checkpoints, and interior defenses but about how a country views and addresses such issues as "birth tourism" and guest workers. It is also about how a country views such issues as illicit drugs. Depending on the perspective of the country, addressing such issues can be very difficult if an effective system of border security is to be put in place. Whether a country has closed or open borders, access to that country by terrorists or criminal or illegal migrants will continue with very few exceptions. Democracies, republics, and industrialized countries cannot survive if they implement the security systems associated with countries such as North Korea.

The European Union Experiment

Since 1985 countries in Europe have been experimenting with an "open borders" concept. By creating a specified area under the Schengen Agreement that allowed residents of member countries to cross borders simply by slowing down, allowing residents along borders to cross outside of formal checkpoints, and harmonizing the visa process to enter the countries, they created the first great experiment in international open borders. In 1990 the Schengen Convention that abolished internal border controls among member nations and established a common visa policy formalized the original Agreement. Essentially, except for those entering or exiting the Schengen Area, there are no border controls between the signatories of the Schengen Convention. Currently, twenty-six European countries with a population more than 400 million are participants in the agreement.

Recent changes to the European Union (EU) experiment in open borders have resulted in a single set of common rules that govern external border checks on persons, entry requirements and duration of stays in the Schengen Area, and standard procedures for the issuing of short-stay (not longer than three months) visas. This commonality has resulted in ease of movement between countries by business travelers and vacationers. For residents of the EU, the impact is even greater. According to the EU website,

> The free movement of persons is a fundamental right guaranteed by the EU to its citizens. It entitles every EU citizen to travel, work and live in any EU country without special formalities. Schengen cooperation enhances this freedom by enabling citizens to cross internal borders without being subjected to border checks. The border-free Schengen Area guarantees free movement to more than 400 million EU citizens, as well as to many non-EU nationals, businessmen, tourists or other persons legally present on the EU territory.[98]

This has not resulted in changes to internal law enforcement by the individual countries. It has fostered the development of cooperative police work and counterterrorism efforts. Additionally, the EU has established standardized visas for visitors and immigrants, standard documents for internal identification, and cooperative efforts in cross-border pursuit by law enforcement, stronger judicial cooperation, and faster extradition systems.

In April 2013 the Schengen Information System II entered service. This is the largest information system for public security in Europe. It allows easy exchange of information between the national border control, customs, and police authorities. The new system also employs biometrics for identification and allows for cross-border responses to cybercrime. Cooperative police work enhances the international effort to stop human trafficking and money laundering in Europe. As part of a multidisciplinary approach to organized crime, the overall EU system, through Europol, assists local law enforcement efforts to interdict criminals and prevent criminal activity.[99]

The European experiment with open borders is fully functioning and has enhanced the travel experience to EU countries for business and recreational travelers. For internal residents of the EU, the open borders allow any member of any EU country

An officer operates the computer system that guards the Portuguese coast, in Almada on April 23, 2012. The monitoring of the Portuguese coast is controlled by the SIVICC (Surveillance Command and Control Integrated System of the Portuguese Coast), a command operation of the Portuguese National Guard (GNR). With the EBF (European Border Fund), coast guards have access to equipment for monitoring the Portuguese coast. European Commission. n.d.

to move, live, and work in any other country without needing special visas or permission. An example: A Spaniard whose job eliminated due to downsizing can apply for work in Germany, relocate there, and do so without any international immigration paperwork.

By recognizing that Europe's natural barriers to illegal immigration and organized crime consisted of oceans and other geographic barriers such as mountains and rivers, Europeans combined forces to move away from a competitive internal system of control for each country and established a common border for all countries with points of entry for external peoples. This resulted in the deployment of border security efforts to ports of entry for ships and aircraft, as well as establishing maritime surveillance on approaches to the EU. The cost savings have been reinvested in better border security and better tracking of those issued visas to visit or immigrate into the EU.

Could a similar system be implemented across North America? There are a lot of objections to such an experiment in border security. They range from maintaining the sovereignty of a country's national culture, territory, politics, and laws to the issue of adapting to the use of three or more languages. Europe overcame twenty-six different languages and the laws of twenty-six different countries. They have agreed to a standardized set of common agreements that govern their relationships with each other. However, it is highly unlikely that the United States would enter into a similar agreement with Mexico. A common agreement with Canada on travel and work is a possibility.

But the Schengen system is under extreme pressure as are the political systems that established it. Today, at the start of 2017, Europe is in conflict. The British have voted to leave the European Union, primarily because of mandates to take a share of war refugees from Islamic Syria, Africa, and other countries, but perhaps more so because the British people have become fed up with the mandated laws and politics of their much more socialist European cousins. Similar movements to leave the EU are being considered in other countries. Again, this is primarily over the problems caused by uncontrolled migration of war refugees from Syria and Africa and the economic, political, environmental, and criminal impact they are creating in the countries that take them. Hungary has even erected a new fence system between itself and Serbia to stop and turn back the migrants. Italy and Spain have begun interdicting Africans off the coasts of Algeria and Libya and turning them back to Africa before they can set foot in the EU and claim the rights of asylum seekers. Greece, already in extreme financial trouble, is facing a massive crisis as Syrian Muslims leave refugee camps in Turkey and make the short trip to the Greek Islands, thus opening the door to full rights of asylum and refugee status in Europe. Somebody needs to pay for the care, shelter, and feeding of these people, and in a world where the recovery from the recession of 2008–9 has been poor to nonexistent over the past eight years, such a burden is too much for many countries to bear.

Conclusion

Humans have always striven to achieve a concept of security, one that has been elusive for most of history. In the modern world, the issue of sovereign nations and their borders has become a point of political contention, particularly in the United States. The problem of establishing effective border security requires a holistic approach that addresses not just the vast geographic expanse of the US-Mexico and US-Canada borders, but also the issues of immigration, human migration, and globalization of crime, terrorism, industry, agriculture, education, technology, energy, and communications.

The best physical borders between nations are those established along natural geographic features that are also barriers. These geographic barriers can change. The Rio Grande River was once a significant barrier to travel. Today, it is barely a stream in most places. In today's world, seaports and airports must also be addressed as points where borders and barriers need to be combined. The dependency of nations on maritime transportation systems has resulted in the extension of border controls away from a country's own ports to the ports where cargo and commodities originate. Border security is not just the Port of Los Angles or the Port of Savannah, but now the factory in Shanghai and the containerization facility in Bangalore, India.

Establishing effective border security has been elusive, if not impossible, across the vast expanse of North America, resulting in a porosity that allows such a large quantity of illegal contraband to cross borders that the seizure of millions of tons of

The Rio Grande River between Las Cruces and Socorro, New Mexico — 1937.
© US Border Patrol Museum. Used with permission.

The Rio Grande River between Eagle Pass, Texas, and
Piedras Negras, Mexico — 2013. James Phelps.

drugs has no effect on market prices. Resolving the causes of this porosity requires political strength, public calls for solutions, and a willingness to look beyond the physical, racial, and cultural walls of the past to a new perspective on what constitutes borders, barriers, and boundaries.

Fixed fortifications are an anachronism in a world of aircraft, ultra-lights, high-speed boats, homemade submarines, and intercontinental ballistic missiles. Fixed fortifications and border fences can be used to direct and divert illegal border crossers to controllable areas but the cost may be more than the effort is worth. As with the

Berlin Wall, desperate people will always try to get across a physical barrier, to escape a totalitarian dictatorship or to access needed work to feed their families.

Are there better ways to secure borders than the construction of fences? Some countries think so and have begun the process to establish common external borders while opening internal borders. These experiments have not yet come to a conclusion that can be determined to be either a success or failure. In the case of the European Union, what appeared to be working is now under extreme pressure and stress due to terrorist attacks and mass migration of refugees. Yet, the two million refugees who have entered the EU are nothing compared with the 11+ million believed to be living illegally in the United States. As continuing economic problems face the EU, accompanied by high youth unemployment, and the real potential of a failure of the Euro as a common currency, only the future will tell if the interior open borders will remain.

The future of border security in the United States appears to be set on a track that will build more fixed fortifications, deploy more personnel, and spend more money. In 1959, just before leaving office, President Dwight Eisenhower warned the American people to be wary of an emerging military-industrial complex. Today the American people should be wary of attempts to maintain the status quo by an emerging border security-industrial complex. Yet the United States' failure to effectively address the issue of its porous southern border over more than 20 years and three two-term presidencies is tantamount to voluntarily ceding territory to another sovereign country. For any country to maintain it's sovereignty the borders must be defined, marked, and recognized by others. Most importantly, control over who crosses those borders must be effective and well established.

A very wise professor once said that the only constant is change. Border security, throughout history, has undergone change with every alteration in technology, travel, politics, culture, and religion in every region of the world. To expect concepts of what constitutes effective border security to remain unchanged in a changing world would be an example of insanity.

Questions for Further Consideration

1. It is common to assign metrics to measure the level of border security. Those metrics often include the number of illegal immigrants stopped from entering a country, the number of criminal aliens who have been arrested and deported, or the tonnage of illegal drugs confiscated by border security agencies. These are all useful measures for political purposes, but do they accurately measure border security?
2. What is it about the relationship between Mexico and the United States that has Mexicans who cross the border talking about visiting the "occupied states of North Mexico"?
3. Where does national sovereignty begin and end if power grids cross international boundaries in our globalized world?

4. When energy systems become globalized and countries become interdependent on each other's energy infrastructure, then border security becomes a problem. Where does the border begin and end when it comes to power distribution systems?

5. Are there better ways to secure borders than the construction of fences? Describe some.

6. What would it take to implement a Schengen-type agreement in North America? What barriers to such an agreement currently exist and would have to be overcome?

7. What should the United States do to stop "birth tourism"? What can be done to bring about this change?

Chapter 12 Endnotes

1. DHS, Border Security Overview. Last accessed 30 Jun 2013 at: http://www.dhs.gov/border-security-overview Remained unchanged as of 24 Feb. 2017.

2. DHS, Secure and Manage Our Borders. Last accessed 30 Jun 2013 at: http://www.dhs.gov/secure-and-manage-borders Remained unchanged as of 24 Feb. 2017.

3. DHS, Border Security. Last accessed 30 Jun 2013 at: http://ipv6.dhs.gov/files/bordersecurity.shtm No clear statement exists as of 24 Feb. 2017.

4. Committee on Homeland Security, US House of Representatives. Border Security. Last accessed 30 Jun 2013 at: http://homeland.house.gov/issue/border-security. A check of the webpage on 24 February 2017 did not show any clear statement on the topic.

5. US Senate Commitztee on Homeland Security & Governmental Affairs. Border Security, Immigration and Ports. Last accessed 30 Jun 2013 at: http://www.hsgac.senate.gov/issues/border-security-and-immigration. A check of the webpage on 24 February 2017 did not show any clear statement on the topic.

6. President George W. Bush. (2002) *Securing the Homeland: Strengthening the nation.* Washington, D.C.: US GPO, 2.

7. Ibid., 3.

8. Official website of the Department of Homeland Security. About DHS, 1 July 2013. Last accessed 1 July 2013 at: http://www.dhs.gov/about-dhs At the time of this revision all the DHS websites are undergoing revision. These statements are from our original research for the first edition. As these websites change and are updated professors and students may find the focus of DHS agencies changing.

9. Official website of the Department of Homeland Security, Our Mission, 1 July 2013. Last accessed 1 July 2013 at: http://www.dhs.gov/our-mission At the time of this revision all the DHS websites are undergoing revision. These statements are from our original research for the first edition. As these websites change and are updated professors and students may find the focus of DHS agencies changing.

10. Ibid.

11. DHS, Home Page. Available at: https://www.dhs.gov Last accessed 24 Feb. 2017. At the time of this revision all the DHS websites are undergoing revision. These statements are from our original research for the first edition. As these websites change and are updated professors and students may find the focus of DHS agencies changing.

12. DHS, About DHS: Mission. Available at: https://www.dhs.gov/mission Last accessed 24 Feb. 2017. At the time of this revision all the DHS websites are undergoing revision. These statements are from our original research for the first edition. As these websites change and are updated professors and students may find the focus of DHS agencies changing.

13. DHS, National Terrorism Advisory System Bulletin. Available at: https://www.dhs.gov/ntas/advisory/ntas_16_1115_0001 Last accessed 24 Feb. 2017. At the time of this revision all the DHS websites are undergoing revision. These statements are from our original research for the first edition. As these websites change and are updated professors and students may find the focus of DHS agencies changing.

14. DHS, Countering Violent Extremism webpage. Accessed July 21, 2017, at: https://www.dhs.gov/

countering-violent-extremism?utm_source=hp_carousel&utm_medium=web&utm_campaign=dhs_hp
. Last accessed 24 Feb. 2017. At the time of this revision all the DHS websites are undergoing revision. These statements are from our original research for the first edition. As these websites change and are updated professors and students may find the focus of DHS agencies changing.

15. Tabirian, Alissa, GAO: Current Method of Measuring Border Security is Incomplete. CNSNEWS.com . 28 June 2013. Accessed July 21, 2017, at: http://cnsnews.com/news/article/gao-current-method-measuring-border-security-incomplete

16. Ibid.

17. Gambler, Rebecca, Border Security: Progress and Challenges in DHS Implementation and Assessment Efforts. Testimony before the Subcommittee on National Security, Committee on Oversight and Government Reform, US House of Representatives. GAO-13-653T, 27 June 2013. Accessed July 21, 2017, at: http://www.gao.gov/assets/660/655539.pdf

18. DHS, Written testimony of CBP Air and Marine Operations Assistant Commissioner Randolph Alles and CBP US Border Patrol Acting Chief Ronald Vitiello for a House Committee on Homeland Security, Subcommittee on Border and Maritime Security hearing titled "Transparency, Trust and Verification: Measuring Effectiveness and Situational Awareness along the Border," March 1, 2016. Accessed July 21, 2017, at: https://www.dhs.gov/news/2016/03/01/written-testimony-cbp-house-homeland-security-subcommittee-border-and-maritime

19. Ibid., 7.

20. Preston, Julia, Officials Concede Failures on Gauging Border Security. *The New York Times,* 21 Mar. 2013. Accessed July 21, 2017, at: http://www.nytimes.com/2013/03/22/us/officials-still-seek-ways-to-assess-border-security.html

21. Ibid.

22. Interestingly, the ONDCP has not published a report on price or purity of drugs since President Obama took office in January 2009.

23. Fries, Arthur, Robert Anthony, Andrew Cseko Jr., Carl Gaither, and Eric Schulman, The Price and Purity of Illicit Drugs: 1981–2007 (Alexandria, VA: Institute for Defense Analyses, October 2008). Here-in-after referred to as: ONDCP, 9.

24. ONDCP, 11.

25. US Inflation Calculator, Current US Inflation Rates: 2003–13. Accessed July 21, 2017, at: http://www.usinflationcalculator.com/inflation/current-inflation-rates/

26. National Drug Threat Assessment 2010, US Department of Justice, National Drug Intelligence Center, Document ID: 2010-Q0317-001 (Archived), February 2010. Available at: http://www.justice.gov/archive/ndic/pubs38/38661/index.htm#Contents . See also National Drug Threat Assessment 2008 (October 2007). US Department of Justice, National Drug Intelligence Center. (Archived; no Document ID). Available at: http://www.justice.gov/archive/ndic/pubs25/25921/25921p.pdf

27. Many of the problems today across the Middle East are the result of British and French diplomats drawing lines on maps without regard to actual geography, or ethnicity or religion of the population. Those drawing the lines were amateur cartographers and had never actually been to the region. The result is continuing ethnic and religious wars between different tribal peoples with different religious beliefs. The simple solution would be to redraw the country lines along demographic and geographic features with the agreement of those people who live there. Unfortunately, nobody in power in any of the Middle Eastern countries is willing to give up territorial control for a potential peace.

28. The CBP and Border Patrol officers who contributed to this section requested to remain anonymous to protect their employment.

29. Bernkopfová, Michala, Ph.D., offers a consolidated and deep reference of the political, economic, historical, and sociological components of the Mexico post revolution government and peoples as part of her course, Government and Politics in Mexico. Accessed July 21, 2017, at Karlova Univerzita's website: https://is.cuni.cz/studium/predmety/index.php?do=predmet&kod=JMM591 The references provided are extensive and offer deeper insight into the issues of U.S.—Mexico relations than do the following paragraphs. To understand the Mexican perspectives that have colored their feelings towards the U.S. one might want to read Rochelle Trotter's doctoral dissertation, ¡EN VOZ ALTA! Mexico's Response to U.S. Imperialism, 1821-1848, accessed July 21, 2017, at: https://d.lib.msu.edu/etd/2779/datastream/OBJ/view The website of M.E.Ch.A. (Movimento Estudiantil Chicanx de Aztlán) makes for interesting, but highly biased reading and is available at: http://www.chicanxdeaztlan.org/p/about-us.html The National Council of La Raza (The Race), recently changed its name to UNIDOSUS (18 July 2017: accessed July 21, 2017, at: http://thehill.com/latino/342623-president-of-latino-group-la-raza-name-was-a-barrier-to-our-mission) and has created a new website that supports similar goals

but without the heavy racial undertones of La Raza. UNIDOSUS can be accessed at: http://www.unidosus.org however to comprehend the underlying political ideology of the movement one should refer to the earlier writing, politics, and claims from the original movement, NCLR. References to this now defunct and removed internet material can be found in: http://www.nationalreview.com/article/224980/la-raza-facts-michelle-malkin http://www.politico.com/blogs/on-congress/2009/05/tancredo-la-raza-is-latino-kkk-018732 https://cis.org/Kammer/Whats-Name-Meaning-La-Raza The best histories of Mexico are written in Spanish. For those wanting an English language history of Mexico up through the implementation of NAFTA, we recommend T.R. Fehrenbach's *Fire and Blood: A history of Mexico*, ISBN 978-0306806285.

30. Bargo, Michael Jr., The Matricula Consular: The Only Card an Illegal Immigrant Will Ever Need, *American Thinker,* 26 Apr. 2012. Accessed July 21, 2017, at: http://www.americanthinker.com/2012/04/the_matricula_consular_the_only_card_an_illegal_immigrant_will_ever_need.html#_edn5

31. Dinerstein, Marti, IDs for Illegals: The 'Matricula Consular' Advances Mexico's Immigration Agenda, Center for Immigration Studies, Jan. 2003.

32. FAIR. Chicano Nationalism, Revanchism and the Aztlan Myth. Accessed July 21, 2017, at: http://www.fairus.org/issue/chicano-nationalism-revanchism-and-the-aztlan-myth

33. Ibid.

34. Ramirez-Dhoore, Dora. Rhetoric of Aztlan: HB 2281, MEChA and Liberatory Education, *New City Community Press,* Jan. 2011. Accessed July 21, 2017, at: http://reflectionsjournal.net/wp-content/uploads/2011/01/The-Rhetoric-of-Aztlán-Dora-Ramirez-Dhoore.pdf

35. For additional information on the issue of cross-border students and financial burdens on school districts see: Viren, Sarah, Mexican Children Cross Border to go to School, *Houston Chronicle,* 29 April 2007. Accessed July 21, 2017, at: http://www.chron.com/opinion/outlook/article/Mexican-children-cross-border-to-go-to-school-1807611.php

36. Benitez, Gina, Woman thrown in jail, Car impounded in Mexico for expired registration, KFOX, 30 May 2013. Available at: http://www.kfoxtv.com/news/news/woman-thrown-jail-car-impounded-mexico-expired-ame/nX7SL/ The original link for this news report has been shifted to the KFOX Facebook Page. Accessed July 21, 2017, at: https://www.facebook.com/KFOXTV/posts/10151704936811424

37. US Bureau of the Census, County Population Estimates by Demographic Characteristics—Age, Sex, Race, and Hispanic Origin; updated annually for states and counties. Accessed July 21, 2017, at: https://www.census.gov/topics/population.html 2010 Census of Population and Housing for places; updated every ten years. http://factfinder2.census.gov

38. Ibid. Accessed July 21, 2017, at: http://www.indexmundi.com/facts/united-states/quick-facts/texas/hispanic-or-latino-population-percentage#map

39. O'Reilly, Bill. Search results for the terms "Mexican+invasion." Accessed July 21, 2017, at: https://www.billoreilly.com/

40. Feere, Jon, Birthright Citizenship in the United States: A Global Comparison, Center for Immigration Studies, August 2010. Accessed July 21, 2017, at: http://www.cis.org/birthright-citizenship

41. Jeff Cox, "What 'are so many of them doing?' 95 million not in US labor force," CNBC TV, 2 Dec. 2016. Accessed July 21, 2017, at: http://www.cnbc.com/2016/12/02/95-million-american-workers-not-in-us-labor-force.html

42. WikiLeaks cable 09STATE15113, para 3. The original cable from Secretary of State Hillary Clinton, to all diplomatic posts and especially the American Embassy in Tripoli, released as P 182318Z FEB 09, SUBJECT: REQUEST FOR INFORMATION: CRITICAL FOREIGN IDEPENDENCIES (CRITICAL INFRASTRUCTURE AND KEY RESOURCES LOCATED ABROAD).

43. Ibid., para 6.

44. Jordan Negotiating to Buy Natural Gas From Israel, JTA online, 26 June 2013. Accessed July 21, 2017, at: http://www.jta.org/2013/06/26/news-opinion/israel-middle-east/jordan-negotiating-to-buy-natural-gas-from-israel

45. STRATFOR, Ethiopia Diverts Water From the Nile River, 28 May 2013.

46. Schiller, Dane, Agents Feared Mexican Drug Cartel Attack on Border Dam, *Houston Chronicle,* 2 June 2010. Accessed July 21, 2017, at: http://www.chron.com/news/houston-texas/article/Agents-feared-Mexican-drug-cartel-attack-on-1617694.php

47. Goldberg, David, James Corless, Nick Donohue, Stephen Davis, and Kevin DeGood, *Fix We're in for: The State of Our Nation's Bridges, 2013,* Transportation for America, 2013. Accessed July 21, 2017, at: http://t4america.org/docs/bridgereport2013/2013BridgeReport.pdf

48. Blackout: A Case Study of the 2003 North American Power Outage with Exercises, George Mason University, 2013. Accessed July 21, 2017, at: https://cip.gmu.edu/wp-content/uploads/2015/08/Blackout-Instructor-Materials-1.pdf

49. Ibid.

50. Demic, Barbara. The Baby Registry of Choice: Thousands of pregnant South Koreans travel to the U.S. to give birth to American citizens. Accessed July 21, 2017, at: http://articles.latimes.com/2002/may/25/world/fg-birth25

51. Doty, Tammy, Chinese top NMI Births, *Marianas Variety*, 14 Mar. 2013. Accessed July 21, 2017, at: http://www.mvariety.com/cnmi/cnmi-news/local/54345-chinese-top-nmi-births

52. Ibid.

53. Encinares, Erwin, Birth by foreign parents skyrockets, *Saipan Tribune*, 23 Nov. 2016. Accessed July 21, 2017, at: http://www.saipantribune.com/index.php/birth-foreign-parents-skyrockets/

54. _____, Births by foreign parents raise questions, 30 Nov. 2016. Accessed July 21, 2017, at: http://www.saipantribune.com/index.php/births-foreign-parents-raise-questions/

55. Newcomb, Alyssa, Chinese Women Pay to Give Birth at California Maternity Mansion, Secure Citizenship for Babies, ABCNews, 2 Dec. 2012. Accessed July 21, 2017, at: http://abcnews.go.com/US/chinese-women-pay-give-birth-california-maternity-mansion/story?id=17862251#

56. Chang, Richard, American Benefits Beget Rise in 'Birth Tourism,' *The Sacramento Bee*, 24 Sep. 2012. Accessed July 21, 2017, at: https://www.amren.com/news/2012/09/in-california-birth-tourism-appears-to-grow/

57. Ibid.

58. Ibid.

59. Is¸ l Eg rikavuk, Birth Tourism in US on the Rise for Turkish Parents. *Hürriyet Daily News*, 12 Mar. 2010. Accessed July 21, 2017, at: http://newadmin.hurriyetdailynews.com/birth-tourism-in-us-on-the-rise-for-turkish-parents.aspx?pageID=438&n=birth-tourism-to-the-usa-explodes-2010-03-12

60. Ibid.

61. Friedman, Thomas L., "The Dell Theory of Conflict Prevention" in *Emerging: A Reader*. Barclay Barrios, ed. (Boston: Bedford, St. Martins, 2008).

62. Boehlje, Michael, Globalization and Agriculture: New Realities, Business Environment, Center for Food and Agricultural Business, Purdue University, n.d. Accessed July 21, 2017, at: http://www.agecon.purdue.edu/extension/sbpcp/resources/globalizationandag.pdf

63. CBP.gov. Agriculture Protection Program, 17 Jun 2013. The original fact sheet from 2013 is no longer available. The current information is available at: https://www.cbp.gov/border-security/protecting-agriculture

64. Food and Agriculture Organization of the United Nations, FAOSTAT. Accessed July 21, 2017, at: http://www.fao.org/statistics/en/

65. Chiquita Bananas website. Accessed July 21, 2017, at: http://www.chiquitabananas.com/Banana-Information/index-yellow-bananas-information.aspx

66. FAOSTAT.

67. Ibid.

68. Ibid.

69. Boehlje, n.d., 1.

70. Ibid., 2.

71. Ibid., 5.

72. USDA, Economic Research Service, Global Food Industry, 31 May 2012. Accessed July 21, 2017, at: http://www.ers.usda.gov/topics/international-markets-trade/global-food-markets/global-food-industry.aspx#

73. FAO, Food Security Information for Action: An Introduction to the Basic Concepts of Food Security. Accessed July 21, 2017, at: http://www.fao.org/docrep/013/al936e/al936e00.pdf

74. From the CBP website. Accessed July 21, 2017, at: https://www.cbp.gov/border-security/protecting-agriculture

75. Executive Order 13112, Invasive Species, Federal Register/Vol. 64, No. 25, 3 Feb. 1999, 6183.

76. USGS. Nonindigenous Aquatic Species by State: Colorado. Accessed July 21, 2017, at: http://nas.er.usgs.gov/queries/SpeciesList.aspx Detailed list for Colorado at: https://nas.er.usgs.gov/queries/SpeciesList.aspx?group=&state=CO&Sortby=1

77. Eastern Forest Environmental Threat Assessment Center, Data & Tools: Colorado. Accessed July 21, 2017, at: https://forestthreats.org/research/tools

78. Office of the President of the United States, *Strategy to Combat Transnational Organized Crime,* July 2011, front matter. Accessed July 21, 2017, at: http://www.justice.gov/criminal/ocgs/org-crime/docs/08-30-11-toc-strategy.pdf

79. Ibid., 6.

80. US Department of Justice,. Child Exploitation & Obscenity Section. Accessed July 21, 2017, at: http://www.justice.gov/criminal/ceos/faqs/faqs.html

81. US Department of Justice, Mass-Marketing Fraud. Accessed July 21, 2017, at: http://www.justice.gov/criminal/fraud/internet/

82. Harris, Andrew, Four Men Found Guilty in Zetas Money Laundering Trial, *Bloomberg,* 9 May 2013. Accessed July 21, 2017, at: http://www.bloomberg.com/news/2013-05-09/four-men-found-guilty-in-zetas-money-laundering-trial.html

83. Office of the President of the United States, *Strategy to Combat Transnational Organized Crime,* July 2011, 13–14.

84. University of Houston Law Center, *Expert Says Borders are Opportunities, not Barriers,* July 2011. Accessed July 21, 2017, at: http://www.law.uh.edu/news/spring2013/0429Zamora.asp

85. Trump, Donald. The Inaugural Address. Accessed July 21, 2017, at: https://www.whitehouse.gov/inaugural-address

86. Seper, Jerry, and Matthew Cella, Signs in Arizona Warn of Smuggler Dangers, *Washington Times,* 31 Aug. 2010. Accessed July 21, 2017, at: http://www.washingtontimes.com/news/2010/aug/31/signs-in-arizona-warn-of-smuggler-dangers/?page=all

87. University of Houston Law Center.

88. Legrain, Philippe, Let Them In, *Forbes,* 10 June 2010. Accessed July 21, 2017, at: http://www.forbes.com/forbes/2010/0628/special-report-immigration-opening-borders-mexico-let-them-in.html

89. Filipowski, Andrew, Immigration and Prosperity: Why Tech Needs Open Borders, *Forbes,* 9 Apr 2012. Accessed July 21, 2017, at: http://www.forbes.com/sites/ciocentral/2012/04/09/immigration-and-prosperity-why-tech-needs-open-borders/

90. Rather than provide a list of 25 different sources for the content of this paragraph, it is simpler to refer the reader to a central clearing house for information: *Wikipedia.* This information was consolidated from: "Dzhokhar and Tamerlan Tsarnaev," available at: http://en.wikipedia.org/wiki/Dzhokhar_and_Tamerlan_Tsarnaev

91. McGovern, Ray, Boston Suspect's Writing on the Wall, Consortiumnews. Com. 17 May 2013. Accessed July 21, 2017, at: https://consortiumnews.com/2013/05/17/boston-suspects-writing-on-the-wall/

92. Bray, Chad, Times Square Bomber Gets Life Sentence, *The Wall Street Journal,* 5 Oct. 2010. Accessed July 21, 2017, at: https://www.wsj.com/articles/SB10001424052748704469004575533902050370826

93. Ibid.

94. Wikipedia, *Nidal Malik Hasan,* accessed July 21, 2017, at: http://en.wikipedia.org/wiki/Nidal_Malik_Hasan

95. Wikipedia, *7 July 2005 London Bombings,* accessed July 21, 2017, at: http://en.wikipedia.org/wiki/7_July_2005_London_bombings

96. Hawkins, Harry, Two Face Murder Trial Over Death of Drummer Lee Rigby, *The Sun,* 28 June 2013. Accessed July 21, 2017, at: http://www.thesun.co.uk/sol/homepage/news/4988667/michael-adebolajo-michael-adebowale-face-trial-over-lee-rigby-killing.html

97. Ibid. See also, Malik, Shiv, Michael Adebolajo tells Old Bailey, "I am a soldier," *The Guardian,* 5 June 2013. Accessed July 21, 2017, at: http://www.guardian.co.uk/uk/2013/jun/05/michael-adebolajo-court-woolwich-murder

98. European Commission, Home Affairs, Schengen Area. Accessed July 21, 2017, at: http://ec.europa.eu/dgs/home-affairs/what-we-do/policies/borders-and-visas/schengen/index_en.htm

99. European Commission, Home Affairs, Organized Crime & Human Trafficking. Accessed July 21, 2017, at: http://ec.europa.eu/dgs/home-affairs/what-we-do/policies/organized-crime-and-human-trafficking/index_en.htm

Index to *Border Security*